# Nature Lover's
# Treasury

THE GREYSTONE

# NATURE LOVER'S
# TREASURY

*Selected and Edited by*

MARSHALL McCLINTOCK

GREYSTONE PRESS

NEW YORK, N. Y.

# CONTENTS

[ v ]

# Contents

# Nature Lover's
# Treasury

# THE SUGAR CAMP

## Louis Bromfield

*Few people write of nature so feelingly as those who have grown up close to it, have abandoned it for many years only to return to it with the full appreciation of its beauties and satisfactions in comparison with the harshness of modern city life. Louis Bromfield grew up in the farm country of Ohio, spent many years in the cities of the world as journalist and novelist (winning the Pulitzer Prize in 1926 for his Early Autumn). He then returned to Ohio and bought a farm. In* Pleasant Valley, *from which this piece is taken, he writes not only of the earth and things of the earth, but of those who live close to the soil.*

THE sugar camp stands on the edge of the woods on the Beck place a little way from Jim Pugh's cabin and his trout pond. It is a big shed with wide cracks between the boards and doors at both ends to permit the air to circulate in boiling time and drive out the smoke and steam. Inside there is a long low brick furnace with a vat on the top where the sap is boiled down into syrup. All through the summer and autumn and winter months the vat lies turned upside down, the inside coated with the thick syrup of last season to keep it from rusting. In autumn the leaves fall and drift inside to cover the earthen floor and pile against the heaps of cordwood left from last spring's boiling. When winter comes the empty shed is frequented by rabbits and raccoons and birds which take shelter there, against the force of the blizzards which sweep down the Valley from the north.

And they come there for the food that is put out for them when the acorns and weed seeds are gone and the ground is covered with snow. Twice a week someone carries up to the sugar camp a bag containing a few ears of corn, some apples and potatoes and a little of the dairy mash mixed in the big barn on the Anson place. Both birds and animals like the mash for it has in it ground corn and oats

[ 1 ]

and wheat and dried green alfalfa. It is a nicely balanced food good
for man, child or beast.

The contents of the bag is scattered inside the shed on the floor
and atop the wood pile where the birds can get it easily. When that
is done you go away wondering how many eyes of wild things have
been watching you on your visit from beneath the old logs or out
of holes in the big trees and from branches overhead. You know
they are all there somewhere near in the myriad dark holes of
refuge that exist in a thick woods. You know they are all there for
if you come back the following morning the record of their presence is in the snow outside the sugar camp.

The tiny tracks come from all directions—the footprints of the
big fox squirrel beginning nowhere at the spot where he has
dropped out of a tree and scurried toward the shed, the triangular
tracks of wild rabbits coming out of old hollow logs and crevices
in the rocks and holes burrowed by the ground hog for his winter
sleep, the tiny footprints of the muskrat dragging his tail along behind him in the snow. He has left his pond during the night and
gone foraging along the creek and up the spring run until his delicate nose told him there were apples in the sugar camp. And there
are in late fall and early spring the prints of sleepy possums with
the yellow eyes that see so well at night. And the prints of the raccoon's little hands pressed into the snow. And here and there in a
crazy pattern are the delicate footprints of birds—the cardinals,
the chickadees, the hedge sparrows, the warblers.

They have all been there in the night or in the early morning
before man is stirring or is busy in the big barns doing his chores.
When you go there in the middle of the day the place is empty,
as empty as all the winter landscape. If it is a fine day you may hear
the distant whistle of a cardinal or the call of a hedge sparrow but
that is all. It is a good place to feed wild things for no owl can
attack them there and I have never seen the tracks of a fox in the
snow, perhaps because he is suspicious of the shed as a place inhabited by his most implacable enemy, the poultryman.

Often I have been tempted to go there at night with an electric
torch to watch the banquet, but I have never done it so far for fear
of frightening the visitors away or making them suspicious. The
story is there the next day written in the snow and on the floor of
the little shed—the teeth marks of the muskrat and the squirrel in
the half-eaten apples and potatoes, the ears of corn shelled and scattered. One of the visitors carries off the apples whole and I suspect

the raccoon who takes his food down to the spring run to wash it before beginning his meal. At any rate that is where his tracks lead. And the squirrel I suspect is the one who likes the seeds of the apples, picking them carefully out of the cores left by the muskrat. And one of them does not nibble his corn off the cob. He shells it all carefully, leaving it scattered about the bare cob. Again I suspect the raccoon.

And all over the piles of dairy mash are the tiny, delicate tracks of the feet of birds.

I should like to see them all feeding there together—the birds, the possum, the raccoons, the squirrels, the muskrat and the rabbits —but I never shall, because the first flash of light or the first foot-fall would destroy the peace and the security of the whole picture. I shall only be able to read the story in the tracks in the snow, in the shelled corn and the tiny teeth marks on the apples and potatoes.

All the year round until late in February the sugar camp belongs to the wild things. Then one morning when the snow begins to melt and the earth to heave and the fields and pastures to stream with water, men come to the place and take it over. There is a great bustle and activity and the evaporator is turned right side up and a big fire built under it to boil out last year's sticky syrup and leave it fresh and clean for the new boiling. Outside the shed the big iron butchering kettle is suspended over another fire and water is heated in it to wash out the sap buckets which have been piled high in a corner of the shed for nearly a year. In my grandfather's day the sap buckets were made of wood and a couple of weeks before an expected run of sap they had to be lined up and filled with melting snow water from the spring run to swell and become watertight again. It was a lot of work but there was something special in the rite which is missing in these days of metal buckets. I think the seasoned ancient wood, soaked year after year with fresh sap, gave a special flavor to the syrup.

Our sugar bush lies all the way along a north slope on the side of the hill where the sandstone crops out among the big beeches and oaks and sugar maples. It is the last place on the whole farm to thaw out and so the sap runs late, but is, I suspect, all the sweeter for its lateness. The crude paths cut among the young trees and underbrush to permit the passage of a wagon to collect the sap from the trees, run up and down, dangerously, across big rocks and through miniature ravines. When the ground is thawing and streaked with melting snow and water streams everywhere, the almighty tractors can't do the job. The front rears up in protest on a steep slope or the big wheels slide helplessly around. Gathering sap is a job that only horses can do and for my money only horses should draw the big sled with the three-hundred gallon tank. A tractor would be a desecration.

There is something beautiful and satisfactory in the sight of the two big iron-blue Percheron mares, Queen and Sylvia, seen from a distance among the bare trunks of the big trees against the snow-streaked hillside. For me it brings back memories of pleasanter times when living was easier and people had a chance to know each other in the leisurely comfortable way of neighbors in a Currier and Ives farm picture. There are lots of reasons why I should like to be twenty years old again, but one of the reasons I am glad I am middle-aged is because it makes me old enough to remember what living was like and what farm life was like before there were automobiles and tractors and airplanes. I am not yet old enough to sit dreaming of the past but I know that life had values in those days which are gone forever, unless someday the world begins all over again. The sight of the big Percherons among the trees brings back all those values which my grandfather knew as well as any man of his time because values were important to him. He did not simply take them for granted. He was intelligent enough to know what a good life he had and to savor it.

And the sight of the big blue mares brings back memories of my grandfather's sugar bush where we used to boil sap round the clock during a big run. It was a big shed, bigger than our own, with bunks built in it where one could sleep or snatch a nap after building up a roaring fire under the evaporator. With him sugar making was a kind of rite celebrating the return of spring. My uncles and my father and friends from town joined him and ate chicken and sweet potatoes roasted in the red-hot coals and they drank hard cider until the sky turned gray and then frosty blue and you went to the barn to harness the big horses and make the rounds of the buckets brimming with sap at sunrise.

There is a kind of excitement which tinges the whole ceremony of sugar making, for it is the symbol of the breaking up of winter and the coming of spring when the sap rises in the trees and the first faint flush of green follows the streaks of melting snow. The cress begins to grow in the spring run and the chickadees and sparrows to call. After the death of winter it is rebirth, the beginning of hope, a new year with the promise of plenty. Even the dogs and horses feel it. The big mares stamp the earth and toss their heads and their breath steams as they snort in the frosty air of early morning or evening. And the dogs go mad running in circles round and round the sled, chasing rabbits and squirrels that never were save in their imaginations.

Few things on earth taste so good as the syrup of the first sugaring off. It is fresh and new, the very essence of the earth and the budding trees and the wakening spring. You can smell it in the steam from the evaporator and taste it in the hot syrup lifted from the vat in the big ladle.

Boiling down at night is the pleasantest of all. The sap boils and the steam smells of syrup and the fire under the evaporator throws shadows against the gray weather-beaten wall of the shed. On the ground, close to the evaporator, lie the dogs, grateful for the pleasant warmth, sleeping heavily after all the foolish running they have done all day. And in the corner is a jug of cider or maybe something stronger and seated on logs or cordwood you sit around and tell stories about the Valley and the people who lived there before you were born and trod this same earth that is beneath your feet and tapped the same big maple trees. A kerosene lantern casts a pleasant yellow glow over the whole scene. If you go outside into the frosty air there is the sound of the rustling and scurrying of the wild things which have come up to stare at the strangers who have invaded their territory. And sometimes if you turn the electric torch in the direction of the big fallen chestnut a hundred yards away the light will catch the reflection of a dozen or more eyes that gleam like green jewels in the darkness—the eyes of the raccoon and rabbits and possum and muskrat that have found the new spot a little way off, where you leave apples and potatoes and corn.

In that weather-beaten shed you are very close to the earth and to security and peace and indeed, very near to God.

# LASSIE COME-HOME

## Eric Knight

*Of animal stories, those about dogs outnumber all others.
There are many fine ones among them, but rarely does a story
appear that is taken to millions of hearts like this simple tale of
a collie whose love for his master is so strong it can surmount
any barrier.*

THE dog had met the boy by the school gate for five years. Now
she couldn't understand that times were changed and she wasn't
supposed to be there any more. But the boy knew.

So when he opened the door of the cottage, he spoke before he
entered.

"Mother," he said, "Lassie's come home again."

He waited a moment, as if in hope of something. But the man
and woman inside the cottage did not speak.

"Come in, Lassie," the boy said.

He held open the door, and the tricolor collie walked in obediently. Going head down, as a collie when it knows something is
wrong, it went to the rug and lay down before the hearth, a black-
white-and-gold aristocrat. The man, sitting on a low stool by the
fireside, kept his eyes turned away. The woman went to the sink
and busied herself there.

"She were waiting at school for me, just like always," the boy
went on. He spoke fast, as if racing against time. "She must ha'
got away again. I thought, happen this time, we might just——"

"No!" the woman exploded.

The boy's carelessness dropped. His voice rose in pleading.

"But this time, mother! Just this time. We could hide her. They
wouldn't ever know."

"Dogs, dogs, dogs!" the woman cried. The words poured from
her as if the boy's pleading had been a signal gun for her own anger.
"I'm sick o' hearing about tykes round this house. Well, she's sold

[6]

and gone and done with, so the quicker she's taken back the better. Now get her back quick, or first thing ye know we'll have Hynes round here again. Mr. Hynes!"

Her voice sharpened in imitation of the Cockney accent of the south: "Hi know you Yorkshiremen and yer come-'ome dogs. Training yer dogs to come 'ome so's yer can sell 'em hover and hover again.

"Well, she's sold, so ye can take her out o' my house and home to them as bought her!"

The boy's bottom lip crept out stubbornly, and there was silence in the cottage. Then the dog lifted its head and nudged the man's hand, as a dog will when asking for patting. But the man drew away and stared, silently, into the fire.

The boy tried again, with the ceaseless guile of a child, his voice coaxing.

"Look, feyther, she wants thee to bid her welcome. Aye, she's that glad to be home. Happen they don't tak' good care on her up there? Look, her coat's a bit poorly, don't ye think? A bit o' linseed strained through her drinking water—that's what I'd gi' her."

Still looking in the fire, the man nodded. But the woman, as if perceiving the boy's new attack, sniffed.

"Aye, tha wouldn't be a Carraclough if tha didn't know more about tykes nor breaking eggs wi' a stick. Nor a Yorkshireman. My goodness, it seems to me sometimes that chaps in this village thinks more on their tykes nor they do o' their own flesh and blood. They'll sit by their firesides and let their own bairns starve so long as t' dog gets fed."

The man stirred, suddenly, but the boy cut in quickly.

"But she does look thin. Look, truly—they're not feeding her right. Just look!"

"Aye," the woman chattered. "I wouldn't put it past Hynes to steal t' best part o' t' dog meat for himself. And Lassie always was a strong eater."

"She's fair thin now," the boy said.

Almost unwillingly the man and woman looked at the dog for the first time.

"My gum, she is off a bit," the woman said. Then she caught herself. "Ma goodness, I suppose I'll have to fix her a bit o' summat. She can do wi' it. But soon as she's fed, back she goes. And never another dog I'll have in my house. Never another. Cooking and nursing for 'em, and as much trouble to bring up as a bairn!"

So, grumbling and chatting as a village woman will, she moved about, warming a pan of food for the dog. The man and boy watched the collie eat. When it was done, the boy took from the mantelpiece a folded cloth and a brush, and began prettying the collie's coat. The man watched for several minutes, and then could stand it no longer.

"Here," he said.

He took the cloth and brush from the boy and began working expertly on the dog, rubbing the rich, deep coat, then brushing the snowy whiteness of the full ruff and the apron, bringing out the heavy leggings on the forelegs. He lost himself in his work, and the boy sat on the rug, watching contentedly. The woman stood it as long as she could.

"Now will ye please tak' that tyke out o' here?"

The man flared in anger.

"Well, ye wouldn't have me tak' her back looking like a mucky Monday wash, wouldta?"

He bent again, and began fluffing out the collie's petticoats.

"Joe!" the woman pleaded. "Will ye tak' her out o' here. Hynes'll be nosing round afore ye know it. And I won't have that man in my house. Wearing his hat inside, and going on like he's the duke himself—him and his leggings!"

"All right, lass."

"And this time, Joe, tak' young Joe wi' ye."

"What for?"

"Well, let's get the business done and over with. It's him that Lassie runs away for. She comes for young Joe. So if he went wi' thee, and told her to stay, happen she'd be content and not run away no more, and then we'd have a little peace and quiet in the home—though heaven knows there's not much hope o' that these days, things being like they are." The woman's voice trailed away, as if she would soon cry in weariness.

The man rose. "Come, Joe," he said. "Get thy cap."

The Duke of Rudling walked along the gravel paths of his place with his granddaughter, Philippa. Philippa was a bright and knowing young woman, allegedly the only member of the duke's family he could address in unspotted language. For it was also alleged that the duke was the most irascible, vile-tempered old man in the three Ridings of Yorkshire.

"Country going to pot!" the duke roared, stabbing at the walk with his great blackthorn stick. "When I was a young man! Hah! Women today not as pretty. Horses today not as fast. As for dogs —ye don't see dogs today like——"

Just then the duke and Philippa came round a clump of rhododendrons and saw a man, a boy and a dog.

"Ah," said the duke, in admiration. Then his brow knotted. "Damme, Carraclough! What're ye doing with my dog?"

He shouted it quite as if the others were in the next county, for it was also the opinion of the Duke of Rudling that people were not nearly so keen of hearing as they used to be when he was a young man.

"It's Lassie," Carraclough said. "She runned away again and I brought her back."

Carraclough lifted his cap, and poked the boy to do the same, not in any servile gesture, but to show that they were as well brought up as the next.

"Damme, ran away again!" the duke roared. "And I told that utter nincompoop Hynes to—where is he? Hynes! Hynes! Damme, Hynes, what're ye hiding for?"

"Coming, your lordship!" sounded a voice, far away behind the shrubberies. And soon Hynes appeared, a sharp-faced man in check coat, riding breeches, and the cloth leggings that grooms wear.

"Take this dog," roared the duke, "and pen her up! And damme, if she breaks out again, I'll—I'll——"

The duke waved his great stick threateningly, and then, without so much as a thank you or kiss the back of my hand to Joe Carraclough, he went stamping and muttering away.

"I'll pen 'er up," Hynes muttered, when the duke was gone. "And if she ever gets awye agyne, I'll——"

He made as if to grab the dog, but Joe Carraclough's hobnailed boot trod heavily on Hynes' foot.

"I brought my lad wi' me to bid her stay, so we'll pen her up this time. Eigh—sorry! I didn't see I were on thy foot. Come, Joe, lad."

They walked down the crunching gravel path, along by the neat kennel buildings. When Lassie was behind the closed door, she raced into the high wire run where she could see them as they went. She pressed close against the wire, waiting.

The boy stood close, too, his fingers through the meshes touching the dog's nose.

"Go on, lad," his father ordered. "Bid her stay!"

The boy looked around, as if for help that he did not find. He swallowed, and then spoke, low and quickly.

"Stay here, Lassie, and don't come home no more," he said. "And don't come to school for me no more. Because I don't want to see ye no more. 'Cause tha's a bad dog, and we don't love thee no more, and we don't want thee. So stay there forever and leave us be, and don't never come home no more."

Then he turned, and because it was hard to see the path plainly, he stumbled. But his father, who was holding his head very high as they walked away from Hynes, shook him savagely, and snapped roughly: "Look where tha's going!"

Then the boy trotted beside his father. He was thinking that he'd never be able to understand why grownups sometimes were so bad-tempered with you, just when you needed them most.

After that, there were days and days that passed, and the dog did not come to the school gate any more. So then it was not like old times. There were so many things that were not like old times.

The boy was thinking that as he came wearily up the path and opened the cottage door and heard his father's voice, tense with anger: ". . . walk my feet off. If tha thinks I like——"

Then they heard his opening of the door and the voice stopped and the cottage was silent.

That's how it was now, the boy thought. They stopped talking in front of you. And this, somehow, was too much for him to bear.

He closed the door, ran out into the night, and onto the moor, that great flat expanse of land where all the people of that village walked in lonesomeness when life and its troubles seemed past bearing.

A long while later, his father's voice cut through the darkness. "What's tha doing out here, Joe lad?"

"Walking."

"Aye."

They went on together, aimlessly, each following his own thoughts. And they both thought about the dog that had been sold.

"Tha maun't think we're hard on thee, Joe," the man said at last. "It's just that a chap's got to be honest. There's that to it. Sometimes, when a chap doesn't have much, he clings right hard to what he's got. And honest is honest, and there's no two ways about it.

"Why, look, Joe. Seventeen year I worked in that Clarabelle Pit till she shut down, and a good collier too. Seventeen year! And butties I've had by the dozen, and never a man of 'em can ever say that Joe Carraclough kept what wasn't his, nor spoke what wasn't true. Not a man in his Riding can ever call a Carraclough mishonest.

"And when ye've sold a man summat, and ye've taken his brass, and ye've spent it—well, then done's done. That's all. And ye've got to stand by that."

"But Lassie was——"

"Now, Joe! Ye can't alter it, ever. It's done—and happen it's for t' best. No two ways, Joe, she was getting hard to feed. Why, ye wouldn't want Lassie to be going around getting peaked and pined, like some chaps round here keep their tykes. And if ye're fond of her, then just think on it that now she's got lots to eat, and a private kennel, and a good run to herself, and living like a varritable princess, she is. Ain't that best for her?"

"We wouldn't pine her. We've always got lots to eat."

The man blew out his breath, angrily. "Eigh, Joe. nowt pleases thee. Well then, tha might as well have it. Tha'll never see Lassie no more. She run home once too often, so the duke's taken her wi' him up to his place in Scotland, and there she'll stay. So it's good-by and good luck to her, and she'll never come home no more, she won't. Now, I weren't off to tell thee, but there it is, so put it in thy pipe and smoke it, and let's never say a word about it no more —especially in front of thy mother."

The boy stumbled on in the darkness. Then the man halted.

"We ought to be getting back, lad. We left thy mother alone."

He turned the boy about, and then went on, but as if he were talking to himself.

"Tha sees, Joe, women's not like men. They have to stay home and manage best they can, and just spend the time in wishing. And when things don't go right, well, they have to take it out in talk and give a man hell. But it don't mean nowt, really, so tha shouldn't mind when thy mother talks hard.

"Ye just got to learn to be patient and let 'em talk, and just let it go up t' chimney wi' th' smoke."

Then they were quiet, until, over the rise, they saw the lights of the village. Then the boy spoke: "How far away is Scotland, feyther?"

"Nay, lad, it's a long, long road."

"But how far, feyther?"

"I don't know—but it's a longer road than thee or me'll ever walk. Now, lad. Don't fret no more, and try to be a man—and don't plague thy mother no more, wilta?"

Joe Carraclough was right. It is a long road, as they say in the North, from Yorkshire to Scotland. Much too far for a man to walk—or a boy. And though the boy often thought of it, he remembered his father's words on the moor, and he put the thought behind him.

But there is another way of looking at it; and that's the distance from Scotland to Yorkshire. And that is just as far as from Yorkshire to Scotland. A matter of about four hundred miles, it would be, from the Duke of Rudling's place far up in the Highlands, to the village of Holdersby. That would be for a man, who could go fairly straight.

To an animal, how much farther would it be? For a dog can study no maps, read no signposts, ask no directions. It could only go blindly, by instinct, knowing that it must keep on to the south, to the south. It would wander and err, quest and quarter, run into firths and lochs that would send it side-tracking and back-tracking before it could go again on its way—south.

A thousand miles, it would be, going that way—a thousand miles over strange terrain.

There would be moors to cross, and burns to swim. And then those great, long lochs that stretch almost from one side of that dour land to another would bar the way and send a dog questing a hundred miles before it could find a crossing that would allow it to go south.

And, too, there would be rivers to cross, wide rivers like the Forth and the Clyde, the Tweed and the Tyne, where one must go miles to find bridges. And the bridges would be in towns. And in the towns there would be officials—like the one in Lanarkshire. In all his life he had never let a captured dog get away—except one. That one was a gaunt, snarling collie that whirled on him right in the pound itself, and fought and twisted loose to race away down the city street—going south.

But there are also kind people, too; ones knowing and understanding in the ways of dogs. There was an old couple in Durham who found a dog lying exhausted in a ditch one night—lying there with its head to the south. They took that dog into their cottage and warmed it and fed it and nursed it. And because it seemed an understanding, wise dog, they kept it in their home, hoping it would learn to be content. But, as it grew stronger, every afternoon toward four o'clock it would go to the door and whine, and then begin pacing back and forth between the door and the window, back and forth as the animals do in their cages at the zoo.

They tried every wile and every kindness to make it bide with them, but finally, when the dog began to refuse food, the old people knew what they must do. Because they understood dogs, they opened the door one afternoon and they watched a collie go, not down the road to the right, or to the left, but straight across a field toward the south; going steadily at a trot, as if he knew it still had a long, long road to travel.

Ah, a thousand miles of tor and brae, of shire and moor, of path and road and plowland, of river and stream and burn and brook and beck, of snow and rain and fog and sun, is a long way, even for a human being. But it would seem too far—much, much too far—for any dog to travel blindly and win through.

And yet—and yet—who shall say why, when so many weeks had passed that hope against hope was dying, a boy coming out of school, out of the cloakroom that always smelled of damp wool drying, across the concrete play yard with the black, waxed slides, should turn his eyes to a spot by the school gate from force of five years of habit, and see there a dog? Not a dog, this one, that lifted glad ears above a proud, slim head with its black-and-gold mask; but a dog that lay weakly, trying to lift a head that would no longer lift, trying to wag a tail that was torn and blotched and matted with dirt and burs, and managing to do nothing much except to whine in a weak, happy, crying way as a boy on his knees threw arms about it, and hands touched it that had not touched it for many a day.

Then who shall picture the urgency of a boy, running, awkwardly, with a great dog in his arms running through the village, past the empty mill, past the Labor Exchange, where the men looked up from their deep ponderings on life and the dole? Or who shall describe the high tones of a voice—a boy's voice, calling as he runs up a path: "Mother! **Oh, mother!** Lassie's come home! Lassie's come home!"

Nor does anyone who ever owned a dog need to be told the sound a man makes as he bends over a dog that has been his for many years; nor how a woman moves quickly, preparing food— which might be the family's condensed milk stirred into warm water; nor how the jowl of a dog is lifted so that raw egg and brandy, bought with precious pence, should be spooned in; nor how bleeding pads are bandaged tenderly.

That was one day. There was another day when the woman in the cottage sighed with pleasure, for a dog lifted itself to its feet for the first time to stand over a bowl of oatmeal, putting its head down and lapping again and again while its pinched flanks quivered.

And there was another day when the boy realized that, even now, the dog was not to be his again. So the cottage rang again with protests and cries, and a woman shrilling: "Is there never to be no more peace in my house and home?" Long after he was in bed that night the boy heard the rise and fall of the woman's voice, and the steady, reiterative tone of the man's. It went on long after he was asleep.

In the morning the man spoke, not looking at the boy, saying the words as if he had long rehearsed them.

"Thy mother and me have decided upon it that Lassie shall stay here till she's better. Anyhow, nobody could nurse her better than us. But the day that t' duke comes back, then back she goes, too. For she belongs to him, and that's honest, too. Now tha has her for a while, so be content."

In childhood, "for a while" is such a great stretch of days when seen from one end. It is a terribly short time seen from the other.

The boy knew how short it was that morning as he went to school and saw a motorcar driven by a young woman. And in the car was a gray-thatched, terrible old man, who waved a cane and shouted: "Hi! Hi, there! Damme, lad! You there! Hi!"

Then it was no use running, for the car could go faster than you, and soon it was beside you and the man was saying: "Damme, Philippa, will you make this smelly thing stand still a moment? Hi, lad!"

"Yes, sir."

"You're What's-'is-Name's lad, aren't you?"

"Ma feyther's Joe Carraclough."

"I know. I know. Is he home now?"

"No, sir. He's away to Allerby. A mate spoke for him at the pit and he's gone to see if there's a chance."

"When'll he be back?"

"I don't know. I think about tea."

"Eh, yes. Well, yes. I'll drop round about fivish to see that father of yours. Something important."

It was hard to pretend to listen to lessons. There was only waiting for noon. Then the boy ran home.

"Mother! T' duke is back and he's coming to take Lassie away."

"Eigh, drat my buttons. Never no peace in this house. Is tha sure?"

"Aye. He stopped me. He said tell feyther he'll be round at five. Can't we hide her? Oh, mother."

"Nay, thy feyther——"

"Won't you beg him? Please, please. Beg feyther to——"

"Young Joe, now it's no use. So stop thy teasing! Thy feyther'll not lie. That much I'll give him. Come good, come bad, he'll not lie."

"But just this once, mother. Please beg him, just this once. Just one lie wouldn't hurt him. I'll make it up to him. I will. When I'm growed up, I'll get a job. I'll make money. I'll buy him things—and you, too. I'll buy you both anything you want if you'll only——"

For the first time in his trouble the boy became a child, and the mother, looking over, saw the tears that ran openly down his contorted face. She turned her face to the fire, and there was a pause. Then she spoke.

"Joe, tha mustn't," she said softly. "Tha must learn never to want nothing in life like that. It don't do, lad. Tha mustn't want things bad, like tha wants Lassie."

The boy shook his clenched fists in impatience.

"It ain't that, mother. Ye don't understand. Don't yer see—it ain't me that wants her. It's her that wants us! Tha's wha made her come all them miles. It's her that wants us, so terrible bad!"

The woman turned and stared. It was as if, in that moment, she were seeing this child, this boy, this son of her own, for the first time in many years. She turned her head down toward the table. It was surrender.

"Come and eat, then," she said. "I'll talk to him. I will that, all right. I feel sure he won't lie. But I'll talk to him, all right. I'll talk to Mr. Joe Carraclough. I will indeed."

At five that afternoon, the Duke of Rudling, fuming and muttering, got out of a car at a cottage gate to find a boy barring his way. This was a boy who stood, stubbornly, saying fiercely: "Away wi' thee! Thy tyke's net here!"

"Damme, Philippa, th' lad's touched," the duke said. "He is. He's touched."

Scowling and thumping his stick, the old duke advanced until the boy gave way, backing down the path out of the reach of the waving blackthorn stick.

"Thy tyke's net here," the boy protested.

"What's he saying?" the girl asked.

"Says my dog isn't here. Damme, you going deaf? I'm supposed to be deaf, and I hear him plainly enough. Now, ma lad, what tyke o' mine's net here?"

As he turned to the boy, the duke spoke in broadest Yorkshire, as he did always to the people of the cottages—a habit which the Duchess of Rudling, and many more members of the duke's family, deplored.

"Coom, coom, ma lad. Whet tyke's net here?"

"No tyke o' thine. Us hasn't got it." The words began running faster and faster as the boy backed away from the fearful old man who advanced. "No tyke could have done it. No tyke can come all them miles. It isn't Lassie. It's another one that looks like her. It isn't Lassie!"

"Why, bless ma heart and sowl," the duke puffed. "Where's thy father, ma lad?"

The door behind the boy opened, and a woman's voice spoke.

"If it's Joe Carraclough ye want, he's out in the shed—and been there shut up half the afternoon."

"What's this lad talking about—a dog of mine being here?"

"Nay," the woman snapped quickly. "He didn't say a tyke o' thine was here. He said it wasn't here."

"Well, what dog o' mine isn't here, then?"

The woman swallowed, and looked about as if for help. The duke stood, peering from under his jutting eyebrows. Her answer, truth or lie, was never spoken, for then they heard the rattle of a door opening, and a man making a pursing sound with his lips, as he will when he wants a dog to follow, and then Joe Carraclough's voice said: "This is t' only tyke us has here. Does it look like any dog that belongs to thee?"

With his mouth opening to cry one last protest, the boy turned. And his mouth stayed open. For there he saw his father, Joe Carraclough, the collie fancier, standing with a dog at his heels—a dog that sat at his left heel patiently, as any well-trained dog should do—as Lassie used to do. But this dog was not Lassie. In fact, it was ridiculous to think of it at the same moment as you thought of Lassie.

For where Lassie's skull was aristocratic and slim, this dog's head was clumsy and rough. Where Lassie's ears stood in twin-lapped symmetry, this dog had one ear draggling and the other standing up Alsatian fashion in a way to give any collie breeder the cold shivers. Where Lassie's coat was rich tawny gold, this dog's coat had ugly patches of black; and where Lassie's apron was a billowing stretch of snow-white, this dog had puddles of off-color blue-merle mixture. Besides, Lassie had four white paws, and this one had one paw white, two dirty-brown, and one almost black.

That is the dog they all looked at as Joe Carraclough stood there, having told no lie, having only asked a question. They all stood, waiting the duke's verdict.

But the duke said nothing. He only walked forward, slowly, as if he were seeing a dream. He bent beside the collie, looking with eyes that were as knowing about dogs as any Yorkshireman alive. And those eyes did not waste themselves upon twisted ears, or blotched marking, or rough head. Instead they were looking at a paw that the duke lifted, looking at the underside of the paw, staring intently at five black pads, crossed and recrossed with the scars where thorns had lacerated, and stones had torn.

For a long time the duke stared, and when he got up he did not speak in Yorkshire accents any more. He spoke as a gentleman should, and he said: "Joe Carraclough. I never owned this dog. 'Pon my soul, she's never belonged to me. Never!"

Then he turned and went stumping down the path, thumping his cane and saying: "Bless my soul. Four hundred miles! Damme, wouldn't ha' believed it. Damme—five hundred miles!"

He was at the gate when his granddaughter whispered to him fiercely.

"Of course," he cried. "Mind your own business. Exactly what I came for. Talking about dogs made me forget. Carraclough! Carraclough! What're ye hiding for?"

"I'm still here, sir."

"Ah, there you are. You working?"

"Eigh, now. Working," Joe said. That's the best he could manage.

"Yes, working, working!" The duke fumed.

"Well, now——" Joe began.

Then Mrs. Carraclough came to his rescue, as a good housewife in Yorkshire will.

"Why, Joe's got three or four things that he's been considering," she said, with proper display of pride. "But he hasn't quite said yes or no to any of them yet."

"Then say no, quick," the old man puffed. "Had to sack Hynes. Didn't know a dog from a drunken filly. Should ha' known all along no damn Londoner could handle dogs fit for Yorkshire taste. How much, Carraclough?"

"Well, now," Joe began.

"Seven pounds a week, and worth every penny," Mrs. Carraclough chipped in. "One o' them other offers may come up to eight," she lied, expertly. For there's always a certain amount of lying to be done in life, and when a woman's married to a man who has made a lifelong cult of being honest, then she's got to learn to do the lying for two.

"Five," roared the duke—who, after all, was a Yorkshireman, and couldn't help being a bit sharp about things that pertained to money.

"Six," said Mrs. Carraclough.

"Five pound ten," bargained the duke, cannily.

"Done," said Mrs. Carraclough, who would have been willing to settle for three pounds in the first place. "But, o' course, us gets the cottage too."

"All right," puffed the duke. "Five pounds ten and the cottage. Begin Monday. But—on one condition. Carraclough, you can live on my land, but I won't have that thick-skulled, screw-lugged, gay-tailed eyesore of a misshapen mongrel on my property. Now never let me see her again. You'll get rid of her?"

He waited, and Joe fumbled for words. But it was the boy who answered, happily, gaily: "Oh, no, sir. She'll be waiting at school for me most o' the time. And, anyway, in a day or so we'll have her fixed up and coped up so's ye'd never, never recognize her."

"I don't doubt that," puffed the duke, as he went to the car. "I don't doubt ye could do just exactly that."

It was a long time afterward, in the car, that the girl said: "Don't sit there like a lion on the Nelson column. And I thought you were supposed to be a hard man."

"Fiddlesticks, m'dear. I'm a ruthless realist. For five years I've sworn I'd have that dog by hook or crook, and now, egad, at last I've got her."

"Pooh! You had to buy the man before you could get his dog."

"Well, perhaps that's not the worst part of the bargain."


### The Trees and the Master

Into the woods my Master went,
Clean forspent, forspent.
Into the woods my Master came,
Forspent with love and shame.
But the olives, they were not blind to Him,
The little gray leaves were kind to Him,
The thorn tree had a mind to Him
When into the woods He came.

Out of the woods my Master went,
And He was well content.
Out of the woods my Master came,
Content with death and shame.
When death and shame would woo Him last,
From under the trees they drew Him last,
'Twas on a tree they slew Him—last
When out of the woods He came.

*Sidney Lanier*

# ON LYING AWAKE AT NIGHT

## Stewart Edward White

*For your next camping trip, you may look forward to a sleep-less night as eagerly as to fishing and hunting. That is, after you've read what Stewart Edward White has to say here. An expert woodsman, Mr. White has camped out on many trails in many countries, and written scores of distinguished pieces on outdoor life. In this one he shows you what new and vital experiences await one in the forest at night—so that hereafter even insomnia, under the right circumstances, may prove pleasant.*

ABOUT once in so often you are due to lie awake at night. Why this is so I have never been able to discover. It apparently comes from no predisposing uneasiness of indigestion, no rashness in the matter of too much tea or tobacco, no excitation of unusual incident or stimulating conversation. In fact, you turn in with the expectation of rather a good night's rest. Almost at once the little noises of the forest grow larger, blend in the hollow bigness of the first drowse; your thoughts drift idly back and forth between reality and dream; when—*snap!*—you are broad awake!

Perhaps the reservoir of your vital forces is full to the overflow of a little waste; or, perhaps, more subtly, the great Mother insists thus that you enter the temple of her larger mysteries.

For, unlike mere insomnia, lying awake at night in the woods is pleasant. The eager, nervous straining for sleep gives way to a de-licious indifference. You do not care. Your mind is cradled in an exquisite poppy-suspension of judgment and of thought. Impres-sions slip vaguely into your consciousness and as vaguely out again. Sometimes they stand stark and naked for your inspection; some-times they lose themselves in the mist of half-sleep. Always they lay soft velvet fingers on the drowsy imagination, so that in their caress-ing you feel the vaster spaces from which they have come. Peaceful-brooding your faculties receive. Hearing, sight, smell—all are preternaturally keen to whatever of sound and sight and woods perfume is abroad through the night; and yet at the same time active appreciation dozes, so these things lie on it sweet and cloying like fallen rose-leaves.

In such circumstance you will hear what the *voyageurs* call the voices of the rapids. Many people never hear them at all. They speak very soft and low and distinct beneath the steady roar and dashing, beneath even the lesser tinklings and gurglings whose quality superimposes them over the louder sounds. They are like the tear-forms swimming across the field of vision, which disappear so quickly when you concentrate your sight to look at them, and which reappear so magically when again your gaze turns vacant. In the stillness of your hazy half-consciousness they speak; when you bend your attention to listen, they are gone, and only the tumults and the tinklings remain.

But in the moments of their audibility they are very distinct. Just as often an odor will wake all a vanished memory, so these voices, by the force of a large impressionism, suggest whole scenes. Far off are the cling-clang-cling of chimes and the swell-and-fall murmur of a multitude *en fête*, so that subtly you feel the gray old town, with its walls, the crowded marketplace, the decent peasant crowd, the booths, the mellow church building with its bells, the warm, dust-moted sun. Or, in the pauses between the swish-dash-dashings of the waters, sound faint and clear voices singing intermittently, calls, distant notes of laughter, as though many canoes were working against the current—only the flotilla never gets any nearer, nor the voices louder. The *voyageurs* call these mist people the Huntsmen; and look frightened. To each is his vision, according to his experience. The nations of the earth whisper to their exiled sons through the voices of the rapids. Curiously enough, by all reports they suggest always peaceful scenes—a harvest-field, a street fair, a Sunday morning in a cathedral town, careless travelers—never the turmoils and struggles. Perhaps this is the great Mother's compensation in a harsh mode of life.

Nothing is more fantastically unreal to tell about, nothing more concretely real to experience, than this undernote of the quick water. And when you do lie awake at night, it is always making its unobtrusive appeal. Gradually its hypnotic spell works. The distant chimes ring louder and nearer as you cross the borderland of sleep. And then outside the tent some little woods noise snaps the thread. An owl hoots, a whippoorwill cries, a twig cracks beneath the cautious prowl of some night creature—at once the yellow sunlit French meadows puff away—you are staring at the blurred image of the moon spraying through the texture of your tent.

The voices of the rapids have dropped into the background, as have the dashing noises of the stream. Through the forest is a great silence, but no stillness at all. The whippoorwill swings down and up the short curve of his regular song; over and over an owl says his rapid *whoo, whoo, whoo*. These, with the ceaseless dash of the rapids, are the web on which the night traces her more delicate embroideries of the unexpected. Distant crashes, single and impressive; stealthy footsteps near at hand; the subdued scratching of claws; a faint *sniff! sniff! sniff!* of inquiry; the sudden clear tin-horn *ko-ko-ko-oh* of the little owl; the mournful, long-drawn-out cry of the loon, instinct with the spirit of loneliness; the ethereal call-note of the birds of passage high in the air; a *patter, patter, patter*, among the dead leaves, immediately stilled; and then at the last, from the thicket close at hand, the beautiful silver purity of the white-throated sparrow—the nightingale of the North—trembling with the ecstasy of beauty, as though a shimmering moonbeam had turned to sound; and all the while the blurred figure of the moon mounting to the ridge-line of your tent—these things combine subtly, until at last the great Silence of which they are a part over-arches the night and draws you forth to contemplation.

No beverage is more grateful than the cup of spring water you drink at such a time; no moment more refreshing than that in which you look about you at the darkened forest. You have cast from you with the warm blanket the drowsiness of dreams. A coolness, physical and spiritual, bathes you from head to foot. All your senses are keyed to the least vibrations. You hear the little night prowlers; you glimpse the greater. A faint, searching woods perfume of dampness greets your nostrils. And somehow, mysteriously, in a manner not to be understood, the forces of the world seem in suspense, as though a touch might crystallize infinite possibilities into infinite power and motion. But the touch lacks. The forces hover on the edge of action, unheeding the little noises. In all humbleness and awe, you are a dweller of the Silent Places.

At such a time you will meet with adventures. One night we put fourteen inquisitive porcupines out of camp. Near McGregor's Bay I discovered in the large grass park of my camp-site nine deer, cropping the herbage like so many beautiful ghosts. A friend tells me of a fawn that every night used to sleep outside his tent and within a foot of his head, probably by way of protection against wolves. Its mother had in all likelihood been killed. The instant my friend moved toward the tent opening the little creature would disappear, and it was always gone by earliest daylight. Nocturnal bears in search of pork are not uncommon. But even though your interest meets nothing but the bats and the woods shadows and the stars, that few moments of the sleeping world forces is a psychical experience to be gained in no other way. You cannot know the night by sitting up; she will sit up with you. Only by coming into her presence from the borders of sleep can you meet her face to face in her intimate mood.

The night wind from the river, or from the open spaces of the wilds, chills you after a time. You begin to think of your blankets. In a few moments you roll yourself in their soft wool. Instantly it is morning.

And, strange to say, you have not to pay by going through the day unrefreshed. You may feel like turning in at eight instead of nine, and you may fall asleep with unusual promptitude, but your journey will begin clear-headedly, proceed springily, and end with much in reserve. No languor, no dull headache, no exhaustion, follows your experience. For this once your two hours of sleep have been as effective as nine.

## The World is Too Much With Us

THE World is too much with us; late and soon,
Getting and spending, we lay waste our powers;
Little we see in Nature that is ours;
We have given our hearts away, a sordid boon!
This Sea that bares her bosom to the moon,
The winds that will be howling at all hours
And are up-gather'd now like sleeping flowers,
For this, for every thing, we are out of tune;
It moves us not.—Great God! I'd rather be
A Pagan suckled in a creed outworn,—
So might I, standing on this pleasant lea,
Have glimpses that would make me less forlorn;
Have sight of Proteus rising from the sea;
Or hear old Triton blow his wreathèd horn.

*William Wordsworth*

# WEIRWOOD MARSH

## Donald Culross Peattie and
## Louise Redfield Peattie

*Everyone has seen a small marsh like the one in this story, and may have noted the dragonflies skimming over it, a turtle sunning himself on a log, a frog diving. But the Peatties, modern masters of nature writing, prove in this selection from* Downwind *that we have never really seen a marsh or known the struggle for life of the myriads of creatures that live in and under and around its placid waters. Here are hunger and fear, love and happiness, in a drama dominated by Stalk, the great blue heron.*

WEIRWOOD marsh is the larch wood's secret. The larch grove is the secret of the dune wilderness; the dunes themselves lie folded between the ice-green waters of the great lake, and the prairies that stretch westward to the sunset. Lost in the heart of that midland country, that lies so ample and so fertile, so candid to the sun, Weirwood marsh has kept its own laws, a tiny, timeless empire that civilization passed by, upon its destroying way, having had no eyes to see it. Nor have there been many eyes that have looked on the lord of that jewel of wilderness—the great blue heron, Stalk. The rare hunter, breaking through the manna grass that rings the marsh's rim, has learned no more of him than the harsh mockery of his cry as he winged to cover in the gloom of the aisles of larch. But he has known, has Stalk, as much of love and death, of fear and fight and hate and joy, as come to most of us in the man-made walks of the world.

There was an early Spring daybreak, lauded in endless canticle by Rana, the great wattled bullfrog, when the little fairy shrimp, new hatched from her egg upon the bottom of the marsh, swam upwards, very slowly. That netherworld, that emerald hell at the oozy bottom of the pond, was a vast breeding ground, and fighting ground and burial ground, where fear pulsed, and the swift and terrible, in miniature, hunted the even lesser meek and helpless. But overhead Spring had come with banners; the wind dappling the shining waters told it; the laughter of the alder catkins, shaking out gold tresses, acknowledged it; the tenderest green in the young larch leaves proclaimed it; and Konkeree, the red-winged blackbird—an unfaithful but enchanting lover—sang it out to Kinkeree, his little mistress in the reeds, over and over.

*"Konkeree-ee-ee!"* he boasted, the first notes like the gurgle of happy water, the last shaken with a rapture he could not contain.

And the fairy shrimp, swimming upon her back, a tiny ripple of translucent rainbow beauty, was answering the seduction of the warm bright waters overhead. Up from the dark sludge of the bottom she rose, from the shards of last year's battles, the seeds and eggs of last year's matings, and as she cleared her moorings where the thin tubifex worms were poised for retreat back into the chimneys of their mud houses, she dodged the shadow of a submarine destroyer cruising about in search of prey—the tigerish nymph of a dragonfly. Up from among the caddis-worms in the muck, centaur-like with their dragging cases hampering half their bodies, she floated, the swimming rows of her delicate legs an undulant shimmer in those dimly lit depths, and suddenly with a convulsive dart she slipped from the jaws of death. The danger that was to her monstrous would not have been noticed in the bill of the swamp's old bittern—a transparent soundless creature the color of water, Leptodora the phantom terror of the deeps. Waving incredibly feathery antennæ, it prowled the jungles of the water-weeds, to overtake and overpower the swiftest of the lowly herds, suck out their softness and discard the shell. Up through the brightening levels rose the fairy shrimp, through drifts of algæ—the green pastures of the most minute, where hid the tiny hydra sponges, and the tidy black snails for whom the sora rails were ravenous—passing through a meteor swarm of gleaming diatoms, plants that seemed sculptured out of crystal, and through a meadow of desmids, bits of exquisite green lace. Dodging an ebony diving beetle encased in a shining air bubble—a silver messenger of death—she reached the top, where the little water-fleas clung, upside down, to the tense surface film, or let themselves down from it, like microscopic spiders, on invisible threads. And there for a bright April hour the fairy shrimp paddled in what for her was ecstasy. Until, by the luck of the marsh, she drifted past the bulging eyes of Rana.

The pæan to the happy hour ceased a moment, and the fairy shrimp was gone.

Lucky for Rana that he had leapt from his choir stall amid the ooze, for Stalk on his hunting was in that moment passing his way, and the bullfrog's song escaped eternal silence by no more than a split second of the lazy time that held the larch-ringed water world. For the life of the marsh was like a great pyramid, whereof the broad base, with its untold billion lives, moved in darkness, a spawning lowly race of slaves on which the hunters of the upper waters fed, to be, in turn, the food of the wild marsh birds that screamed across the surface—the belted kingfisher Rip, that eccentric recluse Ponk the bittern, and Stalk the heron, king of all.

For the marsh knew nothing of pity. Terror it knew, and mother love and mating rapture, and sheer ecstasy, when the dragonflies in intolerable beauty poised over the surface, shimmering on wings of gossamer, tense copper-green and turquoise-blue bodies quivering like the noon heat on the burnished water. Hunger was the driving force of its life, the joy of hunting was a ferocious lust from its dark bottoms to its reedy tops. And it knew cold murder, too.

For Lotor, the old raccoon, the bandit of Weirwood marsh, was more than a hunter. He was a killer born, who slew not merely that he might eat, but because cunning and stealth and the thirst for blood were in his heart. A highwayman was Lotor, and he looked it, with his marking as of a black mask stretched across his bright, malignant eyes. Beneath the mask were elegant white whiskers, but the cruel lower jaw was hidden, when he faced you, and only the deceptive dog-like nose was plainly visible, and his white brows. Under that low skull was room enough for craft and stratagem, for greed and ruthlessness, and above his skull were raised the two small ears—small, but alertly pricked, tingling with the sounds of the marsh and the forest. Lotor heard everything, and there was nothing he forgot.

That faint sound, now, that rippled across the April silences, was Fang the old muskrat, swimming for his hole. Lotor flattened himself upon the high larch bough that held him, his gray fur fading into the shade-mottled bark, and listened. That rainy splash was Chat, the red squirrel, alighting on a branch that shadowed the farther shore; the drilling of Trip the woodpecker half a mile deeper in the dune glooms beat on his sensitive eardrum like a tiny hammer. Scornfully Lotor listened to the wheezy gabble, the eternal sardonic talk of Clack the grackle and his friends, slandering their fellows in a sandy clearing of the wood. For all these sounds he cared nothing; feigning a sleepy torpor he hunted down, with sharp cocked ears, the voice of Rana chanting in the wet grasses where the marsh in its high tide of early Spring was brimming over.

Yes, Rana was there, somewhere in the grasses, piping his deep chorus in sweet, sententious iteration, proclaiming, in the feckless manner of the frog tribe, his position to all the world. Disdain in his dainty, picking gait, greed in his eyes, Lotor descended from the tree and circled the cat-tail crowded bay of the waters.

But though he trod with the stealth of a cat, his going was made known to all the marsh. A dozen sentinels sent up warning, and the soft music of the marsh, the murmur of waters and the hum of flies, was jangled into discord by the anger of its dwellers. Konkeree lifted above the reeds, brilliant epaulettes fluttering, his love song turned to scolding; Chat in his tree stamped and gibbered at the raccoon's passing; and where, in oozy solitude ringed round with whispering rushes, Ponk the bittern, the marsh's meditative eremite, had stood hunched motionless for an hour past, a wild cry broke. *"Haink! Haink!"* cried the bittern, lifting from the reeds and the swirling waters—a call half musical, half the metallic rattle of a chain falling back upon its own coils. A skinny crow on sentinel duty telegraphed warning in his own code, and a black storm of his fellows swept into the wood with an uproar of exaggerated indignation.

And then it was that Stalk, the giant heron, rose slowly out of the shallows where he had been strolling, and took himself away with a leisurely flapping, windy and serene. He had little fear of Lotor, but he loathed disturbance, and at the marsh's uproar he left it, like one who leaves a noisy room. In the midst of the clamor, the croaks and cawings and the shrill bird rage, Rana had quietly plopped into the deep water, in one exultant leap from his strong hind legs, and Lotor's fangs snapped together emptily. It was too late in the morning to be hunting, anyway. A fellow couldn't see in all this blare of daylight. Night! Ah, that was the time for him— velvet, delicious night, cloak of his raids and lusts and hungers, friend of his banditries and murders. Night, his satanic ally.

And blinking in the growing brightness, Lotor picked his clumsy way along the highroads of the air—his path from bough to bough, from tree to tree. He walked there with the cautious

manner of one not native to arboreal life, but as a stranger who has
acquired some familiarity with its ways, a highwayman born of
the lowlands, but choosing the mountain trails for his depredations.
His home, a hollow tree in the larch glooms, was half a mile away,
but Lotor reached it without ever once descending to the ground,
so close together stood the larches and the swamp maples, so intricate their branches, and so well did he know his way. There in
that black abode at last he laid him down to sleep, Lotor the night
prowler, the killer of the marsh.

But for Stalk the heron, who glided down again to the water
once Lotor's ringed brush had vanished among the branches, the
day had just begun. Slowly and carefully he began to stalk his
prey, bending jerky knee joints, wading on into deeper water, with
his long neck pulled backward into his deep shoulders and his black
eyes sharply scanning the surface. Suddenly, with the speed of a
snake, the coiled neck thrust, and the long beak brought up a struggling crayfish that vanished in a gulp.

All around the shallows, where the pale gold of water crowfoot
was in bloom in flowery lanes adown the surface of the water,
stalked the giant heron, a figure of lonely dignity, serene, it seemed,
untroubled as the quiet waters under the sunrise sky. But there was
a surmise trembling through him, a hunger never to be quenched
by the fattest fishing, growing as the rosy light grew in the eastern
deeps beyond the larch tops. He lifted his black tipped wings in
a gesture that sketched magnificent yearning against the sheeny
waters, and let them settle again. The rose brightened to gold, shaking out banners of streaming light across the bosom of Weirwood.
Clearer and clearer grew the call that throbbed through the great
blue heron. A presence was abroad, he knew unerringly, imperative and irresistible.

Profound, unhurried, he stepped down the water lanes, setting
the yellow bloom a-quiver at his coming, turning his high-held
crested head this way and that with quick and graceful jerks. So
he rounded a low shoulder of the land, set with a crown of alders.
There Hyla the little tree toad piped sweet warning. And there he
saw her—Ardea of the fair white crest, loveliest young heron of
the far-off river banks, standing knee-deep in the water, looking
at him. Unthinking, innocently seductive, she waited, exquisite in
her nuptial dress of pale blue, with chestnut on her thighs, with
plumes of pearly gray trailing from her breast and falling over

folded wings. She waited, and he gazed, his black eyes fixed, glittering with steadily rising light.

This for Ardea was the first love season; daughter that she was of freedom she stood all undismayed and candid among the virgin greenery of the shallows, while Stalk approached. His great white crest bordered with black, from which extended the two long trailing black feathers, topped the water by as much as four feet; he wore his marvelous breast plumes as a knight wears his high orders. As he stepped toward Ardea, his gait changed from the haughty jerk of his hunting step to a strange, beautiful prancing—the love dance of his people.

The woman-bird stood watching, critical, coy, her silence and immobility inscrutable to her suitor. And even as Stalk circled round her, he was disturbed by the rush of wings, and two other male herons, with self-conscious flappings, alighted beside him. Another came, and another, each newcomer edging away from his rivals till they accepted him guardedly, until seven made up the company of Ardea's lovers. Then, in her sight, they began their dance, seven eccentric silhouettes. Lifting and closing their mighty pinions, they circled round and round, sometimes about each other, as if feinting at hostility, sometimes all in a wide circle, making common cause of their courtship.

Very softly Ardea spoke, as one who calls the changes in a square dance, and as if by magic a tremor ran through the company and they fell to their places, the ceremonial steps forgotten. Cool, beautiful Ardea, aloof from them, unattained, unattainable by all save one of that rivalry—her voice and presence stirred them, shook their fraternity. Each haughty male opened his beak like a gulf, defying his rival. Wings lifted with a storm; the foes rushed at each other, ruffling feathers, thrusting rapier bills, to meet a swordsman's skill in parrying thrust. One by one, driven off, the young males withdrew, and there was left at last only Stalk and a majestic senior who stood a full inch taller, a wary old creature with more than mimic hatred in his eye.

Up and down on the brown sands, into the shallow water, through the shaken greenery of the bulrushes, driving up Konkeree and Kinkeree in fury, fought the two, until the old bird, pouncing, brought Stalk down to the water in a mass of struggling feathers. And then Stalk thrust, a blow too swift to parry, and the old bird, with a harsh scream of pain, lifted himself on tattered wings away.

No doubt, after the manner of his kind, he bore his wound off to the reeds, to nurse it sulkily.

But Stalk, shaking exultant pinions, uttered his cry of victory, and Ardea rose to meet him. Then the larch boughs closed about them, and there was silence on the sands and shallows where the dance had been. The sun rode high, sank low, but looking down it could not find the wild enchanted lovers deep in the recesses of the forest. At twilight Hyla sang the hymeneal.

The nest, a wide platform of strong sticks, soft lined with the finest twigs, was built in secret. Very fierce and furtive they were then, Ardea and her lover, swift to screen themselves away from all intrusion, in the lost architraves of the larches.

The four eggs of lichen green were laid, and cherished by Ardea, and she and Stalk kept guard above them in turn. And when a moon had waxed and waned, and waxed again, the eternal miracle was reënacted, and out from the fragile shells struggled the four tiny herons—pathetic, naked babes, four mouths to feed, uproarious little hungers whose high piping voices smote the eardrums of the killer, far away.

Chat the squirrel tried to warn the heron parents, scolding and screaming, for he had had a visit lately from the black-masked hunter, and his home was ruin now. But it was not given to Stalk and Ardea to understand the language of the red squirrel. They took it for ill temper.

One night, when Stalk had winged to the river, a sudden higher shriek from the clamoring nest brought Ardea back from the waters where she fished for the pleading mouths. She swooped down, a shining messenger of vengeance, on the stealthy shadow of Lotor seizing two fat squabs in his ravening jaws. Those were enough to glut even his appetite, but at the sight of Ardea the twin flames of lust and hatred flared red in his eyes, and he turned on the mother heron in sheer malice.

They met in a soft shock of claws and feathers, sword bill and fangs, and round and round the nest, over the bleating chicks, dragged to the edge and back again, they fought. And then the cruel teeth found the slender neck; there was an impotent beating of pinions, then silence. Lotor kicked her from the nest, and the four chicks, and then, descending, dragged them to the waters to wash them over and over. The little ones he picked quite clean. But he only sucked at Ardea's throat, and left her.

Left her, a heap of lifeless feathers, a welter of her own bright life blood darkening the ripples, for Stalk to find on his return. Screaming, he rose to search the home of his delight, and found there desolation. In agonized longing he flew off, through the aisles of the larches, hunting all night for a vanished sprite that would not answer him again.

By day he moped in the rushes or dozed in the oozy circles and dreamed of her, the thin film of sorrow dropped over his eyeballs. The days wore on and on. Full Summer had come in, and the long-billed marsh wren twittered gladness from the cat-tails. Ponk the old bittern, whom the shrewd country tongue calls the stake-driver, proclaimed from the marsh's inner silences an "All's well!" for the water-folk. "*Pump-er-LUNK!*" he cried in the drowsy sunshine, dull sucking thunder in the syllables. "All's well! *Pump-er-LUNK!*"

But the march of menace was on the way; it came, out of the sunburnt west, treading on dusty feet. And it was Drought.

June had passed, with only a few drops spattered from a great cumulus castle-cloud. July came in, blown on the breath of the southwest wind, the hot breath of the superheated prairie lands that stretched away and away, there beyond dunes and forest. Utterly empty was the sky; ringing, intolerable heat beat down on the earth from that blue dome where the sun rode. The grass grew so dry that even Lotor, stalking the meadow shrews, made crackling as he went; all day the crickets and the cicadas raised a sizzling chorus, and by night the katydids, rejoicing now in their thin green blood, were stridulent among the trees.

Bit by bit the waters of the marsh went down, and down, and down, and Snap, the old giant turtle, could bask upon a white rock that had not felt the sun for fifteen summers. The alder roots lay drained of water, and put forth naked pleading fingers. The very cat-tails felt the baking air about their rootstocks, and the algæ in the pond, multiplying madly before disaster should find them, grew, and grew, until they became a scummy sargasso, rolling all up the pond in the north wind and down it again in the south wind, making the waters a gaseous fen.

And then the algæ too were gone, and the shallower bottoms stood quite naked now, with the stonewort rotting in chalky webs and the water crowfoot and duckweed stranded in windrows, dying, yielding up their harvest of black snails.

It was Teeter-tip, the little sandpiper, who came at that, with his dapper brothers and their fat wives, and Stalk, standing disconsolate in the hot, foul water, philosophizing on one leg, beheld them with disgust. Omens of drought were they, as surely as the early yellowing of the hickory leaves was its messenger, as surely as the billows of noisome algal slime had foretold it. They came to Weirwood only when the lesser haunts that were home to them had dried to sun-baked desolation.

All around the marsh their little cries rang out, as they wobbled on their toes, flipped their tails and bobbed their heads in search of the black snails. "*Kling, klink! Klink! Kling!*" The sound was like the striking of the thinnest silver anvils, all up and down the muddy shoals. "*Kling! Klink!*"—they tossed it back and forth, till the note grew piercing on the ears, intolerable, and Stalk flapped windy wings and rushed at a knot of them. But they only fluttered feebly up, as if it pained them to fly, and lit again daintily, just out of reach.

"*Kling, klink!*" They beat it out in derision, all day and all the days long.

Rip the kingfisher, brazen with hunger, hawked up and down the water, descending in an airy glide, rattling his war-whoop, to dive, and find nothing. The crayfish were almost gone now, and Rip gave it up at last and departed utterly one burnished, parching day. Stalk watched him go and, blinking, knew another ill omen.

Whole muddy continents, low-lying, spotted the pond now; the water was shrunk to a series of brown, hot pools, where Ponk the bittern still hunted, bitterly, ceaselessly. One could hardly see him at his waddling business among the reeds, so perfectly his stripes of brown and white merged with the shadows of the stems and leaves, the mud and dark water. But he drove unearthly stakes in the woods no more. And his brown mate, frantic between the dying marsh and dying babies, stole on timid toes along her secret pathway through the bulrushes, waiting long, long minutes between little runs, listening for the rustle of a watersnake, or—more fearful dread—the football of Lotor.

Closer and closer together huddled the citizens of the marsh, as the waters went down. Under the meager waters the hunted burrowed in the last sludge at the bottom, only to be caught and brought up, struggling and pleading, to disappear down the cavern of some ravenous gullet.

Then the frog-fruit sprang up upon the muddy, baking bottoms, a thin, penurious weed of evil, scrawling a rune of woe across the cracks and hummocks. And all in and out of the frog-fruit barrens the tracks of Lotor ran, little slim tracks of malice, almost like a child's dainty footprint, with wide toes and narrow heel. For Lotor came down, undaunted, ravening still, under the full blood-red moon, to wash his nightly kill in the waning waters, to cleanse it over and over, like a murderer that would lave away the stains of his misdeed.

Gray clouds came up and hung heavy over the earth, holding the heat down like a blanket. Then they rolled away again, having yielded no relief.

"Rain, rain!" piped Hyla the little green tree toad.

"Water, deep, deep water! Water to steep in, to sleep in, water to keep, to keep, to keep!" echoed Rana.

"*Kling, klink!*" peeped the little sandpipers. "Just think! Not a drop to drink! *Kling, klink!*" They drummed it up and down the baking marl. "*Kling, klink!*" And Lotor, dozing by day in a crow's nest, heard them, and licked his whiskers darkly in his half-sleep.

Then, at a coppery sundown, Stalk was drawn in desperation of hunger from the drought-scourged solitudes of his beloved marsh, to hunt farther afield. Where in the richer fields beyond the sand hills the corn rows glittered and whispered endlessly was food enough for even this famine time—unwary little meadow mice, the less spry of a multitude of grasshoppers, and shrews in their runways among the roots. Up winged Stalk from the brackish pools of Weirwood, his long legs trailing, his strong stroke lifting him over the larch tops, over the dune crests, away to the fields of the white farm that drowsed down the road a half mile beyond them.

The corn was in the milk now. And its sweetness had seduced a glutton tooth to robbery. All up and down the rows the tender young ears had been stripped, and the husks hung tattered among the bright bannerets of leafage. All up and down those moonlit lanes last night Lotor had run thieving, and the night before, and the night before that. The man at the white farm knew it, and knew—or thought he knew—how best to deal with an old villain of a corn-stealing raccoon.

But Lotor of the bright eyes, Lotor of the satanic wisdom, had only bared his pointed little teeth at the steel trap hidden under the hummocks, and had gone away again. Up and down the corn rows he had frolicked, with the harsh leaves clashing and kissing all about him, undeluded, free as the warm breath of the August night.

And now came Stalk, whose lonely meditation in the marshes had brought him no such guile as Lotor had learned from his raids into the man-made world. He settled with a heavy rush of great wings and picked his way delicately down the rows that topped even his proud crest. Down and down the row, stepping with incredibly angular bends of the knee joints, stepping disdainfully, unsuspectingly. With a click the trap sprang, and Stalk was a screaming struggle of slaty feathers, one leg clutched pitilessly to the perilous earth.

They found him there, the men from the white farm, and though this was not the harvest they had sowed to reap, they carried the great heron home, trussed in numbing bonds, to the chicken yard, planning to sell his plumes for the coin or two they might bring.

Here the lord of Weirwood waters was loosed among the fat rabble. He had to endure the bragging of the cock, who had so far forgotten his ancient ancestry, winging in glorious native freedom through the glooms of Java, as to find gusto in the petty supremacy of being a domestic tyrant. He was snubbed by ducks whose water world was nothing wilder than the muddy puddles of the yard. The turkey every so often stretched his wattled neck to gobble insult, and strutted away, preening his feathers.

Even the sky was barred away from Stalk's hungry pinions by a mesh of wires. This was an ungodly spot, where the fetid dog-fennel and squat purslane ran in unhealthy riot over the poultry-scratched dust. This was an ignominy his wild heart could not brook—this was prison, degradation, terror. For hours Stalk flung himself violently about, against this wire wall and that, while the hens fled from him, cackling and frantic. Then when twilight had covered all and the chickens had subsided to muttering sleep on their roosts, he calmed down and found the tin basin that held the poultry water, and stood in it on one leg, miserable and despairing.

Dark fell. The moon was hidden in a wool of clouds, and the air was stifling. In the hot pulses of the night sounds came to him with disturbing keenness—the baying of restless dogs, the distant rattle of slow wheels, and, lifting even his prisoned heart, the dull grumble, very far away, of thunder. He could smell rain in the air. Somewhere, miles to the west, the rain was falling already. The sloughs were filling up with it there; the rivers would be swollen with it. Beautiful, wet, new water, running and gurgling in the ditches. Wonderful, trickling, talking water. Water to drink and wade in; water to slip between the toes and lap liquidly around the knees.

There was a soft, stealthy fumbling at the door of the chicken yard, the faintest dry creak of the crazy boards as they swung open. The thinnest of rank, wicked odors.

And then—a screech of terror from the roosts, a wild squawking and fluttering, and feathers flying. In that instant, when a lurid flash of the first lightning lit the sultry air, Stalk saw that the door of the yard stood open. He half flew, half scrambled under the low wires to the gate of liberty. The next instant he collided with Lotor, making for the gate with a struggling, hapless bantam in his mouth. Lotor the hated, the elusive, Lotor who mocked revenge with sly evasions. Stalk struck, once, with the hammer blow of his bill. In the darkness he heard the flap of the bantam's feathers as the bird, released from deadly jaws, fled for the open. In the next instant the raccoon's body was flung against him, and there in the hot darkness, around and around the yard, the two marsh-dwellers fought and struggled. Hairy legs were around Stalk's body; the breath of the enemy was on his throat. And then the light of another bolt showed him the yellow gleam of the marauder's eye. He needed but that. The rapier beak struck home. The fanged jaws relaxed, and he was free.

There was a crash of thunder, and one stifling second when the whole world held its breath. Then from the high night sky Stalk let fall three harsh and eerie cries, three notes of triumph that drifted down slowly like feathers from his homing wing. With a spatter and a rush, with a thunder, the cloud-burst opened, and coolness, with healing in its breath, filled all the night. The Drought was broken.

# HOW THE MOUNTAIN WAS CLAD

## Björnstjerne Björnson

*Björnson (1832–1910) is considered the father of modern Norwegian literature. The son of a parson of farmer stock, he was born high in the mountains of eastern Norway. Very early in life he decided that the hills and valleys, the fjords and rivers of Norway, should be the strength of her literature. A journalist, orator, playwright, poet, and novelist, in every field he achieved great success, receiving the Nobel Prize for Literature in 1903. Here he relates an old tale of his native land.*

THERE was a deep gorge between two mountains. Through this gorge a large, full stream flowed heavily over a rough and stony bottom. Both sides were high and steep, and so one side was bare; but close to its foot, and so near the stream that the latter sprinkled it with moisture every spring and autumn, stood a group of fresh-looking trees, gazing upward and onward, yet unable to advance this way or that.

"What if we should clothe the mountain?" said the juniper one day to the foreign oak, to which it stood nearer than all the others. The oak looked down to find out who it was that spoke, and then it looked up again without deigning a reply. The river rushed along so violently that it worked itself into a white foam; the north wind had forced its way through the gorge and shrieked in the clefts of the rocks; the naked mountain, with its great weight, hung heavily over and felt cold. "What if we should clothe the mountain?" said the juniper to the fir on the other side. "If anybody is to do it, I suppose it must be we," said the fir, taking hold of its beard and glancing toward the birch. "What do you think?" But the birch peered cautiously up at the mountain, which hung over it so threateningly that it seemed as if it could scarcely breathe. "Let us clothe it, in God's name!" said the birch. And so, though there were but

these three, they undertook to clothe the mountain. The juniper
went first.

When they had gone a little way, they met the heather. The
juniper seemed as though about to go past it. "Nay, take the heather
along," said the fir. And the heather joined them. Soon it began to
glide on before the juniper. "Catch hold of me," said the heather.
The juniper did so, and where there was only a wee crevice, the
heather thrust in a finger, and where it first had placed a finger,
the juniper took hold with its whole hand. They crawled and
crept along, the fir laboring on behind, the birch also. "This is well
worth doing," said the birch.

But the mountain began to ponder on what manner of insignificant objects these might be that were clambering up over it.
And after it had been considering the matter a few hundred years,
it sent a little brook down to inquire. It was yet in the time of the
spring freshets, and the brook stole on until it reached the heather.
"Dear, dear heather, cannot you let me pass? I am so small." The
heather was very busy; only raised itself a little and pressed onward. In, under, and onward went the brook. "Dear, dear juniper,
cannot you let me pass? I am so small." The juniper looked sharply
at it; but if the heather had let it pass, why, in all reason, it must do
so too. Under it and onward went the brook; and now came to the
spot where the fir stood puffing on the hill-side. "Dear, dear fir,
cannot you let me pass? I am really so small," said the brook,—and
it kissed the fir's feet and made itself so very sweet. The fir became
bashful at this, and let it pass. But the birch raised itself before the
brook asked it. "Hi, hi, hi!" said the brook, and grew. "Ha, ha, ha!"
said the brook, and grew. "Ho, ho, ho!" said the brook, and flung
the heather and the juniper and the fir and the birch flat on their
faces and backs, up and down these great hills. The mountain sat
up for many hundred years musing on whether it had not smiled
a little that day.

It was plain enough: the mountain did not want to be clad. The
heather fretted over this until it grew green again, and then it
started forward. "Fresh courage!" said the heather.

The juniper had half raised itself to look at the heather, and
continued to keep this position, until at length it stood upright. It
scratched its head and set forth again, taking such a vigorous foothold that it seemed as though the mountain must feel it. "If you
will not have me, then I will have you." The fir crooked its toes
a little to find out whether they were whole, then lifted one foot,

found it whole, then the other, which proved also to be whole, then both of them. It first investigated the ground it had been over, next where it had been lying, and finally where it should go. After this it began to wend its way slowly along, and acted just as though it had never fallen. The birch had become most wretchedly soiled, but now rose up and made itself tidy. Then they sped onward, faster and faster, upward and on either side, in sunshine and in rain. "What in the world can this be?" said the mountain, all glittering with dew, as the summer sun shone down on it. The birds sang, the wood-mouse piped, the hare hopped along, and the ermine hid itself and screamed.

Then the day came when the heather could peep with one eye over the edge of the mountain. "Oh, dear, oh dear, oh dear!" said the heather, and away it went. "Dear me! what is it the heather sees?" said the juniper, and moved on until it could peer up. "Oh dear, oh dear!" it shrieked, and was gone. "What is the matter with the juniper to-day?" said the fir, and took long strides onward in the heat of the sun. Soon it could raise itself on its toes and peep up. "Oh dear!" Branches and needles stood on end in wonderment. It worked its way forward, came up, and was gone. "What is it all the others see, and not I?" said the birch; and lifting well its skirts, it tripped after. It stretched its whole head up at once. "Oh,—oh!—is not here a great forest of fir and heather, of juniper and birch, standing upon the table-land waiting for us?" said the birch; and its leaves quivered in the sunshine so that the dew trembled. "Ay, this is what it is to reach the goal!" said the juniper.


### Who Has Seen the Wind?

WHO has seen the wind?
　　Neither I nor you:
But when the leaves hang trembling,
　The wind is passing thro'.

Who has seen the wind?
　Neither you nor I:
But when the trees bow down their heads,
　The wind is passing by.

*Christina Rossetti*

# THE CAT

## Mary E. Wilkins Freeman

*When a popular writer of novels and stories for the women's magazines turns her hand to an animal story, one is prepared to be skeptical of the result. But so dramatically has Mrs. Freeman (1852–1930), one of the most widely read authors of her time, portrayed a cat—and not a city cat, either, but one living alone in a shack in the mountains—that this is one of the best animal tales ever written.*

THE snow was falling, and the Cat's fur was stiffly pointed with it, but he was imperturbable. He sat crouched, ready for the death-spring, as he had sat for hours. It was night—but that made no difference—all times were as one to the Cat when he was in wait for prey. Then, too, he was under no constraint of human will, for he was living alone that winter. Nowhere in the world was any voice calling him; on no hearth was there a waiting dish. He was quite free except for his own desires, which tyrannized over him when unsatisfied as now.

The Cat was very hungry—almost famished, in fact. For days the weather had been very bitter, and all the feebler wild things which were his prey by inheritance, the born serfs to his family, had kept, for the most part, in their burrows and nests, and the Cat's long hunt had availed him nothing. But he waited with the inconceivable patience and persistency of his race; besides, he was certain. The Cat was a creature of absolute convictions, and his faith in his deductions never wavered.

The Rabbit had gone in there between those low-hung pine boughs. Now her little doorway had before it a shaggy curtain of snow, but in there she was. The Cat had seen her enter, so like a swift grey shadow that even his sharp and practiced eyes had glanced back for the substance following, and then she was gone. So he sat down and waited; and he waited still in the white night,

[39]

listening angrily to the north wind starting in the upper heights of the mountains with distant screams, then swelling into an awful crescendo of rage, and swooping down with furious white wings of snow like a flock of fierce eagles into the valleys and ravines.

The Cat was on the side of a mountain, on a wooded terrace. Above him a few feet away towered the rock ascent as steep as the wall of a cathedral. The Cat had never climbed it—trees were the ladders to his heights of life. He had often looked with wonder at the rock, and miauled bitterly and resentfully as man does in the face of a forbidding Providence. At his left was the sheer precipice. Behind him, with a short stretch of woody growth between, was the frozen perpendicular wall of a mountain stream. Before him was the way to his home. When the Rabbit came out she was trapped; her little cloven feet could not scale such unbroken steeps. So that Cat waited.

The place in which he was, looked like a maelstrom of the wood. The tangle of trees and bushes clinging to the mountainside with a stern clutch of roots, the prostrate trunks and branches, the vines embracing everything with strong knots and coils of growth, had a curious effect, as of things which had whirled for ages in a current of raging water, only it was not water, but wind, which had disposed everything in circling lines of yielding to its fiercest points of onset.

And now over all this whirl of wood and rock and dead trunks and branches and vines descended the snow. It blew down like smoke over the rock-crest above; it stood in a gyrating column like some death-wraith of nature, on the level, then it broke over the edge of the precipice; and the Cat cowered before the fierce backward set of it. It was as if ice needles pricked his skin through his beautiful thick fur, but he never faltered and never once cried. He had nothing to gain from crying, and everything to lose; the Rabbit would hear him cry, and know he was waiting.

It grew darker and darker, with a strange white smother, instead of the natural blackness of night. It was a night of storm and death superadded to the night of nature. The mountains were all hidden, wrapped about, overawed, and tumultuously overborne by it; but in the midst of it waited, quite unconquered, this little, unswerving, living patience and power under a little coat of grey fur.

A fiercer blast swept over the rock, spun on one mighty foot of whirlwind athwart the level, then was over the precipice.

Then the Cat saw two eyes luminous with terror, frantic with the impulse of flight; he saw a little, quivering, dilating nose, he saw two pointing ears, and he kept still, with every one of his fine nerves and muscles strained like wires. Then the Rabbit was out— there was one long line of incarnate flight and terror—and the Cat had her.

Then the Cat went home, trailing his prey through the snow.

The Cat lived in the house which his master had built, as rudely as a child's block-house, but stanchly enough. The snow was heavy on the low slant of its roof, but it would not settle under it. The two windows and the door were made fast, but the Cat knew a way in. Up a pine-tree behind the house he scuttled, though it was hard work with his heavy Rabbit, and was in his little window under the eaves, then down through the trap to the room below, and on his master's bed with a spring and a great cry of triumph, Rabbit and all. But his master was not there; he had been gone since early fall, and it was now February. He would not return until spring, for he was an old man, and the cruel cold of the mountains clutched at his vitals like a Panther, and he had gone to the village to winter. The Cat had known for a long time that his master was gone, but his reasoning was always sequential and circuitous; always for him what had been would be; and the more easily for marvellous waiting powers, so he always came home expecting to find his master.

When he saw that he was still gone, he dragged the Rabbit off the rude couch which was the bed to the floor, put one little paw on the carcass to keep it steady, and began gnawing with head to one side to bring his strongest teeth to bear.

It was darker in the house than it had been in the wood, and the cold was as deadly, though not so fierce. If the Cat had not received his fur coat unquestioningly of Providence, he would have been thankful that he had it. It was a mottled grey, white on the face and breast, and thick as fur could grow.

The wind drove the snow on the windows with such force that it rattled like sleet, and the house trembled a little. Then all at once the Cat heard a noise, and stopped gnawing his Rabbit, and listened, his shining green eyes fixed upon a window. Then he heard a hoarse shout, a halloo of despair and entreaty; but he knew it was not his master come home, and he waited, one paw still on the Rabbit. Then the halloo came again, and then the Cat answered. He said all that was essential quite plainly to his own comprehension. There was in his cry of response inquiry, information, warning, terror, and finally, the offer of comradeship; but the man outside did not hear him, because of the howling of the storm.

Then there was a great battering pound at the door, then another, and another. The Cat dragged his Rabbit under the bed. The blows came thicker and faster. It was a weak arm which gave them, but it was nerved by desperation. Finally the lock yielded, and the stranger came in. Then the Cat, peering from under the bed, blinked with a sudden light, and his green eyes narrowed. The stranger struck a match and looked about. The Cat saw a face wild and blue with hunger and cold, and a man who looked poorer and older than his poor old master, who was an outcast among men for his poverty and lowly mystery of antecedents; and he heard a muttered, unintelligible voicing of distress from the harsh piteous mouth. There was in it both profanity and prayer, but the Cat knew nothing of that.

The stranger braced the door which he had forced, got some wood from the stock in the corner, and kindled a fire in the old stove as quickly as his half-frozen hands would allow. He shook so pitiably as he worked that the Cat under the bed felt the tremor of it. Then the man, who was small and feeble, and marked with the scars of suffering which he had pulled down upon his own head, sat down in one of the old chairs and crouched over the fire as if it were the one love and desire of his soul, holding out his yellow hands like yellow claws, and he groaned. The Cat came out from under the bed and leaped up on his lap with the Rabbit. The man gave a great shout and start of terror, and sprang, and the Cat slid clawing to the floor, and the Rabbit fell inertly, and the man leaned, gasping with fright, and ghastly, against the wall. The Cat grabbed the Rabbit by the slack of its neck and dragged it to the man's feet. Then he raised his shrill, insistent cry, he arched his back high, his tail was a splendid waving plume. He rubbed against the man's feet, which were bursting out of their torn shoes.

The man pushed the Cat away, gently enough, and began searching about the little cabin. He even climbed painfully the ladder to the loft, lit a match, and peered up in the darkness with straining eyes. He feared lest there might be a man, since there was a Cat. His experience with men had not been pleasant, and neither had the experience of men been pleasant with him. He was an old wandering Ishmael among his kind; he had stumbled upon the house of a brother, and the brother was not at home, and he was glad.

He returned to the Cat, and stooped stiffly and stroked his back, which the animal arched like the spring of a bow.

Then he took up the Rabbit and looked at it eagerly by the firelight. His jaws worked. He could almost have devoured it raw. He fumbled—the Cat close at his heels—around some rude shelves and a table, and found, with a grunt of self-gratulation, a lamp with oil in it. That he lighted; then he found a frying-pan and a knife, and skinned the Rabbit, and prepared it for cooking, the Cat always at his feet.

When the odour of the cooking flesh filled the cabin, both the man and the Cat looked wolfish. The man turned the Rabbit with one hand, and stooped to pat the Cat with the other. The Cat thought him a fine man. He loved him with all his heart, though he had known him such a short time, and though the man had a face both pitiful and sharply set at variance with the best of things.

It was a face with the grimy grizzle of age upon it, with fever hollows in the cheeks, and the memories of wrong in the dim eyes, but the Cat accepted the man unquestioningly and loved him. When the Rabbit was half cooked, neither the man nor the Cat would wait any longer. The man took it from the fire, divided it exactly in halves, gave the Cat one, and took the other himself. Then they ate.

Then the man blew out the light, called the Cat to him, got on the bed, drew up the ragged coverings, and fell asleep with the Cat in his bosom.

The man was the Cat's guest all the rest of the winter, and winter is long in the mountains. The rightful owner of the little hut did not return until May. All that time the Cat toiled hard, and he grew rather thin himself, for he shared everything except Mice with his guest; and sometimes game was wary, and the fruit of patience of days was very little for two. The man was ill and weak, however, and unable to eat much, which was fortunate, since he could not hunt for himself. All day long he lay on the bed, or else sat crouched over the fire. It was a good thing that firewood was ready at hand for the picking up, not a stone's-throw from the door, for that he had to attend to himself.

The Cat foraged tirelessly. Sometimes he was gone for days together, and at first the man used to be terrified, thinking he would never return; then he would hear the familiar cry at the door, and

stumble to his feet and let him in. Then the two would dine together, sharing equally; then the Cat would rest and purr, and
finally sleep in the man's arms.

Towards spring the game grew plentiful; more wild little
quarry were tempted out of their homes, in search of love as well
as food. One day the Cat had luck—a Rabbit, a Partridge, and a
Mouse. He could not carry them all at once, but finally he had
them together at the house door. Then he cried, but no one answered. All the mountain streams were loosened, and the air was
full of the gurgle of many waters, occasionally pierced by a bird-
whistle. The trees rustled with a new sound to the spring wind;
there was a flush of rose and gold-green on the breasting surface of
a distant mountain seen through an opening in the wood. The tips
of the bushes were swollen and glistening red, and now and then
there was a flower; but the Cat had nothing to do with flowers. He
stood beside his booty at the house door, and cried and cried with
his insistent triumph and complaint and pleading, but no one came
to let him in. Then the Cat left his little treasures at the door, and
went around to the back of the house to the pine-tree, and was up
the trunk with a wild scramble, and in through his little window,
and down through the trap to the room; and the man was gone.

The Cat cried again—that cry of the animal for human companionship which is one of the sad notes of the world; he looked in
all the corners; he sprang to the chair at the window and looked
out; but no one came. The man was gone and he never came again.

The Cat ate his Mouse out on the turf beside the house; the
Rabbit and the Partridge he carried painfully into the house, but
the man did not come to share them. Finally, in the course of a day
or two, he ate them up himself; then he slept a long time on the
bed, and when he waked the man was not there.

Then the Cat went forth to his hunting grounds again, and
came home at night with a plump bird, reasoning with his tireless
persistency in expectancy that the man would be there; and there
was a light in the window, and when he cried, his old master
opened the door and let him in.

His master had strong comradeship with the Cat, but not affection. He never patted him like that gentler outcast, but he had a
pride in him and an anxiety for his welfare, though he had left him
alone all winter without scruple. He feared lest some misfortune
might have come to the Cat, though he was so large of his kind,
and a mighty hunter. Therefore, when he saw him at the door in

all the glory of his glossy winter coat, his white breast and face shining like snow in the sun, his own face lit up with welcome, and the Cat embraced his feet with his sinuous body vibrant with rejoicing purrs.

The Cat had his bird to himself, for his master had his own supper already cooking on the stove. After supper the Cat's master took his pipe, and sought a small store of tobacco which he had left in his hut over winter. He had thought often of it; that and the Cat seemed something to come home to in the spring. But the tobacco was gone; not a dust left. The man swore a little in a grim monotone, which made the profanity lose its customary effect. He had been, and was, a hard drinker; he had knocked about the world until the marks of its sharp corners were on his very soul, which was thereby calloused, until his very sensibility to loss was dulled. He was a very old man.

He searched for the tobacco with a sort of dull combativeness of persistency; then he stared with stupid wonder around the room. Suddenly many features struck him as being changed. Another stove-lid was broken; an old piece of carpet was tacked up over a window to keep out the cold; his firewood was gone. He looked and there was no oil left in his can. He looked at the coverings on his bed; he took them up, and again he made that strange remonstrant noise in his throat. Then he looked again for his tobacco.

Finally he gave it up. He sat down beside the fire, for May in the mountains is cold; he held his empty pipe in his mouth, his rough forehead knitted, and he and the Cat looked at each other across that impassable barrier of silence which has been set between man and beast from the creation of the world.

## The Presidents and Fishing

THERE are only two occasions when the American people respect privacy, especially in Presidents—those are prayer and fishing, so some Presidents have gone fishing.

*Herbert Hoover*

# THE HOME TOWN OF
# THE ARMY ANTS

## William Beebe

*Whether describing deep-sea creatures seen through the window of his bathysphere a half mile below the surface, or the flora and fauna of the Galapagos Islands, Beebe has always combined as few other naturalists the careful scientific report with writing of vividness and dramatic power. Here we sit tensely with him as he watches for two days the busy life of millions of ants not two feet from his eyes.*

I SAT at my laboratory table at Kartabe, and looked down river to the pink roof of Kalacoon. I was wondering whether I should ever see the army ants in any guise other than that of scouting, battling searchers for living prey, when a voice of the jungle seemed to hear my unexpressed wish. The sharp, high notes of white-fronted antbirds—those white-crested watchers of the ants—came to my ears, and I left my table to follow up the sound. Physically, I merely walked around the bungalow and approached the edge of the jungle at a point where we had erected a small outhouse a day or two before. But this two hundred feet might have been a single step through quicksilver, hand in hand with Alice, for it took me from a world of hyoids and syrinxes, of vials and lenses and clean-smelling xylol, to the home of the army ants.

The antbirds were chirping and hopping about on the very edge of the jungle. As I passed the doorless entrance of the outhouse I looked up, and saw that an immense mass of some strange material was suspended in the upper corner. It resembled stringy, chocolate-colored tow, studded with hundreds of tiny ivory buttons. I came closer and looked carefully at this mushroom growth which had appeared in a single night, and it was then that my eyes began to perceive and my mind to record things that my reason besought me to reject. Such phenomena were all right in a dream, or one

[ 46 ]

might imagine them and tell them to children on one's knee, with
the wind in the eaves—wild tales to be laughed at and forgotten.
But this was daylight and I was a scientist; my eyes were in excellent order, and my mind was rested after a dreamless sleep; so I
had to record what I saw in that little outhouse.

This chocolate-colored mass with its myriad ivory dots was the
home, the nest, the hearth, the nursery, the bridal suite, the kitchen,
the bed and board of the army ants. It was the focus of all the lines
and files which ravaged the jungle for food, of the battalions which
attacked every living creature in their path, of the unnumbered
rank and file which made them known to every Indian, to every
inhabitant of these vast jungles.

Louis Quatorze once said, *"L'Etat, c'est moi!"* but this figure of
speech becomes an empty, meaningless phrase beside what an
army ant could boast, *"La maison, c'est moi!"* Every rafter, beam,
stringer, window-frame and door-frame, hall-way, room, ceiling,
wall and floor, foundation, superstructure and roof, all were ants—
living ants, distorted by stress, crowded into the dense walls, spread
out to widest stretch across tie-space. I had thought it marvellous
when I saw them arrange themselves as bridged walks, hand-rails,
buttresses, and signboards along the columns; but this new absorp-
tion of environment, this usurpation of wood and stone, this insinuation of themselves into the province of the inorganic world,
was almost too astounding to credit.

Along the upper rim the sustaining structure was more distinctly visible than elsewhere. Here was a maze of taut brown
threads stretching in places across a span of six inches, with here
and there a tiny knot. These were actually tie-strings of living
ants, their legs stretched almost to the breaking-point, their bodies
the inconspicuous knots or nodes. Even at rest and at home, the
army ants are always prepared, for every quiescent individual in
the swarm was standing as erect as possible, with jaws wide-spread
and ready, whether the great curved mahogany scimitars of the
soldiers, or the little black daggers of the smaller workers. With
no eyelids to close, and eyes which were themselves a mockery, the nerve shriveling and never reaching the brain, what could
sleep mean to them? Wrapped in an impenetrable cloak of darkness and silence, life was yet one great activity, directed, ordered,
commanded by scent and odor alone. Hour after hour, as I sat close
to the nest I was aware of this odor, sometimes subtle, again wafted
in strong successive waves. It was musty, like something sweet

which had begun to turn mouldy; not unpleasant, but difficult to describe; and in vain I strove to realize the importance of this faint essence—taking the place of sound, of language, of color, of motion, of form.

I recovered quickly from my first rapt realization, for a dozen ants had lost no time in ascending my shoes and, as if at a preconcerted signal, had simultaneously sunk their jaws into my person. Thus strongly recalled to the realities of life, I realized the opportunity that was offered and planned for my observation. No living thing could long remain motionless within the sphere of influence of these creatures, yet I intended to spend days in close proximity. There was no place to hang a hammock, no over-hanging tree from which I might suspend myself, spider-wise. Therefore I sent Sam for an ordinary chair, four tin cans, and a bottle of disinfectant. I filled the tins with the tarry fluid, and in four carefully timed rushes I placed the tins in a chair-leg square. The fifth time I put the chair in place beneath the nest, but I had misjudged my distances and had to retreat with only two tins in place. Another effort, with Spartan disregard of the fiery bites, and my haven was ready. I hung a bag of vials, note-book, and lens on the chairback, and, with a final rush, climbed on the seat and curled up as comfortably as possible.

Around the tin, swarming to the very edge of the liquid, were the angry hosts. Close to my face were the lines ascending and descending, while immediately above were hundreds of thousands, a bushel-basket of army ants, with only the strength of their thread-like legs as suspension cables. It took some time to get used to my environment, and from first to last I was never entirely relaxed, or quite unconscious of what would happen if a chair-leg broke, or a bamboo fell across the outhouse.

I swiveled round on the chair-seat and counted eight lines of army ants on the ground, converging to the post at my elbow. Each was four or five ranks wide, and the eight lines occasionally divided or coalesced like a nexus of capillaries. As there was a wide expanse of sand and clay, I saw no reason that the various lines of foragers should not approach the nest in a single large column. The dividing and redividing showed how completely free were the columns from any individual dominance. There was no control by specific individuals or soldiers, but, the general route once established, the governing factor was the order of contact.

The law to pass where others have passed is immutable, but freedom of action or individual desire dies with the malleable, plastic ends of the foraging columns. Again and again came to mind the comparison of the entire colony or army with a single organism; and now the home, the nesting swarm, the focus of central control, the body of this strange amorphous organization, housed the spirit of the army. One thinks of a column of foragers as a tendril with only the tip sensitive and growing and moving, while the corpuscle-like individual ants are driven in the current of blind instinct to and fro on their chemical errands; but this theory, this most vivid simile, is upset by the sights I watched in the suburbs of this ant home!

The columns were excellent barometers, and their reaction to passing showers was invariable. The clay surface held water, and after each downfall the pools would be higher, and the contour of the little region altered. At the first few drops the ants would hasten, the throbbing corpuscles speeding up. As the rain came down more heavily, the column melted away, those near each end hurrying to shelter and those in the center crawling beneath fallen leaves and bits of clod and stick. A moment before, hundreds of ants were trudging around a tiny pool, the water lined with ant hand-rails, and in shallow places, veritable formicine pontoons— large ants which stood up to their bodies in water, with the booty laden host passing over them. Now, these had vanished, leaving only a bare expanse of splashing drops and wet clay. The sun broke through and the residue rain tinkled from the bamboos.

As gradually as the growth of the rainbow above the jungle, the lines reformed themselves. Scouts crept from the jungle-edge at one side, and from the post at my end, and felt their way, fan-wise, over the rain-scoured surface, for the odor, which was both sight and sound to these ants, had been washed away—a more serious handicap than mere change in contour. Swiftly the wandering individuals found their bearings again. There was deep water where dry land had been, but, as if by long-planned study of the work of sappers and engineers, new pontoon bridges were thrown across, washouts filled in, new cliffs explored, and easy grades established; and by the time the bamboos ceased their private after-shower, the columns were again running smoothly, battalions of eager light infantry hastening out to battle, and equal hosts of loot-laden warriors hurrying toward the home nest. Four minutes was the average time taken to reform a column across the ten feet of open clay, with all the road-making and engineering feats which I have mentioned, on the part of ants who had never been over this new route before.

Leaning forward within a few inches of the post, I lost all sense of proportion, forgot my awkward human size, and with a new perspective became an equal of the ants, looking on, watching every passer-by with interest, straining with the bearers of the heavy loads, and breathing more easily when the last obstacle had been overcome and home attained. For a period I plucked out every bit of good-sized booty and found that almost all were portions of scorpions from far distant dead logs in the jungle, creatures whose strength and poisonous stings availed nothing against the attacks of these fierce ants. The loads were adjusted equally, the larger pieces carried by the big, white-headed workers, while the smaller ants transported small eggs and larvæ. Often, when a great mandibled soldier had hold of some insect he would have five or six tiny workers surrounding him, each grasping any projecting portion of the loot, as if they did not trust him in this menial capacity—as an anxious mother would watch with doubtful confidence a big policeman wheel her baby across a crowded street. These workers are often diminutive Marcelines, hindering rather than aiding in the progress. But in every phase of activity of these ants there was not an ounce of intentionally lost power, or a moment of time wilfully gone to waste.

Now that I had an opportunity of quietly watching the long, hurrying columns, I came hour by hour to feel a greater intimacy, a deeper enthusiasm for their vigor of existence, their unfailing life at the highest point of achievement. In every direction my former desultory observations were discounted by still greater accomplishments. Elsewhere I have recorded the average speed as two and a half feet in ten seconds, estimating this as a mile in three and a half hours. An observant colonel in the American army has laid bare my congenitally hopeless mathematical inaccuracy, and corrected this to five hours and fifty-two seconds. Now, however, I established a wholly new record for the straight-away dash for home of the army ants. With the handicap of gravity pulling them down, the ants, both laden and unburthened, averaged ten feet in twenty seconds, as they raced up the post. I have now called in an artist and an astronomer to verify my results, these two being the only living beings within hailing distance as I write, except a baby red-howling monkey curled up in my lap, and a toucan, sloth, and green boa, beyond my laboratory table. Our results are identical, and I can safely announce that the amateur record for speed of army ants is equivalent to a mile in two hours and fifty-six seconds; and this when handicapped by gravity and burthens of food, but with the incentive of approaching the end of their long journey.

As once before, I accidentally disabled a big worker that I was robbing of his load, and his entire abdomen rolled down a slope and disappeared. Hours later in the afternoon, I was summoned to see this same soldier unconcernedly making his way along an outward-bound column, guarding it as carefully as if he had not lost the major part of his anatomy. His mandibles were ready and the only difference that I could see was that he could make better speed than others of his caste. That night he joined the general assemblage of cripples quietly awaiting death, halfway up to the nest.

I know of no highway in the world which surpasses that of a big column of army ants in exciting happenings, although I usually had the feeling which inspired Kim as he watched the Great White Road, of understanding so little of all that was going on. Early in the morning, there were only outgoing hosts; but soon eddies were seen in the swift current, vortexes made by a single ant here and there forcing its way against the stream. Unlike penguins and human beings, army ants have no rule of the road to right and left, and there is no lessening of pace or turning aside for a heavily laden drogher. Their blindness caused them to bump squarely into every individual, often sending load and carrier tumbling to the bottom of a vertical path. Another constant loss of energy was a large cockroach leg, or scorpion segment, carried by several ants. Their insistence on trying to carry everything beneath their bodies caused all sorts of comical mishaps. When such a large piece of booty appeared, it was too much of a temptation, and a dozen outgoing ants would rush up and seize hold for a moment, the consequent pulling in all directions reducing progress at once to zero.

Until late afternoon few ants returned without carrying their bit. The exceptions were the cripples, which were numerous and very pitiful. From such fierce strenuousness, such virile activity, as unending as elemental processes, it seemed a terrible drop to disability, to the utilizing of every atom of remaining strength to return to the temporary home nest—that instinct which drives so many creatures to the same homing at the approach of death.

Even in their helplessness they were wonderful. To see a big black-headed worker struggling up a post with five short stumps and only one good hind leg, was a lesson in achieving the impossible. I have never seen even a suspicion of aid given to any cripple, no matter how slight or how complete the disability; but frequently a strange thing occurred, which I have often noticed but can never explain. One army ant would carry another, perhaps of its own size and caste, as if it were a bit of dead provender; and I wondered if cannibalism was to be added to their habits. I would capture both, and the minute they were in the vial, the dead ant would come to life, and with equal vigor and fury both would rush about their prison, seeking to escape, becoming indistinguishable in the twinkling of an eye.

Occasionally an ant would stop and attempt to clean another which had become partly disabled through an accumulation of gummy sap or other encumbering substance. But when the leg or other organ was broken or missing, the odor of the ant-blood seemed to arouse only suspicion and to banish sympathy, and after a few casual wavings of antennæ, all passed by on the other side. Not only this, but the unfortunates were actually in danger of attack within the very lines of traffic of the legionaries. Several times I noticed small rove beetles accompanying the ants, who paid little attention to them. Whenever an ant became suspicious and approached with a raised-eyebrow gesture of antennæ, the beetles turned their backs quickly and raised threatening tails. But I did not suspect the vampire or thug-like character of these guests— tolerated where any other insect would at once have been torn to pieces. A large crippled worker, hobbling along, had slipped a little away from the main line, when I was astonished to see two rove beetles rush at him and bite him viciously, a third coming up at once and joining in. The poor worker had no possible chance against this combination, and he went down after a short futile struggle. Two small army ants now happened to pass, and after a preliminary whiffing, with waving antennæ, rushed joyously into the mêlée. The beetles had a cowardly weapon, and raising their tails, ejected a drop or two of liquid, utterly confusing the ants, which turned and hastened back to the column. For the next few minutes, until the scent wore off, they aroused suspicion wherever they went. Meanwhile the hyena-like rove beetles, having hedged themselves within a barricade of their malodor, proceeded to feast, quarreling with one another as such cowards are wont to do.

Thus I thought, having identified myself with the army ants. From a broader, less biased point of view, I realized that credit should be given to the rove beetles for having established themselves in a zone of such constant danger, and for being able to live and thrive in it.

The columns converged at the foot of the post, and up its surface ran the main artery of the nest. Halfway up, a flat board projected, and here the column divided for the last time, half going directly into the nest and the other half turning aside, skirting the board, ascending a bit of perpendicular canvas, and entering the nest from the rear. The entrance was well guarded by a veritable moat and drawbridge of living ants. A foot away, a flat mat of ants, mandibles outward, was spread, over which every passing individual stepped. Six inches farther, and the sides of the mat thickened, and in the last three inches these sides met overhead, forming a short tunnel at the end of which the nest began.

Here I noticed an interesting thing. Into this organic moat or tunnel, this living mouth of an inferno, passed all the booty-laden foragers or those who for some reason had returned empty-mouthed. But the outgoing host seeped gradually from the outermost nest-layer—a gradual but fundamental circulation, like that of ocean currents. Scorpions, eggs, caterpillars, glass-like wasp pupæ, roaches, spiders, crickets—all were drawn into the nest by a maelstrom of hunger, funneling into the narrow tunnel; while from over the surface of the swarm crept forth layer after layer of invigorated, implacable seekers after food.

The mass of ants composing the nest appeared so loosely connected that it seemed as if a touch must tear a hole, a light wind rend the supports. It was suspended in the upper corner of the doorway, rounded on the free sides, and measured roughly two feet in diameter—an unnumbered host of ants. Those on the surface were in slow but constant motion, with legs shifting and antennæ waving continually. This quivering on the surface of the swarm gave it the appearance of the fur of some terrible animal—fur blowing in the wind from some unknown deadly desert. Yet so cohesive was the entire mass, that I sat close beneath it for the best part of two days and not more than a dozen ants fell upon me. There was, however, a constant rain of egg-cases and pupa-skins and the remains of scorpions and grasshoppers, the residue of the booty which was being poured in. These wrappings and inedible casings were all brought to the surface and dropped. This was reasonable, but what I could not comprehend was a constant falling of small living larvæ. How anything except army ants could emerge alive from such a sinister swarm was inconceivable. It took some resolution to stand up under the nest, with my face only a foot away from this slowly seething mass of widespread jaws. But I had to discover where the falling larvæ came from, and after a time I found that they were immature army ants. Here and there a small worker would appear, carrying in its mandibles a young larvæ; and while most made their way through the maze of mural legs and bodies and ultimately disappeared again, once in a while the burthen was dropped and fell to the floor of the outhouse. I can account for this only by presuming that a certain percentage of the nurses were very young and inexperienced workers and dropped their burthens inadvertently. There was certainly no intentional casting out of these offspring, as was so obviously the case with the débris from the food of the colony. The eleven or twelve ants which fell upon me during my watch were all smaller workers, no larger ones losing their grip.

While recording some of these facts, I dropped my pencil, and it was fully ten minutes before the black mass of enraged insects cleared away, and I could pick it up. Leaning far over to secure it, I was surprised by the uncleanliness of the floor around my chair. My clothes and notepaper had been covered with loose wings, dry skeletons of insects and the other débris, while hundreds of fragments had sifted down past me. Yet now that I looked seeingly, the whole area was perfectly clean. I had to assume a jack-knife pose to get my face near enough to the floor; but achieving it, I found about five hundred ants serving as a street-cleaning squad. They roamed aimlessly about over the floor, ready at once to attack anything of mine, or any part of my anatomy that might come close enough, but otherwise stimulated to activity only when they came across a bit of rubbish from the nest high overhead. This was at once seized and carried off to one of two neat piles in far corners. Before night these kitchen middens were an inch or two deep and nearly a foot in length, composed, literally, of thousands of skins, wings, and insect armor. There was not a scrap of dirt of any kind which had not been gathered into one of the two piles. The nest was nine feet above the floor, a distance (magnifying ant-height to our own) of nearly a mile, and yet the care lavished on the cleanliness of the earth so far below was as thorough and well done as the actual provisioning of the colony.

As I watched the columns and the swarm-nest hour after hour, several things impressed me: the absolute silence in which the ants worked—such ceaseless activity without sound one associates only with a cinema film; all around was tremendous activity, marvelous feats of achievement, superhuman instincts, the ceaseless movement of tens of thousands of legionaries, yet no tramp of feet, no shouts, no curses, no welcomes, no chanties. It was uncanny to think of a race of creatures such as these, dreaded by every living being, wholly dominant in their continent-wide sphere of action, yet born, living out their lives, and dying, dumb and blind, with no possibility of comment on life and its fullness, of censure or of applause.

The sweeping squad on the floor was interesting because of its limited field of work at such a distance from the nest; but close to my chair were a number of other specialized zones of activity, any one of which would have afforded a fertile field for concentrated study. Beneath the swarm on the white canvas, I noticed two large spots of dirt and moisture, where very small flies were collected. An examination showed that this was a second, nearer dumping ground for all the garbage and refuse of the swarm which could not be thrown down on the kitchen middens far below. And here were tiny flies and other insects acting as scavengers, as the hosts of vultures gather about the slaughterhouse at Georgetown.

The most interesting phase of life of the ants' Home Town, was that on the horizontal board which projected from the beam and stretched for several feet to one side of the swarm. This platform was almost on a level with my eyes, and by leaning slightly forward on the chair, I was as close as I dared go. Here many ants came from the incoming columns, and others were constantly arriving from the nest itself. It was here that I realized my good fortune and the achievement of my desires, when I first saw an army ant at rest. One of the first arrivals after I had squatted to my post was a big soldier with a heavy load of roach meat. Instead of keeping on straight up the post, he turned abruptly and dropped his load. It was instantly picked up by two smaller workers and carried on and up toward the nest. Two other big fellows arrived in quick succession, one with a load which he relinquished to a drogher-in-waiting. Then the three weary warriors stretched their legs one after another and commenced to clean their antennæ. This lasted only for a moment, for three or four tiny ants rushed at each of the larger ones and began as thorough a cleaning as masseurs or Turkish-bath attendants. The three arrivals were at once hustled away to a distant part of the board and there cleaned from end to end. I found that the focal length of my 8-diameter lens was out of reach of these ants so I focused carefully on one of the soldiers and watched the entire process. The small ants scrubbed and scraped him with their jaws, licking him and removing every particle of dirt. One even crawled under him and worked away at his upper leg-joints, for all the world as a mechanic will creep under a car. Finally, I was delighted to see him do what no car ever does, turn completely over and lie quietly on his back with his legs in air, while his diminutive helpers overran him and gradually got him into shape for future battles and foraging expeditions.

On this resting-stage, within well-defined limits, were dozens of groups of two cleaning one another, and less numerous parties of the tiny professionals working their hearts out on battle-worn soldiers. It became more and more apparent that in the creed of the army ants, cleanliness comes next to military effectiveness.

Here and there I saw independent individuals cleaning themselves and going through the most un-ant-like movements. They scraped their jaws along the board, pushing forward like a dog trying to get rid of his muzzle; then they turned on one side and passed the opposite legs again and again through the mandibles; while the last performance was to turn over on their backs and roll from side to side, exactly as a horse or donkey loves to do.

One ant, I remember, seemed to have something seriously wrong. It sat up on its bent-under abdomen in a most comical fashion, and was the object of solicitude of every passing ant. Sometimes there were thirty in a dense group, pushing and jostling; and, like most of our city crowds, many seemed to stop only long enough to have a moment's morbid sight, or to ask some silly question as to the trouble, then to hurry on. Others remained, and licked and twiddled him with their antennæ for a long time. He was in this position for at least twenty minutes. My curiosity was so much aroused that I gathered him up in a vial, whereat he became wildly excited and promptly regained full use of his legs and faculties. Later, when I examined him under the lens I could find nothing whatever wrong.

Off to one side of the general cleaning and reconstruction areas was a pitiful assemblage of cripples which had had enough energy to crawl back, but which did not attempt, or were not permitted, to enter the nest proper. Some had one or two legs gone, others had lost an antenna or had an injured body. They seemed not to know what to do—wandering around, now and then giving one another a half-hearted lick. In the midst was one which had died, and two others, each badly injured, were trying to tug the body to the edge of the board. This, after a long series of efforts, they succeeded in doing, and down fell the dead ant. It was promptly picked up by several kitchen-midden-ites and unceremoniously thrown on the pile of nest-débris. A load of booty had been dumped among the cripples, and as each wandered close to it, he seemed to regain strength for a moment, picked up the load and then dropped it. The sight of that which symbolized almost all their life activity aroused them to a momentary forgetfulness of their disabilities. There was no longer any place for them in the home or in the columns of the legionaries. They had been courtmartialed under the most implacable, the most impartial law in the world—the survival of the fit, the elimination of the unfit.

The time came when we had to get at our stored supplies, over which the army ants were such an effective guard. I experimented on a running column with a spray of ammonia and found that it created merely temporary inconvenience, the ants running back and forming a new trail. Formaline was more effective, so I sprayed the nest-swarm with a fifty-per-cent solution, strong enough, one would think, to harden the very boards. It certainly created a terrible commotion, and strings of ants, two feet long, hung dangling from the nest. The heart of the colony came into view, with thousands of eggs and larvæ, looking like heaps of white rice grains. Every ant seized one or the other and sought escape by the nearest way, while the soldiers still defied the world. The gradual disintegration revealed an interior meshed like a wasp's nest, chambered and honey-combed with living tubes and walls. Little by little the taut guy-ropes, lathes, braces, joists, all sagged and melted together, each cell-wall becoming dynamic, now expanding, now contracting; the ceilings vibrant with waving legs, the floors a seething mass of jaws and antennæ. By the time it was dark, the swarm was dropping in sections to the floor.

On the following morning new surprises awaited me. The great mass of the ants had moved in the night, vanishing with every egg and immature larvæ; but there was left in the corner of the flat board a swarm of about one-quarter of the entire number, enshrouding a host of older larvæ. The cleaning zones, the cripples' gathering-room, all had given way to new activities, on the flat board, down near the kitchen middens, and in every horizontal crack.

The cause of all this strange excitement, this braving of the terrible dangers of fumes which had threatened to destroy the entire colony the night before, was made plain as I watched. A critical time was at hand in the lives of the all-precious larvæ, when they could not be moved—the period of spinning, of beginning the transformation from larvæ to pupæ. This evidently was an operation which had to take place outside the nest and demanded some sort of light covering. On the flat board were several thousand ants and a dozen or more groups of full-grown larvæ. Workers of all sizes were searching everywhere for some covering for the tender immature creatures. They had chewed up all available loose splinters of wood, and near the rotten, termite-eaten ends, the sounds of dozens of jaws gnawing all at once was plainly audible. This unaccustomed, unmilitary labor produced a quantity of fine sawdust, which was sprinkled over the larvæ. I had made a partition of a bit of a British officer's tent which I had used in India and China, made of several layers of colored canvas and cloth. The ants found a loose end of this, teased it out and unraveled it, so that all the larvæ nearby were blanketed with a gay, parti-colored covering of fuzz.

This strange work was carried out in a hurry and under great excitement. The scores of big soldiers on guard appeared rather ill at ease, as if they had wandered by mistake into the wrong department. They sauntered about, bumped into larvæ, turned and fled. A constant stream of workers from the nest brought hundreds more larvæ; and no sooner had they been planted and debris of all sorts sifted over them, than they began to spin. A few had already swathed themselves in cocoons—exceedingly thin coverings of pinkish white. As this took place out of the nest—in the jungle they must be covered with wood and leaves—the vital necessity for this was not apparent, for none of this debris was incorporated into the silk of the cocoons which was clean and homogeneous. Yet the hundreds of ants gnawed and tore and laboured to gather this little dust, as if their lives depended on it.

With my hand lens focused beyond mandible reach of the biggest soldier, I leaned forward from my insulated chair, hovering like a great astral eye looking down at this marvelously important business of little lives. Here were thousands of army ants, not killing, not carrying booty, nor even suspended quiescent as organic molecules in the structure of the home, yet in feverish activity equaled only by battles, making ready for the great change of their foster offspring. I watched the first thread of silk being drawn between the larva and the outside world, and in an incredibly short time the cocoon was outlined in a tissue-thin transparent aura, within which the tenant could be seen skilfully weaving its own shroud.

When first brought from the nest, the larvæ lay quite straight and still; but almost at once they bent far over in the spinning position. Then some officious worker would come along, and the unfortunate larva would be snatched up, carried off, and jammed down in some neighboring empty space, like a bolt of cloth that has been rearranged on a shelf. Then another ant would approach, antennæ the larva, disapprove and again shift its position. It was a real survival of the lucky, as to who should avoid being exhausted by kindness and over-solicitude. I uttered many a chuckle at the half-ensilked unfortunates being toted about like mummies, and occasionally giving a sturdy impatient kick which upset their tormentors and for a moment created a little swirl of mild excitement.

There was no order of packing. The larvæ were fitted together any way and meagerly covered with dust of wood and shreds of cloth. One big tissue of wood nearly an inch square was too great a temptation to be let alone, and during the course of my observation it covered in turn almost every group of larvæ in sight, ending by being accidentally shunted over the edge and killing a worker near the kitchen middens. The larvæ were in a single layer; in no case were they piled on each other, and when the platform became crowded, a new column was formed and hundreds taken outside. To the casual eye there was no difference between these legionaries and a column bringing in booty of insects, eggs, and pupæ; yet here all was solicitude, never a bit too severe, or a blunder of undue force.

The sights I saw during this second day's accessible nest-swarm would warrant a season's meditation and study, but one thing impressed me above all others. Sometimes, when I carefully pried open one section and looked deep within, I could see large chambers with the larvæ in piles, besides being held in the mandibles of the components of the walls and ceilings. Now and then a curious little ghost-like form would flit across the chamber, coming to rest, gnome-like, on larva or ant. Again and again I saw these springtails skip through the very scimitar mandibles of a soldier, while the workers paid no attention to them. I wondered if they could be odorless and therefore intangible to the ants, invisible guests which lived close to them, going where, doing what they willed, yet never perceived by the thousands of inhabitants. They seemed to live in a kind of fourth dimensional state, a realm comparable to that which we people with ghosts and spirits. It was a most uncanny, altogether absorbing, intensely interesting relationship; and sometimes, when I ponder on some general aspect of the great jungle,—a forest of greenheart, a mighty rushing river, a crashing, blasting thunderstorm—my mind reverts by way of contrast to the tiny ghosts of springtails flitting silently among the terrible living chambers of the army ants.

On the following morning I expected to achieve still greater intimacy with the lives of the soldier embryos; but at dawn every trace of nesting swarm, larvæ, pupæ, and soldiers, was gone. A few dead workers were being already carried off by small ants which never would have dared approach them in life. A big blue morpho butterfly flapped slowly past out of the jungle, and in its wake came the distant notes—high and sharp—of the white-fronted antbirds; and I knew that the legionaries were again abroad, radiating on their silent dynamic paths of life from some temporary nest deep in the jungle.

### To Autumn

WHERE are the songs of Spring? Ay, where are they?
    Think not of them, thou hast thy music too,—
While barrèd clouds bloom the soft-dying day,
    And touch the stubble-plains with rosy hue;
Then in a wailful choir the small gnats mourn
    Among the river sallows, borne aloft
      Or sinking as the light wind lives or dies;
And full-grown lambs loud bleat from hilly bourn;
    Hedge-crickets sing; and now with treble soft
    The redbreast whistles from a garden-croft;
      And gathering swallows twitter in the skies.

*John Keats*

# THE VOICE OF BUGLE ANN

MacKinlay Kantor

*Fox-hunting in Missouri, without fancy coats and hats, without even horses or the kill—that's the strange sport of men whose chief interest in life seems the breeding and training of hunting dogs. It was natural that old Spring Davis should think little of taking a human life when that of a dog he loved was at stake—especially one he had waited seventy years for.*

H ER voice was something to dream about, on any night when she was running through the hills. The first moment she was old enough to boast an individual voice, Springfield Davis swore that she would be a great dog, and within another month he had given her the name she carried so proudly.

One of her great-grandfathers, many generations removed, had followed Spring Davis away from home when he went off to join General Claiborne Jackson and his homespun army among the prickly-orange hedges, so there was logic in the inheritance which put that trumpet in her throat.

She was slender, like hounds of the Spaulding line, and not as sprawling or cumbersome as the good-natured, long-tongued Walkers. Any one in Missouri who knew anything about fox-hounds had heard of the Davis dogs, but somehow there never came to be a Davis line. It was all in the family, and there existed a haughtiness in the old man which wouldn't permit him to have Davis dogs running anywhere except in the ranges along Heaven Creek. That was why Bugle Ann was still a maiden at five years, long after old Calhoun Royster or the Lanceys would have seen to it that she carried on her business in life.

And Spring Davis was prudish past the point of ridicule, though no one would have dared to laugh at him. He hated the common word for a female dog, and would not let it touch his tongue. He called his she-dogs ladies or girls, and there was a firm beauty about him when he spoke to them. You wouldn't think that a man like that could ever be tried for murder, or become a convict.

Those things did happen to Spring Davis, at eighty-two. They didn't affect him as they would have affected most men of eighty-two. Whenever he heard the gongs and whistles which sent him about his gray routine at Jefferson City, he must have banished those sounds from his consciousness. He must have imagined instead that he was sitting by a fire at the edge of Bachelor's timber, listening to the dogs as they hunted out of Chilly Branch Hollow, with Bugle Ann's cry echoing against the blackness of the sky.

*2*

"Bake," said Old Cal Royster, "put some wood on."

Baker went to the woodpile beyond the red circle and found a piece of rotten stump. "We'll have a good moon by next week," he said, and jammed the wood upon the coals.

"I don't give shucks for moonlight," exclaimed Cal Royster. "Give me a black-dark night, when the fox ain't shadow-shy. Any fool ought to know that. I don't know where my boys get such notions as moonlight nights."

Across the fire, Spring Davis tapped his pipe against the heel of his boot. He stopped, suddenly, head tilted to one side. The fire-light turned his shaggy mustache and eyebrows to fluid metal.

"Listen," he said. "Getting sweet."

His son, Benjy Davis, rose to his feet. He moved like an Indian; so did his father. There was something of the Indian in Benjy's twenty-year-old face, tanned and narrow and bony.

His black eyes glittered. "He's a mighty sweet fox if they've had him away over toward the river! We ain't heard a sound for twenty minutes."

There were five men around that fire at the edge of Bachelor's timber. Four of them—Spring Davis and his only son Benjy, and Calhoun Royster and his oldest son, Baker—were the most ardent fox-hound men in the county. The fifth man was no hound man at all; he was a new insurance agent from Wolf Center. He had eaten supper at the Davises', and he was beside that fire only by invitation and sufferance.

He inquired, "What do you mean, Mr. Davis? 'Getting sweet.' "

"It sweats," Spring told him. "The fox does. They can smell him better after he's been running a while. That's 'getting sweet.' "

Now even the agent's untrained ears could detect a faint distraction amid the common night sounds—the hush of sleeping forests that never sleep, and which is really no hush at all. The sound came from over past the Armstrong place, far past Chilly Branch and across the ridge beyond, and it was as eerie and elusive as the calling of wild geese.

"You'll hear her in a minute," whispered Springfield Davis.

The confused murmur became a tiny baying: the tongues of many dogs, eager and striving in spite of their two-hour run.

"That's Toul Sector," Bake Royster declared. Bake had been in the war, and all the Royster dogs were named Toul Sector or Border Service or General Bullard or some such name.

"It's not Toul Sector," said Benjy. "Not that nearest one."

Calhoun Royster's tone showed the jealous annoyance which he displayed frequently with the self-assured Davises. "It's no Bugle Ann, neither," he snorted. "Nor no Bill Bryan, nor Cox, nor Frances Cleveland, nor any Davis dog."

"Reckon it is a bit turkey-mouthed for one of ours."

Old Spring Davis loved to hear Cal swear in his beard. So he continued, "I'll tell you, Cal. It's an Armstrong dog. They've picked up an Armstrong as they come past."

Royster stood with head wiggling on his humped shoulders, his bearded lips hanging open as he tried to take that baying apart and examine it.

"What Armstrong dog?" he demanded. He seemed to be weakening.

"I'd say it was Jackie Cooper, that little pale-faced two-year-old."

Old man Royster listened a moment longer. He gave a defeated snort. Then his ire mounted. "Where in hell's Bugle Ann, anyway?"

"Maybe she'll quit, and come in," muttered his son.

Benjy whirled, and for a moment the insurance agent thought that he was going to strike Bake Royster. "No Davis dog ever come in without being called, before a fox holed," Benjy said. "Except one. You remember him. We shot him the next day."

Spring nodded. "Easy boy. . . . Guess there's bound to be a black sheep in every tribe, though this dog was white. Don't you folks worry about Bugle Ann. You'll hear her soon enough."

"Pshaw, scat," said Bake, uneasily, "I was just joking."

On such a night as this, with clouds covering the stars and no southeast wind smothering the scent, you could tell that the hounds were running with their heads high. They skirted the eastern boundary of Chilly Branch Hollow, and straightened out along the higher ridge which swung toward Bachelor's woods.

All the men were on their feet.

"You talk moonlight," Royster chided his son. "Never get a fox to keep the high ground except on this kind of night. Lose half the sound when them dogs get in a gulley."

There was a turkey-mouth among those ringing voices; old Spring had been right about the Armstrong dog. The Royster dogs were mainly chop-mouthed, and they sent their clipped bristling bay like a volley across the wooded plateau.

"I don't hear her, Pa," whispered Benjy Davis, with some concern.

The old man held up his hand. Suddenly a new cry was born amid all the hissing of excited crickets.

For some reason, the Wolf Center insurance agent felt the hair prickle on his neck. . . . This was no hound-voice such as he had ever heard before, and he would never hear its like again. It was a bugle—the Davises had a rare poetry in their make-up, thought young Mr. Mayor of the National Emblem Liability. He stood there with his nails cutting his palms, and listened.

"That's her, all right," came Cal Royster's admission, "but why's she kiting off by herself? If she hain't lost it, I'm loony."

Spring Davis repeated the word, "Lost," and smiled into the fire. . . . There had never been a sound like that in the Heaven Creek country until Bugle Ann was born; even now the trumpet-cry knew its own pride, and swung off toward the southeast, far ahead of the *owk-owk-owk-owk* with which the Royster dogs threatened.

The old man whooped, without any warning: "Now, there they go after her!"

Left, around the last spur of Bachelor's woods, the welter of hounds went sweeping after Bugle Ann. Her cry soared ahead— high, round, with that queer and brassy resonance which made you think that ghosts were out there somewhere, sounding Taps without any armies to follow them.

Springfield Davis came back to the fire and squatted on his heels. "You see," he told the insurance agent, "Bugle Ann was running that same fox night-before-last. I reckon she remembered how he likes to feint west along a little draw that's over there, and then double back and cut his own trail. It's a common fox trick if the fox has got the nerve to try it, and easy for him to work when the scent's heavy."

"I'm afraid," said Mr. Mayor, "that I don't understand."

"Well," said Cal Royster, somewhat reluctantly, "the average dog is bound to foller the way he's headed, if the smell is hauling him."

They were silent for a moment, listening to the baying as it swam fainter and fainter into the darkness.

"I'm afraid I don't understand any of this," Mr. Mayor cried with honesty. "I came from the East, just this year. They gave me this Missouri territory and—Fox-hunting! If you hunt every night or two, I don't see how you have any foxes left."

Bake Royster added more wood to the fire, and Benjy Davis brought up the sandwich sack. "We never kill the fox," said Spring sharply. "We don't ride no horses, nor wear funny coats, and caps. We raise dogs, and train them."

*Waken, lords and ladies gay*, thought Mr. Mayor in his baffled mind. *All the jolly chase is here, with* . . . "But it's really just a race between fox and dogs, then?"

"Fox holes up when he gets tired, and the dogs come home."

"And the same fox will run again, another night?"

"There's quite a slew of them around. Plenty of mice and ground-squirrels for them to eat; they never bother no hen roosts. Yes, they run again. Night after night, and year after year."

Benjy opened a battered vacuum bottle and poured a cup of coffee for his father. The gray-headed man touched the hot tin cup with cautious fingers. "Year after year," he repeated, dreamily.

The insurance agent choked over a bacon sandwich. "Are you folks—and you also, Mr. Royster—the only people who do this sort of thing?"

Spring Davis looked up from the fire. "Young man, did you ever hear of Old Man Spaulding? Reckon not. Or Gentry German, or Alex Parrish, or Colonel Trigg?"

"I suppose," Mr. Mayor replied, "that those are dogs."

"Those are men who made fox-hound history in America. And Wash Maupin, and Robert Rodes, and James Kanatzar. You see, sir, it's a matter of breeding good dogs—and understanding them—and—kind of loving them. It—" He broke off suddenly.

Cal Royster blinked at the gems of flame which shone through the whisky flask in his hand. "Speaking of names, Spring," he began, "you ought to take our friend here, over to the Armstrongs. You see, mister, Ed Armstrong is mighty religious and his boys are mighty the other way."

"Always going to town," put in Bake, "to dances and moving pictures and rotation pool, and things."

His father insisted, "But they do hunt. They name their dogs after moving picture actors. Old Ed Armstrong, he names his after religious folks. Until you've heard the Armstrong pack after a good, sweet fox, you hain't heard a thing. All turkey-mouthed, or squawl-horn-chop-mouthed at the best. Until you've heard Billy Sunday and Jackie Cooper and Dwight L. Moody and Zasu Pitts and Hoot Gibson and Mary Magdalene all driving a fox at once, you never have had no treat give to you."

"They're good bench dogs," said Spring Davis. He didn't like to hear too much laughter directed at the Armstrongs. "They mostly got stylish tails and compact feet and good stifles. If you like bench, the Armstrong dogs just hustle in the points."

He held up his hand, and Cal Royster put away the whisky bottle.

"Coming in," Davis prophesied. "I can get it, from 'way south, at the top of Heaven Creek."

Benjy swore; his face was very dark. "Blame fox won't give them more'n three hours any more."

"That's a fact," nodded his father. "We'll have to try farther up Heaven Creek to-morrow."

Mr. Mayor burst out, "Good Lord, do you do this all night, every night? When do you do your farm work?" He began to understand why Spring Davis had been unable to renew his fire insurance policy.

"Not every night," said Springfield. "Sometimes it rains. Or just the opposite, sometimes the weather's been too dry. Or we get long damp spells—too damp—or we get low southeast winds. We don't come out every night."

"Mr. Davis," cried Mr. Mayor of the National Emblem Liability, "how old are you?"

Spring smiled into the fire. "Seventy years ago this season, I ran off to join the Confederate army. I was only twelve, but I had done a sight of fox-hunting before that."

The hounds came closer, and once more Bugle Ann's blare was riding high above their hooted chorus.

"He's striking for his hole," Bake said. "In a minute he'll hand them the raspberry."

Spring Davis leaned back and closed his eyes. He drew a deep breath. "Waited seventy years to have a dog like that," he whispered to nobody in particular.

The fox uttered his shout of defiance—that strange yelp which was half a cat-cry, half a dog-bark, and wholly insulting. Then baffled shrieks told that he had holed.

"Fetch the horn, Benjy," ordered old Davis. "I don't want her sporting around."

Cal Royster bristled. "This ain't August nor yet February. You talk like our dogs was a pack of hoodlums."

"I just like to have her to home, Cal."

From beside a rolled up sweater, Benjy Davis brought a battered army bugle and gave it to his father. The old man wet his lips, fitted the mouthpiece carefully beneath his shaggy mustache, and blew two notes: the *ta-da* of galloping Valkyries, forever a summons and a challenge.

"Will she come for that?" Mr. Mayor asked in amazement.

"Always."

Benjy peered toward the crossing at Heaven Creek. "Looks like some other folks are coming, too."

The dull, yellow lights of an old Ford were rocking toward them, and they could hear the chatter of its motor. "That'll be Tom and Delbert, I reckon," said Cal Royster. "Don't know what's got into them. Been to see the Lancey girls again. They'd ruther spark around with two flibberty-jibbets than be out with the dogs."

Slowly the Ford rattled up the hill, and stopped at the wood road. The two younger Royster boys got out with cheers of greeting, which were stilled hastily when they saw a stranger at the fire.

"How's the calf market?" taunted their elder brother.

"Never you mind," grunted Delbert Royster. He and Tom were sunburned, strapping youngsters who would have looked happier in overalls than in the Sunday suits they had worn for their squiring.

Their faces were unwontedly serious, and neither of them headed for the sandwiches.

"What in time ails you two?" demanded Cal.

"You heard about the old Camden place?" countered Delbert.

Every one except the insurance agent looked automatically toward the northwest. A mile down the valley of Heaven Creek stood an abandoned house and farm buildings, which in daylight showed plainly from their hill.

"I did hear that somebody was moving on it," said the father.

"Some of the Camdens, coming back," added Baker.

Old Spring Davis stood fingering his bugle. "The Camdens was great dog people in their day. That's twenty-thirty year ago."

"Well," said Tom, "we heard about it over at Lancey's. It's a son-in-law of the old Camdens, and his name is Terry, and he aims to raise sheep."

For a long moment no one spoke.

"Fence," said Spring Davis. There was an odd whine in his tone.

Delbert brought out a sack of Bull Durham, and began to make a cigarette. "Martin Lancey was at the lumberyard to-day, and this Terry was there. He was ordering posts and wire. Wove-wire, Lancey said."

"Hog-tight, bull-strong and horse-high," added Tom.

A coal popped in the fire, and a shower of sparks blew up.

Spring Davis said, thoughtfully: "Man's name is Jacob Terry. I remember him."

"Sure enough," agreed Calhoun Royster, "and he married Effie Camden. I heard she died, up in Jackson County. Had one daughter, seems to me."

Spring Davis put down the bugle. His knee-joints creaked as he stood up. "I wouldn't call this Jake Terry a pleasant man. Once he whipped a horse with a piece of board . . . going to put up a wove-wire fence, hey?"

"They're moving in, this week," went on Delbert. "Mrs. Lancey said there was a light in the house early to-night."

Something twitched outside the last reaches of firelight, and Spring Davis went down on one knee. "Come on, little lady," he cried. Bugle Ann trotted into the light, her long ears flapping, her elbows plastered with mud. She was a small hound, but with a strong, well-arched coupling, and she carried her tail like a banner.

Davis took her in his arms. "This here's the angel song you heard, Mr. Mayor."

"She didn't come very prompt," scoffed old Royster.

"Prompt enough," said the veteran. "She set out there past the light, until she was sure about that car. You didn't know the

Royster boys would come driving up in their smoke-wagon, did you, honey?"

She wiped his chin with her limp tongue.

"What do you feed her?" asked Mr. Mayor.

"Best cornmeal, bran, and pork cracklings," answered Benjy. "Ma boils it to a thick mush. All our dogs get that."

His father rubbed Bugle Ann's head with his stubbled chin. "I puke out," growled the saturnine neighbor. "Spring, you're plumb foolish over that dog."

The older man shrugged. "I've run dogs for seventy-odd year, but I never heard a voice like this. Nor did you, Cal, nor anybody else. She's galloped forty-five miles to-night. She's the sweetest-mouthed hound in Missouri, and sometimes I reckon I don't deserve her."

Baker asked, "What do you say about the fence, Spring?"

The other hounds were coming in—tan and white, wet ears, drooling jowls—a muddle of tails and snorts and sneezes in the fire-light. Benjy took charge of the Davises. There were six of them out, this night, and he handled them with skill and deference and firmness . . . his father still held Bugle Ann wrapped in his gaunt arms.

"I reckon," decided Spring, "that we'd better make a visit on this Jake Terry to-morrow. Call the Armstrongs and Lanceys and everybody together; even get the Pettigrews down from Big Panther Creek. Nobody has ever put up such a fence in these parts, and this is a mighty poor time to start."

Again Mr. Frank Mayor prayed for information.

"First place," explained Davis, "a fox hates such a fence. He's liable to shy off and leave the country because of it. But some of the foxes do like it, and that's even worse. Because a dog runs about fifteen mile an hour—and he hits a wove-wire fence in the dark. The fox is little—he's gone through without choking to death. The dog is liable to get killed."

He rubbed the home-made collar on Bugle Ann's neck. The collar plate was made from a silver dollar stamped flat, and silver dollars were none too plentiful with Springfield Davis any more.

"You can't get good hunting in a country where they put such fences across the fox range," Baker Royster summed up.

Bugle Ann was snoring happily in old Spring's arms.

Mr. Mayor had to drive all the way to Wolf Center, and he didn't arrive at home until four A.M., and his wife was worried to death. He told her that he had just attended the strangest fox hunt in the world; it was a kind of fox-hunting in which no killing took place. He was a discerning man, but in this case he spoke too soon.

The men of the Heaven Creek neighborhood waited upon Jacob Terry the next day.

*3*

That was June. By July, everybody knew that young Benjy Davis was tarnishing some mysterious code which existed among them all, and which no one of them could have explained or accounted for. Benjy was keeping company with Jacob Terry's daughter, and he made no secret of it.

She was named after her mother's people: Camden. She was eighteen, and she had the shaded hazel eyes of her mother's family, the dainty nostrils and firm lower lip which had marked the Camdens as quality folks when they first came to that country on horseback.

From her father Camden inherited the Terry stature, the Terry red hair. All Heaven Creek hoped that she hadn't inherited his surliness, loose tongue and ugly disposition. Benjy believed that she hadn't.

The crisis began to develop, one night when the grass still reeked from a July flood, and the southeast wind would have drowned any fox-smell which rose from last autumn's leaves. Springfield Davis sat on the front porch with his shoes off, and Bugle Ann dreamed on the step beside him.

Spring noticed that Benjy disappeared immediately after the evening chores were done, and later he smelled shoe polish. About eight o'clock Benjy came around the corner of the house, and he was wearing his good trousers and the blue necktie which Grandma Duncan had sent him for Christmas, and which he had never worn.

"It's a wet night," Spring said. He began to fill his pipe.

"I reckon the wind will change," said Benjy. "But anyway it's unlike to dry off the grass before midnight."

Spring put his hand on Bugle Ann. "If it does dry up enough, Cal will be out."

"I'll listen when I get back," Benjy told him. "If I hear you up in the woods, I'll come over. I thought," he said, "that I might go with Camden Terry to see the moving pictures in town."

McKee's Crossing was five miles to the north. . . . Spring thought, "I've counted, each time they was together. This is eight times." He said aloud, "That's a long way for a buggy. You plowed pretty steady all day, too."

"I wanted to lay-by that slow corn," Benjy said. "Camden can drive her Ford. We talked about it out in the field, when she came past to-day."

"Well," his father muttered. He thought, "So I was wrong. Nine times." He cleared his throat. "You might bring me a sack of Sweet Burley from town."

Benjy waved good-by. "I'll bring it," he said, and went away like a war-chief in the dusk.

A long while later, Spring leaned down and blew softly against Bugle Ann's ear, and she roused up to wash his face for him. The April pups, by Billy Bryan out of Miss Wilson, came to tumble across his lap. "I reckon there would be no way to stop that," decided old Davis, "even if I wanted to. She looks more like the Camdens, and they was fine folks. Used to have a beautiful line of Irish-Maryland stock. I hope Benjy has sense enough to pay for the gasoline, if he rides in a Terry car. He will, though."

He sat for hours, thinking of Jacob Terry and how he had greeted the deputation which waited on him a few weeks before. They were men with sober faces, but they were not men who would shoot unless they were called by a certain name, and that was one curse which Jacob Terry had not dared to invoke. He had talked some of shooting dogs, but people didn't believe he really meant it. No man who had married a Camden could be perverted enough to shoot a fox-hound wantonly, they thought.

The fence was solidly in place: bull-strong, hog-tight and horse-high, just as the Royster boys had foretold. It ran across the creek, up the west slope of Heaven Hump, swung its yellow posts to the north and went down hill for another half mile. On the other two sides it paralleled Heaven Creek and Welsh Run. Jake Terry hadn't bought many sheep yet, but folks said that he was dickering here and there.

It seemed that recently he had inherited some money from an elderly aunt, and likely he would run through with that just as he had done with his wife's share of the Camden property.

When that woven belt of wire encompassed the slope of Heaven Hump, the Davises and Roysters had gone up into the woods and had dug out all the nearer fox dens. Several foxes were captured alive, and later were liberated miles away, east of the Armstrong farm. Their dens were broken in, or stopped with boulders and saturated with chemicals. Now it was hoped that no fox would venture toward that menacing wire sash. The north range of Heaven Creek became a victory for Jacob Terry.

As a matter of fact, the foxes were quick to learn what Terry had done to the hills. Certain of them seemed to take a fiendish delight in slipping through the meshes, whereat the dogs would howl and scramble perilously, knotting themselves in the wire squares.

This night, Spring Davis dozed on the steps until after eleven, and his wife slept on the sofa in the living room. Mrs. Davis was thirty years younger than her husband, eighteen inches shorter, a few degrees less talkative, and she knew that after his dogs Spring loved her well. . . . The breeze did change, and when the old man awoke he found a steady west wind breathing its dryness against his face.

He went out into the yard and felt of the ground. He sniffed several times. Bugle Ann came behind him, stretching and yawning.

"I think a fox would hang on the high ground, after all. The scent'd be fairly free. Reckon you wouldn't have to grind your nose against the ground, little girl," said the master.

She swung her tail, and lifted her muzzle. "Now, hush!" he said, and waited with delight for her to disobey him.

She blew her trumpet.

"What is it?" called Mrs. Davis, sleepily.

The other hounds were answering, from out by the barn, and far in the southwest you could hear the Royster hounds casting about. "We had bugles in the rebel army," said Spring, "but I tell you, Adelaide, I waited a long time to hear the noise that this little girl has got snuggled inside her, all ready to let out when God is willing."

"Are you going up the creek?" asked his wife. They didn't say "down the creek" any more.

"I reckon I will. Cal is out. I hear General Bullard; sounds like he's striking. Will you fetch me a snack, while I get the lantern?"

She had a lunch ready when the old man came up from the corncrib, with his hands full of Frances Cleveland and Billy Bryan and Old Hickory. "I can't mind more than four, what with Benjy gone," he told Adelaide, and put his lunch in his pocket and the bugle under his suspender strap. He went across the cabbage patch, with the rest of the Davis dogs wailing their grief behind him.

"Poor little folks," he commiserated. "You'll just have to be patient, I reckon. Benjy sure is gone a long time. It must be a mighty good moving picture."

He saw the Royster lanterns opposite the line fence, and he let the dogs loose, one by one. Bugle Ann shot into the lead. "You find the pack, little lady!" Spring shouted at her. "Find the pack if they come high. They got a long jump on you."

Cal Royster chuckled in the shadows. "Talk like she understood every word you said."

"I wager she'll be up with them inside thirty minutes," Spring responded. "And anyway, likely she does know what's what. How could she help it, with that silver cornet the Lord bequeathed her?"

Del and Thomas were off with the Lancey girls again, but Bake and old Cal and Spring Davis all waded Heaven Creek and went up on the south end of the Divide to build their fire. The bugs were bad, and it was more of a smudge than a camp-blaze.

"What's become of Benjy?" asked Bake, who knew well enough what had become of Benjy. "Is he still taking that mail-school lesson about new ways of farming?"

"No, that's been done up for some time," Spring replied. He hesitated, then said: "He's gone to McKee's Crossing to the Wednesday night moving picture." This seemed neither the time nor the place to elaborate on his statement.

## 4

The hounds came down the valley soon after midnight, with the fox at a tantalizing short lead. The men descended the Divide when the baying sounded first from above them, and they felt rather than saw the truant varmint squeeze past them into the north.

White blur after white blur—like snowy hands whisking before the eyes—the dogs went by.

Cal Royster voiced the apprehension of the others when he spoke. "Fox'll go right up Chilly Branch Holler," he said, and Spring hoped that he was right, for it was hard to forget the menace of the wire which lay beyond.

They heard the dogs crossing Chilly Branch near its mouth, and then Bugle Ann singled out ahead of them all, booming up the steep terraces of Heaven Hump. And Springfield Davis recognized another sound in the universe beyond: the faint clatter of an old Ford rocking along a narrow lane.

He thought, "So they're back from the moving pictures. I hope to God the fox switches east to the hill-top. The girl looks more like the Camdens than she does like Jacob. I reckon most of my dogs would be small enough to squeeze through that fence without getting hung up."

Then Bake cracked out, savagely, "They never went up the Hollow. Let's get over there!" and he lumbered away through the darkness. The two older men fumbled after him until their feet touched a deep cattle trail at the base of the hill, and then they could travel rapidly.

They splashed through the rapids near the mouth of Chilly Branch, and far ahead the hounds were rearing and yelling against Jacob Terry's hog-tight fence. One dog (he must have been Wound Stripe, and well-named, for Bake Royster swore about it) kiyied, and told the world that an end of the wire had been sharp and gashing.

When the men reached the fence, waving their lanterns, the fox was long since gone. The pack danced and strutted in hysteria beside the barrier.

Wound Stripe's left fore-leg was drenched with blood.

"Bugle Ann ain't here," muttered Cal Royster.

The lantern beams had gone their anxious round.

"No," Spring Davis replied, "reckon she sailed right through." He walked up to the fence and tested its strength with his shoe, and prepared to climb over. You couldn't see his face in the lantern light.

Bake was thirty-four, and heavy enough, but he was standing inside Terry's sheep pasture before old Springfield had managed to put his stiff legs astride the fence. Baker was thinking that Benjy should be there, and probably the others were thinking the same thing. . . . The far-away chugging of the Ford car had ceased, but a bright light moved rapidly toward them from the Terry farmhouse.

Sheep scampered here and there in distracted little coteries, appearing suddenly, and vanishing into the thick night amid a rattle of hillside pebbles.

"She'd come up to me, if she was inside the lot," said Spring. "It's possible she squeezed out at the other side, too."

Cal Royster put his arms in the fence meshes, trying vainly to stop their trembling. "She ain't giving voice no more. Maybe you better use your horn, Spring."

The old soldier had the bugle against his lips when Jacob Terry loomed up the hillside, an electric flashlight in his fist.

"Get out of this pasture," Terry said. He did not yell, and there was added menace in his voice on that account.

"Look out," Cal Royster warned. He saw a shotgun in the curve of the farmer's arm.

Spring Davis turned around and took down the bugle. He rubbed a finger across his mouth. "Jacob," he said, "I come in here after my dog."

"If your damn dog is here, he's got no good business among my sheep." Terry held the flashlight steadily on old Springfield's face, and somehow Bake Royster thought of big searchlights he had seen weaving above the Argonne woods, on another night when hatred paraded on a grander scale.

Spring told Terry, "It's Bugle Ann. She wouldn't hurt your sheep, but she's small enough to come through your fence when a fox brings her here."

In the next silence, they listened for her voice, but could hear only the thudding of sheep which scampered along the slope. The rest of the dogs panted and mourned outside the fence.

"Get this straight, old boy." The flashlight held its unblinking stare in Terry's hand. "I'm gonna raise sheep, and I don't care a stink for all the dogs in Missouri. You keep yours off of my land, or they'll get a dose of Number Ten shot in the high end."

Benjy got there a moment later. He had left Camden at the lane entrance, and he had started across a spur of the Davis timber when he heard the hounds working straight down the creek. He had no lantern; the woods were black, so was the creek valley, and it had taken him longer than he anticipated.

Somehow there had been a menace in the entire evening, from the moment when Camden first cried against his clean green shirt.

He asked, "What's the matter?" and his voice sounded like a youth's voice, breaking as it essayed the inflection. He snatched Cal Royster's lantern and investigated the hounds outside the pen. "Pa," he called, "where's Bugle Ann?" and then he came over.

Terry took a couple of steps closer. "There's more than just dogs that give me a peeve, anyway, and you know what I mean."

Get out, all of you, and don't bend down my fence when you go over it, neither."

"One of my hounds got cut open," said Bake Royster. "I don't reckon you could be decent enough to staple down those ragged ends of wire, could you? Well, I'll sure come around and staple them for you."

Terry called him a name, and turned the muzzle of the gun toward him, but Benjy stepped out to meet it. He swung wide and openly, for he was not a trained boxer, but he was quicker than a cat in any movement. His fist lifted Terry off his heels and threw him heavily.

The shotgun flew wide; it was still uncocked, and that kept it from going off.

"Take care, Benjy," was all his father said. There were grief and resignation in Spring's voice.

Terry rolled over and got up on his haunches.

"Don't you make a pass at me!" Benjy cried. "If you've killed Bugle Ann, I'll sure kill you."

"No," Spring said, "that'd be my job. But he hasn't, Benjy, he hasn't. . . . I'm plumb certain she went out the other side." Then, all in an instant, he stepped back and flung his arms high; one hand held the bugle.

He appealed, huskily, "For God's sake, listen to that!"

. . . She was far beyond Heaven Hump, far in the timber that blanketed Welsh Run. And she must have passed successfully through the north fence of Terry's pasture, for she had found the fox-smell again, and she was telling the whole state of Missouri about it.

It was a bugle, and every man knew that he would never hear its like again after she died.

Bake Royster had Terry's shotgun, and Benjy had his flashlight, and together they eyed the big farmer. "Terry," said Bake, "it's mighty fortunate for you that she's out there running safe and sound."

"You talk smart enough," whispered Jacob Terry. "Four against one! It's easy to talk smart."

"Your having this gun kind of evened it up."

"I'll even up any of your dogs, if they come on my land again." He went on to say what kind of dogs they were.

The hunters returned across the fence—all except Benjy.

"Come on, boy," Spring ordered him.

"Here's your light," said Benjy to Jacob. "I reckoned you had something else to say."

Terry came close to him. "I'm not afraid of no Davises," he bellowed, "but I like to choose my friends! Don't you come near Camden no more—hear me? I'm particular about who my little girl goes places with."

"I reckoned that was it," replied Benjy. The others knew from the drawl with which he spoke that he was enraged almost beyond control. "Well, you can go to hell and fry in your own lard. You know well enough that fox-hounds don't go around pulling the hide off of sheep."

The man's voice rose in one shouting shriek. "Why, you young blacksnake, I'll kill every God damn cur that steps on this grass!"

"Jacob," Spring called to him, steadily enough, "I can't speak for the Roysters or Lanceys or Armstrongs or anybody else. But if you shoot a Davis dog, I'll blow you clean to glory. Now come out of that hog-pen, Benjy Davis."

Benjy climbed over the fence. Terry turned off the flashlight, and stood there like the black stub of a tree, watching him. "How about my gun?" he asked. "Are you folks going around stealing honest people's guns, too?"

"Here," said Bake. He clicked the breech and threw something far into the valley. He passed the shotgun back through the fence. "Both barrels empty. If you look careful, down by the creek, you'll maybe find the shells."

"Remember what I said!" yelled Jacob Terry. "I got an old cistern needs filling in, and I'd just as soon fill it up with dog-meat."

Spring Davis said nothing more, but Cal Royster spat out his tobacco and declared that nobody would forget a word that had been said. He doubted Spring Davis's ability to blow Jacob Terry to glory, and remarked that another destination would be more easy to promise.

They gathered up the dogs and went back to the Divide. Their fire was nearly out, but Bake soon kicked it into activity, and his father found some dry wood stowed away in a hollow basswood at the head of the ravine.

They waited until two-thirty o'clock, and still Bugle Ann didn't come back, nor did they hear her metal baying any more. Baker took all the Royster dogs home to their straw beds, and then returned to the fireside. The Davis animals lay near the fire and sprawled like the dead, as only hounds can ever do, but there was a nervousness haunting their dreams and you could imagine that the eldest of them moaned in his sleep for Bugle Ann.

Benjy sat like bronze, his arms locked around his knees. From where he watched, Cal Royster studied him and wondered if a strain of Shawnee had not been dropped into the Davis blood a century before. . . . The whisky got lower and lower in Cal's flask.

Spring Davis walked up and down outside the firelight, tramping a path from the basswood to the nearest clump of hickory sprouts. Once he came back to the fire and spat into the coals.

"Wonder how far the gamest fox would travel, if he set his mind to go in a bee-line?" he asked, but Cal Royster couldn't tell him. Then Spring climbed to the highest point of the Divide, and awakened the dozing whippoorwills with his urgent bugle.

### 5

In the darkest half-hour, immediately before the sky above the Armstrong farm turned gray, the men heard Jacob Terry's Ford beginning to hiccough. By that time they were scattered far and wide through the hills, but Bake Royster was on top of the Divide. He saw the car lights twist out of Terry's barnyard, and stop for awhile, and then go on, smudging away toward the county road.

Bake listened until the car had chugged in the direction of McKee's Crossing. He had started back toward the fire, when a gnome with a lantern waylaid him at the edge of the timber.

"Bake," whispered his father's voice, "I heard a yip."

He asked, "What kind of a yip?" with the unreasoning annoyance of a young man who shuns the mumbling vagaries of the aged.

"A dog yip," said Cal. "I was down the crick, plumb inside Terry's pasture again. And I heard it, up toward the house."

"Just once?"

In the growing fog of dawn, the old man clutched Baker's arm; his fingers tightened and relaxed. "The dog was struck dead, if you ask me. Terry might of done it with an ax, so's Spring wouldn't hear the gun."

Far along the upper twist of Chilly Branch Hollow, Spring Davis's bugle chanted stubbornly. . . . Bake felt stuffed up inside, as he considered what his father had just told him. "Benjy went to take his dogs home, Pa. You wait here for Spring, and I'll go for Del and Tom."

"Don't bring 'em back direct," commanded his father. "Send Tom across fields for the Lanceys, and have Del take the car and go up to the Armstrong place. He can ring the Pettigrews from there. I wish to God I was rich and could afford a telephone."

Bake swallowed. "You want the whole tribe?"

"We can't go off half-cocked, boy. Maybe it was just a notion I had, or something. I would of sworn it was a yip—just one quick one. Don't you dare tell Spring about it. But if that little bitch—"

"Lady," muttered Bake, not realizing he had said it.

"If she's hung up on bob-wire somewhere, we got to find her soon. It'll take a sight of searching. She never was one to try and dig up a fox-hole. Maybe she got clear over east on the slab, and some foreigners picked her up in a car."

Bake started for home like a good soldier, with crisp obedience in his mind. At all this talk of killing, he began to tremble inside with a nervousness which had never possessed him since his discharge from the U. S. Veterans' hospital in 1921. *Too much . . .* his big feet found the trampled mire beside Heaven Creek . . . *too much of that sort of thing.* Just now he didn't like the name Springfield. It didn't make him think of a town there in Missouri, but it did make him think of a rifle. Cartridges began to glint in his mind: pointed clips of them, clicking one against the other in a webbed pouch.

Suddenly, he thought he could feel the cold stolidity of a Springfield bolt in the curve of his right index-finger.

He decided, "She's got to be caught in the wire somewhere. It'll be the best thing that could happen."

He routed Tom and Delbert out, and sent them flying. His mother and Lucy stood in their nightgowns and stared at him with cold, pale eyes, and said they'd do the milking if the men weren't back in an hour and a half. . . . There was a mess of cornmeal in the smelly summer kitchen, stirred up in a huge crock, and Bake took it out to the hounds. Halfway to the barn, he imagined that he heard a frightened voice yapping: "I'm runner—Brigade Headquarters—where's Sixtieth Infantry?" and the rifle bolts clicked in a machine-gun chorus. His throat was dusty, and he smelled pepper in his nose, as if some one had given him a blow that fractured the little blood vessels inside. . . . Then he pulled his nerves together, and went on to feed the dogs.

On the Divide behind his farm, Spring Davis came back to the dead fire with the sunrise smoking behind him. He walked, not like an old man who has been up and on his feet all night, but like a solemn pontiff who has sat in the cruelest judgment.

"It's the first time she ever disobeyed the horn," he said to Cal Royster and Benjy, who were waiting for him.

Cal kicked his empty bottle into the ashes. "Spring, you ought to drink at least a cup of coffee and maybe have a snack, before you go further."

"Why," said Spring, "I don't need—"

Benjy said: "They'll be gathering at the house. Bake and Tom and Del are getting folks."

"I heard her," said Spring. "So did you. She had got through that second fence. I heard her plain, over past the outside of his pasture."

"Sure we heard her," crooned old Royster, "and if she ain't found by high noon—maybe just got a toe caught somewhere, or something, like when she was a pup—I'll give you a four-headed Shorthorn rooster!"

Benjy looked at his father. "Anyway, you got to stop by the house first."

Spring nodded. "Guess that's so. Come along with you."

Roy and Joe Lancey were sitting on the well-curb when they got to the house, and Tom Royster was up at the kitchen door, talking with Mrs. Davis. The Lanceys stood up, awkwardly, as untutored men do at funerals, when Spring strode across the yard.

"Ma," asked Benjy, "you got some coffee?"

She nodded. "I kept hearing the horn, even after you was here, Benjy. The dogs have been just wild. I got a big coffeepot on the stove, and a couple skillets of eggs for anybody that wants them."

Bake Royster was coming across the south pasture, and another Lancey—Patterson, the sixteen-year-old one—was advancing up the front road on horseback.

At the back step, Spring Davis surveyed the men in his yard. His eyes were hot enough, but it was a slow and sturdy heat, infinitely ferocious. . . . An orange sun lifted above the Divide and found a whole jewelry store scattered over the clover behind the yard fence. All the remaining Davis dogs seemed to sense the import of this hour, except the April pups. They were smelling around Roy Lancey's legs.

"How about the ears on this one?" muttered Roy.

"They're well set," said Joe, "but she'll never have a stylish tail."

Cal Royster cackled. "Don't ask me! I ain't much on bench, but I'm the darndest Home-plate Judge you kids ever seen." The men all tried to laugh, as if he had said something very funny.

They heard the drone of the Armstrongs' old Studebaker from the road, and the rattle of Delbert Royster's Ford behind it. . . . When Spring Davis came out of the house five minutes later, there were thirteen men in the yard, including Benjy.

Spring had a lever action 30–30 Winchester in his hands. He tried it a couple of times, sliding shells into the breech, lowering the hammer with his thumb while he released the trigger, and flicking the cartridges out again. The sun discovered the Winchester; for a moment its barrel looked like mother-of-pearl.

"I'd just as soon go alone," Spring said, mildly.

Benjy cried, "No."

"You might say I'd prefer it."

Benjy said, "I'll go with you."

Cal Royster tried to make an explosion of laughter, but it was only a vague squawl. "Why, of course we all got to go with you, Spring. It'll take all the men we can raise, to comb real thorough. Maybe that fox took her—" His throat crackled.

"Maybe the fox went clean to the Indian River," supplied young Tom, and there was a murmur of assent.

Spring clamped the rifle under his arm. "Very well, neighbors. . . . I might be wrong, but I reckon I can learn in a hurry when I get there." He stepped down into the yard. "Good-by, Mother," he said to his wife, and in the doorway she made a sound. The pups scampered to meet him, ears flopping and tails swinging. "Get 'em into the crib or kitchen or somewhere," he requested of the world, and kept going.

The unkempt mob of men started after him. Benjy hustled the pups into the kitchen, and his mother hooked the sagging screen door.

Down in the barn, Frances Cleveland began to bay, and her relatives took up the song. Benjy sprinted ahead and opened the plank gate for his father; the old man headed along the edge of the corn-field, but after twenty yards he struck off between the green fronds, his feet sinking deep into the damp earth and leaving the prints of his heel-corners bright and compressed.

The neighbors followed, all of them; they talked a little about corn. The thinnest corner of the Davis timber swayed forward to meet them, and beyond that lay the lane, and beyond that the Terry house.

They came out into the jet lane, with its golden, morning pools of mud and the grooved ruts where Terry's Ford had plowed through. Nobody tried to avoid the deeper mire; the farmers marched in uneven phalanx behind Spring Davis, and anybody would have guessed that the old man didn't know whether he was walking through mud or last year's oat stubble.

Cal Royster had fallen to the rear, but not through choice. A little pageant walked with him, and impeded his footsteps . . . it was when he was eighteen, some fifty years earlier, and the neighbors all went up Welsh Run to prosecute Big Cass Strickland when he beat his two children to death. They prosecuted him at the end of his own wagon-harness, wrapped around the limb of a white-oak tree, and he hung there seven hours before any one cut him down. . . .

You couldn't see a soul moving in the Terry yard, and now the men believed most certainly that Jacob Terry had gone far away in the Ford, before dawn. Bake Royster and his father began to watch for tracks, as soon as they came opposite the weed-grown orchard, and it was impossible for them to conceal their search.

Cal felt Spring Davis turning and staring at him, and he held his face closer than ever to the ground.

Then all the men had stopped. Benjy Davis came back and stood between the two Roysters, with his hands clamped over his hip-bones.

"The pack never got up this high," he said. "They weren't out of the creek valley, except on the other side."

"No," whispered old Cal. "We was just a-looking."

Benjy grabbed Bake's shoulder and turned him around. "What do you know, Bake?"

"It ain't me," said Bake. "It's Pa. He heard it. I didn't."

Cal stammered, "Now, Benjy Davis. My ears are mighty old and mighty tricky. I can't depend on them no way."

"You better speak up," drawled Benjy. Spring Davis had come back to stand beside them; the rest of the neighbors waited in uneasy silence beyond.

"Well," Cal told them, "it did sound like a yip."

"Up here?" persisted Benjy.

"It was kind of in this general direction. I guess it was a short while before sun-up."

Benjy turned to his father, and tried to take the gun. The old man pushed him away with sudden and amazing strength. "You remember, boy," he said, as if there wasn't another man within twenty miles, "how she got her foot caught in that rat-trap before she was weaned."

Bake Royster yowled, without being asked, "Sure, sure! Everybody knows that. But one gone toe never bothered her, because it happened when she was young enough. You'd never pick her as belonging to a Casual Outfit."

"All right, Father," Benjy Davis said. Nobody had ever heard him say Father before. "I reckon any tracks that are here would be like cement in the mud. Quite—" He hunted for the word. "Quite unmistakable."

"I'll warrant you," his father replied. Spring drew down the lever of his Winchester the barest part of its arc; there was a shell in the breech. He clicked it back. Then he turned and started east along the lane, with his eyes boring against the ground.

Benjy looked at him as if he were just seeing him for the first time. "Wait," he cried, and the old man turned. Benjy brought out a sack of Sweet Burley, its blue seal blazing in the fresh sunlight. "I just remembered that you wanted me to bring this from town, and I been carrying it in my pants all this time."

Spring nodded. "I'm obliged, Benjy." He thrust the tobacco into his hip pocket. "Before Cal talked about that yip," he told his neighbors, "I had been quite divided. I thought that probably she was in wire, or else somebody had stole her, over on the slab highway. Just possibly."

They didn't find any tracks until they came to the yard gate, almost directly in front of the house. Then there were a few. The imprints were made by the feet of a hound coming from the east, coming slowly and wearily a few inches outside the thick grass which bordered the wood road.

Everybody moved off upon the turf, and let the Davises handle this matter in their own way.

Benjy stood looking into the deserted barnyard, but his father got down on his knees and examined the smoother patches of drying mud near the intersection of the wheel ruts.

"How about that toe?" asked the boy.

"I think so," answered Spring, haltingly. "I'm not right certain: so many car wheels, and other tracks. She must of turned off on the grass at this point. . . . Wait'll I find a good one."

Then at last he stood up, and took the rifle in both hands. "Oh, I reckon it would stand in court," he declared. "Just like fingerprints and such. That gone toe is as plain as copper plate. And the tracks don't pass this gateway. She did get this far, on the way home."

A drop of water bobbed over his crusty eyelid and spent itself in a quick streak on his face, dividing and splitting when it came to a nest of wrinkles.

Benjy said, "She was all alone, and likely the fox holed over in Lester's timber near the creek mouth. She knew this old wood road come back, and was easier traveling. She knew enough not to go through those wove-wire fences unless a fox took her that way."

"Cal Royster," said Spring, "you owe me a four-headed Shorthorn rooster." He faced the Terry house for the first time.

Old Ed Armstrong cried, "Now, Springfield. Now, Brother, wait a spell! The Lord don't smile on wrath in unguarded moments of haste."

"You and the Lord can hold your horses," Spring said, without turning his head. "If I'm looking for rats in my granary, I don't set down and pray on it."

Benjy pleaded, "Give me that Winchester, Pa."

"Pshaw, scat," said his father, and started into the farmyard. "You never bred her, did you? She was mine."

Benjy swung around and glared at the neighbors. "He don't want to go in with a whole parade. I'll stay by this gate. Don't nobody try to come past me."

"Spring!" howled Cal Royster. "He's gone! Spring, I tell you he went away in the car. We all heard it go. We—"

"If he ain't at home," said Benjy. "Pa'll wait."

Jacob Terry came out on the kitchen porch. In the barn lot, his two cows were lowing: they had not yet been milked, and none of the neighbors was surprised to know that Jacob had put off his milking until that hour. There were young chickens on the porch, and in the yard below.

Terry held his shotgun in his hands; of course there had been plenty of other shells in the house. Number Ten shot, Baker remembered. Little bright lights flickered in Bake's eyes, and again he smelled that pepper of a painful smash against his nose.

"Get out of here, you old devil," said Terry.

"What'd you do with her?" asked Spring. His tone was flat. "The tracks are to the gate. Did you haul her inside, then?"

Terry mouthed, "I never killed your damn dog, but I'll put some slugs through you if you don't get out of here." He began to hoist the shotgun toward his shoulder.

Springfield Davis fired from his hip. Terry dropped the shotgun and looked surprised and horrified; a dishpan behind him rang like a gong, and fell from its nail, rolling unsteadily across the floor of the porch. Terry's knees bent; he tried to get hold of his chest, and failed. He fell forward into the mud below the porch, with his arms doubled under him.

A lot of half-feathered chickens scurried away from him, peeping shrilly. When the men had rolled him over, they found that one chicken was dead beneath him—crushed flat when he fell upon it.

Benjy went into the house, but Camden wasn't there, and he was dumbly grateful—even in this calamity, and in the mystery of her absence. But the Ford was gone. She must have driven away in it.

That afternoon, after Springfield Davis had ridden to Wolf Center with the Sheriff, the authorities were able to telephone to the Camdens up in Jackson County. Camden Terry had arrived there about noon, but had driven on to an isolated farm belonging to a bachelor uncle. It was twenty-four hours before she could be notified and could complete the return trip as far as Wolf Center.

On the first day when people sat in the big, hot room among the scarred oak desks, Benjy Davis thought Camden looked prettier than she had ever looked before. Her pallor was the cold pallor of hepaticas; her eyes were excessively deep and shaded and secret.

Benjy didn't look her way when he thought she might be looking at him, but he studied her often when she was watching old Spring and the Coroner and the other people. Her story was calm, distant, told without emotion—it might have been translated from some ancient book. Yes, she had been with Benjy Davis the night before the shooting. Yes, she knew that her father had had trouble with the neighbors over his fence and their fox-hounds. She knew that there had been threats. . . . After her father came back to the house from the sheep pasture, they had engaged in an argument.

He had slapped her; just once, she said; not very hard. She

packed some clothes, and took the Ford. He dared not stop her, because the Ford was hers—not his. Her Aunt Nancy had given it to her after Uncle Newt died; Aunt Nancy couldn't drive.

(She didn't look at Benjy, either, when she thought that he might be observing her. Sometimes their glances crossed, but never seemed to meet and hold. Each understood that Jacob Terry was still between them, standing or lying dead, it didn't make any difference. In a way, Spring Davis also was between them now. And Bugle Ann.)

Her voice continued soberly, a little-girl voice. She thought that she wouldn't stay with her father any more, after that night. She drove up to Jackson County, and went out to Uncle Elnathan's place, and that was where the news had reached her.

Benjy Davis and the Royster boys spent days in going over the Terry farm, both before and after the sale of farm animals and machinery and household goods. They couldn't find a trace of Bugle Ann's body, even though they took up wooden slabs and explored the old cistern. She could have been buried in any loose earth of the barnyard or hog-lot, and no one would have known the difference.

Spring Davis was tried in September; the trial was in no way notable except for the oration on fox-hounds by a young attorney who volunteered to assume the defense without pay. The young attorney quoted, "Senator Vest's Tribute to the Dog," and added tributes of his own. He discussed fox-hunting as practiced in Missouri, and offered a biographical sketch of Old Man Spaulding, who was still alive in those days. In the eastern part of these great United States, said the young attorney, fox-hunting was an Anglicized pose of the idle rich, and they had many strange fetishes, not the least of which was the custom never to refer to a fox-hound as a "dog." They were all "hounds." Most of his listeners thought that very odd, but they did remember with interest how Spring Davis always called his female dogs Little Ladies or Little Girls.

Fifty years before, certainly, he would never have been convicted. But in this age you must not kill a man, even when another man talks of shooting and has a shotgun in his hands. It was proved that Spring Davis went into the Terry yard armed and ready to kill—he said as much himself. It was proved that Jacob Terry did not fire the first shot, nor did he have his gun at his shoulder when he was struck down.

The most important *corpus delicti*—the body of Bugle Ann— was not available. In short, no one could swear beyond all doubt that Jacob Terry had killed her. Spring Davis had usurped the prerogatives of the Sovereign State of Missouri, and the Sovereign State of Missouri brought that out very pointedly.

Girls made fudge for Spring while he was in jail; women sent in basket dinners. He gave the fudge away, of course, and some of the dinners. There was muttering at his conviction, and men talked darkly of a jail delivery. But such a rebellion belonged fifty years in the past. Springfield Davis went to Jefferson City and served three years, eight months and twenty-one days, and then he was pardoned by the governor.

## 6

During the first June which Spring spent in prison, the voice of Bugle Ann came back to ring across the dark valleys. Adelaide Davis was the first to hear this banshee, and she ran and told Benjy, and then they were both awake. Over on the next farm, Cal Royster started from his bed screaming, "Bake! Bake! It's her—" and even the youngest Lancey, who was up with a toothache, declared that there was no mistake in the identity.

And from that night rose the sprout of a legend which spread itself over the whole county, and farther than that. It was the legend of a white dog—lean, like hounds of the Spaulding line— who bugled her way through the brush at night, who ran with her head high, calling and hunting for the master who had been carried away from the hills he loved.

They said she ran at the head of a silent pack in which there were thirty-four dogs, all the great and noble sires who had galloped those ranges before the Civil War. There were the hounds brought into Missouri when Daniel Boone came, great sword-mouthed brutes who could pull down a deer if they wanted to. But they all ran silently—their feet made not even a whisper in the dryest leaves of last year, and their baying was not the kind which ordinary people could hear. Only if you were about to die, you might hear them crying all at once.

But the Davises and the Roysters and one Lancey, and even old Ed Armstrong's hired man—all had heard Bugle Ann on that solitary night, and though they didn't hear her again, it was said that

Benjy Davis spent more hours roving the woods than was wise for a young man with a farm on his hands.

No one lived at the Terry farm now. Shortly after Springfield Davis had gone to the penitentiary, men from McKee's Crossing came and took down the hog-tight wire fence. When questioned, they declared that a lawyer had told them they could have the wire and posts if they'd take them down. It was easy to pry out the staples, and they bore the wire away in huge rolls atop their trucks. But the posts were another matter; they quit digging after they had uprooted a few. Still, the wire was the main thing.

And there were those who swore that the pack led by Bugle Ann could go through a hog-tight fence like so much dishwater, but young Benjy Davis was hard to convince. After he had searched and yelled through every ravine between the Indian River and Big Panther Hollow, he declared that it had all been a mistake. Bugle Ann lay somewhere beneath the fresh weeds that grew in Terry's hog-lot, and as for her baying—it was another dog, that was all.

"It was her," insisted Adelaide Davis. "If your Pa had been here, he would of got up out of bed and gone for his lantern."

"Well," said Benjy, "I did that, didn't I?"

"But she quit giving voice," his mother said, "and whoever stole her took her away again." Her hands shook, in their cerements of bread dough. "Or else—"

He chided, awkwardly, "I got to get out to the field. . . . It's mighty unnatural to believe in ghosts."

Then he returned to his cultivator seat, and combed the black earth of the cornfield; he combed the rows early and late, and this year he had planted extra acreage. It was too bad, perhaps, for the price of corn got lower—so low that Benjy said there was no sense in selling. He didn't sell his corn, but he did sell the April pups of the year before, to the Lanceys. He took a corn-crib in payment— one fairly new. They moved it over to the Davis place with teams and cables and turnstiles: a three-day job. The Davises were hard put to scratch for a living, and that new corn-crib did look like a lot of foolishness.

Benjy stored his 1933 corn, too, and then came the next summer and the drouth, and corn at seventy cents. . . . Benjy carried an important slip of pink paper out of the office of the Wolf Center Farmers Grain Company, and shoved it under a grille at the Wolf Center Savings Bank.

Mr. Mayor came after him and talked of insurance, but the only expenditures which Benjy was known to have made were subscriptions to *The Red Ranger* and *The Hunter's Horn*. You couldn't expect the library at the state prison to have those periodicals in stock.

It was the night of Wednesday, September 26th, when Bake Royster came around to the Davis place and got Benjy out of bed. Bake could remember the date forever; that day, sixteen years removed, marked the opening of the Meuse-Argonne offensive. Bake had a great head for names and dates.

He looked green around the gills when Benjy padded out across the kitchen in his night-shirt, and wanted to know what was up.

"I've found something," announced Bake. "Found it in the dark, and I guess you better come and see it."

Benjy's sharp glance made a hole in Royster's face. "I'll get my clothes, Bake. Keep soft, so's not to wake Ma. Her sciatica has been bothering her again."

He came out promptly, and sat on the back step to draw on his shoes. "Where is this—what you found?"

"It's clear in the east side of Bachelor's timber, where the Bachelor used to have a shack. It's a smart piece, but I got my lantern."

"I better take mine, too," said Benjy. He brought a square, scarlet-enameled electric lantern from the porch shelf; Bake thought of that check for the seventy-cent corn.

They went across the yard, with the white disk dancing around their feet and ahead of them. "Maybe you'll want a spade, too," muttered Bake.

"A spade?" Benjy stopped and looked at him in the dark.

Bake said, "Or else a grain sack."

After a moment, Benjy replied, "I'll get a sack, I think," and he found one hanging inside the barn door. Together they crossed the garden patch, and up across the Divide they could hear the Royster dogs and a couple of Armstrongs working intently north into the tangles along Chilly Branch. One or two of the Davis hounds wailed at them, but half-heartedly: the Davis hounds had forgotten what a black-dark night was like, with a fox spraying his oily perfume through the thickets.

"Wound Stripe and Toul Sector had him across the corner of Bachelor's," explained Royster. "Some young dogs was along with them, and that little Elsie Janis got herself twisted in some rusty wire. That's how I come to go down there and—"

He gargled in the dimness, and added with an attempt at being casual, "Tom and Pa are there now."

When they crossed Heaven Creek (its widest pool could have flowed between your shoes, after the drouth) Baker began to remonstrate with Benjy Davis.

"I don't see what ails you, Benjy. It's a shame to have good stock tied up and molting away the way yours are."

"You can't sashay around the woods all night, if you're busy farming," the younger man told him.

Bake growled, "Now I know all about that corn! You don't need to rub it into me. But you ain't had nothing but dried-up crops to worry you, this year, and since the fall rains began to come there's been *beaucoup* fox around here."

For a while Benjy climbed the incline without speaking, loose pebbles rolling down around Bake Royster as he plodded an arm's length behind. "No stomach for it," Benjy said, at last, and Baker knew that was really the explanation. "Not until he's out of that damn place. I can't set beside a fire and listen to the baying, and know he's at Jefferson City in a cell-house."

It was eerie, passing through the oak woods, with a few katydids throbbing in secret dens under the stiff green leaves, and occasional yellow leaves sailing down into the straight electric ray. There was a feel of frost in the air, and Blake kept thinking of what he had found an hour before . . . a dog like Bugle Ann could take a thousand ghost hounds across the prairies among the stars, and still her baying would come back to you. Bake had ceased worrying about Springfield rifles and cartridges in webbed pouches, long before; sometimes still he thought of Jacob Terry and the chicken which had been crushed beneath his tumbling body, and he wouldn't get enthusiastic about half-feathered chickens ever again, especially if they made a shrill peeping.

But the death of Jacob Terry had come with its own certain violence, justified and canceled by a rifle bullet, the same as the many deaths Baker had seen in the valley of the Meuse. In Bugle Ann's passing there was too much mystery for any man to ponder. Any man who had ever been a patient in a government hospital.

The Bachelor's cabin was nothing but a heap of mossy shingles and broken crockery among the hickory saplings, for the Bachelor had left the country before Bake Royster was born. Some of his wire existed still: thick, old-fashioned plaits of bent rust amid the stumps. And near one of those barricades Cal Royster and young Tom waited with their lantern.

"Pa," called Bake.

"I'm right here," said the old man. "Evening, Benjy." Tom Royster didn't offer any greeting; embarrassment had frozen him into silence.

Benjy stood beside them and took what Cal Royster handed him. It was a leather collar, now stiff as iron with winter and summer and rain and mold, but the flattened silver dollar on it was unmistakable—you could even scrape away what had gathered over it, and see the Liberty head all flatly distorted, with its crudely-scratched legend.

The men waited silently.

"Where's the rest?" asked Benjy, after a long time. He slid the collar, with leaves still clinging to it, inside his shirt.

"Right here, in the bushes. They're a little scattered."

Benjy got down on his knees. If you had seen him, and had not known why he was there, you would have thought that he was praying. . . . Cal Royster had a vague notion that he ought to remove his hat, but Cal had never done such a thing for a dog.

"How long would you say?" asked Benjy presently.

The others murmured, hazarding several opinions. You couldn't tell much about bones. Maybe a doctor could. Animals had been there, probably, and birds. Maybe a year, maybe two, or three, or—"

It was the collar which first had attracted Bake's attention. He saw it sticking up out of the leaves while he was releasing Elsie Janis from the wire. The young hound had left some of her blood there, from a lacerated elbow, and it seemed strangely appropriate to have that ground moistened with the blood of a fox-hound, even if she wasn't a Davis dog.

"The point is," said Benjy, speaking slowly and gravely, "whether she was here all the time, that night, or whether she come later. Somehow or other. The point is whether we heard her voice two year ago last June, or whether—"

Cal Royster said, "By God, it was her voice. Reckon I heard it."

"And by God," whispered Benjy, "those were her tracks at the edge of Terry's barnyard, in July of 'thirty-one."

"So what?" asked young Tom. It was slang such as he always picked up at the moving pictures, but it seemed unusually apt.

Benjy said, "I reckon there's nothing I can do except tote her home in the grain sack. I'm glad I didn't bring the spade, Blake, because now I'd be tempted to use it: just seem like a lot of old sticks, somehow, and I always did think a dog skull was powerful ugly."

They helped him pick up the relics, and he carried them back home while Bake Royster went ahead with the elctric lantern. The men brought a shovel from the woodshed and buried the fragments, grain sack and all, beneath the sweet-crab tree at the corner of Mrs. Davis's little orchard. Benjy washed the collar and wiped it clean, using several dish towels in the process, and then he took it upstairs and hung it over the pointed, upright support of his bureau mirror, on top of his five neckties.

He told his mother the next morning, and of course through the Roysters the story was well around the neighborhood before noon. But Benjy and his mother were positive that no word of it would reach the ears of Springfield Davis at Jefferson City, and they were correct. It was the sort of a tale which might not be welcomed in print, so the *Weekly Clarion-Advocate* held no mention of it. No person except members of the family carried on any correspondence with Spring Davis, anyway, and thus the old man did not learn of how Bugle Ann's skeleton had been found until after he was released from prison.

It gave Bake Royster a fever, however, and he spent four days in bed. His family thought it was a kind of flu, but Baker knew the truth. He'd lie there at night, until he got over it, and watch the whole insane puzzle exploding before his eyes. Desperately he tried to align the formations—to put each separate element in the nook where it belonged; and this was lunacy to attempt.

Camden Terry: take her, now. She was living up in Jackson County, folks said, and she had never offered to sell the farm. Just let it grow to weeds. Nobody seemed to know whether or not she was married, and naturally it would take a hardy soul to mention her name to Benjy. Blake reckoned that Benjy had been mighty sweet on Camden.

Everybody had seen the tracks at Jake Terry's gate; there was no doubt about that missing toe. Not another hound in the neighborhood had a toe gone. So there were her tracks, and why would Bugle Ann have gone across Heaven Creek from the Terry farm— why would she have climbed Heaven Hump, or gone through

Chilly Branch Hollow, and south into the timber land to get herself strangled in the Bachelor's wire? Spring Davis was making the hills quiver with his trumpet, and people all knew how Bugle Ann would come to such a summons.

No, she must have lived somehow, somewhere—and then she must have come back to the woods she loved, on another night, in June of 1932. Then they had heard her calling, and then she had met her death, alone beside the windfall of curling shingles.

No, she must have been a ghost, all along. It was not natural for any dog to have a voice like hers, and perhaps she had been sired by one of the silent pack which followed her so willingly in popular imagination. Even now her bones lay wadded in the Davis orchard, but Bugle Ann was up and gone, baying in ranges where no horns could ever summon her, and it would be death to hear her bugling again. . . . It was this surmise, however hysterical, which comforted Baker Royster and let him sleep with no more fever. Yet it was hard for him to forget how Benjy Davis had looked in the lantern light, coming down from the Divide with that sack of bones swinging from his shoulder and Bugle Ann's collar nestling inside his shirt.

### 7

They had less than twenty-four hours' warning, the next June when Springfield Davis was sent home from the penitentiary. There hadn't been such a tornado of festivity in the neighborhood since Delbert Royster and La Vonne Lancey were married two years before, and even then the Davises could not have felt very festive.

At five-thirty P.M. of the great day, Benjy and Bake started for McKee's Crossing in the old Royster car, but the fan-belt parted and as a result the train was just pulling out when they careened up to the station. They saw Spring Davis sitting there with a straw suitcase beside him.

His hair and mustache were snow-white and his face sagged, as if its fleshy sub-structure had dried up. His pointed shoulders came forward more noticeably and tried to meet across the front of his chest, but otherwise his appearance was the same as it had been. Benjy expected him to be as pale as a tallow candle, but he was not;

Spring explained later that he had worked out of doors a good deal. The worst thing about the whole prison experience, he thought, was having so many of the convicts call him Pop.

He was eighty-six years old, and walked stiffly, and sometime he'd open his mouth for a moment before he could say anything when he wanted to talk.

They got him into the car, with twenty townspeople staring quietly at him, and started for home. Spring didn't talk much on the way. He took off his old slouch hat and let the wind blow his hair—soft as milkweed silk. Once he said, "I see they've cut down that willow row on the Collins place," and again, "Well, there's no use in my not saying that I was surprised—terribly surprised. It come so sudden! I didn't expect them to let me out for years and years."

He glanced keenly toward the Terry place as they passed its burdock-grown lane, and he seemed about to ask a question. But the next moment the north field of the Davises had swum past, and the car was crunching in at the gate. Adelaide Davis was just opening the screen door: others of the neighborhood women huddled behind her, and a lot of men were squatting on their heels beneath the cottonwood tree. Benjy always remembered how Cal Royster snapped his knife shut and put it into his pocket before he turned. Cal had been whittling a toy dart for one of the Lancey kids.

A long table had been arranged beside the peony bushes, and you could smell everything from fried chicken to beet pickles. After the greetings were made, Spring said that he'd like to put on some other clothes, and Benjy went behind him as he toiled up the narrow stairway to the hot rooms under the eaves. Spring's old work-clothes were there, but washed and smooth and foreign to him; he would not feel at home until his crooked knees and elbows had made their appropriate dents in the cloth.

Mrs. Davis had disposed of his old suspenders, and he couldn't get a satisfactory adjustment on the ones he was wearing. He came into Benjy's room for help, and the first thing he saw was Bugle Ann's collar hanging beside the mirror.

If he lived to be a hundred, Benjy would never cease blaming himself for that.

Finally, after working his mouth for a long time, Spring managed to say, "Then you did find her. You never wrote it to me."

"Pa," Benjy groaned, "now you set down, Pa. Set down." And at last the old man sank deep into the narrow feather-bed.

He wanted to know, "Where was it? Where?"

"Up in Bachelor's timber. We never found her until last September."

"Bachelor's," echoed Spring. And then: "No, no, couldn't have been there."

"It was right beside the old shack," said his son, as gently as he could.

Spring stared for a while. Downstairs they were yelling and laughing, and La Vonne Lancey Royster was ringing a dinner bell. Out in the yard, old Billy Bryan began to challenge with excitement.

"Then Terry never did it," said Spring.

"Maybe she run up there—after he shot her—or—"

The old man hissed, "Ah, stop your foolish talk!" His eyes were wet and blazing. "Nevertheless," he declared in a rapid whisper. "I'm thankful I done it when I did, for certainly I'd had to do it sometime. He meant it, Benjy. He would of killed her in a minute."

"Sure he would!" cried Benjy. "You don't think anybody in this world is blaming you, do you?"

Springfield had the collar in his hand, turning it slowly around and around.

Benjy mopped his perspiring forehead. "Pa," he began, "that ain't the whole story. There was a time, first June after you went up there—"

He told briefly of the dog's bugling which had echoed in the woods beyond Heaven Creek, and how the neighborhood had taken it, and of the phantom pack which was said to hunt so silently at night, unattended by any hunters.

Spring blew his nose when Benjy was through. "There was a time when I would of laughed my head off at that," he said, simply enough, "but I've had plenty of time to think, these last four years. There were funny things in the War, boy, and there's been funny things other times. My mother knew that brother Rufus was killed by a snapped log-cabin, long before they ever brung her the news. She saw it in a kind of dream. . . . I don't say you heard Bugle Ann up there in the timber, that night, but you did hear something. Mighty often I thought I heard her, clear off in Jefferson City."

Then they went downstairs and out into the yard, to the fried chicken and other food, and all the talk, and all the people.

Supper stretched far into the dusk; then the table was cleared, and women began chattering and packing their baskets in the vicious heat of the kitchen. The men sat on the front porch and on the grass, and children shrieked at mysterious games among the berry bushes.

They had tried to enthrone Springfield Davis in the big splint-bottomed rocker, but he preferred to sit with his angular spine against a porch post. The dogs came to pay their respects; there was no one of them that he loved well enough to let it sleep across his lap, though Benjy watched hopefully.

In the first hush of twilight, when conversation had labored away from fox-hunting a dozen times, Spring astonished the crowd by rising to his feet and walking slowly down into the yard to feel the grass.

"It's not real wet," he said, so distinctly that all could hear him, "but there's a promising feel of dampness between the blades. When did it rain here?"

Somebody coughed. "Must of been night-before-last."

The pipes and cigarettes glowed spasmodically, and in the kitchen the younger Lancey girls were trying to harmonize with *Sometimes I'm happy, sometimes I'm blue.*

"This night'll be black-dark and that's a fact," came from Cal Royster.

Spring stood listening to the girls' song. "Radio," he muttered. "Well, we had radio music up there, too." He called to Royster, "Cal, I've been smelling at black-dark nights for nigh onto four years."

"I didn't think you'd feel—" Bake started to say, and then he chewed his nervous lip.

Spring Davis echoed, "Feel what?" He looked like a tall, guerrilla ghost in the thickening dusk, and the scent of June flowers was heavy as at a funeral. "Why, when a relative dies we all go on living, don't we? We all have to. I'd like, just as quick as possible, to set beside a fire again."

Benjy stood up. He felt his knees quivering. "The dogs are rusty, Pa. You know I've been farming pretty steady."

"They'll get the kinks out of their noses, once a fox is good and sweet," said Spring. It was as if he alone were trying to whistle up the courage of his neighbors. "I hate to see a good, sticky night go to waste. And there ain't any southeast wind."

There was a stir among the farmers, and more than one stood up. But for all their eagerness a certain delicacy possessed them now. They realized that this pathetic rite—the first journeying

of old Spring to the hills of Heaven Creek—was something sacred
to the Davises and Roysters, who had hunted together time out
of mind.

"I'm afraid Gabe won't look after that colt proper," said old Ed
Armstrong. "Awful hard to keep a hock bandaged." The Lanceys
spoke of a big day in the field to-morrow, and Henry Pettigrew
made lugubrious mention of his rheumatic knee.

"Well," Bake Royster announced, in a sweeping gesture of
exclusion. "looks like everybody else has to go home and do chores
or go to bed early, but Pa and I might trail up in the timber a spell
with you, Spring."

Davis said, "Fetch the hounds, Benjy. I don't reckon we'll need
a snack to-night, we're so full of good supper."

In half an hour the four of them had crossed the narrow clover
field and were wading the valley darkness: Spring, Benjy, Cal and
Baker. A solid bank of clouds rose slowly out of the west, and rain
would come before morning. The air was one great, mossy cellar
of humidity.

On the high crest of the Divide, the hounds went loose—four
Davis dogs and five Roysters. All of the Davis dogs were elderly
hounds whose voices Spring Davis knew as well as his own name.
The white blots went speeding, zigzagging toward the shadows
where foxes most often made their path.

The men sat on their haunches and waited.

"One's struck," said Cal, when a haunting moan came from the
hilltop. The moan stopped suddenly. "No," Benjy grunted, "you
just thought so. If that was Toul Sector . . . has he run on his own
trail lately, Bake?"

Bake grinned, in spite of himself. "Not for a good month. Wait
awhile."

The insects skirmished around them. At last little Elsie Janis
found exciting evidence; she talked about it. Billy Bryan and Old
Hickory joined her, and the whole mob went hooting melodiously
toward the south slope.

"Good voice she's got," said Spring. "She one of your new ones,
Cal?"

"Just small fry," replied Royster, with pride which he couldn't
conceal, "and she'll run as long as a fox makes tracks."

Baker thought. "Good voice? Well, the old guy said so," and
yet Bake was well aware that her yelps were not qualified for a
chorus of the best Royster voices, let alone to bring praise from the

man who had bred Bugle Ann. He wondered whether it was merely
a mistaken kindness on Spring's part, or whether the old man had
really lost his ear. Three years, eight months and twenty-one days
were an awful long time.

Bake began to hum *I stood in the jailhouse*, and stopped in horror when he realized what he was humming.

He heard the bubbling of his father's whisky bottle. "Let's have
a fire," Cal ordered.

The first curling flame, nursed tenderly through drying twigs,
showed Benjy Davis something which made him catch his breath.
He had to build the fire higher before he was sure. . . . Yes, old
Springfield had gone upstairs before he left the house, but Benjy
hadn't given it any thought at the time. And now he saw that the
old man wore the battered bugle, tucked neatly beneath his suspender strap.

Stiff little needles rose on Benjy's scalp. He kept fooling with
the fire.

"They're well toward Big Panther Holler," Cal estimated.

Spring inclined his head critically. "Yes, that's a bee-line fox to-
night. Doesn't let no crops grow under his feet." He spoke without
a tremor of madness, but this old bugle glowed and shimmered and
caught dull flashes from the firelight at every snap of the flames.

Then Benjy saw the shaking of Baker Royster's hands, and he
knew that Bake too had seen the trumpet. . . . The son thought
crazily, "Christ in the Mountains, what would we do if he stood up
and started to blow that thing?"

Bake was shivering with the same wonder. This was June . . . he
knew the month, and the year, and the farm—he knew every scrap
of sod beneath his feet—and yet the first blast of that horn would
turn the commonplace world to madness. No person could estimate
what tribes might come sweeping through the underbrush in
answer.

After a few moments, it was impossible to hear the dogs any
more. They had gone deep into the crooked defile of Big Panther
Creek; there was no telling just when they might return. The Roysters knew this fox well enough: their dogs had run him frequently
during the year. He was a bee-liner from the word Go, as Cal often
remarked, and he'd just as soon venture into the next county as not.
But always he holed at the south end of Bachelor's timber, so they
knew the pack would come howling back eventually.

No one talked. The log on the fire shrank to the thinness of a charred bone, and Benjy arose to see whether he could find another one dry enough to burn. There was a V of discarded fence posts nearby, and under their shelter perhaps—

He stopped, frozen in his tracks as the sound pierced them. It was a faint and elvish cry, half lost amid the buzz of tree-toads, and it might have been fathered by one of those nighthawks which rode high overhead. . . . Still, it never came from the throat of a bird, and in the first second Benjy wondered what sort of a throat it had come from.

Before the sudden blurring of his gaze, he watched his father's head lifting, nodding. Spring's mouth had opened slightly, in the reflex of one who listens without half knowing. . . .

Again the thin, silver measure—the horn of something which searched the forest away over beyond Heaven Hump. Bake Royster crawled up on his elbow, and his face became yellow instead of red in the firelight.

"Benjy," whispered Spring Davis, "I reckon she's struck."

The young man made a harsh sound. "It's a dog," he said. "Foxhound that belongs to— Running all off by himself, that way. I reckon he's an Armstrong."

The sockets beneath Spring's eyebrows were blank and dark and empty; the weaving shadows did strange things to the contour of his face. He said, "No Armstrong ever had that kind of music in him." Then, creakily, he was on his feet and fingering the lip of his bugle.

"For pity sake," mumbled Cal Royster, "it's just a kind of echo. . . ."

"Cal," said Spring, "if she comes real close to us, I'll blow the bugle for her."

Benjy didn't know why she should have been up again, loping through that timber. It was her voice, of course—no other dog had ever lived with such a melody hidden in its throat. He ventured to suppose that Bugle Ann had loved Spring Davis, much as a woman might have loved him, but it was a cruel and selfish devotion which would rob them all of their sanity, and never let them live in the same world with other men again.

He was repeating, again and again, "Pa! Pa—set down—set down—" and that was the same plea he had made in the bedroom.

Old Spring laughed at them all, and he seemed to tower against

the sky. "Are you plumb certain that was her collar, Benjy? . . . I
reckon nobody but God seen her bones hop up out of the orchard
to-night."

He ceased speaking, then, because the dog's howling was closer
and more distinct, as if the trail had swung toward the Hollow;
even now the fox might be leaping the gorge of Chilly Branch.
But Bugle Ann had learned the last trick of any fox that ever
jumped.

Bake Royster was trying to stand up, but for the moment his
legs wouldn't support him. He thought, "She won't need any help
to-night. Spring Davis is in the woods, and naturally she knows it."
When he was far off in the penitentiary it had been kind of the
Boone dogs, the hounds buried and dust a hundred years ago, to
come out and hunt with her and cast in enormous circles to locate
the scent . . . big, gobbling shapes, they could drag down the fast-
est deer in the hills. They could make the black bears afraid of
them, and every catamount would slink along the tree-tops when
they went by.

In sudden relief, Bake wanted to laugh out loud. He had hoped
that she was a ghost, all along, for that made the whole tale so much
easier to understand.

"Sweet mouth," he heard old Davis saying, "the sweetest mouth
that ever lived."

Cal groped for his friend's arm. "Now, Spring," he quavered,
"you got to get holt of yourself."

Spring laughed.

That clear, baying voice rocketed against the cloudy ceiling,
and came down to wash all around them.

"Get holt? Why, I bred the most beautiful tune ever played in
these parts, and I ain't ashamed! Maybe you laughed when you seen
me bring this bugle, but I reckoned it would come handy." He
paused, grinning slyly, and nodding again as the round pealing
broke loose anew.

Then, from blackest distance and seeming to rise behind the
hound notes, sounded the yell of a bugle. It blew the same chords
which Springfield Davis had always blown for his dog.

The hound's cry ceased, quickly, and the woods seemed to hold
out empty hands.

The men looked at one another, pale face reflecting pale face,
and for the first time you could see Springfield's eyes. They were
bright with bewilderment, and with rage.

Once more the *ta-da*, the shrill witchery and command of it.
The strings of old Davis's neck stood out tight against his skin. "I
never done it," he cried. "I never gave no one else leave to blow
her in!"

"Where was it?" asked Bake, hoarsely.

"Up on Heaven Hump, or past," Benjy answered him. Then he
started away through the timber like a runaway steer, with Bake
after him.

### 8

Spring and Cal stumbled cruelly in the underbrush, until the
younger men called to each other, remembering, and came back to
help them. Only when they had worked their way across Chilly
Branch and had crept to the summit beyond, did any one say a
complete sentence. It was Spring who spoke.

"Put out your lights," he ordered. "I see another fire."

A faint ruddiness lived in the north and east, and they went
toward it. Benjy grasped his father's arm, pulling him along. The
old man moved like a wooden image, but he breathed steadily, and
Benjy was certain he'd never drop dead in those woods, no matter
who or what they found beside that fire.

Again the tree-toads buzzed; the crickets sawed and chuckled,
and betty-millers came to kiss the hunters' perspiring faces; these
creatures could be merry and could exalt their whispers again, with
all those mighty trumpet notes echoed beyond recall.

The woods thinned away. Here was a clearing, stockaded with
lonely fence posts, where once Jacob Terry's sheep had lain down
in a green pasture.

A black shape grew against the distant core of firelight.

"It's a woman," said Bake.

For a moment he weaved, dizzy, as in the dawn before Jacob
Terry was killed.

Camden Terry sat beside the blaze. She was motionless, even as
the dry sticks crackled under approaching feet; she must have been
expecting this invasion, all along. A dog was with her. The dog
bayed, briefly, and Springfield Davis whispered, ". . . World, and
they that dwell therein," and his arm tried to twist out of Benjy's
manacling grasp.

The girl looked up at them. Benjy thought that she was more
beautiful than ever—more beautiful than that day in court, for the

fire made red gilt of her hair. Her eyes held dignity and fearlessness, but undoubtedly she was waiting for some immense judgment.

Spring stepped up against the fire, and looked down at the hound which crouched within the curve of the girl's arm. "You blew them notes," were the first words he said, for he saw the bugle in Camden Terry's lap.

She said, "Yes. Twice. Yes, I did."

"That hound . . ." His throat went to pieces on the word. He seemed to build it up again. "What dog is that?"

"I raised her."

"But it's got—her voice."

"Yes, I know. I used to hear her."

He said, scornfully, "I tell you, God never made no two hound-voices alike. Same kind of mouth, and all. He never."

The girl looked up at him. "This—She was hers. She's Bugle Ann's. She's by Proctor Pride out of Bugle Ann. There were four more, but only this one had the real bugle-mouth."

Springfield staggered. Benjy held him. "She never had no pups," said Spring, thickly.

Camden passed her hand over the little hound's ears, and the dog watched Spring Davis with soft, sad eyes. Her nostrils reached out for the smell of him. . . . Camden Terry stood up; the bugle rolled across the ground. Firelight made her blue dress seem purple, and it did kindly with her eyes, and for a moment Benjy couldn't breathe.

"Mr. Davis," the girl said, "my father never killed her."

Spring cried, "Aw, we know that! The boys found her skeleton over by Bachelor's, and they heard her voice in the woods, but I still say she never was bred to any dog."

"That night—" Camden's voice was very low; her hands struggled together. "I drove out of the yard, just like I told in court. She was coming past the gate; I couldn't see her in time. I couldn't —It was an awful sharp turn. . . . I got out and picked her up. . . . She wasn't dead, and even—hurt—she— She didn't seem to blame me. I was afraid there'd be trouble over it: Bugle Ann's being hurt."

Somewhere in the world beyond, Cal Royster was saying, "Car lights. They stopped for a minute. Then they went on. It was when I heard the yip."

"This hound never was hers," Spring Davis snarled. "Where in hell did it get her voice?"

"Wait, Pa," said Benjy.

The girl's hands separated; the fingers flattened stiffly together. "I took her along in the car. The rest of my folks didn't know I'd brought her; just Uncle Elnathan. I told them I had found a run-over dog, on the way, and I hustled her out to Uncle's place. . . . After we heard what had happened, I didn't dare tell the truth. It would have been worse for you, if the jury knew Bugle Ann wasn't really dead at all."

She gasped, "Oh, I hated Pa. He killed my mother with pure meanness. It's the awfulest thing in the world to have a father you've got to hate."

Spring eyed her grimly, and told her to go on.

"Well, it was Bugle Ann's shoulder and leg. . . . She was kind of crippled, but I nursed her to health. When she came in heat in February, I bred her to Proctor Pride. He was a Spaulding hound; the only good one Uncle had, any more. There were five pups. But this was the one—like her."

Camden paused, and there were tears all over her face, but this time it was Benjy who asked her to go on.

"She waited till they were weaned. Then she left one night— there was a moon—She wasn't dried up yet, and she wasn't strong enough to run. But she did go away. We traced her fifteen miles, next day, and then lost her for good. Likely she was heading for home when she struck a fox, and you folks heard her. We never knew she was dead, for sure, but I always thought she'd been killed trying to get back home."

Spring exclaimed, "Benjy, I got to set," and his son eased him quickly to the ground. . . . Cal Royster fumbled around. It took him a long while to find his flask, but at last he did find it.

Soon, Spring opened his eyes and nodded at the girl. "You see," he murmured, "they let me out of Jefferson City."

Her chin trembled. "I knew. That's how I come to be here to-night. I thought you'd maybe be out in the timber."

Benjy stared at her with fierce intensity. "*You* knew. How did you know? They don't talk those things around."

"Well," she told him, "I knew beforehand."

Benjy said, "It wasn't a parole. He was pardoned."

"Yes. The parole board. Sometimes they—kind of recommend. Folks write letters. And talk."

He had taken her hand—both of her hands. He came between her and the Roysters, and he seemed even to have forgotten his father. Camden said, rapidly: "Jacob Terry was my father. I'd like to forget that, but it counted for something when they come to considering and—All my folks weren't Terrys," she cried at him. "Half of them were Camdens, and Camdens mean something in this state, even yet. Some of them are in the legislature."

Bake Royster exploded, "My God! You done it, didn't you?"

She shook her head. "No. I couldn't of done it myself. I just— did what I could. They all knew what kind of a man my father was. And I told them about Mr. Davis."

Inch by inch, the hound had hitched forward to sniff around Spring Davis's feet. At first the old man twisted his legs away, but finally he lay still and watched the dog. "I'm all right, boy," he muttered to Benjy, and then he raised up on his elbow. His eyes took in the whole color and shape and hide of the hound; they studied her slenderness, her strong and well-arched coupling, the stifle built far out from her body. . . . The hound sneezed. She looked at old Davis with curiosity, and then stepped across his legs with tail waving politely, and smelled him from the other side.

"I reckon she could run," said Spring.

"I trained her to the horn. Same as— It seemed like the best thing to do." Camden looked at Benjy, and he nodded slowly, and his face came close to hers.

Spring asked, "What do you call her?"

"Little Lady."

The old man said, "Got a deeper tan, but it's spotted much the same." Stiffly, reluctantly, he put out his hand and touched the hound's muzzle. His eyes were still hard and dry, but he whispered, "Little Lady. You got quite a mouth, Little Lady."

Cal Royster was crying like his own grandchild, but more quietly. Bake took him away from the fire. "Come on, Pa," he grunted, "we got to get out of here. I think I hear the pack coming north again." Baker was certain in his heart that before the other hounds had ever come in, Spring Davis would have sent Little Lady out with Camden and Benjy, to see what she was made of. He prophesied to himself that she would run as long as any fox made tracks; she would be a twenty-hour dog, given to mighty journey-ings and chasings, but always she would come back to those black-dark hills when the bugle called her home.

# JIM BAKER'S BLUE-JAY YARN

## Mark Twain

*Can birds and animals talk? Men have thought so since pre-*
*historic days, when they worshipped beasts as gods, or, like the*
*Indians, claimed them as ancestors. The speech and thoughts*
*of the inhabitants of the woodland have been recorded for us*
*many times from Aesop to Ernest Thompson Seton, but sel-*
*dom more delightfully than in this tall tale by Mark Twain.*

ONE afternoon I got lost in the woods about a mile from the
hotel, and presently fell into a train of dreamy thought about
animals which talk, and kobolds, and enchanted folk, and the rest
of this pleasant legendary stuff; and so, by stimulating my fancy, I
finally got to imagining I glimpsed small flitting shapes here and
there down the columned aisles of the forest. It was a place which
was peculiarly meet for the occasion. It was a pine wood, with so
thick and soft a carpet of brown needles that one's footfall made
no more sound than if he were treading on wool; the tree-trunks
were as round and straight and smooth as pillars, and stood close
together; they were bare of branches to a point about twenty-five
feet above-ground, and from there upward so thick with boughs
that not a ray of sunlight could pierce through. The world was
bright with sunshine outside, but a deep and mellow twilight
reigned in there, and also a silence so profound that I seemed to
hear my own breathings.

When I had stood ten minutes, thinking and imagining, and
getting my spirit in tune with the place, and in the right mood to
enjoy the supernatural, a raven suddenly uttered a hoarse croak
over my head. It made me start; and then I was angry because I
started. I looked up, and the creature was sitting on a limb right
over me, looking down at me. I felt something of the same sense
of humiliation and injury which one feels when he finds that a
human stranger has been clandestinely inspecting him in his pri-

vacy and mentally commenting upon him. I eyed the raven, and the raven eyed me. Nothing was said during some seconds. Then the bird stepped a little way along his limb to get a better point of observation, lifted his wings, stuck his head down below his shoulders toward me, and croaked again—a croak with a distinctly insulting expression about it. If he had spoken in English he could not have said any more plainly than he did say in raven, "Well, what do *you* want here?" I felt as foolish as if I had been caught in some mean act by a responsible being, and reproved for it. However, I made no reply; I would not bandy words with a raven. The adversary waited a while, with his shoulders still lifted, his head thrust down between them, and his keen bright eye fixed on me; then he threw out two or three more insults, which I could not understand, further than that I knew a portion of them consisted of language not used in church.

I made no reply. Now the adversary raised his head and called. There was an answering croak from a little distance in the wood— evidently a croak of inquiry. The adversary explained with enthusiasm, and the other raven dropped everything and came. The two sat side by side on the limb and discussed me as freely and offensively as two great naturalists might discuss a new kind of bug. The thing became more and more embarrassing. They called in another friend. This was too much. I saw that they had the advantage of me, and so I concluded to get out of the scrape by walking out of it. They enjoyed my defeat as much as any low white people could have done. The craned their necks and laughed at me (for a raven *can* laugh, just like a man), and they squalled insulting remarks after me as long as they could see me. They were nothing but ravens—I knew that—what they thought about me could be a matter of no consequence—and yet when even a raven shouts after you, "What a hat!" "Oh, pull down your vest!" and that sort of thing, it hurts you and humiliates you, and there is no getting around it with fine reasoning and pretty arguments.

Animals talk to each other, of course. There can be no question about that; but I suppose there are very few people who can understand them. I never knew but one man who could. I knew he could, however, because he told me so himself. He was a middle-aged, simple-hearted miner, who had lived in a lonely corner of California, among the woods and mountains, a good many years, and had studied the ways of his only neighbours, the beasts and the birds, until he believed he could accurately translate any remark which they made. This was Jim Baker. According to Jim Baker, some animals have only a limited education and use only very simple words, and scarcely ever a comparison or a flowery figure; whereas, certain other animals have a large vocabulary, a fine command of language and a ready and fluent delivery; consequently this latter talk a great deal; they like it; they are conscious of their talent, and they enjoy "showing off." Baker said that, after long and careful observation, he had come to the conclusion that the blue-jays were the best talkers he had found among birds and beasts. Said he:

"There's more *to* a blue-jay than any other creature. He has got more moods and more different kinds of feelings than other creatures; and, mind you, whatever a blue-jay feels, he can put into language. And no mere commonplace language, either, but rattling, out-and-out book-talk—and bristling with metaphor, too—just bristling! And as for command of language—why, *you* never see a blue-jay get stuck for a word. No man ever did. They just boil out of him! And another thing: I've noticed a good deal and there's no bird, or cow, or anything that uses as good grammar as a blue-jay. You may say a cat uses good grammar. Well, a cat does—but you let a cat get excited, once; you let a cat get to pulling fur with another cat on a shed, nights, and you'll hear grammar that will give you the lockjaw. Ignorant people think it's the *noise* which fighting cats make that is so aggravating, but it ain't so; it's the sickening grammar they use. Now I've never heard a jay use bad grammar but very seldom; and when they do, they are as ashamed as a human; they shut right down and leave.

"You may call a jay a bird. Well, so he is, in a measure—because he's got feathers on him, and don't belong to no church, perhaps; but otherwise he is just as much a human as you be. And I'll tell you for why. A jay's gifts, and instincts, and feelings, and interests cover the whole ground. A jay hasn't got any more principle than a Congressman. A jay will lie, a jay will steal, a jay will deceive, a jay will betray; and, four times out of five, a jay will go back on his solemnest promise. The sacredness of an obligation is a thing which you can't cram into no blue-jay's head. Now, on top of all this, there's another thing: a jay can out-swear any gentleman in the mines. You think a cat can swear. Well, a cat can; but you give a blue-jay a subject that calls for his reserve powers, and where is your cat? Don't talk to *me*—I know too much about this thing. And there's yet another thing: in the one little particular of scolding—just good, clean, out-and-out scolding—a blue-jay can lay **over** anything, human or divine. Yes, sir, a jay is everything that a man is. A jay can cry, a jay can laugh, a jay can feel shame, a jay can reason and plan and discuss, a jay likes gossip and scandal, a jay has got a sense of humour, a jay knows when he is an ass just as well as you do—maybe better. If a jay ain't human, he better take in his sign, that's all. Now I am going to tell you a perfectly true fact about some blue-jays.

"When I first begun to understand jay language correctly, there was a little incident happened here. Seven years ago, the last man in this region but me moved away. There stands his house—been empty ever since; a log house, with a plank roof—just one big room, and no more; no ceiling—nothing between the rafters and the floor. Well, one Sunday morning I was sitting out here in front of my cabin with my cat, taking the sun, and looking at the blue hills, and listening to the leaves rustling so lonely in the trees, and thinking of the home away yonder in the States, that I hadn't heard from in thirteen years, when a blue-jay lit on that house, with an acorn in his mouth, and says, 'Hello, I reckon I've struck something!' When he spoke the acorn fell out of his mouth and rolled down the roof, of course, but he didn't care; his mind was all on the thing he had struck. It was a knot-hole in the roof. He cocked his head to one side, shut one eye and put the other one to the hole, like a 'possum looking down a jug; then he glanced up with his bright eyes, gave a wink or two with his wings—which signifies gratification, you understand—and says, 'It looks like a hole, it's located like a hole—blamed if I don't believe it *is* a hole!'

"Then he cocked his head down and took another look; he glances up perfectly joyful this time; winks his wings and his tail both, and says, ' Oh, no, this ain't no fat thing, I reckon! If I ain't in luck!—why, it's a perfectly elegant hole!' So he flew down and got that acorn, and fetched it up and dropped it in, and was just tilting his head back with the heavenliest smile on his face, when all of a sudden he was paralyzed into a listening attitude, and that smile faded gradually out of his countenance like breath off'n a razor, and the queerest look of surprise took its place. Then he says, 'Why, I didn't hear it fall!' He cocked his eye at the hole again and took a long look; raised up and shook his head; stepped around to the other side of the hole, and took another look from that side; shook his head again. He studied a while, then he just went into the *details*—walked round and round the hole, and spied into it from every point of the compass. No use. Now he took a thinking attitude on the comb of the roof, and scratched the back of his head with his right foot a minute, and finally says, 'Well, it's too many for *me*, that's certain; must be a mighty long hole; however, I ain't got no time to fool around here; I got to 'tend to business; I reckon it's all right—chance it, anyway!'

"So he flew off and fetched another acorn and dropped it in, and tried to flirt his eyes to the hole quick enough to see what become of it, but he was too late. He held his eyes there as much as a minute; then he raised up and sighed, and says, 'Confound it, I don't seem to understand this thing, no way; however, I'll tackle her again.' He fetched another acorn, and done his level best to see what become of it, but he couldn't. He says, 'Well, *I* never struck no such hole as this before; I'm of the opinion it's a totally new kind of a hole.' Then he begun to get mad. He held in for a spell, walking up and down the comb of the roof, and shaking his head and muttering to himself; but his feelings got the upper hand of him presently, and he broke loose and cussed himself black in the face. I never see a bird take on so about a little thing. When he got through, he walks to the hole and looks in again for a half a minute; then he says, 'Well, you're a long hole, and a deep hole, and a mighty singular hole altogether—but I've started in to fill you, and I'm d——d if I *don't* fill you, if it takes a hundred years!'

"And with that, away he went. You never see a bird work so since you was born. He laid into his work like a nigger, and the way he hove acorns into that hole for about two hours and a half was one of the most exciting and astonishing spectacles I ever struck. He never stopped to take a look any more—he just hove 'em in, and went for more. Well, at last he could hardly flop his wings, he was so tuckered out. He comes a-dropping down, once more, sweating like an ice-pitcher, drops his acorn in and says, '*Now* I guess I've got the bulge on you by this time!' So he bent down for a look. If you'll believe me, when his head come up again he was just pale with rage. He says, 'I've shoveled acorns enough in there to keep the family thirty years, and if I can see a sign of one of 'em I wish I may land in a museum with a belly full of sawdust in two minutes!'

"He just had strength enough to crawl up on to the comb and lean his back agin the chimbly, and then he collected his impressions and begun to free his mind. I see in a second that what I had mistook for profanity in the mines was only just the rudiments, as you may say.

"Another jay was going by, and heard him doing his devotions, and stops to inquire what was up. The sufferer told him the whole circumstance, and says, 'Now, yonder's the hole, and if you don't believe me, go and look for yourself.' So this fellow went and looked, and comes back and says, 'How many did you say you put in there?' 'Not any less than two tons,' says the sufferer. The other jay went and looked again. He couldn't seem to make it out, so he raised a yell, and three more jays come. They all examined the hole, they all made the sufferer tell it over again, then they all discussed it, and got off as many leather-headed opinions about it as an average crowd of humans could have done.

"They called in more jays; then more and more, till pretty soon this whole region 'peared to have a blue flush about it. There must have been five thousand of them; and such another jawing and disputing and ripping and cussing, you never heard. Every jay in the whole lot put his eye to the hole, and delivered a more chuckle-headed opinion about the mystery than the jay that went there before him. They examined the house all over, too. The door was standing half-open, and at last one old jay happened to go and light on it and look in. Of course, that knocked the mystery galley-west in a second. There lay the acorns, scattered all over the floor. He flopped his wings and raised a whoop. 'Come here!' he says, 'Come here, everybody; hang'd if this fool hasn't been trying to fill up a house with acorns!' They all came a-swooping down like a blue cloud, and as each fellow lit on the door and took a glance, the whole absurdity of the contract that that first jay had tackled hit him home, and he fell over backwards suffocating with laughter, and the next jay took his place and done the same.

"Well, sir, they roosted around here on the house-top and the trees for an hour, and guffawed over that thing like human beings. It ain't no use to tell me a blue-jay hasn't got a sense of humour, because I know better. And memory, too. They brought jays here from all over the United States to look down that hole, every summer for three years. Other birds, too. And they could all see the point, except an owl that come from Nova Scotia to visit the Yo Semite, and he took this thing in on his way back. He said he couldn't see anything funny in it. But then, he was a good deal disappointed about Yo Semite, too."

# UNUSUAL TAMENESS

## Charles Darwin

*On December 27, 1831, a small British vessel, H.M.S. Beagle, sailed from England on a charting voyage that was to circle the globe and last five years. On board as the expedition's naturalist was a young man named Charles Darwin (1809–1882), who had previously tried the study of medicine and then thought of becoming a clergyman. But at Cambridge University he had come under the influence of Henslow, the botanist, who later recommended him for the Beagle's trip, called by Darwin "the most important event of my life." His journal of the voyage, published in 1839, was the foundation of all his thinking, the sourcebook of his later masterpieces* The Origin of Species *and* The Descent of Man. *Here are two selections from it, one about birds on the Galapagos Islands, the second about the first condor he shot.*

I WILL conclude my description of the natural history of these islands by giving an account of the extreme tameness of the birds.

This disposition is common to all the terrestrial species—namely, to the mocking-thrushes, the finches, wrens, tyrant fly-catchers, the dove, and carrion-buzzard. All of them often approached sufficiently near to be killed with a switch, and sometimes, as I myself tried, with a cap or hat. A gun is here almost superfluous, for with the muzzle I pushed a hawk off the branch of a tree. One day, whilst lying down, a mocking-thrush alighted on the edge of a pitcher made of the shell of a tortoise, which I held in my hand, and began very quietly to sip the water. It allowed me to lift it from the ground whilst seated on the vessel. I often tried, and very nearly succeeded, in catching these birds by their legs. Formerly the birds appear to have been even tamer than at present. Cowley (in the year 1684) says that the 'turtle-doves were so tame that they would often alight upon our hats and arms, so that we could take them alive; they not fearing man, until such time as some of our company did fire at them, whereby they were rendered more shy.' Dampier also, in the same year, says that a man in a morning's walk might kill six or seven dozen of these doves. At present, although certainly very tame, they do not alight on people's arms, nor do they suffer themselves to be killed in such large numbers. It is surprising that they have not become wilder; for these islands during the last hundred and fifty years have been frequently visited by buccaneers and whalers, and the sailors, wandering through the woods in search of tortoises, always take cruel delight in knocking down the little birds.

These birds, although now still more persecuted, do not readily become wild. In Charles Island, which had then been colonized about six years, I saw a boy sitting by a well with a switch in his hand, with which he killed the doves and finches as they came to drink. He had already procured a little heap of them for his dinner; and he said that he had constantly been in the habit of waiting by this well for the same purpose. It would appear that the birds of this archipelago, not having as yet learned that man is a more dangerous animal than the tortoise or the amblyrhynchus, disregard him, in the same manner as in England shy birds, such as magpies, disregard the cows and horses grazing in our fields.

The Falkland Islands offer a second instance of birds with a similar disposition. The extraordinary tameness of the little opetiorhynchus has been remarked by Pernety, Lesson, and other voyagers. It is not, however, peculiar to that bird. The polyborus, snipe, upland and lowland goose, thrush, bunting, and even some true hawks, are all more or less tame. As the birds are so tame there, where foxes, hawks, and owls occur, we may infer that the absence of all rapacious animals at the Galapagos is not the cause of their tameness here. The upland geese at the Falklands show, by the precaution they take in building on the islets, that they are aware of their danger from the foxes; but they are not by this rendered wild towards man. This tameness of the birds, especially of the water-fowl, is strongly contrasted with the habits of the same species in Tierra del Fuego, where for ages past they have been persecuted by the wild inhabitants. In the Falklands, the sportsman may sometimes kill more of the upland geese in one day than he can carry home; whereas in Tierra del Fuego it is nearly as difficult to kill one as it is in England to shoot the common wild goose.

In the time of Pernety (1763), all the birds there appear to have been much tamer than at present. He states that the opetiorhynchus would almost perch on his finger; and that with a wand he killed ten in half an hour. At that period the birds must have been about as tame as they now are at the Galapagos. They appear to have learned caution more slowly at these latter islands than at the Falklands, where they have had proportionate means of experience, for besides frequent visits from vessels, those islands have been at intervals colonized during the entire period. Even formerly, when all the birds were so tame, it was impossible, by Pernety's account, to kill the black-necked swan—a bird of passage, which probably brought with it the wisdom learned in foreign countries.

I may add that, according to Du Bois, all the birds at Bourbon in 1571–72, with the exception of the flamingoes and geese, were so extremely tame that they could be caught by the hand or killed in any number with a stick. Again, at Tristan d'Acunha, in the Atlantic, Carmichael states that the only two land-birds, a thrush and a bunting, were 'so tame as to suffer themselves to be caught with a hand-net.' From these several facts we may, I think, conclude—first, that the wildness of birds, with regard to man, is a particular instinct directed against *him*, and not dependent on any general degree of caution arising from other sources of danger; secondly, that it is not acquired by individual birds in a short time, even when much persecuted, but that in the course of successive generations it becomes hereditary. With domesticated animals we are accustomed to see new mental habits or instincts acquired and rendered hereditary; but with animals in a state of nature it must always be most difficult to discover instances of acquired hereditary knowledge. In regard to the wildness of birds towards man, there is no way of accounting for it, except as an inherited habit. Comparatively few young birds, in any one year, have been injured by man in England; yet almost all, even nestlings, are afraid of him. Many individuals, on the other hand, both at the Galapagos and at the Falklands, have been pursued and injured by man, but yet have not learned a salutary dread of him. We may infer from these facts what havoc the introduction of any new beast of prey must cause in a country, before the instincts of the indigenous inhabitants have become adapted to the stranger's credit or power.

# THE CONDOR

## Charles Darwin

THIS day I shot a condor. It measured from tip to tip of the wings eight and a half feet, and from beak to tail four feet. This bird is known to have a wide geographical range, being found on the west coast of South America, from the Strait of Magellan along the Cordillera, as far as eight degrees north of the Equator. The steep cliff near the mouth of the Rio Negro is its northern limit on the Patagonian coast; and they have there wandered about four hundred miles from the great central line of their habitation in the Andes. Further south, among the bold precipices at the head of Port Desire, the condor is not uncommon; yet only a few stragglers occasionally visit the sea-coast. A line of cliff near the mouth of the Santa Cruz is frequented by these birds; and about eighty miles up the river, where the sides of the valley are formed by steep basaltic precipices, the condor reappears. From these facts it seems that the condors require perpendicular cliffs. In Chili they haunt, during the greater part of the year, the lower country near the shores of the Pacific, and at night several roost together in one tree; but in the early part of summer they retire to the most inaccessible parts of the inner Cordillera, there to breed in peace.

With respect to their propagation, I was told by the country people in Chili that the condor makes no sort of nest, but in the months of November and December lays two large white eggs on a shelf of bare rock. It is said that the young condors cannot fly for an entire year; and long after they are able, they continue to roost by night and hunt by day with their parents. The old birds generally live in pairs; but among the inland basaltic cliffs of the Santa Cruz I found a spot where scores must usually haunt. On coming suddenly to the brow of the precipice, it was a grand spectacle to see between twenty and thirty of these great birds start heavily from their resting-place and wheel away in majestic circles. From the quantity of dung on the rocks they must long have frequented this cliff for roosting and breeding. Having gorged themselves with carrion on the plains below, they retire to these favourite ledges to digest their food. From these facts the condor, like the gallinazo, must to a certain degree be considered as a gregarious bird. In this part of the country they live altogether on the guanacos which have died a natural death, or, as more commonly happens, have been killed by the pumas. I believe, from what I saw in Patagonia, that they do not on ordinary occasions extend their daily excursions to any great distance from their regular sleeping-places.

The condors may oftentimes be seen at a great height, soaring over a certain spot in the most graceful circles. On some occasions I am sure that they do this only for pleasure; but on others, the Chileno countryman tells you that they are watching a dying animal, or the puma devouring its prey. If the condors glide down, and then suddenly all rise together, the Chileno knows that it is the puma which, watching the carcass, has sprung out to drive away the robbers. Besides feeding on carrion, the condors frequently attack young goats and lambs; and the shepherd-dogs are trained, whenever they pass over, to run out, and looking upwards, to bark violently. The Chilenos destroy and catch numbers. Two methods are used. One is to place a carcass on a level piece of ground within an enclosure of sticks with an opening, and when the condors are gorged, to gallop up on horseback to the entrance and thus enclose them; for when this bird has not space to run, it cannot give its body sufficient momentum to rise from the ground. The second method is to mark the trees in which, frequently to the number of five or six together, they roost, and then at night to climb up and noose them. They are such heavy sleepers, as I have myself witnessed, that this is not a difficult task. At Valparaiso I have seen a living condor sold for sixpence, but the common price is eight or ten shillings. One which I saw brought in had been tied with rope and was much injured; yet the moment the line was cut by which its bill was secured, although surrounded by people, it began ravenously to tear a piece of carrion. In a garden, at the same place, between twenty and thirty were kept alive. They were fed only once a week, but they appeared in pretty good health. The Chileno countrymen assert that the condor will live and retain its vigour between five and six weeks without eating. I cannot answer for the truth of this; but it is a cruel experiment, which very likely has been tried.

When an animal is killed in the country, it is well known that the condors, like other carrion-vultures, soon gain intelligence of it, and congregate in an inexplicable manner. In most cases it must not be overlooked that the birds have discovered their prey, and have picked the skeleton clean, before the flesh is in the least degree tainted. Remembering the experiments of M. Audubon on the little smelling powers of carrion-hawks, I tried in the above-mentioned garden the following experiment: the condors were tied, each by a rope, in a long row at the bottom of a wall; and having folded up a piece of meat in white paper, I walked backwards and forwards, carrying it in my hand at the distance of about three yards from them; but no notice whatever was taken. I then threw it on the ground, within one yard of an old male bird. He looked at it for a moment with attention, but then regarded it no more. With a stick I pushed it closer and closer, until at last he touched it with his beak. The paper was then instantly torn off with fury, and at the same moment every bird in the long row began struggling and flapping its wings. Under the same circumstances it would have been quite impossible to have deceived a dog. The evidence in favour of and against the acute smelling powers of carrion-vultures is singularly balanced. Professor Owen has demonstrated that the olfactory nerves of the turkey-buzzard (*Cathartes aura*) are highly developed; and on the evening when Mr. Owen's paper was read at the Zoological Society, it was mentioned by a gentleman that he had seen the carrion-hawks in the West Indies on two occasions collect on the roof of a house, when a corpse had become offensive from not having been buried. In this case, the intelligence could hardly have been acquired by sight. On the other hand, besides the experiments of Audubon and that one by myself, Mr. Bachman has tried in the United States many varied plans, showing that neither the turkey-buzzard (the species dissected by Professor Owen) nor the gallinazo finds its food by smell. He covered portions of highly offensive offal with a thin canvas cloth, and strewed pieces of meat on it. These the carrion-vultures ate up, and then remained quietly standing, with the beaks within the eighth of an inch of the putrid mass, without discovering it. A small rent was made in the canvas, and the offal was immediately discovered. The canvas was replaced by a fresh piece, and meat again put on it, and was again devoured by the vultures without their discovering the hidden mass on which they were trampling. These facts are attested by the signatures of six gentlemen, besides that of Mr. Bachman.

Often when lying down to rest on the open plains, on looking upwards I have seen carrion-hawks sailing through the air at a great height. Where the country is level, I do not believe a space of the heavens, of more than fifteen degrees above the horizon, is commonly viewed with any attention by a person either walking or on horseback. If such be the case, and the vulture is on the wing at a height of between three and four thousand feet, before it could come within the range of vision, its distance in a straight line from the beholder's eye would be rather more than two British miles. Might it not thus readily be overlooked? When an animal is killed by the sportsman in a lonely valley, may he not all the while be watched from above by the sharp-sighted bird? And will not the manner of its descent proclaim throughout the district to the whole family of carrion-feeders that their prey is at hand?

When the condors are wheeling in a flock round and round any spot their flight is beautiful. Except when rising from the ground, I do not recollect ever having seen one of these birds flap its wings. Near Lima I watched several for nearly half an hour, without once taking off my eyes. They moved in large curves, sweeping in circles, descending and ascending without giving a single flap. As they glided close over my head, I intently watched from an oblique position the outlines of the separate and great terminal feathers of each wing, and these separate feathers, if there had been the least vibratory movement, would have appeared as if blended together; but they were seen distinct against the blue sky. The head and neck were moved frequently, and apparently with force; and the extended wings seemed to form the fulcrum on which the movements of the neck, body, and tail acted. If the bird wished to descend, the wings were for a moment collapsed; and when again expanded with an altered inclination the momentum gained by the rapid descent seemed to urge the bird upwards with the even and steady movement of a paper kite. In the case of any bird *soaring*, its motion must be sufficiently rapid, so that the action of the inclined surface of its body on the atmosphere may counter-balance its gravity. The force to keep up the momentum of a body moving in a horizontal plane in the air (in which there is so little friction) cannot be great, and this force is all that is wanted. The movement of the neck and body of the condor, we must suppose, is sufficient for this. However this may be, it is truly wonderful and beautiful to see so great a bird, hour after hour, without any apparent exertion, wheeling and gliding over mountain and river.

# THE GREAT KAAN HUNTS

## Marco Polo

*When hunters long for something new and different in the practice of their sport, they will perhaps envy the Great Kaan of China, who had leopards and lions trained to catch game, who had twenty thousand men in charge of his hounds, and ten thousand falconers. The famous Venetian traveler of the thirteenth century tells of such fabulous facts in* The Travels of Marco Polo.

You must know that the Great Kaan has many leopards, all excellent for the chase and for catching game. He also has a large number of lynxes trained to hunt, and very good for the chase. He has many very big lions, too, much bigger than those of Babylon; they have very fine coats, and are of a beautiful colour, being striped lengthways in black, red, and white. They are trained to take wild boars, wild oxen, bears, wild asses, stags, fallow-deer, and other beasts. And I assure you it is a splendid sight to see those lions catch their quarries. When lions are taken to the chase, each lion is put in a cage on a cart, and a little dog with him. The reason they are placed in cages is that otherwise they would be too fierce and anxious to fall on the game, and it would be impossible to hold them. They have, moreover, to be led to the windward of the game, for if the latter scented them, they would flee, and not wait for them to approach.

He also has a multitude of eagles, trained to catch wolves, foxes, deer and roes; and they take many of them. Those trained to catch wolves are remarkably big and powerful. For you may be sure there is not a wolf, however big, that can escape them.

You are now informed of these things. I will next tell you how the Great Kaan keeps an enormous number of excellent hounds.

You must know that among the barons at court there are two who are own brothers, one called Baian, and the other Mingan.

Their title is that of *Cuiuci*, a word that means "those who look after the mastiffs." Each of these brothers has ten thousand men at his orders, and each group of ten thousand is dressed in one colour, the two colours being vermilion and yellow. Every time they go out hunting with the Great Lord, they wear this livery I have told you of. Out of the ten thousand, two thousand have, each of them, charge of one, two, or more mastiffs; so the number of mastiffs is immense. When the Great Kaan goes out hunting, one of these two brothers goes on one side of him, with his ten thousand men and quite five thousand hounds, and the other brother goes on the other side, with his ten thousand and their hounds. They all go abreast, and at a short distance of one another, so as to occupy the space of more than a day's march, and then they gradually converge. No wild animal they come across can escape. It is truly marvellous to see this hunt, and the behaviour of those hounds and hunters. For I assure you that when the Great Kaan rides out with his barons hunting over these plains, you will see these hounds, some here, some there, hunting down bears or stags or other animals; it is really a glorious sight.

It is part of the duty of these brothers to furnish the Great Kaan's court every day, from the beginning of the month of October to the end of March, with a thousand head of beasts and birds, except quails. Fish, too, they have to provide, as best as they may, counting as one "head" as much fish as three persons could eat at a meal.

I have now told you of those who look after the hounds. We will next tell you what the Great Kaan does during the other three months.

After passing the three months of December, January, and February in the city I have mentioned, the Great Kaan leaves in the month of March, and goes south, keeping at a short distance from the Ocean Sea, which is only two days' journey away. He takes with him no less than ten thousand falconers, and quite five hundred gerfalcons, besides a multitude of peregrine and saker falcons. He also takes numbers of goshawks for catching water-fowl. You must not, however, suppose that he keeps all these falconers near him in one place, he distributes them here and there, in groups of a hundred or two hundred or more. These groups go out fowling, and the greater part of the birds caught, they take to the Great Kaan. And when the Great Lord goes fowling with his gerfalcons and other birds, he takes with him no less than ten thousand men, disposed in twos, who are called *Toscaor*, a word that in our language signifies "men who watch." And that indeed they do, for they are posted here and there, in couples, so as to cover between them a large tract of land; and each of them has a whistle and a hood, to call in the birds, if necessary, and hold them. So when the Great Kaan gives orders to let his birds fly, there is no need for those who do so to go after them, since there are these men I have mentioned, scattered about the country, who keep their eye on them so well that the birds can go nowhere without the men going there too. And if the birds need help, the men straightway give it.

All the Great Kaan's birds, as well as those of the barons, have a little silver tablet attached to their legs, bearing the name of the owner and of the keeper. In this way the birds are recognised as soon as they are taken, and returned to their owners. And if one does not know whose the bird is, it is brought to a baron called *Bularguchi*, a word signifying "the keeper of things without an owner." For you must know that if a horse or a sword or a bird or anything else is found, without its owner being known, it must at once be brought to that baron, and he has it taken and put away. If he who finds it does not straightway give it up, he is held to be a thief. And those who have lost something go to that baron; if he has the object, he at once has it handed over. He is always stationed at the highest point of the camp with his banner, so that those who have lost or found anything, may see at once where he is. In this way all that is lost cannot but be found again and returned.

And when the Great Kaan goes on this expedition I have told you of, in the neighborhood of the Ocean Sea, there is no lack of fine sights in the way of the hunting of birds and beasts. There is no amusement in the world equal to it. And the Great Kaan always goes on four elephants, in a beautiful wooden chamber, all lined inside with cloths of beaten gold, and covered outside with lions' skins. He always remains inside it when fowling, as he is troubled with the gout. The Great Lord always keeps in it twelve of his best gerfalcons. There are also many barons and ladies to amuse him and keep him company. And when he goes journeying in that chamber placed on the elephants, you must know that if the barons who ride round him, cry out: "Sire, cranes are passing!" then he has the chamber uncovered above, and, on seeing the cranes, he has the gerfalcons he wants, brought to him, and casts them. The gerfalcons fight at length with the cranes, and generally take them. The Great Lord watches the sight, remaining in his bed, and finds great pleasure and amusement in it. And all the barons and knights ride round their Lord. And truly there never was, nor do I believe there is now, any man on earth able to have so much pleasure and delight as the Kaan, and to procure it with such ease.

So the Great Lord travels on until he reaches a place called Cachar Modum. Here he finds his tents pitched, and those of his sons, barons, and concubines; more than ten thousand tents in all, and every one richly adorned and beautiful. And I will tell you how the Great Kaan's tents are made.

They are more than one, as I shall tell you. The tent in which he holds his court is so large that it can contain a thousand knights; its door opens to the south, and in it, as in a pavilion, stand the barons and other people. Then there is another tent, connected with this one, facing west, in which the Lord lives; it is a kind of pavilion reserved for his use. When he wishes to speak to anyone, he summons him within. Behind the large hall, is a spacious and fine chamber where the Great Lord sleeps. There are also other chambers and tents, but they do not communicate with the large one. The large halls and the chamber are built as I shall tell you. Each of the two halls has three pillars of spice-wood, very cunningly carved and gilt. On the outside, they are all covered with lions' skins, which are most beautiful, for they are all striped in black and red and white; and they are so well arranged that the rain and the wind can do no injury within. Inside they are all lined with ermine and sable, which are the most beautiful, fine, and costly furs in existence. For you must know that a sable fur sufficient for a man's mantle is worth 2000 gold bezants, if good, and 1000 if of the ordinary kind. The Tartars call it the queen of furs. The animals are of the size of a weasel. Now, those two halls of the Great Kaan are lined with these skins, worked and decorated in a marvellous way. And the chamber in which the Kaan sleeps, and which is connected with the two large halls, is also covered outside with lions' skins, and lined inside with sable and ermine. It is most cunningly constructed and arranged. And the ropes that brace the halls and the chamber are all made of silk. Those three tents are so valuable and costly, that no petty king could pay for them.

Around these tents stand all the other tents, excellently constructed and arranged. The Lord's concubines also have splendid tents. And the gerfalcons and hawks and other birds and beasts

have many immense tents. What more shall I tell you? Know in
very truth that there are so many people in that camp that verily
it is a marvel. One would think the Kaan was in his finest city. For
people flock from all sides. And, further, he brings all his servants
with him, and with him are also his leeches, and astrologers, and
falconers, and other officers in great number. And everything is as
orderly as in his capital.

And you must know that he remains there till spring, that is to
say, till about the season of our Easter. And during all that time he
never ceases fowling in the lakes and rivers, catching cranes, swans,
and other birds in abundance. His people, too, scattered on all sides
around him, send him plenty of venison and game. And, all the
time, he lives there in the midst of the greatest pleasure and entertainment; nor would anyone believe it, who had not seen it, for
his splendour and delight are much greater than I have told you.

Another thing I will add, too; no merchant or artisan or peasant
dare keep any falcon, or other bird for fowling, or any dog fit for
the chase throughout the whole of the Great Kaan's dominions.
And no baron or knight or any nobleman whatsoever dare hunt
or fowl near the place where the Great Kaan lives, in some parts to
a distance of five days' journey, and elsewhere to a distance of ten
or even fifteen days' journey, unless he be entered in the rolls of
the Captain of the Falconers, or have a special privilege. But beyond the limit of twenty days' journey, in all the other provinces
and lands, barons, knights, and noblemen can hunt, and keep birds
and hounds as they please. Know, too, that throughout all the lands
where the Great Kaan holds sway, no king, no baron, no one, in
a word, dare take or chase hares, fallow-deer, roe-bucks, stags, or
any other animal of this kind, between the months of March and
October; and this is in order that they may breed. And who should
transgress this order, would be made bitterly to rue it, for so the
Great Kaan has decreed. But I assure you that his commands are
so respected, that often enough hares and deer and the other animals I have mentioned come right up to people, and no one touches
them or does them any harm.

Even as you have heard, then, does the Great Lord remain in
that place till, more or less, the time of our Easter. Then he goes
away with all his people, and returns straight to the city of Cam-
baluc, along the same road by which he came, ever hunting and
fowling, to his great entertainment and delight.

# JUNGLE LIFE

## Charles Waterton

*One of the first naturalists to penetrate the South American jungles and report on the strange and colorful living things there was Charles Waterton (1782–1865), an Englishman who lived for eight years in British Guiana and later traveled up the Orinoco River and over much of the continent. Some of the creatures described and the adventures he narrated were so different from anything previously known that many naturalists doubted his accuracy until other expeditions confirmed him as a genuine scientist as well as a colorful writer. The following piece is taken from his* Wanderings in South America.

H E whose eye can distinguish the various beauties of unculti- vated nature, and whose ear is not shut to the wild sound in the woods, will be delighted in passing up the River Demerara. Every now and then the Maam or Tinamou sends forth one long and plaintive whistle from the depths of the forest, and then stops; whilst the yelping of the Toucan, and the shrill voice of the bird called Pi-pi-yo, is heard during the interval. The Campanero never fails to attract the attention of the passenger: at a distance of nearly three miles, you may hear this snow-white bird tolling every four or five minutes, like the distant convent bell. From six to nine in the morning, the forests resound with the mingled cries and strains of the feathered race; after this, they gradually die away. From eleven to three all nature is hushed as in a midnight silence, and scarce a note is heard, saving that of the Campanero and the Pi-pi-yo; it is then that, oppressed by the solar heat, the birds retire to the thickest shade, and wait for the refreshing cool of evening.

At sundown the Vampires, Bats, and Goat-suckers dart from their lonely retreat, and skim along the trees on the river's bank. The different kinds of Frogs almost stun the ear with their coarse and hollow-sounding croaking, while the Owls and Goat-suckers lament and mourn all night long.

About two hours before daybreak you will hear the red monkey moaning as though in deep distress; the Houtou, a solitary bird, and only found in the thickest recesses of the forest, distinctly articulates, 'houtou, houtou,' in a low and plaintive tone, an hour before sunrise; the Maam whistles about the same hour; the Hannaquoi, Pataca, and Maroudi announce his near approach to the eastern horizon, and the Parrots and Paroquets confirm his arrival there.

The Crickets chirp from sunset to sunrise, and often during the day, when the weather is cloudy. The Bête-rouge is exceedingly numerous in these extensive wilds, and not only man, but beasts and birds, are tormented by it. Mosquitoes are very rare after you pass the third island in the Demerara, and Sand-flies but seldom appear.

Courteous reader, here thou hast the outlines of an amazing landscape given thee; thou wilt see that the principal parts of it are but faintly traced, some of them scarcely visible at all, and that the shades are wholly wanting. If thy soul partakes of the ardent flame which the persevering Mungo Park's did, these outlines will be enough for thee; they will give thee some idea of what a noble country this is; and if thou hast but courage to set about giving the world a finished picture of it, neither materials to work on, nor colours to paint it in its true shades, will be wanting to thee. It may appear a difficult task at a distance; but look close at it, and it is nothing at all; provided thou hast but a quiet mind, little more is necessary, and the genius which presides over these wilds will kindly help thee through the rest. She will allow thee to slay the fawn, and cut down the Mountain-cabbage for thy support, and to select from every part of her domain whatever may be necessary for the work thou art about; but having killed a pair of Doves in order to enable thee to give mankind a true and proper description of them, thou must not destroy a third through wantonness, or to show what a good marksman thou art; that would only blot the picture thou art finishing, not colour it.

Though retired from the haunts of men, and even without a friend with thee, thou wouldst not find it solitary. The crowing of the Hannaquoi will sound in thine ears like the daybreak town-clock; and the Wren and the Thrush will join with thee in thy matin hymn to thy Creator, to thank Him for thy night's rest.

At noon thy Genius will lead thee to the Troely, one leaf of which will defend thee from both sun and rain. And if, in the cool of the evening, thou hast been tempted to stray too far from thy place of abode, and art deprived of light to write down the information thou hast collected, the Firefly, which thou wilt see in almost every bush around thee, will be thy candle. Hold it over thy pocket book, in any position which thou knowest will not hurt it, and it will afford thee ample light. And when thou hast done with it, put it kindly back again on the next branch to thee. It will want no other reward for its services.

When in thy hammock, should the thought of thy little crosses and disappointments, in thy ups and downs through life, break in upon thee, and throw thee into a pensive mood, the Owl will bear thee company. She will tell thee that hard has been her fate too; and at intervals, 'Whip-poor-Will' and 'Willy come go,' will take up the tale of sorrow. Ovid has told thee how the owl once boasted the human form, and lost it for a very small offence; and were the poet alive now, he would inform thee, that 'Whip-poor-Will,' and 'Willy come go,' are the shades of those poor African and Indian slaves, who died worn out and broken-hearted. They wail and cry, 'Whip-poor-Will,' and "Willy come go,' all night long; and often, when the moon shines, you see them sitting on the green turf, near the houses of those whose ancestors tore them from the bosom of their helpless families, which all probably perished through grief and want, after their support was gone.

## The Grass

A CHILD said *What is the grass?* fetching it to me with full hands;
How could I answer the child? I do not know what it is any
more than he.
I guess it must be the flag of my disposition, out of hopeful green
stuff woven.
Or I guess it is the handkerchief of the Lord,
A scented gift and remembrancer designedly dropt,
Bearing the owner's name someway in the corners, that we may see
and remark, and say *Whose?*

*Walt Whitman*

# THE STORM

## Lafcadio Hearn

*This "American" author was born in Greece of an English
father and a Greek mother, was educated in France and England, and passed the last fourteen years of his life as a Japanese
citizen, married to a Japanese girl of a Samurai family. But in
between these events he spent a good part of twenty years in
the United States as a journalist and author, in Cincinnati, New
Orleans, and New York. Partly blind, ridden by poverty, and
of a morbid temperament, he nevertheless had the soul of a
great painter who used the pen instead of a brush. In* Chita:
A Memory of Last Island, *he tells of the destruction by a tidal
wave of a Caribbean island which was the fashionable watering place of aristocratic New Orleans families.*

THIRTY years ago, Last Island lay steeped in the enormous light
of even such magical days. July was dying: for weeks no fleck
of cloud had broken the heaven's blue dream of eternity; winds
held their breath; slow wavelets caressed the bland brown beach
with a sound as of kisses and whispers. To one who found himself
alone, beyond the limits of the village and beyond the hearing of
its voices, the vast silence, the vast light, seemed full of weirdness.
And these hushes, these transparencies, do not always inspire a
causeless apprehension: they are omens sometimes—omens of
coming tempest. Nature,—incomprehensible Sphinx!—before her
mightiest bursts of rage ever puts forth her divinest witchery,
makes more manifest her awful beauty.

But in that forgotten summer the witchery lasted many long
days,—days born in rose-light, buried in gold. It was the height of
the season. The long myrtle-shadowed village was thronged with
its summer population; the big hotel could hardly accommodate all
its guests; the bathing-houses were too few for the crowds who
flocked to the water morning and evening. There were diversions
for all: hunting and fishing parties, yachting excursions, rides,

[ 126 ]

music, games, promenades. Carriage wheels whirled flickering along the beach, seaming its smoothness noiselessly, as if muffled. Love wrote its dreams upon the sand.

Then one great noon, when the blue abyss of day seemed to yawn over the world more deeply than ever before, a sudden change touched the quicksilver smoothness of the waters—the swaying shadow of a vast motion. First the whole sea circle appeared to rise up bodily at the sky; the horizon curve lifted to a straight line; the line darkened and approached,—a monstrous wrinkle, an immeasurable fold of green water, moving swift as a cloud shadow pursued by sunlight. But it had looked formidable only by startling contrast with the previous placidity of the open: it was scarcely two feet high; it curled slowly as it neared the beach, and combed itself out in sheets of woolly foam with a low, rich roll of whispered thunder. Swift in pursuit another followed—a third—a feebler fourth; then the sea only swayed a little, and stilled again. Minutes passed, and the immeasurable heaving recommenced—one, two, three, four—seven long swells this time; and the Gulf smoothed itself once more. Irregularly the phenomenon continued to repeat itself, each time with heavier billowing and briefer intervals of quiet, until at last the whole sea grew restless, and shifted color and flickered green; the swells became shorter and changed form. Then from horizon to shore ran one uninterrupted heaving, one vast green swarming of snaky shapes, rolling in to hiss and flatten upon the sand. Yet no single cirrus speck revealed itself through all the violet heights; there was no wind! You might have fancied the sea had been upheaved from beneath.

And indeed, the fancy of a seismic origin for a windless surge would not appear in these latitudes to be utterly without foundation. On the fairest days a southeast breeze may bear you an odor singular enough to startle you from sleep,—a strong, sharp smell as of fish-oil; and gazing at the sea, you might be still more startled at the sudden apparition of great oleaginous patches spreading over the water, sheeting over the swells. That is, if you had never heard of the mysterious submarine oil wells, the volcanic fountains, unexplored, that well up with the eternal pulsing of the Gulf Stream.

But the pleasure-seekers of Last Island knew there must have been a "great blow" somewhere that day. Still the sea swelled; and a splendid surf made the evening bath delightful. Then just at sundown a beautiful cloud bridge grew up and arched the sky with a single span of cottony pink vapor, that changed and deepened color with the dying of the iridescent day. And the cloud bridge approached, stretched, strained, and swung round at last to make way for the coming of the gale,—even as the light bridges that traverse the dreamy Têche swing open when luggermen sound through their conch-shells the long, bellowing signal of approach.

Then the wind began to blow, with the passing of July. It blew from the northeast,—clear, cool. It blew in enormous sighs, dying away at regular intervals, as if pausing to draw breath. All night it blew; and in each pause could be heard the answering moan of the rising surf,—as if the rhythm of the sea molded itself after the rhythm of the air,—as if the waving of the water responded precisely to the waving of the wind,—a billow for every puff, a surge for every sigh.

The August morning broke in a bright sky; the breeze still came cool and clear from the northeast. The waves were running now at a sharp angle to the shore; they began to carry fleeces, an innumerable flock of vague green shapes, wind-driven to be despoiled of their ghostly wool. Far as the eye could follow the line of the beach, all the slope was white with the great shearing of them. Clouds came, flew as in a panic against the face of the sun, and passed. All that day and through the night and into the morning again the breeze continued from the northeast, blowing like an equinoctial gale.

Then day by day the vast breath freshened steadily, and the waters heightened. A week later sea-bathing had become perilous; colossal breakers were herding in, like moving leviathan backs, twice the height of a man. Still the gale blew, and the billowing waxed mightier, and faster and faster overhead flew the tatters of torn cloud. The gray morning of the 9th wanly lighted a surf that appalled the best swimmers: the sea was one wild agony of foam, the gale was rending off the heads of the waves and veiling the horizon with a fog of salt spray. Shadowless and gray the day remained; there were mad bursts of lashing rain. Evening brought with it a sinister apparition, looming through a cloud-rent in the west—a scarlet sun in a green sky. His sanguine disk, enormously magnified, seemed barred like the body of a belted planet. A moment, and the crimson spectre vanished, and the moonless night came.

Then the wind grew weird. It ceased being a breath; it became a voice moaning across the world, hooting, uttering nightmare sounds,—*Whoo!—whoo!—whoo!*—and with each stupendous owl-cry the mooing of the waters seemed to deepen, more and more abysmally, through all the hours of darkness. From the northwest the breakers of the bay began to roll high over the sandy slope, into the salines; the village bayou broadened to a bellowing flood. So the tumult swelled and the turmoil heightened until morning—a morning of gray gloom and whistling rain. Rain of bursting clouds and rain of wind-blown brine from the great spuming agony of the sea.

The steamer Star was due from St. Mary's that fearful morning. Could she come? No one really believed it,—no one. And nevertheless men struggled to the roaring beach to look for her, because hope is stronger than reason.

Even to-day, in these Creole islands, the advent of the steamer is the great event of the week. There are no telegraph lines, no telephones: the mail packet is the only trustworthy medium of communication with the outer world, bringing friends, news, letters. The magic of steam has placed New Orleans nearer to New York than to the Timbaliers, nearer to Washington than to Wine Island, nearer to Chicago than to Barataria Bay. And even during the deepest sleep of waves and winds, there will come betimes to sojourners in this unfamiliar archipelago a feeling of lonesomeness that is a fear, a feeling of isolation from the world of men,—totally unlike that sense of solitude which haunts one in the silence of mountain heights, or amid the eternal tumult of lofty granitic coasts: a sense of helpless insecurity. The land seems but an undulation of the sea-bed; its highest ridges do not rise more than the height of a man above the salines on either side; the salines themselves lie almost level with the level of the flood-tides; the tides are variable, treacherous, mysterious. But when all around and above these ever-changing shores the twin vastnesses of heaven and sea begin to utter the tremendous revelation of themselves as infinite forces in contention, then indeed this sense of separation from humanity appalls. Perhaps it was such a feeling which forced men, on the tenth day of August, eighteen hundred and fifty-six, to hope against hope for the coming of the Star, and to strain their eyes towards far-off Terrebonne. "It was a wind you could lie down on," said my friend the pilot.

"Great God!" shrieked a voice above the shouting of the storm, *"she is coming!"* It was true. Down the Atchafalaya, and thence through strange mazes of bayou, lakelet, and pass, by a rear route familiar only to the best of pilots, the frail river craft had toiled into

Caillou Bay, running close to the main shore; and now she was heading right for the island, with the wind aft, over the monstrous sea. On she came, swaying, rocking, plunging, with a great whiteness wrapping her about like a cloud, and moving with her moving,—a tempest-whirl of spray; ghost-white and like a ghost she came, for her smoke-stacks exhaled no visible smoke—the wind devoured it!

The excitement on shore became wild; men shouted themselves hoarse; women laughed and cried. Every telescope and opera-glass was directed upon the coming apparition; all wondered how the pilot kept his feet; all marveled at the madness of the captain.

But Captain Abraham Smith was not mad. A veteran American sailor, he had learned to know the great Gulf as scholars know deep books by heart; he knew the birthplace of its tempests, the mystery of its tides, the omens of its hurricanes. While lying at Brashear City he felt the storm had not yet reached its highest, vaguely foresaw a mighty peril, and resolved to wait no longer for a lull. "Boys," he said, "we've got to take her out in spite of hell!" And they "took her out." Through all the peril, his men stayed by him and obeyed him. By mid-morning the wind had deepened to a roar,—lowering sometimes to a rumble, sometimes bursting upon the ears like a measureless and deafening crash. Then the captain knew the Star was running a race with Death. "She'll win it," he muttered; "she'll stand it. Perhaps they'll have need of me to-night."

She won! With a sonorous steam chant of triumph the brave little vessel rode at last into the bayou, and anchored hard by her accustomed resting-place, in full view of the hotel, though not near enough to shore to lower her gang-plank.

But she had sung her swan song. Gathering in from the northeast, the waters of the bay were already marbling over the salines and half across the island; and still the wind increased its paroxysmal power.

Cottages began to rock. Some slid away from the solid props upon which they rested. A chimney tumbled. Shutters were wrenched off; verandas demolished. Light roofs lifted, dropped again, and flapped into ruin. Trees bent their heads to the earth. And still the storm grew louder and blacker with every passing hour.

The Star rose with the rising of the waters, dragging her anchor. Two more anchors were put out, and still she dragged— dragged in with the flood, twisting, shuddering, careening in her

agony. Evening fell; the sand began to move with the wind, stinging faces like a continuous fire of fine shot; and frenzied blasts came
to buffet the steamer forward, sideward. Then one of her hog-
chains parted with a clang like the boom of a big bell. Then another!—Then the captain bade his men to cut away all her upper
works, clean to the deck. Overboard into the seething went her
stacks, her pilot-house, her cabins—and whirled away. And the
naked hull of the Star, still dragging her three anchors, labored on
through the darkness, nearer and nearer to the immense silhouette
of the hotel, whose hundred windows were now all aflame. The
vast timber building seemed to defy the storm. The wind, roaring
round its broad verandas, hissing through every crevice with the
sound and force of steam, appeared to waste its rage. And in the
half-lull between two terrible gusts there came to the captain's ears
a sound that seemed strange in that night of multitudinous terrors—
a sound of music!

Almost every evening throughout the season there had been
dancing in the great hall; there was dancing that night also. The
population of the hotel had been augmented by the advent of families from other parts of the island, who found their summer cottages insecure places of shelter; there were nearly four hundred
guests assembled. Perhaps it was for this reason that the entertainment had been prepared upon a grander plan than usual, that it
assumed the form of a fashionable ball. And all those pleasure-
seekers, representing the wealth and beauty of the Creole parishes,
—whether from Ascension or Assumption, St. Mary's or St. Lan-
dry's, Iberville or Terrebonne, whether inhabitants of the multi-
colored and many-balconied Creole quarter of the quaint metrop-
olis, or dwellers in the dreamy paradises of the Têche,—mingled
joyously, knowing each other, feeling in some sort akin; whether
affiliated by blood, connaturalized by caste, or simply interasso-
ciated by traditional sympathies of class sentiment and class interest. Perhaps in the more than ordinary merriment of that evening
something of nervous exaltation might have been discerned,—something like a feverish resolve to oppose apprehension with gayety,
to combat uneasiness by diversion. But the hours passed in mirth-
fulness; the first general feeling of depression began to weigh less
and less upon the guests: they had found reason to confide in the
solidity of the massive building; there were no positive terrors, no
outspoken fears; and the new conviction of all had found expres-

sion in the words of the host himself, "Il n'y a rien de mieux à faire que de s'amuser!" Of what avail to lament the prospective devastation of cane-fields, to discuss the possible ruin of crops? Better to seek solace in choregraphic harmonies, in the rhythm of gracious motion and of perfect melody, than hearken to the discords of the wild orchestra of storms; wiser to admire the grace of Parisian toilets, the eddy of trailing robes with its fairy foam of lace, the ivorine loveliness of glossy shoulders and jeweled throats, the glimmering of satin-slippered feet, than to watch the raging of the flood without, or the flying of the wrack.

So the music and the mirth went on: they made joy for themselves, those elegant guests; they jested and sipped rich wines; they pledged, and hoped, and loved, and promised, with never a thought of the morrow, on the night of the tenth of August, eighteen hundred and fifty-six. Observant parents were there, planning for the future bliss of their nearest and dearest; mothers and fathers of handsome lads, lithe and elegant as young pines, and fresh from the polish of foreign university training; mothers and fathers of splendid girls whose simplest attitudes were witcheries. Young cheeks flushed; young hearts fluttered with an emotion more puissant than the excitement of the dance; young eyes betrayed the happy secret discreeter lips would have preserved. Slave-servants circled through the aristocratic press, bearing dainties and wines, praying permission to pass in terms at once humble and officious,— always in the excellent French which well-trained house-servants were taught to use on such occasions.

Night wore on: still the shining floor palpitated to the feet of the dancers; still the pianoforte pealed, and still the violins sang; and the sound of their singing shrilled through the darkness, in gasps of the gale, to the ears of Captain Smith, as he strove to keep his footing on the spray-drenched deck of the Star.

"Christ!" he muttered,—"a dance! If that wind whips round south, there'll be another dance! But I guess the Star will stay."

Half an hour might have passed; still the lights flamed calmly, and the violins trilled, and the perfumed whirl went on.

And suddenly the wind veered!

Again the Star reeled, and shuddered, and turned, and began to drag all her anchors. But she now dragged away from the great building and its lights,—away from the voluptuous thunder of the grand piano, even at that moment outpouring the great joy of

Weber's melody orchestrated by Berlioz, 'L'Invitation à la Valse,' with its marvelous musical swing!

"Waltzing!" cried the captain. "God help them! God help us all now! *The Wind waltzes to-night, with the Sea for his partner!*"

Oh the stupendous Valse Tourbillon! Oh the mighty Dancer! One—two—three! From northeast to east, from east to southeast, from southeast to south; then from the south he came, whirling the Sea in his arms.

Some one shrieked in the midst of the revels,—some girl who found her pretty slippers wet. What could it be? Thin streams of water were spreading over the level planking, curling about the feet of the dancers. What could it be? All the land had begun to quake, even as but a moment before the polished floor was trembling to the pressure of circling steps; all the building shook now; every beam uttered its groan. What could it be?

There was a clamor, a panic, a rush to the windy night. Infinite darkness above and beyond; but the lantern beams danced far out over an unbroken circle of heaving and swirling black water. Stealthily, swiftly, the measureless sea flood was rising.

"Messieurs—mesdames, ce n'est rien. Nothing serious, ladies, I assure you. Mais nous en avons vu bien souvent, les inondations comme celle-ci; ça passe vite! The water will go down in a few hours, ladies: it never rises higher than this; il n'y a pas le moindre danger, je vous dis! Allons! il n'y a— My God! what is that?"

For a moment there was a ghastly hush of voices. And through that hush there burst upon the ears of all a fearful and unfamiliar sound, as of a colossal cannonade—rolling up from the south with volleying lightnings. Vastly and swiftly, nearer and nearer it came, a ponderous and unbroken thunder roll, terrible as the long muttering of an earthquake.

The nearest mainland, across mad Caillou Bay to the sea marshes, lay twelve miles north; west, by the Gulf, the nearest solid ground was twenty miles distant. There were boats, yes! but the stoutest swimmer might never reach them now!

Then rose a frightful cry: the hoarse, hideous, indescribable cry of hopeless fear; the despairing animal cry man utters when suddenly brought face to face with Nothingness, without preparation, without consolation, without possibility of respite. "*Sauve qui peut!*" Some wrenched down the doors; some clung to the heavy

banquet tables, to the sofas, to the billiard tables; during one terrible instant, against fruitless heroisms, against futile generosities,
raged all the frenzy of selfishness, all the brutalities of panic. And
then—then came, thundering through the blackness, the giant
swells, boom on boom! One crash! the huge frame building rocks
like a cradle, seesaws, crackles. What are human shrieks now? the
tornado is shrieking! Another! chandeliers splinter; lights are
dashed out; a sweeping cataract hurls in; the immense hall rises,
oscillates, twirls as upon a pivot, crepitates, crumbles into ruin.
Crash again! the swirling wreck dissolves into the wallowing of
another monster billow; and a hundred cottages overturn, spin in
sudden eddies, quiver, disjoint, and melt into the seething.

So the hurricane passed, tearing off the heads of the prodigious
waves to hurl them a hundred feet in air, heaping up the ocean
against the land, upturning the woods. Bays and passes were swollen
to abysses; rivers regorged; the sea marshes were changed to raging
wastes of water. Before New Orleans the flood of the mile-broad
Mississippi rose six feet above highest water-mark. One hundred
and ten miles away, Donaldsonville trembled at the towering tide
of the Lafourche. Lakes strove to burst their boundaries. Far-off
river steamers tugged wildly at their cables, shivering like tethered
creatures that hear by night the approaching howl of destroyers.
Smoke-stacks were hurled overboard, pilot-houses torn away,
cabins blown to fragments.

And over roaring Kaimbuck Pass, over the agony of Caillou
Bay, the billowing tide rushed unresisted from the Gulf, tearing
and swallowing the land in its course, plowing out deep-sea channels where sleek herds had been grazing but a few hours before,
rending islands in twain, and ever bearing with it, through the
night, enormous vortex of wreck and vast wan drift of corpses.

But the Star remained. And Captain Abraham Smith, with a
long, good rope about his waist, dashed again and again into that
awful surging to snatch victims from death,—clutching at passing
hands, heads, garments, in the cataract-sweep of the seas; saving,
aiding, cheering, though blinded by spray and battered by drifting
wreck, until his strength failed in the unequal struggle at last, and
his men drew him aboard senseless, with some beautiful half-
drowned girl safe in his arms. But well-nigh twoscore souls had
been rescued by him; and the Star stayed on through it all.

Long years after, the weed-grown ribs of her graceful skeleton could still be seen, curving up from the sand-dunes of Last Island, in valiant witness of how well she stayed.

DAY breaks through the flying wrack, over the infinite heaving of the sea, over the low land made vast with desolation. It is a spectral dawn; a wan light, like the light of a dying sun.

The wind has waned and veered; the flood sinks slowly back to its abysses, abandoning its plunder, scattering its piteous waifs over bar and dune, over shoal and marsh, among the silences of the mango swamps, over the long low reaches of sand grasses and drowned weeds, for more than a hundred miles. From the shell reefs of Pointe-au-Fer to the shallows of Pelto Bay the dead lie mingled with the high-heaped drift; from their cypress groves the vultures rise to dispute a share of the feast with the shrieking frigate-birds and squeaking gulls. And as the tremendous tide withdraws its plunging waters, all the pirates of air follow the great white-gleaming retreat—a storm of billowing wings and screaming throats.

And swift in the wake of gull and frigate-bird the Wreckers come, the Spoilers of the dead,—savage skimmers of the sea, hurricane-riders wont to spread their canvas pinions in the face of storms; Sicilian and Corsican outlaws, Manila men from the marshes, deserters from many navies, Lascars, marooners, refugees of a hundred nationalities, fishers and shrimpers by name, smugglers by opportunity, wild channel-finders from obscure bayous and unfamiliar *chénières*, all skilled in the mysteries of these mysterious waters beyond the comprehension of the oldest licensed pilot.

There is plunder for all, birds and men. There are drowned sheep in multitude, heaped carcasses of kine. There are casks of claret and kegs of brandy and legions of bottles bobbing in the surf. There are billiard tables overturned upon the sand; there are sofas, pianos, footstools and music-stools, luxurious chairs, lounges of bamboo. There are chests of cedar, and toilet tables of rosewood, and trunks of fine stamped leather stored with precious apparel. There are *objets de luxe* innumerable. There are children's playthings: French dolls in marvelous toilets, and toy carts, and wooden horses, and wooden spades, and brave little wooden ships that rode out the gale in which the great Nautilus went down. There is money in notes and in coin—in purses, in pocket-books, and in pockets; plenty of it! There are silks, satins, laces, and fine linen to be stripped from the bodies of the drowned, and necklaces, bracelets, watches, finger-rings and fine chains, brooches and trinkets. "Chi bidizza! Oh! chi bedda mughieri! Eccu, la bidizza!" That ball-dress was made in Paris by— But you never heard of him, Sicilian Vicenzu.

"Che bella sposina!" Her betrothal ring will not come off, Giuseppe: but the delicate bone snaps easily; your oyster-knife can sever the tendon. "Guardate! chi bedda picciota!" Over her heart you will find it, Valentino—the locket held by that fine Swiss chain of woven hair—"Caya manan!" And it is not your quadroon bondsmaid, sweet lady, who now disrobes you so roughly: those Malay hands are less deft than hers; but she slumbers very far away from you, and may not be aroused from her sleep. "Na quita mo! dalaga!—na quita maganda!" Juan, the fastenings of those diamond ear-drops are much too complicated for your peon fingers: tear them out!—"Dispense, chulita!"

Suddenly a long, mighty silver trilling fills the ears of all; there is a wild hurrying and scurrying; swiftly, one after another, the overburdened luggers spread wings and flutter away.

Thrice the great cry rings rippling through the gray air, and over the green sea, and over the far-flooded shell reefs, where the huge white flashes are,—sheet-lightning of breakers,—and over the weird wash of corpses coming in.

It is the steam-call of the relief boat, hastening to rescue the living, to gather in the dead.

The tremendous tragedy is over!

### The Ocean

Roll on, thou deep and dark blue ocean—roll!
　　Ten thousand fleets sweep over thee in vain;
Man marks the earth with ruin—his control
Stops with the shore;—upon the watery plain
The wrecks are all thy deed, nor doth remain
A shadow of man's ravage, save his own,
When, for a moment, like a drop of rain,
He sinks into thy depth with bubbling groan,
Without a grave, unknelled, uncoffined, and unknown.
*Lord Byron*

# BENNY AND THE BIRD-DOGS

## Marjorie Kinnan Rawlings

*A remnant of the American frontier, in the hummock country of Florida, has become familiar to millions of readers—and moviegoers—through* The Yearling *and other stories by Marjorie Kinnan Rawlings, who adopted the region as her own. This tale shows that she knows the humor, as well as the drama, in the people and animals she writes about.*

You can't change a man, no-ways. By the time his mammy turns him loose and he takes up with some innocent woman and marries her, he's what he is. If it's his nature to set by the hearthfire and stretch hisself, you just as good to let him set and scratch. If it's his nature, like Will Dover, my man, to go to the garage in his Sunday clothes and lay down under some backwoods Cracker's old greasy Ford and tinker with it, you just as good to let him lay and tinker. And if it's his nature, like Uncle Benny, to prowl; if it's his nature to cut the fool; why, it's interfering in the ways of Providence even to stop to quarrel with him about it. Some women is born knowing this. Sometimes a woman, like the Old Hen (Uncle Benny's wife, poor soul!), has to quarrel a lifetime before she learns it. Then when it does come to her, she's like a cow has tried to jump a high fence and has got hung up on it—she's horn-swoggled.

The Old Hen's a mighty fine woman—one of the finest I know. She looks just the way she did when she married Uncle Benny Mathers thirty years ago, except her hair has turned gray, like the feathers on an Irish Gray game hen. She's plump and pretty and kind of pale from thirty years' fretting about Uncle Benny. She has a disposition, by nature, as sweet as new cane syrup. When she settled down for a lifetime's quarreling at him, it was for the same reason syrup sours—the heat had just been put to her too long.

I can't remember a time when the Old Hen wasn't quarreling at Uncle Benny. It begun a week after they was married. He went

[ 137 ]

off prowling by hisself, to a frolic or such as that, and didn't come home until four o'clock in the morning. She was setting up waiting for him. When she crawled him about it, he said, "Bless Katy, wife, let's sleep now and quarrel in the morning." So she quarrelled in the morning and just kept it up. For thirty years. Not for meanness—she just kept hoping she could change him.

Change him? When he takened notice of the way she was fussing and clucking and ruffling her feathers, he quit calling her by her given name and began calling her the Old Hen. That's all I could ever see she changed him.

Uncle Benny's a sight. He's been constable here at Oak Bluff, Florida, for twenty years. We figure it keeps him out of worse trouble to let him be constable. He's the quickest shot in three counties and the colored folks is all as superstitious of him as if he was the devil himself. He's a comical-appearing somebody. He's small and quick and he don't move—he prances. He has a little bald sun-tanned head with a rim of white hair around the back of it. Where the hair ends at the sides of his head, it sticks straight up over his ears in two little white tufts like goat-horns. He's got bright blue eyes that look at you quick and wicked, the way a goat looks. That's exactly what he looks and acts like—a mischievous little old billy-goat. And he's been popping up under folks' noses and playing tricks on them as long as Oak Bluff has knowed him. Doc in particular. He loved to torment Doc.

And stay home? Uncle Benny don't know what it is to stay home. The Old Hen'll cook hot dinner for him and he won't come. She'll start another fire in the range and warm it up for him about dusk-dark and he won't come. She'll set up till midnight, times till daybreak, and maybe just about the time the east lightens and the birds gets to whistling good, he'll come home. Where's he been? He's been with somebody 'gatoring, or with somebody catching crabs to Salt Springs; he's been to a square-dance twenty miles away in the flat-woods; he's been on the highway in that Ford car, just rambling as long as his gas held out—and them seven pied bird-dogs setting up in the back keeping him company.

It was seven years ago, during the Boom, that he bought the Model-T and began collecting bird-dogs. Everybody in Florida was rich for a whiles, selling gopher holes to the Yankees. Now putting an automobile under Uncle Benny was like putting wings on a wild cat—it just opened up new territory. Instead of rambling

over one county, he could ramble over ten. And the way he drove
—like a bat out of Torment. He's one of them men just loves to
cover the ground. And that car and all them bird-dogs worked on
the Old Hen like a quart of gasoline on a camp-fire. She really went
to raring. I tried to tell her then 'twasn't no use to pay him no mind,
but she wouldn't listen.

I said, "It's just his nature. You can't do a thing about it but take
it for your share and go on. You and Uncle Benny is just made different. You want him home and he don't want to be home. You're
a barnyard fowl and he's a wild fowl."

"Mis' Dover," she said, "it's easy for you to talk. Your man runs
a garage and comes home nights. You don't know how terrible it
is to have a man that prowls."

I said, "Leave him prowl."

She said, "Yes, but when he's on the prowl, I don't no more
know where to look for him than somebody's tom-cat."

I said, "If 'twas me, I wouldn't look for him."

She said, "Moonlight nights he's the worst. Just like the var-
mints."

I said, "Don't that tell you nothing?"

She said, "If he'd content hisself with prowling—But he ain't
content until he cuts the fool. He takes that Ford car and them
seven bird-dogs and maybe a pint of moonshine, and maybe picks
up Doc to prowl with him, and he don't rest until he's done something crazy. What I keep figuring is, he'll kill hisself in that Ford
car, cutting the fool."

I said, "You don't need to fret about him and that Ford. What's
unnatural for one man is plumb natural for another. And cutting
the fool is so natural for Uncle Benny, it's like a bird in the air
or a fish in water—there won't no harm come to him from it."

She said, "Mis' Dover, what the devil throws over his back has
got to come down under his belly."

I said, "Uncle Benny Mathers is beyond rules and sayings. I
know men-folks, and if you'll listen to me, you'll settle down and
quit quarrelling and leave him to go his way in quiet."

I happened to be in on it this spring, the last time the Old Hen
ever quarrelled at Uncle Benny. Me and Doc was both in on it. It
was the day of old lady Weller's burying. Doc carried me in his
car to the cemetery. My Will couldn't leave the garage, because

the trucks hauling the Florida oranges north was bringing in pretty good business. Doc felt obliged to go to the burying. He's a patent-medicine salesman—a big fat fellow with a red face and yellow hair. He sells the Little Giant line of remedies. Old lady Weller had been one of his best customers. She'd taken no nourishment the last week of her life except them remedies, and Doc figured he ought to pay her the proper respect and show everybody he was a man was always grateful to his customers.

Uncle Benny and the Old Hen went to the burying in the Model-T. And the seven bird-dogs went, setting up in the back seat. They always went to the buryings.

Uncle Benny said, "Walls nor chains won't hold 'em. Better to have 'em go along riding decent and quiet, than to bust loose and foller the Model-T like a daggone pack of bloodhounds."

That was true enough. Those bird-dogs could hear that old Ford crank up and go off in low gear, clear across the town. They'd always hope it was time to go bird-hunting again, and here they'd come, trailing it. So there were the bird-dogs riding along to old lady Weller's burying, with their ears flopping and their noses in the air for quail. As constable, Uncle Benny sort of represented the town, and he was right in behind the hearse. I mean, that car was a pain, to be part of a funeral procession. In the seven years he'd had it, he'd all but drove it to pieces, and it looked like a rusty, mangy razor-back hog. The hood was thin and narrow, like a shoat's nose —you remember the way all Model-T Fords were built. It had no top to it, nor no doors to the front seat, and the back seat rose up in a hump where the bird-dogs had squeezed the excelsior chitlin's out of it.

The Old Hen sat up stiff and proud, not letting on she minded. Doc and I figured she's been quarrelling at Uncle Benny about the bird-dogs, because when one of them put his paws on her shoulders and begun licking around her ears, she turned and smacked the breath out of him.

The funeral procession had just left the Oak Bluff dirt road and turned onto No. 9 Highway, when the garage keeper at the bend ran out.

He hollered, "I just got a 'phone call for Uncle Benny Mathers from the high sheriff!"

So Uncle Benny cut out of the procession and drove over to the pay station by the kerosene tank to take the message. He caught up again in a minute and called to Doc, "A drunken nigger is headed this way in a Chevrolet and the sheriff wants I should stop him."

About that time here comes the Chevrolet and started to pass the procession, wobbling back and forth as if it had the blind staggers. You may well know the nigger was drunk or he wouldn't have passed a funeral. Uncle Benny cut out of line and took out after him. When he saw who was chasing him, the nigger turned around and headed back the way he'd come from. Uncle Benny was gaining on him when they passed the hearse. The bird-dogs begun to take an interest and rared up, barking. What does Uncle Benny do but go to the side of the Chevrolet so the nigger turns around—and then Uncle Benny crowded him so all he could do was to shoot into line in the funeral procession. Uncle Benny cut right in after him and the nigger shot out of line and Uncle Benny crowded him in again.

I'll declare, I was glad old lady Weller wasn't alive to see it. She'd had no use for Uncle Benny, she'd hated a nigger, and she'd despised dogs so to where she kept a shotgun by her door to shoot at them if one so much as crossed her cornfield. And here on the way to her burying, where you'd figure she was entitled to have things the way she liked them, here was Uncle Benny chasing a nigger in and out of line, and seven bird-dogs were going Ki-yippity-yi! Ki-yippity-yi! Ki-yippity-yi! I was mighty proud the corpse was no kin to me.

The Old Hen was plumb mortified. She put her hands over her face and when the Ford would swerve by or cut in ahead of us, Doc and me could see her swaying back and forth and suffering. I don't scarcely need to say Uncle Benny was enjoying hisself. If he'd looked sorrowful-like, as if he was just doing his duty, you could of forgive him. Near a filling-station the Chevrolet shot ahead and stopped and the nigger jumped out and started to run. Uncle Benny stopped and climbed out of the Ford and drew his pistol and called "Stop!" The nigger kept on going.

Now Uncle Benny claims that shooting at niggers in the line of duty is what keeps him in practice for bird-shooting. He dropped a ball to the right of the nigger's heel and he dropped a ball to the left of it. He called "Stop!" and the nigger kept on going. Then Uncle Benny took his pistol in both hands and took a slow aim and he laid the third ball against the nigger's shin-bone. He dropped like a string-haltered mule.

Uncle Benny said to the man that ran the filling-station, "Get your gun. That there nigger is under arrest and I deputize you to keep him that-a-way. The sheriff'll be along to pick him up direckly."

He cut back into the funeral procession between us and the hearse, and we could tell by them wicked blue eyes he didn't know when he'd enjoyed a burying like old lady Weller's. When we got back from the burying, he stopped by Will's garage. The Old Hen was giving him down-the-country.

She said, "That was the most scandalous thing I've ever knowed you to do, chasing that nigger in and out of Mis' Weller's funeral."

Uncle Benny's eyes begun to dance and he said, "I know it, wife, but I couldn't help it. 'Twasn't me done the chasing—it was the Model-T."

Doc got in to it then and sided with the Old Hen. He gets excited, the way fat men do, and he swelled up like a spreading adder.

"Benny," he said, "you shock my modesty. This ain't no occasion for laughing or lying."

Uncle Benny said, "I know it, Doc. I wouldn't think of laughing nor lying. You didn't know I've got that Ford trained? I've got it trained to where it'll do two things. It's helped me chase so many niggers, I've got it to where it just naturally takes out after 'em by itself."

Doc got red in the face and asked, real sarcastic, "And what's the other piece of training?"

Uncle Benny said, "Doc, that Ford has carried me home drunk so many times, I've got it trained to where it'll take care of me and carry me home safe when I ain't fitten."

Doc spit halfway across the road and he said, "You lying old jaybird."

Uncle Benny said, "Doc, I've got a pint of moonshine and if you'll come go camping with me to Salt Springs this evening, I'll prove it."

The Old Hen spoke up and she said, "Benny, Heaven forgive you for I won't, if you go on the prowl again before you've cleaned the weeds out of my old pindar field. I'm a month late now, getting it planted."

Doc loves Salt Springs crab and mullet as good as Uncle Benny does, and I could see he was tempted.

But he said, "Benny, you go along home and do what your wife wants, and when you're done—when she says you're done—then we'll go to Salt Springs."

So Uncle Benny and the Old Hen drove off. Doc watched after them.

He said, "Anyways, cutting the fool at a burying had ought to last Benny quite a while."

I said, "You don't know him. Cutting the fool don't last him no time at all."

I was right. I ain't so special wise a woman, but if I once know a man, I can come right close to telling you what he'll do. Uncle Benny hadn't been gone hardly no time, when somebody come by the garage hollering that he'd done set the Old Hen's pindar field on fire.

I said to Doc, "What did I tell you? The last thing in the world was safe for that woman to do, was to turn him loose on them weeds. He figured firing was the quickest way to get shut of them."

Doc said, "Let's go see."

We got in his car and drove out to Uncle Benny's place. Here was smoke rolling up back of the house, and the big live oak in the yard was black with soldier blackbirds the grass fire had drove out of the pindar field. The field hadn't had peanuts in it since fall, but bless Katy, it was full of something else. Uncle Benny's wife had it plumb full of setting guinea-hens. She hadn't told him, because he didn't like guineas.

Far off to the west corner of the field was the Old Hen, trying to run the guineas into a coop. They were flying every which-a-way and hollering *Pod-rac! Pod-rac!* the way guineas holler. All the young uns in the neighborhood were in the middle of the field, beating out the grass fire with palmettos. And setting up on top of the east gate, just as unconcerned, was Uncle Benny, with them two little horns of white hair curling in the heat. Now what do you reckon he was doing? He had all seven of them bird-dogs running back and forth retrieving guinea eggs. He'd say now and again, "Dead—fetch!" and they'd wag their tails and go hunt up another nest and here they'd come, with guinea eggs carried gentle in their mouths. He was putting the eggs in a basket.

When the commotion was over, and the fire out, and every-body gone on but Doc and me, we went to the front porch to set down and rest. The Old Hen was wore out. She admitted it was her fault not letting Uncle Benny know about the setting guinea-hens. She was about to forgive him setting the field a-fire, because him and the bird-dogs had saved the guinea eggs. But when we got to the porch, here lay the bird-dogs in the rocking chairs. There was one to every chair, rocking away and cutting their eyes at her. Their coats and paws were smuttied from the burnt grass—and the Old Hen had put clean sugar-sacking covers on every blessed chair that morning. That settled it. She was stirred up anyway about the way he'd cut the fool at the burying, and she really set in to quarrel at Uncle Benny. And like I say, it turned out to be the last piece of quarrelling she ever done.

She said to him, "You taught them bird-dogs to rock in a rocking chair just to torment me. Ever' beast or varmint you've brought home, you've learned to cut the fool as bad as you do."

"Now wife, what beast or varmint did I ever learn to cut the fool?"

"You learned the 'coon to screw the tops off my syrup cans. You learned the 'possum to hang upside down in my cupboards, and I'd go for a jar of maybe pepper relish and put my hand on him. . . . There's been plenty of such as that. I've raised ever'thing in the world for you but a stallion horse."

Doc said, "Give him time, he'll have one of them stabled in the kitchen."

"Bird-dogs is natural to have around," she said. "I was raised to bird-dogs. But it ain't natural for 'em to rock in a rocking-chair. There's so terrible many of them, and when they put in the night on the porch laying in the rocking-chairs and rocking, I don't close my eyes for the fuss."

Uncle Benny said, "You see, Doc? You see, Mis' Dover? She's always quarrelling that me and the dogs ain't never home at night. Then when we do come in, she ain't willing we should all be comf'table.

"We just as good to go on to Salt Springs, Doc. Wait while I go in the house and get my camping outfit and we'll set out."

He went in the house and came out with his camping stuff. She knowed he was gone for nobody knew how long.

We walked on down to the gate and the Old Hen followed, sniffling a little and twisting the corner of her apron.

"Benny," she said, "please don't go to Salt Springs. You always lose your teeth in the Boil."

"I ain't lost 'em but three times," he said, and he cranked up the Model-T and climbed in. "I couldn't help losing 'em the first time. That was when I was laughing at the Yankee casting for bass, and his plug caught me in the open mouth and lifted my teeth out. Nor I couldn't help it the second time, when Doc and me was rassling in the rowboat and he pushed me in."

"Yes," she said, "an how'd you lose 'em the third time?"

His eyes twinkled and he shoved the Ford in low. "Cuttin' the fool," he said.

"That's just it," she said, and the tears begun to roll out of her eyes. "Anybody with false teeth hadn't ought to cut the fool!"

Now I always thought it was right cute, the way Uncle Benny fooled Doc about the trained Ford. You know how the old-timey Fords get the gas—it feeds from the hand-throttle on the wheel. Well, Uncle Benny had spent the day before old lady Weller's funeral at Will's garage, putting in a foot accelerator. He didn't say a word to anybody, and Will and me was the only ones knowed he had it. Doc and Uncle Benny stayed three-four days camping at Salt Springs. Now the night they decided to come home, they'd both had something to drink, but Uncle Benny let on like he was in worse shape than he was.

Doc said, "Benny, you better leave me drive."

Uncle Benny pretended to rock on his feet and roll his head and he said, "I've got that Model-T trained to carry me home, drunk or sober."

Doc said, "Never mind that lie again. You get up there in the seat and whistle in the dogs. I'm fixing to drive us home."

Well, I'd of give a pretty to of been in the back seat with them bird-dogs that night when Doc drove the Ford back to Oak Bluff. It's a treat, any ways, to see a fat man get excited. The first thing Doc knowed, the Ford was running away with him. The Ford lights were none too good, and Doc just did clear a stump by the roadside, and he run clean over a blackjack sapling. He looked at the hand-throttle on the wheel and here it was where the car had ought to be going about twenty miles an hour and it was going forty-five. That rascal of an Uncle Benny had his foot on the foot accelerator.

Doc shut off the gas altogether and the Ford kept right on going.

He said, "Something's the matter."

Uncle Benny seemed to be dozing and didn't pay no mind. The Ford whipped back and forth in the sand road like a 'gator's tail. Directly they got on to the hard road and the Model-T put on speed. They begun to get near a curve. It was a dark night and the carlights wobbling, but Doc could see it coming. He took a tight holt of the wheel and begun to sweat. He felt for the brakes, but Uncle Benny never did have any.

He said, "We'll all be kilt."

When they started to take the curve, the Model-T was going nearly fifty-five—and then just as they got there, all of a sudden it slowed down as if it knowed what it was doing, and went around the curve as gentle as a day-old kitten. Uncle Benny had eased his foot off the accelerator. Doc drawed a breath again.

It's a wonder to me that trip didn't make Doc a nervous wreck. On every straightway the Ford would rare back on its haunches and stretch out like a greyhound. Every curve they come to, it would go to it like a jack-rabbit. Then just as the sweat would pour down Doc's face and the drops would splash on the wheel, and he'd gather hisself together ready to jump, the Ford would slow down. It was a hot spring night, but Uncle Benny says Doc's teeth were chattering. The Model-T made the last mile lickety-brindle with the gas at the hand-throttle shut off entirely—and it coasted down in front of Will's garage and of its own free will come to a dead stop.

It was nine o'clock at night. Will was just closing up and I had locked the candy and cigarette counter and was waiting for him. There was a whole bunch of men and boys around, like always, because the garage is the last place in Oak Bluff to put the lights out. Doc climbed out of the Ford trembling like a dish of custard. Uncle Benny eased out after him and I looked at him and right away I knowed he'd been up to mischief.

Doc said, "I don't know how he done it—but dogged if he wasn't telling the truth when he said he had that blankety-blank Model-T trained to carry him home when he ain't fitten."

Will asked, "How come?" and Doc told us. Will looked at me and begun to chuckle and we knowed what Uncle Benny had done to him. I think maybe I would of let Uncle Benny get away with it, but Will couldn't keep it.

"Come here, Doc," he said. "Here's your training."

I thought the bunch would laugh Doc out of town. He swelled

up like a toadfish and he got in his car without a word and drove away.

It's a wonderful thing just to set down and figure out how many different ways there are to be crazy. We never thought of Uncle Benny as being really crazy. We'd say, "Uncle Benny's cutting the fool again," and we'd mean he was just messing around some sort of foolishness like a daggone young un. We figured his was what you might call the bottom kind of craziness. The next would be the half-witted. The next would be the senseless. The next would be what the colored folks call "mindless." And clear up at the top would be what you'd call cold-out crazy. With all his foolishness, we never figured Uncle Benny was cold-out crazy.

Well, we missed Uncle Benny from Oak Bluffs a day or two. When I came to ask questions, I found he'd gone on a long prowl and was over the Withlacoochie River camping with some oyster fishermen. I didn't think much of it, because he was liable to stay off that-a-way. But time rocked on and he didn't show up. I dropped by his house to ask the Old Hen about him. She didn't know a blessed thing.

She said, "Ain't it God's mercy we've got no young uns? The pore things would be as good as fatherless."

And then a few days later Doc came driving up to the garage. He got out and blew his nose and we could see his eyes were red.

He said, "Ain't it awful! I can't hardly bear to think about it."

Will said, "Doc, if you know bad news, you must be carrying it. Ain't nothing sorrowful I know of, except the prohi's have found Philbin's still."

Doc said, "Don't talk about such little accidents at a time like this. You don't mean you ain't heerd about Benny?"

The bunch was there and they all perked up, interested. They knowed if it was Uncle Benny, they could expect 'most any news.

I said, "We ain't heerd a word since he went off to the west coast."

"You ain't heerd about him going crazy?"

I said, "Doc, you mean being crazy. He's always been that-a-way."

"I mean being crazy and going crazy, pore ol' Benny Mathers has gone really cold-out crazy."

"Well, we all just looked at him and we looked at one another. And it came over the whole bunch of us that we weren't surprised. A nigger setting by the free air hose said, "Do, Jesus!" and eased away to tell the others.

Doc blew his nose and wiped his eyes and he said, "I'm sure we all forgive the pore ol' feller all the things he done. He wasn't responsible. I feel mighty bad, to think the hard way I've often spoke to him."

Will asked, "How come it to finally happen?"

Doc said, "He'd been up to some foolishness all night, raring through some of them Gulf coast flat-woods. Him and the fellers he was camping with was setting on the steps of the camp-house after breakfast. All of a sudden Uncle Benny goes to whistling, loud and shrill like a jay-bird. Then he says, 'I'm Sampson,' and he begun to tear down the camp-house."

Will asked, "What'd they do with him?"

Doc said, "You really ain't heerd? I declare, I can't believe the news has come so slow. They had a terrible time holding him and tying him. They got in the doctors and the sheriff and they takened pore ol' Uncle Benny to the lunatic asylum at Chattahoochie."

Doc wiped his eyes and we all begun to sniffle and our eyes to burn. I declare, it was just as if Uncle Benny Mathers had died on us.

I said, "Oh, his poor wife—"

Will said, "We'll have to be good to him and go see him and take him cigarettes and maybe slip him a pint of 'shine now and again."

I said, "The way he loved his freedom—shutting him up in the crazy-house will be like putting a wild-cat in a crocus sack."

Doc said, "Oh, he ain't in the asylum right now. He's broke loose. That's what makes me feel so bad. He's headed this way, and no telling the harm he'll do before he's ketched again."

Everybody jumped up and begun feeling in their hip pockets for their guns.

Doc said, "No use to try to put no guns on him. He's got his'n and they say he's shooting just as accurate as ever."

That was enough for me. I ran back of the counter at the garage and begun locking up.

I said, "Doc, you're a sight. 'Tain't no time to go to feeling sorry for Uncle Benny and our lives and property in danger."

Doc said, "I know, but I knowed him so long and I knowed him so good. I can't help feeling bad about it."

I said, "Do something about it. Don't just set there, and him liable to come shooting his way in any minute."

Doc said, "I know, but what can anybody do to stop him? Pore man, with all them deputies after him."

Will said, "Deputies?"

Doc said, "Why, yes. The sheriff at Ocala asked me would I stop along the road and leave word for all the deputies to try and ketch him. Pore ol' Benny, I'll swear. I hated doing it the worst way."

I scooped the money out of the cash register and I told them, "Now, men, I'm leaving. I've put up with Uncle Benny Mathers when he was drunk and I've put up with him when he was cutting the fool. But the reckless way he drives that Ford and the way he shoots a pistol, I ain't studying on messing up around him and him gone cold-out crazy."

Doc said, "Ain't a thing in the world would stop him when he goes by, and all them deputies after him, but a barricade across the road."

I said, "Then for goodness' sake, you sorry, low-down, no-account, varminty white men, tear down the wire fence around my chicken yard and fix Uncle Benny a barricade."

Doc said, "I just hated to suggest it."

Will said, "He'd slow down for the barricade and we could come in from behind and hem him in."

Doc said, "It'll be an awful thing to hem him in and have to see him sent back to Chattahoochie."

Will said, "I'll commence pulling out the posts and you-all can wind up the fencing."

They worked fast and I went out and looked up the road now and again to see if Uncle Benny was coming. Doc had stopped at the Standard filling-station on his way, to leave the news, and we could see the people there stirring around and going out to look, the same as we were doing. When we dragged the roll of wire fencing out into the road we hollered to them so they could see what we were doing and they all cheered and waved their hats. The word had spread, and the young uns begun traipsing barefooted down to the road, until some of their mammies ran down and cuffed them and hurried them back home out of the way of

Uncle Benny. The men strung the fencing right across the road between the garage on one side and our smokehouse on the other. They nailed it firm at both ends.

Doc said, "Leave me drive the last nail, men—it may be the last thing I can do for Benny this side of Chattahoochie."

I talked the men into unloading their guns.

"He'll have to stop when he sees the barricade," I said, "and then you can all go in on him with your guns drawed and capture him. I just can't hear to a loaded gun being drawed on him, for fear of somebody getting excited and shooting him."

Doc wiped the sweat off his forehead and he said, "Men, this is a mighty serious occasion. I'd be mighty proud if you'd all have a little snort on me," and he passed the bottle.

"Here's to Uncle Benny, the way we all knowed him before he went cold-out crazy," he said.

And then we heerd a shouting up the dirt road and young uns whistling and women and girls screaming and chickens scattering.

"Yonder comes Uncle Benny!"

And yonder he came.

The Model-T was swooping down like a bull-bat after a mosquito. The water was boiling up out of the radiator in a foot-high stream. The seven pieded bird-dogs were hanging out of the back seat and trembling as if they craved to tell the things they'd seen. And behind Uncle Benny was a string of deputy sheriffs in Fords and Chevrolets and motorcycles that had gathered together from every town between Oak Bluff and Ocala. And Uncle Benny was hunched over the steering wheel with them two tufts of goat-horn hair sticking up in the breeze—and the minute I laid eyes on him I knowed he wasn't one mite crazier than he ever had been. I knowed right then Doc had laid out to get even with him and had lied on him all the way down the road.

It was too late then. I knowed, whatever happened, there'd be people to the end of his life would always believe it. I knowed there'd be young uns running from him and niggers hiding. And I knowed there wasn't a thing in the world now could keep him out of Chattahoochie for the time being. I know'd he fight when he was taken, and all them mad and hot and dusty deputies would get him to the lunatic asylum quicker than a black snake can cross hot ashes. And once a man that has cut the fool all his life, like Uncle Benny, is in the crazy-house, there'll be plenty of folks to say to keep him there.

It was too late. Uncle Benny was bearing down toward the garage and right in front of him was the barricade.

Doc hollered, "Be ready to jump on him when he stops!"

Stop? Uncle Benny stop? He kept right on coming. The sight of that chicken-wire barricade was no more to him than an aggravation. Uncle Benny and the Model-T dived into the barricade like a water-turkey into a pool. The barricade held. And the next thing we knowed, the Ford had somersaulted over the fencing and crumpled up like a paper shoe-box and scattered bird-dogs over ten acres and laid Uncle Benny in a heap over against the wall of the smoke-house. I was raised to use the language of a lady, but I could hold in.

"Doc," I said, "you low-down son of a ——"

He said, 'Mis' Dover, the name's too good. I've killed my friend."

Killed him? Killed Uncle Benny? It can't be done until the Almighty Hisself hollers "Sooey!" Uncle Benny was messed up considerable, but him nor none of the bird-dogs was dead.

The doctor took a few stitches in him at the garage before he come to, and tied up his head right pretty in a white bandage. We left Will to quiet the deputies and we put Uncle Benny in Doc's car and carried him home to the Old Hen. Naturally, I figured it would set her to quarrelling. Instead, it just brought out all her sweetness. I can guess a man, but I can't guess another woman.

"The pore ol' feller," she said. "I knowed he had it coming to him. What the devil throws over his back——. I knowed he'd kill hisself in that Ford car, cutting the fool and prowling. The biggest load is off my mind. Now," she said, "now, by God's mercy, when it did come to him, he got out alive."

She begun fanning him with a palmetto fan where he lay on the bed, and Doc poured out a drink of 'shine to have ready for him when he come to. Doc's hand was trembling. Uncle Benny opened his eyes. He eased one hand up to the bandage across his head and he groaned and grunted. He looked at Doc as if he couldn't make up his mind whether or not to reach for his pistol. Doc put the 'shine to his mouth and Uncle Benny swallowed. Them wicked blue eyes begun to dance.

"Doc," he said, "how will I get home when I'm drunk, now you've tore up my trained Ford?"

Doc broke down and cried like a little baby.

"I ain't got the money to replace it," he said, "but I'll give you my car. I'll carry the Little Giant line of remedies on foot."

Uncle Benny said, "I don't want your car. It ain't trained."

Doc said, "Then I'll tote you on my back, anywheres you say."

The Old Hen let in the bird-dogs, some of them limping a little, and they climbed on the bed and beat their tails on the counterpane and licked Uncle Benny. We felt mighty relieved things had come out that way.

Uncle Benny was up and around in a few days, with his head bandaged, and him as pert as a woodpecker. He just about owned Oak Bluff—all except the people that did like I figured, never did get over the idea he'd gone really crazy. Most people figured he'd had a mighty good lesson and it would learn him not to cut the fool. The Old Hen was as happy as a bride. She was so proud to have the Ford torn up, and no money to get another, that she'd even now and again pet one of the bird-dogs. She waited on Uncle Benny hand and foot and couldn't do enough to please him.

She said to me, "The pore ol' feller sure stays home nights now."

Stay home? Uncle Benny stay home? Two weeks after the accident the wreck of the Model-T disappeared from behind the garage where Will had dragged it. The next day the seven bird-dogs disappeared. The day after that Doc and Uncle Benny went to Ocala in Doc's car. Will wouldn't answer me when I asked him questions. The Old Hen stopped by the garage and got a Coca-Cola and she didn't know any more than I did. Then Will pointed down the road.

He said, "Yonder he comes."

And yonder he came. You could tell him way off by the white bandage with the tufts of hair sticking up over it. He was scrooched down behind the wheel of what looked like a brand-new automobile. Doc was following behind him. They swooped into the garage.

Will said, "It's a new second-hand body put on the chassis and around the engine of the old Ford."

Uncle Benny got out and he greeted us.

He said, "Will, it's just possible it was the motor of the Model-T that had takened the training. The motor ain't hurt, and me and Doc are real hopeful."

The Old Hen said, "Benny, where'd you get the money to pay for it?"

He said, "Why, a daggone bootlegger in a truck going from Miami to New York bought the bird-dogs for twenty-five dollars apiece. The low-down rascal knowed good and well they was worth seventy-five."

She brightened some. Getting shut of the bird-dogs was a little progress. She walked over to the car and begun looking around it.

"Benny," she said, and her voice come kind of faintified, "if you sold the bird-dogs, what's this place back here looks like it was fixed for 'em?"

We all looked, and here was a open compartment-like in the back, fixed up with seven crocus sacks stuffed with corn shucks. About that time here come a cloud of dust down the road. It was the seven bird-dogs. They were about give out. Their tongues were hanging out and their feet looked blistered.

Uncle Benny said, "I knowed they'd jump out of that bootlegger's truck. I told him so."

I tell you, what's in a man's nature you can't change. It takened the Old Hen thirty years and all them goings-on to learn it. She went and climbed in the front seat of the car and just sat there waiting for Uncle Benny to drive home for his dinner. He lifted the bird-dogs up and set them down to rest on the corn-shucks cushions, and he brought them a pan of water.

He said, "I figure they busted loose just about Lawtey."

The Old Hen never opened her mouth. She hasn't quarrelled at him from that day to this. She was hornswoggled.

## Rhodora

RHODORA! if the sages ask thee why
   This charm is wasted on the earth and sky,
Tell them, dear, that if eyes were made for seeing
Then Beauty is its own excuse for being:
Why thou wert there, O rival of the rose!
I never thought to ask, I never knew:
But, in my simple ignorance, suppose
The self-same Power that brought me there brought you.
                  *Ralph Waldo Emerson*

# THE MALLARD

## John James Audubon

*The most famous painter of birds took a long road before he
began the work for which he is best known. Audubon (1785–
1851) was born in Haiti and educated in France, where he
studied art under the painter David. When he came to the
United States in 1804, he settled down on his father's estate
near Philadelphia, painted some portraits and engaged unsuc-
cessfully in various business ventures. Finally he turned seriously to bird study and drew his four hundred and thirty-five
magnificent pictures of American birds in their natural states.
The following piece is one he wrote to accompany his pictures.*

ALTHOUGH it is commonly believed that the Mallard is found
abundantly everywhere in the United States, I have received
sufficient proof to the contrary. If authors had acknowledged that
they state so on report, or had said that in the tame state the bird is
common, I should not have blamed them. According to my observation, and I may be allowed to say that I have had good opportunities, this valuable species is extremely rare in the wild state in
the neighbourhood of Boston in Massachusetts. Farther eastward,
this bird is so rare that it is scarcely known, and not one was seen by
myself or my party beyond Portland in Maine. On the western
coast of Labrador none of the inhabitants that we conversed with
had ever seen the Mallard, and in Newfoundland the people were
equally unacquainted with it, the species being in those countries
replaced by the Black Duck, *Anas fusca*. From New York southward, the Mallards become more plentiful, and numbers of them
are seen in the markets of Philadelphia, Baltimore, Richmond in
Virginia, and other towns. Although they are very abundant in the
Carolinas and Florida, as well as in Lower Louisiana, they are much
more so in the Western Country. The reason of this is merely that
the Mallard, unlike the sea Ducks, is rarely seen on salt water, and
that its course from the countries where it chiefly breeds is across

[154]

the interior of the continent. From our great lakes, they spread along the streams, betake themselves to the ponds, wet meadows, submersed savannahs, and inland swamps, and are even found in the thick beech woods, in early autumn, and indeed long before the males have acquired the dark green colour of the head. Many of them proceed beyond the limits of the United States.

Be not startled, good reader, when I tell you that many of these Ducks are bred in the lakes near the Mississippi, nay even in some of the small ponds in the low lands or bottoms of the States of Kentucky, Indiana and Illinois; for in many parts of those districts I have surprised the females on their eggs, have caught the young when their mother was cautiously and with anxiety leading them for greater safety to some stream, and have shot many a fat one before the poor thing could fly, and when it was so plump, tender and juicy, that I doubt much whether you, like myself, would not much prefer them to the famed Canvass-backed Duck.

Look at that Mallard as he floats on the lake; see his elevated head glittering with emerald-green, his amber eyes glancing in the light! Even at this distance, he has marked you and suspects that you bear no good will towards him, for he sees that you have a gun, and he has many a time been frightened by its report, or that of some other. The wary bird draws his feet under his body, springs upon them, opens his wings, and with loud quacks bids you farewell.

Now another is before you, on the margin of that purling streamlet. How brisk are all his motions compared with those of his brethren that waddle across your poultry-yard! how much more graceful in form and neat in apparel! The Duck at home is the descendant of a race of slaves, and has lost his native spirit: his wings have been so little used that they can hardly raise him from the ground. But the free-born, the untamed Duck of the swamps,— see how he springs on wing, and hies away over the woods.

The mallards generally arrive in Kentucky and other parts of the Western Country, from the middle of September to the first of October, or as soon as the acorns and beech-nuts are fully ripe. In a few days they are to be found in all the ponds that are covered with seed-bearing grasses. Some flocks, which appear to be guided by an experienced leader, come directly down on the water with a rustling sound of their wings that can be compared only to the noise produced by an Eagle in the act of swooping upon its prey, while other flocks, as if they felt uneasy respecting the safety of the place, sweep around and above it several times in perfect silence, before they alight. In either case, the birds immediately bathe themselves, beat their bodies with their wings, dive by short plunges, and cut so many capers that you might imagine them to be stark mad. The fact, however, seems to be, that all this alacrity and gaiety only shows the necessity they feel of clearing themselves of the insects about their plumage, as well as the pleasure they experience on finding themselves in a milder climate, with abundance of food around them, after a hard journey of perhaps a day and a night. They wash themselves and arrange their dress, before commencing their meal; and in this other travellers would do well to imitate them.

Now, towards the grassy margins they advance in straggling parties. See how they leap from the water to bend the loaded tops of the tall reeds. Woe be to the slug or snail that comes in their way. Some are probing the mud beneath, and waging war against the leech, frog, or lizard that is within reach of their bills; while many of the older birds run into the woods, to fill their crops with beech-nuts and acorns, not disdaining to swallow also, should they come in their way, some of the wood-mice that, frightened by the approach of the foragers, hie towards their burrows. The cackling they keep up would almost deafen you, were you near them; but it is suddenly stopped by the approach of some unusual enemy, and at once all are silent. With heads erected on out-stretched necks, they anxiously look around. It is nothing, however, but a bear, who being, like themselves, fond of mast, is ploughing up the newly fallen leaves with his muzzle, or removing an old rotting log in search of worms. The Ducks resume their employment. But another sound is now heard, one more alarming. The bear raises himself on his hind legs, snuffs the air, and with a loud snort gallops off towards the depths of his cane-brake. The Ducks retreat to the water, betake themselves to the centre of the pool, and uttering half-stifled notes await the sight of the object they dread. There the enemy cunningly advances, first covered by one tree, then by another. He has lost his chance of the bear, but as he is pushed by hunger, a Mallard will do for the bullet of his rusty rifle. It is an Indian, as you perceive by his red skin and flowing black hair, which, however, has been cut close from the sides of his head. In the centre of his dearly purchased blanket, a hole has been cut, through which he has thrust his bare head, and the ragged garment, like a horse's netting, is engaged as it were in flapping off the last hungry mosquitoes of the season that are fast sucking the blood from his limbs. Watch him, Mallard. Nay, wait no longer, for I see him taking aim; better for you all to fly! No—well, one of you will certainly furnish him with a repast. Amid the dark wood rises the curling smoke, the report comes on my ear, the Ducks all rise save a pair, that, with back downwards and feet kicking against the air, have been hit by the prowler. The free son of the forest slowly approaches the pool, judges at a glance of the depth of the mire, and boldly advances, until with a cane he draws the game towards him. Returning to the wood, he now kindles a little fire, the feathers fill the air around; from each wing he takes a quill, to clean the touch-hole of his gun in damp weather; the entrails he saves to bait some trap. In a short time the Ducks are ready, and the hunter enjoys his meal, although brief time does he take in swallowing the savoury morsels. Soon, the glimmering light of the moon will see him again on his feet, and lead him through the woods, as he goes in pursuit of other game.

The Mallards that remain with us during the whole year, and breed on the banks of the Mississippi or Lake Michigan, or in the beautiful meadows that here and there border the Schuylkill in Pennsylvania, begin to pair in the very heart of winter; and although Ducks are quite destitute of song, their courtships are not devoid of interest. The males, like other gay deceivers, offer their regards to the first fair one that attracts their notice, promise unremitting fidelity and affection, and repeat their offers to the next they meet. See that drake, how he proudly shows, first the beauty of his silky head, then the brilliancy of his wing-spots, and, with honeyed jabberings, discloses the warmth of his affection. He plays around this one, then around another, until the passion of jealousy is aroused in the breasts of the admired and flattered. Bickerings arise; the younger Duck disdains her elder sister, and a third, who conceives herself a coquette of the first order, interposes, as if to ensure the caresses of the feathered beau. Many tricks are played by Ducks, good reader, but ere long the females retire in search of a safe place in which they may deposit their eggs and rear their young. They draw a quantity of weeds around them, and form an ill-arranged sort of nest, in which from seven to ten eggs are laid. From their bodies they pluck the softest down, and placing it beneath the eggs, begin the long process of incubation, which they intermit only for short periods, when it becomes absolutely necessary to procure a little sustenance.

At length, in about three weeks, the young begin to cheep in the shell, from which, after a violent struggle, they make their escape. What beautiful creatures! See how, with their little bills, they dry their downy apparel! Now, in a long line, one after another, they follow their glad mother to the water, on arriving at which they take to swimming and diving, as if elated with joy for having been introduced into existence. The male, wearied and emaciated, is far away on some other pond. The unnatural barbarian cares nothing about his progeny, nor has a thought arisen in his mind respecting the lonely condition of his mate, the greatness of her cares, or the sadness that she may experience under the idea that she has been utterly forsaken by him who once called her his only and truly beloved. No, reader, not a thought of this kind has he wasted on her whom he has left alone in charge of a set of eggs, and now of a whole flock of innocent ducklings, to secure which from danger, and see them all grow up apace, she manifests the greatest care and anxiety. She leads them along the shallow edges of grassy ponds, and teaches them to seize the small insects that abound there, the flies, the mosquitoes, the giddy beetles that skim along the surface in circles and serpentine lines. At the sight of danger they run as it were on the water, making directly for the shore, or dive and disappear. In about six weeks, those that have escaped from the ravenous fishes and turtles have attained a goodly size; the quills appear on their wings; their bodies are encased with feathers; but as yet none are able to fly. They now procure their food by partial immersions of the head and neck in the manner of the old bird. At this period they are already fit for the table, and delicate as well as savoury food they afford. By the time that the leaves are changing their hues, the young Mallards take freely to their wings, and the old males join the congregated flocks.

I have found the Mallard breeding on large prostrate and rotten logs, three feet above the ground, and in the centre of a cane-brake, nearly a mile distant from any water. Once I found a female leading her young through the woods, and no doubt conducting them towards the Ohio. When I first saw her, she had already observed me, and had squatted flat among the grass, with her brood around her. As I moved onwards, she ruffled her feathers, and hissed at me in the manner of a Goose, while the little ones scampered off in all directions. I had an excellent dog, well instructed to catch young birds without injuring them, and I ordered him to seek for them. On this the mother took to wing, and flew through the woods as if about to fall down at every yard or so. She passed and repassed over the dog, as if watching the success of his search; and as one after another of the ducklings were brought to me, and struggled in my bird-bag, the distressed parent came to the ground near me, rolled and tumbled about, and so affected me by her despair, that I ordered my dog to lie down, while, with a pleasure that can be felt only by those who are parents themselves, I restored to her the innocent brood, and walked off. As I turned round to observe her, I really thought I could perceive gratitude expressed in her eye; and a happier moment I never felt while rambling in search of knowledge through the woods.

The flight of the Mallard is swift, strong, and well sustained. It rises either from the ground or from the water at a single spring and flies almost perpendicularly for ten or fifteen yards, or, if in a thick wood, until quite above the tops of the tallest trees, after which it moves horizontally. If alarmed, it never rises without uttering several *quacks;* but on other occasions it usually leaves its place in silence. While travelling to any distance, the whistling sound of their wings may be heard a great way off, more especially in the quiet of night. Their progress through the air I have thought might be estimated at a mile or a mile and a half in the minute; and I feel very confident that when at full speed and on a long journey, they can fly at the rate of a hundred and twenty miles an hour.

## Sunrise

DAY!
   Faster and more fast,
O'er night's brim, day boils at last:
Boils, pure gold, o'er the cloud-cup's brim
Where spurting and suppressed it lay,
For not a froth-flake touched the rim
Of yonder gap in the solid gray
Of the eastern cloud, an hour away;
But forth one wavelet, then another, curled,
Till the whole sunrise, not to be suppressed,
Rose, reddened, and its seething breast
Flickered in bounds, grew gold, then overflowed the world.
*Robert Browning*

# THE CHUB

## Izaak Walton

*The Compleat Angler appeared nearly three hundred years ago and is still widely read with great enjoyment. Yet it was written by a man whose chief occupation was neither fishing nor writing. Izaak Walton (1593–1683) was a successful London ironmonger. Much of his long life was spent traveling, writing, fishing, and compiling biographies of famous men he liked. His lovable and kindly personality pervaded all he wrote, as it does the following selection, in which Piscator, the fisherman, speaks to Venator, the hunter.*

WELL, scholar, you see what pains I have taken to recover the lost credit of the poor despised chub. And now I will give you some rules how to catch him; and I am glad to enter you into the art of fishing by catching a chub, for there is no fish better to enter a young angler,—he is so easily caught, but then it must be this particular way:

Go to the same hole in which I caught my chub, where in most hot days you will find a dozen or twenty chevens floating near the top of the water. Get two or three grasshoppers as you go over the meadow, and get secretly behind the tree, and stand as free from motion as possible; then put a grasshopper on your hook, and let your hook hang a quarter of a yard short of the water, to which end you must rest your rod on some bough of the tree. But it is likely the chubs will sink down towards the bottom of the water at the first shadow of your rod (for a chub is the fearfullest of fishes), and will do so if but a bird flies over him and makes the least shadow on the water; but they will presently rise up to the top again, and there lie soaring till some shadow affrights them again. I say, when they lie upon the top of the water, look out the best chub; which you, setting yourself in a fit place, may very easily see, and move your rod, as softly as a snail moves, to that chub you intend to catch; let your bait fall gently upon the water three or four inches before him, and he will infallibly take the bait. And you will be as sure to catch him, for he is one of the leather-mouthed fishes, of which a hook doth scarce ever lose its hold; and therefore give him play enough before you offer to take him out of the water. Go your way presently, take my rod, and do as I bid you, and I will sit down and mend my tackling till you return back.

VENATOR. Truly, my loving master, you have offered me as fair as I could wish. I'll go and observe your directions.

Look you, master, what I have done! that which joys my heart, caught just such another chub as yours was.

PISCATOR. Marry, and I am glad of it: I am like to have a to-wardly scholar of you. I now see, that with advice and practice you will make an angler in a short time. Have but a love to it, and I'll warrant you.

VENATOR. But, master! what if I could not have found a grass-hopper?

PISCATOR. Then I may tell you, that a black snail, with his belly slit, to show his white; or a piece of soft cheese, will usually do as well: nay, sometimes a worm, or any kind of fly, as the ant-fly, the flesh-fly, or wall-fly; or the dor or beetle, which you may find under a cowturd; or a bob, which you will find in the same place, and in time will be a beetle; it is a short white worm, like to and bigger than a gentle, or a cod-worm, or a case-worm, any of these will do very well to fish in such a manner. And after this manner you may catch a trout in a hot evening: when, as you walk by a brook, and shall see or hear him leap at flies, then, if you get a grasshopper, put it on your hook, with your line about two yards long, standing behind a bush or tree where his hole is, and make your bait stir up and down on the top of the water: you may, if you stand close, be sure of a bite, but not sure to catch him, for he is not a leather-mouthed fish: and after this manner you may fish for him with almost any kind of live fly, but especially with a grasshopper.

VENATOR. But before you go further, I pray, good master, what mean you by a leather-mouthed fish?

PISCATOR. By a leather-mouthed fish, I mean such as have their teeth in their throat, as the chub or cheven, and so the barbel, the gudgeon, and carp, and divers others have: and the hook, being stuck into the leather or skin of the mouth of such fish, does very seldom or never lose its hold; but on the contrary, a pike, a perch, or trout, and so some other fish, which have not their teeth in their throats, but in their mouths (which you shall observe to be very full of bones, and the skin very thin, and little of it); I say, of these fish the hook never takes so sure hold, but you often lose your fish, unless he have gorged it.

VENATOR. I thank you, good master, for this observation; but now what shall be done with my chub or cheven that I have caught?

PISCATOR. Marry, Sir, it shall be given away to some poor body, for I'll warrant you I'll give you a trout for your supper: and it is a good beginning of your art to offer your first-fruits to the poor, who will both thank God and you for it, which I see by your silence you seem to consent to. And for your willingness to part with it so charitably, I will also teach more concerning chub-fishing. You are to note, that in March and April he is usually taken with worm; in May, June and July he will bite at any fly, or at cherries, or at beetles with their legs and wings cut off, or at any kind of snail, or at the black bee that breeds in clay walls; and he never refuses a grasshopper on the top of a swift stream, nor, at the bottom, the young humble-bee that breeds in long grass, and is ordinarily found by the mower of it. In August, and in the cooler months, a yellow paste, made of the strongest cheese, and pounded in a mortar, with a little butter and saffron (so much of it as, being beaten small, will turn it to a lemon colour). And some make a paste for the winter months, at which time the chub is accounted best (for then it is observed, that the forked bones are lost, or turned into a kind of gristle, especially if he be baked) of cheese and turpentine. He will bite also at a minnow or penk, as a trout will: of which I shall tell you more hereafter, and of divers other baits. But take this for a rule, that in hot weather he is to be fished for towards the mid-water, or near the top; and in colder weather nearer the bottom; and if you fish for him on the top, with a beetle or any fly, then be sure to let your line be very long, and to keep out of sight. And having told you that his spawn is excellent meat, and that the head of a large cheven, the throat being well washed, is the best part of him, I will say no more of this fish at the present, but wish you may catch the next you fish for.

# THE BISON STAMPEDE

## James Fenimore Cooper

*Cooper (1789–1851) was thirty years old when he exclaimed to his wife one evening, as he was reading an English novel, that even he could write a better book than that. His wife challenged him to back up the statement, and Cooper turned out a book called* Precaution, *which was indeed superior to the book which had provoked him. His second story,* The Spy, *was an immediate success—and Cooper went on to write thirty-two novels in the next twenty-nine years, plus a scholarly history of the American Navy, travel letters and pungent social essays. Most popular were his adventure stories of the western frontier, called* The Leather-Stocking Tales, *featuring the scout Natty Bumppo. The fifth of these was* The Prairie, *in which Natty, now almost ninety years old, helps Duncan Middleton, son of an old friend, rescue his fiancee, Inez, from kidnappers on a wagon train heading west. With them are a naturalist, Dr. Battius, and two others from the wagon train—Ellen Wade and Paul Hover. Natty saves them from Indians, a prairie fire, and many other dangers, among them the stampede described below.*

THE warrior suddenly paused and bent his face aside, like one who listened with all his faculties absorbed in the act. Then turning the head of his horse, he rode to the nearest angle of the thicket, and looked intently across the bleak prairie in a direction opposite to the side on which the party stood. Returning slowly from this unaccountable, and, to his observers, startling procedure, he riveted his eyes on Inez, and paced back and forth several times with the air of one who maintained a warm struggle on some difficult point in the recesses of his own thoughts. He had drawn the reins of his impatient steed, and was seemingly about to speak when his head again sank on his chest, and he resumed his former attitude of attention. Galloping like a deer to the place of his former observations, he rode for a moment swiftly in short and rapid circles as if still uncertain of his course, and then darted away like a bird that had been fluttering around its nest before it takes a distant flight. After scouring the plain for a minute he was lost to the eye behind a swell of the land.

The hounds, who had also manifested great uneasiness for some time, followed him for a little distance, and then terminated their chase by seating themselves on the ground and raising their usual low, whining, and warning howls.

These movements had passed in so short a space of time that the old man, while he neglected not to note the smallest incident, had no opportunity of expressing his opinion concerning the stranger's motives. After the Pawnee had disappeared, however, he shook his head and muttered, while he walked slowly to the angle of the thicket that the Indian had just quitted:—

"There are both scents and sounds in the air, though my miserable senses are not good enough to hear the one or to catch the taint of the other."

"There is nothing to be seen," cried Middleton, who kept close at his side. "My ears and my eyes are good, and yet I can assure you that I neither hear nor see anything."

"Your eyes are good! and you are not deaf!" returned the other, with a slight air of contempt; "no, lad, no; they may be good to see across a church, or to hear a town bell, but afore you had passed a year in these prairies you would find yourself taking a turkey for a buffalo, or conceiting fifty times that the roar of a buffalo bull was the thunder of the Lord! There is a deception of natur' in these naked plains in which the air throws up the images like water, and then it is hard to tell the prairies from a sea. But yonder is a sign that a hunter never fails to know."

The trapper pointed to a flight of vultures that were sailing over the plain at no great distance, and apparently in the direction in which the Pawnee had riveted his eyes. At first Middleton could not distinguish the small dark objects that were dotting the dusky clouds; but as they came swiftly onward, first their forms and then their heavy waving wings became distinctly visible.

"Listen!" said the trapper, when he had succeeded in making Middleton see the moving column of birds. "Now you hear the buffaloes, or bisons, as your knowing Doctor sees fit to call them; though buffaloes is their name among all the hunters of these regions. And I conclude that a hunter is a better judge of a beast and of its name," he added, winking at the young soldier, "than any man who has turned over the leaves of a book instead of traveling over the face of the 'arth, in order to find out the natur's of its inhabitants."

"Of their habits, I will grant you," cried the naturalist, who rarely missed an opportunity to agitate any disputed point in his favorite studies. "That is, provided always deference is had to the proper use of definitions, and that they are contemplated with scientific eyes."

"Eyes of a mole! as if any man's eyes were not as good for names as the eyes of any other creatur'! Who named the works of His hand? can you tell me that, with your book and college wisdom? Was it not the first man in the Garden, and is it not a plain consequence that his children inherit his gifts?"

"That is certainly the Mosaic account of the event," said the Doctor; "though your reading is by far too literal!"

"My reading! nay, if you suppose that I have wasted my time in schools, you do such a wrong to my knowledge as one mortal should never lay to the door of another without sufficient reason. If I have ever craved the art of reading, it has been that I might better know the sayings of the book you name, for it is a book which speaks in every line according to human feelings, and therein according to reason."

"And do you then believe," said the Doctor, a little provoked by the dogmatism of his stubborn adversary, and perhaps secretly too confident in his own more liberal, though scarcely as profitable attainments, "do you then believe that all these beasts were literally collected in a garden to be enrolled in the nomenclature of the first man?"

"Why not? I understand your meaning; for it is not needful to live in towns to hear all the devilish devices that the conceit of man can invent to upset his own happiness. What does it prove, except indeed it may be said to prove that the garden He made was not after the miserable fashions of our times, thereby directly giving the lie to what the world calls its civilizing? No, no, the garden of the Lord was the forest then, and is the forest now, where the fruits do grow and the birds do sing, according to his own wise ordering. Now, lady, you may see the mystery of the vultures! There come the buffaloes themselves, and a noble herd it is! I warrant me that Pawnee has a troop of his people in some of the hollows nigh by; and as he has gone scampering after them, you are about to see a glorious chase. It will serve to keep the squatter and his brood under cover, and for ourselves there is little reason to fear. A Pawnee is not apt to be a malicious savage."

Every eye was now drawn to the striking spectacle that succeeded. Even the timid Inez hastened to the side of Middleton to gaze at the sight, and Paul summoned Ellen from her culinary labors to become a witness of the lively scene.

Throughout the whole of those moving events which it has been our duty to record, the prairies had lain in the majesty of perfect solitude. The heavens had been blackened with the passage of the migratory birds, it is true; but the dogs of the party and the ass of the Doctor were the only quadrupeds that had enlivened the broad surface of the waste beneath. There was now a sudden exhibition of animal life which changed the scene, as it were by magic, to the very opposite extreme.

A few enormous bison bulls were first observed scouring along the most distant rolls of the prairie, and then succeeded long files of single beasts, which in their turns were followed by a dark mass of bodies, until the dun-colored herbage of the plain was entirely lost in the deeper hue of their shaggy coats. The herd, as the column spread and thickened, was like the endless flocks of the smaller birds whose extended flanks are so often seen to heave up out of the abyss of the heavens, until they appear as countless as the leaves in those forests over which they wing their endless flight. Clouds of dust shot up in little columns from the centre of the mass, as some animal, more furious than the rest, plowed the plain with his horns; and from time to time a deep hollow bellowing was borne along on the wind, as if a thousand throats vented their plaints in a discordant murmuring.

A long and musing silence reigned in the party as they gazed on this spectacle of wild and peculiar grandeur. It was at length broken by the trapper, who, having been long accustomed to similar sights, felt less of its influence, or rather felt it in a less thrilling and absorbing manner, than those to whom the scene was more novel.

"There go ten thousand oxen in one drove, without keeper or master, except Him who made them and gave them these open plains for their pasture! Ay, it is here that man may see the proofs of his wantonness and folly! Can the proudest governor in all the States go into his fields and slaughter a nobler bullock than is here offered to the meanest hand; and when he has gotten his sirloin or his steak, can he eat it with as good a relish as he who has sweetened his food with wholesome toil, and earned it according to the law of natur', by honestly mastering that which the Lord hath put before him?"

"If the prairie platter is smoking with a buffalo's hump, I answer no," interrupted the luxurious bee-hunter.

"Ay, boy, you have tasted, and you feel the genuine reasoning of the thing! But the herd is heading a little this-away, and it behooves us to make ready for their visit. If we hide ourselves altogether, the horned brutes will break through the place and trample us beneath their feet like so many creeping worms; so we will just put the weak ones apart, and take post, as becomes men and hunters, in the van."

As there was but little time to make the necessary arrangements, the whole party set about them in good earnest. Inez and Ellen were placed in the edge of the thicket on the side furthest from the approaching herd. Asinus [the ass] was posted in the centre, in consideration of his nerves; and then the old man with his three male companions divided themselves in such a manner as they thought would enable them to turn the head of the rushing column, should it chance to approach too nigh their position. By the vacillating movements of some fifty or a hundred bulls that led the advance, it remained questionable for many moments what course they intended to pursue. But a tremendous and painful roar which came from behind the cloud of dust that rose in the centre of the herd, and which was horridly answered by the screams of the carrion-birds that were greedily sailing directly above the flying drove, appeared to give a new impulse to their flight and at once to remove every symptom of indecision. As if glad to seek the smallest signs of the forest, the whole of the affrighted herd became steady in its direction, rushing in a straight line toward the little cover of bushes which has already been so often named.

The appearance of danger was now in reality of a character to try the stoutest nerves. The flanks of the dark moving mass were advanced in such a manner as to make a concave line of the front; and every fierce eye that was glaring from the shaggy wilderness of hair in which the entire heads of the males were enveloped, was riveted with mad anxiety on the thicket. It seemed as if each beast strove to outstrip his neighbor in gaining this desired cover; and as thousands in the rear pressed blindly on those in front, there was the appearance of an imminent risk that the leaders of the herd would be precipitated on the concealed party, in which case the destruction of every one of them was certain. Each of our adventurers felt the danger of his situation in a manner peculiar to his individual character and circumstances.

Middleton wavered. At times he felt inclined to rush through the bushes, and seizing Inez, attempt to fly. Then recollecting the impossibility of outstripping the furious speed of an alarmed bison, he felt for his arms, determined to make head against the countless drove. The faculties of Dr. Battius were quickly wrought up to the very summit of mental delusion. The dark forms of the herd lost their distinctness, and then the naturalist began to fancy he beheld a wild collection of all the creatures of the world rushing upon him in a body, as if to revenge the various injuries which, in the course of a life of indefatigable labor in behalf of the natural sciences, he had inflicted on their several genera. The paralysis it occasioned in his system was like the effect of the incubus. Equally unable to fly or to advance, he stood riveted to the spot, until the infatuation became so complete that the worthy naturalist was beginning, by a desperate effort of scientific resolution, even to class the different specimens. On the other hand, Paul shouted, and called on Ellen to come and assist him in shouting, but his voice was lost in the bellowings and trampling of the herd. Furious, and yet strangely excited by the obstinacy of the brutes and the wildness of the sight, and nearly maddened by sympathy and a species of unconscious apprehension in which the claims of nature were singularly mingled with concern for his mistress, he nearly split his throat in exhorting his aged friend to interfere.

"Come forth, old trapper," he shouted, "with your prairie inventions! or we shall be all smothered under a mountain of buffalo humps!"

The old man, who had stood all this while leaning on his rifle and regarding the movements of the herd with a steady eye, now deemed it time to strike his blow. Leveling his piece at the foremost bull, with an agility that would have done credit to his youth, he fired. The animal received the bullet on the matted hair between his horns, and fell to his knees; but shaking his head he instantly arose, the very shock seeming to increase his exertions. There was now no longer time to hesitate. Throwing down his rifle, the trapper stretched forth his arms, and advanced from the cover with naked hands directly towards the rushing column of the beasts.

The figure of a man, when sustained by the firmness and steadiness that intellect can only impart, rarely fails of commanding respect from all the inferior animals of the creation. The leading bulls recoiled, and for a single instant there was a sudden stop to their speed, a dense mass of bodies rolling up in front until hundreds were seen floundering and tumbling on the plain. Then came another of those hollow bellowings from the rear, and set the herd again in motion. The head of the column, however, divided, the immovable form of the trapper cutting it as it were into two gliding streams of life. Middleton and Paul instantly profited by his example, and extended the feeble barrier by a similar exhibition of their own persons.

For a few moments the new impulse given to the animals in front served to protect the thicket. But as the body of the herd pressed more and more upon the open line of its defenders, and the dust thickened so as to obscure their persons, there was at each instant a renewed danger of the beasts breaking through. It became necessary for the trapper and his companions to become still more and more alert; and they were gradually yielding before the headlong multitude, when a furious bull darted by Middleton so near as to brush his person, and at the next instant swept through the thicket with the velocity of the wind.

"Close, and dive for the ground," shouted the old man, "or a thousand of the devils will be at his heels!"

All their efforts would have proved fruitless however against the living torrent, had not Asinus, whose domains had just been so rudely entered, lifted his voice in the midst of the uproar. The most sturdy and furious of the bulls trembled at the alarming and unknown cry, and then each individual brute was seen madly pressing from that very thicket which the moment before he had endeavored to reach, with the eagerness with which the murderer seeks the sanctuary.

As the stream divided the place became clear; the two dark columns moving obliquely from the copse, to unite again at the distance of a mile, on its opposite side. The instant the old man saw the sudden effect which the voice of Asinus had produced, he coolly commenced reloading his rifle, indulging at the same time in a heartfelt fit of his silent and peculiar merriment.

"There they go, like dogs with so many half-filled shot-pouches dangling at their tails, and no fear of their breaking their order; for what the brutes in the rear didn't hear with their own ears, they'll conceit they did: besides, if they change their minds, it may be no hard matter to get the jack to sing the rest of his tune!"

"The ass has spoken, but Balaam is silent!" cried the bee-hunter, catching his breath after a repeated burst of noisy mirth, that might possibly have added to the panic of the buffaloes by its vociferation. "The man is as completely dumfounded as if a swarm of young bees had settled on the end of his tongue, and he not willing to speak for fear of their answer."

"How now, friend," continued the trapper, addressing the still motionless and entranced naturalist; "how now, friend; are you, who make your livelihood by booking the names and natur's of the beasts of the fields and the fowls of the air, frightened at a herd of scampering buffaloes? Though perhaps you are ready to dispute my right to call them by a word that is in the mouth of every hunter and trader on the frontier!"

The old man was however mistaken in supposing he could excite the benumbed faculties of the Doctor by provoking a discussion. From that time henceforth he was never known, except on one occasion, to utter a word that indicated either the species or the genus of the animal. He obstinately refused the nutritious food of the whole ox family; and even to the present hour, now that he is established in all the scientific dignity and security of a savant in one of the maritime towns, he turns his back with a shudder on those delicious and unrivaled viands that are so often seen at the suppers of the craft, and which are unequaled by anything that is served under the same name at the boasted chop-houses of London or at the most renowned of the Parisian restaurants.

### Forbearance

H AST thou named all the birds without a gun?
　　Loved the wood-rose, and left it on its stalk?
At rich men's tables eaten bread and pulse?
Unarmed, faced danger with a heart of trust?
And loved so well a high behavior,
In man or maid, that thou from speech refrained,
Nobility more nobly to repay?
O, be my friend, and teach me to be thine!
　　　　　　　　　　*Ralph Waldo Emerson*

# A-HUNTING OF THE DEER

## Charles Dudley Warner

*Deer hunters are warned away from this story, because they may never enjoy their sport quite so fully once they have read it. But all lovers of nature will take it to their hearts, not only because of the understanding and sympathy it shows for wild life, but also for the steadily mounting drama of the tale itself. Charles Dudley Warner (1829–1900) was probably the leading editor of his day, a famous essayist who turned to fiction and realism after collaborating on* The Gilded Age *with his friend Mark Twain.*

IF civilization owes a debt of gratitude to the self-sacrificing sportsmen who have cleared the Adirondack region of Catamounts and savage trout, what shall be said of the army which has so nobly relieved them of the terror of the Deer? The deer-slayers have somewhat celebrated their exploits in print; but I think that justice has never been done them. . . .

The pleasurable excitement of a deer-hunt has never, I believe, been regarded from the Deer's point of view. I happen to be in a position, by reason of a lucky Adirondack experience, to present it in that light.

Early on the morning of the 23d of August, 1877, a doe was feeding on Basin Mountain. The night had been warm and showery, and the morning opened in an undecided way. The wind was southerly; it is what the Deer call a dog-wind, having come to know quite well the meaning of "a southerly wind and a cloudy sky." The sole companion of the doe was her only child, a charming little fawn, whose brown coat was mottled with the beautiful spots which make this young creature as lovely as the Gazelle. The buck, its father, had been that night on a long tramp across the mountain to Clear Pond and had not yet returned: he went ostensibly to feed on the succulent lily-pads there. "He feedeth among the lilies until the day break and the shadows flee away, and he should be here by this hour; but he cometh not," she said, "leaping upon the mountains, skipping upon the hills."

Clear Pond was too far off for the young mother to go with her fawn for a night's pleasure. It was a fashionable watering-place at this season among the Deer; and the doe may have remembered, not without uneasiness, the moonlight meetings of a frivolous society there. But the buck did not come; he was very likely sleeping under one of the ledges on Tight Nippin. Was he alone? "I charge you, by the roes and by the hinds of the field, that ye stir not nor awake my love till he please."

The doe was feeding, daintily cropping the tender leaves of the young shoots, and turning from time to time to regard her offspring. The fawn had taken his morning meal, and now lay curled up on a bed of moss, watching contentedly, with his large soft brown eyes, every movement of his mother. The great eyes followed her with an alert entreaty; and, if the mother stepped a pace or two farther away in feeding, the fawn made a half-movement, as if to rise and follow her. You see, she was his sole dependence in all the world. But he was quickly reassured when she turned her gaze on him; and if, in alarm, he uttered a plaintive cry, she bounded to him at once, and, with every demonstration of affection, licked his mottled skin till it shone again.

It was a pretty picture,—maternal love on the one part, and happy trust on the other. The doe was a beauty, and would have been so considered anywhere, as graceful and winning a creature as the sun that day shone on,—slender limbs, not too heavy flanks, round body, and aristocratic head, with small ears, and luminous, intelligent, affectionate eyes. How alert, supple, free, she was! What untaught grace in every movement! What a charming pose when she lifted her head, and turned it to regard her child! You would have had a companion-picture, if you had seen, as I saw that morning, a baby kicking about among the dry pine-needles on a ledge above the Ausable, in the valley below, while its young mother sat near, with an easel before her touching in the color of a reluctant landscape, giving a quick look at the sky and the outline of the Twin Mountains, and bestowing every third glance upon the laughing boy,—art in its infancy.

The doe lifted her head a little with a quick motion, and turned her ear to the south. Had she heard something? Probably it was only the south winds in the balsams. There was silence all about in the forest. If the doe had heard anything, it was one of the distant noises of the world. There are in the woods occasional moanings, premonitions of change, which are inaudible to the dull ears of men, but which, I have no doubt, the forest-folk hear and understand. If the doe's suspicions were excited for an instant, they were gone as soon. With an affectionate glance at her fawn, she continued picking up her breakfast.

But suddenly she started, head erect, eyes dilated, a tremor in her limbs. She took a step; she turned her head to the south; she listened intently. There was a sound,—a distant, prolonged note, bell-toned, pervading the woods, shaking the air in smooth vibrations. It was repeated. The doe had no doubt now. She shook like the sensitive mimosa when a footstep approaches. It was the baying of a Hound! It was far off,—at the foot of the mountain. Time enough to fly; time enough to put miles between her and the Hound, before he should come upon her fresh trail; time enough to escape away through the dense forest, and hide in the recesses of Panther Gorge; yes, time enough.

But there was the fawn. The cry of the Hound was repeated, more distinct this time. The mother instinctively bounded away a few paces. The fawn started up with an anxious bleat. The doe turned; she came back; she couldn't leave it. She bent over it, and licked it, and seemed to say, "Come, my child; we are pursued; we must go." She walked away towards the west, and the little thing skipped after her. It was slow going for the slender legs, over the fallen logs, and through the rasping bushes. The doe bounded in advance, and waited; the fawn scrambled after her, slipping and tumbling along, very groggy yet on his legs, and whining a good deal because its mother kept always moving away from it. The fawn evidently did not hear the Hound; the little innocent would even have looked sweetly at the Dog, and tried to make friends with it, if the brute had been rushing upon him. By all the means at her command, the doe urged her young one on; but it was slow work. She might have been a mile away while they were making a few rods. Whenever the fawn caught up he was quite content to frisk about. He wanted more breakfast, for one thing; and his mother wouldn't stand still. She moved on continually; and his weak legs were tangled in the roots of the narrow deer-path.

Shortly came a sound that threw the doe into a panic of terror,— a short, sharp yelp, followed by a prolonged howl, caught up and re-echoed by other bayings along the mountainside. The doe knew what that meant. One Hound had caught her trail; and the whole pack responded to the "view-halloo." The danger was certain now; it was near. She could not crawl on in this way; the Dogs would soon be upon them. She turned again for flight; the fawn, scrambling after her, tumbled over, and bleated piteously. The baying, now emphasized by the yelp of certainty, came nearer. Flight with the fawn was impossible. The doe returned and stood by it, head erect, and nostrils distended. She stood perfectly still, but trembling. Perhaps she was thinking. The fawn took advantage of the situation, and began to draw his luncheon ration. The doe seemed to have made up her mind. She let him finish. The fawn, having taken all he wanted, lay down contentedly, and the doe licked him for a moment. Then, with the swiftness of a bird, she dashed away, and in a moment was lost in the forest. She went in the direction of the Hounds.

According to all human calculations, she was going into the jaws of death. So she was: all human calculations are selfish. She kept straight on, hearing the baying every moment more distinctly. She descended the slope of the mountain till she reached the more open forest of hard-wood. It was freer going here, and the cry of the pack echoed more resoundingly in the great spaces. She was going due east, when (judging by the sound, the Hounds were not far off, though they were still hidden by a ridge) she turned away towards the north, and kept on at a good pace. In five minutes more she heard the sharp, exultant yelp of discovery, and the deep-mouthed howl of pursuit. The Hounds had struck her trail where she turned, and the fawn was safe.

The doe was in good running condition, the ground was not bad, and she felt the exhilaration of the chase. For the moment, fear left her, and she bounded on with the exaltation of triumph. For a quarter of an hour she went on at a slapping pace, clearing the moose-bushes with bound after bound, flying over the fallen logs, pausing neither for brook or ravine. The baying of the Hounds grew fainter behind her. But she struck a bad piece of going, a dead-wood slash. It was marvellous to see her skim over it, leaping among its intricacies, and not breaking her slender legs. No other living animal could do it. But it was killing work. She began to pant fearfully; she lost ground. The baying of the Hounds was nearer. She climbed the hard-wood hill at a slower gait; but, once on more level, free ground, her breath came back to her, and she stretched away with new courage, and may be a sort of contempt of her heavy pursuers.

After running at a high speed perhaps half a mile farther, it occurred to her that it would be safe now to turn to the west, and, by a wide circuit, seek her fawn. But, at the moment, she heard a sound that chilled her heart. It was the cry of a Hound to the west of her. The crafty brute had made the circuit of the slash, and cut off her retreat. There was nothing to do but to keep on; and on she went, still to the north, with the noise of the pack behind her. In five minutes more she had passed into a hillside clearing. Cows and young Steers were grazing there. She heard a tinkle of bells. Below her, down the mountain slope, were other clearings, broken by patches of woods. Fences intervened; and a mile or two down lay the valley, the shining Ausable, and the peaceful farmhouses. That way also her hereditary enemies were. Not a merciful heart in all that lovely valley.

She hesitated; it was only for an instant. She must cross the Slidebrook Valley if possible, and gain the mountain opposite. She bounded on; she stopped. What was that? From the valley ahead came the cry of a searching Hound. All the devils were loose this morning. Every way was closed but one, and that led straight down the mountain to the cluster of houses. Conspicuous among them was a slender white wooden spire. The doe did not know it was the spire of a Christian chapel, but perhaps she thought that human pity dwelt there, and would be more merciful than the teeth of the Hounds.

"The hounds are baying on my track:
O White man! will you send me back?"

In a panic, frightened animals will always flee to human-kind from the danger of more savage foes. They always make a mistake in doing so. Perhaps the trait is the survival of an era of peace on earth; perhaps it is a prophecy of the golden age of the future. The business of this age is murder,—the slaughter of animals, the slaughter of fellow-men, by the wholesale. Hilarious poets who never fire a gun write hunting songs,—*Ti-ra-la* and good bishops write war-songs,—*Ave the Czar!*

The hunted doe went down "the open," clearing the fences splendidly, flying along the stony path. It was a beautiful sight. But consider what a shot it was! If the Deer, now, could only have been caught! No doubt there were tender-hearted people in the valley who would have spared her life, shut her up in a stable, and petted her. Was there one who would have let her go back to her waiting fawn? It is the business of civilization to tame or kill.

The doe went on; she left the saw-mill on John's Brook to her right; she turned into a wood-path. As she approached Slide Brook, she saw a boy standing by a tree with a raised rifle. The Dogs were not in sight, but she could hear them coming down the hill. There was no time for hesitation. With a tremendous burst of speed she cleared the stream, and, as she touched the bank, heard the "ping" of a rifle bullet in the air above her. The cruel sound gave wings to the poor thing. In a moment more she was in the opening: she leaped into the travelled road. Which way? Below her in the wood was a load of hay: a man and a boy, with pitchforks in their hands, were running towards her. She turned south, and flew along the street. The town was up. Women and children ran to the doors and windows; men snatched their rifles; shots were fired; at the big boarding-houses, the summer boarders, who never have anything to do, came out and cheered; a camp-stool was thrown from a verandah. Some young fellows shooting at a mark in the meadow saw the flying Deer, and popped away at her: but they were accustomed to a mark that stood still. It was all so sudden! There were twenty people who were just going to shoot her, when the doe leaped the road fence, and went away across a marsh towards the foothills. It was a fearful gauntlet to run. But nobody except the Deer considered it in that light. Everybody told what he was just going to do; everybody who had seen the performance was a kind of hero,—everybody except the Deer. For days and days it was the subject of conversation; and the summer boarders kept their guns at hand, expecting another Deer would come to be shot at.

The doe went away to the foothills, going now slower, and evidently fatigued, if not frightened half to death. Nothing is so appalling to a recluse as a half a mile of summer boarders. As the Deer entered the thin woods, she saw a rabble of people start across the meadow in pursuit. By this time, the Dogs, panting and lolling out their tongues, came swinging along, keeping the trail, like stupids, and consequently losing ground when the Deer doubled. But, when the doe had got into the timber, she heard the savage brutes howling across the meadow. (It is well enough, perhaps, to say that nobody offered to shoot the Dogs.)

The courage of the panting fugitive was not gone: she was game to the tip of her high-bred ears. But the fearful pace at which she had just been going told on her. Her legs trembled, and her heart beat like a trip-hammer. She slowed her speed perforce, but still fled industriously up the right bank of the stream. When she had gone a couple of miles, and the Dogs were evidently gaining again, she crossed the broad, deep brook, climbed the steep, left bank, and fled on in the direction of the Mount Marcy Trail. The fording of the river threw the Hounds off for a time. She knew, by their uncertain yelping up and down the opposite bank, that she had a little respite: she used it, however, to push on until the baying was faint in her ears; and then she dropped, exhausted, upon the ground.

This rest, brief as it was, saved her life. Roused again by the baying pack, she leaped forward with better speed, though without that keen feeling of exhilarating flight that she had in the morning. It was still a race for life; but the odds were in her favor, she thought. She did not appreciate the dogged persistence of the Hounds, nor had any inspiration told her that the race is not to the swift. She was a little confused in her mind where to go; but an instinct kept her course to the left, and consequently farther away from her fawn. Going now slower, and now faster, as the pursuit seemed more distant or nearer, she kept to the southwest, crossed the stream again, left Panther Gorge on her right, and ran on by Haystack and Skylight in the direction of the Upper Ausable Pond. I do not know her exact course through this maze of mountains, swamps, ravines, and frightful wildernesses. I only know that the poor thing worked her way along painfully, with sinking heart and unsteady limbs, lying down "dead-beat" at intervals, and then spurred on by the cry of the remorseless Dogs, until, late in the afternoon she staggered down the shoulder of Bartlett, and stood upon the shore of the lake. If she could put that piece of water between her and her pursuers, she would be safe. Had she strength to swim it?

At her first step into the water, she saw a sight that sent her back with a bound. There was a boat midlake; two men were in it. One was rowing: the other had a gun in his hand. They were looking towards her: they had seen her. (She did not know that they had heard the baying of Hounds on the mountains, and had been lying in wait for her an hour.) What should she do? The Hounds were drawing near. No escape that way, even if she could still run. With only a moment's hesitation, she plunged into the lake, and struck obliquely across. Her tired legs could not propel the body rapidly. She saw the boat headed for her. She turned towards the center of the lake. The boat turned. She could hear the rattle of the oar-locks. It was gaining on her. Then there was a silence. Then there was a splash of the water just ahead of her, followed by a roar round the lake, the words, "Confound it all!" and a rattle of the oars again. The doe saw the boat nearing her. She turned irresolutely to the shore whence she came: the Dogs were lapping the water, and howling there. She turned again to the center of the lake.

The brave, pretty creature was quite exhausted now. In a moment more, with a rush of water, the boat was on her, and the man at the oars had leaned over and caught her by the tail.

"Knock her on the head with that paddle!" he shouted to the gentleman in the stern.

The gentleman *was* a gentleman, with a kind, smooth-shaven face, and might have been a minister of some sort of everlasting gospel. He took the paddle in his hand. Just then the doe turned her head, and looked at him with her great, appealing eyes.

"I can't do it! my soul, I can't do it!" and he dropped the paddle. "Oh, let her go!"

"Let thunder go!" was the only response of the guide as he slung the Deer round, whipped out his hunting-knife, and made a pass that severed her jugular.

And the gentleman ate that night of the venison.

The buck returned about the middle of the afternoon. The fawn was bleating piteously, hungry and lonesome. The buck was surprised. He looked about in the forest. He took a circuit and came back. His doe was nowhere to be seen. He looked down at the fawn in a helpless sort of way. The fawn appealed for his supper. The buck had nothing whatever to give his child,—nothing but his sympathy. If he said anything, this is what he said: "I'm the head of this family; but, really, this is a novel case. I've nothing whatever for you. I don't know what to do. I've the feelings of a father; but you can't live on *them*. Let us travel."

The buck walked away; the little one toddled after him. They disappeared in the forest.

# SILVERSPOT: THE STORY OF A CROW

## Ernest Thompson Seton

*Many people are personally acquainted with certain animals—
a dog, a cat, a rabbit we can readily know as an individual. But
it is not easy to acquire a close familiarity with some creatures,
like the crow—a single crow in a flock of crows. Only someone with the acute perception of an Ernest Thompson Seton
(1860–1946) possesses that ability—as well as the skill of giving
his knowledge to others vividly and memorably, as this story
shows.*

How many of us have ever got to know a wild animal? I do not
mean merely to meet with one once or twice, or to have one
in a cage, but to really know it for a long time while it is wild, and
to get an insight into its life and history. The trouble usually is to
know one creature from his fellow. One fox or crow is so much
like another that we cannot be sure that it really is the same next
time we meet. But once in awhile there arises an animal who is
stronger or wiser than his fellow, who becomes a great leader, who
is, as we would say, a genius, and if he is bigger, or has some mark
by which men can know him, he soon becomes famous in his country, and shows us that the life of a wild animal may be far more
interesting and exciting than that of many human beings.

Of this class were Courtant, the bob-tailed wolf that terrorized
the whole city of Paris for about ten years in the beginning of
the fourteenth century; Clubfoot, the lame grizzly bear that left
such a terrific record in the San Joaquin Valley of California;
Lobo, the king-wolf of New Mexico, that killed a cow every day
for five years, and the Seonee panther that in less than two years
killed nearly three hundred human beings—and such also was Silverspot, whose history, so far as I could learn it, I shall now briefly
tell.

Silverspot was simply a wise old crow; his name was given
because of the silvery white spot that was like a nickel, stuck on

[ 179 ]

his right side, between the eye and the bill, and it was owing to this spot that I was able to know him from the other crows, and put together the parts of his history that came to my knowledge.

Crows are, as you must know, our most intelligent birds—'Wise as an old crow' did not become a saying without good reason. Crows know the value of organization, and are as well drilled as soldiers—very much better than some soldiers, in fact, for crows are always on duty, always at war, and always dependent on each other for life and safety. Their leaders not only are the oldest and wisest of the band, but also the strongest and bravest, for they must be ready at any time with sheer force to put down an upstart or a rebel. The rank and file are the youngsters and the crows without special gifts.

Old Silverspot was the leader of a large band of crows that made their headquarters near Toronto, Canada, in Castle Frank, which is a pine-clad hill on the northeast edge of the city. This band numbered about two hundred, and for reasons that I never understood did not increase. In mild winters they stayed along the Niagara River; in cold winters they went much farther south. But each year in the last week of February, Old Silverspot would muster his followers and boldly cross the forty miles of open water that lies between Toronto and Niagara; not, however, in a straight line would he go, but always in a curve to the west, whereby he kept in sight of the familiar landmark of Dundas Mountain, until the pine-clad hill itself came in view. Each year he came with his troop, and for about six weeks took up his abode on the hill. Each morning thereafter the crows set out in three bands to forage. One band went southeast to Ashbridge's Bay. One went north up the Don, and one, the largest, went northwestward up the ravine. The last, Silverspot led in person. Who led the others I never found out.

On calm mornings they flew high and straight away. But when it was windy the band flew low, and followed the ravine for shelter. My windows overlooked the ravine, and it was thus that in 1885 I first noticed this old crow. I was a new-comer in the neighborhood, but an old resident said to me then "that there old crow has been a-flying up and down this ravine for more than twenty years." My chances to watch were in the ravine, and Silverspot doggedly clinging to the old route, though now it was edged with houses and spanned by bridges, became a very familiar acquaintance. Twice each day in March and part of April, then again in the late summer and the fall, he passed and repassed, and gave me chances to see his movements, and hear his orders to his bands, and so, little by little, opened my eyes to the fact that the crows, though a little people, are of great wit, a race of birds with a language and a social system that is wonderfully human in many of its chief points, and in some is better carried out than our own.

One windy day I stood on the high bridge across the ravine, as the old crow, heading his long, straggling troop, came flying down homeward. Half a mile away I could hear the contented

'*All's well, come right along!*' as we should say, or as he put it, and as also his lieutenant echoed it at the rear of the band. They were flying very low to be out of the wind, and would have to rise a little to clear the bridge on which I was. Silverspot saw me standing there, and as I was closely watching him he didn't like it. He checked his flight and called out, '*Be on your guard,*' or

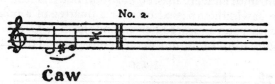

and rose much higher in the air. Then seeing that I was not armed he flew over my head about twenty feet, and his followers in turn did the same, dipping again to the old level when past the bridge.

Next day I was at the same place, and as the crows came near I raised my walking stick and pointed it at them. The old fellow at

once cried out '*Danger,*' and rose fifty feet higher than before. Seeing that it was not a gun, he ventured to fly over. But on the third day I took with me a gun, and at once he cried out, '*Great danger—a gun.*' His lieutenant repeated the cry, and every crow

**ca ca ca ca   Caw**

in the troop began to tower and scatter from the rest, till they were far above gunshot, and so passed safely over, coming down again to the shelter of the valley when well beyond reach. Another time, as the long, straggling troop came down the valley, a red-tailed hawk alighted on a tree close by their intended route. The leader

**Caw      Caw**

cried out, '*Hawk, hawk,*' and stayed his flight, as did each crow on nearing him, until all were massed in a solid body. Then, no longer fearing the hawk, they passed on. But a quarter of a mile farther on a man with a gun appeared below, and the cry, '*Great danger— a gun, a—gun; scatter for your lives,*' at once caused them to scatter

**ca ca ca ca   Caw**

widely and tower till far beyond range. Many others of his words of command I learned in the course of my long acquaintance, and found that sometimes a very little difference in the sound makes a very great difference in meaning. Thus while No. 5 means hawk, or any large, dangerous bird, this means '*wheel around,*' evidently

**Caw      Caw    ca ca ca ca**

a combination of No. 5, whose root idea is danger, and of No. 4, whose root idea is retreat, and this again is a mere '*good day*,' to a

**No. 8.**

**Caw     Caw**

far away comrade. This is usually addressed to the ranks and means '*attention*.'

**No. 9.**

Early in April there began to be great doings among the crows. Some new cause of excitement seemed to have come on them. They spent half the day among the pines, instead of foraging from dawn till dark. Pairs and trios might be seen chasing each other, and from time to time they showed off in various feats of flight. A favorite sport was to dart down suddenly from a great height toward some perching crow, and just before touching it to turn at a hairbreadth and rebound in the air so fast that the wings of the swooper whirred with a sound like distant thunder. Sometimes one crow would lower his head, raise every feather, and coming close to another would gurgle out a long note like

**No. 10.**

**C - r - r - r - a - w**

What did it all mean? I soon learned. They were making love and pairing off. The males were showing off their wing powers and their voices to the lady crows. And they must have been highly appreciated, for by the middle of April all had mated and had scattered over the country for their honeymoon, leaving the sombre old pines of Castle Frank deserted and silent.

2

The Sugar Loaf hill stands alone in the Don Valley. It is still covered with woods that join with those of Castle Frank, a quarter of a mile off. In the woods, between the two hills, is a pine-tree on whose top is a deserted hawk's nest. Every Toronto school-boy knows the nest, and, excepting that I had once shot a black squirrel on its edge, no one had ever seen a sign of life about it. There it was year after year, ragged and old, and falling to pieces. Yet, strange to tell, in all that time it never did drop to pieces, like other old nests.

One morning in May I was out at gray dawn, and stealing gently through the woods, whose dead leaves were so wet that no rustle was made. I chanced to pass under the old nest, and was surprised to see a black tail sticking over the edge. I struck the tree a smart blow, off flew a crow, and the secret was out. I had long suspected that a pair of crows nested each year about the pines, but now I realized that it was Silverspot and his wife. The old nest was theirs, and they were too wise to give it an air of spring-cleaning and housekeeping each year. Here they had nested for long, though guns in the hands of men and boys hungry to shoot crows were carried under their home every day. I never surprised the old fellow again, though I several times saw him through my telescope.

One day while watching I saw a crow crossing the Don Valley with something white in his beak. He flew to the mouth of the Rosedale Brook, then took a short flight to the Beaver Elm. There he dropped the white object, and looking about gave me a chance to recognize my old friend Silverspot. After a minute he picked up the white thing—a shell—and walked over past the spring, and here, among the docks and the skunk-cabbages, he unearthed a pile of shells and other white, shiny things. He spread them out in the sun, turned them over, lifted them one by one in his beak, dropped them, nestled on them as though they were eggs, toyed with them and gloated over them like a miser. This was his hobby, his weakness. He could not have explained *why* he enjoyed them, any more than a boy can explain why he collects postage-stamps, or a girl why she prefers pearls to rubies, but his pleasure in them was very real, and after half an hour he covered them all, including the new one, with earth and leaves, and flew off. I went at once to the spot and examined the hoard; there was about a hatful in all, chiefly white pebbles, clam-shells, and some bits of tin, but there was also the handle of a china cup, which must have been the gem of the collection. That was the last time I saw them. Silverspot knew that I had found his treasures, and he removed them at once; where, I never knew.

During the space that I watched him so closely he had many little adventures and escapes. He was once severely handled by a sparrowhawk, and often he was chased and worried by king-birds. Not that these did him much harm, but they were such noisy pests that he avoided their company as quickly as possible, just as a grown man avoids a conflict with a noisy and impudent small boy. He had some cruel tricks, too. He had a way of going the round of the small birds' nests each morning to eat the new laid eggs, as regularly as a doctor visiting his patients. But we must not judge him for that, as it is just what we ourselves do to the hens in the barnyard.

His quickness of wit was often shown. One day I saw him flying down the ravine with a large piece of bread in his bill. The stream below him was at this time being bricked over as a sewer. There was one part of two hundred yards quite finished, and, as he flew over the open water just above this, the bread fell from his bill, and was swept by the current out of sight into the tunnel. He flew down and peered vainly into the dark cavern, then, acting upon a happy thought, he flew to the downstream end of the tunnel, and awaiting the reappearance of the floating bread, as it was swept onward by the current, he seized and bore it off in triumph.

Silverspot was a crow of the world. He was truly a successful crow. He lived in a region that, though full of dangers, abounded with food. In the old, unrepaired nest he raised a brood each year with his wife, whom, by the way, I never could distinguish, and when the crows again gathered together he was their acknowledged chief.

The reassembling takes place about the end of June—the young crows with their bobtails, soft wings, and falsetto voices are brought by their parents, whom they nearly equal in size, and introduced to society at the old pine woods, a woods that is at once their fortress and college. Here they find security in numbers and in lofty yet sheltered perches, and here they begin their schooling

and are taught all the secrets of success in crow life, and in crow
life the least failure does not simply mean begin again. It means
*death.*

The first week or two after their arrival is spent by the young
ones in getting acquainted, for each crow must know personally
all the others in the band. Their parents meanwhile have time to
rest a little after the work of raising them, for now the youngsters
are able to feed themselves and roost on a branch in a row, just
like big folks.

In a week or two the moulting season comes. At this time the
old crows are usually irritable and nervous, but it does not stop
them from beginning to drill the youngsters, who, of course, do
not much enjoy the punishment and nagging they get so soon
after they have been mamma's own darlings. But it is all for their
good, as the old lady said when she skinned the eels, and old Silverspot is an excellent teacher. Sometimes he seems to make a speech
to them. What he says I cannot guess, but judging by the way
they receive it, it must be extremely witty. Each morning there is
a company drill, for the young ones naturally drop into two or
three squads according to their age and strength. The rest of the
day they forage with their parents.

When at length September comes we find a great change. The
rabble of silly little crows have begun to learn sense. The delicate
blue iris of their eyes, the sign of a fool-crow, has given place to the
dark brown eye of the old stager. They know their drill now and
have learned sentry duty. They have been taught guns and traps
and taken a special course in wire-worms and greencorn. They
know that a fat old farmer's wife is much less dangerous, though
so much larger, than her fifteen-year-old son, and they can tell
the boy from his sister. They know that an umbrella is not a gun,
and they can count up to six, which is fair for young crows, though
Silverspot can go up nearly to thirty. They know the smell of gunpowder and the south side of a hemlock-tree, and begin to plume
themselves upon being crows of the world. They always fold
their wings three times after alighting, to be sure that it is neatly
done. They know how to worry a fox into giving up half his dinner, and also that when the kingbird or the purple martin assails
them they must dash into a bush, for it is as impossible to fight the
little pests as it is for the fat apple-woman to catch the small boys
who have raided her basket. All these things do the young crows
know; but they have taken no lessons in egg-hunting yet, for it is

not the season. They are unacquainted with clams, and have never tasted horses' eyes, or seen sprouted corn, and they don't know a thing about travel, the greatest educator of all. They did not think of that two months ago, and since then they have thought of it, but have learned to wait till their betters are ready.

September sees a great change in the old crows, too. Their moulting is over. They are now in full feather again and proud of their handsome coats. Their health is again good, and with it their tempers are improved. Even old Silverspot, the strict teacher, becomes quite jolly, and the youngsters, who have long ago learned to respect him, begin really to love him.

He has hammered away at drill, teaching them all the signals and words of command in use, and now it is a pleasure to see them in the early morning.

'*Company 1!*' the old chieftain would cry in crow, and Company 1 would answer with a great clamor.

'*Fly!*' and himself leading them, they would all fly straight forward.

'*Mount!*' and straight upward they turned in a moment.

'*Bunch!*' and they all massed into a dense black flock.

'*Scatter!*' and they spread out like leaves before the wind.

'*Form line!*' and they strung out into the long line of ordinary flight.

'*Descend!*' and they all dropped nearly to the ground.

'*Forage!*' and they alighted and scattered about to feed, while two of the permanent sentries mounted duty—one on a tree to the right, the other on a mound to the far left. A minute or two later Silverspot would cry out, '*A man with a gun!*' The sentries repeated the cry and the company flew at once in open order as quickly as possible toward the trees. Once behind these, they formed line again in safety and returned to the home pines.

Sentry duty is not taken in turn by all the crows, but a certain number whose watchfulness has been often proved are the perpetual sentries, and are expected to watch and forage at the same time. Rather hard on them it seems to us, but it works well and the crow organization is admitted by all birds to be the very best in existence.

Finally, each November sees the troop sail away southward to learn new modes of life, new landmarks and new kinds of food, under the guidance of the everwise Silverspot.

3

There is only one time when a crow is a fool, and that is at night. There is only one bird that terrifies the crow, and that is the owl. When, therefore, these come together it is a woeful thing for the sable birds. The distant hoot of an owl after dark is enough to make them withdraw their heads from under their wings, and sit trembling and miserable till morning. In very cold weather the exposure of their faces thus has often resulted in a crow having one or both of his eyes frozen, so that blindness followed and therefore death. There are no hospitals for sick crows.

But with the morning their courage comes again, and arousing themselves they ransack the woods for a mile around till they find that owl, and if they do not kill him they at least worry him half to death and drive him twenty miles away.

In 1893 the crows had come as usual to Castle Frank. I was walking in these woods a few days afterward when I chanced upon the track of a rabbit that had been running at full speed over the snow and dodging about among the trees as though pursued. Strange to tell, I could see no track of the pursuer. I followed the trail and presently saw a drop of blood on the snow, and a little farther on found the partly devoured remains of a little brown bunny. What had killed him was a mystery until a careful search showed in the snow a great double-toed track and a beautifully pencilled brown feather. Then all was clear—*a horned owl*. Half an hour later, in passing again by the place, there, in a tree, within ten feet of the bones of his victim, was the fierce-eyed owl himself. The murderer still hung about the scene of his crime. For once circumstantial evidence had not lied. At my approach he gave a guttural '*grrr-oo*' and flew off with low flagging flight to haunt the distant sombre woods.

Two days afterward, at dawn, there was a great uproar among the crows. I went out early to see, and found some black feathers drifting over the snow. I followed up the wind in the direction from which they came and soon saw the bloody remains of a crow and the great double-toed track which again told me that the murderer was the owl. All around were signs of the struggle, but the fell destroyer was too strong. The poor crow had been dragged from his perch at night, when the darkness had put him at a hopeless disadvantage.

I turned over the remains, and by chance unburied the head—
then started with an exclamation of sorrow. Alas! It was the head
of old Silverspot. His long life of usefulness to his tribe was over—
slain at last by the owl that he had taught so many hundreds of
young crows to beware of.

The old nest on the Sugar Loaf is abandoned now. The crows
still come in spring-time to Castle Frank, but without their famous
leader their numbers are dwindling, and soon they will be seen no
more about the old pine-grove in which they and their forefathers
had lived and learned for ages.

### Geology

THIS ball was once a glowing mass
   Of mixed and superheated gas
Which cooled to liquid, shrank in girth,
Solidified and turned to earth.
For several thousand endless ages
It muddled through its early stages
Of heat, eruptions, floods, and quakes
And other infant belly-aches.
Surviving all such pains and notions
It settled down to land and oceans.
In eras which are known as "glacials"
The planet then got several facials . . .
Four geological massages
In four successive ice barrages
Which filled its unbecoming dimples
And leveled off some rocky pimples.
If, sometimes, there's a recrudescence,
It's due, no doubt, to adolescence,
But in the main, we now are able
To say the earth is fairly stable
And, in most geologic features,
Is better balanced than its creatures.

                             *Joseph S. Newman*

# THE INDIAN WELL

## Walter Van Tilburg Clark

*Some few years ago a novel called* The Ox-Bow Incident *lifted
the western story out of the dime-novel class and proved that
it could be literature. The author, Walter Van Tilburg Clark,
born in Maine, was taken to Nevada at an early age. He came
to know and love Nevada's deserts, mountains, ghost mining
towns, and the men who are themselves ghosts, relics of a dead
pioneer age. Jim Suttler, who comes to the old Indian water
hole with his burro, Jenny, is one of these men.*

I N THIS dead land the only allegiance was to sun. Even night was
not strong enough to resist; earth stretched gratefully when
night came, but had no hope that day would not return. Such living things as hoarded a little juice at their cores were secret about
it, and only the most ephemeral existences, the air at dawn and
sunset, the amethyst shadows in the mountains, had any freedom.
The Indian Well alone, of lesser creations, was in constant revolt.
Sooner or later all minor breathing rebels came to its stone basin
under the spring in the cliff, and from its overflow grew a tiny
meadow delta and two columns of willows and aspens, holding a
tiny front against the valley. The pictograph of a starving, ancient
journey, cut in rock above the basin, a sun-warped shack on the
south wing of the canyon, and an abandoned mine above it, were
the only tokens of man's participation in the well's cycles, each of
which was an epitome of centuries, and perhaps of the wars of the
universe.

The day before Jim Suttler came up, in the early spring, to take
his part in one cycle, was a busy day. The sun was merely lucid
after four days of broken showers, and, under the separate cloud
shadows sliding down the mountain and into the valley, the canyon
was alive. A rattler emerged partially from a hole in the mound on
which the cabin stood, and having gorged in the darkness, rested

with his head on a stone. A road-runner, stepping long and always about to sprint, came down the morning side of the mound, and his eye, quick to perceive the difference between the live and the inanimate of the same color, discovered the coffin-shaped head on the stone. At once he broke into a reaching sprint, his neck and tail stretched level, his beak agape with expectation. But his shadow arrived a step before him. The rattler recoiled, his head scarred by the sharp beak but his eye intact. The road-runner said nothing, but peered warily into the hole without stretching his neck, then walked off stiffly, leaning forward again as if about to run. When he had gone twenty feet he turned, balanced for an instant, and charged back, checking abruptly just short of the hole. The snake remained withdrawn. The road-runner paraded briefly before the hole, talking to himself, and then ran angrily up to the spring, where he drank at the overflow, sipping and stretching his neck, lifting his feet one at a time, ready to go into immediate action. The road-runner lived a dangerous and exciting life.

In the upper canyon the cliff swallows, making short harp notes, dipped and shot between the new mud under the aspens and their high community on the forehead of the cliff. Electrical blue-birds appeared to dart the length of the canyon at each low flight, turned up tilting. Lizards made unexpected flights and stops on the rocks, and when they stopped did rapid push-ups, like men exercising on a floor. They were variably pugnacious and timid.

Two of them arrived simultaneously upon a rock below the road-runner. One of them immediately skittered to a rock two feet off, and they faced each other, exercising. A small hawk coming down over the mountain, but shadowless under a cloud, saw the lizards. Having overfled the difficult target, he dropped to the canyon mouth swiftly and banked back into the wind. His trajectory was cleared of swallows, but one of them, fluttering hastily up, dropped a pellet of mud between the lizards. The one who had retreated disappeared. The other flattened for an instant, then sprang and charged. The road-runner was on him as he struck the pellet, and galloped down the canyon in great, tense strides, on his toes, the lizard lashing the air from his beak. The hawk swooped at the road-runner, thought better of it, and rose against the wind to the head of the canyon, where he turned back and coasted over the desert, his shadow a little behind him and farther and farther below.

The swallows became the voice of the canyon again, but in moments when they were all silent, the lovely smaller sounds emerged,

their own feathering, the liquid overflow, the snapping and clicking of insects, a touch of wind in the new aspens. Under these lay
still more delicate tones, erasing, in the most silent seconds, the
difference between eye and ear, a white cloud shadow passing under the water of the well, a dark cloud shadow on the cliff, the
aspen patterns on the stones. Silentest of all were the rocks, the lost
on the canyon floor, and the strong, thinking cliffs. The swallows
began again.

At noon a red and white cow with one new calf, shining and
curled, came slowly up from the desert, stopping often to let the
calf rest. At each stop the calf would try vigorously to feed, but
the cow would go on. When they reached the well the cow drank
slowly for a long time; then she continued to wrinkle the water
with her muzzle, drinking a little and blowing, as if she found it
hard to leave. The calf worked under her with spasmodic nudgings.
When she was done playing with the water, she nosed and licked
him out from under her and up to the well. He shied from the surprising coolness and she put him back. When he stayed, she drank
again. He put his nose into the water too, and bucked up as if bitten.
He returned, got water up his nostrils and took three jumps away.
The cow was content and moved off toward the canyon wall,
tonguing grass tufts from among the rocks. Against the cliff she
rubbed gently and continuously with a mild voluptuous look,
occasionally lapping her nose with a serpent tongue. The loose
winter shag came off in tufts on the rock. The calf lost her, became
panicked and made desperate noises which stopped prematurely,
and when he discovered her, complicated her toilet. Finally she
led him down to the meadow where, moving slowly, they both
fed until he was full and went to sleep in a ball in the sun. At sunset
they returned to the well, where the cow drank again and gave him
a second lesson. After this they went back into the brush and northward into the dusk. The cow's size and relative immunity to sudden
death left an aftermath of peace, rendered gently humorous by the
calf.

Also at sunset, there was a resurgence of life among the swallows. The thin golden air at the cliff tops, in which there were now
no clouds so that the eastern mountains and the valley were flooded
with unbroken light, was full of their cries and quick maneuvers
among a dancing myriad of insects. The direct sun gave them,
when they perched in rows upon the cliff, a dramatic significance
like that of men upon an immensely higher promontory. As dusk

rose out of the canyon, while the eastern peaks were still lighted, the swallows gradually became silent. At twilight, the air was full of velvet, swooping bats.

In the night jack-rabbits multiplied spontaneously out of the brush of the valley, drank in the rivulet, their noses and great ears continuously searching the dark, electrical air, and played in fits and starts on the meadow, the many young ones hopping like rubber, or made thumping love among the aspens and the willows.

A coyote came down canyon on his belly and lay in the brush with his nose between his paws. He took a young rabbit in a quiet spring and snap, and went into the brush again to eat it. At the slight rending of his meal the meadow cleared of leaping shadows and lay empty in the starlight. The rabbits, however, encouraged by new-comers, returned soon, and the coyote killed again and went off heavily, the jack's great hind legs dragging.

In the dry-wash below the meadow an old coyote, without family, profited by the second panic, which came over him. He ate what his loose teeth could tear, leaving the open remnant in the sand, drank at the basin and, carefully circling the meadow, disappeared into the dry wilderness.

Shortly before dawn, when the stars had lost luster and there was no sound in the canyon but the rivulet and the faint, separate clickings of mice in the gravel, nine antelope in loose file, with three silently flagging fawns, came on trigger toe up the meadow and drank at the well, heads often up, muzzles dripping, broad ears turning. In the meadow they grazed and the fawns nursed. When there was as much gray as darkness in the air, and new wind in the canyon, they departed, the file weaving into the brush, merging into the desert, to nothing, and the swallows resumed the talkative day shift.

Jim Suttler and his burro came up into the meadow a little after noon, very slowly, though there was only a spring-fever warmth. Suttler walked pigeon-toed, like an old climber, but carefully and stiffly, not with the loose walk natural to such a long-legged man. He stopped in the middle of the meadow, took off his old black sombrero, and stared up at the veil of water shining over the edge of the basin.

"We're none too early, Jenny," he said to the burro.

The burro had felt water for miles, but could show no excitement. She stood with her head down and her four legs spread unnaturally, as if to postpone a collapse. Her pack reared higher than

Suttler's head, and was hung with casks, pans, canteens, a pick, two shovels, a crowbar, and a rifle in a sheath. Suttler had the cautious uncertainty of his trade. His other burro had died two days before in the mountains east of Beatty, and Jenny and he bore its load.

Suttler shifted his old six-shooter from his rump to his thigh, and studied the well, the meadow, the cabin and the mouth of the mine as if he might choose not to stay. He was not a cinema prospector. If he looked like one of the probably mistaken conceptions of Christ, with his red beard and red hair to his shoulders, it was because he had been away from barbers and without spare water for shaving. He was unlike Christ in some other ways.

"It's kinda run down," he told Jenny, "but we'll take it."

He put his sombrero back on, let his pack fall slowly to the ground, showing the sweat patch in his bleached brown shirt, and began to unload Jenny carefully, like a collector handling rare vases, and put everything into one neat pile.

"Now," he said, "we'll have a drink." His tongue and lips were so swollen that the words were unclear, but he spoke casually, like a club-man sealing a minor deal. One learns to do business slowly with deserts and mountains. He picked up a bucket and started for the well. At the upper edge of the meadow he looked back. Jenny was still standing with her head down and her legs apart. He did not particularly notice her extreme thinness, for he had seen it coming on gradually. He was thinner himself, and tall, and so round-shouldered that when he stood his straightest he seemed to be peering ahead with his chin out.

"Come on, you old fool," he said. "It's off you now."

Jenny came, stumbling in the rocks above the meadow, and stopping often as if to decide why this annoyance recurred. When she became interested, Suttler would not let her get to the basin, but for ten minutes gave her water from his cupped hands, a few licks at a time. Then he drove her off and she stood in the shade of the canyon wall watching him. He began on his thirst in the same way, a gulp at a time, resting between gulps. After ten gulps he sat on a rock by the spring and looked up at the meadow and the big desert, and might have been considering the courses of the water through his body, but noticed also the antelope tracks in the mud.

After a time he drank another half dozen gulps, gave Jenny half a pail full, and drove her down to the meadow, where he spread a dirty blanket in the striped sun and shadow under the willows. He sat on the edge of the blanket, rolled a cigarette and smoked it

while he watched Jenny. When she began to graze with her rump
to the canyon, he flicked his cigarette onto the grass, rolled over
with his back to the sun and slept until it became chilly after sunset. Then he woke, ate a can of beans, threw the can into the
willows and led Jenny up to the well, where they drank together
from the basin for a long time. While she resumed her grazing, he
took another blanket and his rifle from the pile, removed his heel-
worn boots, stood his rifle against a fork, and rolling up in both
blankets, slept again.

In the night many rabbits played in the meadow in spite of the
strong sweat and tobacco smell of Jim Suttler lying under the
willows, but the antelope, when they came in the dead dark before
dawn, were nervous, drank less, and did not graze but minced
quickly back across the meadow and began to run at the head of
the dry wash. Jenny slept with her head hanging, and did not hear
them come or go.

Suttler woke lazy and still red-eyed, and spent the morning
drinking at the well, eating and dozing on his blanket. In the afternoon, slowly, a few things at a time, he carried his pile to the cabin.
He had a bachelor's obsession with order, though he did not mind
dirt, and puttered until sundown, making a brush bed and arranging his gear. Much of this time, however, was spent studying the
records on the cabin walls of the recent human life of the well. He
had to be careful, because among the still legible names and dates,
after Frank Davis, 1893, Willard Harbinger, 1893, London, England, John Mason, June 13, 1887, Bucksport, Maine, Mathew Ken-
ling, from Glasgow, 1891, Penelope and Martin Reave, God Guide
Us, 1885, was written Frank Hayward, 1492, feeling my age. There
were other wits too. John Barr had written, Giv it back to the in-
juns, and Kenneth Thatcher, two years later, had written under
that, Pity the noble redskin, while another man, whose second name
was Evans, had written what was already a familiar libel, since it
was not strictly true, Fifty miles from water, a hundred miles from
wood, a million miles from God, three feet from hell. Someone un-
named had felt differently, saying, God is kind. We may make it
now. Shot an antelope here July 10, 188—and the last number
blurred. Arthur Smith, 1881, had recorded, Here berried my beloved wife Semantha, age 22, and my soul. God let me keep the
child. J.M. said cryptically, Good luck, John, and Bill said, Ralph,
if you come this way, am trying to get to Los Angeles. B. Westover
said he had recovered from his wound there in 1884, and Galt said,

enigmatically and without date, Bart and Miller burned to death
in the Yellow Jacket. I don't care now. There were poets too, of
both parties. What could still be read of Byron Cotter's verses,
written in 1902, said,

> . . . . . here alone
> Each shining dawn I greet,
> The Lord's wind on my forehead
> And where he set his feet
> One mark of heel remaining
> Each day filled up anew,
> To keep my soul from burning,
> With clear, celestial dew.
> Here in His Grace abiding
> The mortal years and few
> I shall . . .

but you can't tell what he intended, while J. A. had printed,

> My brother came out in '49
> I came in '51
> At first we thought we liked it fine
> But now, by God, we're done.

Suttler studied these records without smiling, like someone
reading a funny paper, and finally, with a heavy blue pencil, registered, Jim and Jenny Suttler, damn dried out, March—and paused,
but had no way of discovering the day—1940.

In the evening he sat on the steps watching the swallows in the
golden upper canyon turn bats in the dusk, and thought about the
antelope. He had seen the new tracks also, and it alarmed him a
little that the antelope could have passed twice in the dark without
waking him.

Before false dawn he was lying in the willows with his carbine
at ready. Rabbits ran from the meadow when he came down, and
after that there was no movement. He wanted to smoke. When he
did see them at the lower edge of the meadow, he was startled, yet
made no quick movement, but slowly pivoted to cover them. They
made poor targets in that light and backed by the pale desert, appearing and disappearing before his eyes. He couldn't keep any
one of them steadily visible, and decided to wait until they made
contrast against the meadow. But his presence was strong. One of
the antelope advanced onto the green, but then threw its head up,

spun, and ran back past the flank of the herd, which swung after him. Suttler rose quickly and raised the rifle, but let it down without firing. He could hear the light rattle of their flight in the wash, but had only a belief that he could see them. He had few cartridges, and the ponderous echo under the cliffs would scare them off for weeks.

His energies, however, were awakened by the frustrated hunt. While there was still more light than heat in the canyon, he climbed to the abandoned mine tunnel at the top of the alluvial wing of the cliff. He looked at the broken rock in the dump, kicked up its pack with a boot toe, and went into the tunnel, peering closely at its sides, in places black with old smoke smudges. At the back he struck two matches and looked at the jagged dead end and the fragments on the floor, then returned to the shallow beginning of a side tunnel. At the second match here he knelt quickly, scrutinized a portion of the rock, and when the match went out at once lit another. He lit six matches, and pulled at the rock with his hand. It was firm.

"The poor chump," he said aloud.

He got a loose rock from the tunnel and hammered at the projection with it. It came finally, and he carried it into the sun on the dump.

"Yessir," he said aloud, after a minute.

He knocked his sample into three pieces and examined each minutely.

"Yessir, yessir," he said with malicious glee, and, grinning at the tunnel, "the poor chump."

Then he looked again at the dump, like the mound before a gigantic gopher hole. "Still, that's a lot of digging," he said.

He put sample chips into his shirt pocket, keeping a small black, heavy one that had fallen neatly from a hole like a borer's, to play with in his hand. After trouble he found the claim pile on the side hill south of the tunnel, its top rocks tumbled into the shale. Under the remaining rocks he found what he wanted, a ragged piece of yellow paper between two boards. The writing was in pencil, and not diplomatic. "I hereby clame this hole damn side hill as far as I can dig in. I am a good shot. Keep off. John Barr, April 11, 1897."

Jim Suttler grinned. "Tough guy, eh?" he said.

He made a small ceremony of burning the paper upon a stone from the cairn. The black tinsel of ash blew off and broke into flakes.

"O.K., John Barr?" he asked.

"O.K., Suttler," he answered himself.

In blue pencil, on soiled paper from his pocket, he slowly printed, "Becus of the lamented desease of the late clamant, John Barr, I now clame these diggins for myself and partner Jenny. I can shoot too." And wrote, rather than printed, "James T. Suttler, March—" and paused.

"Make it an even month," he said, and wrote, "11, 1940." Underneath he wrote, "Jenny Suttler, her mark," and drew a skull with long ears.

"There," he said, and folded the paper, put it between the two boards, and rebuilt the cairn into a neat pyramid above it.

In high spirit he was driven to cleanliness. With scissors, soap, and razor he climbed to the spring. Jenny was there, drinking.

"When you're done," he said, and lifted her head, pulled her ears and scratched her. "Maybe we've got something here, Jenny," he said.

Jenny observed him soberly and returned to the meadow.

"She doesn't believe me," he said, and began to perfect himself. He sheared off his red tresses in long hanks, then cut closer, and went over yet a third time, until there remained a brush, of varying density, of stiff red bristles, through which his scalp shone whitely. He sheared the beard likewise, then knelt to the well for mirror and shaved painfully. He also shaved his neck and about his ears. He arose younger and less impressive, with jaws as pale as his scalp, so that his sunburn was a red domino. He burned tresses and beard ceremoniously upon a sage bush, and announced, "It is spring."

He began to empty the pockets of his shirt and breeches onto a flat stone, yelling, "In the spring a young man's fancy," to a kind of tune, and paused, struck by the facts.

"Oh yeah?" he said. "Fat chance."

"Fat," he repeated with obscene consideration. "Oh, well," he said, and finished piling upon the rock notebooks, pencil stubs, cartridges, tobacco, knife, stump pipe, matches, chalk, samples, and three wrinkled photographs. One of the photographs he observed at length before weighting it down with a .45 cartridge. It showed a round, blonde girl with a big smile on a stupid face, in a patterned calico house dress in front of a blossoming rhododendron bush.

He added to this deposit his belt and holster with the big .45.

Then he stripped himself, washed and rinsed his garments in the spring, and spread them upon stones and brush, and carefully arranged four flat stones into a platform beside the trough. Standing there he scooped water over himself, gasping, made it a lather, and at last, face and copper bristles also foaming, gropingly entered the basin and submerged, flooding the water over in a thin and soapy sheet. His head emerged at once. "My God," he whispered. He remained under, however, till he was soapless, and goose pimpled as a file, he climbed out cautiously onto the rock platform and performed a dance of small, revolving patterns with a great deal of up and down.

At one point in his dance he observed the pictograph journey upon the cliff, and danced nearer to examine it.

"Ignorant," he pronounced. "Like a little kid," he said.

He was intrigued, however, by some more recent records, names smoked and cut upon the lower rock. One of these, in script, like a gigantic handwriting deeply cut, said ALVAREZ BLANCO DE TOLEDO, Anno Di 1624. A very neat, upright cross was chiselled beneath it.

Suttler grinned. "Oh yeah?" he asked, with his head upon one side. "Nuts," he said, looking at it squarely.

But it inspired him, and with his jack-knife he began scraping beneath the possibly Spanish inscription. His knife, however, made scratches, not incisions. He completed a bad Jim and Jenny and quit, saying, "I should kill myself over a phony wop."

Thereafter, for weeks, while the canyon became increasingly like a furnace in the daytime and the rocks stayed warm at night, he drove his tunnel farther into the gully, making a heap of ore to be worked, and occasionally adding a peculiarly heavy pebble to the others in his small leather bag with a draw string. He and Jenny thrived upon this fixed and well-watered life. The hollows disappeared from his face and he became less stringy, while Jenny grew round, her battleship-gray pelt even lustrous and its black markings distinct and ornamental. The burro found time from her grazing to come to the cabin door in the evenings and attend solemnly to Suttler playing with his samples and explaining their future.

"Then, old lady," Suttler said, "you will carry only small children, one at a time, for never more than half an hour. You will have a bedroom with French windows and a mattress, and I will paint your feet gold.

"The children," he said, "will probably be red-headed, but maybe blonde. Anyway, they will be beautiful.

"After we've had a holiday, of course," he added. "For one

hundred and thirty-three nights," he said dreamily. "Also," he said, "just one hundred and thirty-three quarts. I'm no drunken bum. For you, though," he said, "for one hundred and thirty-three nights a quiet hotel with other old ladies. I should drag my own mother in the gutter." He pulled her head down by the ears and kissed her loudly upon the nose. They were very happy together.

Nor did they greatly alter most of the life of the canyon. The antelope did not return, it is true, the rabbits were fewer and less playful because he sometimes snared them for meat, the little, clean mice and desert rats avoided the cabin they had used, and the road-runner did not come in daylight after Suttler, for fun, narrowly missed him with a piece of ore from the tunnel mouth. Suttler's violence was disproportionate perhaps, when he used his .45 to blow apart a creamy rat who did invade the cabin, but the loss was insignificant to the pattern of the well, and more than compensated when he one day caught the rattler extended at the foot of the dump in a drunken stupor from rare young rabbit, and before it could recoil held it aloft by the tail and snapped its head off, leaving the heavy body to turn slowly for a long time among the rocks. The dominant voices went undisturbed, save when he sang badly at his work or said beautiful things to Jenny in a loud voice.

There were, however, two more noticeable changes, one of which, at least, was important to Suttler himself. The first was the execution of the range cow's calf in the late fall, when he began to suggest a bull. Suttler felt a little guilty about this because the calf might have belonged to somebody, because the cow remained near the meadow bawling for two nights, and because the calf had come to meet the gun with more curiosity than challenge. But when he had the flayed carcass hung in the mine tunnel in a wet canvas, the sensation of providence overcame any qualms.

The other change was more serious. It occurred at the beginning of such winter as the well had, when there was sometimes a light rime on the rocks at dawn, and the aspens held only a few yellow leaves. Suttler thought often of leaving. The nights were cold, the fresh meat was eaten, his hopes had diminished as he still found only occasional nuggets, and his dreams of women, if less violent, were more nostalgic. The canyon held him with a feeling he would have called lonesome but at home, yet he probably would have gone except for this second change.

In the higher mountains to the west, where there was already snow, and at dawn a green winter sky, hunger stirred a buried memory in a cougar. He had twice killed antelope at the well, and felt there had been time enough again. He came down from the dwarfed trees and crossed the narrow valley under the stars, sometimes stopping abruptly to stare intently about, like a house-cat in a strange room. After each stop he would at once resume a quick, noiseless trot. From the top of the mountain above the spring he came down very slowly on his belly, but there was nothing at the well. He relaxed, and leaning on the rim of the basin, drank, listening between laps. His nose was clean with fasting, and he knew of the man in the cabin and Jenny in the meadow, but they were strange, not what he remembered about the place. But neither had his past made him fearful. It was only his habitual hunting caution which made him go down into the willows carefully, and lie there head up, watching Jenny, but still waiting for antelope, which he had killed before near dawn. The strange smells were confusing and therefore irritating. After an hour he rose and went silently to the cabin, from which the strangest smell came strongly, a carnivorous smell which did not arouse appetite, but made him bristle nervously. The tobacco in it was like pins in his nostrils. He circled the cabin, stopping frequently. At the open door the scent was violent. He stood with his front paws up on the step, moving his head in serpent motions, the end of his heavy tail furling and unfurling constantly. In a dream Suttler turned over without waking, and muttered. The cougar crouched, his eyes intent, his ruff lifting. Then he swung away from the door again and lay in the willows, but where he could watch the cabin also.

When the sky was alarmingly pale and the antelope had not come, he crawled a few feet at a time, behind the willows, to a point nearer Jenny. There he crouched, working his hind legs slowly under him until he was set, and sprang, raced the three or four jumps to the drowsy burro, and struck. The beginning of her mortal scream was severed, but having made an imperfect leap, and from no height, the cat did not at once break her neck, but drove her to earth, where her small hooves churned futilely in the sod, and chewed and worried until she lay still.

Jim Suttler was nearly awakened by the fragment of scream, but heard nothing after it, and sank again.

The cat wrestled Jenny's body into the willows, fed with uncertain relish, drank long at the well, and went slowly over the crest, stopping often to look back. In spite of the light and the beginning talk of the swallows, the old coyote also fed and was gone before Suttler woke.

When Suttler found Jenny, many double columns of regimented ants were already at work, streaming in and out of the interior and mounting like bridge workers upon the ribs. Suttler stood and looked down. He desired to hold the small muzzle in the hollow of his hand, feeling that this familiar gesture would get through to Jenny, but couldn't bring himself to it because of what had happened to that side of her head. He squatted and lifted one hoof on its stiff leg and held that. Ants emerged hurriedly from the fetlocks, their lines of communication broken. Two of them made disorganized excursions on the back of his hand. He rose, shook them off, and stood staring again. He didn't say anything because he spoke easily only when cheerful or excited, but a determination was beginning in him. He followed the drag to the spot torn by the small hoofs. Among the willows again, he found the tracks of both the cougar and the coyote, and the cat's tracks again at the well and by the cabin doorstep. He left Jenny in the willows with a canvas over her during the day, and did not eat.

At sunset he sat on the doorstep, cleaning his rifle and oiling it until he could spring the lever almost without sound. He filled the clip, pressed it home, and sat with the gun across his knees until dark, when he put on his sheepskin, stuffed a scarf into the pocket, and went down to Jenny. He removed the canvas from her, rolled it up and held it under his arm.

"I'm sorry, old woman," he said. "Just tonight."

There was a little cold wind in the willows. It rattled the upper branches lightly.

Suttler selected a spot thirty yards down wind, from which he could see Jenny, spread the canvas and lay down upon it, facing toward her. After an hour he was afraid of falling asleep and sat up against a willow clump. He sat there all night. A little after midnight the old coyote came into the dry-wash below him. At the top of the wash he sat down, and when the mingled scents gave him a clear picture of the strategy, let his tongue loll out, looked at the stars for a moment with his mouth silently open, rose and trotted into the desert.

At the beginning of daylight the younger coyote trotted in from the north, and turned up toward the spring, but saw Jenny. He sat down and looked at her for a long time. Then he moved to

the west and sat down again. In the wind was only winter, and the
water, and faintly the acrid bat dung in the cliffs. He completed
the circle, but not widely enough, walking slowly through the
willows, down the edge of the meadow and in again not ten yards
in front of the following muzzle of the carbine. Like Jenny, he felt
his danger too late. The heavy slug caught him at the base of the
skull in the middle of the first jump, so that it was amazingly accelerated for a fraction of a second. The coyote began it alive, and
ended it quite dead, but with a tense muscular movement conceived
which resulted in a grotesque final leap and twist of the hind-quarters alone, leaving them propped high against a willow clump while
the head was half buried in the sand, red welling up along the lips
of the distended jaws. The cottony underpelt of the tail and rump
stirred gleefully in the wind.

When Suttler kicked the body and it did not move, he suddenly
dropped his gun, grasped it by the upright hind legs, and hurled it
out into the sage-brush. His face appeared slightly insane with fury
for that instant. Then he picked up his gun and went back to the
cabin, where he ate, and drank half of one of his last three bottles
of whiskey.

In the middle of the morning he came down with his pick and
shovel, dragged Jenny's much-lightened body down into the dry-
wash, and dug in the rock and sand for two hours. When she was
covered, he erected a small cairn of stone, like the claim post, above
her.

"If it takes a year," he said, and licked the salt sweat on his lips.

That day he finished the half bottle and drank all of a second
one, and became very drunk, so that he fell asleep during his vigil
in the willows, sprawled wide on the dry turf and snoring. He was
not disturbed. There was a difference in his smell after that day
which prevented even the rabbits from coming into the meadow.
He waited five nights in the willows. Then he transferred his watch
to a niche in the cliff, across from and just below the spring.

All winter, while the day wind blew long veils of dust across
the desert, regularly repeated, like waves or the smoke of line artillery fire, and the rocks shrank under the cold glitter of night, he
did not miss a watch. He learned to go to sleep at sundown, wake
within a few minutes of midnight, go up to his post, and become at
once clear headed and watchful. He talked to himself in the mine
and the cabin, but never in the niche. His supplies ran low, and he
ate less, but would not risk a startling shot. He rationed his tobacco,

and when it was gone worked up to a vomiting sickness every three days for nine days, but did not miss a night in the niche. All winter he did not remove his clothes, bathe, shave, cut his hair or sing. He worked the dead mine only to be busy, and became thin again, with sunken eyes which yet were not the eyes he had come with the spring before. It was April, his food almost gone, when he got his chance.

There was a half moon that night, which made the canyon walls black, and occasionally gleamed on wrinkles of the overflow. The cat came down so quietly that Suttler did not see him until he was beside the basin. The animal was suspicious. He took the wind, and twice started to drink, and didn't, but crouched. On Suttler's face there was a set grin which exposed his teeth.

"Not even a drink, you bastard," he thought.

The cat drank a little though, and dropped again, softly, trying to get the scent from the meadow. Suttler drew slowly upon his soul in the trigger. When it gave, the report was magnified impressively in the canyon. The cougar sprang straight into the air and screamed outrageously. The back of Suttler's neck was cold and his hand trembled, but he shucked the lever and fired again. This shot ricocheted from the basin and whined away thinly. The first, however, had struck near enough. The cat began to scramble rapidly on the loose stone, at first without voice, then screaming repeatedly. It doubled upon itself, snarling and chewing in a small furious circle, fell and began to throw itself in short, leaping spasms upon the stones, struck across the rim of the tank and lay half in the water, its head and shoulders raised in one corner and resting against the cliff. Suttler could hear it breathing hoarsely and snarling very faintly. The soprano chorus of swallows gradually became silent.

Suttler had risen to fire again, but lowered the carbine and advanced, stopping at every step to peer intently and listen for the hoarse breathing, which continued. Even when he was within five feet of the tank the cougar did not move, except to gasp so that the water again splashed from the basin. Suttler was calmed by the certainty of accomplishment. He drew the heavy revolver from his holster, aimed carefully at the rattling head, and fired again. The canyon boomed, and the east responded faintly and a little behind, but Suttler did not hear them, for the cat thrashed heavily in the tank, splashing him as with a bucket, and then lay still on its side over the edge, its muzzle and forepaws hanging. The water was settling quietly in the tank, but Suttler stirred it again, shooting five more times with great deliberation into the heavy body, which did not move except at the impact of the slugs.

The rest of the night, even after the moon was gone, he worked fiercely, slitting and tearing with his knife. In the morning, under the swallows, he dragged the marbled carcass, still bleeding a little in places, onto the rocks on the side away from the spring, and dropped it. Dragging the ragged hide by the neck, he went unsteadily down the canyon to the cabin, where he slept like a drunkard, although his whiskey had been gone for two months.

In the afternoon, with dreaming eyes, he bore the pelt to Jenny's grave, took down the stones with his hands, shoveled the earth from her, covered her with the skin, and again with earth and the cairn.

He looked at this monument. "There," he said.

That night, for the first time since her death, he slept through.

In the morning, at the well, he repeated the cleansing ritual of a year before, save that they were rags he stretched to dry, even to the dance upon the rock platform while drying. Squatting naked and clean, shaven and clipped, he looked for a long time at the grinning countenance, now very dirty, of the plump girl in front of the blossoming rhododendrons, and in the resumption of his dance he made singing noises accompanied by the words, "Spring, spring, beautiful spring." He was a starved but revived and volatile spirit. An hour later he went south, his boot soles held on by canvas strips, and did not once look back.

The disturbed life of the spring resumed. In the second night the rabbits loved in the willows, and at the end of the week the rats played in the cabin again. The old coyote and a vulture cleaned the cougar, and his bones fell apart in the shale. The road-runner came up one day, tentatively, and in front of the tunnel snatched up a horned toad and ran with it around the corner, but no farther. After a month the antelope returned. The well brimmed, and in the gentle sunlight the new aspen leaves made a tiny music of shadows.

# SHARP EYES

## John Burroughs

*When Burroughs (1837–1921) was a young man, he fell under the influence of Emerson and Thoreau, and became the greatest writer of nature essays after them. His first works, of a poetic nature, were gradually supplanted by writings showing more careful scientific observation. In this selection from* Locusts and Wild Honey *he reveals his appreciation of a keen eye for tiny details, so necessary to the student and lover of nature.*

NOTING how one eye seconds and reinforces the other, I have often amused myself by wondering what the effect would be if one could go on opening eye after eye, to the number, say, of a dozen or more. What would he see? Perhaps not the invisible—not the odors of flowers or the fever germs in the air—not the infinitely small of the microscope or the infinitely distant of the telescope. This would require not so much more eyes as an eye constructed with more and different lenses; but would he not see with augmented power within the natural limits of vision? At any rate, some persons seem to have opened more eyes than others, they see with such force and distinctness; their vision penetrates the tangle and obscurity where that of others fails, like a spent or impotent bullet. How many eyes did Gilbert White open? how many did Henry Thoreau? how many did Audubon? how many does the hunter, matching his sight against the keen and alert senses of a deer, or a moose, or a fox, or a wolf? Not outward eyes, but inward. We open another eye whenever we see beyond the first general features or outlines of things—whenever we grasp the special details and characteristic markings that this mask covers. Science confers new powers of vision. Whenever you have learned to discriminate the birds, or the plants, or the geological features of a country, it is as if new and keener eyes were added.

Of course one must not only see sharply, but read aright what he sees. The facts in the life of nature that are transpiring about us are like written words that the observer is to arrange into sentences. Or, the writing is a cipher and he must furnish the key. A female oriole was one day observed very much preoccupied under a shed where the refuse from the horse stable was thrown. She hopped about among the barn fowls, scolding them sharply when they came too near her. The stable, dark and cavernous, was just beyond. The bird, not finding what she wanted outside, boldly ventured into the stable, and was presently captured by the farmer. What did she want? was the query. What but a horse-hair for her nest, which was in an apple-tree near by? and she was so bent on having one that I have no doubt she would have tweaked one out of the horse's tail had he been in the stable. Later in the season I examined her nest, and found it sewed through and through with several long horse-hairs, so that the bird persisted in her search till the hair was found.

Little dramas and tragedies and comedies, little characteristic scenes, are always being enacted in the lives of the birds, if our eyes are sharp enough to see them. Some clever observer saw this little comedy played among some English sparrows, and wrote an account of it in his newspaper. It is too good not to be true: A male bird brought to his box a large, fine goose-feather, which is a great find for a sparrow and much coveted. After he had deposited his prize and chattered his gratulations over it, he went away in quest of his mate. His next-door neighbor, a female bird, seeing her chance, quickly slipped in and seized the feather,—and here the wit of the bird came out, for instead of carrying it into her own box she flew with it to a near tree and hid it in a fork of the branches, then went home, and when her neighbor returned with his mate, was innocently employed about her own affairs. The proud male, finding his feather gone, came out of his box in a high state of excitement, and with wrath in his manner and accusation on his tongue, rushed into the cot of the female. Not finding his goods and chattels there as he had expected, he stormed around awhile, abusing everybody in general and his neighbor in particular, and then went away as if to repair the loss. As soon as he was out of sight, the shrewd thief went and brought the feather home and lined her own domicile with it. . . .

The bluebird is a home bird, and I am never tired of recurring to him. His coming or reappearance in the spring marks a new chapter in the progress of the season; things are never quite the same after one has heard that note. The past spring the males came about a week in advance of the females. A fine male lingered about my grounds and orchard all that time, apparently awaiting the arrival of his mate. He called and warbled every day, as if he felt sure she was within earshot and could be hurried up. Now he warbled half angrily or upbraidingly; then coaxingly; then cheerily and confidently, the next moment in a plaintive and far-away manner. He would half open his wings, and twinkle them caressingly as if beckoning his mate to his heart. One morning she had come, but was shy and reserved. The fond male flew to a knot-hole in an old apple-tree and coaxed her to his side. I heard a fine confidential warble—the old, old story. But the female flew to a near tree and uttered her plaintive, homesick note. The male went and got some dry grass or bark in his beak and flew again to the hole in the old tree, and promised unremitting devotion; but the other said "Nay," and flew away in the distance. When he saw her going, or rather heard her distant note, he dropped his stuff and cried out in a tone that said plainly enough, "Wait a minute: one word, please!" and flew swiftly in pursuit. He won her before long, however, and early in April the pair were established in one of the four or five boxes I had put up for them, but not until they had changed their minds several times. As soon as the first brood had flown, and while they were yet under their parents' care, they began to nest in one of the other boxes, the female as usual doing all the work and the male all the complimenting. A source of occasional great distress to the mother-bird was a white cat that sometimes followed me about. The cat had never been known to catch a bird, but she had a way of watching them that was very embarrassing to the bird. Whenever she appeared, the mother bluebird set up that pitiful melodious plaint. One morning the cat was standing by me, when the bird came with her beak loaded with building material, and alighted above me to survey the place before going into the box. When she saw the cat she was greatly disturbed, and in her agitation could not keep her hold upon all her material. Straw after straw came eddying down, till not half her original burden remained. After the cat had gone away the bird's alarm subsided; till presently, seeing the coast clear, she flew quickly to the box and pitched in her remaining straws with the greatest precipitation, and without going in to arrange them as was her wont, flew away in evident relief.

In the cavity of an apple-tree but a few yards off, and much nearer the house than they usually build, a pair of high-holes, or golden-shafted woodpeckers, took up their abode. A knot-hole which led to the decayed interior was enlarged, the live wood being cut away as clean as a squirrel would have done it. The inside preparations I could not witness, but day after day as I passed near I heard the bird hammering away, evidently beating down obstructions and shaping and enlarging the cavity. The chips were not brought out, but were used rather to floor the interior. The woodpeckers are not nest-builders, but rather nest-carvers.

The time seemed very short before the voices of the young were heard in the heart of the old tree,—at first feebly, but waxing stronger day by day, until they could be heard many rods distant. When I put my hand upon the trunk of the tree they would set up an eager, expectant chattering; but if I climbed up it toward the opening, they soon detected the unusual sound and would hush quickly, only now and then uttering a warning note. Long before they were fully fledged they clambered up to the orifice to receive their food. As but one could stand in the opening at a time, there was a good deal of elbowing and struggling for this position. It was a very desirable one, aside from the advantages it had when food was served; it looked out upon the great shining world, into which the young birds seemed never tired of gazing. The fresh air must have been a consideration also, for the interior of a high-hole's dwelling is not sweet. When the parent birds came with food, the young one in the opening did not get it all; but after he had received a portion, either on his own motion or on a hint from the old one, he would give place to the one behind him. Still, one bird evidently outstripped his fellows, and in the race of life was two or three days in advance of them. His voice was the loudest and his head oftenest at the window. But I noticed that when he had kept the position too long, the others evidently made it uncomfortable in his rear, and after "fidgeting" about awhile he would be compelled to "back down." But retaliation was then easy, and I fear his mates spent few easy moments at the outlook. They would close their eyes and slide back into the cavity as if the world had suddenly lost all its charms for them.

This bird was of course the first to leave the nest. For two days before that event he kept his position in the opening most of the time, and sent forth his strong voice incessantly. The old ones abstained from feeding him almost entirely, no doubt to encourage his exit. As I stood looking at him one afternoon and noticing his progress, he suddenly reached a resolution,—seconded, I have no doubt, from the rear,—and launched forth upon his untried wings. They served him well, and carried him about fifty yards up-hill the first heat. The second day after, the next in size and spirit left in the same manner; then another, till only one remained. The parent birds ceased their visits to him, and for one day he called and called till our ears were tired of the sound. His was the faintest heart of all: then he had none to encourage him from behind. He left the nest and clung to the outer bole of the tree, and yelped and piped for an hour longer; then he committed himself to his wings and went his way like the rest.

A young farmer in the western part of New York sends me some interesting observations about the cuckoo. He says a large gooseberry-bush, standing in the border of an old hedge-row in the midst of the open fields, and not far from his house, was occupied by a pair of cuckoos for two seasons in succession; and after an interval of a year, for two seasons more. This gave him a good chance to observe them. He says the mother-bird lays a single egg and sits upon it a number of days before laying the second, so that he has seen one young bird nearly grown, a second just hatched, and a whole egg all in the nest at once. "So far as I have seen, this is the settled practice,—the young leaving the nest one at a time, to the number of six or eight. The young have quite the look of the young of the dove in many respects. When nearly grown they are covered with long blue pin-feathers as long as darning needles, without a bit of plumage on them. They part on the back and hang down on each side by their own weight. With its curious feathers and misshapen body the young bird is anything but handsome. They never open their mouths when approached, as many young birds do, but sit perfectly still, hardly moving when touched." He also notes the un-natural indifference of the mother-bird when her nest and young are approached. She makes no sound, but sits quietly on a near branch in apparent perfect unconcern.

These observations, together with the fact that the egg of the cuckoo is occasionally found in the nest of other birds, raise the inquiry whether our bird is slowly relapsing into the habit of the European species, which always foists its egg upon other birds; or whether on the other hand it be not mending its manners in this respect. It has but little to unlearn or forget in the one case, but great progress to make in the other. How far is its rudimentary nest —a mere platform of coarse twigs and dry stalks of weeds—from the deep, compact, finely woven and finely modeled nest of the goldfinch or king-bird, and what a gulf between its indifference toward its young and their solicitude! Its irregular manner of laying also seems better suited to a parasite like our cow-bird, or the European cuckoo, than to a regular nest-builder.

This observer, like most sharp-eyed persons, sees plenty of interesting things as he goes about his work. He one day saw a white swallow, which is of rare occurrence. He saw a bird, a sparrow, he thinks, fly against the side of a horse and fill his beak with hair from the loosened coat of the animal. He saw a shrike pursue a chickadee, when the latter escaped by taking refuge in a small hole in a tree. One day in early spring he saw two hen-hawks that were circling and screaming high in air, approach each other, extend a claw, and grasping them together, fall toward the earth flapping and struggling as if they were tied together; on nearing the ground they separated and soared aloft again. He supposed that it was not a passage of war but of love, and that the hawks were toying fondly with each other.

When the air is damp and heavy, swallows frequently hawk for insects about cattle and moving herds in the field. My farmer describes how they attended him one foggy day, as he was mowing in the meadow with a mowing-machine. It had been foggy for two days, and the swallows were very hungry and the insects stupid and inert. When the sound of his machine was heard, the swallows appeared and attended him like a brood of hungry chickens. He says there was a continual rush of purple wings over the "cutter-bar," and just where it was causing the grass to tremble and fall. Without his assistance the swallows would have gone hungry yet another day.

Of the hen-hawk he has observed that both the male and female take part in incubation. "I was rather surprised," he says, "on one occasion, to see how quickly they change places on the nest. The nest was in a tall beech, and the leaves were not yet fully out. I could see the head and neck of the hawk over the edge of the nest, when I saw the other hawk coming down through the air at full speed. I expected he would alight near by, but instead of that he struck directly upon the nest, his mate getting out of the way barely in time to avoid being hit; it seemed almost as if he had knocked her off the nest. I hardly see how they can make such a rush on the nest without danger to the eggs."

The kingbird will worry the hawk as a whiffet dog will worry a bear. It is by his persistence and audacity, not by any injury he is capable of dealing his great antagonist. The kingbird seldom more than dogs the hawk, keeping above and between his wings and making a great ado; but my correspondent says he once "saw a kingbird riding on a hawk's back. The hawk flew as fast as possible, and the kingbird sat upon his shoulders in triumph until they had passed out of sight,"—tweaking his feathers, no doubt, and threatening to scalp him the next moment.

That near relative of the kingbird, the great crested fly-catcher, has one well-known peculiarity: he appears never to consider his nest finished until it contains a cast-off snake-skin. My alert correspondent one day saw him eagerly catch up an onion skin and make off with it, either deceived by it or else thinking it a good substitute for the coveted material.

One day in May, walking in the woods, I came upon a nest of whippoorwill, or rather its eggs,—for it builds no nest,—two elliptical whitish spotted eggs lying upon the dry leaves. My foot was within a yard of the mother-bird before she flew. I wondered what a sharp eye would detect curious or characteristic in the ways of the bird, so I came to the place many times and had a look. It was always a task to separate the bird from her surroundings, though I stood within a few feet of her, and knew exactly where to look. One had to bear on with his eye, as it were, and refuse to be baffled. The sticks and leaves, and bits of black or dark-brown bark, were all exactly copied in the bird's plumage. And then she did sit so close and simulate so well a shapeless decaying piece of wood or bark! Twice I brought a companion, and guiding his eye to the spot, noted how difficult it was for him to make out there, in full view upon the dry leaves, any semblance to a bird. When the bird returned after being disturbed, she would alight within a few inches of her eggs and then, after a moment's pause, hobble awkwardly upon them.

After the young had appeared, all the wit of the bird came into play. I was on hand the next day, I think. The mother-bird sprang up when I was within a pace of her, and in doing so fanned the leaves with her wings till they sprang up too; as the leaves started the young started, and, being of the same color, to tell which was the leaf and which the bird was a trying task to any eye. I came the next day, when the same tactics were repeated. Once a leaf fell upon one of the young birds and nearly hid it. The young are covered with a reddish down like a young partridge, and soon follow their mother about. When disturbed they gave but one leap, then settled down, perfectly motionless and stupid, with eyes closed. The parent bird, on these occasions, made frantic efforts to decoy me away from her young. She would fly a few paces and fall upon her breast, and a spasm like that of death would run through her tremulous outstretched wings and prostrate body. She kept a sharp eye out the meanwhile to see if the ruse took, and if it did not she was quickly cured, and moving about to some other point tried to draw my attention as before. When followed she always alighted upon the ground, dropping down in a sudden peculiar way. The second or third day both old and young had disappeared.

The whippoorwill walks as awkwardly as a swallow, which is as awkward as a man in a bag, and yet she manages to lead her young about the woods. The latter, I think, move by leaps and sudden spurts, their protective coloring shielding them most effectively. Wilson once came upon the mother-bird and her brood in the woods, and though they were at his very feet, was so baffled by the concealment of the young that he was about to give up the search, much disappointed, when he perceived something "like a slight moldiness among the withered leaves, and, on stooping down, discovered it to be a young whippoorwill, seemingly asleep." Wilson's description of the young is very accurate, as its downy covering does look precisely like a "slight moldiness." Returning a few moments afterward to the spot to get a pencil he had forgotten, he could find neither old nor young.

It takes an eye to see a partridge in the woods, motionless upon the leaves; this sense needs to be as sharp as that of smell in hounds and pointers, and yet I know an unkempt youth that seldom fails to see the bird and shoot it before it takes wing. I think he sees it as soon as it sees him, and before it suspects itself seen. What a training to the eye is hunting! To pick out the game from its surroundings, the grouse from the leaves, the gray squirrel from the mossy oak limb it hugs so closely, the red fox from the ruddy or brown or gray field, the rabbit from the stubble, or the white hare from the snow, requires the best powers of this sense. A woodchuck motionless in the fields or upon a rock looks very much like a large stone or bowlder, yet a keen eye knows the difference at a glance, a quarter of a mile away.

A man has a sharper eye than a dog, or a fox, or than any of the wild creatures; but not so sharp an ear or nose. But in the birds he finds his match. How quickly the old turkey discovers the hawk, a

mere speck against the sky, and how quickly the hawk discovers
you if you happen to be secreted in the bushes, or behind the fence
near which he alights! One advantage the bird surely has; and that
is, owing to the form, structure, and position of the eye, it has a
much larger field of vision—indeed, can probably see in nearly
every direction at the same instant; behind as well as before. Man's
field of vision embraces less than half a circle horizontally, and still
less vertically; his brow and brain prevent him from seeing within
many degrees of the zenith without a movement of the head; the
bird, on the other hand, takes in nearly the whole sphere at a glance.

I find I see, almost without effort, nearly every bird within sight
in the field or wood I pass through (a flit of the wing, a flirt of the
tail, are enough, though the flickering leaves do all conspire to hide
them), and that with like ease the birds see me, though unquestion-
ably the chances are immensely in their favor. The eye sees what it
has the means of seeing, truly. You must have the bird in your heart
before you can find it in the bush. The eye must have purpose and
aim. No one ever yet found the walking-fern who did not have the
walking-fern in his mind. A person whose eye is full of Indian relics
picks them up in every field he walks through.

One season I was interested in the tree-frogs, especially the tiny
pipers that one hears about the woods and brushy fields—the hylas
of the swamps become a denizen of trees; I had never seen him in
this new rôle. But this season having them in mind, or rather being
ripe for them, I several times came across them. One Sunday, walking amid some bushes, I captured two. They leaped before me as
doubtless they had done many times before, but though not looking
for or thinking of them, yet they were quickly recognized, because
the eye had been commissioned to find them. On another occasion,
not long afterward, I was hurriedly loading my gun in the October
woods in hopes of overtaking a gray squirrel that was fast escaping
through the treetops, when one of these Lilliput frogs, the color of
the fast-yellowing leaves, leaped near me. I saw him only out of the
corner of my eye, and yet bagged him, because I had already made
him my own.

Nevertheless, the habit of observation is the habit of clear and
decisive gazing; not by a first casual glance, but by a steady, deliberate aim of the eye are the rare and characteristic things discovered. You must look intently and hold your eye firmly to the spot,
to see more than do the rank and file of mankind. The sharpshooter
picks out his man and knows him with fatal certainty from a stump,

or a rock, or a cap on a pole. The phrenologists do well to locate not only form, color, weight, etc., in the region of the eye, but a faculty which they call individuality—that which separates, discriminates, and sees in every object its essential character. This is just as necessary to the naturalist as to the artist or the poet. The sharp eye notes specific points and differences,—it seizes upon and preserves the individuality of the thing.

We think we have looked at a thing sharply until we are asked for its specific features. I thought I knew exactly the form of the leaf of the tulip-tree, until one day a lady asked me to draw the outlines of one. A good observer is quick to take a hint and to follow it up. Most of the facts of nature, especially in the life of the birds and animals, are well screened. We do not see the play, because we do not look intently enough.

Birds, I say, have wonderfully keen eyes. Throw a fresh bone or a piece of meat upon the snow in winter, and see how soon the crows will discover it and be on hand. If it be near the house or barn, the crow that first discovers it will alight near it, to make sure that he is not deceived; then he will go away and soon return with a companion. The two alight a few yards from the bone, and after some delay, during which the vicinity is sharply scrutinized, one of the crows advances boldly to within a few feet of the coveted prize. Here he pauses, and if no trick is discovered, and the meat be indeed meat, he seizes it and makes off.

One midwinter I cleared away the snow under an apple-tree near the house, and scattered some corn there. I had not seen a bluejay for weeks, yet that very day they found my corn, and after that they came daily and partook of it, holding the kernels under their feet upon the limbs of the trees and pecking them vigorously.

Of course the woodpecker and his kind have sharp eyes. Still I was surprised to see how quickly Downy found out some bones that were placed in a convenient place under the shed to be pounded up for the hens. In going out to the barn I often disturbed him making a meal off the bits of meat that still adhered to them.

"Look intently enough at anything," said a poet to me one day, "and you will see something that would otherwise escape you." I thought of the remark as I sat on a stump in the opening of the woods one spring day. I saw a small hawk approaching; he flew to a tall tulip-tree and alighted on a large limb near the top. He eyed me and I eyed him. Then the bird disclosed a trait that was new to me; he hopped along the limb to a small cavity near the trunk, when he thrust in his head and pulled out some small object and fell to eating it. After he had partaken of it some minutes he put the remainder back in his larder and flew away. I had seen something like feathers eddying slowly down as the hawk ate, and on approaching the spot found the feathers of a sparrow here and there clinging to the bushes beneath the tree. The hawk then—commonly called the chicken hawk—is as provident as a mouse or squirrel, and lays by a store against a time of need; but I should not have discovered the fact had I not held my eye to him.

An observer of the birds is attracted by any unusual sound or commotion among them. In May and June, when other birds are most vocal, the jay is a silent bird; he goes sneaking about the orchards and the groves as silent as a pickpocket; he is robbing birds'-nests and he is very anxious that nothing should be said about it, but in the fall none so quick and loud to cry "Thief, thief" as he. One December morning a troop of them discovered a little screech-owl secreted in the hollow trunk of an old apple-tree near my house. How they found the owl out is a mystery, since it never ventures forth in the light of day; but they did, and proclaimed the fact with great emphasis. I suspect the bluebirds first told them, for these birds are constantly peeping into holes and crannies, both spring and fall. Some unsuspecting bird probably entered the cavity, prospecting for a place for next year's nest, or else looking out a likely place to pass a cold night, when it has rushed with very important news. A boy who should unwittingly venture into a bear's den when Bruin was at home could not be more astonished and alarmed than a bluebird would be on finding itself in the cavity of a decayed tree with an owl. At any rate, the bluebirds joined the jays, in calling the attention of all whom it might concern to the fact that a culprit of some sort was hiding from the light of day in the old apple-tree. I heard the notes of warning and alarm and approached to within eyeshot. The bluebirds were cautious, and hovered about uttering their peculiar twittering calls; but the jays were bolder, and took turns looking in at the cavity and deriding the poor shrinking owl. A jay would alight in the entrance of the hole, and flirt and peer and attitudinize, and then fly away crying "Thief, thief, thief," at the top of his voice.

I climbed up and peered into the opening, and could just descry the owl clinging to the inside of the tree. I reached in and took him out, giving little heed to the threatening snapping of his beak. He was as red as a fox and as yellow-eyed as a cat. He made no effort to escape, but planted his claws in my forefinger and clung there with a grip that soon grew uncomfortable. I placed him in the loft of an out-house in hopes of getting better acquainted with him. By day he was a very willing prisoner, scarcely moving at all even when approached and touched with the hand, but looking out upon the world with half-closed sleepy eyes. But at night what a change; how alert, how wild, how active! He was like another bird; he darted about with wild fearful eyes, and regarded me like a cornered cat. I opened the window, and swiftly, but as silently as a shadow, he glided out into the congenial darkness, and perhaps ere this has revenged himself upon the sleeping jay or bluebird that first betrayed his hiding-place.

## Quiet Work

ONE lesson, Nature, let me learn of thee,
   One lesson which in every wind is blown,
One lesson of two duties kept at one
Though the loud world proclaim their enmity—
Of toil unsevered from tranquillity!
Of labor, that in lasting fruit outgrows
Far noisier schemes, accomplished in repose,
Too great for haste, too high for rivalry!
Yes, while on earth a thousand discords ring,
Man's fitful uproar mingling with his toil,
Still do thy sleepless ministers move on,
Their glorious tasks in silence perfecting;
Still working, blaming still our vain turmoil,
Laborers that shall not fail, when man is gone.

*Matthew Arnold*

# THE ISLE OF ST. PETER

## Jean Jacques Rousseau

*The French-Swiss philosopher and man of letters, Rousseau (1712–1778) spent the first half of his life as footman, gigolo, secretary, music copyist, and professional guest of wealthy people. The great fame that came to him when he began writing seemed to turn his head—he fought with old friends, believed himself persecuted and his life actually in danger. Once, panic-stricken, he fled to a small island in Lake Bienne in Switzerland, where he was for a brief while supremely happy and unfearful, devoting himself to botany. He writes of this time in his* Reveries.

I FOUND my existence so charming, and led a life so agreeable to my humor, that I resolved here to end my days. My only source of disquiet was whether I should be allowed to carry my project out. In the midst of the presentiments that disturbed me, I would fain have had them make a perpetual prison of my refuge, to confine me in it for all the rest of my life. I longed for them to cut off all chance and all hope of leaving it; to forbid my holding any communication with the mainland, so that knowing nothing of what was going on in the world, I might have forgotten the world's existence, and people might have forgotten mine too. They suffered me to pass only two months in the island, but I could have passed two years, two centuries, and all eternity, without a moment's weariness; though I had not, with my companion, any other society than that of the steward, his wife, and their servants. They were in truth honest souls and nothing more, but that was just what I wanted. . . . Carried thither in a violent hurry, alone and without a thing, I afterwards sent for my housekeeper, my books, and my scanty possessions,—of which I had the delight of unpacking nothing,—leaving my boxes and chests just as they had come, and dwelling in the house where I counted on ending my days exactly as if it were an inn whence I must set forth on the morrow. All things went so well, just as they were, that to think of ordering them better were to spoil them. One of my greatest joys was to leave my books fastened up in their boxes, and to be without even a case for writing. When any luckless letter forced me to take up a pen for an answer, I grumblingly borrowed the steward's inkstand, and hurried to give it back to him with all the haste I could, in the vain hope that I should never have need of the loan any more. Instead of meddling with those weary quires and reams and piles of old books, I filled my chamber with flowers and grasses; for I was then in my first fervor for botany. Having given up employment that would be a task to me, I needed one that would be an amusement, nor cause me more pains than a sluggard might choose to take.

I undertook to make the 'Flora Petrinsularis'; and to describe every single plant on the island, in detail enough to occupy me for the rest of my days. In consequence of this fine scheme, every morning after breakfast, which we all took in company, I used to go with a magnifying-glass in my hand, and my 'Systema Naturæ' under my arm, to visit some district of the island. I had divided it for that purpose into small squares, meaning to go through them one after another in each season of the year. At the end of two or three hours I used to return laden with an ample harvest,—a provision for amusing myself after dinner indoors, in case of rain. I spent the rest of the morning in going with the steward, his wife, and Theresa, to see the laborers and the harvesting, and I generally set to work along with them: many a time when people from Berne came to see me, they found me perched on a high tree, with a bag fastened round my waist; I kept filling it with fruit, and then let it down to the ground with a rope. The exercise I had taken in the morning, and the good-humor that always comes from exercise, made the repose of dinner vastly pleasant to me. But if dinner was kept up too long, and fine weather invited me forth, I could not wait; but was speedily off to throw myself all alone into a boat, which, when the water was smooth enough, I used to pull out to the middle of the lake. There, stretched at full length in the boat's bottom, with my eyes turned up to the sky, I let myself float slowly hither and thither as the water listed, sometimes for hours together; plunged in a thousand confused delicious musings, which, though they had no fixed nor constant object, were not the less on that account a hundred times dearer to me than all that I had found sweetest in what they call the pleasures of life. Often warned by

the going down of the sun that it was time to return, I found myself
so far from the island that I was forced to row with all my might
to get in before it was pitch dark. At other times, instead of losing
myself in the midst of the waters, I had a fancy to coast along the
green shores of the island, where the clear waters and cool shadows
tempted me to bathe.

But one of my most frequent expeditions was from the larger
island to the less: there I disembarked and spent my afternoon,—
sometimes in mimic rambles among wild elders, persicaries, willows, and shrubs of every species; sometimes settling myself on the
top of a sandy knoll, covered with turf, wild thyme, flowers, even
sainfoin and trefoil that had most likely been sown there in old days,
making excellent quarters for rabbits. They might multiply in
peace without either fearing anything or harming anything. I spoke
of this to the steward. He at once had male and female rabbits
brought from Neuchâtel, and we went in high state—his wife, one
of his sisters, Theresa, and I—to settle them in the little islet. The
foundation of our colony was a feast-day. The pilot of the Argo-
nauts was not prouder than I, as I bore my company and the rabbits
in triumph from our island to the smaller one.

When the lake was too rough for me to sail, I spent my afternoon in going up and down the island, gathering plants to right and
left; seating myself now in smiling lonely nooks to dream at my
ease, now on little terraces and knolls, to follow with my eyes the
superb and ravishing prospect of the lake and its shores, crowned on
one side by the neighboring hills, and on the other melting into rich
and fertile plains up to the feet of the pale-blue mountains on their
far-off edge.

As evening drew on, I used to come down from the high
ground, and sit on the beach at the water's brink in some hidden
sheltering-place. There the murmur of the waves and their agitation
charmed all my senses, and drove every other movement away
from my soul: they plunged it into delicious dreamings, in which
I was often surprised by night. The flux and reflux of the water, its
ceaseless stir, swelling and falling at intervals, striking on ear and
sight, made up for the internal movements which my musings
extinguished; they were enough to give me delight in mere existence, without taking any trouble of thinking. From time to time
arose some passing thought of the instability of the things of this
world, of which the face of the waters offered an image: but such
light impressions were swiftly effaced in the uniformity of the

ceaseless motion, which rocked me as in a cradle; it held me with such fascination that even when called at the hour and by the signal appointed, I could not tear myself away without summoning all my force.

After supper, when the evening was fine, we used to go all together for a saunter on the terrace, to breathe the freshness of the air from the lake. We sat down in the arbor,—laughing, chatting, or singing some old song,—and then we went home to bed, well pleased with the day, and only craving another that should be exactly like it on the morrow. . . .

All is a continual flux upon the earth. Nothing in it keeps a form constant and determinate; our affections—fastening on external things—necessarily change and pass just as they do. Ever in front of us or behind us, they recall the past that is gone, or anticipate a future that in many a case is destined never to be. There is nothing solid to which the heart can fix itself. Here we have little more than a pleasure that comes and passes away; as for the happiness that endures, I cannot tell if it be so much as known among men. There is hardly in the midst of our liveliest delights a single instant when the heart could tell us with real truth, "*I would this instant might last forever.*" And how can we give the name of happiness to a fleeting state that all the time leaves the heart unquiet and void,—that makes us regret something gone, or still long for something to come?

But if there is a state in which the soul finds a situation solid enough to comport with perfect repose, and with the expansion of its whole faculty, without need of calling back the past or pressing on towards the future; where time is nothing for it, and the present has no ending; with no mark for its own duration, and without a trace of succession; without a single other sense of privation or delight, of pleasure or pain, of desire or apprehension, than this single sense of existence,—so long as such a state endures, he who finds himself in it may talk of bliss, not with a poor, relative, and imperfect happiness such as people find in the pleasures of life, but with a happiness full, perfect, and sufficing, that leaves in the soul no conscious unfilled void. Such a state was many a day mine in my solitary musings in the isle of St. Peter, either lying in my boat as it floated on the water, or seated on the banks of the broad lake, or in other places than the little isle,—on the brink of some broad stream, or a rivulet murmuring over a gravel bed.

What is it that one enjoys in a situation like this? Nothing outside of one's self, nothing except one's self and one's own existence.

But most men, tossed as they are by unceasing passion, have little knowledge of such a state: they taste it imperfectly for a few moments, and then retain no more than an obscure confused idea of it, that is too weak to let them feel its charm. It would not even be good, in the present constitution of things, that in their eagerness for these gentle ecstasies, they should fall into a disgust for the active life in which their duty is prescribed to them by needs that are ever on the increase. But a wretch cut off from human society, who can do nothing here below that is useful and good either for himself or for other people, may in such a state find for all lost human felicities many recompenses, of which neither fortune nor men can ever rob him.

'Tis true that these recompenses cannot be felt by all souls, nor in all situations. The heart must be in peace, nor any passion come to trouble its calm. There must be in the surrounding objects neither absolute repose nor excess of agitation; but a uniform and moderated movement, without shock, without interval. With no movement, life is only a lethargy. If the movement be unequal or too strong, it awakes us; by recalling us to the objects around, it destroys the charm of our musing, and plucks us from within ourselves, instantly to throw us back under the yoke of fortune and man, in a moment to restore us to all the consciousness of misery. Absolute stillness inclines one to gloom. It offers an image of death: then the help of a cheerful imagination is necessary, and presents itself naturally enough to those whom Heaven has endowed with such a gift. The movement which does not come from without then stirs within us. The repose is less complete, it is true; but it is also more agreeable when light and gentle ideas, without agitating the depths of the soul, only softly skim the surface. This sort of musing we may taste whenever there is tranquillity about us; and I have thought that in the Bastille, and even in a dungeon where no object struck my sight, I could have dreamed away many a thrice pleasurable day.

But it must be said that all this came better and more happily in a fruitful and lonely island, where nothing presented itself to me save smiling pictures, where nothing recalled saddening memories, where the fellowship of the few dwellers there was gentle and obliging, without being exciting enough to busy me incessantly; where, in short, I was free to surrender myself all day long to the promptings of my taste or to the most luxurious indolence. As I came out from a long and most sweet musing fit, seeing myself surrounded by verdure and flowers and birds, and letting my eyes wander far over romantic shores that fringed a wide expanse of water bright as crystal, I fitted all these attractive objects into my dreams; and when at last I slowly recovered myself, and recognized what was about me, I could not mark the point that cut off dream from reality, so equally did all things unite to endear to me the lonely retired life I led in this happy spot! Why can that life not come back to me again? Why can I not go finish my days in the beloved island, never to quit it, never again to see in it one dweller from the mainland, to bring back to me the memory of all the woes of every sort that they have delighted in heaping on my head for all these long years? Freed from the earthly passions engendered by the tumult of social life, my soul would many a time lift itself above this atmosphere, and commune beforehand with the heavenly intelligences, into whose number it trusts to be ere long taken.

## Les Silhouettes

THE sea is flecked with bars of gray,
  The dull dead wind is out of tune,
And like a withered leaf the moon
Is blown across the stormy bay.

Etched clear upon the pallid sand
Lies the black boat; a sailor boy
Clambers aboard in careless joy
With laughing face and gleaming hand.

And overhead the curlews cry,
Where through the dusky upland grass
The young brown-throated reapers pass
Like silhouettes against the sky.

*Oscar Wilde*

# THE CHARACTER OF DOGS

## Robert Louis Stevenson

*Here is an exposé of the vanities and foibles of dogs. In the eyes of most writers, the animal is "man's best friend"—to R. L. S., the dog is a snob pure and simple. But the gentle author presents his case with such affection and understanding that one ends by loving dogs more than ever. This delightful piece is from Stevenson's* Memories and Portraits.

THE civilization, the manners, and the morals of dog-kind are to a great extent subordinated to those of his ancestral master, man. This animal, in many ways so superior, has accepted a position of inferiority, shares the domestic life, and humors the caprices of the tyrant. But the potentate, like the British in India, pays small regard to the character of his willing client, judges him with listless glances, and condemns him in a byword. Listless have been the looks of his admirers, who have exhausted idle terms of praise, and buried the poor soul below exaggerations. And yet more idle and, if possible, more unintelligent has been the attitude of his express detractors; those who are very fond of dogs "but in their proper place"; who say "poo' fellow, poo' fellow," and are themselves far poorer; who whet the knife of the vivisectionist or heat his oven; who are not ashamed to admire "the creature's instinct"; and flying far beyond folly, have dared to resuscitate the theory of animal machines. The "dog's instinct" and the "automaton-dog," in this age of psychology and science, sound like strange anachronisms. An automaton he certainly is; a machine working independently of his control, the heart like the mill-wheel, keeping all in motion, and the consciousness, like a person shut in the mill garret, enjoying the view out of the window and shaken by the thunder of the stones; an automaton in one corner of which a living spirit is confined: an automaton like man. Instinct again he certainly possesses.

Inherited aptitudes are his, inherited frailties. Some things he at once views and understands, as though he were awakened from a sleep, as though he came "trailing clouds of glory." But with him, as with man, the field of instinct is limited; its utterances are obscure and occasional; and about the far larger part of life both the dog and his master must conduct their steps by deduction and observation.

The leading distinction between dog and man, after and perhaps before the different duration of their lives, is that the one can speak and that the other cannot. The absence of the power of speech confines the dog in the development of his intellect. It hinders him from many speculations, for words are the beginning of metaphysic. At the same blow it saves him from many superstitions and his silence has won for him a higher name for virtue than his conduct justifies. The faults of the dog are many. He is vainer than man, singularly greedy of notice, singularly intolerant of ridicule, suspicious like the deaf, jealous to the degree of frenzy, and radically devoid of truth. The day of an intelligent small dog is passed in the manufacture and the laborious communication of falsehood; he lies with his tail, he lies with his eye, he lies with his protesting paw; and when he rattles his dish or scratches at the door his purpose is other than appears. But he has some apology to offer for the vice. Many of the signs which form his dialect have come to bear an arbitrary meaning, clearly understood both by his master and himself; yet when a new want arises he must either invent a new vehicle of meaning or wrest an old one to a different purpose; and this necessity frequently recurring must tend to lessen his idea of the sanctity of symbols. Meanwhile the dog is clear in his own conscience, and draws, with a human nicety, the distinction between formal and essential truth. Of his punning perversions, his legitimate dexterity with symbols, he is even vain; but when he has told and been detected in a lie, there is not a hair upon his body but confesses guilt. To a dog of gentlemanly feeling theft and falsehood are disgraceful vices. The canine, like the human, gentleman demands in his misdemeanours Montaigne's *"je ne sais quoi de généreux."* His is never more than half ashamed of having barked or bitten; and for those faults into which he has been led by the desire to shine before a lady of his race, he retains, even under physical correction, a share of pride. But to be caught lying, if he understands it, instantly uncurls his fleece.

Just as among dull observers he preserves a name for truth, the

dog has been credited with modesty. It is amazing how the use of
language blunts the faculties of man—that because vainglory finds
no vent in words, creatures supplied with eyes have been unable to
detect a fault so gross and obvious. If a small spoiled dog were suddenly to be endowed with speech, he would prate interminably,
and still about himself; when we had friends, we should be forced
to lock him in a garret; and what with his whining jealousies and his
foible for falsehood, in a year's time he would have gone far to
weary out our love. I was about to compare him to Sir Willoughby
Patterne, but the Patternes have a manlier sense of their own merits;
and the parallel, besides, is ready. Hans Christian Andersen, as we
behold him in his startling memoirs, thrilling from top to toe with
an excruciating vanity, and scouting even along the street for shadows of offence—here was the talking dog.

It is just this rage for consideration that has betrayed the dog
into his satellite position as the friend of man. The cat, an animal of
franker appetites, preserves his independence. But the dog, with
one eye ever on the audience, has been wheedled into slavery, and
praised and patted into the renunciation of his nature. Once he
ceased hunting and became man's plate-licker, the Rubicon was
crossed. Thenceforth he was a gentleman of leisure; and except the
few whom we keep working, the whole race grew more and more
self-conscious, mannered and affected. The number of things that
a small dog does naturally is strangely small. Enjoying better spirits
and not crushed under material cares, he is far more theatrical than
average man. His whole life, if he be a dog of any pretension to
gallantry, is spent in a vain show, and in the hot pursuit of admiration. Take out your puppy for a walk, and you will find the little
ball of fur clumsy, stupid, bewildered, but natural. Let but a few
months pass, and when you repeat the process you will find nature
buried in convention. He will do nothing plainly; but the simplest
processes of our material life will all be bent into the forms of an
elaborate and mysterious etiquette. Instinct, says the fool, has
awakened. But it is not so. Some dogs—some, at the very least—if
they be kept separate from others, remain quite natural; and these,
when at length they meet with a companion of experience, and have
the game explained to them, distinguish themselves by the severity
of their devotion to its rules. I wish I were allowed to tell a story
which would radiantly illuminate the point; but men, like dogs,
have an elaborate and mysterious etiquette. It is their bond of sympathy that both are the children of convention.

The person, man or dog, who has a conscience is eternally condemned to some degree of humbug; the sense of law in their members fatally precipitates either towards a frozen and affected bearing. And the converse is true; and in the elaborate and conscious manners of the dog, moral opinions and the love of the ideal stand confessed. To follow for ten minutes in the street some swaggering, canine cavalier, is to receive a lesson in dramatic art and the cultured conduct of the body; in every act and gesture you see him true to a refined conception; and the dullest cur, beholding him, pricks up his ear and proceeds to imitate and parody that charming ease. For to be a high-mannered and high-minded gentleman, careless, affable, and gay, is the inborn pretension of the dog. The large dog, so much lazier, so much more weighed upon with matter, so majestic in repose, so beautiful in effort, is born with the dramatic means to wholly represent the part. And it is more pathetic and perhaps more instructive to consider the small dog in his conscientious and imperfect efforts to outdo Sir Philip Sidney. For the ideal of the dog is feudal and religious; the ever-present polytheism, the whip-bearing Olympus of mankind, rules them on the one hand; on the other, their singular difference of size and strength among themselves effectually prevents the appearance of the democratic notion. Or we might more exactly compare their society to the curious spectacle presented by a school—ushers, monitors, and big and little boys—qualified by one circumstance, the introduction of the other sex. In each, we should observe a somewhat similar tension of manner, and somewhat similar points of honor. In each the large animal keeps a contemptuous good humor; in each the smaller annoys him with wasp-like impudence, certain of practical immunity; in each we shall find a double life producing double characters, and an excursive and noisy heroism combined with a fair amount of practical timidity. I have known dogs, and I have known school heroes that, set aside the fur, could hardly have been told apart; and if we desire to understand the chivalry of old, we must turn to the school playfields or the dungheap where the dogs are trooping.

Woman, with the dog, has been long enfranchised. Incessant massacre of female innocents has changed the proportions of the sexes and perverted their relations. Thus, when we regard the manners of the dog, we see a romantic and monogamous animal, once perhaps as delicate as the cat, at war with impossible conditions. Man has much to answer for; and the part he plays is yet more damnable and parlous than Corin's in the eyes of Touchstone. But his intervention has at least created an imperial situation for the rare surviving ladies. In that society they reign without a rival: conscious queens; and in the only instance of a canine wife-beater that has ever fallen under my notice, the criminal was somewhat excused by the circumstances of his story. He is a little, very alert, well-bred, intelligent Skye, as black as a hat, with a wet bramble for a nose and two cairngorms for eyes. To the human observer, he is decidedly well-looking; but to the ladies of his race he seems abhorrent. A thorough elaborate gentleman, of the plume and sword-knot order, he was born with a nice sense of gallantry to women. He took at their hands the most outrageous treatment; I have heard him bleating like a sheep, I have seen him streaming blood, and his ear tattered like a regimental banner; and yet he would scorn to make reprisals. Nay more, when a human lady up-raised the contumelious whip against the very dame who had been so cruelly misusing him, my little greatheart gave but one hoarse cry and fell upon the tyrant tooth and nail. This is the tale of a soul's tragedy. After three years of unavailing chivalry, he suddenly, in one hour, threw off the yoke of obligation; had he been Shake-speare he would then have written *Troilus and Cressida* to brand the offending sex; but being only a little dog, he began to bite them. The surprise of the ladies whom he attacked indicated the monstrosity of his offence; but he had fairly beaten off his better angel, fairly committed moral suicide; for almost in the same hour, throwing aside the last rags of decency, he proceeded to attack the aged also. The fact is worth remark, showing, as it does, that ethical laws are common both to dogs and men; and that with both a single deliberate violation of the conscience loosens all. "But while the lamp holds on to burn," says the paraphrase, "the greatest sin-ner may return." I have been cheered to see symptoms of effectual penitence in my sweet ruffian; and by the handling that he ac-cepted uncomplainingly the other day from an indignant fair one, I began to hope the period of *Sturm und Drang* is closed.

All these little gentlemen are subtle casuists. The duty to the fe-male dog is plain; but where competing duties rise, down they will sit and study them out, like Jesuit confessors. I knew another little Skye, somewhat plain in manner and appearance, but a creature compact of amiability and solid wisdom. His family going abroad for a winter, he was received for that period by an uncle in the same city. The winter over, his own family home again, and his own house (of which he was very proud) reopened, he found himself in a dilemma between two conflicting duties of loyalty and gratitude. His old friends were not to be neglected, but it seemed hardly decent to desert the new. This was how he solved the problem. Every morning, as soon as the door was opened, off posted Coolin to his uncle's, visited the children in the nursery, saluted the whole family, and was back at home in time for breakfast and his bit of fish. Nor was this done without a sacrifice on his part, sharply felt; for he had to forego the particular honor and jewel of his day—his morning's walk with my father. And, perhaps from this cause, he gradually wearied of and relaxed the practice, and at length returned entirely to his ancient habits. But the same decision served him in another and more distressing case of divided duty, which happened not long after. He was not at all a kitchen dog, but the cook had nursed him with unusual kindness during the distemper; and though he did not adore her as he adored my father—although (born snob) he was critically conscious of her position as "only a servant"—he still cherished for her a special gratitude. Well, the cook left, and retired some streets away to lodgings of her own; and there was Coolin in precisely the same situation with any young gentleman who has had the inestimable benefit of a faithful nurse. The canine conscience did not solve the problem with a pound of tea at Christmas. No longer content to pay a flying visit, it was the whole forenoon that he dedicated to his solitary friend. And so, day by day, he continued to comfort her solitude until (for some reason which I could never understand and cannot approve) he was kept locked up to break him of the graceful habit. Here, it is not the similarity, it is the difference, that is worthy of remark; the clearly marked degrees of gratitude and the proportional duration of his visits. Anything further removed from instinct it were hard to fancy; and one is even stirred to a certain impatience with a character so destitute of spontaneity, so passionless in justice, and so priggishly obedient to the voice of reason.

There are not many dogs like this good Coolin, and not many people. But the type is one well marked, both in the human and the canine family. Gallantry was not his aim, but a solid and somewhat oppressive respectability. He was a sworn foe to the unusual and the conspicuous, a praiser of the golden mean, a kind of city uncle modified by Cheeryble. And as he was precise and conscientious in all the steps of his own blameless course, he looked for the same precision and an even greater gravity in the bearing of his deity, my

father. It was no sinecure to be Coolin's idol: he was exacting like a
rigid parent; and at every sign of levity in the man whom he respected, he announced loudly the death of virtue and the proximate
fall of the pillars of the earth.

I have called him a snob; but all dogs are so, though in varying
degrees. It is hard to follow their snobbery among themselves; for
though I think we can perceive distinctions of rank, we cannot
grasp what is the criterion. Thus in Edinburgh, in a good part of
the town, there were several distinct societies or clubs that met in
the morning to—the phrase is technical—to "rake the backets" in a
troop. A friend of mine, the master of three dogs, was one day surprised to observe that they had left one club and joined another;
but whether it was a rise or a fall, and the result of an invitation or
an expulsion, was more than he could guess. And this illustrates
pointedly our ignorance of the real life of dogs, their social ambitions and their social hierarchies. At least, in their dealings with
men they are not only conscious of sex, but of the difference of
station. And that in the most snobbish manner; for the poor man's
dog is not offended by the notice of the rich, and keeps all his ugly
feeling for those poorer or more ragged than his master. And again,
for every station they have an ideal of behavior, to which the master, under pain of derogation, will do wisely to conform. How
often has not a cold glance of an eye informed me that my dog was
disappointed; and how much more gladly would he not have taken
a beating than to be thus wounded in the seat of piety!

I knew one disrespectable dog. He was far liker a cat; cared little
or nothing for men, with whom he merely coexisted as we do with
cattle, and was entirely devoted to the art of poaching. A house
would not hold him, and to live in a town was what he refused. He
led, I believe, a life of troubled but genuine pleasure, and perished
beyond all question in a trap. But this was an exception, a marked
reversion to the ancestral type; like the hairy human infant. The
true dog of the nineteenth century, to judge by the remainder of
my fairly large acquaintance, is in love with respectability. A street-
dog was once adopted by a lady. While still an Arab, he had done
as Arabs do, gambolling in the mud, charging into butchers' stalls,
a cat-hunter, a sturdy beggar, a common rogue and vagabond; but
with his rise into society he laid aside these inconsistent pleasures.
He stole no more, he hunted no more cats; and conscious of his
collar, he ignored his old companions. Yet the canine upper class
was never brought to recognize the upstart, and from that hour,

except for human countenance, he was alone. Friendless, shorn of his sports and the habits of a lifetime, he still lived in a glory of happiness, content with his acquired respectability, and with no care but to support it solemnly. Are we to condemn or praise this self-made dog? We praise his human brother. And thus to conquer vicious habits is as rare with dogs as with men. With the most part, for all their scruple-mongering and moral thought, the vices that are born with them remain invincible throughout; and they live all their years, glorying in their virtues, but still the slaves of their defects. Thus the sage Coolin was a thief to the last; among a thousand peccadilloes, a whole goose and a whole cold leg of mutton lay upon his conscience; but Woggs,[1] whose soul's shipwreck in the matter of gallantry I have recounted above, has only twice been known to steal, and has often nobly conquered the temptation. The eighth is his favorite commandment. There is something painfully human in these unequal virtues and moral frailties of the best. Still more painful is the bearing of those "stammering professors" in the house of sickness and under the terror of death. It is beyond a doubt to me that, somehow or other, the dog connects together, or confounds, the uneasiness of sickness and the consciousness of guilt. To the pains of the body he often adds the tortures of the conscience; and at these times his haggard protestations form, in regard to the human deathbed, a dreadful parody or parallel.

I once supposed that I had found an inverse relation between the double etiquette which dogs obey; and that those who were most addicted to the showy street life among other dogs were less careful in the practice of home virtues for the tyrant man. But the female dog, that mass of carneying affections, shines equally in either sphere; rules her rough posse of attendant swains with unwearying tact and gusto; and with her master and mistress pushes the arts of insinuation to their crowning point. The attention of man and the regard of other dogs flatter (it would thus appear) the same sensibility; but perhaps, if we could read the canine heart, they would be found to flatter it in very different degrees. Dogs live with man as courtiers round a monarch, steeped in the flattery of his notice and enriched with sinecures. To push their favor in this world of pickings and caresses is, perhaps, the business of their

[1] Walter, Watty, Woggy, Woggs, Wogg, and lastly Bogue; under which last name he fell in battle some twelve months ago. Glory was his aim and he attained it; for his icon, by the hand of Caldecott, now lies among the treasures of the nation.

lives; and their joys may lie outside. I am in despair at our persistent ignorance. I read in the lives of our companions the same processes of reason, the same antique and fatal conflicts of the right against the wrong, and of unbitted nature with too rigid custom; I see them with our weaknesses, vain, false, inconstant against appetite, and with our one stalk of virtue, devoted to the dream of an ideal; and yet, as they hurry by me on the street with tail in air, or come singly to solicit my regard, I must own the secret purport of their lives is still inscrutable to man. Is man the friend, or is he the patron only? Have they indeed forgotten nature's voice? or are those moments snatched from courtiership when they touch noses with the tinker's mongrel, the brief reward and pleasure of their artificial lives? Doubtless, when man shares with his dog the toils of a profession and the pleasures of an art, as with the shepherd or the poacher, the affection warms and strengthens till it fills the soul. But doubtless, also, the masters are, in many cases, the object of a merely interested cultus, sitting aloft like Louis Quatorze, giving and receiving flattery and favor; and the dogs, like the majority of men, have but foregone their true existence and become the dupes of their ambition.

### The Crocodile

How doth the little crocodile
　Improve his shining tail,
And pour the waters of the Nile
　On every shining scale!

How cheerfully he seems to grin,
　How neatly spreads his claws,
And welcomes little fishes in
　With gently smiling jaws.

*Lewis Carroll*

# LIFE AMONG THE INDIANS

## Colonel James Smith

*In May, 1755, the colony of Pennsylvania sent out a body of men to cut a new road through the forest. In an encounter between the party and hostile Indians, an eighteen-year-old colonist, James Smith (1737–1814), was wounded and captured. The natives took him to an Indian town called Tullihas, inhabited by Delawares, Caughnewagas, and Mohicans. Here he was rather forcibly adopted into the tribe, and for five years lived as an Indian. The following selection from his book,* An Account of Remarkable Occurrences in the Life and Travels of Col. James Smith, *shows what a thorough Indian he became.*

THE day after my arrival at the aforesaid town a number of Indians collected about me, and one of them began to pull the hair out of my head. He had some ashes on a piece of bark, in which he frequently dipped his fingers in order to take the firmer hold, and so he went on, as if he had been plucking a turkey, until he had all the hair clean out of my head except a small spot about three or four inches square on my crown; this they cut off with a pair of scissors, excepting three locks, which they dressed up in their own mode. Two of these they wrapped round with a narrow beaded garter made by themselves for that purpose, and the other they plaited at full length, and then stuck it full of silver brooches. After this they bored my nose and ears, and fixed me off with earrings and nose jewels; then they ordered me to strip off my clothes and put on a breech-clout, which I did; they then painted my head, face, and body in various colors. They put a large belt of wampum on my neck, and silver bands on my hands and right arm; and so an old chief led me out in the street, and gave the alarm halloo, *coo-wigh,* several times repeated quick; and on this, all that were in the town came running and stood round the old chief, who held me by the hand in the midst. As I at that time knew nothing of their mode of adoption, and had seen them put to death all they had taken, and as I never could find that they saved a man alive at Braddock's defeat, I made no doubt but they were about putting me to death in some cruel manner. The old chief, holding me by the hand, made a long speech, very loud, and when he had done, he handed me to three young squaws, who led me by the hand down the bank, into the river, until the water was up to our middle. The squaws then made signs to me to plunge myself into the water, but I did not understand them; I thought that the result of the council was that I should be drowned, and that these young ladies were to be the executioners. They all three laid violent hold of me, and I for some time opposed them with all my might, which occasioned loud laughter by the multitude that were on the bank of the river. At length one of the squaws made out to speak a little English (for I believe they began to be afraid of me), and said *no hurt you*. On this I gave myself up to their ladyships, who were as good as their word; for though they plunged me under water, and washed and rubbed me severely, yet I could not say they hurt me much.

These young women then led me up to the council-house, where some of the tribe were ready with new clothes for me. They gave me a new ruffled shirt, which I put on, also a pair of leggings done off with ribbons and beads, likewise a pair of moccasons and garters dressed with beads, porcupine quills, and red hair—also a tinsel-laced cappo. They again painted my head and face with various colors, and tied a bunch of red feathers to one of those locks they had left on the crown of my head, which stood up five or six inches. They seated me on a bearskin, and gave me a pipe, tomahawk, and polecat-skin pouch, which had been skinned pocket fashion, and contained tobacco, killegenico, or dry sumach leaves, which they mix with their tobacco; also spunk, flint, and steel. When I was thus seated, the Indians came in dressed and painted in their grandest manner. As they came in they took their seats, and for a considerable time there was a profound silence—every one was smoking; but not a word was spoken among them. At length one of the chiefs made a speech, which was delivered to me by an interpreter, and was as followeth: "My son, you are now flesh of our flesh, and bone of our bone. By the ceremony which was performed this day every drop of white blood was washed out of your veins; you are taken into the Caughnewaga nation, and initiated into a warlike tribe; you are adopted into a great family, and now received with great seriousness and solemnity in the room and place of a great man. After what has passed this day, you are now one of us by an old strong law and custom. My son, you have now nothing to fear—we are now under the same obligations to love, support, and defend you that we are to love and to defend one another; therefore, you are to consider yourself as one of our people." At this time I did not believe this fine speech, especially that of the white blood being washed out of me; but since that time I have found out that there was much sincerity in said speech; for, from that day, I never knew them to make any distinction between me and themselves in any respect whatever until I left them. If they had plenty of clothing, I had plenty; if we were scarce, we all shared one fate.

After this ceremony was over I was introduced to my new kin, and told that I was to attend a feast that evening, which I did. And as the custom was, they gave me also a bowl and a wooden spoon, which I carried with me to the place, where there was a number of large brass kettles full of boiled venison and green corn; every one advanced with his bowl and spoon, and had his share given him. After this, one of the chiefs made a short speech, and then we began to eat.

Shortly after this I went out to hunt in company with Mohawk Solomon, some of the Caughnewagas, and a Delaware Indian that was married to a Caughnewaga squaw. We travelled about south from this town, and the first night we killed nothing, but we had with us green corn, which we roasted and ate that night. The next day we encamped about twelve o'clock, and the hunters turned out to hunt, and I went down the run that we encamped on, in company with some squaws and boys, to hunt plums, which we found in great plenty. On my return to camp I observed a large piece of fat meat; the Delaware Indian, that could talk some English, observed me looking earnestly at this meat, and asked me, "What meat you think that is?" I said I supposed it was bear meat; he laughed, and said, "Ho, all one fool you, beal now elly pool," and pointing to the other side of the camp, he said, "Look at that skin, you think that beal skin?" I went and lifted the skin, which appeared like an ox-hide; he then said, "What skin you think that?" I replied, that I thought it was a buffalo-hide; he laughed, and said, "You fool again, you know nothing, you think buffalo that colo'?" I acknowledged I did not know much about these things, and told him I never saw a buffalo, and that I had not heard what color they were. He replied, "By and by you shall see gleat many buffalo; he now go to gleat

lick. That skin no buffalo-skin, that skin buck-elk-skin." They went
out with horses, and brought in the remainder of this buck-elk,
which was the fattest creature I ever saw of the tallow kind.

We remained at this camp about eight or ten days, and killed a
number of deer. Though we had neither bread nor salt at this time,
yet we had both roast and boiled meat in great plenty, and they
were frequently inviting me to eat when I had no appetite.

We then moved to the buffalo lick, where we killed several buffalo, and in their small brass kettles they made about half a bushel
of salt. I suppose this lick was about thirty or forty miles from the
aforesaid town, and somewhere between the Muskingum, Ohio,
and Sciota. About the lick was clear, open woods, and thin white-
oak land, and at that time there were large roads leading to the lick,
like wagon-roads. We moved from this lick about six or seven
miles, and encamped on a creek.

Some time after this, I was told to take the dogs with me, and
go down the creek, perhaps I might kill a turkey; it being in the
afternoon, I was also told not to go far from the creek, and to come
up the creek again to the camp, and to take care not to get lost.
When I had gone some distance down the creek, I came upon fresh
buffalo tracks, and as I had a number of dogs with me to stop the
buffalo, I concluded I would follow after and kill one; and as the
grass and weeds were rank, I could readily follow the track. A little
before sundown I despaired of coming up with them. I was then
thinking how I might get to camp before night. I concluded, as the
buffalo had made several turns, if I took the track back to the creek
it would be dark before I could get to camp; therefore I thought I
would take a near way through the hills, and strike the creek a little
below the camp; but as it was cloudy weather, and I a very young
woodsman, I could find neither creek nor camp. When night came
on I fired my gun several times, and hallooed, but could have no
answer. The next morning, early, the Indians were out after me,
and as I had with me ten or a dozen dogs, and the grass and weeds
rank, they could readily follow my track. When they came up with
me they appeared to be in very good humor. I asked Solomon if he
thought I was running away; he said, "No, no, you go too much
clooked." On my return to camp they took my gun from me, and
for this rash step I was reduced to a bow and arrows for near two
years. We were out on this tour for about six weeks.

This country is generally hilly, though intermixed with considerable quantities of rich upland and some good bottoms.

When we returned to the town, Pluggy and his party had arrived, and brought with them a considerable number of scalps and prisoners from the south branch of the Potomac; they also brought with them an English Bible, which they gave to a Dutch woman who was a prisoner; but as she could not read English, she made a present of it to me, which was very acceptable.

I remained in this town until some time in October, when my adopted brother, called Tontileaugo, who had married a Wyandot squaw, took me with him to Lake Erie. On this route we had no horses with us, and when we started from the town all the pack I carried was a pouch containing my books, a little dried venison, and my blanket. I had then no gun, but Tontileaugo, who was a first-rate hunter, carried a rifle gun, and every day killed deer, raccoons, or bears. We left the meat, excepting a little for present use, and carried the skins with us until we encamped, and then stretched them with elm bark, in a frame made with poles stuck in the ground, and tied together with lynn or elm bark; and when the skins were dried by the fire, we packed them up and carried them with us the next day.

As Tontileaugo could not speak English, I had to make use of all the Caughnewaga I had learned, even to talk very imperfectly with him; but I found I learned to talk Indian faster this way than when I had those with me who could speak English.

As we proceeded down the Canesadooharie waters, our packs increased by the skins that were daily killed, and became so very heavy that we could not march more than eight or ten miles per day. We came to Lake Erie about six miles west of the mouth of Canesadooharie. As the wind was very high the evening we came to the lake, I was surprised to hear the roaring of the water, and see the high waves that dashed against the shore, like the ocean. We encamped on a run near the lake, and, as the wind fell that night, the next morning the lake was only in a moderate motion, and we marched on the sand along the side of the water, frequently resting ourselves, as we were heavily laden. I saw on the sand a number of large fish, that had been left in flat or hollow places; as the wind fell and the waves abated they were left without water, or only a small quantity; and numbers of bald and gray eagles, etc., were along the shore devouring them.

Some time in the afternoon we came to a large camp of Wyandots, at the mouth of Canesadooharie, where Tontileaugo's wife was. Here we were kindly received; they gave us a kind of rough, brown potatoes, which grew spontaneously, and were called by the Caughnewagas *ohnenata*. These potatoes, peeled and dipped in raccoon's fat, taste nearly like our sweet potatoes. They also gave us what they call *canaheanta*, which is a kind of hominy, made of green corn, dried, and beans, mixed together.

We continued our camp at the mouth of Canesadooharie for some time, where we killed some deer and a great many raccoons; the raccoons here were remarkably large and fat. At length we all embarked in a large birch-bark canoe. This vessel was about four feet wide and three feet deep, and about five-and-thirty feet long; and though it could carry a heavy burden, it was so artfully and curiously constructed that four men could carry it several miles, or from one landing-place to another, or from the waters of the lake to the waters of the Ohio. We proceeded up Canesadooharie a few miles, and went on shore to hunt; but, to my great surprise, they carried the vessel we all came in up the bank, and inverted it, or turned the bottom up, and converted it to a dwelling-house, and kindled a fire before us to warm ourselves by and cook. With our baggage and ourselves in this house we were very much crowded, yet our little house turned off the rain very well.

While we remained here I left my pouch with my books in camp, wrapped up in my blanket, and went out to hunt chestnuts. On my return to camp my books were missing. I inquired after them, and asked the Indians if they knew where they were; they told me that they supposed the puppies had carried them off. I did not believe them, but thought they were displeased at my poring over my books, and concluded that they had destroyed them, or put them out of my way.

After this I was again out after nuts, and on my return beheld a new erection, composed of two white-oak saplings, that were forked about twelve feet high, and stood about fifteen feet apart. They had cut these saplings at the forks, and laid a strong pole across, which appeared in the form of a gallows; and the poles they had shaved very smooth, and painted in places with vermilion. I could not conceive the use of this piece of work, and at length concluded it was a gallows. I thought that I had displeased them by reading my books, and that they were about putting me to death. The next morning I observed them bringing their skins all to this place, and hanging them over this pole, so as to preserve them from being injured by the weather. This removed my fears. They also buried their large canoe in the ground, which is the way they took to preserve this sort of a canoe in the winter season.

As we had at this time no horse, every one got a pack on his back, and we steered an east course about twelve miles and encamped. The next morning we proceeded on the same course about ten miles to a large creek that empties into Lake Erie, betwixt Canesadooharie and Cayahoga. Here they made their winter cabin in the following form: they cut logs about fifteen feet long, and laid these logs upon each other, and drove posts in the ground at each end to keep them together; the posts they tied together at the top with bark, and by this means raised a wall fifteen feet long and about four feet high, and in the same manner they raised another wall opposite to this, at about twelve feet distance; then they drove forks in the ground in the centre of each end, and laid a strong pole from end to end on these forks; and from these walls to the poles they set up poles instead of rafters, and on these they tied small poles in place of laths; and a cover was made of lynn-bark, which will run even in the winter season.

It was some time in December when we finished this winter-cabin; but when we had got into this comparatively fine lodging another difficulty arose—we had nothing to eat. While I was travelling with Tontileaugo, as was before mentioned, and had plenty of fat venison, bear's meat, and raccoons, I then thought it was hard living without bread or salt; but now I began to conclude that, if I had anything that would banish pinching hunger, and keep soul and body together, I would be content.

While the hunters were all out, exerting themselves to the utmost of their ability, the squaws and boys (in which class I was) were scattered out in the bottoms, hunting red haws, black haws, and hickory-nuts. As it was too late in the year we did not succeed in gathering haws, but we had tolerable success in scratching up hickory-nuts from under a light snow, which we carried with us lest the hunters should not succeed. After our return the hunters came in, who had killed only two small turkeys, which were but little among eight hunters and thirteen squaws, boys, and children; but they were divided with the greatest equity and justice; every one got their equal share.

The next day the hunters turned out again, and killed one deer and three bears. One of the bears was very large and remarkably fat. The hunters carried in meat sufficient to give us all a hearty supper and breakfast. The squaws and all that could carry turned out to bring in meat; every one had their share assigned them, and my load was among the least; yet, not being accustomed to carrying in this way, I got exceedingly weary, and told them my load was too heavy; I must leave part of it and come for it again. They made a halt, and only laughed at me, and took part of my load, and added it to a young squaw's, who had as much before as I carried.

This kind of reproof had a greater tendency to excite me to exert myself in carrying without complaining than if they had whipped me for laziness. After this the hunters held a council, and concluded that they must have horses to carry their loads; and that they would go to war, even in this inclement season, in order to bring in horses.

Tontileaugo wished to be one of those who should go to war; but the votes went against him, as he was one of our best hunters; it was thought necessary to leave him at this winter-camp to provide for the squaws and children. It was agreed upon that Tontileaugo and three others should stay and hunt, and the other four go to war.

They then began to go through their common ceremony. They sung their war-songs, danced their war-dances, etc. And when they were equipped they went off singing their marching-song and firing their guns. Our camp appeared to be rejoicing; but I was grieved to think that some innocent persons would be murdered, not thinking of danger.

After the departure of these warriors we had hard times; and though we were not altogether out of provisions, we were brought to short allowance. At length Tontileaugo had considerable success, and we had meat brought into camp sufficient to last ten days. Tontileaugo then took me with him in order to encamp some distance from this winter-cabin, to try his luck there. We carried no provisions with us; he said he would leave what was there for the squaws and children, and that we could shift for ourselves. We steered about a south course up the waters of this creek, and encamped about ten or twelve miles from the winter-cabin. As it was still cold weather, and a crust upon the snow, which made a noise as we walked, and alarmed the deer, we could kill nothing, and consequently went to sleep without supper. The only chance we had, under these circumstances, was to hunt bear-holes; as the bears, about Christmas, search out a winter lodging-place, where they lie about three or four months without eating or drinking. This may appear to some incredible, but it is well known to be the case by those who live in the remote western parts of North America.

The next morning early we proceeded on, and when we found a tree scratched by the bears climbing up, and the hole in the tree sufficiently large for the reception of the bear, we then felled a sapling or small tree against or near the hole, and it was my business to climb up and drive out the bear, while Tontileaugo stood ready with his gun and bow. We went on in this manner until evening without success. At length we found a large elm scratched, and a hole in it about forty feet up, but no tree nigh suitable to lodge against the hole. Tontileaugo got a long pole and some dry rotten wood, which he tied in bunches with bark; and as there was a tree that grew near the elm, and extended up near the hole, but leaned the wrong way, so that we could not lodge it to advantage, to remedy this inconvenience he climbed up this tree and carried with him his rotten wood, fire, and pole. The rotten wood he tied to his belt, and to one end of the pole he tied a hook and a piece of rotten wood, which he set fire to, as it would retain fire almost like punk, and reached this hook from limb to limb as he went up. When he got up with his pole he put dry wood on fire into the hole; after he put in the fire he heard the bear snuff, and he came speedily down, took his gun in his hand, and waited until the bear would come out; but it was some time before it appeared, and when it did appear he attempted taking sight with his rifle; but it being then too dark to see the sights, he set it down by a tree, and instantly bent his bow, took hold of an arrow, and shot the bear a little behind the shoulder. I was preparing also to shoot an arrow, but he called to me to stop, there was no occasion; and with that the bear fell to the ground.

Being very hungry, we kindled a fire, opened the bear, took out the liver, and wrapped some of the caul-fat round, and put it on a wooden spit, which we stuck in the ground by the fire to roast; then we skinned the bear, got on our kettle, and had both roast and boiled, and also sauce to our meat, which appeared to me to be delicate fare. After I was fully satisfied I went to sleep; Tontileaugo awoke me, saying, "Come, eat hearty, we have got meat plenty now."

The next morning we cut down a lynn-tree, peeled bark and made a snug little shelter, facing the southeast, with a large log betwixt us and the northwest; we made a good fire before us, and scaffolded up our meat at one side. When we had finished our camp we went out to hunt; searched two trees for bears, but to no purpose. As the snow thawed a little in the afternoon, Tontileaugo killed a deer, which we carried with us to camp.

Some time in February the four warriors returned, who had taken two scalps and six horses from the frontiers of Pennsylvania. The hunters could then scatter out a considerable distance from the winter-cabin and encamp, kill meat, and bring it in upon horses; so that we commonly, after this, had plenty of provision.

In this month we began to make sugar. As some of the elm-bark will strip at this season, the squaws, after finding a tree that would do, cut it down, and with a crooked stick, broad and sharp at the end, took the bark off the tree, and of this bark made vessels, in a curious manner, that would hold about two gallons each; they made above one hundred of these kind of vessels. In the sugar-tree they cut a notch, sloping down, and at the end of the notch stuck in a tomahawk; in the place where they stuck the tomahawk they drove a long chip, in order to carry the water out from the tree, and under this they set their vessel to receive it. As sugar-trees were plenty and large here, they seldom or never notched a tree that was not two or three feet over. They also made bark vessels for carrying the water that would hold about four gallons each. They had two brass-kettles that held about fifteen gallons each, and other smaller kettles in which they boiled the water. But as they could not at times boil away the water as fast as it was collected, they made vessels of bark that would hold about one hundred gallons each for retaining the water; and though the sugar-trees did not run every day, they had always a sufficient quantity of water to keep them boiling during the whole sugar-season.

About the latter end of March we began to prepare for moving into town in order to plant corn. The squaws were then frying the last of their bear's fat and making vessels to hold it; the vessels were made of deer-skins, which were skinned by pulling the skin off the neck without ripping. After they had taken off the hair they gathered it in small plaits round the neck, and, with a string, drew it together like a purse; in the centre a pin was put, below which they tied a string, and while it was wet they blew it up like a bladder, and let it remain in this manner until it was dry, when it appeared nearly in the shape of a sugar-loaf, but more rounding at the lower end. One of these vessels would hold about four or five gallons. In these vessels it was they carried their bear's oil.

When all things were ready we moved back to the falls of Canesadooharie. In our arrival at the falls (as we had brought with us on horseback about two hundred weight of sugar, a large quantity of bear's oil, skins, etc.) the canoe we had buried was not sufficient to carry all; therefore we were obliged to make another one of elm-bark. While we lay here a young Wyandot found my books. On this they collected together; I was a little way from the camp, and saw the collection, but did not know what it meant. They called me by my Indian name, which was Scoouwa, repeatedly. I ran to see what was the matter; they showed me my books, and said they were glad they had been found, for they knew I was grieved at the loss of them, and that they now rejoiced with me because they were found. As I could then speak some Indian, especially Caughnewaga (for both that and the Wyandot tongue were spoken in this camp), I told them that I thanked them for the kindness they had always shown to me, and also for finding my books. They asked if the books were damaged. I told them not much. They then showed how they lay, which was in the best manner to turn off the water. In a deer-skin pouch they lay all winter. The print was not much injured, though the binding was. This was the first time that I felt my heart warm towards the Indians. Though they had been exceedingly kind to me, I detested them as before on account of the barbarity I beheld after Braddock's defeat. Neither had I ever before pretended kindness, or expressed myself in a friendly manner; but I began now to excuse the Indians on account of their want of information.

We staid at this camp about two weeks, and killed a number of bears, raccoons, and some beavers. We made a canoe of elm-bark, and Tontileaugo embarked in it. He arrived at the falls that night; while I, mounted on horseback, with a bear-skin saddle and bark stirrups, proceeded by land to the falls. I came there the next morning, and we carried our canoe and loading past the falls.

We again proceeded towards the lakes; I on horseback and Tontileaugo by water. Here the land is generally good, but I found some difficulty in getting round swamps and ponds. When we came to the lake I proceeded along the strand and Tontileaugo near the shore, sometimes paddling and sometimes poling his canoe along.

After some time the wind arose, and he went into the mouth of a small creek and encamped. Here we staid several days on account of high wind, which raised the lake in great billows. While we were here Tontileaugo went out to hunt, and when he was gone a Wyandot came to our camp; I gave him a shoulder of venison which I had by the fire well roasted, and he received it gladly; told me he was hungry, and thanked me for my kindness. When Tontileaugo came home I told him that a Wyandot had been at camp, and that I gave him a shoulder of roasted venison; he said that was very well, and I suppose you gave him also sugar and bear's oil to eat with his venison. I told him I did not, as the sugar and bear's oil were down in the canoe, I did not go for it. He replied, "You have behaved just like a Dutchman. Do you not know that when strangers come to our camp we ought always to give them the best that we have?" I acknowledged that I was wrong. He said that he could excuse this, as I was but young; but I must learn to behave like a warrior, and do great things, and never be found in any such little actions.

The lake being again calm, we proceeded, and arrived safe at Sunyendeand, which was a Wyandot town that lay upon a small creek which empties into the little lake below the mouth of Sandusky.

The town was about eighty rood above the mouth of the creek, on the south side of a large plain, on which timber grew, and nothing more but grass or nettles. In some places there were large flats where nothing but grass grew, about three feet high when grown, and in other places nothing but nettles, very rank, where the soil is extremely rich and loose; here they planted corn. In this town there were also French traders, who purchased our skins and fur, and we all got new clothes, paint, tobacco, etc.

After I had got my new clothes, and my head done off like a red-headed woodpecker, I, in company with a number of young Indians, went down to the corn-field to see the squaws at work. When we came there they asked me to take a hoe, which I did, and hoed for some time. The squaws applauded me as a good hand at the business; but when I returned to the town the old men, hearing of what I had done, chid me, and said that I was adopted in the place of a great man, and must not hoe corn like a squaw. They never had occasion to reprove me for anything like this again; as I never was extremely fond of work, I readily complied with their orders.

# THE ELEPHANT REMEMBERS

## Edison Marshall

*Edison Marshall grew up in Oregon, becoming city editor of a newspaper when he was only nineteen years old. But he gave up this promising career to write fiction and to travel to the loneliest corners of Alaska, Africa, India, French Indo-China, Siam, and elsewhere. In this tale of the great Muztagh, he tells of the most fascinating trait of the animal Juggernaut, its memory, and of its most fabulous breed—the white elephant.*

IN A remote section of British India, in a strange wild province called Burma, Muztagh was born. And although he was born in captivity, the property of a mahout, in his first hour he heard the far-off call of the wild elephants in the jungle.

The Burmans always watch the first hour of a baby's life very closely. They know some incident will occur that will point, as a weather-vane points in the wind, to the baby's future. No one knows whether or not the prophecy works the same with baby elephants, but this wild far-carrying call did seem a token and an omen in the life of Muztagh. And it is a fact that the baby lifted his ears at the sound and rocked back and forth on his pillar legs.

Little Muztagh weighed a flat two hundred pounds at birth. But this was not the queerest thing about him. Elephant babies, though usually weighing not more than one hundred and eighty, often touch two hundred. The queerest thing was a peculiarity that probably was completely overlooked by his mother. If she saw it out of her dull eyes, she took no notice of it. It was not definitely discovered until the mahout came out of his hut with a lighted fagot for a first inspection.

He had been awakened by the sound of the mother's pain. "Hai!" he had exclaimed to his wife, "who has ever heard a cow bawl so loud in labour? The little one that tomorrow you will see beneath her belly must weigh more than you."

This was rather a compliment to his plump wife, for Burman women love to be well-rounded: but the mahout was not weighing the effect of his words. Rather he was already weighing the profits of little Muztagh. He was an elephant-catcher by trade, in the employ of Dugan Sahib, and the cao that was at this moment bringing a son into the world was his own property. If the baby should be of the Kumeria—

The mahout knew elephants from head to tail, and he was well acquainted with the three grades that compose that breed. The least valuable are the Mierga—a light, small-headed, thin-skinned, weak-trunked and unintelligent variety. They are often born of the most noble parents, and they are as big a problem to elephant-men as razor-backs to hog-breeders. The second variety, the Dwasala, which compose the bulk of the herd, is a good, substantial, strong, intelligent grade of elephant. But the Kumeria is the best of all; he is a perfect elephant—heavy, symmetrical, trustworthy, and fearless—fitted for the pageantry of kings.

He hurried out to the lines for now he knew that the baby was born. The mother's cries had ceased. The jungle, dark and savage, lay just beyond. He could feel its heavy air, and as he stood, lifting the fagot high, he heard the wild elephants trumpeting from the hills.

He turned his head in amazement. A Burman, and especially one who chases the wild elephants in their jungles, is superstitious and it seemed to him that the trumpeting must have some meaning. It was like the far-famed salute that the elephants offer on certain occasions.

"Are you saluting this little one?" he cried. "He is not a wild tusker like you. He is born in bonds such as you too will wear after the next drive."

They trumpeted again as the man turned back to the lines and lifted higher his light.

Yes—the little elephant was a Kumeria. Never had there been a more perfect calf. As he held the fagot nearer so that the beams played on his coat, the mahout sat down and was still, lest the gods observe his good luck and, being jealous, turn it into evil.

For the coat was not pinky dark, as is usual in baby elephants. It was light-coloured—only a few degrees darker than white.

The man understood at once. In elephants, as in other animals, an albino is sometimes born. Up to a few years ago, a perfectly white elephant had never been seen, but occasionally elephants are born with light coloured or clouded hides. Such creatures are bought at fabulous prices by Malay and Siamese princes, for to them a white elephant is the greatest treasure a king can possess.

Muztagh was not an albino, yet a tendency in that direction had bleached his skin. And the mahout knew that Dugan Sahib would pay him a lifetime's wages for the little wobbly calf whose welcome had been the wild cries of the tuskers in the jungle.

2

Little Muztagh (*i.e.*, White Mountain) did not enjoy his babyhood. He was born with the memory of jungle kingdoms, and the life in the elephant lines almost killed him with dullness.

He had never anything to do but nurse at the strong elephant milk and roam about in the keddah or along the lines. He had been bought the second day of his life by Dugan Sahib, who saw to it that he underwent none of the risks that are the happy fate of most baby elephants. His mother was not taken on the elephant drives into the jungle so he never got a taste of this exciting sport. Mostly she was kept chained in the lines, and Langur Dass, the low-caste hillman in Dugan's employ, grubbed grass for her in the valleys. All night, except for the regular four hours of sleep, he would hear her grumble the discontent which her little son shared.

Muztagh's second year was little better. He had reached the age when he could eat grass and young sugar-cane, but these dainties did not make up for the fun he was missing in the hills. He would stand for long hours watching their purple tops. He would see the haze steam up from the wet vines, and he would tingle and scratch for the feel of its wetness on his skin. And often when the night came down, it seemed to him that he would go mad. He would hear the wild tuskers trumpeting in the jungles and at such time even his mother looked at him in wonder.

"Oh, little restless one," Langur Dass would say, "thou and that old cow thy mother and I have one heart between us. We know the burning—we understand, we three!"

Langur Dass understood more of the ways of the forest people than any other hillman in the encampment. But his caste was low, and he was drunken and idle and lazy and the hunters called him Langur after a grey-bearded breed of monkeys along the slopes of the Himalayas. He never wanted to join in the drives and one day they asked him about it. "If thy name speaks true," they said, "thou art brother to many monkey-folk and who knows the jungle better than thou or they? How is it that when we go hunting thou art afraid to come?"

Langur evaded their questions as long as he could. "Have you forgotten the tales you heard on your mothers' breasts?" he asked at last. "Elephants are of the jungle. You are of the cooking-pots and thatch. How should such folks as ye are understand?"

This was flat heresy from their viewpoint. There is an old legend among the elephant-catchers that at one time men were subject to the elephants.

Mostly the elephants that these men knew were patient and contented in their bonds, but little Muztagh was an exception. Even though he had been born in captivity, his desire for liberty was with him as constantly as his trunk or his ears.

He had no love for the mahout that rode his mother. He took little interest in the little brown boys and girls that played before his stall. He would stand and look over their heads into the wild dark heart of the jungle. Being a beast he did not know anything about caste but he did know that Langur Dass, ragged, dirty, and despised, awoke a responsive chord in his lonely heart.

They would have long talks together, that is Langur would talk and Muztagh would mumble. "Little calf, little fat one," the man would say, "thy heart speaks through those sleepless eyes of thine. Shalt thou never lie the day long in the cool mud? Never see a storm break on the hills? Nor feel a warm rain dripping through the branches? Or are these matters part of thee that none may steal? I think already thou knowest how the tiger steals away at thy shrill note; how thickets feel that crash beneath thy hurrying weight. How knowest thou these things? Not as I know them, who have seen—nay, but as a king, it is in thy blood. Shall some fat rajah of the plains make a beast of burthen of thee? Answer, lord of mighty memories!"

Most of the mahouts and catchers noticed the rapidity with which Muztagh acquired weight and strength. He outweighed, at the age of three, any calf of his season by a full two hundred pounds. And of course three in an elephant is no more than three in a child. He would probably have fulfilled the plans Dugan had made for him but for a mistake the sahib made in the little calf's ninth year.

He sold Muztagh's mother to an elephant-breeder from a distant province. Little Muztagh watched her march away between two tuskers—down the long elephant trail into the valley of the shadow.

"Watch the little one closely tonight," Dugan said to his mahout; so, when they led him back and forth along the lines, they saw that the end of his ropes were pegged down tightly. They were horsehair ropes, beyond the strength of any normal nine-year-old elephant to break. Then they went to the huts and to their women and left him to shift restlessly from foot to foot, and think.

Probably he would have been satisfied with thinking, for Muztagh did not know his strength, and thought he was securely tied. The incident that upset the mahout's plans was simply that the wild elephants trumpeted again from the hills.

Muztagh heard the sound, long drawn and strange, from the silence of the jungle. He grew motionless. The great ears pricked forward, the whipping tail stood. It was a call not to be denied. The blood leapt in his veins. He rocked forward with all his strength. The rope spun tight, hummed and snapped, and he padded out among the huts. Nobody who had not seen him do it would believe how silently an elephant can move when he sees fit.

There was no thick jungle here—just soft grass, huts, approaching dark fringe that was the jungle. None of the mahouts was awake to see him. The grass gave way to bamboo thickets, the smell of the huts to the wild perfumes of the jungle.

Muztagh walked forward with his trunk outstretched into the primordial jungle and was born again.

### 3

Muztagh's reception was cordial. The great bulls of the herd stood still and lifted their ears when they heard him grunting up the hills. But he slipped among them and was forgotten at once. They had no dealings with the princes of Malay and Siam, and his light-coloured coat meant nothing to them. If they did anything about him it was to wonder why a calf with the marks of a nine-year-old should be so tall and weigh so much.

The great old wrinkled tusker that led the herd peered at him now and then out of his little red eyes and wondered. A herd-leader begins to think about future contestants for his place as soon as he acquires the leadership. But *Hai!* This little one would not have his greatest strength for fifteen years.

It was a compact, medium-sized herd—vast males, mothers, old-maid elephants, long-legged and ungainly young males, learning their strength and proud of it beyond words, and many calves. They ranged in size from the leader, who stood ten feet and weighed nearly nine thousand pounds, to little two-hundred-and-fifty-pound babies that had been born that season. And before long the herd began its cautious advance into the deeper hills.

The first night in the jungle—Muztagh found it wonderful past all dreams. The mist on his skin was a cool joy; there were sounds that set his muscles a-quiver; and he knew, because it was his heritage, what everyone of these sounds meant.

The herd threaded through the jungle and descended into a river. A herd of deer—either the dark sambur or black buck—sprang from the misty shore-line and leaped away into the bamboos. Further down he could hear the grunt of buffalo.

It was simply a caress—the touch of the soft cool water on his flanks. The herd reared out, like sea-gods rising from the deep, and grunted and squealed their way up the banks into the jungle again. When dawn burst over the eastern hills, he was weary in every muscle of his young body but too happy to admit it.

That day was the first of three thousand joyous days. The herd was never still. They ranged from one hill to another, to the ranges of the Himalayas and back again. There were no rivers that they did not swim, no jungles that they did not penetrate, no elephant trails that they did not follow, in the whole northeastern corner of British India. And all the time Muztagh's strength grew upon him till it became too vast to measure or control, and he would have broken any scales in the Indian Empire that tried to weigh him.

He had had his share of adventures, yet he knew that life in reality had only begun. The time would come when he would want to fight the great arrogant bull for the leadership of the herd. He was tired of fighting the young bulls of his own age. He always won and constant winning is almost as dull as constant losing.

India is too thickly populated for a wild elephant to escape observation. Many natives had caught sight of him and at last the tales reached a circle of trackers and hunters in camp on a distant range of hills. One night they sat and talked softly over their fire.

"You will go, Khusru," said the leader, "for there are none here half so skillful with the horsehair rope as you. If you do not come back within twelve months, we shall know that you have failed."

If a man failed in the effort to capture a wild elephant by the hair-rope method, he very rarely lived to tell of it.

"And in that case," Ahmad Din went on, "we will have a drive after the monsoon of next year. It will cost more but it will be sure. And our purses will be fat from the selling-price of this king of elephants with a white coat!"

### 4

Khusru was an able hunter and, after countless days, he crept up within a half dozen feet of Muztagh as he slept. He intended to loop a horsehair rope about one of his great feet. But Muztagh wakened in time.

Then a curious thing happened. The native could never entirely believe it but it was one of his best stories till he died. Any other wild tusker would have charged in fury and there would have been a quick and certain death beneath his knees. Muztagh started out as if he had intended to charge. He lifted his trunk out of the way—the elephant trunk is for a thousand uses, but fighting is not one of them—and sprang forward. He went just two paces. Then his little eyes caught sight of the brown figure fleeing through the bamboos. At once the elephant set his feet to brace himself, and drew to a sliding halt six feet beyond. He did not know why. He was aware that this man was an enemy and that it was his intention to put him back into bonds. He did not feel fear. It seemed to him that memories came thronging from long ago, memories so insistent that he could not think of charging.

He remembered his days in the elephant lines. The hill people say that the elephant memory is the greatest single marvel in the jungle and it was that memory that saved Khusru.

Those were the days when Muztagh lived apart from the herd. He did it from choice. He liked the silence, the solitary mud-baths, the constant watchfulness against danger.

One day a rhino charged him—without warning or reason. This is quite a common thing for a rhino to do. They have the worst tempers in the jungle, and they would as soon charge a mountain if they did not like the look of it. Muztagh had awakened the rhino from his sleep and he came bearing down like a tank over "no man's land."

Muztagh met him squarely, with the full shock of his tusks, and the battle ended promptly. Muztagh's trunk, driven by his five tons of might would have pierced a ship's side, and the rhino limped away to let his hurt grow well and meditate revenge. There-after for a full year, he looked carefully out of his bleary eyes, and chose a smaller objective before he charged.

Month after month Muztagh went his way alone. He swam in the deep holes, and sometimes shut his eyes and stood on the bottom, just keeping the end of his trunk out of the water. One day he was obliged to kneel on the broad back of an alligator who was trying to bite off his foot. He drove the long body down into the muddy bottom, and no living creature, except possibly the catfish that burrow in the mud, ever saw it again.

He loved the rains that flashed through the jungles, the swift-climbing dawns, the strange, tense, breathless nights. At twenty-five he had reached maturity; and no more magnificent specimen of the elephant could be found in India.

Of course he had known for years his mastery over inanimate things, but he did not know that he had developed a craft and skill that would avail him in battle against the greatest of his own kind. He made the discovery one sunlit day beside the Manipur River.

He was in the mud-bath, grunting and bubbling with content. And seeing that he was young, and perhaps failing to measure his size, obscured as it was in the mud, a "rogue" elephant came out of the jungle to take the bath for himself.

He was a huge creature—wrinkled and yellow-tusked and scarred from a thousand fights. He confidently expected Muztagh would yield at once because as a rule twenty-five-year-olds do not care to mix in battle with veterans of sixty years. But he did not know Muztagh.

The latter had been enjoying the bath and he had no desire to give it up. Something hot and raging exploded in his brain and it was as if a red glare had fallen over the stretch of river and jungle before his eyes. He squealed once, reared with one lunge out of the bath—and charged!

Of all the expressions of power in the animal world, an elephant fight is the most terrible. It is as if two mountains rose up from their roots of strata and went to war. The jungle people were asleep. A thunder-storm could not have broken more quickly or created a wilder pandemonium.

They squealed and bellowed and trumpeted and grunted and charged. Their tusks clicked like the noise of a giant's game of billiards. The thickets cracked and broke beneath their feet.

It lasted only a moment. In a few seconds the old rogue became aware that he had made a dangerous mistake. There were better mud-baths in the river, anyway.

He had not been able to land a single blow. And his wrath gave way to startled amazement when Muztagh sent home his third. The rogue did not wait for the fourth.

Muztagh chased him into the thickets. But he was too proud to chase a beaten elephant for long. He halted, trumpeting, and swung back to his mud-bath.

But he did not enter it again. All at once he remembered the herds and the fights of his childhood. All at once he knew that his craft and strength were beyond that of any elephant in the jungle. Who was the herd-leader to stand against him?

His little eyes grew ever more red as he stood rocking back and forth. Why should he abide alone when he could be ruler of the herd? He grunted softly and started away down the river.

## 5

"Khusru has failed to catch White-Skin," said Ahmad Din to the little band of elephant-catchers, sitting round the night-fire. "He comes tonight."

"Do you mean the white elephant of which the Manipur people tell so many lies?" asked Langur Dass, who sat on the edge of the circle.

"The Manipur people tell of him," was the reply, "but for once they tell the truth. He is the greatest elephant, the richest prize in Burma. Too many people have seen him to doubt, thou son of immortality!"

Langur Dass's face lit suddenly. "Then it could be none but Muztagh, escaped from Dugan Sahib fifteen years ago. That calf was white, also he was overgrown for his years."

"Then," gasped one of the trackers, "that was why he spared Khusru! He remembered men."

The others nodded gravely. "They never forget," said Langur Dass.

"He is now with the herd," Ahmad Din went on, "a day's journey beyond the river. There is no time to be lost."

His fellows nodded in agreement.

"Tomorrow we will break camp, but the white sahib who holds the license is not to know that White-Coat is in the herd at all."

The circle nodded again, and contracted towards the speaker.

"We will hire beaters and drivers, the best that can be found. Tomorrow we will take the elephants and go."

"If a drive is on," said Langur Dass humbly, "perhaps you will give your servant a place among the beaters?"

The circle turned and stared, for it was one of the stories of Langur Dass that he never joined in elephant hunts.

"You shall have your wish," replied Ahmad Din. "Indeed you can watch the flame tonight. And remember—a gipsy died in a tiger's claws on this very slope not six months past."

For another hour they sat perfecting their plans. Then they lay down by the fire and sleep dropped over them one by one. At last Langur Dass sat by the fire alone. Soon he got up and stole out into the darkness.

"Have I followed the tales of your greatness all these years for this?" he muttered. "Thou, who art of the breed of masters, not of slaves! Muztagh, we will see what can be done. Thy Langur Dass is old, and his whole strength is not that of thy trunk, and men look upon him as a worm in the grass, but perhaps thou wilt find him an ally not to be despised."

6

The night had just fallen, moist and heavy over the jungle, when Muztagh caught up with the herd. The old bull that led them, seventy years of age, and scarred and yellow-tusked past any elephant patriarch in the jungle, curled up his trunk. He knew what would happen. And because no one knows better than the jungle people what a good thing it is to take the offensive he uttered the challenge himself.

The silence dropped as something from the sky. The little pink calves, who had never seen the herd grow still in the same way before, felt the dawn of the storm that they could not understand, and took shelter beneath their mothers' bellies. They did not squeal. The silence was too deep for them to dare to break.

When a young bull contests for the leadership it is always an epoch in the life of the herd. It is more serious than in the herds of deer and buffalo. A great bull who has attained strength and wisdom enough to obtain the leadership of an elephant herd may keep it for forty years. As most men know, an elephant is not really old until he has seen a hundred summers come and go. He will live fifty years more, wise and grey and wrinkled and full of memories of a time no man can remember.

Long years had passed since the leader's place had been questioned. The aristocracy of strength is drawn on inflexible lines. Elephants of the Dwasila and Mierga grades do not covet the leadership. Only the Kumeria ever make a trial at it.

The herd stood like figures in stone for a long moment—until Muztagh had replied to the challenge. He was so surprised that at first he could not make a sound. He had expected to do the challenging himself. That the leader had done it, shook his self-confidence to some degree. Evidently the old fellow still felt able to handle any young and arrogant bulls that desired his place.

Then the herd began to shift. The cows drew back with their calves, the bulls surged forward, and slowly they made a hollow ring, not greatly different from the pugilistic ring known to fight fans. The calves began to squeal, but their mothers silenced them. Slowly Muztagh stamped into the circle. His tusks gleamed. His eyes glowed red. And these appraising old bulls in the ring knew that such an elephant had not been born since the time of their grandfathers.

They looked him over from tail to trunk. They marked the symmetrical form, legs like pillars, sloping back, wide-apart eyes. His shoulders were an expression of latent might—power to break a tree-trunk at its base by the conformity of his muscles—he was agile and quick as a tiger. And knowing these things they threw their trunks in the air till they touched their foreheads and blared their full-voiced salute.

They gave it the same instant—as musicians strike the same note at their leader's signal. It was a perfect explosion of sound, a terrible blare, that crashed out through the jungles and wakened every sleeping thing. The dew fell from the trees. A tiger, lingering in hope of an elephant calf, slipped silently away.

Not only the jungle people marvelled at the sound. At an encampment three miles distant, Ahmad Din and his men heard the wild call.

"My lord Muztagh has come back to his herd," said Langur Dass. "That is his salute."

Ahmad Din looked darkly about the circle. "And how long shall he stay?" he asked.

The trap was almost ready. The hour to strike had almost come.

Meanwhile the old leader, stamping into the circle, appeared unconscious of the eyes upon him.

Again the salute sounded—shattering out like a thunder-clap over the jungle. The challenger and challenged closed.

At first the watchers were silent. Then, as the battle grew fiercer they began to grunt and squeal, surging back and forth, stamping the earth and crashing the underbrush. And Ahmad Din wished his *keddah* were completed, for never could there be a better opportunity to surround the herd than at the present moment, when they had forgotten everything but the fight.

The two bulls were evenly matched. The patriarch knew more of fighting, had learned more wiles, but he had neither the strength nor the agility of Muztagh. The late twilight deepened into dark, and the stars of midnight rose above the eastern hills.

All at once Muztagh went to his knees. But, as might a tiger, he sprang aside in time to avoid a tusk blow to his shoulder. His counter-blow, a lashing cut with the head, shattered the leader to the earth. The elephants bounded forward, but the old leader had a trick left in his trunk. As Muztagh bore down upon him he reared up beneath, and only the youngster's superior strength saved him from defeat.

As the night drew to morning, the bulls saw that the tide of battle had turned. The rushes of the patriarch were weakening. He could still inflict punishment, and the hides of both were in a terrible state but he was no longer able to take advantage of openings. Then Muztagh did a thing which reassured the old bulls as to his wisdom. As a pugilist will invite a blow to draw his opponent within range, Muztagh pretended to leave his shoulder exposed. The old bull bore down, and Muztagh was ready with flashing tusk.

The great bull went down, Muztagh stood over him, lunging. The battle was over.

The old leader, seriously hurt, backed away into the jungle. His trunk was lowered in token of defeat. The ring was empty, except for a great red-eyed elephant, whose hide was no longer white, standing blaring his triumph to the stars.

Three times the elephant salute crashed out into the jungle silence—the full-voiced salaam to a new king. Muztagh had come into his birthright.

## 7

The *keddah* was built at last. It was a stockade, opening with wings that spread out a hundred yards, and equipped with a gate which dropped like a portcullis at the funnel end of the wings. The herd had been surrounded by drivers and beaters and driven slowly, for days, towards the *keddah* mouth. The men had guns loaded with blank cartridges, and firebrands ready to light. At a given signal they would close down quickly about the herd, and stampede it into the yawning mouth of the stockade.

No detail had been overlooked and the profit was assured, not only from the matchless Muztagh, but from the herd as well. He had led the herd through the hills and had known the rapture of living as never before. It had been his work to clear the trail of all dangers, to find the coolest watering-places, the greenest hills. One night a tiger had tried to kill a calf which had wandered from its mother's side. Muztagh lifting his trunk high had charged down with great, driving strides—four tons and over of majestic wrath. The tiger leaped to meet him but the elephant was ready. He avoided the terrible stroke of outstretched claws, and his tusks lashed to one side as the tiger was in midspring. Then he lunged out, and the great knees descended slowly, as a hydraulic press descends on yellow apples. Soon after the kites were dropping out of the sky for a feast.

His word was law and slowly he began to overcome the doubt that the bulls had of him—doubt of his youth and experience. If he had had three months more of leadership, their trust would have been absolute. But in the meantime the drive towards the *keddah* had begun.

"We will need brave men to stand at the end of the wings," said Ahmad Din, speaking no less than the truth. The man who stands at the end of the wings or widespreading gates of the *keddah* is in danger of being charged and killed. The herd, mad with fear, is only slightly less afraid of the wings of the stockade than of the yelling, whooping beaters behind. Often they will try to break through the circle rather than enter the wings.

"For two rupees additional I will hold one of the wings," said old Langur Dass.

Ahmad Din peered at his hard bright eyes and determined face, trying to read the thoughts behind the eyes. "You shall lie behind the right-wing men to pass them torches," he said.

Within the hour the signal of "*Mail, mail!*" (Go on, go on!) was given, and the final laps of the drive began.

The hills grew full of sound. The beaters sprang up with firebrand and rifle and closed swiftly about the herd. The animals moved slowly at first. Many times the herd would leave their trail and start to dip into a valley or creek-bed, but always there was a new crowd of beaters to block their path. Presently the beaters began to close in. The animals began a wild descent toward the mouth of the *keddah*.

"*Hai!*" the wild men cried. "On, on! Block the way through that valley, you sons of jackals. Stand close. Watch, Puran! Guard your post, Khusru! Now on, on—do not let them halt! *Arre! Aihai!*"

Firebrands waved, rifles cracked, the wild shout of beaters increased in volume. The men drove the beasts before them.

Only one man did not raise his voice. Throughout the turmoil he crouched at the end of the stockade, tense and silent. It was Langur Dass waiting for the instant when the herd would come thundering down the hill. He would then have to pass lighted firebrands to the men who held that corner.

Muztagh had lost control of his herd. At their head ran the old leader whom he had worsted. In their hour of fear they had turned back to him. What did this youngster know of elephant drives? The waving firebrands drew nearer, the drivers lessened their circle, the avenues of escape became more narrow. Beyond stretched the yawning arms of the stockade.

"Close down, close down!" Ahmad Din was shouting. "Hasten, pigs of the hills! Raise your voice! Now, *Aihai!*"

The herd was at the very wings of the stockade. They had halted an instant, milling, and the beaters increased their shouts. Only one of the herd seemed to know the danger—Muztagh himself, and he had dropped from the front rank to the very rear. He stood with uplifted trunk, facing the approaching rows of beaters. And there seemed to be no break in the line.

The herd started to move on into the wings of captivity. They did not heed his warning squeals to turn.

The circle of fire drew nearer. His trunk drooped. He, too, turned. He couldn't break the line. He turned toward the mouth of the *keddah*.

Even as he turned, a brown figure darted towards him from the end of the wing. A voice known long ago was calling to him—a voice which penetrated the babble of the beaters. "Muztagh!" it was crying. "Muztagh!"

It was not the words that turned Muztagh but the smell of the man, remembered from long ago, and the sound of his voice, never quite forgotten.

"Muztagh! Muztagh!"

The elephant knew him now. He remembered his one friend among the human beings that he had known in his calfhood.

"More firebrands!" yelled the men who held that corner of the wing. "Firebrands! Where is Langur Dass?"

But instead of firebrands that would have frightened beast and aided men, Langur Dass stepped out from behind a tree and beat at the heads of the right-wing guards with a bamboo cane that whistled and whacked and scattered them in panic, yelling the while—"Muztagh! Oh, my Muztagh! Here is an opening, Muztagh, come!"

And Muztagh came—trumpeting—crashing like an avalanche, with Langur Dass hard after him, afraid, now that he had done the trick. And hot on the trail of Langur Dass ran Ahmad Din, with his knife drawn.

But it was not written that that knife should enter the flesh of Langur Dass.

An elephant never forgets. Muztagh turned back two paces and struck with his trunk. Ahmad Din was knocked aside as the wind whips a straw.

For an instant elephant and man stood front to front. To the left of them the gate of the stockade dropped shut behind the herd. The elephant stood with trunk slightly lifted, the long-haired man, who had saved him, stood lifting upstretched arms.

Langur Dass spoke to my lord the elephant. "Take me with thee, Muztagh! Thou and I are not of the world of men, but of the jungle, and the rain, the silence and the cold touch of rivers. We are brothers—and wilt thou leave me here to die?"

The elephant slowly turned his head, and saw the group of beaters who were bearing down on Langur Dass, murder shining no less from their knives than from their lighted eyes.

"Take me," pleaded the old man. "Thy herd is gone!"

The elephant knew what he was asking. He had lifted him to his shoulders many times in the last days of his service. This was not one of the man-herd that stood pleading to him. It was one of his own jungle people, deep in his heart as he had always known. With one motion light as air, he swung Langur Dass gently to his shoulder.

The jungle, vast and mysterious and still, closed its gates behind them.


*Bonie Doon*

YE FLOWERY banks o' bonie Doon,
   How can ye blume sae fair?
How can ye chant, ye little birds,
   And I sae fu' o' care?

Thou'll break my heart, thou bonie bird,
   That sings upon the bough;
Thou minds me o' the happy days,
   When my fause luve was true.

Thou'll break my heart, thou bonie bird,
   That sings beside thy mate;
For sae I sat, and sae I sang,
   And wist na o' my fate.

Aft hae I roved by bonie Doon
   To see the woodbine twine,
And ilka bird sang o' its luve
   And sae did I o' mine.

With lightsome heart I pu'd a rose
   Frae aff its thorny tree;
And my fause luver staw my rose
   But left the thorn wi' me.

                *Robert Burns*

# THE WINDS OF HEAVEN

## Richard Jefferies

*The son of a poor English farmer, Richard Jefferies (1848–1887), against great odds, educated himself, determined to become an author. He wrote for the local newspapers, then for magazines, and later published several novels. His finest work, however, was the nature essay, of which he wrote many volumes. Like the American, John Burroughs, Jefferies turned more and more from poetic writing about the beauties of nature to scientific reporting, combining both skills admirably.*

THE window rattled, the gate swung; a leaf rose, and the kitten chased it, 'whoo-oo'—the faintest sound in the keyhole. I looked up, and saw the feathers on a sparrow's breast ruffled for an instant. It was quiet for some time; after a while it came again with heavier purpose. The folded shutters shook; the latch of the kitchen door rattled as if someone were lifting it and dropped it; indefinite noises came from upstairs: there was a hand in the house moving everything. Another pause. The kitten was curled up on the window-ledge outside in the sunshine, just as the sleek cats curled up in the warmth at Thebes of old Egypt five or six thousand years ago; the sparrow was happy at the rose tree; a bee was happy on a broad dandelion disc. 'Soo-hoo!'—a low whistle came through the chink; a handful of rain was flung at the window; a great shadow rushed up the valley and strode the house in an instant as you would get over a stile. I put down my book and buttoned my coat. Soo-hoo! the wind was here and the cloud—soo-hoo! drawing out longer and more plaintive in the thin mouthpiece of the chink. The cloud had no more rain in it, but it shut out the sun; and all that afternoon and all that night the low plaint of the wind continued in sorrowful hopelessness, and little sounds ran about the floors and round the rooms.

Still soo-hoo all the next day and sunlessness, turning the mind, through work and conversation, to pensive notes. At even the edge of the cloud lifted over the forest hill westwards, and a yellow glow, the great beacon fire of the sun, burned out, a conflagration at the verge of the world. In the night, awakening gently as one who is whispered to—listen! Ah! all the orchestra is at work—the keyhole, the chink, and the chimney; whoo-hooing in the keyhole, whistling shrill whew-w-w! in the chink, moaning long and deep in the chimney. Over in the field the row of pines was sighing; the wind lingered and clung to the close foliage, and each needle of the million million leaflets drew its tongue across the organ blast. A countless multitude of sighs made one continued distant undertone to the wild roar of the gable close at hand. Something seemed to be running with innumerable centipede feet over the mouth of the chimney, for the long deep moan, as I listened, resolved itself into a quick succession of touches, just as you might play with your finger-tips fifty times a second tattooing on the hollow table. In the midst of the clangour, the hearing settled down to the sighing of the pines, which drew the mind towards it, and soothed the senses to sleep.

Towards dawn, awake again—another change: the battering-ram at work now against the walls. Swinging back, the solid thickness of the wind came forward—crush! as the iron-shod ram's head hanging from its chains rushed to the tower. Crush! It sucked back again as if there had been a vacuum—a moment's silence, and crush! Blow after blow—the floor heaved; the walls were ready to come together—alternate sucking back and heavy billowy advance. Crush! crush! Blow after blow, heave and batter and hoist, as if it would tear the house up by the roots. Forty miles that battering-ram wind had travelled without so much as a bough to check it till it struck the house on the hill. Thud! thud! as if it were iron and not air. I looked from the window, and the bright morning star was shining—the sky was full of the wind and the star. As light came, the thud, thud sank away, and nothing remained but the whoo-hoo-hoo of the keyhole and the moan of the chimney. These did not leave us; for four day and nights the whoo-hoo-hoo-whoo never ceased a moment. Whoo-hoo! whoo! and this is the wind on the hill indoors.

Out of doors, sometimes in the morning, deep in the valley, over the tree-tops of the forest, there stays a vapour, lit up within by sunlight. A glory hovers over the oaks—a cloud of light hundreds of feet thick, the air made visible by surcharge and heaviness of sunbeams, pressed together till you can see them in themselves and not reflected. The cloud slants down the sloping wood, till in a moment it is gone, and the beams are now focussed in the depth of the narrow valley. The mirror has been tilted, and the glow has shifted; in a moment more it has vanished into space, and the dream has gone from the wood. In the arms of the wind, vast bundles of mist are borne against the hill; they widen and slip, and lengthen, drawing out; the wind works quickly with moist colours ready and a wide brush laying broadly. Colour comes up in the wind; the thin mist disappears, drunk up in the grass and trees, and the air is full of blue behind the vapour. Blue sky at the far horizon—rich deep blue overhead—a dark-brown blue deep yonder in the gorge among the trees. I feel a sense of blue colour as I face the strong breeze; the vibration and blow of its force answer to that hue, the sound of the swinging branches and the rush-rush in the grass is azure in its note; it is wind-blue, not the night-blue, or heaven-blue, a colour of air. To see the colour of the air it needs great space like this—a vastness of concavity and hollow—an equal cauldron of valley and plain under, to the dome of the sky over, for no vessel of earth and sky is too large for the air-colour to fill. Thirty, forty, and more miles of eye-sweep, and beyond that the limitless expanse over the sea—the thought of the eye knows no butt, shooting on with stellar penetration into the unknown. In a small space there seems a vacuum, and nothing between you and the hedge opposite, or even across the valley; in a great space the void is filled, and the wind touches the sight like a thing tangible. The air becomes itself a cloud, and is coloured—recognized as a thing suspended; something real exists between you and the horizon. Now full of sun, and now of shade, the air-cloud rests in the expanse.

It is summer, and the wind-birds top the furze; the bright stone-chat, velvet-black and red and white, sits on the highest spray of the gorse, as if he were painted there. He is always in the wind on the hill, from the hail of April to August's dry glow. All the mile-long slope of the hill under me is purple-clad with heath down to the tree-filled gorge where the green boughs seem to join the purple. The corn-fields and the pastures of the plain—count them one by one till the hedges and squares close together and cannot be separated. The surface of the earth melts away as if the eyes insensibly shut and grew dreamy in gazing, as the soft clouds melt and lose their outline at the horizon. But dwelling there, the glance slowly finds and fills out something that interposes its existence between us and the further space. Too shadowy for the substance of a cloud, too delicate for outline against the sky, fainter than haze, something of which the eye has consciousness, but cannot put into a word to itself. Something is there. It is the air-cloud adhering like a summer garment to the great downs by the sea. I cannot see the substance of the hills nor their exact curve along the sky; all I can see is the air that has thickened and taken to itself form about them. The atmosphere has collected as the shadow collects in the distant corner of a room—it is the shadow of the summer wind. At times it is so soft, so little more than the air at hand, that I almost fancy I can look through the solid boundary. There is no cloud so faint; the great hills are but a thought at the horizon; I *think* them there rather than see them; if I were not thinking of them, I should scarce know there was even a haze, with so dainty a hand does the atmosphere throw its covering over the massy downs. Riding or passing quickly perhaps you would not observe them; but stay among the heath-bells, and the sketch appears in the south. Up from the sea over the corn-fields, through the green boughs of the forest, along the slope, comes a breath of wind, of honey-sweetened air, made more delicate by the fanning of a thousand wings.

The labour of the wind: the cymbals of the aspen clashing, from the lowest to the highest bough, each leaf twirling first forwards and then backwards and swinging to and fro, a double motion. Each lifts a little and falls back like a pendulum, twisting on itself; and as it rises and sinks, strikes its fellow-leaf. Striking the side of the dark pines, the wind changes their colour and turns them paler. The oak leaves slide one over the other, hand above hand, laying shadow upon shadow upon the white road. In the vast net of the wide elm-tops the drifting shadow of the cloud which the wind brings is caught for a moment. Pushing aside the stiff ranks of the wheat with both arms, the air reaches the sun-parched earth. It walks among the mowing-grass like a farmer feeling the crop with his hand one side, and opening it with his walking-stick the other. It rolls the wavelets carelessly as marbles to the shore; the red cattle redden the pool and stand in their own colour. The green caterpillar swings as he spins his thread and lengthens his cable to the tide of air, descending from the tree; before he can slip it the white-throat takes him. With a thrust the wind hurls the swift fifty miles faster on his way; it ruffles back the black velvet of the mole peeping forth from his burrow. Apple bloom and crab-apple bloom have been blown long since athwart the furrows over the orchard wall; May petals and June roses scattered; the pollen and the seeds of the meadow-grasses thrown on the threshing-floor of earth in basketfuls. Thistle-down and dandelion-down, the brown down of the goat's-beard; by and by the keys of the sycamores twirling aslant—the wind carries them all on its back, gossamer web and great heron's vanes—the same weight to the wind; the drops of the waterfall blown aside sprinkle the bright green ferns. The voice of the cuckoo in his season travels on the zephyr, and the note comes to the most distant hill, and deep into the deepest wood.

The light and fire of summer are made beautiful by the air, without whose breath the glorious summer were all spoiled. Thick are the hawthorn leaves, many deep on the spray; and beneath them is a twisted and intertangled winding in and out of boughs, such as no curious ironwork of ancient artist could equal; through the leaves and metalwork of boughs the soft west wind wanders at its ease. Wild wasp and tutored bee sing sideways on their course as the breeze fills their vanes; with broad coloured sails boomed out, the butterfly drifts a-lee. Beside a brown-coated stone in the shadowed stream a brown trout watches for the puffs that slay the mayflies. Their ephemeral wings were made for a more exquisite life; they endure but one sun; they bear not the touch of the water; they die like a dream dropping into the river. To the amethyst in the deep ditch the wind comes; no petal so hidden under green it cannot find; to the blue hill-flower up by the sky; it lifts the guilty head of the passionate poppy that has sinned in the sun for love. Sweet in the rain the wind brings to the wallflower browned in the heat, a-dry on the crumbling stone. Pleasant the sunbeams to the marigold when the wind has carried the rain away and his sun-disc glows on the bank. Acres of perfume come on the wind from the black and white of the bean-field; the firs fill the air by the copse with perfume. I know nothing to which the wind has not some happy use. Is there a grain of dust so small the wind shall not find it out? Ground in the mill-wheel of the centuries, the iron of the distant mountain floats like gossamer, and is drunk up as dew by leaf and living lung. A thousand miles of cloud go by from morn till night, passing overhead without a sound; the immense packs, a mile square, succeed to each other, side by side, laid parallel, book-shape, coming up from the horizon and widening as they approach. From morn till night the silent footfalls of the ponderous vapours travel overhead, no sound, no creaking of the wheels and rattling of the chains; it is calm at the earth, but the wind labours without an effort above, with such ease, with such power. Grey smoke hangs on the hillside where the couch-heaps are piled, a cumulus of smoke; the wind comes, and it draws its length along like the genii from the earthen pot; there leaps up a great red flame shaking its head; it shines in the bright sunlight; you can see it across the valley.

### November in England

No sun—no moon!
　　No morn—no noon!
No dawn—no dusk—no proper time of day—
No sky—no earthly view—
No distance looking blue—
No road—no street—no "t'other side the way"—
No end to any "Row"—
No indications where the Crescents go—
No top to any steeple—
No recognitions of familiar people—
No courtesies for showing 'em—
No knowing 'em!
No travelling at all—no locomotion,
No inkling of the way—no notion—
"No go"—by land or ocean—
No mail—no post—
No news from any foreign coast—
No park—no ring—no afternoon gentility—
No company—no nobility—
No warmth, no cheerfulness, no healthful ease,
No comfortable feel in any member—
No shade, no shine, no butterflies, no bees,
No fruits, no flowers, no leaves, no birds,
November!

*Thomas Hood*

# WINTER AT WALDEN

## Henry David Thoreau

*There has never been anyone to match Thoreau (1817–1862), who, besides being poet, naturalist, and philosopher, was a very individual individualist. He studied at Harvard, taught school, helped make pencils in his father's factory, and served as general handyman to Ralph Waldo Emerson. But the most important event in his life was the building of a shack on the shores of Walden Pond, near Concord, Massachusetts, where he lived alone in the woods for more than two years. Here he figured out a simple life for himself, and observed the animals and natural things around him, reporting his experiences in his masterpiece,* Walden, or Life in the Woods, *from which these chapters are taken.*

WHEN the ponds were firmly frozen, they afforded not only new and shorter routes to many points, but new views from their surfaces of the familiar landscape around them. When I crossed Flint's Pond, after it was covered with snow, though I had often paddled about and skated over it, it was so unexpectedly wide and so strange that I could think of nothing but Baffin's Bay. The Lincoln hills rose up around me at the extremity of a snowy plain, in which I did not remember to have stood before; and the fishermen, at an indeterminable distance over the ice, moving slowly about with their wolfish dogs, passed for sealers or Esquimaux, or in misty weather loomed like fabulous creatures, and I did not know whether they were giants or pigmies. I took this course when I went to lecture in Lincoln in the evening, travelling in no road and passing no house between my own hut and the lecture-room. In Goose Pond, which lay in my way, a colony of musk-rats dwelt, and raised their cabins high above the ice, though none could be seen abroad when I crossed it. Walden, being like the rest usually bare of snow, or with only shallow and interrupted drifts on it, was

my yard where I could walk freely when the snow was nearly two
feet deep on a level elsewhere and the villagers were confined to
their streets. There, far from the village street, and, except at very
long intervals, from the jingle of sleigh-bells, I slid and skated, as in
a vast moose-yard well trodden, overhung by oak woods and solemn pines bent down with snow or bristling with icicles.

For sounds in winter nights, and often in winter days, I heard
the forlorn but melodious notes of a hooting owl indefinitely far;
such a sound as the frozen earth would yield if struck with a suitable plectrum, the very *lingua vernacula* of Walden Wood, and
quite familiar to me at last, though I never saw the bird while it was
making it. I seldom opened my door in a winter evening without
hearing it; *Hoo hoo hoo, hoorer hoo*, sounded sonorously, and the
first three syllables accented somewhat like *how der do;* or sometimes *hoo hoo* only. One night in the beginning of winter, before
the pond froze over, about nine o'clock, I was startled by the loud
honking of a goose, and, stepping to the door, heard the sound of
their wings like a tempest in the woods as they flew low over my
house. They passed over the pond toward Fair-Haven, seemingly
deterred from settling by my light, their commodore honking all
the while with a regular beat. Suddenly an unmistakable cat-owl
from very near me, with the most harsh and tremendous voice I
ever heard from any inhabitant of the woods, responded at regular
intervals to the goose, as if determined to expose and disgrace this
intruder from Hudson's Bay by exhibiting a greater compass and
volume of voice in a native, and *boo-hoo* him out of Concord
horizon. What do you mean by alarming the citadel at this time of
night consecrated to me? Do you think I am ever caught napping
at such an hour, and that I have not got lungs and a larynx as well
as yourself? *Boo-hoo, boo-hoo, boo-hoo!* It was one of the most
thrilling discords I ever heard. And yet, if you had a discriminating
ear, there were in it the elements of a concord such as these plains
never saw nor heard.

I also heard the whooping of the ice in the pond, my great bed-
fellow in that part of Concord, as if it were restless in its bed and
would fain turn over—were troubled with flatulency and bad
dreams; or I was waked by the cracking of the ground by the frost,
as if some one had driven a team against my door, and in the morning would find a crack in the earth a quarter of a mile long and a
third of an inch wide.

Sometimes I heard the foxes as they ranged over the snow crust, in moonlight nights, in search of a partridge or other game, barking raggedly and demoniacally like forest dogs, as if labouring with some anxiety, or seeking expression, struggling for light and to be dogs outright and run freely in the streets; for if we take the ages into our account, may there not be a civilisation going on among brutes as well as men? They seemed to me to be rudimental, burrowing men, still standing on their defence, awaiting their transformation. Sometimes one came near to my window, attracted by my light, barked a vulpine curse at me, and then retreated.

Usually the red squirrel (*Sciurus Hudsonius*) waked me in the dawn, coursing over the roof and up and down the sides of the house, as if sent out of the woods for this purpose. In the course of the winter I threw out half a bushel of ears of sweet-corn, which had not got ripe, on to the snow crust by my door, and was amused by watching the motions of the various animals which were baited by it. In the twilight and the night the rabbits came regularly and made a hearty meal. All day long the red squirrels came and went, and afforded me much entertainment by their manœuvres. One would approach at first warily through the shrub-oaks, running over the snow crust by fits and starts like a leaf blown by the wind, now a few paces this way, with wonderful speed and waste of energy, making inconceivable haste with his "trotters," as if it were for a wager, and now as many paces that way, but never getting on more than half a rod at a time; and then suddenly pausing with a ludicrous expression and a gratuitous somerset, as if all the eyes in the universe were fixed on him,—for all the motions of a squirrel, even in the most solitary recesses of the forest, imply spectators as much as those of a dancing girl,—wasting more time in delay and circumspection than would have sufficed to walk the whole distance,—I never saw one walk,—and then suddenly, before you could say Jack Robinson, he would be in the top of a young pitch-pine, winding up his clock and chiding all imaginary spectators, soliloquising and talking to all the universe at the same time,—for no reason that I could ever detect, or he himself was aware of, I suspect. At length he would reach the corn, and selecting a suitable ear, brisk about in the same uncertain trigonometrical way to the topmost stick of my wood-pile, before my window, where he looked me in the face, and there sit for hours, supplying himself with a new ear from time to time, nibbling at first voraciously and throwing the half-naked cobs about; till at length he grew more dainty still and played with his food, tasting only the inside of the kernel, and the ear, which was held balanced over the stick by one paw, slipped from his careless grasp and fell to the ground, when he would look over at it with a ludicrous expression of uncertainty, as if suspecting that it had life, with a mind not made up whether to get it again, or a new one, or be off; now thinking of corn, then listening to hear what was in the wind. So the little impudent fellow would waste many an ear in a forenoon; till at last, seizing some longer and plumper one, considerably bigger than himself, and skilfully balancing it, he would set out with it to the woods, like a tiger with a buffalo, by the same zig-zag course and frequent pauses, scratching along with it as if it were too heavy for him and falling all the while, making its fall a diagonal between a perpendicular and horizontal, being determined to put it through at any rate;—a singularly frivolous and whimsical fellow;—and so he would get off with it to where he lived, perhaps carry it to the top of a pine tree forty or fifty rods distant, and I would afterwards find the cobs strewn about the woods in various directions.

At length the jays arrive, whose discordant screams were heard long before, as they were warily making their approach an eighth of a mile off, and in a stealthy and sneaking manner they flit from tree to tree, nearer and nearer, and pick up the kernels which the squirrels have dropped. Then, sitting on a pitch-pine bough, they attempt to swallow in their haste a kernel which is too big for their throats and chokes them; and after great labour they disgorge it, and spend an hour in the endeavour to crack it by repeated blows with their bills. They were manifestly thieves, and I had not much respect for them; but the squirrels, though at first shy, went to work as if they were taking what was their own.

Meanwhile also came the chickadees in flocks, which, picking up the crumbs the squirrels had dropped, flew to the nearest twig, and, placing them under their claws, hammered away at them with their little bills, as if it were an insect in the bark, till they were sufficiently reduced for their slender throats. A little flock of these titmice came daily to pick a dinner out of my wood-pile, or the crumbs at my door, with faint, flitting, lisping notes, like the tinkling of icicles in the grass, or else with sprightly *day, day, day,* or more rarely, in spring-like days, a wiry summery *phe-be* from the wood-side. They were so familiar that at length one alighted on an armful of wood which I was carrying in and pecked at the sticks without fear. I once had a sparrow alight upon my shoulder for a moment while I was hoeing in a village garden, and I felt that I was more distinguished by that circumstance than I should have been by any epaulet I could have worn. The squirrels also grew at last to be quite familiar, and occasionally stepped upon my shoe, when that was the nearest way.

When the ground was not yet quite covered, and again near the end of winter, when the snow was melted on my south hill-side and about my wood-pile, the partridges came out of the woods morning and evening to feed there. Whichever side you walk in the woods the partridge bursts away on whirring wings, jarring the snow from the dry leaves and twigs on high, which comes sifting down in the sunbeams like golden dust, for this brave bird is not to be scared by winter. It is frequently covered up by drifts, and, it is said, "sometimes plunges from on wing into the soft snow, where it remains concealed for a day or two." I used to start them in the open land also, where they had come out of the woods at sunset to "bud" the wild apple trees. They will come regularly every evening to particular trees, where the cunning sportsman lies in wait for them, and the distant orchards next the woods suffer thus not a little. I am glad that the partridge gets fed, at any rate. It is Nature's own bird, which lives on buds and diet-drink.

In dark winter mornings, or in short winter afternoons, I sometimes heard a pack of hounds threading all the woods with hounding cry and yelp, unable to resist the instinct of the chase, and the note of the hunting-horn at intervals, proving that man was in the rear. The woods ring again, and yet no fox bursts forth on to the open level of the pond, nor following pack pursuing their Actæon. And perhaps at evening I see the hunters returning with a single brush trailing from their sleigh for a trophy, seeking their inn. They tell me that if the fox would remain in the bosom of the frozen earth he would be safe, or if he would run in a straight line away no fox-hound could overtake him; but, having left his pursuers far behind, he stops to rest and listen till they come up, and when he runs he circles round to his old haunts, where the hunters await him. Sometimes, however, he will run upon a wall many rods, and then leap off far to one side, and he appears to know that water will not retain his scent. A hunter told me that he once saw a fox pursued by hounds burst out on to Walden when the ice was covered with shallow puddles, run part way across, and then return to the same shore. Ere long the hounds arrived, but here they lost the scent. Sometimes a pack hunting by themselves would pass my door, and circle round my house, and yelp and hound without regarding me, as if afflicted by a species of madness, so that nothing could divert them from the pursuit. Thus they circle until they fall upon the recent trail of a fox, for a wise hound will forsake everything else for this. One day a man came to my hut from Lexington to inquire after his hound that made a large track, and had been hunting for a week by himself. But I fear that he was not the wiser for all I told him, for every time I attempted to answer his questions he interrupted me by asking, "What do you do here?" He had lost a dog, but found a man.

One old hunter who has a dry tongue, who used to come to bathe in Walden once every year when the water was warmest, and at such times looked in upon me, told me, that many years ago he took his gun one afternoon and went out for a cruise in Walden Wood; and as he walked the Wayland road he heard the cry of hounds approaching, and ere long a fox leaped the wall into the road, and as quick as thought leaped the other wall out of the road, and his swift bullet had not touched him. Some way behind came an old hound and her three pups in full pursuit, hunting on their own account, and disappeared again in the woods. Late in the afternoon, as he was resting in the thick woods south of Walden, he heard the voice of the hounds far over toward Fair-Haven still pursuing the fox; and on they came, their hounding cry, which made all the woods ring, sounding nearer and nearer, now from Well-Meadow, now from the Baker Farm. For a long time he stood still and listened to their music, so sweet to a hunter's ear, when suddenly the fox appeared, threading the solemn aisles with an easy coursing pace, whose sound was concealed by a sympathetic rustle of the leaves, swift and still, keeping the ground, leaving his pursuers far behind; and leaping upon a rock amid the woods, he sat erect and listening, with his back to the hunter. For a moment compassion restrained the latter's arm; but that was a short-lived mood, and as quick as thought can follow thought his piece was levelled, and *whang!*—the fox rolling over the rock lay dead on the ground. The hunter still kept his place and listened to the hounds. Still on they came, and now the near woods resounded through all their aisles with their demoniac cry. At length the old hound burst into view with muzzle to the ground, and snapping the air as if possessed, and ran directly to the rock; but spying the dead fox she suddenly ceased her hounding, as if struck dumb with amazement, and walked round and round him in silence; and one by one her pups arrived, and, like their mother, were sobered into silence by the mystery. Then the hunter came forward and stood in their midst, and the mystery was solved. They waited in silence while he skinned the fox, then followed the brush a while, and at length turned off into the woods again. That evening a Weston Squire came to the Concord hunter's cottage to inquire for his hounds, and told how for a week they had been hunting on their own account from Weston woods. The Concord hunter told him what he knew and offered him the skin; but the other declined it and departed. He did not find his hounds that night, but the next day learned that they had crossed the river and put up at a farm-house for the night, whence, having been well fed, they took their departure early in the morning.

The hunter who told me this could remember one Sam Nutting, who used to hunt bears on Fair-Haven Ledges, and exchange their skins for rum in Concord village—who told him, even, that he had seen a moose there. Nutting had a famous fox-hound named Burgoyne—he pronounced it Bugine—which my informant used to borrow. In the "Waste Book" of an old trader of this town, who was also a captain, town-clerk, and representative, I find the following entry:—Jan. 18th, 1742–3, "John Melven Cr. by 1 Grey Fox 0—2—3"; they are not now found here; and in his ledger, Feb. 7th, 1743, Hezekiah Stratton has credit "by ½ a Catt skin 0—1—4½"; of course, a wild-cat, for Stratton was a sergeant in the old French war, and would not have got credit for hunting less noble game. Credit is given for deer-skins also, and they were daily sold. One man still preserves the horns of the last deer that was killed in this vicinity, and another party has told me the particulars of the hunt in which his uncle was engaged. The hunters were formerly a numerous and merry crew here. I remember well one gaunt Nimrod who would catch up a leaf by the roadside, and play a strain on it wilder and more melodious, if my memory serves me, than any hunting-horn.

At midnight, when there was a moon, I sometimes met with hounds in my path prowling about the woods, which would skulk out of my way, as if afraid, and stand silent amid the bushes till I had passed.

Squirrels and wild mice disputed for my store of nuts. There were scores of pitch-pines around my house, from one to four inches in diameter, which had been gnawed by mice the previous winter,—a Norwegian winter for them, for the snow lay long and deep, and they were obliged to mix a large proportion of pine bark

with their other diet. These trees were alive and apparently flourishing at midsummer, and many of them had grown a foot, though
completely girdled; but after another winter such were without
exception dead. It is remarkable that a single mouse should thus be
allowed a whole pine tree for its dinner, gnawing round instead of
up and down it; but perhaps it is necessary in order to thin these
trees, which are wont to grow up densely.

The hares (*Lepus Americanus*) were very familiar. One hid
her form under my house all winter, separated from me only by the
flooring, and she startled me each morning by her hasty departure
when I began to stir,—thump, thump, thump, striking her head
against the floor timbers in her hurry. They used to come round
my door at dusk to nibble the potato parings which I had thrown
out, and were so nearly the colour of the ground that they could
hardly be distinguished when still. Sometimes in the twilight I
alternately lost and recovered sight of one sitting motionless under
my window. When I opened my door in the evening, off they
would go with a squeak and a bounce. Near at hand they only excited my pity. One evening one sat by my door two paces from
me, at first trembling with fear, yet unwilling to move; a poor wee
thing, lean and bony, with ragged ears and sharp nose, scant tail
and slender paws. It looked as if Nature no longer contained the
breed of nobler bloods, but stood on her last toes. Its large eyes
appeared young and unhealthy, almost dropsical. I took a step, and
lo, away it scud with an elastic spring over the snow crust, straight-
ening its body and its limbs into graceful length, and soon put the
forest between me and itself,—the wild free venison, asserting its
vigour and the dignity of Nature. Not without reason was its
slenderness. Such then was its nature. (*Lepus, livipes*, light-foot,
some think.)

What is a country without rabbits and partridges? They are
among the most simple and indigenous animal products; ancient and
venerable families known to antiquity as to modern times; of the
very hue and substance of Nature, nearest allied to leaves and to the
ground,—and to one another; it is either winged or it is legged. It is
hardly as if you had seen a wild creature when a rabbit or a partridge bursts away, only a natural one, as much to be expected as
rustling leaves. The partridge and the rabbit are still sure to thrive,
like true natives of the soil, whatever revolutions occur. If the forest is cut off, the sprouts and bushes which spring up afford them

concealment, and they become more numerous than ever. That must be a poor country indeed that does not support a hare. Our woods teem with them both, and around every swamp may be seen the partridge or rabbit walk, beset with twiggy fences and horse-hair snares, which some cow-boy tends.

### Good-bye

GOOD-BYE, proud world! I'm going home:
Thou art not my friend, and I'm not thine.
Long through thy weary crowds I roam;
A river-ark on the ocean brine,
Long I've been tossed like the driven foam;
But now, proud world! I'm going home.

Good-bye to flattery's fawning face;
To Grandeur with his wise grimace;
To upstart wealth's averted eye;
To supple Office, low and high;
To crowded halls, to court and street;
To frozen hearts and hasting feet;
To those who go, and those who come;
Good-bye, proud world! I'm going home.

I am going to my own hearth stone,
Bosomed in yon green hills alone,—
A secret nook in a pleasant land,
Whose groves the frolic fairies planned;
Where arches green, the livelong day,
Echo the blackbird's roundelay,
And vulgar feet have never trod
A spot that is sacred to thought and God.

O, when I am safe in my sylvan home,
I tread on the pride of Greece and Rome;
And when I am stretched beneath the pines,
Where the evening star so holy shines,
I laugh at the lore and the pride of man,
At the sophist schools, and the learned clan;
For what are they all, in their high conceit,
When man in the bush with God may meet?

*Ralph Waldo Emerson*

# THE POND IN WINTER

## Henry David Thoreau

AFTER a still winter night I awoke with the impression that some question had been put to me, which I had been endeavouring in vain to answer in my sleep, as what—how—when—where? But there was dawning Nature, in whom all creatures live, looking in at my broad windows with serene and satisfied face, and no question on *her* lips. I awoke to an answered question, to Nature and daylight. The snow lying deep on the earth dotted with young pines, and the very slope of the hill on which my house is placed seemed to say, Forward! Nature puts no question, and answers none which we mortals ask. She has long ago taken her resolution. "O Prince, our eyes contemplate with admiration and transmit to the soul the wonderful and varied spectacle of this universe. The night veils without doubt a part of this glorious creation; but day comes to reveal to us this great work, which extends from earth even into the plains of the ether."

Then to my morning work. First I take an axe and pail and go in search of water, if that be not a dream. After a cold and snowy night it needed a divining rod to find it. Every winter the liquid and trembling surface of the pond, which was so sensitive to every breath, and reflected every light and shadow, becomes solid to the depth of a foot or a foot and a half, so that it will support the heaviest teams, and perchance the snow covers it to an equal depth, and it is not to be distinguished from any level field. Like the marmots in the surrounding hills, it closes its eyelids and becomes dormant for three months or more. Standing on the snow-covered plain, as if in a pasture amid the hills, I cut my way first through a foot of snow, and then a foot of ice, and open a window under my feet, where, kneeling to drink, I look down into the quiet parlour of the fishes, pervaded by a softened light as through a window of ground glass, with its bright sanded floor the same as in summer; there a

perennial waveless serenity reigns as in the amber twilight sky,
corresponding to the cool and even temperament of the inhabitants.
Heaven is under our feet as well as over our heads.

Early in the morning, while all things are crisp with frost, men
come with fishing reels and slender lunch, and let down their fine
lines through the snowy field to take pickerel and perch; wild men,
who instinctively follow other fashions and trust other authorities
than their townsmen, and by their goings and comings stitch towns
together in parts where else they would be ripped. They sit and
eat their luncheon in stout fear-naughts on the dry oak leaves on
the shore, as wise in natural lore as the citizen is in artificial. They
never consulted with books, and know and can tell much less than
they have done. The things which they practise are said not yet to
be known. Here is one fishing for pickerel with grown perch for
bait. You look into his pail with wonder as into a summer pond, as
if he kept summer locked up at home, or knew where she had retreated. How, pray, did he get these in mid-winter? Oh, he got
worms out of rotten logs since the ground froze, and so he caught
them. His life itself passes deeper in Nature than the studies of the
naturalist penetrate, himself a subject for the naturalist. The latter
raises the moss and bark gently with his knife in search of insects;
the former lays open logs to their core with his axe, and moss and
bark fly far and wide. He gets his living by barking trees. Such a
man has some right to fish, and I love to see Nature carried out in
him. The perch swallows the grub-worm, the pickerel swallows the
perch, and the fisherman swallows the pickerel; and so all the chinks
in the scale of being are filled.

When I strolled around the pond in misty weather I was sometimes amused by the primitive mode which some ruder fisherman
had adopted. He would perhaps have placed alder branches over
the narrow holes in the ice, which were four or five rods apart and
an equal distance from the shore, and having fastened the end of the
line to a stick to prevent its being pulled through, have passed the
slack line over a twig of the alder, a foot or more above the ice,
and tied a dry oak leaf to it, which, being pulled down, would
show when he had a bite. These alders loomed through the mist
at regular intervals as you walked half-way round the pond.

Ah, the pickerel of Walden! when I see them lying on the ice,
or in the well which the fisherman cuts in the ice, making a little
hole to admit the water, I am always surprised by their rare beauty,
as if they were fabulous fishes, they are so foreign to the streets,

even to the woods, foreign as Arabia to our Concord life. They possess a quite dazzling and transcendent beauty, which separates them by a wide interval from the cadaverous cod and haddock whose fame is trumpeted in our streets. They are not green like the pines, nor grey like the stones, nor blue like the sky; but they have, to my eyes, if possible, yet rarer colours, like flowers and precious stones, as if they were the pearls, the animalised *nuclei* or crystals of the Walden water. They, of course, are Walden all over and all through; are themselves small Waldens in the animal kingdom, Waldenses. It is surprising that they are caught here,—that in this deep and capacious spring, far beneath the rattling teams and chaises and tinkling sleighs that travel the Walden road, this great gold and emerald fish swims. I never chanced to see its kind in any market; it would be the cynosure of all eyes there. Easily, with a few convulsive quirks, they give up their watery ghosts, like a mortal translated before his time to the thin air of heaven.

As I was desirous to recover the long lost bottom of Walden Pond, I surveyed it carefully, before the ice broke up, early in '46, with compass and chain and sounding line. There have been many stories told about the bottom, or rather no bottom, of this pond, which certainly had no foundation for themselves. It is remarkable how long men will believe in the bottomlessness of a pond without taking the trouble to sound it. I have visited two such Bottomless Ponds in one walk in this neighbourhood. Many have believed that Walden reached quite through to the other side of the globe. Some who have lain flat on the ice for a long time, looking down through the illusive medium, perchance with watery eyes into the bargain, and driven to hasty conclusions by the fear of catching cold in their breasts, have seen vast holes "into which a load of hay might be driven," if there were anybody to drive it, the undoubted source of the Styx and entrance to the Infernal Regions from these parts. Others have gone down from the village with a "fifty-six" and a waggon load of inch rope, but yet have failed to find any bottom; for while the "fifty-six" was resting by the way, they were paying out the rope in the vain attempt to fathom their truly immeasurable capacity for marvellousness. But I can assure my readers that Walden has a reasonably tight bottom at a not unreasonable, though at an unusual depth. I fathomed it easily with a cod-line and a stone weighing about a pound and a-half, and could tell accurately when the stone left the bottom, by having to pull so much harder before the water got underneath to help me. The greatest depth was exactly one hundred and two feet; to which may be added the five feet which it has risen since, making one hundred and seven. This is a remarkable depth for so small an area; yet not an inch of it can be spared by the imagination. What if all ponds were shallow? Would it not react on the minds of men? I am thankful that this pond was made deep and pure for a symbol. While men believe in the infinite, some ponds will be thought to be bottomless.

A factory owner, hearing what depth I had found, thought that it could not be true, for, judging from his acquaintance with dams, sand would not lie at so steep an angle. But the deepest ponds are not so deep in proportion to their area as most suppose, and, if drained, would not leave very remarkable valleys. They are not like cups between the hills; for this one, which is so unusually deep for its area, appears in a vertical section through its centre not deeper than a shallow plate. Most ponds, emptied, would leave a meadow no more hollow than we frequently see. William Gilpin, who is so admirable in all that relates to landscapes, and usually so correct, standing at the head of Loch Fyne, in Scotland, which he describes as "a bay of salt water, sixty or seventy fathoms deep, four miles in breadth," and about fifty miles long, surrounded by mountains, observes, "If we could have seen it immediately after the diluvian crash, or whatever convulsion of Nature occasioned it, before the waters gushed in, what a horrid chasm it must have appeared!

> " 'So high as heaved the tumid hills, so low
>   Down sunk a hollow bottom, broad, and deep,
>   Capacious bed of waters.—' "

But if, using the shortest diameter of Loch Fyne, we apply these proportions to Walden, which, as we have seen, appears already in a vertical section only like a shallow plate, it will appear four times as shallow. So much for the *increased* horrors of the chasm of Loch Fyne when emptied. No doubt many a smiling valley with its stretching corn-fields occupies exactly such a "horrid chasm," from which the waters have receded, though it requires the insight and the far sight of the geologist to convince the unsuspecting inhabitants of this fact. Often an inquisitive eye may detect the shores of a primitive lake in the low horizon hills, and no subsequent elevation of the plain has been necessary to conceal their history. But

it is easiest, as they who work on the highways know, to find the
hollows by the puddles after a shower. The amount of it is, the
imagination, give it the least license, dives deeper and soars higher
than Nature goes. So, probably, the depth of the ocean will be
found to be very inconsiderable compared with its breadth.

As I sounded through the ice I could determine the shape of the
bottom with greater accuracy than is possible in surveying harbours which do not freeze over, and I was surprised at its general
regularity. In the deepest part there are several acres more level
than almost any field which is exposed to the sun, wind, and plough.
In one instance, on a line arbitrarily chosen, the depth did not vary
more than one foot in thirty rods; and generally, near the middle, I
could calculate the variation of each one hundred feet in any direction beforehand within three or four inches. Some are accustomed
to speak of deep and dangerous holes even in quiet sandy ponds like
this, but the effect of water under these circumstances is to level all
inequalities. The regularity of the bottom and its comformity to
the shores and the range of the neighbouring hills were so perfect
that a distant promontory betrayed itself in the soundings quite
across the pond, and its direction could be determined by observing
the opposite shore. Cape becomes bar, and plain shoal, and valley
and gorge deep water and channel.

When I had mapped the pond by the scale of ten rods to an inch,
and put down the soundings, more than a hundred in all, I observed
this remarkable coincidence. Having noticed that the number indi-
cating the greatest depth was apparently in the centre of the map, I
laid a rule on the map lengthwise, and then breadthwise, and found,
to my surprise, that the line of greatest length intersected the line
of greatest breadth *exactly* at the point of the greatest depth, notwithstanding that the middle is so nearly level, the outline of the
pond far from regular, and the extreme length and breadth were
got by measuring into the coves; and I said to myself, Who knows
but this hint would conduct to the deepest part of the ocean as
well as of a pond or puddle? Is not this the rule also for the height
of mountains, regarded as the opposite of valleys? We know that a
hill is not highest at its narrowest part.

Of five coves, three, or all which had been sounded, were observed to have a bar quite across their mouths and deeper water
within, so that the bay tended to be an expansion of water within
the land not only horizontally but vertically, and to form a basin
or independent pond, the direction of the two capes showing the

course of the bar. Every harbour on the sea-coast, also, has its bar at its entrance. In proportion as the mouth of the cove was wider compared with its length, the water over the bar was deeper compared with that in the basin. Given, then, the length and breadth of the cove, and the character of the surrounding shore, and you have almost elements enough to make out a formula for all cases.

In order to see how nearly I could guess, with this experience, at the deepest point in a pond, by observing the outlines of its surface and the character of its shores alone, I made a plan of White Pond, which contains about forty-one acres, and, like this, has no island in it, nor any visible inlet or outlet; and as the line of greatest breadth fell very near the line of least breadth, where two opposite capes approached each other and two opposite bays receded, I ventured to mark a point a short distance from the latter line, but still on the line of greatest length, as the deepest. The deepest part was found to be within one hundred feet of this, still farther in the direction to which I had inclined, and was only one foot deeper, namely, sixty feet. Of course a stream running through, or an island in the pond, would make the problem much more complicated.

If we knew all the laws of Nature, we should need only one fact, or the description of one actual phenomenon, to infer all the particular results at that point. Now we know only a few laws, and our result is vitiated, not, of course, by any confusion or irregularity in Nature, but by our ignorance of essential elements in the calculation. Our notions of law and harmony are commonly confined to those instances which we detect; but the harmony which results from a far greater number of seemingly conflicting, but really concurring, laws, which we have not detected, is still more wonderful. The particular laws are as our points of view, as, to the traveller, a mountain outline varies with every step, and it has an infinite number of profiles, though absolutely but one form. Even when cleft or bored through it is not comprehended in its entireness.

What I have observed of the pond is no less true in ethics. It is the law of average. Such a rule of the two diameters not only guides us toward the sun in the system and the heart in man, but draw lines through the length and breadth of the aggregate of a man's particular daily behaviours and waves of life into his coves and inlets, and where they intersect will be the height or depth of his character. Perhaps we need only to know how his shores trend and his adjacent country or circumstances, to infer his depth and concealed bottom. If he is surrounded by mountainous circumstances, an

Achillean shore, whose peaks overshadow and are reflected in his bosom, they suggest a corresponding depth in him. But a low and smooth shore proves him shallow on that side. In our bodies, a bold projecting brow falls off to and indicates a corresponding depth of thought. Also there is a bar across the entrance of our every cove, or particular inclination; each is our harbour for a season, in which we are detained and partially land-locked. These inclinations are not whimsical usually, but their form, size, and direction are determined by the promontories of the shore, the ancient axis of elevation. When this bar is gradually increased by storms, tides, or currents, or there is a subsidence of the waters, so that it reaches to the surface, that which was at first but an inclination in the shore in which a thought was harboured becomes an individual lake, cut off from the ocean, wherein the thought secures its own conditions, changes, perhaps, from salt to fresh, becomes a sweet sea, dead sea, or a marsh. At the advent of each individual into this life, may we not suppose that such a bar has risen to the surface somewhere? It is true, we are such poor navigators that our thoughts, for the most part, stand off and on upon a harbourless coast, are conversant only with the bights of the bays of poesy, or steer for the public ports of entry, and go into the dry docks of science, where they merely refit for this world, and no natural currents concur to individualise them.

As for the inlet or outlet of Walden, I have not discovered any but rain and snow and evaporation, though perhaps, with a thermometer and a line, such places may be found, for where water flows into the pond it will probably be coldest in summer and warmest in winter. When the icemen were at work here in '46-7, the cakes sent to the shore were one day rejected by those who were stacking them up there, not being thick enough to lie side by side with the rest; and the cutters thus discovered that the ice over a small space was two or three inches thinner than elsewhere, which made them think that there was an inlet there. They also showed me in another place what they thought was a "leach hole," through which the pond leaked out under a hill into a neighbouring meadow, pushing me out on a cake of ice to see it. It was a small cavity under ten feet of water; but I think that I can warrant the pond not to need soldering till they find a worse leak than that. One has suggested that if such a "leach hole" should be found, its connection with the meadow might be proved by conveying some coloured powder or sawdust to the mouth of the hole, and then putting a strainer over the spring in the meadow, which would catch some of the particles carried through by the current.

While I was surveying, the ice, which was sixteen inches thick, undulated under a slight wind like water. It is well known that a level cannot be used on ice. At one rod from the shore its greatest fluctuation, when observed by means of a level on land directed toward a graduated staff on the ice, was three-quarters of an inch, though the ice appeared firmly attached to the shore. It was probably greater in the middle. Who knows but if our instruments were delicate enough we might detect an undulation in the crust of the earth? When two legs of my level were on the shore and the third on the ice, and the sights were directed over the latter, a rise or fall of the ice of an almost infinitesimal amount made a difference of several feet on a tree across the pond. When I began to cut holes for sounding, there were three or four inches of water on the ice under a deep snow which had sunk it thus far; but the water began immediately to run into these holes, and continued to run for two days in deep streams, which wore away the ice on every side, and contributed essentially, if not mainly, to dry the surface of the pond; for, as the water ran in, it raised and floated the ice. This was somewhat like cutting a hole in the bottom of a ship to let the water out. When such holes freeze, and a rain succeeds, and finally a new freezing forms a fresh smooth ice over all, it is beautifully mottled internally by dark figures, shaped somewhat like a spider's web, what you may call ice rosettes, produced by the channels worn by the water flowing from all sides to a centre. Sometimes, also, when the ice was covered with shallow puddles, I saw a double shadow of myself, one standing on the head of the other—one on the ice, the other on the trees or hill-side.

While yet it is cold January, and snow and ice are thick and solid, the prudent landlord comes from the village to get ice to cool his summer drink; impressively, even pathetically wise, to foresee the heat and thirst of July now in January,—wearing a thick coat and mittens! when so many things are not provided for. It may be that he lays up no treasures in this world which will cool his summer drink in the next. He cuts and saws the solid pond, unroofs the house of fishes, and carts off their very element and air, held fast by chains and stakes like corded wood through the favouring winter air, to wintry cellars, to underlie the summer there. It looks like solidified azure, as, far off, it is drawn through the streets. These ice-cutters are a merry race, full of jest and sport, and when I went among them they were wont to invite me to saw pit-fashion with them, I standing underneath.

In the winter of '46–7 there came a hundred men of Hyperborean extraction swoop down on to our pond one morning, with many car-loads of ungainly-looking farming tools, sleds, ploughs, drill-barrows, turf-knives, spades, saws, rakes, and each man was armed with a double-pointed pike-staff, such as is not described in the "New-England Farmer" or the "Cultivator." I did not know whether they had come to sow a crop of winter rye, or some other kind of grain recently introduced from Iceland. As I saw no manure, I judged that they meant to skim the land, as I had done, thinking the soil was deep and had lain fallow long enough. They said that a gentleman farmer, who was behind the scenes, wanted to double his money, which, as I understood, amounted to half a million already; but in order to cover each one of his dollars with another, he took off the only coat, ay, the skin itself, of Walden Pond in the midst of a hard winter. They went to work at once, ploughing, harrowing, rolling, furrowing, in admirable order, as if they were bent on making this a model farm; but when I was looking sharp to see what kind of seed they dropped into the furrow, a gang of fellows by my side suddenly began to hook up the virgin mould itself, with a peculiar jerk, clean down to the sand, or rather the water,—for it was a very springy soil,—indeed all the *terra firma* there was,—and haul it away on sleds, and then I guessed that they must be cutting peat in a bog. So they came and went every day, with a peculiar shriek from the locomotive, from and to some point of the polar regions, as it seemed to me, like a flock of arctic snow-birds. But sometimes Squaw Walden had her revenge, and a hired man, walking behind his team, slipped through a crack in the ground down toward Tartarus, and he who was so brave before suddenly became but the ninth part of a man, almost gave up his animal heat, and was glad to take refuge in my house, and acknowledged that there was some virtue in a stove; or sometimes the frozen soil took a piece of steel out of a ploughshare, or a plough got set in the furrow and had to be cut out.

To speak literally, a hundred Irishmen, with Yankee overseers, came from Cambridge every day to get out the ice. They divided it into cakes by methods too well known to require description, and these, being sledded to the shore, were rapidly hauled off on to an ice platform, and raised by grappling irons and block and tackle, worked by horses, on to a stack, as surely as so many barrels of flour, and there placed evenly side by side, and row upon row, as if they formed the solid base of an obelisk designed to pierce the clouds. They told me that in a good day they could get out a thousand tons, which was the yield of about one acre. Deep ruts and "cradle holes" were worn in the ice, as on *terra firma*, by the passage of the sleds over the same track, and the horses invariably ate their oats out of cakes of ice hollowed out like buckets. They stacked up the cakes thus in the open air in a pile thirty-five feet high on one side and six or seven rods square, putting hay between the outside layers to exclude the air; for when the wind, though never so cold, finds a passage through, it will wear large cavities, leaving slight supports or studs only here and there, and finally topple it down. At first it looked like a vast blue fort or Valhalla; but when they began to tuck the coarse meadow hay into the crevices, and this became covered with rime and icicles, it looked like a venerable moss-grown and hoary ruin, built of azure-tinted marble, the abode of Winter, that old man we see in the almanac— his shanty, as if he had a design to estivate with us. They calculated that not twenty-five per cent. of this would reach its destination, and that two or three per cent. would be wasted in the cars. However, a still greater part of this heap had a different destiny from what was intended; for, either because the ice was found not to keep so well as was expected, containing more air than usual, or for some other reason, it never got to market. This heap, made in the winter of '46-7, and estimated to contain ten thousand tons, was finally covered with hay and boards; and though it was unroofed the following July, and a part of it carried off, the rest remaining exposed to the sun, it stood over that summer and the next winter, and was not quite melted till September 1848. Thus the pond recovered the greater part.

Like the water, the Walden ice, seen near at hand, has a green tint, but at a distance is beautifully blue, and you can easily tell it from the white ice of the river or the merely greenish ice of some ponds, a quarter of a mile off. Sometimes one of those great cakes slips from the ice-man's sled into the village street, and lies there for a week like a great emerald, an object of interest to all passers. I have noticed that a portion of Walden which in the state of water was green, will often, when frozen, appear from the same point of view blue. So the hollows about this pond will, sometimes, in the winter, be filled with a greenish water somewhat like its own, but the next day will have frozen blue. Perhaps the blue colour of water and ice is due to the light and air they contain, and the most transparent is the bluest. Ice is an interesting subject for contemplation. They told me that they had some in the ice-houses at Fresh Pond five years old which was as good as ever. Why is it that a bucket of water soon becomes putrid, but frozen remains sweet for ever? It is commonly said that this is the difference between the affections and the intellect.

Thus for sixteen days I saw from my window a hundred men at work like busy husbandmen, with teams and horses and apparently all the implements of farming, such a picture as we see on the first page of the almanac; and as often as I looked out I was reminded of the fable of the lark and the reapers, or the parable of the sower, and the like; and now they are all gone; and in thirty days more, probably, I shall look from the same window on the pure sea-green Walden water there, reflecting the clouds and the trees, and sending up its evaporations in solitude, and no traces will appear that a man has ever stood there. Perhaps I shall hear a solitary loon laugh as he dives and plumes himself, or shall see a lonely fisher in his boat, like a floating leaf, beholding his form reflected in the waves, where lately a hundred men securely laboured.

Thus it appears that the sweltering inhabitants of Charleston and New Orleans, of Madras and Bombay and Calcutta, drink at my well. In the morning I bathe my intellect in the stupendous and cosmogonal philosophy of the Bhagvat Geeta, since whose composition years of the gods have elapsed, and in comparison with which our modern world and its literature seem puny and trivial; and I doubt if that philosophy is not to be referred to a previous state of existence, so remote is its sublimity from our conceptions. I lay down the book and go to my well for water, and lo! there I meet the servant of the Brahmin, priest of Brahma and Vishnu and Indra, who still sits in his temple on the Ganges reading the Vedas, or dwells at the root of a tree with his crust and water-jug. I meet his servant come to draw water for his master, and our buckets, as it were, grate together in the same well. The pure Walden water is mingled with the sacred water of the Ganges. With favouring winds it is wafted past the site of the fabulous islands of Atlantis and the Hesperides, makes the periplus of Hanno, and, floating by Ternate and Tidore, and the mouth of the Persian Gulf, melts in the tropic gales of the Indian seas, and is landed in ports of which Alexander only heard the names.

# FROGS IN THE HORSE-POND

## Francis Trevelyan Buckland

*A fine English humorist was lost—but not completely—when Buckland (1826–1880) became a naturalist. Although his observations of living things were scientific, the humor he saw in them, in himself, and in other human beings, could not be kept entirely from his reports nor from his life—he loved practical jokes and had as permanent guests in his home many of the creatures he was studying, until friends hesitated to enter "his menagerie." Denizens of the pond and the cellar interested him as much as more exotic fauna, as these selections from* Curiosities of Natural History *show.*

WELL, let us have a look at the pond-world; choose a dry place at the side, and fix our eyes steadily upon the dirty water: what shall we see? Nothing at first; but wait a minute or two: a little round black knob appears in the middle; gradually it rises higher and higher, till at last you can make out a frog's head, with his great eyes staring hard at you, like the eyes of the frog in the woodcut facing Æsop's fable of the frog and the bull. Not a bit of his body do you see: he is much too cunning for that; he does not know who or what you are; you may be a heron, his mortal enemy, for aught he knows. You move your arm: he thinks it is the heron's bill coming; down he goes again, and you see him not: a few seconds, he regains courage and reappears, having probably communicated the intelligence to the other frogs; for many big heads and many big eyes appear, in all parts of the pond, looking like so many hippopotami on a small scale. Soon a conversational "Wurk, wurk, wurk," begins: you don't understand it; luckily, perhaps, as from the swelling in their throats it is evident that the colony is outraged by the intrusion, and the remarks passing are not complimentary to the intruder. These frogs are all respectable, grown-up, well-to-do frogs, and they have in this pond duly deposited their spawn, and then, hard-hearted creatures! left it to its fate; it has, however, taken care of itself, and is now hatched, at least that part of it which has escaped the hands of the gipsies, who not unfrequently prescribe baths of this natural jelly for rheumatism. . . .

In some places, from their making this peculiar noise, frogs have been called "Dutch nightingales." In Scotland, too, they have a curious name, Paddock or Puddick; but there is poetical authority for it:—

> "The water-snake whom fish and paddocks feed,
> With staring scales lies poisoned."—DRYDEN.

Returning from the University of Giessen, I brought with me about a dozen green tree-frogs, which I had caught in the woods near the town. The Germans call them *laub-frosch*, or leaf-frog; they are most difficult things to find, on account of their color so much resembling the leaves on which they live. I have frequently heard one singing in a small bush, and though I have searched carefully, have not been able to find him: the only way is to remain quite quiet till he again begins his song. After much ambush-work, at length I collected a dozen frogs and put them in a bottle. I started at night on my homeward journey by the diligence, and I put the bottle containing the frogs into the pocket inside the diligence. My fellow-passengers were sleepy old smoke-dried Germans: very little conversation took place, and after the first mile every one settled himself to sleep, and soon all were snoring. I suddenly awoke with a start, and found all the sleepers had been roused at the same moment. On their sleepy faces were depicted fear and anger. What had woke us all up so suddenly? The morning was just breaking, and my frogs, though in the dark pocket of the coach, had found it out; and with one accord, all twelve of them had begun their morning song. As if at a given signal, they one and all of them began to croak as loud as ever they could. The noise their united concert made, seemed, in the closed compartment of the coach, quite deafening. Well might the Germans look angry: they wanted to throw the frogs, bottle and all, out of the window; but I gave the bottle a good shaking, and made the frogs keep quiet. The Germans all went to sleep again, but I was obliged to remain awake, to shake the frogs when they began to croak. It was lucky that I did so, for they tried to begin their concert again two or three times. These frogs came safely to Oxford; and the day after their arrival, a stupid housemaid took off the top of the bottle to see what was inside; one of the frogs croaked at that instant, and so frightened her that she dared not put the cover on again. They all got loose in the garden, where I believe the ducks ate them, for I never heard or saw them again.

## ON RATS

On one occasion, when a boy, I recollect secretly borrowing an old-fashioned flint gun from the bird-keeper of the farm to which I had been invited. I ensconced myself behind the door of the pig-sty, determined to make a victim of one of the many rats that were accustomed to disport themselves among the straw that formed the bed of the farmer's pet bacon-pigs. In a few minutes out came an old patriarchal-looking rat, who, having taken a careful survey, quietly began to feed. After a long aim, bang went the gun—I fell backwards, knocked down by the recoil of the rusty old piece of artillery. I did not remain prone long, for I was soon roused by the most unearthly squeaks, and a dreadful noise as of an infuriated animal madly rushing round and round the sty. Ye gods! what had I done? I had not surely, like the tailor in the old song of the 'Carrion Crow,'

> "Shot and missed my mark,
> And shot the old sow right bang through the heart."

But I had nearly performed a similar sportsman-like feat. There was poor piggy, the blood flowing in streamlets from several small punctures in that part of his body destined, at no very distant period, to become ham; in vain attempting, by dismal cries and by energetic waggings of his curly tail, to appease the pain of the charge of small shot which had so unceremoniously awaked him from his porcine dreams of oatmeal and boiled potatoes. But where was the rat? He had disappeared unhurt; the buttocks of the unfortunate pig, the rightful owner of the premises, had received the charge of shot intended to destroy the daring intruder.

To appease piggy's wrath I gave him a bucketful of food from the hog-tub; and while he was thus consoling his inward self, wiped off the blood from the wounded parts, and said nothing about it to anybody. No doubt, before this time, some frugal housewife has been puzzled and astonished at the unwonted appearance of a charge of small shot in the centre of the breakfast ham which she procured from Squire Morland, of Sheepstead, Berks.

Rats are very fond of warmth, and will remain coiled up for hours in any snug retreat where they can find this very necessary element of their existence. The following anecdote well illustrates this point:—

My late father, when fellow of Corpus College, Oxford, many years ago, on arriving at his rooms late one night, found that a rat was running about among the books and geological specimens, behind the sofa, under the fender, and poking his nose into every hiding-place he could find. Being studiously inclined, and wishing to set to work at his books, he pursued him, armed with the poker in one hand, and a large dictionary, big enough to crush any rat, in the other; but in vain; Mr. Rat was not to be caught, particularly when such "arma scholastica" were used.

No sooner had the studies recommenced than the rat resumed his gambols, squeaking and rushing about the room like a mad creature. The battle was renewed, and continued at intervals, to the destruction of all studies, till quite a late hour at night, when the pursuer, angry and wearied, retired to his adjoining bedroom; though he listened attentively he heard no more of the enemy, and soon fell asleep. In the morning he was astonished to find something warm lying on his chest; carefully lifting up the bed-clothes, he discovered his tormentor of the preceding night quietly and snugly ensconced in a fold in the blanket, and taking advantage of the bodily warmth of his two-legged adversary. These two lay looking daggers at each other for some minutes, the one unwilling to leave his warm berth, the other afraid to put his hand out from under the protection of the coverlid, particularly as the stranger's aspect was anything but friendly, his little sharp teeth and fierce little black eyes seeming to say, "Paws off from me, if you please!"

At length, remembering the maxim that "discretion is the better part of valor"—the truth of which, I imagine, rats understand as well as most creatures,—he made a sudden jump off the bed, scuttled away into the next room, and was never seen or heard of afterwards. . . .

Rats are not selfish animals: having found out where the feast is stored, they will kindly communicate the intelligence to their friends and neighbors. The following anecdote will confirm this fact. A certain worthy old lady named Mrs. Oke, who resided at Axminster several years ago, made a cask of sweet wine, for which she was celebrated, and carefully placed it on a shelf in the cellar. The second night after this event she was frightened almost to death by a strange unaccountable noise in the said cellar. The household was called up and a search made, but nothing was found to clear up the mystery. The next night, as soon as the lights were extinguished and the house quiet, this dreadful noise was heard again. This time it was most alarming: a sound of squeaking, crying, knocking, pattering feet; then a dull scratching sound, with many other such ghostly noises, which continued throughout the livelong night. The old lady lay in bed with the candle alight, pale and sleepless with fright, anon muttering her prayers, anon determined to fire off the rusty old blunderbuss that hung over the chimney-piece. At last the morning broke, and the cock began to crow. "Now," thought she, "the ghosts must disappear." To her infinite relief, the noise really did cease, and the poor frightened dame adjusted her nightcap and fell asleep. Great preparations had she made for the next night; farm servants armed with pitchforks slept in the house; the maids took the family dinner-bell and the tinder-box into their rooms; the big dog was tied to the hall-table. Then the dame retired to her room, not to sleep, but to sit up in the arm-chair by the fire, keeping a drowsy guard over the neighbor's loaded horse-pistols, of which she was almost as much afraid as she was of the ghost in the cellar. Sure enough, her warlike preparations had succeeded; the ghost was certainly frightened; not a noise, not a sound, except the heavy snoring of the bumpkins and the rattling of the dog's chain in the hall, could be heard. She had gained a complete victory; the ghost was never heard again on the premises, and the whole affair was soon forgotten. Some weeks afterward some friends dropped in to take a cup of tea and talk over the last piece of gossip. Among other things the wine was mentioned, and the maid sent to get some from the cellar. She soon returned, and gasping for breath, rushed into the room, exclaiming, " 'Tis all gone, ma'am;" and sure enough it was all gone. "The ghost has taken it"—not a drop was left, only the empty cask remained; the side was half eaten away, and marks of sharp teeth were visible round the ragged margins of the newly made bungholes.

This discovery fully accounted for the noise the ghost had made, which caused so much alarm. The aboriginal rats in the dame's cellar had found out the wine, and communicated the joyful news to all the other rats in the parish; they had assembled there to enjoy the fun, and get very tipsy (which, judging from the noise they made, they certainly did) on this treasured cask of wine. Being quite a family party, they had finished it in two nights; and having got all they could, like wise rats they returned to their respective homes, perfectly unconscious that their merry-making had nearly been the death of the rightful owner and "founder of the feast." They had first gnawed out the cork, and got as much as they could: they soon found that the more they drank the lower the wine became. Perseverance is the motto of the rat; so they set to work and ate away the wood to the level of the wine again. This they continued till they had emptied the cask; they must then have got into it and licked up the last drains, for another and less agreeable smell was substituted for that of wine. I may add that this cask, with the side gone, and the marks of the rats' teeth, is still in my possession.

## Under the Greenwood Tree

UNDER the greenwood tree
  Who loves to lie with me,
And turn his merry note
Unto the sweet bird's throat,
Come hither! come hither! come hither!
  Here shall he see
  No enemy
But winter and rough weather.

  Who doth ambition shun
  And loves to live i' the sun,
  Seeking the food he eats
  And pleased with what he gets,
Come hither! come hither! come hither!
  Here shall he see
  No enemy
But winter and rough weather.

*William Shakespeare*

# A STORY OF THE STONE AGE

## H. G. Wells

*Between jobs as a druggist's or draper's apprentice, Wells
(1866–1946) worked his way through school, finally winning
a scholarship at the Royal College of Science. He became a
science teacher and his first book was a biology text. Recover-
ing from a severe illness, he turned to journalism and the writing of science-fiction—finally, novels of realism and social
significance. After 1895, Wells averaged a book a year or
better, including such tremendous achievements as* The Outline of History *and* The Science of Life. *This story of fifty
thousand years ago, the reader may be certain, is as scientifi-
cally sound as it is exciting.*

### I. Ugh-lomi and Uya

THIS story is of a time beyond the memory of man, before the
beginning of history, a time when one might have walked dry-
shod from France (as we call it now) to England, and when a
broad and sluggish Thames flowed through its marshes to meet its
father Rhine, flowing through a wide and level country that is
under water in these latter days, and which we know by the name
of the North Sea. In that remote age the valley which runs along
the foot of the Downs did not exist, and the south of Surrey was a
range of hills, fir-clad on the middle slopes, and snow-capped for
the better part of the year. The cores of its summits still remain as
Leith Hill, and Pitch Hill, and Hindhead. On the lower slopes of
the range, below the grassy spaces where the wild horses grazed,
were forests of yew and sweet-chestnut and elm, and the thickets
and dark places hid the grizzly bear and the hyæna, and the grey
apes clambered through the branches. And still lower amidst the
woodland and marsh and open grass along the Wey did this little
drama play itself out to the end that I have to tell. Fifty thousand

years ago it was, fifty thousand years—if the reckoning of geologists is correct.

And in those days the spring-time was as joyful as it is now, and sent the blood coursing in just the same fashion. The afternoon sky was blue with piled white clouds sailing through it, and the south-west wind came like a soft caress. The new-come swallows drove to and fro. The reaches of the river were spangled with white ranunculus, the marshy places were starred with lady's-smock and lit with marshmallow wherever the regiments of the sedges lowered their swords, and the northward moving hippopotami, shiny black monsters, sporting clumsily, came floundering and blundering through it all, rejoicing dimly and possessed with one clear idea, to splash the river muddy.

Up the river and well in sight of the hippopotami, a number of little buff-coloured animals dabbled in the water. There was no fear, no rivalry, and no enmity between them and the hippopotami. As the great bulks came crashing through the reeds and smashed the mirror of the water into silvery splashes, these little creatures shouted and gesticulated with glee. It was the surest sign of high spring. "Boloo!" they cried. "Baayah. Boloo!" They were the children of the men folk, the smoke of whose encampment rose from the knoll at the river's bend. Wild-eyed youngsters they were, with matted hair and little broad-nosed impish faces, covered (as some children are covered even nowadays) with a delicate down of hair. They were narrow in the loins and long in the arms. And their ears had no lobes, and had little pointed tips, a thing that still, in rare instances, survives. Stark-naked vivid little gipsies, as active as monkeys and as full of chatter, though a little wanting in words.

Their elders were hidden from the wallowing hippopotami by the crest of the knoll. The human squatting-place was a trampled area among the dead brown fronds of Royal Fern, through which the crosiers of this year's growth were unrolling to the light and warmth. The fire was a smouldering heap of char, light grey and black, replenished by the old women from time to time with brown leaves. Most of the men were asleep—they slept sitting with their foreheads on their knees. They had killed that morning a good quarry, enough for all, a deer that had been wounded by hunting dogs; so that there had been no quarreling among them, and some of the women were still gnawing the bones that lay scattered about. Others were making a heap of leaves and sticks to feed Brother Fire when the darkness came again, that he might grow strong and tall therewith, and guard them against the beasts. And two were piling flints that they brought, an armful at a time, from the bend of the river where the children were at play.

None of these buff-skinned savages were clothed, but some wore about their hips rude girdles of adder-skin or crackling, undressed hide, from which depended little bags, not made, but torn from the paws of beasts, and carrying the rudely-dressed flints that were men's chief weapons and tools. And one woman, the mate of Uya the Cunning Man, wore a wonderful necklace of perforated fossils—that others had worn before her. Beside some of the sleeping men lay the big antlers of the elk, with the tines chipped to sharp edges, and long sticks, hacked at the ends with flints into sharp points. There was little else save these things and the smouldering fire to mark these human beings off from the wild animals that ranged the country. But Uya the Cunning did not sleep, but sat with a bone in his hand and scraped busily thereon with a flint, a thing no animal would do. He was the oldest man in the tribe, beetle-browed, prognathous, lank-armed; he had a beard and his cheeks were hairy; and his chest and arms were black with thick hair. And by virtue both of his strength and cunning he was master of the tribe, and his share was always the most and the best.

Eudena had hidden herself among the alders, because she was afraid of Uya. She was still a girl, and her eyes were bright and her smile pleasant to see. He had given her a piece of the liver, a man's piece, and a wonderful treat for a girl to get; but as she took it the other woman with the necklace had looked at her, an evil glance, and Ugh-lomi had made a noise in his throat. At that, Uya had looked at him long and steadfastly, and Ugh-lomi's face had fallen. And then Uya had looked at her. She was frightened and she had stolen away, while the feeding was still going on, and Uya was busy with the marrow of a bone. Afterwards he had wandered about as if looking for her. And now she crouched among the alders, wondering mightily what Uya might be doing with the flint and the bone. And Ugh-lomi was not to be seen.

Presently a squirrel came leaping through the alders, and she lay so quiet the little man was within six feet of her before he saw her. Whereupon he dashed up a stem in a hurry and began to chatter and scold her. "What are you doing here," he asked, "away from the other men beasts?" "Peace," said Eudena, but he only chattered more, and then she began to break off the little black cones to throw at him. He dodged and defied her, and she grew excited and rose up to throw better, and then she saw Uya coming down the knoll. He had seen the movement of her pale arm amidst the thicket—he was very keen-eyed.

At that she forgot the squirrel and set off through the alders and reeds as fast as she could go. She did not care where she went so long as she escaped Uya. She splashed nearly knee-deep through a swampy place, and saw in front of her a slope of ferns—growing more slender and green as they passed up out of the light into the shade of the young chestnuts. She was soon amidst the trees—she was very fleet of foot, and she ran on and on until the forest was old and the vales great, and the vines about their stems where the light came were thick as young trees, and the ropes of ivy stout and tight. On she went, and she doubled and doubled again, and then at last lay down amidst some ferns in a hollow place near a thicket, and listened with her heart beating in her ears.

She heard footsteps presently rustling among the dead leaves, far off, and they died away and everything was still again, except the scandalising of the midges—for the evening was drawing on—and the incessant whisper of the leaves. She laughed silently to think the cunning Uya should go by her. She was not frightened. Sometimes, playing with the other girls and lads, she had fled into the wood, though never so far as this. It was pleasant to be hidden and alone.

She lay a long time there, glad of her escape, and then she sat up listening.

It was a rapid pattering growing louder and coming towards her, and in a little while she could hear grunting noises and the snapping of twigs. It was a drove of lean grisly wild swine. She turned about her, for a boar is an ill fellow to pass too closely, on account of the sideway slash of his tusks, and she made off slantingly through the trees. But the patter came nearer, they were not feeding as they wandered, but going fast—or else they would not overtake her—and she caught the limb of a tree, swung on to it, and ran up the stem with something of the agility of a monkey.

Down below the sharp bristling backs of the swine were already passing when she looked. And she knew the short, sharp grunts they made meant fear. What were they afraid of? A man? They were in a great hurry for just a man.

And then, so suddenly it made her grip on the branch tighten involuntarily, a fawn started in the brake and rushed after the swine. Something else went by, low and grey, with a long body, she did not know what it was, indeed she saw it only momentarily through the interstices of the young leaves; and then there came a pause.

She remained stiff and expectant, as rigid almost as though she was a part of the tree she clung to, peering down.

Then, far away among the trees, clear for a moment, then hidden, then visible knee-deep in ferns, then gone again, ran a man. She knew it was young Ugh-lomi by the fair colour of his hair, and there was red upon his face. Somehow his frantic flight and that scarlet mark made her feel sick. And then nearer, running heavily and breathing hard, came another man. At first she could not see, and then she saw, foreshortened and clear to her, Uya, running with great strides and his eyes staring. He was not going after Ugh-lomi. His face was white. It was Uya—*afraid!* He passed, and was still loud hearing, when something else, something large and with grizzled fur, swinging along with soft swift strides, came rushing in pursuit of him.

Eudena suddenly became rigid, ceased to breathe, her clutch convulsive, and her eyes starting.

She had never seen the thing before, she did not even see him clearly now, but she knew at once it was the Terror of the Wood-shade. His name was a legend, the children would frighten one another, frighten even themselves with his name, and run screaming to the squatting-place. No man had ever killed any of his kind. Even the mighty mammoth feared his anger. It was the grizzly bear, the lord of the world as the world went then.

As he ran he made a continuous growling grumble. "Men in my very lair! Fighting and blood. At the very mouth of my lair. Men, men, men. Fighting and blood." For he was the lord of the wood and of the caves.

Long after he had passed she remained, a girl of stone, staring down through the branches. All her power of action had gone from her. She gripped by instinct with hands and knees and feet It was some time before she could think, and then only one thing was clear in her mind, that the Terror was between her and the tribe—that it would be impossible to descend.

Presently, when her fear was a little abated, she clambered into a more comfortable position, where a great branch forked. The trees rose about her, so that she could see nothing of Brother Fire, who is black by day. Birds began to stir, and things that had gone into hiding for fear of her movements crept out. . . .

After a time the taller branches flamed out at the touch of the sunset. High overhead the rooks, who were wiser than men, went cawing home to their squatting-places among the elms. Looking down, things were clearer and darker. Eudena thought of going back to the squatting-place; she let herself down some way, and then the fear of the Terror of the Woodshade came again. While she hesitated a rabbit squealed dismally, and she dared not descend farther.

The shadows gathered, and the deeps of the forest began stirring. Eudena went up the tree again to be nearer the light. Down below the shadows came out of their hiding places and walked abroad. Overhead the blue deepened. A dreadful stillness came, and then the leaves began whispering.

Eudena shivered and thought of Brother Fire.

The shadows now were gathering in the trees, they sat on the branches and watched her. Branches and leaves were turned to ominous, quiet black shapes that would spring on her if she stirred. Then the white owl, flitting silently, came ghostly through the shades. Darker grew the world and darker, until the leaves and twigs against the sky were black, and the ground was hidden.

She remained there all night, an age-long vigil, straining her ears for the things that went on below in the darkness, and keeping motionless lest some stealthy beast should discover her. Man in those days was never alone in the dark, save for such rare accidents as this. Age after age he had learnt the lesson of its terror—a lesson we poor children of his have nowadays painfully to unlearn. Eudena, though in age a woman, was in heart like a little child. She kept as still, poor little animal, as a hare before it is started.

The stars gathered and watched her—her one grain of comfort. In one bright one she fancied there was something like Ugh-lomi. Then she fancied it *was* Ugh-lomi. And near him, red and duller, was Uya, and as the night passed Ugh-lomi fled before him up the sky.

She tried to see Brother Fire, who guarded the squatting-place from beasts, but he was not in sight. And far away she heard the mammoths trumpeting as they went down to the drinking-place, and once some huge bulk with heavy paces hurried along, making a noise like a calf, but what it was she could not see. But she thought from the voice it was Yaaa, the rhinoceros, who stabs with his nose, goes always alone, and rages without cause.

At last the little stars began to hide, and then the larger ones. It was like all the animals vanishing before the Terror. The Sun was coming, lord of the sky, as the grizzly was lord of the forest. Eudena wondered what would happen if one star stayed behind. And then the sky paled to the dawn.

When the daylight came the fear of lurking things passed, and she could descend. She was stiff, but not so stiff as you would have been, dear young lady (by virtue of your upbringing), and as she had not been trained to eat at least once in three hours, but instead had often fasted three days, she did not feel uncomfortably hungry. She crept down the tree very cautiously, and went her way stealthily through the wood, and not a squirrel sprang or deer started but the terror of the grizzly bear froze her marrow.

Her desire was now to find her people again. Her dread of Uya the Cunning was consumed by a greater dread of loneliness. But she had lost her direction. She had run heedlessly overnight, and she could not tell whether the squatting-place was sunward or where it lay. Ever and again she stopped and listened. And at last, very far away, she heard a measured chinking. It was so faint even in the morning stillness that she could tell it must be far away. But she knew the sound was that of a man sharpening a flint.

Presently the trees began to thin out, and then came a regiment of nettles barring the way. She turned aside, and then she came to a fallen tree that she knew, with a noise of bees about it. And so presently she was in sight of the knoll, very far off, and the river under it, and the children and the hippopotami just as they had been yesterday, and the thin spire of smoke swaying in the morning breeze. Far away by the river was the cluster of alders where she had hidden. And at the sight of that the fear of Uya returned, and she crept into a thicket of bracken, out of which a rabbit scuttled, and lay awhile to watch the squatting-place.

The men were mostly out of sight, saving Wau, the flint-chopper; and at that she felt safer. They were away hunting food, no doubt. Some of the women, too, were down in the stream, stooping intent, seeking mussels, crayfish, and watersnails, and at the sight of their occupation Eudena felt hungry. She rose, and ran through the fern, designing to join them. As she went she heard a voice among the bracken calling softly. She stopped. Then suddenly she heard a rustle behind her, and turning saw Ugh-lomi rising out of the fern. There were streaks of brown blood and dirt on his face, and his eyes were fierce, and the white stone of Uya, the white Fire Stone, that none but Uya dared to touch, was in his hand. In a stride he was beside her, and gripped her arm. He swung her about, and thrust her before him towards the woods. "Uya," he said, and waved his arms about. She heard a cry, looked back, and saw all the women standing up, and two wading out of the stream. Then came a nearer howling, and the old woman with the beard, who watched the fire on the knoll, was waving her arms, and Wau, the man who had been chipping the flint, was getting to his feet. The little children too were hurrying and shouting.

"Come!" said Ugh-lomi, and dragged her by the arm.

She still did not understand.

"Uya has called the death word," said Ugh-lomi, and she glanced back at the screaming curve of figures, and understood.

Wau and all the women and children were coming towards them, a scattered array of buff, shock-headed figures, howling, leaping, and crying. Over the knoll two youths hurried. Down among the ferns to the right came a man, heading them off from the wood. Ugh-lomi left her arm, and the two began running side by side, leaping the bracken and stepping clear and wide. Eudena, knowing her fleetness and the fleetness of Ugh-lomi, laughed aloud at the unequal chase. They were an exceptionally straight-limbed couple for those days.

They soon cleared the open, and drew near the wood of chest-nut-trees again—neither afraid now because neither was alone. They slackened their pace, already not excessive. And suddenly Eudena cried and swerved aside, pointing, and looking up through the tree-stems. Ugh-lomi saw the feet and legs of men running towards him. Eudena was already running off at a tangent. And as he, too, turned to follow her they heard the voice of Uya coming through the trees, and roaring out his rage at them.

Then terror came in their hearts, not the terror that numbs, but the terror that makes one silent and swift. They were cut off now on two sides. They were in a sort of corner of pursuit. On the right hand, and near by them, came the men swift and heavy, with bearded Uya, antler in hand, leading them; and on the left, scattered as one scatters corn, yellow dashes among the fern and grass, ran Wau and the women; and even the little children from the shallow had joined the chase. The two parties converged upon them. Off they went, with Eudena ahead.

They knew there was no mercy for them. There was no hunting so sweet to these ancient men as the hunting of men. Once the fierce passion of the chase was lit, the feeble beginnings of humanity in them were thrown to the winds. And Uya in the night had marked Ugh-lomi with the death word. Ugh-lomi was the day's quarry, the appointed feast.

They ran straight—it was their only chance—taking whatever ground came in the way—a spread of stinging nettles, an open glade, a clump of grass out of which a hyæna fled snarling. Then woods again, long stretches of shady leaf-mould and moss under the green trunks. Then a stiff slope, tree-clad, and long vistas of trees, a glade, a succulent green area of black mud, a wide-open space again, and then a clump of lacerating brambles, with beast tracks through it. Behind them the chase trailed out and scattered, with Uya ever at their heels. Eudena kept the first place, running light and with her breath easy, for Ugh-lomi carried the Fire Stone in his hand.

It told on his pace—not at first, but after a time. His footsteps behind her suddenly grew remote. Glancing over her shoulder as they crossed another open space, Eudena saw that Ugh-lomi was many yards behind her and Uya close upon him, with antler already raised in the air to strike him down. Wau and the others were but just emerging from the shadow of the woods.

Seeing Ugh-lomi in peril, Eudena ran sideways, looking back, threw up her arms and cried aloud, just as the antler flew. And young Ugh-lomi, expecting this and understanding her cry, ducked his head, so that the missile merely struck his scalp lightly, making but a trivial wound, and flew over him. He turned forthwith, the quartzite Fire Stone in both hands, and hurled it straight at Uya's body as he ran loose from the throw. Uya shouted, but could not dodge it. It took him under the ribs, heavy and flat, and he reeled and went down without a cry. Ugh-lomi caught up the antler—one tine of it was tipped with his own blood—and came running on again with a red trickle just coming out of his hair.

Uya rolled over twice, and lay a moment before he got up, and then he did not run fast. The colour of his face was changed. Wau overtook him, and then others, and he coughed and laboured in his breath. But he kept on.

At last the two fugitives gained the bank of the river, where the stream ran deep and narrow, and they still had fifty yards in hand of Wau, the foremost pursuer, the man who made the smiting stones. He carried one, a large flint, the shape of an oyster and double the size, chipped to a chisel edge, in either hand.

They sprang down the steep bank into the stream, rushed through the water, swam the deep current in two or three strokes, and came out wading again, dripping and refreshed, to clamber up the farther bank. It was undermined, and with willows growing thickly therefrom, so that it needed clambering. And while Eudena was still among the silvery branches and Ugh-lomi still in the water —for the antler had encumbered him—Wau came up against the sky on the opposite bank, and the smiting stone, thrown cunningly, took the side of Eudena's knee. She struggled to the top and fell.

They heard the pursuers shout to one another, and Ugh-lomi climbing to her and moving jerkily to mar Wau's aim, felt the second smiting stone graze his ear, and heard the water splash below him.

Then it was Ugh-lomi, the stripling, proved himself to have come to man's estate. For running on, he found Eudena fell behind, limping, and at that he turned, and crying savagely and with a face terrible with sudden wrath and trickling blood, ran swiftly past her back to the bank, whirling the antler round his head. And Eudena kept on, running stoutly still, though she must needs limp at every step, and the pain was already sharp.

So that Wau, rising over the edge and clutching the straight willow branches, saw Ugh-lomi towering over him, gigantic against the blue; saw his whole body swing round, and the grip of his hands upon the antler. The edge of the antler came sweeping through the air, and he saw no more. The water under the osiers whirled and eddied and went crimson six feet down the stream. Uya following stopped knee-high across the stream, and the man who was swimming turned about.

The other men who trailed after—they were none of them very mighty men (for Uya was more cunning than strong, brooking no sturdy rivals)—slackened momentarily at the sight of Ugh-lomi standing there above the willows, bloody and terrible, between them and the halting girl, with the huge antler waving in his hand. It seemed as though he had gone into the water a youth, and come out of it a man full grown.

He knew what there was behind him. A broad stretch of grass, and then a thicket, and in that Eudena could hide. That was clear in his mind, though his thinking powers were too feeble to see what should happen thereafter. Uya stood knee-deep, undecided and unarmed. His heavy mouth hung open, showing his canine teeth, and he panted heavily. His side was flushed and bruised under the hair. The other man beside him carried a sharpened stick. The rest of the hunters came up one by one to the top of the bank, hairy, long-armed men clutching flints and sticks. Two ran off along the bank down stream, and then clambered to the water, where Wau had come to the surface struggling weakly. Before they could reach him he went under again. Two others threatened Ugh-lomi from the bank.

He answered back, shouts, vague insults, gestures. Then Uya, who had been hesitating, roared with rage, and whirling his fists plunged into the water. His followers splashed after him.

Ugh-lomi glanced over his shoulder and found Eudena already vanished into the thicket. He would perhaps have waited for Uya, but Uya preferred to spar in the water below him until the others were beside him. Human tactics in those days, in all serious fighting, were the tactics of the pack. Prey that turned at bay they gathered around and rushed. Ugh-lomi felt the rush coming, and hurling the antler at Uya, turned about and fled.

When he halted to look back from the shadow of the thicket he found only three of his pursuers had followed him across the river, and they were going back again. Uya, with a bleeding mouth, was on the farther side of the stream again, but lower down, and holding his hand to his side. The others were in the river dragging something to shore. For a time at least the chase was intermitted.

Ugh-lomi stood watching for a space, and snarled at the sight of Uya. Then he turned and plunged into the thicket.

In a minute, Eudena came hastening to join him, and they went on hand in hand. He dimly perceived the pain she suffered from the cut and bruised knee, and chose the easier ways. But they went on all that day, mile after mile, through wood and thicket, until at last they came to the chalk-land, open grass with rare woods of beech, and the birch growing near water, and they saw the Wealden mountains nearer, and groups of horses grazing together. They went circumspectly, keeping always near thicket and cover, for this was a strange region—even its ways were strange. Steadily the ground rose, until the chestnut forests spread wide and blue below them, and the Thames marshes shone silvery, high and far. They saw no men, for in those days men were still only just come into this part of the world, and were moving but slowly along the riverways. Towards evening they came on the river again, but now it ran in a gorge, between high cliffs of white chalk that sometimes overhung it. Down the cliffs was a scrub of birches and there were many birds there. And high up the cliff was a little shelf by a tree, whereon they clambered to pass the night.

They had had scarcely any food; it was not the time of year for berries, and they had no time to go aside to snare or waylay. They tramped in a hungry, weary silence, gnawing at twigs and leaves. But over the surface of the cliffs were a multitude of snails, and in a bush were the freshly-laid eggs of a little bird, and then Ugh-lomi threw at and killed a squirrel in a beech-tree, so that at last they fed well. Ugh-lomi watched during the night, his chin on his knees; and he heard young foxes crying hard by, and the noise of mammoths down the gorge, and the hyænas yelling and laughing far away. It was chilly, but they dared not light a fire. Whenever he dozed, his spirit went abroad, and straightway met with the spirit of Uya, and they fought. And always Ugh-lomi was paralysed so that he could not smite nor run, and then he would awake suddenly. Eudena, too, dreamt evil things of Uya, so that they both awoke with the fear of him in their hearts, and by the light of the dawn they saw a woolly rhinoceros go blundering down the valley.

During the day they caressed one another and were glad of the sunshine, and Eudena's leg was so stiff she sat on the ledge all day. Ugh-lomi found great flints sticking out of the cliff face, greater than any he had seen, and he dragged some to the ledge and began chipping, so as to be armed against Uya when he came again. And at one he laughed heartily, and Eudena laughed, and they threw it about in derision. It had a hole in it. They stuck their fingers through it, it was very funny indeed. Then they peeped at one another through it. Afterwards, Ugh-lomi got himself a stick, and thrusting by chance at this foolish flint, the stick went in and stuck there. He had rammed it in too tightly to withdraw it. That was still stranger—scarcely funny, terrible almost, and for a time Ugh-lomi did not greatly care to touch the thing. It was as if the flint had bit and held with its teeth. But then he got familiar with the odd combination. He swung it about, and perceived that the stick with the heavy stone on the end struck a better blow than anything he knew. He went to and fro swinging it, and striking with it; but later he tired of it and threw it aside. In the afternoon he went up over the brow of the white cliff, and lay watching by a rabbit-warren until the rabbits came out to play. There were no men thereabouts, and the rabbits were heedless. He threw a smiting stone he had made and got a kill.

That night they made a fire from flint sparks and bracken fronds, and talked and caressed by it. And in their sleep Uya's spirit came again, and suddenly, while Ugh-lomi was trying to fight vainly, the foolish flint on the stick came into his hand, and he struck Uya with it, and behold! it killed him. But afterwards came other dreams of Uya—for spirits take a lot of killing, and he had to be killed again. Then after that the stone would not keep on the stick. He awoke tired and rather gloomy, and was sulky all the forenoon, in spite of Eudena's kindliness, and instead of hunting he sat chipping a sharp edge to the singular flint, and looking strangely at her. Then he bound the perforated flint on to the stick with strips of rabbit skin. And afterwards he walked up and down the ledge, striking with it, and muttering to himself, and thinking of Uya. It felt very fine and heavy in the hand.

Several days, more than there was any counting in those days, five days, it may be, or six, did Ugh-lomi and Eudena stay on that shelf in the gorge of the river, and they lost all fear of men, and their fire burnt redly of a night. And they were very merry together; there was food every day, sweet water, and no enemies. Eudena's knee was well in a couple of days, for those ancient savages had quick-healing flesh. Indeed, they were very happy.

On one of those days Ugh-lomi dropped a chunk of flint over the cliff. He saw it fall, and go bounding across the river bank into the river, and after laughing and thinking it over a little he tried another. This smashed a bush of hazel in the most interesting way. They spent all the morning dropping stones from the ledge, and in the afternoon they discovered this new and interesting pastime was also possible from the cliff-brow. The next day they had forgotten this delight. Or at least, it seemed they had forgotten.

But Uya came in dreams to spoil the paradise. Three nights he came fighting Ugh-lomi. In the morning after these dreams Ugh-lomi would walk up and down, threatening him and swinging the axe, and at last came the night after Ugh-lomi brained the otter, and they had feasted. Uya went too far. Ugh-lomi awoke, scowling under his heavy brows, and he took his axe, and extending his hand towards Eudena he bade her wait for him upon the ledge. Then he clambered down the white declivity, glanced up once from the foot of it and flourished his axe, and without looking back again went striding along the river bank until the overhanging cliff at the bend hid him.

Two days and nights did Eudena sit alone by the fire on the ledge waiting, and in the night the beasts howled over the cliffs and down the valley, and on the cliff over against her the hunched hyænas prowled black against the sky. But no evil thing came near her save fear. Once, far away, she heard the roaring of a lion, following the horses as they came northward over the grass lands with the spring. All the time she waited—the waiting that is pain.

And the third day Ugh-lomi came back, up the river. The plumes of a raven were in his hair. The first axe was red-stained, and had long dark hairs upon it, and he carried the necklace that had marked the favourite of Uya in his hand. He walked in the soft places, giving no heed to his trail. Save a raw cut below his jaw there was not a wound upon him. "Uya!" cried Ugh-lomi exultant, and Eudena saw it was well. He put the necklace on Eudena, and they ate and drank together. And after eating he began to rehearse the whole story from the beginning, when Uya had cast his eyes on Eudena, and Uya and Ugh-lomi, fighting in the forest, had been chased by the bear, eking out his scanty words with abundant pantomime, springing to his feet and whirling the stone axe round when it came to the fighting. The last fight was a mighty one, stamping and shouting, and once a blow at the fire that sent a torrent of sparks up into the night. And Eudena sat red in the light of the fire, gloating on him, her face flushed and her eyes shining, and the necklace Uya had made about her neck. It was a splendid time, and the stars that look down on us looked down on her, our ancestor—who has been dead now these fifty thousand years.

## II.   The Cave Bear

In the days when Eudena and Ugh-lomi fled from the people of Uya towards the fir-clad mountains of the Weald, across the forests of sweet-chestnut and the grass-clad chalkland, and hid themselves at last in the gorge of the river between the chalk cliffs, men were few and their squatting-places far between. The nearest men to them were those of the tribe, a full day's journey down the river, and up the mountains there were none. Man was indeed a newcomer to this part of the world in that ancient time, coming slowly along the rivers, generation after generation, from one squatting place to another, from the south-westward. And the animals that held the land, the hippopotamus and rhinoceros of the river valleys, the horses of the grass plains, the deer and swine of the woods, the grey apes in the branches, the cattle of the uplands, feared him but little—let alone the mammoths in the mountains and the elephants that came through the land in the summer-time out of the south.

For why should they fear him, with but the rough, chipped flints that he had not learnt to haft and which he threw but ill, and the poor spear of sharpened wood, as all the weapons he had against hoof and horn, tooth and claw?

Andoo, the huge cave bear, who lived in the cave up the gorge, had never even seen a man in all his wise and respectable life, until midway through one night, as he was prowling down the gorge along the cliff edge, he saw the glare of Eudena's fire upon the ledge, and Eudena red and shining, and Ugh-lomi, with a gigantic shadow mocking him upon the white cliff, going to and fro, shaking his mane of hair, and waving the axe of stone—the first axe of stone—while he chanted of the killing of Uya. The cave bear was far up the gorge, and he saw the thing slanting-ways and far off. He was so surprised he stood quite still upon the edge, sniffing the novel odour of burning bracken, and wondering whether the dawn was coming up in the wrong place.

He was the lord of the rocks and caves, was the cave bear, as his slighter brother, the grizzly, was lord of the thick woods below, and as the dappled lion—the lion of those days was dappled—was lord of the thorn-thickets, reed-beds, and open plains. He was the greatest of all meat-eaters; he knew no fear, none preyed on him, and none gave him battle; only the rhinoceros was beyond his strength. Even the mammoth shunned his country. This invasion perplexed him. He noticed these new beasts were shaped like monkeys, and sparsely hairy like young pigs. "Monkey and young pig," said the cave bear. "It might not be so bad. But that red thing that jumps, and the black thing jumping with it yonder! Never in my life have I seen such things before!"

He came slowly along the brow of the cliff towards them, stopping thrice to sniff and peer, and the reek of the fire grew stronger. A couple of hyænas also were so intent upon the thing below that Andoo, coming soft and easy, was close upon them before they knew of him or he of them. They stared guiltily and went lurching off. Coming round in a wheel, a hundred yards off, they began yelling and calling him names to revenge themselves for the start they had had. "Ya-ha!" they cried. "Who can't grub his own burrow? Who eats roots like a pig? . . . Ya-ha!" for even in those days the hyæna's manners were just as offensive as they are now.

"Who answers the hyæna?" growled Andoo, peering through the midnight dimness at them, and then going to look at the cliff edge.

There was Ugh-lomi still telling his story, and the fire getting low, and the scent of the burning hot and strong.

Andoo stood on the edge of the chalk cliff for some time, shifting his vast weight from foot to foot, and swaying his head to and fro, with his mouth open, his ears erect and twitching, and the nostrils of his big, black muzzle sniffing. He was very curious, was the cave bear, more curious than any of the bears that live now, and the flickering fire and the incomprehensible movements of the man, let alone the intrusion into his indisputable province, stirred him with a sense of strange new happenings. He had been after red deer fawn that night, for the cave bear was a miscellaneous hunter, but this quite turned him from that enterprise.

"Ya-ha!" yelled the hyænas behind. "Ya-ha-ha!"

Peering through the starlight, Andoo saw there were now three or four going to and fro against the grey hillside. "They will hang about me now all the night. . . . until I kill," said Andoo. "Filth of the world!" And mainly to annoy them, he resolved to watch the red flicker in the gorge until the dawn came to drive the hyæna scum home. And after a time they vanished, and he heard their voices, like a party of Cockney beanfeasters, away in the beech-woods. Then they came slinking near again. Andoo yawned and went on along the cliff, and they followed. Then he stopped and went back.

It was a splendid night, beset with shining constellations, the same stars, but not the same constellations we know, for since those days all the stars have had time to move into new places. Far away across the open space beyond where the heavy-shouldered, lean-bodied hyænas blundered and howled, was a beech-wood, and the mountain slopes rose beyond, a dim mystery, until their snow-capped summits came out white and cold and clear, touched by the first rays of the yet unseen moon. It was a vast silence, save when the yell of the hyænas flung a vanishing discordance across its peace, or when from down the hills the trumpeting of the new-come elephants came faintly on the faint breeze. And below now, the red flicker had dwindled and was steady, and shone a deeper red, and Ugh-lomi had finished his story and was preparing to sleep, and Eudena sat and listened to the strange voices of unknown beasts, and watched the dark eastern sky growing deeply luminous at the advent of the moon. Down below, the river talked to itself, and things unseen went to and fro.

After a time the bear went away, but in an hour he was back

again. Then, as if struck by a thought, he turned, and went up the gorge. . . .

The night passed, and Ugh-lomi slept on. The waning moon rose and lit the gaunt white cliff overhead with a light that was pale and vague. The gorge remained in a deeper shadow and seemed all the darker. Then by imperceptible degrees, the day came stealing in the wake of the moonlight. Eudena's eyes wandered to the cliff brow overhead once, and then again. Each time the line was sharp and clear against the sky, and yet she had a dim perception of something lurking there. The red of the fire grew deeper and deeper, grey scales spread upon it, its vertical column of smoke became more and more visible, and up and down the gorge things that had been unseen grew clear in a colourless illumination. She may have dozed.

Suddenly she started up from her squatting position, erect and alert, scrutinising the cliff up and down.

She made the faintest sound, and Ugh-lomi too, light-sleeping like an animal, was instantly awake. He caught up his axe and came noiselessly to her side.

The light was still dim, the world now all in black and dark grey, and one sickly star still lingered overhead. The ledge they were on was a little grassy space, six feet wide, perhaps, and twenty feet long, sloping outwardly, and with a handful of St. John's wort growing near the edge. Below it the soft white rock fell away in a steep slope of nearly fifty feet to the thick bush of hazel that fringed the river. Down the river this slope increased, until some way off a thin grass held its own right up to the crest of the cliff. Overhead, forty or fifty feet of rock bulged into the great masses characteristic of chalk, but at the end of the ledge a gully, a precipitous groove of discoloured rock, slashed the face of the cliff, and gave a footing to a scrubby growth, by which Eudena and Ugh-lomi went up and down.

They stood as noiseless as startled deer, with every sense expectant. For a minute they heard nothing, and then came a faint rattling of dust down the gully, and the creaking of twigs.

Ugh-lomi gripped his axe, and went to the edge of the ledge, for the bulge of the chalk overhead had hidden the upper part of the gully. And forthwith, with a sudden contraction of the heart, he saw the cave bear halfway down from the brow, and making a gingerly backward step with his flat hind-foot. His hind-quarters were towards Ugh-lomi, and he clawed at the rock and bushes so that he seemed flattened against the cliff. He looked none the less for that. From his shining snout to his stumpy tail he was a lion and a half, the length of two tall men. He looked over his shoulder, and his huge mouth was open with the exertion of holding up his great carcase, and his tongue lay out. . . .

He got his footing, and came down slowly, a yard nearer.

"Bear," said Ugh-lomi, looking round with his face white.

But Eudena, with terror in her eyes, was pointing down the cliff.

Ugh-lomi's mouth fell open. For down below, with her big fore-feet against the rock, stood another big brown-grey bulk—the she-bear. She was not so big as Andoo, but she was big enough for all that.

Then suddenly Ugh-lomi gave a cry, and catching up a handful of the litter of ferns that lay scattered on the ledge, he thrust it into the pallid ash of the fire. "Brother Fire!" he cried. "Brother Fire!" And Eudena, starting into activity, did likewise. "Brother Fire! Help, help! Brother Fire!"

Brother Fire was still red in his heart, but he turned to grey as they scattered him. "Brother Fire!" they screamed. But he whispered and passed, and there was nothing but ashes. Then Ugh-lomi danced with anger and struck the ashes with his fist. But Eudena began to hammer the firestone against a flint. And the eyes of each were turning ever and again towards the gully by which Andoo was climbing down. Brother Fire!

Suddenly the huge furry hind-quarters of the bear came into view, beneath the bulge of the chalk that had hidden him. He was still clambering gingerly down the nearly vertical surface. His head was yet out of sight, but they could hear him talking to himself. "Pig and monkey," said the cave bear. "It ought to be good."

Eudena struck a spark and blew at it; it twinkled brighter and then—went out. At that she cast down flint and firestone and stared blankly. Then she sprang to her feet and scrambled a yard or so up the cliff above the ledge. How she hung on even for a moment I do not know, for the chalk was vertical and without grip for a monkey. In a couple of seconds she had slid back to the ledge again with bleeding hands.

Ugh-lomi was making frantic rushes about the ledge—now he would go to the edge, now to the gully. He did not know what to do, he could not think. The she-bear looked smaller than her mate—much. If they rushed down on her together, *one* might live. "Ugh?"

said the cave bear, and Ugh-lomi turned again and saw his little eyes peering under the bulge of the chalk.

Eudena, cowering at the end of the ledge, began to scream like a gripped rabbit.

At that a sort of madness came upon Ugh-lomi. With a mighty cry, he caught up his axe and ran towards Andoo. The monster gave a grunt of surprise. In a moment Ugh-lomi was clinging to a bush right underneath the bear, and in another he was hanging to its back half buried in fur, with one fist clutched in the hair under its jaw. The bear was too astonished at this fantastic attack to do more than cling passive. And then the axe, the first of all axes, rang on its skull.

The bear's head twisted from side to side, and he began a petulant scolding growl. The axe bit within an inch of the left eye, and the hot blood blinded that side. At that the brute roared with surprise and anger, and his teeth gnashed six inches from Ugh-lomi's face. Then the axe, clubbed close, came down heavily on the corner of the jaw.

The next blow blinded the right side and called forth a roar, this time of pain. Eudena saw the huge, flat feet slipping and sliding, and suddenly the bear gave a clumsy leap sideways, as if for the ledge. Then everything vanished, and the hazels smashed, and a roar of pain and a tumult of shouts and growls came up from far below.

Eudena screamed and ran to the edge and peered over. For a moment, man and bears were a heap together, Ugh-lomi uppermost; and then he had sprung clear and was scaling the gully again, with the bears rolling and striking at one another among the hazels. But he had left his axe below, and three knob-edged streaks of carmine were shooting down his thigh. "Up!" he cried, and in a moment Eudena was leading the way to the top of the cliff.

In half a minute they were at the crest, their hearts pumping noisily, with Andoo and his wife far and safe below them. Andoo was sitting on his haunches, both paws at work, trying with quick, exasperated movements to wipe the blindness out of his eyes, and the she-bear stood on all-fours a little way off, ruffled in appearance and growling angrily. Ugh-lomi flung himself flat on the grass, and lay panting and bleeding with his face on his arms.

For a second Eudena regarded the bears, then she came and sat beside him, looking at him. . . .

Presently she put forth her hand timidly and touched him, and made the guttural sound that was his name. He turned over and raised himself on his arm. His face was pale, like the face of one who is afraid. He looked at her steadfastly for a moment, and then suddenly he laughed. "Waugh!" he said exultantly.

"Waugh!" she said—a simple but expressive conversation.

Then Ugh-lomi came and knelt beside her, and on hands and knees peered over the brow and examined the gorge. His breath was steady now, and the blood on his leg had ceased to flow, though the scratches the she-bear had made were open and wide. He squatted up and sat staring at the footmarks of the great bear as they came to the gully—they were as wide as his head and twice as long. Then he jumped up and went along the cliff face until the ledge was visible. Here he sat down for some time thinking, while Eudena watched him. Presently she saw the bears had gone.

At last Ugh-lomi rose, as one whose mind is made up. He returned towards the gully, Eudena keeping close by him, and together they clambered to the ledge. They took the firestone and a flint, and then Ugh-lomi went down to the foot of the cliff very cautiously, and found his axe. They returned to the cliff as quietly as they could, and set off at a brisk walk. The ledge was a home no longer, with such callers in the neighbourhood. Ugh-lomi carried the axe and Eudena the firestone. So simple was a Palæolithic removal.

They went up stream, although it might lead to the very lair of the cave bear, because there was no other way to go. Down the stream was the tribe, and had not Ugh-lomi killed Uya and Wau? By the stream they had to keep—because of drinking.

So they marched through beech-trees, with the gorge deepening until the river flowed, a frothing rapid, five hundred feet below them. Of all the changeful things in this world of change, the courses of rivers in deep valleys change least. It was the river Wey, the river we know to-day, and they marched over the very spots where nowadays stand little Guildford and Godalming—the first human beings to come into the land. Once a grey ape chattered and vanished, and all along the cliff edge, vast and even, ran the spoor of the great cave bear.

And then the spoor of the bear fell away from the cliff, showing, Ugh-lomi thought, that he came from some place to the left, and keeping to the cliff's edge, they presently came to an end. They found themselves looking down on a great semicircular space caused by the collapse of the cliff. It had smashed right across the gorge, banking the up-stream water back in a pool which over-flowed in a rapid. The slip had happened long ago. It was grassed over, but the face of the cliffs that stood about the semicircle was still almost fresh-looking and white as on the day when the rock must have broken and slid down. Starkly exposed and black under the foot of these cliffs were the mouths of several caves. And as they stood there, looking at the space, and disinclined to skirt it, because they thought the bears' lair lay somewhere on the left in the direction they must needs take, they saw suddenly first one bear and then two coming up the grass slope to the right and going across the amphitheatre towards the caves. Andoo was first; he dropped a little on his fore-foot and his mien was despondent, and the she-bear came shuffling behind.

Eudena and Ugh-lomi stepped back from the cliff until they could just see the bears over the verge. Then Ugh-lomi stopped. Eudena pulled his arm, but he turned with a forbidding gesture, and her hand dropped. Ugh-lomi stood watching the bears, with his axe in his hand, until they had vanished into the cave. He growled softly, and shook the axe at the she-bear's receding quarters. Then to Eudena's terror, instead of creeping off with her, he lay flat down and crawled forward into such a position that he could just see the cave. It was bears—and he did it as calmly as if it had been rabbits he was watching!

He lay still, like a bared log, sun-dappled, in the shadow of the trees. He was thinking. And Eudena had learnt, even when a little girl, that when Ugh-lomi became still like that, jaw-bone on fist, novel things presently began to happen.

It was an hour before the thinking was over; it was noon when the two little savages had found their way to the cliff brow that overhung the bears' cave. And all the long afternoon they fought desperately with a great boulder of chalk; trundling it, with nothing but their unaided sturdy muscles, from the gully where it had hung like a loose tooth, towards the cliff top. It was full two yards about, it stood as high as Eudena's waist, it was obtuse-angled and toothed with flints. And when the sun set it was poised, three inches from the edge, above the cave of the great cave bear.

In the cave conversation languished during that afternoon. The she-bear snoozed sulkily in her corner—for she was fond of pig and monkey—and Andoo was busy licking the side of his paw and smearing his face to cool the smart and inflammation of his wounds. Afterwards he went and sat just within the mouth of the cave, blinking out at the afternoon sun with his uninjured eye, and thinking.

"I never was so startled in my life," he said at last. "They are the most extraordinary beasts. Attacking *me!*"

"I don't like them," said the she-bear, out of the darkness behind.

"A feebler sort of beast I *never* saw. I can't think what the world is coming to. Scraggy, weedy legs. . . . Wonder how they keep warm in winter?"

"Very likely they don't," said the she-bear.

"I suppose it's a sort of monkey gone wrong."

"It's a change," said the she-bear.

A pause.

"The advantage he had was merely accidental," said Andoo. "These things *will* happen at times."

"*I* can't understand why you let go," said the she-bear.

That matter had been discussed before, and settled. So Andoo, being a bear of experience, remained silent for a space. Then he resumed upon a different aspect of the matter. "He has a sort of claw—a long claw that he seemed to have fi st on one paw and then on the other. Just one claw. They're very odd things. The bright thing, too, they seemed to have—like that glare that comes in the sky in daytime—only it jumps about—it's really worth seeing. It's a thing with a root, too—like grass when it is windy."

"Does it bite?" asked the she-bear. "If it bites it can't be a plant."

"No—— I don't know," said Andoo. "But it's curious, anyhow."

"I wonder if they *are* good eating?" said the she-bear.

"They look it," said Andoo, with appetite—for the cave bear, like the polar bear, was an incurable carnivore—no roots or honey for *him*.

The two bears fell into a meditation for a space. Then Andoo resumed his simple attention to his eye. The sunlight up the green slope before the cave mouth grew warmer in tone and warmer, until it was a ruddy amber.

"Curious sort of thing—day," said the cave bear. "Lot too much of it, I think. Quite unsuitable for hunting. Dazzles me always. I can't smell nearly so well by day."

The she-bear did not answer, but there came a measured crunching sound out of the darkness. She had turned up a bone.

Andoo yawned. "Well," he said. He strolled to the cave mouth and stood with his head projecting, surveying the amphitheatre. He found he had to turn his head completely round to see objects on his right-hand side. No doubt that eye would be all right tomorrow.

He yawned again. There was a tap overhead, and a big mass of chalk flew out from the cliff face, dropped a yard in front of his nose, and starred into a dozen unequal fragments. It startled him extremely.

When he had recovered a little from his shock, he went and sniffed curiously at the representative pieces of the fallen projectile. They had a distinctive flavour, oddly reminiscent of the two drab animals of the ledge. He sat up and pawed the larger lump, and walked round it several times, trying to find a man about it somewhere. . . .

When night had come he went off down the river gorge to see if he could cut off either of the ledge's occupants. The ledge was empty, there were no signs of the red thing, but as he was rather hungry he did not loiter long that night, but pushed on to pick up a red deer fawn. He forget about the drab animals. He found a fawn, but the doe was close by and made an ugly fight for her young. Andoo had to leave the fawn, but as her blood was up she stuck to the attack, and at last he got in a blow of his paw on her nose, and so got hold of her. More meat but less delicacy, and the she-bear, following, had her share. The next afternoon, curiously enough, the very fellow of the first white rock fell, and smashed precisely according to precedent.

The aim of the third, that fell the night after, however, was better. It hit Andoo's unspeculative skull with a crack that echoed up the cliff, and the white fragments went dancing to all the points of the compass. The she-bear, coming after him and sniffing curiously at him, found him lying in an odd sort of attitude, with his head wet and all out of shape. She was a young she-bear, and inexperienced, and having sniffed about him for some time and licked him a little, and so forth, she decided to leave him until the odd mood had passed, and went on her hunting alone.

She looked up the fawn of the red doe they had killed two nights ago, and found it. But it was lonely hunting without Andoo, and she returned caveward before dawn. The sky was grey and overcast, the trees up the gorge were black and unfamiliar, and into her ursine mind came a dim sense of strange and dreary happenings. She lifted up her voice and called Andoo by name. The sides of the gorge reëchoed her.

As she approached the caves she saw in the half-light, and heard a couple of jackals scuttle off, and immediately after a hyæna howled and a dozen clumsy bulks went lumbering up the slope, and stopped and yelled derision. "Lord of the rocks and caves—ya-ha!" came down the wind. The dismal feeling in the she-bear's mind became suddenly acute. She shuffled across the amphitheatre.

"Ya-ha!" said the hyænas, retreating. "Ya-ha!"

The cave bear was not lying quite in the same attitude, because the hyænas had been busy, and in one place his ribs showed white. Dotted over the turf about him lay the smashed fragments of the three great lumps of chalk. And the air was full of the scene of death.

The she-bear stopped dead. Even now that the great and wonderful Andoo was killed was beyond her believing. Then she heard far overhead a sound, a queer sound, a little like the shout of a hyæna but fuller and lower in pitch. She looked up, her little dawn-blinded eyes seeing little, her nostrils quivering. And there, on the cliff edge, far above her against the bright pink of dawn, were two little shaggy round dark things, the heads of Eudena and Ugh-lomi, as they shouted derision at her. But though she could not see them very distinctly she could hear, and dimly she began to apprehend. A novel feeling as of imminent strange evils came into her heart.

She began to examine the smashed fragments of chalk that lay about Andoo. For a space she stood still, looking about her and making a low continuous sound that was almost a moan. Then she went back incredulously to Andoo to make one last effort to rouse him.

### III.  *The First Horseman*

In the days before Ugh-lomi there was little trouble between the horses and men. They lived apart—the men in the river swamps and thickets, the horses on the wide grassy uplands between the chestnuts and the pines. Sometimes a pony would come straying into the clogging marshes to make a flint-hacked meal, and sometimes the tribe would find one, the kill of a lion, and drive off the jackals, and feast heartily while the sun was high. These horses of the old time were clumsy at the fetlock and dun-coloured, with a rough tail and big head. They came every spring-time north-westward into the country after the swallows and before the hippopotami, as the grass on the wide downland stretches grew long. They came only in small bodies thus far, each herd, a stallion and two or three mares and a foal or so, having its own stretch of country, and they went again when the chestnut-trees were yellow and the wolves came down the Wealden mountains.

It was their custom to graze right out in the open, going into cover only in the heat of the day. They avoided the long stretches of thorn and beech-wood, preferring an isolated group of trees void of ambuscade, so that it was hard to come upon them. They were never fighters; their heels and teeth were for one another, but in the clear country, once they were started, no living thing came near them, though perhaps the elephant might have done so had he felt the need. And in those days man seemed a harmless thing enough. No whisper of prophetic intelligence told the species of the terrible slavery that was to come, of the whip and spur and bearing-rein, the clumsy load and the slippery street, the insufficient food, and the knacker's yard, that was to replace the wide grass-land and the freedom of the earth.

Down in the Wey marshes Ugh-lomi and Eudena had never seen the horses closely, but now they saw them every day as the two of them raided out from their lair on the ledge in the gorge, raiding together in search of food. They had returned to the ledge after the killing of Andoo; for of the she-bear they were not afraid. The she-bear had become afraid of them, and when she winded them she went aside. The two went together everywhere; for since they had left the tribe Eudena was not so much Ugh-lomi's woman as his mate; she learnt to hunt even—as much, that is, as any woman could. She was indeed a marvellous woman. He would lie for hours watching a beast, or planning catches in that shock head of his, and she would stay beside him, with her bright eyes upon him, offering no irritating suggestions—as still as any man. A wonderful woman!

At the top of the cliff was an open grassy lawn and then beech-woods, and going through the beech-woods one came to the edge of the rolling grassy expanse, and in sight of the horses. Here, on the edge of the wood and bracken, were the rabbit-burrows, and here among the fronds Eudena and Ugh-iomi would lie with their throwing-stones ready, until the little people came out to nibble and play in the sunset. And while Eudena would sit, a silent figure of watchfulness, regarding the burrows, Ugh-lomi's eyes were ever away across the greensward at those wonderful grazing strangers.

In a dim way he appreciated their grace and their supple nimbleness. As the sun declined in the evening-time, and the heat of the day passed, they would become active, would start chasing one another, neighing, dodging, shaking their manes, coming round in great curves, sometimes so close that the pounding of the turf sounded like hurried thunder. It looked so fine that Ugh-lomi wanted to join in badly. And sometimes one would roll over on the turf, kicking four hoofs heavenward, which seemed formidable and was certainly much less alluring.

Dim imaginings ran through Ugh-lomi's mind as he watched —by virtue of which two rabbits lived the longer. And sleeping, his brains were clearer and bolder—for that was the way in those days. He came near the horses, he dreamt, and fought, smiting-stone against hoof, but then the horses changed to men, or, at least, to men with horses' heads, and he awoke in a cold sweat of terror.

Yet the next day in the morning, as the horses were grazing, one of the mares whinnied, and they saw Ugh-lomi coming up the wind. They all stopped their eating and watched him. Ugh-lomi was not coming towards them, but strolling obliquely across the open, looking at anything in the world but horses. He had stuck three fern-fronds into the mat of his hair, giving him a remarkable appearance, and he walked very slowly. "What's up now?" said the Master Horse, who was capable but inexperienced.

"It looks more like the first half of an animal than anything else in the world," he said. "Fore-legs and no hind."

"It's only one of those pink monkey things," said the Eldest Mare. "They're a sort of river monkey. They're quite common on the plains."

Ugh-lomi continued his oblique advance. The Eldest Mare was struck with the want of motive in his proceedings.

"Fool!" said the Eldest Mare, in a quick, conclusive way she had. She resumed her grazing. The Master Horse and the Second Mare followed suit.

"Look! he's nearer," said the Foal with a stripe.

One of the younger foals made uneasy movements. Ugh-lomi squatted down, and sat regarding the horses fixedly. In a little while he was satisfied that they meant neither flight nor hostilities. He began to consider his next procedure. He did not feel anxious to kill, but he had his axe with him, and the spirit of sport was upon him. How would one kill one of these creatures?—these great beautiful creatures!

Eudena, watching him with a fearful admiration from the cover of the bracken, saw him presently go on all fours, and so proceed again. But the horses preferred him a biped to a quadruped, and the Master Horse threw up his head and gave the word to move. Ugh-lomi thought they were off for good, but after a minute's gallop they came round in a wide curve, and stood winding him. Then, as a rise in the ground hid him, they tailed out, the Master Horse leading, and approached him spirally.

He was as ignorant of the possibilities of a horse as they were of his. And at this stage it would seem he funked. He knew this kind of stalking would make red deer or buffalo charge, if it were persisted in. At any rate, Eudena saw him jump up and come walking towards her with the fern plumes held in his hand.

She stood up, and he grinned to show that the whole thing was an immense lark, and that what he had done was just what he had planned to do from the very beginning. So that incident ended. But he was very thoughtful all that day.

The next day this foolish drab creature with the leonine mane, instead of going about the grazing or hunting he was made for, was prowling round the horses again. The Eldest Mare was all for silent contempt. "I suppose he wants to learn something from us," she said, and "*Let* him." The next day he was at it again. The Master Horse decided he meant absolutely nothing. But as a matter of fact, Ugh-lomi, the first of men to feel that curious spell of the horse that binds us even to this day, meant a great deal. He admired them unreservedly. There was a rudiment of the snob in him, I am afraid, and he wanted to be near these beautifully-curved animals. Then there were vague conceptions of a kill. If only they would let him come near them! But they drew the line, he found, at fifty yards. If he came nearer than that they moved off—with dignity. I suppose it was the way he had blinded Andoo that made him think of leaping on the back of one of them. But though Eudena after a time came out in the open too, and they did some unobtrusive stalking, things stopped there.

Then one memorable day a new idea came to Ugh-lomi. The horse looks down and level, but he does not look up. No animals

look up—they have too much common sense. It was only that
fantastic creature, man, could waste his wits skyward. Ugh-lomi
made no philosophical deductions, but he perceived the thing was
so. So he spent a weary day in a beech that stood in the open, while
Eudena stalked. Usually the horses went into the shade in the heat
of the afternoon, but that day the sky was overcast, and they
would not, in spite of Eudena's solicitude.

It was two days after that that Ugh-lomi had his desire. The
day was blazing hot, and the multiplying flies asserted themselves.
The horses stopped grazing before mid-day, and came into the
shadow below him, and stood in couples nose to tail, flapping.

The Master Horse, by virtue of his heels, came closest to the
tree. And suddenly there was a rustle and a creak, a *thud*. . . . Then
a sharp chipped flint bit him on the cheek. The Master Horse stumbled, came on one knee, rose to his feet, and was off like the wind.
The air was full of the whirl of limbs, the prance of hoofs, and
snorts of alarm. Ugh-lomi was pitched a foot in the air, came
down again, up again, his stomach was hit violently, and then his
knees got a grip of something between them. He found himself
clutching with knees, feet, and hands, careering violently with
extraordinary oscillation through the air—his axe gone Heaven
knows whither. "Hold tight," said Mother Instinct, and he did.

He was aware of a lot of coarse hair in his face, some of it
between his teeth, and of green turf streaming past in front of his
eyes. He saw the shoulder of the Master Horse, vast and sleek, with
the muscles flowing swiftly under the skin. He perceived that his
arms were round the neck, and that the violent jerkings he experienced had a sort of rhythm.

Then he was in the midst of a wild rush of tree-stems, and then
there were fronds of bracken about, and then more open turf.
Then a stream of pebbles rushing past, little pebbles flying sideways athwart the stream from the blow of the swift hoofs. Ugh-
lomi began to feel frightfully sick and giddy, but he was not the
stuff to leave go simply because he was uncomfortable.

He dared not leave his grip, but he tried to make himself more
comfortable. He released his hug on the neck, gripping the mane
instead. He slipped his knees forward, and pushing back, came
into a sitting position where the quarters broaden. It was nervous
work, but he managed it, and at last he was fairly seated astride,
breathless indeed, and uncertain, but with that frightful pounding
of his body at any rate relieved.

Slowly the fragments of Ugh-lomi's mind got into order again. The pace seemed to him terrific, but a kind of exultation was beginning to oust his first frantic terror. The air rushed by, sweet and wonderful, the rhythm of the hoofs changed and broke up and returned into itself again. They were on turf now, a wide glade—the beech-trees a hundred yards away on either side, and a succulent band of green starred with pink blossom and shot with silver water here and there, meandered down the middle. Far off was a glimpse of blue valley—far away. The exultation grew. It was man's first taste of pace.

Then came a wide space dappled with flying fallow deer scattering this way and that, and then a couple of jackals, mistaking Ugh-lomi for a lion, came hurrying after him. And when they saw it was not a lion they still came on out of curiosity. On galloped the horse, with his one idea of escape, and after him the jackals, with pricked ears and quickly barked remarks. "Which kills which?" said the first jackal. "It's the horse being killed," said the second. They gave the howl of following, and the horse answered to it as a horse answers nowadays to the spur.

On they rushed, a little tornado through the quiet day, putting up startled birds, sending a dozen unexpected things darting to cover, raising a myriad of indignant dung-flies, smashing little blossoms, flowering complacently, back into their parental turf. Trees again, and then splash, splash across a torrent; then a hare shot out of a tuft of grass under the very hoofs of the Master Horse, and the jackals left them incontinently. So presently they broke into the open again, a wide expanse of turfy hillside—the very grassy downs that fall northward nowadays from the Epsom Stand.

The first hot bolt of the Master Horse was long since over. He was falling into a measured trot, and Ugh-lomi, albeit bruised exceedingly and quite uncertain of the future, was in a state of glorious enjoyment. And now came a new development. The pace broke again, the Master Horse came round on a short curve, and stopped dead. . . .

Ugh-lomi became alert. He wished he had a flint, but the throwing flint he had carried in a thong about his waist was—like the axe—Heaven knows where. The Master Horse turned his head, and Ugh-lomi became aware of an eye and teeth. He whipped his leg into a position of security, and hit at the cheek with his fist. Then the head went down somewhere out of existence apparently, and

the back he was sitting on flew up into a dome. Ugh-lomi became
a thing of instinct again—strictly prehensile; he held by knees and
feet, and his head seemed sliding towards the turf. His fingers
were twisted into the shock of mane, and the rough hair of the
horse saved him. The gradient he was on lowered again, and then
—"Whup!" said Ugh-lomi, astonished, and the slant was the other
way up. But Ugh-lomi was a thousand generations nearer the primordial than man: no monkey could have held on better. And the
lion had been training the horse for countless generations against
the tactics of rolling and rearing back. But he kicked like a master,
and buck-jumped rather neatly. In five minutes Ugh-lomi lived a
lifetime. If he came off the horse would kill him, he felt assured.

Then the Master Horse decided to stick to his old tactics again,
and suddenly went off at a gallop. He headed down the slope, taking the steep places at a rush, swerving neither to the right nor to
the left, and, as they rode down, the wide expanse of valley sank
out of sight behind the approaching skirmishers of oak and hawthorn. They skirted a sudden hollow with the pool of a spring, rank
weeds and silver bushes. The ground grew softer and the grass
taller, and on the righthand side and the left came scattered bushes
of May—still splashed with belated blossom. Presently the bushes
thickened until they lashed the passing rider, and little flashes and
gouts of blood came out on horse and man. Then the way opened
again.

And then came a wonderful adventure. A sudden squeal of unreasonable anger rose amidst the bushes, the squeal of some creature
bitterly wronged. And crashing after them appeared a big, grey-
blue shape. It was Yaaa, the big-horned rhinoceros, in one of those
fits of fury of his, charging full tilt, after the manner of his kind.
He had been startled at his feeding, and someone, it did not matter
who, was to be ripped and trampled therefor. He was bearing down
on them from the left, with his wicked little eye red, his great horn
down, and his tail like a jury-mast behind him. For a minute Ugh-
lomi was minded to slip off and dodge, and then behold! the stac-
cato of the hoofs grew swifter, and the rhinoceros and his stumpy
hurrying little legs seemed to slide out at the back corner of Ugh-
lomi's eye. In two minutes they were through the bushes of May,
and out in the open, going fast. For a space he could hear the
ponderous paces in pursuit receding behind him, and then it was
just as if Yaaa had not lost his temper, as if Yaaa had never existed.

The pace never faltered, on they rode and on.

Ugh-lomi was now all exultation. To exult in those days was to insult. "Ya-ha! big nose!" he said, trying to crane back and see some remote speck of a pursuer. "Why don't you carry your smiting-stone in your fist?" he ended with a frantic whoop.

But that whoop was unfortunate, for coming close to the ear of the horse, and being quite unexpected, it startled the stallion extremely. He shied violently. Ugh-lomi suddenly found himself uncomfortable again. He was hanging on to the horse, he found, by one arm and one knee.

The rest of the ride was honourable but unpleasant. The view was chiefly of blue sky, and that was combined with the most unpleasant physical sensations. Finally, a bush of thorn lashed him and he let go.

He hit the ground with his cheek and shoulder, and then, after a complicated and extraordinarily rapid movement, hit it again with the end of his backbone. He saw splashes and sparks of light and colour. The ground seemed bouncing about just like the horse had done. Then he found he was sitting on turf, six yards beyond the bush. In front of him was a space of grass, growing greener and greener, and a number of human beings in the distance, and the horse was going round at a smart gallop quite a long way off to the right.

The human beings were on the opposite side of the river, some still in the water, but they were all running away as hard as they could go. The advent of a monster that took to pieces was not the sort of novelty they cared for. For quite a minute Ugh-lomi sat regarding them in a purely spectacular spirit. The bend of the river, the knoll among the reeds and royal ferns, the thin streams of smoke going up to Heaven, were all perfectly familiar to him. It was the squatting-place of the Sons of Uya, of Uya from whom he had fled with Eudena, and whom he had waylaid in the chestnut-woods and killed with the first axe.

He rose to his feet, still dazed from his fall, and as he did so the scattering fugitive turned and regarded him. Some pointed to the receding horse and chattered. He walked slowly towards them, staring. He forgot the horse, he forgot his own bruises, in the growing interest of this encounter. There were fewer of them than there had been—he supposed the others must have hid—the heap of fern for the night fire was not so high. By the flint heaps should have sat Wau—but then he remembered he had killed Wau. Suddenly brought back to this familiar scene, the gorge and the bears and Eudena seemed things remote, things dreamt of.

He stopped at the bank and stood regarding the tribe. His mathematical abilities were of the slightest, but it was certain there were fewer. The men might be away, but there were fewer women and children. He gave the shout of home-coming. His quarrel had been with Uya and Wau—not with the others. "Children of Uya!" he cried. They answered with his name, a little fearfully because of the strange way he had come.

For a space they spoke together. Then an old woman lifted a shrill voice and answered him, "Our Lord is a Lion."

Ugh-lomi did not understand that saying. They answered him again several together, "Uya comes again. He comes as a Lion. Our Lord is a Lion. He comes at night. He slays whom he will. But none other may slay us, Ugh-lomi, none other may slay us."

Still Ugh-lomi did not understand.

"Our Lord is a Lion. He speaks no more to men."

Ugh-lomi stood regarding them. He had had dreams—he knew that though he had killed Uya, Uya still existed. And now they told him Uya was a Lion.

The shrivelled old woman, the mistress of the fire-minders, suddenly turned and spoke softly to those next to her. She was a very old woman indeed, she had been the first of Uya's wives, and he had let her live beyond the age to which it is seemly a woman should be permitted to live. She had been cunning from the first, cunning to please Uya and to get food. And now she was great in counsel. She spoke softly, and Ugh-lomi watched her shrivelled form across the river with a curious distaste. Then she called aloud, "Come over to us, Ugh-Lomi."

A girl suddenly lifted up her voice. "Come over to us, Ugh-lomi," she said. And they all began crying, "Come over to us, Ugh-lomi."

It was strange how their manner changed after the old woman called.

He stood quite still watching them all. It was pleasant to be called, and the girl who had called first was a pretty one. But she made him think of Eudena.

"Come over to us, Ugh-lomi," they cried, and the voice of the shrivelled old woman rose above them all. At the sound of her voice his hesitation returned.

He stood on the river bank, Ugh-lomi—Ugh the Thinker—with his thoughts slowly taking shape. Presently one and then another paused to see what he would do. He was minded to go back, he was minded not to. Suddenly his fear or his caution got the upper hand. Without answering them he turned, and walked back towards the distant thorn-trees, the way he had come. Forthwith the whole tribe started crying to him again very eagerly. He hesitated and turned, then he went on, then he turned again, and then once again, regarding them with troubled eyes as they called. The last time he took two paces back, before his fear stopped him. They saw him stop once more, and suddenly shake his head and vanish among the hawthorn-trees.

Then all the women and children lifted up their voices together, and called to him in one last vain effort.

Far down the river the reeds were stirring in the breeze, where, convenient for his new sort of feeding, the old lion, who had taken to man-eating, had made his lair.

The old woman turned her face that way, and pointed to the hawthorn thickets. "Uya," she screamed, "there goes thine enemy! There goes thine enemy, Uya! Why do you devour us nightly? We have tried to snare him! There goes thine enemy, Uya!"

But the lion who preyed upon the tribe was taking his siesta. The cry went unheard. That day he had dined on one of the plumper girls, and his mood was a comfortable placidity. He really did not understand that he was Uya or that Ugh-lomi was his enemy.

So it was that Ugh-lomi rode the horse, and heard first of Uya the Lion, who had taken the place of Uya the Master, and was eating up the tribe. And as he hurried back to the gorge his mind was no longer full of the horse, but of the thought that Uya was still alive, to slay or be slain. Over and over again he saw the shrunken band of women and children crying that Uya was a lion. Uya was a lion!

And presently, fearing the twilight might come upon him, Ugh-lomi began running.

### IV. Uya the Lion

The old lion was in luck. The tribe had a certain pride in their ruler, but that was all the satisfaction they got out of it. He came the very night that Ugh-lomi killed Uya the Cunning, and so it

was they named him Uya. It was the old woman, the fire-minder,
who first named him Uya. A shower had lowered the fires to a
glow, and made the night dark. And as they conversed together,
and peered at one another in the darkness, and wondered fearfully
what Uya would do to them in their dreams now that he was dead,
they heard the mounting reverberations of the lion's roar close
at hand. Then everything was still.

They held their breath, so that almost the only sounds were
the patter of the rain and the hiss of the raindrops in the ashes.
And then, after an interminable time, a crash, and a shriek of fear,
and a growling. They sprang to their feet, shouting, screaming,
running this way and that, but brands would not burn, and in a
minute the victim was being dragged away through the ferns. It
was Irk, the brother of Wau.

So the lion came.

The ferns were still wet from the rain the next night, and he
came and took Click with the red hair. That sufficed for two nights.
And then in the dark between the moons he came three nights,
night after night, and that though they had good fires. He was
an old lion with stumpy teeth, but very silent and very cool; he
knew of fires before; these were not the first of mankind that had
ministered to his old age. The third night he came between the
outer fire and the inner, and he leapt the flint heap, and pulled down
Irm the son of Irk, who had seemed like to be the leader. That was
a dreadful night, because they lit great flares of fern and ran
screaming, and the lion missed his hold of Irm. By the glare of the
fire they saw Irm struggle up, and run a little way towards them,
and then the lion in two bounds had him down again. That was
the last of Irm.

So fear came, and all the delight of spring passed out of their
lives. Already there were five gone out of the tribe, and four nights
added three more to the number. Food-seeking became spiritless,
none knew who might go next, and all day the women toiled, even
the favourite women, gathering litter and sticks for the night-fires.
And the hunters hunted ill: in the warm spring-time hunger came
again as though it was still winter. The tribe might have moved,
had they had a leader, but they had no leader, and none knew
where to go that the lion could not follow them. So the old lion
waxed fat and thanked heaven for the kindly race of men. Two of
the children and a youth died while the moon was still new, and
then it was the shrivelled old fire-minder first bethought herself

in a dream of Eudena and Ugh-lomi, and of the way Uya had been slain. She had lived in fear of Uya all her days, and now she lived in fear of the lion. That Ugh-lomi could kill Uya for good—Ugh-lomi whom she had seen born—was impossible. It was Uya still seeking his enemy!

And then came the strange return of Ugh-lomi, a wonderful animal seen galloping far across the river, that suddenly changed into two animals, a horse and a man. Following this portent, the vision of Ugh-lomi on the farther bank of the river. . . . Yes, it was all plain to her. Uya was punishing them, because they had not hunted down Ugh-lomi and Eudena.

The men came straggling back to the chances of the night while the sun was still golden in the sky. They were received with the story of Ugh-lomi. She went across the river with them and showed them his spoor hesitating on the farther bank. Siss the Tracker knew the feet for Ugh-lomi's. "Uya needs Ugh-lomi," cried the old woman, standing on the left of the bend, a gesticulating figure of flaring bronze in the sunset. Her cries were strange sounds, flitting to and fro on the borderland of speech, but this was the sense they carried: "The lion needs Eudena. He comes night after night seeking Eudena and Ugh-lomi. When he cannot find Eudena and Ugh-lomi, he grows angry and he kills. Hunt Eudena and Ugh-lomi, Eudena whom he pursued, and Ugh-lomi for whom he gave the death-word! Hunt Eudena and Ugh-lomi!"

She turned to the distant reed-bed, as sometimes she had turned to Uya in his life. "Is it not so, my lord?" she cried. And, as if in answer, the tall reeds bowed before a breath of wind.

Far into the twilight the sound of hacking was heard from the squatting-places. It was the men sharpening their ashen spears against the hunting of the morrow. And in the night, early before the moon rose, the lion came and took the girl of Siss the Tracker.

In the morning before the sun had risen, Siss the Tracker, and the lad Wau-hau, who now chipped flints, and One Eye, and Bo, and the Snail-Eater, the two red-haired men, and Cat's-skin and Snake, all the men that were left alive of the Sons of Uya, taking their ash spears and their smiting-stones, and with throwing-stones in the beast-paw bags, started forth upon the trail of Ugh-lomi through the hawthorn thickets where Yaaa the Rhinoceros and his brothers were feeding, and up the bare downland towards the beech-woods.

That night the fires burnt high and fierce, as the waxing moon set, and the lion left the crouching women and children in peace.

And the next day, while the sun was still high, the hunters returned—all save One Eye, who lay dead with a smashed skull at the foot of the ledge. (When Ugh-lomi came back that evening from stalking the horses, he found the vultures already busy over him.) And with them the hunters brought Eudena, bruised and wounded, but alive. That had been the strange order of the shrivelled old woman, that she was to be brought alive—"She is no kill for us. She is for Uya the Lion." Her hands were tied with thongs, as though she had been a man, and she came weary and drooping—her hair over her eyes and matted with blood. They walked about her, and ever and again the Snail-Eater, whose name she had given, would laugh and strike her with his ashen spear. And after he had struck her with his spear, he would look over his shoulder like one who had done an over-bold deed. The others, too, looked over their shoulders ever and again, and all were in a hurry save Eudena. When the old woman saw them coming, she cried aloud with joy.

They made Eudena cross the river with her hands tied, although the current was strong and when she slipped the old woman screamed, first with joy and then for fear she might be drowned. And when they had dragged Eudena to shore, she could not stand for a time, albeit they beat her sore. So they let her sit with her feet touching the water, and her eyes staring before her, and her face set, whatever they might do or say. All the tribe came down to the squatting-place, even curly little Haha, who as yet could scarcely toddle and stood staring at Eudena and the old woman, as now we should stare at some strange wounded beast and its captor.

The old woman tore off the necklace of Uya that was about Eudena's neck, and put it on herself—she had been the first to wear it. Then she tore at Eudena's hair, and took a spear from Siss and beat her with all her might. And when she had vented the warmth of her heart on the girl she looked closely into her face. Eudena's eyes were closed and her features were set, and she lay so still that for a moment the old woman feared she was dead. And then her nostrils quivered. At that the old woman slapped her face and laughed and gave the spear to Siss again, and went a little way off from her and began to talk and jeer at her after her manner.

The old woman had more words than any in the tribe. And her talk was a terrible thing to hear. Sometimes she screamed and moaned incoherently, and sometimes the shape of her guttural cries was the mere phantom of thoughts. But she conveyed to Eudena, nevertheless, much of the things that were yet to come, of the Lion and of the torment he would do her. "And Ugh-lomi! Ha, ha! Ugh-lomi is slain?"

And suddenly Eudena's eyes opened and she sat up again, and her look met the old woman's fair and level. "No," she said slowly, like one trying to remember, "I did not see my Ugh-lomi slain. I did not see my Ugh-lomi slain."

"Tell her," cried the old woman, "Tell her—he that killed him. Tell her how Ugh-lomi was slain."

She looked, and all the women and children there looked, from man to man.

None answered her. They stood shamefaced.

"Tell her," said the old woman. The men looked at one another. Eudena's face suddenly lit.

"Tell her," she said. "Tell her, mighty men! Tell her the killing of Ugh-lomi."

The old woman rose and struck her sharply across her mouth.

"We could not find Ugh-lomi," said Siss the Tracker, slowly. "Who hunts two, kills none."

Then Eudena's heart leapt, but she kept her face hard. It was as well, for the old woman looked at her sharply, with murder in her eyes.

Then the old woman turned her tongue upon the men because they had feared to go on after Ugh-lomi. She dreaded no one now Uya was slain. She scolded them as one scolds children. And they scowled at her, and began to accuse one another. Until suddenly Siss the Tracker raised his voice and bade her hold her peace.

And so when the sun was setting they took Eudena and went—though their hearts sank within them—along the trail the old lion had made in the reeds. All the men went together. At one place was a group of alders, and here they hastily bound Eudena where the lion might find her when he came abroad in the twilight, and having done so they hurried back until they were near the squatting-place. Then they stopped. Siss stopped first and looked back again at the alders. They could see her head even from the squatting-place, a little black shock under the limb of the larger tree. That was as well.

All the women and children stood watching upon the crest of

the mound. And the old woman stood and screamed for the lion to take her whom he sought, and counselled him on the torments he might do her.

Eudena was very weary now, stunned by beatings and fatigue and sorrow, and only the fear of the thing that was still to come upheld her. The sun was broad and blood-red between the stems of the distant chestnuts, and the west was all on fire; the evening breeze had died to a warm tranquillity. The air was full of midge swarms, the fish in the river hard by would leap at times, and now and again a cockchafer would drone through the air. Out of the corner of her eye Eudena could see a part of the squatting-knoll, and little figures standing and staring at her. And—a very little sound but very clear—she could hear the beating of the firestone. Dark and near to her and still was the reed-fringed thicket of the lair.

Presently the firestone ceased. She looked for the sun and found he had gone, and overhead and growing brighter was the waxing moon. She looked towards the thicket of the lair, seeking shapes in the reeds, and then suddenly she began to wriggle and wriggle, weeping and calling upon Ugh-lomi.

But Ugh-lomi was far away. When they saw her head moving with her struggles, they shouted together on the knoll, and she desisted and was still. And then came the bats, and the star that was like Ugh-lomi crept out of its blue hiding place in the west. She called to it, but softly, because she feared the lion. And all through the coming of the twilight the thicket was still.

So the dark crept upon Eudena, and the moon grew bright, and the shadows of things that had fled up the hillside and vanished with the evening came back to them short and black. And the dark shapes in the thicket of reeds and alders where the lion lay, gathered, and a faint stir began there. But nothing came out therefrom all through the gathering of the darkness.

She looked at the squatting-place and saw the fires glowing smoky-red, and the men and women going to and fro. The other way, over the river, a white mist was rising. Then far away came the whimpering of young foxes and the yell of a hyæna.

There were long gaps of aching waiting. After a long time some animal splashed in the water, and seemed to cross the river at the ford beyond the lair, but what animal it was she could not see. From the distant drinking-pools she could hear the sound of splashing, and the noise of elephants—so still was the night.

The earth was now a colourless arrangement of white reflections and impenetrable shadows, under the blue sky. The silvery moon was already spotted with the filigree crests of the chestnut-woods, and over the shadowy eastward hills the stars were multiplying. The knoll fires were bright red now, and black figures stood waiting against them. They were waiting for a scream. . . . Surely it would be soon.

The night suddenly seemed full of movement. She held her breath. Things were passing—one, two, three—subtly sneaking shadows. . . . Jackals.

Then a long waiting again.

Then, asserting itself as real at once over all the sounds her mind had imagined, came a stir in the thicket, then a vigorous movement. There was a snap. The reeds crashed heavily, once, twice, thrice, and then everything was still save a measured swishing. She heard a low tremulous growl, and then everything was still again. The stillness lengthened—would it never end? She held her breath; she bit her lips to stop screaming. Then something scuttled through the undergrowth. Her scream was involuntary. She did not hear the answering yell from the mound.

Immediately the thicket woke up to vigorous movement again. She saw the grass stems waving in the light of the setting moon, the alders swaying. She struggled violently—her last struggle. But nothing came towards her. A dozen monsters seemed rushing about in that little place for a couple of minutes, and then again came silence. The moon sank behind the distant chestnuts and the night was dark.

Then an odd sound, a sobbing panting, that grew faster and fainter. Yet another silence, and then dim sounds and the grunting of some animal.

Everything was still again. Far away eastwards an elephant trumpeted, and from the woods came a snarling and yelping that died away.

In the long interval the moon shone out again, between the stems of the trees on the ridge, sending two great bars of light and a bar of darkness across the reedy waste. Then came a steady rustling, a splash, and the reeds swayed wider and wider apart. And at last they broke open, cleft from root to crest. . . . The end had come.

She looked to see the thing that had come out of the reeds. For a moment it seemed certainly the great head and jaw she expected, and then it dwindled and changed. It was a dark low thing, that remained silent, but it was not the lion. It became still—everything became still. She peered. It was like some gigantic frog, two limbs and a slanting body. Its head moved about searching the shadows. . . .

A rustle, and it moved clumsily, with a sort of hopping. And as it moved it gave a low groan.

The blood rushing through her veins was suddenly joy. "*Ugh-lomi!*" she whispered.

The thing stopped. "*Eudena*," he answered softly with pain in his voice, and peering into the alders.

He moved again, and came out of the shadow beyond the reeds into the moonlight. All his body was covered with dark smears. She saw he was dragging his leg, and that he gripped his axe, the first axe, in one hand. In another moment he had struggled into the position of all fours, and had staggered over to her. "The lion," he said in a strange mingling of exultation and anguish. "Wau!— I have slain a lion. With my own hand. Even as I slew the great bear." He moved to emphasise his words, and suddenly broke off with a faint cry. For a space he did not move.

"Let me free," whispered Eudena. . . .

He answered her no words but pulled himself up from his crawling attitude by means of the alder stem, and hacked at her thongs with the sharp edge of his axe. She heard him sob at each blow. He cut away the thongs about her chest and arms, and then his hand dropped. His chest struck against her shoulder and he slipped down beside her and lay still.

But the rest of her release was easy. Very hastily she freed herself. She made one step from the tree, and her head was spinning. Her last conscious movement was towards him. She reeled, and dropped. Her hand fell upon his thigh. It was soft and wet, and gave way under her pressure; he cried out at her touch, and writhed and lay still again.

Presently a dark dog-like shape came very softly through the reeds. Then stopped dead and stood sniffing, hesitated, and at last turned and slunk back into the shadows.

Long was the time they remained there motionless, with the light of the setting moon shining on their limbs. Very slowly, as slowly as the setting of the moon, did the shadow of the reeds towards the mound flow over them. Presently their legs were hidden, and Ugh-lomi was but a bust of silver. The shadow crept to his neck, crept over his face, and so at last the darkness of the night swallowed them up.

The shadow became full of instinctive stirrings. There was a patter of feet, and a faint snarling—the sound of a blow.

There was little sleep that night for the women and children at the squatting-place until they heard Eudena scream. But the men were weary and sat dozing. When Eudena screamed they felt assured of their safety, and hurried to get the nearest places to the fires. The old woman laughed at the scream, and laughed again because Si, the little friend of Eudena, whimpered. Directly the dawn came they were all alert and looking towards the alders. They could see that Eudena had been taken. They could not help feeling glad to think that Uya was appeased. But across the minds of the men the thought of Ugh-lomi fell like a shadow. They could understand revenge, for the world was old in revenge, but they did not think of rescue. Suddenly a hyæna fled out of the thicket, and came galloping across the reed space. His muzzle and paws were dark-stained. At that sight all the men shouted and clutched at throwing-stones and ran towards him, for no animal is so pitiful a coward as the hyæna by day. All men hated the hyæna because he preyed on children, and would come and bite when one was sleeping on the edge of the squatting-place. And Cat's-skin, throwing fair and straight, hit the brute shrewdly on the flank, whereat the whole tribe yelled with delight.

At the noise they made there came a flapping of wings from the lair of the lion, and three white-headed vultures rose slowly and circled and came to rest amidst the branches of an alder, overlooking the lair. "Our lord is abroad," said the old woman, pointing. "The vultures have their share of Eudena." For a space they remained there, and then first one and then another dropped back into the thicket.

Then over the eastern woods, and touching the whole world of life and colour, poured, with the exaltation of a trumpet blast, the light of the rising sun. At the sight of him the children shouted together, and clapped their hands and began to race off towards the water. Only little Si lagged behind and looked wonderingly at the alders where she had seen the head of Eudena overnight.

But Uya, the old lion, was not abroad, but at home, and he lay very still, and a little on one side. He was not in his lair, but a little way from it in a place of trampled grass. Under one eye was a little wound, the feeble little bite of the first axe. But all the ground beneath his chest was ruddy brown with a vivid streak, and in his chest was a little hole that had been made by Ugh-lomi's stabbing-spear. Along his side and at his neck the vultures had marked their claims. For so Ugh-lomi had slain him, lying stricken under his paw and thrusting haphazard at his chest. He had driven the spear in with all his strength and stabbed the giant to the heart. So it was the reign of the lion, of the second incarnation of Uya the Master, came to an end.

From the knoll the bustle of preparation grew, the hacking of spears and throwing-stones. None spake the name of Ugh-lomi for fear that it might bring him. The men were going to keep together, close together, in the hunting for a day or so. And their hunting was to be Ugh-lomi, lest instead he should come a-hunting them.

But Ugh-lomi was lying very still and silent, outside the lion's lair, and Eudena squatted beside him, with the ash spear, all smeared with lion's blood, gripped in her hand.

### V. *The Fight in the Lion's Thicket*

Ugh-lomi lay still, his back against an alder, and his thigh was a red mass terrible to see. No civilised man could have lived who had been so sorely wounded, but Eudena got him thorns to close his wounds, and squatted beside him day and night, smiting the flies from him with a fan of reeds by day, and in the night threatening the hyænas with the first axe in her hand; and in a little while he began to heal. It was high summer, and there was no rain. Little food they had during the first two days his wounds were open. In the low place where they hid were no roots nor little beasts, and the stream, with its water-snails and fish, was in the open a hundred yards away. She could not go abroad by day for fear of the tribe, her brothers and sisters, nor by night for fear of the beasts, both on his account and hers. So they shared the lion with the vultures. But there was a trickle of water near by, and Eudena brought him plenty in her hands.

Where Ugh-lomi lay was well hidden from the tribe by a thicket of alders, and all fenced about with bulrushes and tall reeds. The dead lion he had killed lay near his old lair on a place of trampled reeds fifty yards away, in sight through the reed-stems, and the vultures fought each other for the choicest pieces and kept the jackals off him. Very soon a cloud of flies that looked like bees hung over him, and Ugh-lomi could hear their humming. And when Ugh-lomi's flesh was already healing—and it was not many days before that began—only a few bones of the lion remained scattered and shining white.

For the most part Ugh-lomi sat still during the day, looking before him at nothing; sometimes he would mutter of the horses and bears and lions, and sometimes he would beat the ground with the first axe and say the names of the tribe—he seemed to have no fear of bringing the tribe—for hours together. But chiefly he slept, dreaming little because of his loss of blood and the slightness of his food. During the short summer night both kept awake. All the while the darkness lasted things moved about them, things they never saw by day. For some nights the hyænas did not come, and then one moonless night near a dozen came and fought for what was left of the lion. The night was a tumult of growling, and Ugh-lomi and Eudena could hear the bones snap in their teeth. But they knew the hyæna dare not attack any creature alive and awake, and so they were not greatly afraid.

Of a daytime Eudena would go along the narrow path the old lion had made in the reeds until she was beyond the bend, and then she would creep into the thicket and watch the tribe. She would lie close by the alders where they had bound her to offer her up to the lion, and thence she could see them on the knoll by the fire, small and clear, as she had seen them that night. But she told Ugh-lomi little of what she saw, because she feared to bring them by their names. For so they believed in those days, that naming called.

She saw the men prepare stabbing-spears and throwing-stones on the morning after Ugh-lomi had slain the lion, and go out to hunt him, leaving the women and children on the knoll. Little they knew how near he was as they tracked off in single file towards the hills, with Siss the Tracker leading them. And she watched the women and children, after the men had gone, gathering fern-fronds and twigs for the night-fire, and the boys and girls running and playing together. But the very old woman made her feel afraid. Towards noon, when most of the others were down at the stream by the bend, she came and stood on the hither side of the knoll, a gnarled brown figure, and gesticulated so that Eudena could scarce believe she was not seen. Eudena lay like a hare in its form, with shining eyes fixed on the bent witch away there, and presently she dimly understood it was the lion the old woman was worshipping— the lion Ugh-lomi had slain.

And the next day the hunters came back weary, carrying a fawn, and Eudena watched the feast enviously. And then came a strange thing. She saw—distinctly she heard—the old woman shrieking and gesticulating and pointing towards her. She was afraid, and crept like a snake out of sight again. But presently curiosity overcame her and she was back at her spying-place, and as she peered her heart stopped, for there were all the men, with their weapons in their hands, walking together towards her from the knoll.

She dared not move lest her movement should be seen, but she pressed herself close to the ground. The sun was low and the golden light was in the faces of the men. She saw they carried a piece of rich red meat thrust through by an ashen stake. Presently they stopped. "Go on!" screamed the old woman. Cat's-skin grumbled, and they came on, searching the thicket with sun-dazzled eyes. "Here!" said Siss. And they took the ashen stake with the meat upon it and thrust it into the ground. "Uya!" cried Siss, "behold thy portion. And Ugh-lomi we have slain. Of a truth we have slain Ugh-lomi. This day we slew Ugh-lomi, and to-morrow we will bring his body to you." And the others repeated the words.

They looked at each other and behind them, and partly turned and began going back. At first they walked half-turned to the thicket, then, facing the mound, they walked faster, looking over their shoulders, then faster; soon they ran, it was a race at last, until they were near the knoll. Then Siss, who was hindmost, was first to slacken his pace.

The sunset passed and the twilight came, the fires glowed red against the hazy blue of the distant chestnut-trees, and the voices over the mound were merry. Eudena lay scarcely stirring, looking from the mound to the meat and then to the mound. She was hungry, but she was afraid. At last she crept back to Ugh-lomi.

He looked round at the little rustle of her approach. His face was in shadow. "Have you got me some food?" he said.

She said she could find nothing, but that she would seek farther, and went back along the lion's path until she could see the mound again, but she could not bring herself to take the meat; she had the brute's instinct of a snare. She felt very miserable.

She crept back at last towards Ugh-lomi and heard him stirring and moaning. She turned back to the mound again; then she saw something in the darkness near the stake, and peering distinguished a jackal. In a flash she was brave and angry; she sprang up, cried out, and ran towards the offering. She stumbled and fell, and heard the growling of the jackal going off.

When she arose only the ashen stake lay on the ground, the meat was gone. So she went back, to fast through the night with Ugh-lomi; and Ugh-lomi was angry with her, because she had no food for him; but she told him nothing of the things she had seen.

Two days passed and they were near starving, when the tribe slew a horse. Then came the same ceremony, and a haunch was left on the ashen stake; but this time Eudena did not hesitate.

By acting and words she made Ugh-lomi understand, but he ate most of the food before he understood; and then as her meaning passed to him he grew merry with his food. "I am Uya," he said; "I am the Lion. I am the Great Cave Bear, I who was only Ugh-lomi. I am Wau the Cunning. It is well that they should feed me, for presently I will kill them all."

Then Eudena's heart was light, and she laughed with him; and afterwards she ate what he had left of the horseflesh with gladness.

After that it was he had a dream, and the next day he made Eudena bring him the lion's teeth and claws—so much of them as she could find—and hack him a club of alder. And he put the teeth and claws very cunningly into the wood so that the points were outward. Very long it took him, and he blunted two of the teeth hammering them in, and was very angry and threw the thing away; but afterwards he dragged himself to where he had thrown it and finished it—a club of a new sort set with teeth. That day there was more meat for them both, an offering to the lion from the tribe.

It was one day—more than a hand's fingers of days, more than anyone had skill to count—after Ugh-lomi had made the club, that Eudena while he was asleep was lying in the thicket watching the squatting-place. There had been no meat for three days. And the old woman came and worshipped after her manner. Now while she worshipped, Eudena's little friend Si and another, the child of the first girl Siss had loved, came over the knoll and stood regarding her skinny figure, and presently they began to mock her. Eudena found this entertaining, but suddenly the old woman turned on them quickly and saw them. For a moment she stood and they stood motionless, and then with a shriek of rage, she rushed towards them, and all three disappeared over the crest of the knoll.

Presently the children reappeared among the ferns beyond the shoulder of the hill. Little Si ran first, for she was an active girl, and the other child ran squealing with the old woman close upon her.

And over the knoll came Siss with a bone in his hand, and Bo and Cat's-skin obsequiously behind him, each holding a piece of food, and they laughed aloud and shouted to see the old woman so angry. And with a shriek the child was caught and the old woman set to work slapping and the child screaming, and it was very good after-dinner fun for them. Little Si ran on a little way and stopped at last between fear and curiosity.

And suddenly came the mother of the child, with hair streaming, panting, and with a stone in her hand, and the old woman turned about like a wild cat. She was the equal of any woman, was the chief of the fire-minders, in spite of her years; but before she could do anything Siss shouted to her and the clamour rose loud. Other shock heads came into sight. It seemed the whole tribe was at home and feasting. But the old woman dared not go on wreaking herself on the child Siss befriended.

Everyone made noises and called names—even little Si. Abruptly the old woman let go of the child she had caught and made a swift run at Si, for Si had no friends; and Si, realising her danger when it was almost upon her, made off headlong, with a faint cry of terror, not heeding whither she ran, straight to the lair of the lion. She swerved aside into the reeds presently, realising now whither she went.

But the old woman was a wonderful old woman, as active as she was spiteful, and she caught Si by the streaming hair within thirty yards of Eudena. All the tribe now was running down the knoll and shouting and laughing, ready to see the fun.

Then something stirred in Eudena; something that had never stirred in her before; and, thinking all of little Si and nothing of her fear, she sprang up from her ambush and ran swiftly forward. The old woman did not see her, for she was busy beating little Si's face with her hand, beating with all her heart, and suddenly something hard and heavy struck her cheek. She went reeling, and saw Eudena with flaming eyes and cheeks between her and little Si. She shrieked with astonishment and terror, and little Si, not understanding, set off towards the gaping tribe. They were quite close now, for the sight of Eudena had driven their fading fear of the lion out of their heads.

In a moment Eudena had turned from the cowering old woman and overtaken Si. "Si!" she cried, "Si!" She caught the child up in her arms as it stopped, pressed the nail-lined face to hers, and turned about to run towards her lair, the lair of the old lion. The old woman stood waist-high in the reeds, and screamed foul things and inarticulate rage, but did not dare to intercept her; and at the bend of the path Eudena looked back and saw all the men of the tribe crying to one another and Siss coming at a trot along the lion's trail.

She ran straight along the narrow way through the reeds to the shady place where Ugh-lomi sat with his healing thigh, just awakened by the shouting and rubbing his eyes. She came to him, a woman, with little Si in her arms. Her heart throbbed in her throat. "Ugh-lomi!" she cried. "Ugh-lomi, the tribe comes!"

Ugh-lomi sat staring in stupid astonishment at her and Si.

She pointed with Si in one arm. She sought among her feeble store of words to explain. She could hear the men calling. Apparently they had stopped outside. She put down Si and caught up the new club with the lion's teeth, and put it into Ugh-lomi's hand, and ran three yards and picked up the first axe.

"Ah!" said Ugh-lomi, waving the new club, and suddenly he perceived the occasion and, rolling over, began to struggle to his feet.

He stood but clumsily. He supported himself by one hand against the tree, and just touched the ground gingerly with the toe of his wounded leg. In the other hand he gripped the new club. He looked at his healing thigh; and suddenly the reeds began whispering, and ceased and whispered again, and coming cautiously along the track, bending down and holding his fire-hardened stabbing-stick of ash in his hand, appeared Siss. He stopped dead, and his eyes met Ugh-lomi's.

Ugh-lomi forgot he had a wounded leg. He stood firmly on both feet. Something trickled. He glanced down and saw a little gout of blood had oozed out along the edge of the healing wound. He rubbed his hand there to give him the grip of his club, and fixed his eyes again on Siss.

"Wau!" he cried, and sprang forward, and Siss, still stooping and watchful, drove his stabbing-stick up very quickly in an ugly thrust. It ripped Ugh-lomi's guarding arm and the club came down in a counter that Siss was never to understand. He fell, as an ox falls to the pole-axe, at Ugh-lomi's feet.

To Bo it seemed the strangest thing. He had a comforting sense of tall reeds on either side, and an impregnable rampart, Siss, between him and any danger. Snail-eater was close behind and there was no danger there. He was prepared to shove behind and send

Siss to death or victory. That was his place as second man. He saw the butt of the spear Siss carried leap away from him, and suddenly a dull whack and the broad back fell away forward, and he looked Ugh-lomi in the face over his prostrate leader. It felt to Bo as if his heart had fallen down a well. He had a throwing-stone in one hand and an ashen stabbing-stick in the other. He did not live to the end of his momentary hesitation which to use.

Snail-eater was a readier man, and besides Bo did not fall forward as Siss had done, but gave at his knees and hips, crumpling up with the toothed club upon his head. The Snail-eater drove his spear forward swift and straight, and took Ugh-lomi in the muscle of the shoulder, and then he drove him hard with the smiting-stone in his other hand, shouting out as he did so. The new club swished ineffectually through the reeds. Eudena saw Ugh-lomi come staggering back from the narrow path into the open space, tripping over Siss and with a foot of ashen stake sticking out of him over his arm. And then the Snail-eater, whose name she had given, had his final injury from her, as his exultant face came out of the reeds after his spear. For she swung the first axe swift and high, and hit him fair and square on the temple; and down he went on Siss at prostrate Ugh-lomi's feet.

But before Ugh-lomi could get up, the two red-haired men were tumbling out of the reeds, spears and smiting-stones ready, and Snake hard behind them. One she struck on the neck, but not to fell him, and he blundered aside and spoilt his brother's blow at Ugh-lomi's head. In a moment Ugh-lomi dropped his club and had his assailant by the waist, and had pitched him sideways sprawling. He snatched at his club again and recovered it. The man Eudena had hit stabbed at her with his spear as he stumbled from her blow, and involuntarily she gave ground to avoid him. He hesitated between her and Ugh-lomi, half-turned, gave a vague cry at finding Ugh-lomi so near, and in a moment Ugh-lomi had him by the throat, and the club had its third victim. As he went down Ugh-lomi shouted—no words, but an exultant cry.

The other red-haired man was six feet from her with his back to her, and a darker red streaking his head. He was struggling to his feet. She had an irrational impulse to stop his rising. She flung the axe at him, missed, saw his face in profile, and he had swerved beyond little Si, and was running through the reeds. She had a transitory vision of Snake standing in the throat of the path, half-turned away from her, and then she saw his back. She saw the club whirling through the air, and the shock head of Ugh-lomi, with blood in the hair and blood upon the shoulder, vanishing below the reeds in pursuit. Then she heard Snake scream like a woman.

She ran past Si to where the handle of the axe stuck out of a clump of fern, and turning, found herself panting and alone with three motionless bodies. The air was full of shouts and screams. For a space she was sick and giddy, and then it came into her head that Ugh-lomi was being killed along the reed-path, and with an inarticulate cry she leapt over the body of Bo and hurried after him. Snake's feet lay across the path, and his head was among the reeds. She followed the path until it bent round and opened out by the alders, and thence she saw all that was left of the tribe in the open, scattering like dead leaves before a gale, and going back over the knoll. Ugh-lomi was hard upon Cat's-skin.

But Cat's-skin was fleet of foot and got away, and so did young Wau-Hau when Ugh-lomi turned upon him, and Ugh-lomi pursued Wau-Hau far beyond the knoll before he desisted. He had the rage of battle on him now, and the wood thrust through his shoulder stung him like a spur. When she saw he was in no danger she stopped running and stood panting, watching the distant active figures run up and vanish one by one over the knoll. In a little time she was alone again. Everything had happened very swiftly. The smoke of Brother Fire rose straight and steady from the squatting-place, just as it had done ten minutes ago, when the old woman had stood yonder worshipping the lion.

And after a long time, as it seemed, Ugh-lomi reappeared over the knoll, and came back to Eudena, triumphant and breathing heavily. She stood, her hair about her eyes and hot-faced, with the blood-stained axe in her hand, at the place where the tribe had offered her as a sacrifice to the lion. "Wau!" cried Ugh-lomi at the sight of her, his face alight with the fellowship of battle, and he waved his new club, red now and hairy; and at the sight of his glowing face her tense pose relaxed somewhat, and she stood sobbing and rejoicing.

Ugh-lomi had a queer, unaccountable pang at the sight of her tears; but he only shouted "Wau!" the louder and shook the axe east and west. He called manfully to her to follow him and turned back, striding, with the club swinging in his hand, towards the squatting-place, as if he had never left the tribe; and she ceased her weeping and followed quickly as a woman should.

So Ugh-lomi and Eudena came back to the squatting-place from

which they had fled many days before from the face of Uya; and
by the squatting-place lay a deer half-eaten, just as there had been
before Ugh-lomi was man or Eudena woman. So Ugh-lomi sat
down to eat, and Eudena beside him like a man, and the rest of the
tribe watched them from safe hiding places. And after a time one
of the elder girls came back timorously, carrying little Si in her
arms, and Eudena called to them by name, and offered them food.
But the elder girl was afraid and would not come, though Si struggled to come to Eudena. Afterwards, when Ugh-lomi had eaten,
he sat dozing, and at last he slept, and slowly the others came out
of the hiding places and drew near. And when Ugh-lomi woke,
save that there were no men to be seen, it seemed as though he had
never left the tribe.

Now, there is a thing strange but true: that all through this
fight Ugh-lomi forgot that he was lame, and was not lame, and after
he had rested behold! he was a lame man; and he remained a lame
man to the end of his days.

Cat's-skin and the second red-haired man and Wau-Hau, who
chipped flints cunningly, as his father had done before him, fled
from the face of Ugh-lomi, and none knew where they hid. But
two days after they came and squatted a good way off from the
knoll among the bracken under the chestnuts and watched. Ugh-
lomi's rage had gone, he moved to go against them and did not,
and at sundown they went away. That day, too, they found the
old woman among the ferns, where Ugh-lomi had blundered upon
her when he had pursued Wau-Hau. She was dead and more ugly
than ever, but whole. The jackals and vultures had tried her and
left her;—she was ever a wonderful old woman.

The next day the three men came again and squatted nearer,
and Wau-Hau had two rabbits to hold up, and the red-haired man
a wood-pigeon, and Ugh-lomi stood before the women and mocked
them.

The next day they sat again nearer—without stones or sticks,
and with the same offerings, and Cat's-skin had a trout. It was rare
men caught fish in those days, but Cat's-skin would stand silently
in the water for hours and catch them with his hand. And the
fourth day Ugh-lomi suffered these three to come to the squatting-
place in peace, with the food they had with them. Ugh-lomi ate the
trout. Thereafter for many moons Ugh-lomi was master and had
his will in peace. And on the fulness of time he was killed and eaten
even as Uya had been slain.

# THE SANDWICH ISLANDS

## Captain James Cook

*The South Pacific was almost bare on the maps when James Cook (1728–1779) was a young man. But, before Cook died, he had given the world Australia, New Zealand, hundreds of islands in the South Seas, and the first accurate charts of the Antarctic. He made three great voyages of exploration—to the South Pacific, to the Antarctic, and one in search of a north-west passage from the Atlantic to the Pacific. On this last trip he discovered the Hawaiian Islands—named by him the Sandwich Islands. He was killed by natives on his return from the Arctic when they found out he was not their great god Lono.*

ON THE 2d of January 1778, at daybreak, we weighed anchor, and resumed our course to the north. We discovered no land till daybreak in the morning of the 18th, when an island made its appearance, and soon after we saw more land, entirely detached from the former.

On the 19th, at sunrise, the island first seen bore east several leagues distant. This being directly to windward, which prevented our getting near it, I stood for the other, and not long after discovered a third island in the direction of west-north-west, as far distant as land could be seen. Soon after, we saw some canoes coming off from the shore toward the ships. I immediately brought to to give them time to join us. They had from three to six men each, and on their approach we were agreeably surprised to find that they spoke the language of Otaheite, and of the other islands we had lately visited. It required but very little address to get them to come alongside, but no entreaties could prevail upon any of them to come on board. I tied some brass medals to a rope, and gave them to those in one of the canoes, who, in return, tied some small mackerel to the rope as an equivalent. This was repeated, and some small nails, or bits of iron, which they valued more than any other article, were given them.

These people were of a brown colour, and though of the common size, were stoutly made. There was little difference in the casts of their colour, but a considerable variation in their features—some of their visages not being very unlike those of Europeans. They seemed very mild, and had no arms of any kind, if we except some small stones, which they had evidently brought for their own defence, and these they threw overboard, when they found that they were not wanted.

Seeing no signs of an anchoring place at this eastern extreme of the island, I ranged along the south-east side, at the distance of half a league from the shore. As soon as we made sail the canoes left us, but others came off as we proceeded along the coast, bringing with them roasting pigs, and some very fine potatoes, which they exchanged, as the others had done, for whatever was offered to them. Several small pigs were purchased for a sixpenny nail, so that we again found ourselves in a land of plenty.

The next morning we stood in for the land, and were met by several canoes filled with people, some of whom took courage and ventured on board.

In the course of my several voyages I never before met with the natives of any place so much astonished as these people were upon entering a ship. Their eyes were continually flying from object to object—the wildness of their looks and gestures fully expressing their entire ignorance about everything they saw, and strongly marking to us that till now they had never been visited by Europeans, nor been acquainted with any of our commodities except iron, which, however, it was plain they had only heard of, or had known it in some small quantity, brought to them at some distant period. They seemed only to understand that it was a substance much better adapted to the purposes of cutting or of boring holes than anything their own country produced. They asked for it by the name of hamaite, probably referring to some instrument, in the making of which iron could be usefully employed. For the same reason they frequently called iron by the name of toe, which, in their language, signifies a hatchet, or rather a kind of adze. When we shewed them some beads, they asked first what they were, and then whether they should eat them. But on their being told that they were to be hung in their ears, they returned them as useless. They were equally indifferent as to a looking-glass which was offered them, and returned it for the same reason, but sufficiently expressed their desire for hamaite and toe, which they wished might be very large. They were in some respect naturally well-bred, or at least fearful of giving offence, asking where they should sit down, whether they might spit upon the deck, and the like. Some of them repeated a long prayer before they came on board, and others afterwards sung and made motions with their hands, such as we had been accustomed to see in the dances of the islands we had lately visited. There was another circumstance in which they also perfectly resembled those other islanders. At first on their entering the ship they endeavoured to steal everything they came near, or rather to take it openly, as what we either should not resent or not hinder. We soon convinced them of their mistake; and if they after some time became less active in appropriating to them-selves whatever they took a fancy to, it was because they found that we kept a watchful eye over them.

At nine o'clock, being pretty near to the shore, I sent three armed boats, under the command of Lieutenant Williamson, to look for a landing-place and for fresh water. I ordered him that if he should find it necessary to land in search of the latter, not to suffer more than one man to go with him out of the boats.

While the boats were occupied in examining the coast, we stood on and off with the ships, waiting for their return. About noon Mr. Williamson came back, and reported that he had seen a large pond near one of the villages which contained fresh water. He also re-ported that he had attempted to land in another place, but was pre-vented by the natives, who, coming down to the boats in great numbers, attempted to take away the oars, muskets, and in short everything that they could lay hold of, and pressed so thick upon him that he was obliged to fire, by which one man was killed. But this unhappy circumstance I did not know till after we had left the island, so that all my measures were directed as if nothing of the kind had happened.

Between three and four o'clock I went ashore with three armed boats to examine the water, and to try the disposition of the in-habitants, several hundreds of whom were assembled on the beach.

The very instant I leaped on shore the collected body of the natives all fell flat upon their faces, and remained in that very hum-ble posture till, by expressive signs, I prevailed upon them to rise. They then brought a great many small pigs which they presented to me, with plantain trees, using much the same ceremonies that we had seen practised on such occasions at the Society and other is-lands; and a long prayer being spoken by a single person, in which others of the assembly sometimes joined, I expressed my acceptance of their proffered friendship by giving them in return such presents as I had brought with me from the ship for that purpose. When this introductory business was finished, I stationed a guard upon the beach, and got some of the natives to conduct me to the water, which proved to be very good, and in a proper situation for our purpose. Having satisfied myself about this very essential point, and about the peaceable disposition of the natives, I returned on board, and then gave orders that everything should be in readiness for landing and filling our water-casks in the morning, when again I went ashore.

As soon as we landed a trade was set on foot for hogs and potatoes, which the people of the island gave us in exchange for nails and pieces of iron, formed into something like chisels. We met with no obstruction in watering; on the contrary, the natives assisted our men in rolling the casks to and from the pool, and readily performed whatever we required.

Everything thus going on to my satisfaction, and considering my presence on the spot as unnecessary, I left the command to Mr. Williamson, who had landed with me, and made an excursion into the country up the valley, accompanied by Mr. Anderson and Mr. Webber. A numerous train of natives followed us; and one of them, whom I had distinguished for his activity in keeping the rest in order, I made choice of as our guide. Every one whom we met fell prostrate upon the ground, and remained in that position till we had passed. This, as I afterwards understood, is the mode of paying their respect to their own great chiefs. As we ranged down the coast from the east in the ships we had observed at every village one or more elevated white objects, like pyramids, or rather obelisks; and one of these, which I guessed to be at least fifty feet high, was very conspicuous from the ship's anchoring station, and seemed to be at no great distance up this valley. To have a nearer inspection of it was the principal object of my walk. The moment we got to it we saw that it stood in a burying-ground or morai, the resemblance of which, in many respects, to those we were so well acquainted with at other islands in this ocean could not but strike us; and we also soon found that the several parts that compose it were called by the same names.

After we had examined very carefully everything that was to be seen about the morai, we returned by a different route. At noon I went on board to dinner, having procured in the course of the day nine tuns of water; and by exchanges, chiefly for nails and pieces of iron, about seventy or eighty pigs and a few fowls. These people merited our best commendations, never once attempting to cheat us, either ashore or alongside the ships. Some of them, indeed, at first betrayed a thievish disposition; but they soon laid aside a conduct which we convinced them they could not persevere in with impunity.

Amongst the articles which they brought to barter this day, we could not help taking notice of a particular sort of cloak and cap. The first are nearly of the size and shape of the short cloaks worn by the women in England. The ground of them is a net-work, upon which the most beautiful red and yellow feathers are so closely fixed, that the surface might be compared to the thickest and richest velvet, which they resemble, both as to the feel and the glossy appearance.

The cap is made almost exactly like a helmet, with the middle part or crest sometimes of a hand's breadth, and it sits very close upon the head, having notches to admit the ears. It is a frame of twigs and osiers covered with a network, into which are wrought feathers in the same manner as upon the cloaks, though rather closer and less diversified. These probably complete the dress with the cloaks, for the natives sometimes appeared in both together.

We were at a loss to guess whence they could get such a quantity of these beautiful feathers, but were soon informed, for they afterwards brought great numbers of skins of small red birds for sale.

Next day one of our visitors, who offered some fishhooks for sale, was observed to have a very small parcel tied to the string of one of them, which he separated with great care and reserved for himself when he parted with the hook. Being asked what it was, he pointed to his belly. It struck us that it might be human flesh. The question being put to him, he answered that the flesh was part of a man. Another of his countrymen who stood by him, was then asked whether it was their custom to eat those killed in battle, and he immediately answered in the affirmative.

After leaving Atooi, as this island was named, we proceeded to Oneeheow, on the coast of which we anchored.

Six or seven canoes had come off to us before we anchored, bringing some small pigs and potatoes, and a good many yams and mats. The people in them resembled those of Atooi, and seemed to be equally well acquainted with the use of iron, which they asked for also by the names of hamaite and toe, parting readily with all their commodities for pieces of this precious metal.

These visitors furnished us with an opportunity of agitating again the curious inquiry whether they were cannibals. One of the islanders, who wanted to get in at the gun-room port was refused, and at the same time asked whether, if he should come in, we would kill and eat him? This gave a proper opening to retort the question as to this practice; and a person behind the other in the canoe, who paid great attention to what was passing, immediately answered that if we were killed on shore they would certainly eat us; but that their eating us would be the consequence of our being at enmity with them. I cannot see the least reason to hesitate in pronouncing it to be certain that the horrid banquet of human flesh is as much relished here amidst plenty as it is in New Zealand.

On the 30th, I sent Mr. Gore ashore with a guard of marines, and a party to trade with the natives for refreshments. The weather soon became very unpropitious, and the sea ran so high that we had no manner of communication with our party on shore, and even the natives themselves durst not venture out to the ships in their canoes. In the evening of next day I sent the master in a boat up to the south-east head or point of the island to try if he could land under it. He returned with a favourable report, but it was too late now to send for our party till the next morning; and thus they had another night to improve their intercourse with the natives.

Encouraged by the master's report, I went myself with the pinnace and launch up to the point to bring the party on board, taking with me a ram-goat and two ewes, a boar and sow-pig of the English breed, and the seeds of melons, pumpkins, and onions, being very desirous of benefiting these poor people by furnishing them with some additional articles of food. I found my party already there with some of the natives in company. To one of them, whom Mr. Gore had observed assuming some command, I gave the goats, pigs, and seeds.

The ground through which I passed was in a state of nature, very stony, and the soil seemed poor. It was, however, covered with shrubs and plants, some of which perfumed the air with a more delicious fragrancy than I had met with at any other of the islands in this ocean. The habitations of the natives were thinly scattered about, and it was supposed that there could not be more than five hundred people upon the island. Our people had an opportunity of observing the method of living amongst the natives, and it appeared to be decent and cleanly. They did not, however, see any instance of the men and women eating together, and the latter seemed generally associated in companies by themselves. It was found that they burnt here the oily nuts of the dooe dooe for lights in the night, as at Otaheite, and that they baked their hogs in ovens. A particular veneration seemed to be paid here to owls, which they have very tame; and it was observed to be a pretty general practice amongst them to pull out one of their teeth, for which odd custom, when asked the reason, the only answer that could be got was, that it was teeha.

On Monday, the 2d of February, we stood away to the northward, in prosecution of our voyage. Our ship procured from these islands provisions sufficient for three weeks at least; and Captain Clerke, more fortunate, obtained of their vegetable productions a supply that lasted his people upwards of two months.

It is worthy of observation, that the islands in the Pacific Ocean, which our late voyages have added to the geography of the globe, have been generally found lying in groups or clusters, the single intermediate islands, as yet discovered, being few in proportion to the others, though probably there are many more of them still unknown, which serve as steps between the several clusters. Of what number this newly-discovered archipelago consists must be left for future investigation. We saw five of them, whose names, as given to us by the natives, are Wohaoo, Atooi, Oneeheow, Oreehoua, and Tahoora.

The temperature of the climate may be easily guessed from the situation. Were we to judge of it from our experience, it might be said to be very variable, notwithstanding it was now the season of the year when the weather is supposed to be most settled, the sun being at his greatest annual distance. The heat was at this time very moderate, and few of those inconveniences which many of those tropical countries are subject to, either from heat or moisture, seem to be experienced here.

Besides the vegetable articles bought by us as refreshments, amongst which were at least five or six varieties of plantains, the island produces bread-fruit, though it seems to be scarce, as we saw only one tree, which was large and had some fruit upon it.

The scarlet birds which were brought for sale were never met with alive; but we saw a single small one, about the size of a canary-bird, of a deep crimson colour, a large owl, two large brown hawks or kites, and a wild duck; and it is probable there are a great many sorts, judging by the quantity of fine yellow, green, and very small velvet-like black feathers, used upon the cloaks, and other ornaments worn by the inhabitants.

Fish and other marine productions were, to appearance, not various.

The hogs, dogs, and fowls, which were the only tame or domestic animals that we found here, were all of the same kind that we met with at the South Pacific Islands.

The inhabitants are of a middling stature, firmly made. Their visage, especially amongst the women, is sometimes round; but we cannot say that they are distinguished as a nation by any general cast of countenance. Their colour is nearly of a nut-brown. The women are little more delicate than the men in their formation; and I may say that, with a very few exceptions, they have little claim to those peculiarities that distinguish the sex in other countries. There is, indeed, a more remarkable equality in the size, colour, and figure of both sexes, than in most places I have visited.

They are very expert swimmers. It was very common to see women with infants at the breast, when the surf was so high that they could not land in the canoes, leap overboard, and without endangering their little ones, swim to the shore through a sea that looked dreadful.

They seem to be blest with a frank, cheerful disposition; they live very sociably in their intercourse with one another, and, except the propensity to thieving, which seems innate in most of the people we have visited in this ocean, they were exceedingly friendly to us. It was a pleasure to observe with how much affection the women manage their infants, and how readily the men lent their assistance to such a tender office, thus sufficiently distinguishing themselves from those savages who esteem a wife and child as things rather necessary than desirable, or worthy of their notice.

Though they seem to have adopted the mode of living in villages, there is no appearance of defence or fortification near any of them; and the houses are scattered about without any order. Some are large and commodious, from forty to fifty feet long, and twenty or thirty broad, while others of them are mere hovels. They are well thatched with long grass, which is laid on slender poles, disposed with some regularity. The entrance is made indifferently in the end or side, and is an oblong hole, so low, that one must rather creep than walk in. No light enters the house but by this opening; and though such close habitations may afford a comfortable retreat in bad weather, they seem but ill adapted to the warmth of the climate. Of animal food they can be in no want, as they have abundance of hogs, which run without restraint about the houses; and if they eat dogs, which is not improbable, their stock of these seemed to be very considerable. The great number of fishing-hooks found amongst them, shewed that they derived no inconsiderable supply of animal food from the sea.

They bake their vegetable food with heated stones, in the same manner as the inhabitants of the southern islands. The only artificial dish we met with was a taro pudding, which, though a disagreeable mess, from its sourness, was greedily devoured by the natives.

In everything manufactured by these people, there appears to be an uncommon degree of neatness and ingenuity. Their cloth, which is the principal manufacture, is made from the *Morus papyrifera;* and, doubtless, in the same manner as at Otaheite and Tongataboo; in colouring or staining it, the people of Atooi display a superiority of taste, by the endless variation of figures which they execute.

They fabricate a great many white mats, which are strong, with many red stripes, rhombuses, and other figures interwoven on one side, and often pretty large.

They stain their gourd-shells prettily with undulated lines, triangles, and other figures of a black colour; instances of which we saw practised at New Zealand. Their wooden dishes and bowls, out of which they drink their ava, are of the etooa-tree, or cordia, as neat as if made in our turning-lathe, and perhaps better polished. A great variety of fishing-hooks are ingeniously made of pearl shell. One fishing-hook was procured, nine inches long, of a single piece of bone, which, doubtless, belonged to some large fish. The elegant form and polish of this could not certainly be outdone by any European artist, even if he should add all his knowledge in design to the number and convenience of his tools.

The only iron tools, or rather bits of iron, seen amongst them, and which they had before our arrival, were a piece of iron hoop, about two inches long, fitted into a wooden handle; and another edge-tool, which our people guessed to be made of the point of a broadsword. How they came by them I cannot account for.

Though I did not see a chief of any note, there were, however, several, as the natives informed us, who reside upon Atooi, and to whom they prostrate themselves as a mark of submission. After I had left the island, one of the chiefs made his appearance, and paid a visit to Captain Clerke on board the Discovery. His attendants helped him into the ship and placed him on the gangway. Their care of him did not cease then, for they stood round him, holding each other by the hands; nor would they suffer any one to come near him but Captain Clerke himself. He was a young man, clothed from head to foot, accompanied by a young woman, supposed to be his wife. His name was said to be Tamahano. Captain Clerke made him some suitable presents, and received from him, in return, a large bowl, supported by two figures of men, the carving of which, both as to the design and the execution, shewed some degree of skill.

In their language they had not only adopted the soft mode of the Otaheitans in avoiding harsh sounds, but the whole idiom of their language, using not only the same affixes and suffixes to their words, but the same measure and cadence in their songs, though in a manner somewhat less agreeable.

### Had I the Choice

HAD I the choice to tally greatest bards,
　To limn their portraits, stately, beautiful, and emulate at will,
Homer with all his wars and warriors—Hector, Achilles, Ajax,
Or Shakspere's woe-entangled Hamlet, Lear, Othello—Tennyson's
　fair ladies,
Metre or wit the best, or choice conceit to wield in perfect rhyme,
　delight of singers;
These, these, O sea, all these I'd gladly barter,
Would you the undulation of one wave, its trick to me transfer,
Or breathe one breath of yours upon my verse,
　And leave its odor there.

*Walt Whitman*

# AN ADVENTURE WITH A DOG AND A GLACIER

## John Muir

*One of America's most noted naturalist-authors, John Muir (1838–1914), was born in Scotland. With true devotion to his chosen study, he traveled over much of the United States by foot. The greatest part of Muir's writings were reports of his explorations among the mountains and glaciers of the Far West and Alaska, or impassioned pleas for the conservation of our forests. But in telling of one hazardous experience on a glacier, when his only companion was an insignificant little dog, he has written one of the best but least-known animal stories in our literature.*

IN THE summer of 1880 I set out from Fort Wrangel in a canoe, with the Rev. S. H. Young, my former companion, and a crew of Indians, to continue the exploration of the icy region of southeastern Alaska, begun in the fall of 1879. After the necessary provisions, blankets, etc., had been collected and stowed away, and the Indians were in their places ready to dip their paddles, while a crowd of their friends were looking down from the wharf to bid them good-by and good luck, Mr. Young, for whom we were waiting, at length came aboard, followed by a little black dog that immediately made himself at home by curling up in a hollow among the baggage. I like dogs, but this one seemed so small, dull, and worthless that I objected to his going, and asked the missionary why he was taking him. "Such a helpless wisp of hair will only be in the way," I said; "you had better pass him up to one of the Indian boys on the wharf, to be taken home to play with the children. This trip is not likely to be a good one for toy dogs. He will be rained on and snowed on for weeks, and will require care like a baby." But the missionary assured me that he would be no trouble

[ 353 ]

at all; that he was a perfect wonder of a dog—could endure cold and hunger like a polar bear, could swim like a seal, and was wondrous wise, etc., making out a list of virtues likely to make him the most interesting of the company.

Nobody could hope to unravel the lines of his ancestry. He was short-legged, bunchy-bodied, and almost featureless—something like a muskrat. Though smooth, his hair was long and silky, so that when the wind was at his back it ruffled, making him look shaggy. At first sight his only noticeable feature was his showy tail, which was about as shady and airy as a squirrel's, and was carried curling forward nearly to his ears. On closer inspection you might see his thin, sensitive ears and his keen dark eyes with cunning tan spots. Mr. Young told me that when the dog was about the size of a wood-rat he was presented to his wife by an Irish prospector at Sitka, and that when he arrived at Fort Wrangel he was adopted by the Stickeen Indians as a sort of new good-luck totem, and named "Stickeen" for the tribe, with whom he became a favorite. On our trip he soon proved himself a queer character—odd, concealed, independent, keeping invincibly quiet, and doing many inexplicable things that piqued my curiosity. Sailing week after week through the long, intricate channels and inlets among the innumerable islands and mountains of the coast, he spent the dull days in sluggish ease, motionless, and apparently as unobserving as a hibernating marmot. But I discovered that somehow he always knew what was going forward. When the Indians were about to shoot at ducks or seals, or when anything interesting was to be seen along the shore, he would rest his chin on the edge of the canoe and calmly look out. When he heard us talking about making a landing, he roused himself to see what sort of place we were coming to, and made ready to jump overboard and swim ashore as soon as the canoe neared the beach. Then, with a vigorous shake to get rid of the brine in his hair, he went into the woods to hunt small game. But though always the first out of the canoe, he was always the last to get into it. When we were ready to start he could never be found, and refused to come to our call. We soon found out, however, that though we could not see him at such times, he saw us, and from the cover of the briers and huckleberry-bushes in the fringe of the woods was watching the canoe with wary eye. For as soon as we were fairly off, he came trotting down the beach, plunged into the surf, and swam after us, knowing well that we would cease rowing and take him in. When the contrary little vagabond came alongside, he was lifted by the neck, held at arm's length a moment to drip, and dropped aboard. We tried to cure him of this trick by compelling him to swim farther before stopping for him; but this did no good: the longer the swim, the better he seemed to like it.

Though capable of most spacious idleness, he was always ready for excursions or adventures of any sort. When the Indians went into the woods for a deer, Stickeen was sure to be at their heels, provided I had not yet left camp. For though I never carried a gun, he always followed me, forsaking the hunting Indians, and even his master, to share my wanderings. The days that were too stormy for sailing I spent in the woods, or on the mountains or glaciers, wherever I chanced to be; and Stickeen always insisted on following me, gliding through the dripping huckleberry-bushes and prickly *Panax* and *Rubus* tangles like a fox, scarce stirring their close-set branches, wading and wallowing through snow, swimming ice-cold streams, jumping logs and rocks and the crusty hummocks and crevasses of glaciers with the patience and endurance of a determined mountaineer, never tiring or getting discouraged. Once he followed me over a glacier the surface of which was so rough that it cut his feet until every step was marked with blood; but he trotted on with Indian fortitude until I noticed his pain and, taking pity on him, made him a set of moccasins out of a handkerchief. But he never asked help or made any complaint, as if, like a philosopher, he had learned that without hard work and suffering there could be no pleasure worth having.

Yet nobody knew what Stickeen was good for. He seemed to meet danger and hardships without reason, insisted on having his own way, never obeyed an order, and the hunters could never set him on anything against his will, or make him fetch anything that was shot. I tried hard to make his acquaintance, guessing there must be something in him; but he was as cold as a glacier, and about as invulnerable to fun, though his master assured me that he played at home, and in some measure conformed to the usages of civilization. His equanimity was so immovable it seemed due to unfeeling ignorance. Let the weather blow and roar, he was as tranquil as a stone; and no matter what advances you made, scarce a glance or a tail-wag would you get for your pains. No superannuated mastiff or bulldog grown old in office surpassed this soft midget in stoic dignity. He sometimes reminded me of those plump, squat, unshakable cacti of the Arizona deserts that give no sign of feeling. A true child of the wilderness, holding the even tenor of his hidden life with the silence and serenity of nature, he never displayed a trace of the elfish vivacity and fun of the terriers and collies that we all know, nor of their touching affection and devotion. Like children, most small dogs beg to be loved and allowed to love, but Stickeen seemed a very Diogenes, asking only to be let alone. He seemed neither old nor young. His strength lay in his eyes. They looked as old as the hills, and as young and as wild. I never tired looking into them. It was like looking into a landscape; but they were small and rather deep-set, and had no explaining puckers around them to give out particulars. I was accustomed to look into the faces of plants and animals, and I watched the little sphinx more and more keenly as an interesting study. But there is no estimating the wit and wisdom concealed and latent in our lower fellow-mortals until made manifest by profound experiences; for it is by suffering that dogs as well as saints are developed and made perfect.

After we had explored the glaciers of the Sumdum and Tahkoo inlets, we sailed through Stephen's Passage into Lynn Canal, and thence through Icy Strait into Cross Sound, looking for unexplored inlets leading toward the ice-fountains of the Fairweather Range. While the tide was in our favor in Cross Sound we were accompanied by a fleet of icebergs drifting out to the ocean from Glacier Bay. Slowly we crawled around Vancouver's Point, Wimbleton, our frail canoe tossed like a feather on the massive swells coming in past Cape Spenser. For miles the Sound is bounded by precipitous cliffs which looked terribly stern in gloomy weather. Had our canoe been crushed or upset, we could have gained no landing here; for the cliffs, as high as those of Yosemite, sink perfectly sheer into deep water. Eagerly we scanned the immense wall on the north side for the first sign of an opening, all of us anxious except Stickeen, who dozed in peace or gazed dreamily at the tremendous precipices when he heard us talking about them. At length we discovered the entrance of what is now called Taylor Bay, and about five o'clock reached the head of it, and encamped near the front of a large glacier which extends as an abrupt barrier all the way across from wall to wall of the inlet, a distance of three or four miles.

On first observation the glacier presented some unusual features, and that night I planned a grand excursion for the morrow. I awoke early, called not only by the glacier, but also by a storm. Rain, mixed with trailing films of scud and the ragged, drawn-out nether surfaces of gray clouds, filled the inlet, and was sweeping forward in a thick, passionate, horizontal flood, as if it were all passing over the country instead of falling on it. Everything was streaming with life and motion—woods, rocks, waters, and the sky. The main perennial streams were booming, and hundreds of new ones, born of the rain, were descending in gray and white cascades on each side of the inlet, fairly streaking their rocky slopes, and roaring like the sea. I had intended making a cup of coffee before starting, but when I heard the storm I made haste to join it; for in storms nature has always something extra fine to show us, and if we have wit to keep in right relations with them the danger is no more than in home-keeping, and we can go with them rejoicing, sharing their enthusiasm, and chanting with the old Norsemen, "The blast of the tempest aids our oars; the hurricane is our servant, and drives us whither we wish to go." So I took my ice-ax, buttoned my coat, put a piece of bread in my pocket, and set out. Mr. Young and the Indians were asleep, and so, I hoped, was Stickeen; but I had not gone a dozen rods before he left his warm bed in the tent, and came boring through the blast after me. That a man should welcome storms for their exhilarating music and motion, and go forth to see God making landscapes, is reasonable enough; but what fascination could there be in dismal weather for this poor, feeble wisp of a dog, so pathetically small? Anyhow, on he came, breakfastless, through the choking blast. I stopped, turned my back to the wind, and gave him a good, dissuasive talk. "Now don't," I said, shouting to make myself heard in the storm—"now don't, Stickeen. What has got into your queer noddle now? You must be daft. This wild day has nothing for you. Go back to camp and keep warm. There is no game abroad—nothing but weather. Not a foot or wing is stirring. Wait and get a good breakfast with your master, and be sensible for once. I can't feed you or carry you, and this storm will kill you." But nature, it seems, was at the bottom of the affair; and she gains her ends with dogs as well as with men, making us do as she likes, driving us on her ways, however rough. So after ordering him back again and again to ease my conscience, I saw that he was not to be shaken off; as well might the earth try to shake off the moon. I had once led his master into trouble, when he fell on one of the topmost jags of a mountain, and dislocated his arms. Now the turn of his humble companion was coming. The dog just stood there in the wind, drenched and blinking, saying doggedly, "Where thou goest I will go." So I told him to come on, if he must, and gave him a piece of the bread I had put in my pocket for breakfast. Then we pushed on in company, and thus began the most memorable of all my wild days.

The level flood, driving straight in our faces, thrashed and washed us wildly until we got into the shelter of the trees and ice-cliffs on the east side of the glacier, where we rested and listened and looked on in comfort. The exploration of the glacier was my main object, but the wind was too high to allow excursions over its open surface, where one might be dangerously shoved while balancing for a jump on the brink of a crevasse. In the meantime the storm was a fine study. Here the end of the glacier, descending over an abrupt swell of resisting rock about five hundred feet high, leans forward and falls in majestic ice-cascades. And as the storm came down the glacier from the north, Stickeen and I were beneath the main current of the blast, while favorably located to see and hear it. A broad torrent, draining the side of the glacier, now swollen by scores of new streams from the mountains, was rolling boulders along its rocky channel between the glacier and the woods with thudding, bumping, muffled sounds, rushing toward the bay with tremendous energy, as if in haste to get out of the mountains, the waters above and beneath calling to each other, and all to the ocean, their home. Looking southward from our shelter, we had this great torrent on our left, with mossy woods on the mountain slope above it, the glacier on our right, the wild, cascading portion of it forming a multitude of towers, spires, and flat-topped battlements seen through the trees, and smooth gray gloom ahead. I tried to draw the marvelous scene in my note-book, but the rain fell on my page in spite of all that I could do to shelter it, and the sketch seemed miserably defective.

When the wind began to abate I traced the east side of the glacier. All the trees standing on the edge of the woods were barked and bruised, showing high ice-mark in a very telling way, while tens of thousands of those that had stood for centuries on the bank of the glacier farther out lay crushed and being crushed. In many places I could see, down fifty feet or so beneath, the margin of the glacier mill, where trunks from one to two feet in diameter were being ground to pulp against outstanding rock-ribs and bosses of the bank. About three miles above the front of the glacier, I climbed to the surface of it by means of ax-steps, made easy for Stickeen; and as far as the eye could reach, the level, or nearly level, glacier stretched away indefinitely beneath the gray sky, a seemingly boundless prairie of ice. The rain continued, which I did not mind; but a tendency to fogginess in the drooping clouds made me hesitate about venturing far from land. No trace of the west shore was visible, and in case the misty clouds should settle, or the wind again become violent, I feared getting caught in a tangle of crevasses. Lingering undecided, watching the weather, I sauntered about on the crystal sea. For a mile or two out I found the ice remarkably safe. The marginal crevasses were mostly narrow, while the few wider ones were easily avoided by passing around them, and the clouds began to open here and there. Thus encouraged, I at last pushed out for the other side; for nature can make us do anything she likes, luring us along appointed ways for the fulfilment of her plans. At first we made rapid progress, and the sky was not very threatening, while I took bearings occasionally with a pocket-compass, to enable me to retrace my way more surely in case the storm should become blinding; but the structure-lines of the ice were my main guide. Toward the west side we came to a closely crevassed section, in which we had to make long, narrow tacks and doublings, tracing the edges of tremendous longitudinal crevasses, many of which were from twenty to thirty feet wide, and perhaps a thousand feet deep, beautiful and awful. In working a way through them I was severely cautious, but Stickeen came on as unhesitatingly as the flying clouds. Any crevasse that I could jump he would leap without so much as halting to examine it. The weather was bright and dark, with quick flashes of summer and winter close together. When the clouds opened and the sun shone, the glacier was seen from shore to shore, with a bright array of encompassing mountains partly revealed, wearing the clouds as garments, black in the middle, burning on the edges, and the whole icy prairie seemed to burst into a bloom of iris colors from myriads of crystals. Then suddenly all the glorious show would be again smothered in gloom. But Stickeen seemed to care for none of these things, bright or dark, nor for the beautiful wells filled to the brim with water so pure that it was nearly invisible, the rumbling, grinding moulins, or the quick-flashing, glinting, swirling streams in frictionless channels of living ice. Nothing seemed novel to him. He showed neither caution nor curiosity. His courage was so unwavering that it seemed due to dullness of perception, as if he were only blindly bold; and I warned him that he might slip or fall short. His bunchy body seemed all one skipping muscle, and his peg legs appeared to be jointed only at the top.

We gained the west shore in about three hours, the width of the glacier here being about seven miles. Then I pushed northward, in order to see as far back as possible into the fountains of the Fairweather Mountains, in case the clouds should rise. The walking was easy along the margin of the forest, which, of course, like that on the other side, had been invaded and crushed by the swollen glacier. In an hour we rounded a massive headland and came suddenly on another outlet of the glacier, which, in the form of a wild ice-cascade, was pouring over the rim of the main basin toward the ocean with the volume of a thousand Niagaras. The surface was broken into a multitude of sharp blades and pinnacles leaning forward, something like the updashing waves of a flood of water descending a rugged channel. But these ice-waves were many times higher than those of river cataracts, and to all appearance motionless. It was a dazzling white torrent two miles wide, flowing between high banks black with trees. Tracing its left bank three or four miles, I found that it discharged into a fresh-water lake, filling it with icebergs.

I would gladly have followed the outlet, but the day was waning, and we had to make haste on the return trip to get off the ice before dark. When we were about two miles from the west shore the clouds dropped misty fringes, and snow soon began to fly. Then I began to feel anxiety as to finding a way in the storm through the intricate net-work of crevasses which we had entered. Stickeen showed no fear. He was still the same silent, sufficient, uncomplaining Indian philosopher. When the storm-darkness fell he kept close behind me. The snow warned us to make haste, but at the same time hid our way. At rare intervals the clouds thinned, and mountains, looming in the gloom, frowned and quickly vanished. I pushed on as best I could, jumping innumerable crevasses, and for every hundred rods or so of direct advance traveling a mile in doubling up and down in the turmoil of chasms and dislocated masses of ice. After an hour or two of this work we came to a series of longitudinal crevasses of appalling width, like immense furrows. These I traced with firm nerve, excited and strengthened by the danger, making wide jumps, poising cautiously on the dizzy edges after cutting hollows for my feet before making the spring, to avoid slipping or any uncertainty on the farther sides, where only one trial is granted—exercise at once frightful and inspiring. Stickeen flirted across every gap I jumped, seemingly without effort. Many a mile we thus traveled, mostly up and down, making but little real headway in crossing, most of the time running instead of walking, as the danger of spending the night on the glacier became threatening. No doubt we could have weathered the storm for one night, and I faced the chance of being compelled to do so; but we were hungry and wet, and the north wind was thick with snow and bitterly cold, and of course that night would have seemed a long one. Stickeen gave me no concern. He was still the wonderful, inscrutable philosopher, ready for anything. I could not see far enough to judge in which direction the best route lay, and had simply to grope my way in the snow-choked air and ice. Again and again I was put to my mettle, but Stickeen followed easily, his nerves growing more unflinching as the dangers thickened; so it always is with mountaineers.

At length our way was barred by a very wide and straight crevasse, which I traced rapidly northward a mile or so without finding a crossing or hope of one, then southward down the glacier about as far, to where it united with another crevasse. In all this distance of perhaps two miles there was only one place where I could possibly jump it; but the width of this jump was nearly the utmost I dared attempt, while the danger of slipping on the farther side was so great that I was loath to try it. Furthermore, the side I was on was about a foot higher than the other, and even with this advantage it seemed dangerously wide. One is liable to underestimate the width of crevasses where the magnitudes in general are great. I therefore measured this one again and again, until satisfied that I could jump it if necessary, but that in case I should be compelled to jump back to the higher side, I might fail. Now a cautious mountaineer seldom takes a step on unknown ground which seems at all dangerous, that he cannot retrace in case he should be stopped by unseen obstacles ahead. This is the rule of mountaineers who live long; and though in haste, I compelled myself to sit down and deliberate before I broke it. Retracing my devious path in imagination, as if it were drawn on a chart, I saw that I was recrossing the glacier a mile or two farther up-stream, and was entangled in a section I had not before seen. Should I risk this dangerous jump, or try to regain the woods on the west shore, make a fire, and have only hunger to endure while waiting for a new day? I had already crossed so broad a tangle of dangerous ice that I saw it would be difficult to get back to the woods through the storm; while the ice just beyond the present barrier seemed more promising, and the east shore was now perhaps about as near as the west. I was therefore eager to go on; but this wide jump was a tremendous obstacle. At length, because of the dangers already behind me, I determined to venture against those that might be ahead, jumped, and landed well, but with so little to spare that I more than ever dreaded being compelled to take that jump back from the lower side. Stickeen followed, making nothing of it. But within a distance of a few hundred yards we were stopped again by the widest crevasse yet encountered. Of course I made haste to explore it, hoping all might yet be well. About three fourths of a mile up-stream it united with the one we had just crossed, as I feared it would. Then, tracing it down, I found it joined the other great crevasse at the lower end, maintaining a width of forty to fifty feet. We were on an island about two miles long and from one hundred to three hundred yards wide, with two barely possible ways of escape—one by the way we came, the other by an almost inaccessible sliver-bridge that crossed the larger crevasse from near the middle of the island. After tracing the brink, I ran back to the sliver-bridge and cautiously studied it. Crevasses caused by strains from variations of the rate of motion of different parts of the glacier and by convexities in the channel are mere cracks when they first open,—so narrow as hardly to admit the blade of a pocket-knife,—and widen gradually, according to the extent of the strain. Now some of these cracks are interrupted like the cracks in wood, and, in opening, the strip of ice between overlapping ends is dragged out; and if the flow of the glacier there is such that no strain is made on the sliver, it maintains a continuous connection between the sides, just as the two sides of a slivered crack in wood that is being split are connected. Some crevasses remain open for years, and by the melting of their sides continue to increase in width long after the opening strain has ceased, while the sliver-bridges, level on top at first, and perfectly safe, are at length melted to thin, knife-edged blades, the upper portion being most exposed to the weather; and since the exposure is greatest in the middle, they at length curve downward like the cables of suspension-bridges. This one was evidently very old, for it had been wasted until it was the worst bridge I ever saw. The width of the crevasse was here about fifty feet, and the sliver, crossing diagonally, was about seventy feet long, was depressed twenty-five or thirty feet in the middle, and the up-curving ends were attached to the sides eight or ten feet below the surface of the glacier. Getting down the nearly vertical wall to the end of it and up the other side were the main difficulties, and they seemed all but insurmountable. Of the many perils encountered in my years of wandering in mountain altitudes, none seemed so plain and stern and merciless as this. And it was presented when we were wet to the skin and hungry, the sky was dark with snow, and the night near, and we had to fear the snow in our eyes and the disturbing action of the wind in any movement we might make. But we were forced to face it. It was a tremendous necessity.

Beginning not immediately above the sunken end of the bridge, but a little to one side, I cut nice hollows on the brink for my knees to rest in; then, leaning over, with my short-handled ax cut a step sixteen or eighteen inches below, which, on account of the sheerness of the wall, was shallow. That step, however, was well made; its floor sloped slightly inward, and formed a good hold for my heels. Then, slipping cautiously upon it, and crouching as low as possible, with my left side twisted toward the wall, I steadied myself with my left hand in a slight notch, while with the right I cut other steps and notches in succession, guarding against glinting of the ax, for life or death was in every stroke, and in the niceness of finish of every foothold. After the end of the bridge was reached, it was a delicate thing to poise on a little platform which I had chipped on its up-curving end, and, bending over the slippery surface, get astride of it. Crossing was easy, cutting off the sharp edge with careful strokes, and hitching forward a few inches at a time, keeping my balance with my knees pressed against its sides. The tremendous abyss on each side I studiously ignored. The surface of that blue sliver was then all the world. But the most trying part of the adventure was, after working my way across inch by inch, to rise from the safe position astride that slippery strip of ice, and to cut a ladder in the face of the wall—chipping, climbing, holding on with feet and fingers in mere notches. At such times one's whole body is eye, and common skill and fortitude are replaced by power beyond our call or knowledge. Never before had I been so long under deadly strain. How I got up the cliff at the end of the bridge I never could tell. The thing seemed to have been done by somebody else. I never have had contempt of death, though in the course of my explorations I oftentimes felt that to meet one's fate on a mountain, in a grand cañon, or in the heart of a crystal glacier would be blessed as compared with death from disease, a mean accident in a street, or from a sniff of sewer-gas. But the sweetest, cleanest death, set thus calmly and glaringly clear before us, is hard enough to face, even though we feel gratefully sure that we have already had happiness enough for a dozen lives.

But poor Stickeen, the wee, silky, sleekit beastie—think of him! When I had decided to try the bridge, and while I was on my knees cutting away the rounded brow, he came behind me, pushed his head past my shoulder, looked down and across, scanned the sliver and its approaches with his queer eyes, then looked me in the face with a startled air of surprise and concern, and began to mutter and whine, saying as plainly as if speaking with words, "Surely you are not going to try that awful place?" This was the first time I had seen him gaze deliberately into a crevasse or into my face with a speaking look. That he should have recognized and appreciated the danger at the first glance showed wonderful sagacity. Never before had the quick, daring midget seemed to know that ice was slippery, or that there was such a thing as danger anywhere. His looks and the tones of his voice when he began to complain and speak his fears were so human that I unconsciously talked to him as I would to a boy, and in trying to calm his fears perhaps in some measure moderated my own. "Hush your fears, my boy," I said; "we will get across safe, though it is not going to be easy. No right way is easy in this rough world. We must risk our lives to save them. At the worst we can only slip; and then how grand a grave we shall have! And by and by our nice bones will do good in the terminal moraine." But my sermon was far from reassuring him; he began to cry, and after taking another piercing look at the tremendous gulf, ran away in desperate excitement, seeking some other crossing. By the time he got back, baffled, of course, I had made a step or two. I dared not look back, but he made himself heard; and when he saw that I was certainly crossing, he cried aloud in despair. The danger was enough to daunt anybody, but it seems wonderful that he should have been able to weigh and appreciate it so justly. No mountaineer could have seen it more quickly or judged it more wisely, discriminating between real and apparent peril.

After I had gained the other side he howled louder than ever, and after running back and forth in vain search for a way of escape, he would return to the brink of the crevasse above the bridge, moaning and groaning as if in the bitterness of death. Could this be the silent, philosophic Stickeen? I shouted encouragement, telling him the bridge was not so bad as it looked, that I had left it flat for his feet, and he could walk it easily. But he was afraid to try it.

Strange that so small an animal should be capable of such big, wise fears! I called again and again in a reassuring tone to come on and fear nothing; that he could come if he would only try. Then he would hush for a moment, look again at the bridge, and shout his unshakable conviction that he could never, never come that way; then lie back in despair, as if howling: "Oh-o-o, what a place! No-o-o; I can never go-o-o down there!" His natural composure and courage had vanished utterly in a tumultuous storm of fear. Had the danger been less, his distress would have seemed ridiculous. But in this gulf—a huge, yawning sepulcher big enough to hold every-body in the territory—lay the shadow of death, and his heartrend-ing cries might well have called Heaven to his help. Perhaps they did. So hidden before, he was transparent now, and one could see the workings of his mind like the movements of a clock out of its case. His voice and gestures were perfectly human, and his hopes and fears unmistakable, while he seemed to understand every word of mine. I was troubled at the thought of leaving him. It seemed impossible to get him to venture. To compel him to try by fear of being left, I started off as if leaving him to his fate, and disappeared back of a hummock; but this did no good, for he only lay down and cried. So after hiding a few minutes, I went back to the brink of the crevasse, and in a severe tone of voice shouted across to him that now I must certainly leave him—I could wait no longer; and that if he would not come, all I could promise was that I would re-turn to seek him next day. I warned him that if he went back to the woods the wolves would kill him, and finished by urging him once more by words and gestures to come on. He knew very well what I meant, and at last, with the courage of despair, hushed and breath-less, he lay down on the brink in the hollow I had made for my knees, pressed his body against the ice to get the advantage of the friction, gazed into the first step, put his little feet together, and slid them slowly down into it, bunching all four in it, and almost standing on his head. Then, without lifting them, as well as I could see through the snow, he slowly worked them over the edge of the step, and down into the next and the next in succession in the same way, and gained the bridge. Then lifting his feet with the regular-ity and slowness of the vibrations of a seconds' pendulum, as if counting and measuring one, two, three, holding himself in dainty poise, and giving separate attention to each little step, he gained the foot of the cliff, at the top of which I was kneeling to give him a lift should he get within reach. Here he halted in dead silence, and it was here I feared he might fail, for dogs are poor climbers. I had no cord. If I had had one, I would have dropped a noose over his head and hauled him up. But while I was thinking whether an available cord might be made out of clothing, he was looking keenly into the series of notched steps and finger-holds of the ice-ladder I had made, as if counting them and fixing the position of each one in his mind. Then suddenly up he came, with a nervy, springy rush, hooking his paws into the notches and steps so quickly that I could not see how it was done, and whizzed past my head, safe at last!

And now came a scene! "Well done, well done, little boy! Brave boy!" I cried, trying to catch and caress him; but he would not be caught. Never before or since have I seen anything like so passionate a revulsion from the depths of despair to uncontrollable, exultant, triumphant joy. He flashed and darted hither and thither as if fairly demented, screaming and shouting, swirling round and round in giddy loops and circles like a leaf in a whirlwind, lying down and rolling over and over, sidewise and heels over head, pouring forth a tumultuous flood of hysterical cries and sobs and gasping mutterings. And when I ran up to him to shake him, fearing he might die of joy, he flashed off two or three hundred yards, his feet in a mist of motion; then, turning suddenly, he came back in wild rushes, and launched himself at my face, almost knocking me down, all the time screeching and screaming and shouting as if saying, "Saved! saved! saved!" Then away again, dropping suddenly at times with his feet in the air, trembling, and fairly sobbing. Such passionate emotion was enough to kill him. Moses's stately song of triumph after escaping the Egyptians and the Red Sea was nothing to it. Who could have guessed the capacity of the dull, enduring little fellow for all that most stirs this mortal frame? Nobody could have helped crying with him.

But there is nothing like work for toning down either excessive fear or joy. So I ran ahead, calling him, in as gruff a voice as I could command, to come on and stop his nonsense, for we had far to go, and it would soon be dark. Neither of us feared another trial like this. Heaven would surely count one enough for a lifetime. The ice ahead was gashed by thousands of crevasses, but they were common ones. The joy of deliverance burned in us like fire, and we ran without fatigue, every muscle, with immense rebound, glorying in its strength. Stickeen flew across everything in his way, and not till dark did he settle into his normal fox-like, gliding trot. At last the mountains crowned with spruce came in sight, looming faintly in the gloaming, and we soon felt the solid rock beneath our feet, and were safe. Then came weariness. We stumbled down along the lateral moraine in the dark, over rocks and tree-trunks, through the bushes and devil-club thickets and mossy logs and boulders of the woods where we had sheltered ourselves in the morning. Then out on the level mud-slope of the terminal moraine. Danger had vanished, and so had our strength. We reached camp about ten o'clock, and found a big fire and a big supper. A party of Hoona Indians had visited Mr. Young, bringing a gift of porpoise-meat and wild strawberries, and hunter Joe had brought in a wild goat. But we lay down, too tired to eat much, and soon fell into a troubled sleep. The man who said, "The harder the toil the sweeter the rest," never was profoundly tired. Stickeen kept springing up and muttering in his sleep, no doubt dreaming that he was still on the brink of the crevasse; and so did I—that night and many others, long afterward, when I was nervous and overtired.

Thereafter Stickeen was a changed dog. During the rest of the trip, instead of holding aloof, he would come to me at night, when all was quiet about the camp-fire, and rest his head on my knee, with a look of devotion, as if I were his god. And often, as he caught my eye, he seemed to be trying to say, "Wasn't that an awful time we had together on the glacier?"

None of his old friends know what finally became of him. When my work for the season was done I departed for California, and never saw the dear little fellow again. Mr. Young wrote me that in the summer of 1883 he was stolen by a tourist at Fort Wrangel, and taken away on a steamer. His fate is wrapped in mystery. If alive he is very old. Most likely he has left this world—crossed the last crevasse—and gone to another. But he will not be forgotten. Come what may, to me Stickeen is immortal.

# GREY EAGLE

## Herbert Ravenel Sass

*Wild ducks streaking across the sky in long wedges—the man
with the shotgun is not the only foe they have to fear. A charge
of shot had broken the wing of the shoveller drake in this
story; on the ground he found other enemies, and, hovering in
airy ambush, the tyrannous grey eagle. One of the most popular tellers of stories about nature's creatures, Mr. Sass was
born in Charleston, South Carolina, and has always lived there.*

THE tyrant was coming. He was coming like a tyrant—announced
by the tribute of thousands. In the heart of a myrtle thicket in
the swamp woods, a whitetail buck, half-asleep on a bed of dry
leaves, heard the tumult and flicked an ear. Knowing what it was
he dozed on, scarcely conscious of the distant turmoil.

A gray fox, trailing a rabbit along a bush-grown peninsula, extending into a wilderness of marsh, crouched close to the ground as
that air-shaking hubbub rolled down upon her. She was directly
in its path and, lover of silence that she was, for an instant the
clamor startled and disconcerted her. Her fright, however, was
only momentary. Although her sensitive ears, accustomed to the
faint, furtive sounds of the wood, throbbed with the din, already
her calculating brain was occupied with the business of the moment, the stalking of the marsh hare whose scent was strong in her
nostrils.

These, however—the whitetail buck and the fox—were exceptions. To them the coming of the tyrant meant nothing, because
he was not their oppressor; but they were two among many. Under
the white blanket of mist hanging over the watery flats that morning huddled a multitude of living creatures—ducks and coots in
regiments and legions, mallard and pintail, blue-winged teal and
widgeon; and these were subject to the tyrant's will and power.
To these his coming brought panic; and that hollow, drumming

thunder, which rolled along the flats and filled the air and shook the
mist blanket spread above the marshes, was the roar of their myriad opinions as, regiment after regiment, they rocketed upward
and fled on swiftly whirring wing before the great gray eagle who
was their scourge.

He came rather slowly, sailing on set rigid pinions immediately under the opaque stratum of vapor which veiled the marshes
from the morning sun. Ahead the shallow waters had been packed
and crammed with life; under him they were empty, for no duck
of all those thousands had been bold enough to await his arrival.
Once fairly launched in flight they were comparatively safe, for
this gray eagle, like most others of his kind, seldom undertook a
straightforward chase. They had learned, however, that to delay
their start one instant too long might be fatal. Hence that thunder
of wings which rolled down the flats well in advance of the eagle
as he swept on under the sheet of mist; and long before they saw
him the hundreds of mallards, pintails and coots, dabbing and feeding in a certain long marsh-encircled lagoon bordering the river,
had warning of his approach.

To those hundreds of birds the warning brought terror which
in nearly all was instantly manifest. The squadrons of big, green-
headed mallards ceased their busy dabbing for food and, with low
excited quacks and apprehensive upward glances, bunched together in preparation for flight. The high-riding, swanlike pintails
settled lower in the water and bent their long necks over their
backs, searching the air for the enemy. A black fleet of coots, which
a moment before had rested almost motionless on the surface, split
suddenly down the middle, half making for one side of the lagoon
and half for the other. Of the feathered multitude floating on those
placid shallow waters, only a gaudy shoveller drake, more brilliantly coloured than the mallards and except for his broad ungainly-looking bill, more beautiful even than the pintails, remained,
to all appearances, indifferent to the peril.

The shoveller, an adult male already attired in full nuptial
plumage of green and shining white and rich russet, floated near
the middle of the lagoon, in water free from weeds and sedge. A
moment before he had been surrounded by the legions of the coots;
but they had melted away, hastening with a bobbing of blue-black
heads and a flashing of white bills towards the reedy margin. The
mallards were massed towards the northern end of the lagoon, the
pintails toward the southern and along the eastern edge. For a space

of yards around the shoveller the water was empty. An enemy looking down from the air could not fail to see the lone drake floating quietly and with apparent unconcern in the middle of the lagoon.

It was not indifference that held him there. Instinct was wrestling with terror in the shoveller's brain. Instinct bade him be still. Terror urged him to flee. Because instinct had at first prevailed, the shoveller for some moments had not stirred.

A week previously, a charge of duck shot had broken his right wing. The shattered bone had not yet knit. He could not fly and, since the power of flight had thus been taken from him, instinct had more than once saved his life, by freezing him into immobility in the presence of danger. This instinct, gripping him now, held him motionless as an anchored billet of wood on the glassy surface of the lagoon. Little by little, however, as the surging thunder of wings rolled nearer along the flats, and the panic of the ducks and coots around him flared, the grip of instinct weakened until terror gained the upper hand.

From a marsh pool a quarter of a mile away another flock of mallards vaulted into the air. As the throbbing roar of their pinions smote the shoveller's ears, he leaped forward in the water and began swimming desperately toward the margin of the lagoon.

Fifty yards behind him, a squadron of pintail took wing with a sibilant noise as of wind rushing through bare tree-tops. In front a regiment of a hundred coots scurried across the water with a clatter of lobed feet pattering on the surface. Next moment, to the right, the left and ahead, the lagoon heaved thunderously as the main body of the pintails and the vast array of the mallards rose in an opaque mass.

For a space of seconds the air glittered and swirled with the flash of whirring wings, while the water falling from their bodies shimmered in the pale morning light. Then, above and behind him, dark against the mist, the crippled shoveller saw the wide-pinioned shape of doom for which, even as he swam, his round, brilliant, golden eyes had been searching.

If the keener eyes of the gray eagle had already picked out the lone duck swimming across the lagoon ahead of him, for some moments he gave no heed to it. Possibly he may have mistaken the shoveller for a coot, many hundreds of which dotted the pools and ponds within sight. Possibly his attention was distracted momentarily by the armies of pintails and mallards which surging up from the lagoon bordering the river were racing away, the mallards swinging to the right, the pintails to the left. At any rate, some seconds elapsed before the eagle, with a slight motion of his tail, altered his line of flight until he would pass directly over the center of the lagoon. Not until he was nearly over that center did he show unmistakably that he had found a victim suited to his fancy.

Until that moment he had sailed on without appearance of haste, his long marble wings extended and apparently as rigid as the lifeless wings of a monoplane. The broad dark pinions were then bent slightly upward, curving so sharply that they appeared half-closed, the long stiff-shafted tail opened like a fan, the burly body of the bird tilted forward, the strong yellow feet were thrust forward and downward with widely opened claws, and the cloven air sang the wild keen song of the eagle plunging for his prey.

The shoveller drake, swimming desperately, was now some twenty feet from the eastern margin. A willow-grown bank, bordered with tall dense reeds which sprang from the marginal water, extended between the lagoon and the river. If the drake could reach the close-growing reeds, they would provide a respite and perhaps safety; but that sanctuary seemed as unattainable as if it were twenty miles instead of twenty feet away.

The drake had made a mistake, a mistake likely to prove fatal. Minutes earlier he should have sought safety beneath the surface. He could have clung to some submerged grass root or reed stem until his breath failed or the eagle had passed on. It was too late now for this expedient. His broken pinion hampered him seriously whenever he sought to force his buoyant body under water, and only an infinitesimal moment was still his. If he tried to dive, those trenchant talons already stretching toward him would sink deep into his back before he could force himself down.

In that final moment chance intervened. The shoveller did not know that, in the reeds close to the water's edge, round yellow eyes, set in a long narrow snake-like head, had watched, at first with languid interest, this drama of the river flats. He did not know that, at the moment when the gray tyrant half-closed his wings and shot downward through the singing air, fear had flamed in those eyes, and the javelin bill in front of the snake-like head had sagged open with fright. Neither the fleeting duck nor the plunging eagle was aware that a great blue heron had been standing motionless in the reeds, until, with a terrified squawk, the tall bird spread its ash-

blue wings and, with craning neck and trailing legs, flapped upward.

The heron had been facing the lagoon. Either there was not
time to change his position before flight, or the stiff dense stems,
hedging him in, governed the direction of his take-off. At any
rate, when he flapped upward with a hoarse, long-drawn croak of
panic, the first hurried strokes of his pinions placed him squarely in
the plunging eagle's path.

For the hundredth of a second his ash-blue bulk, the wings
spread wide, the long neck stretched to its utmost, loomed almost
directly over the swimming shoveller, and not more than fifteen
feet above him. Next moment the eagle, hurtling downward,
crashed full into the heron.

The great, loosely-knit bird crumpled, collaped—a shapeless
mass of blood-spattered, ashy feathers. Before the gray tyrant,
lashing the air furiously, had recovered from the surprise and shock
of the collision, the shoveller drake was hidden among the crowding reed-stems.

With the wild things fear is a shadow that falls suddenly and as
quickly passes. For perhaps ten minutes the shoveller remained in
the cover of the reeds, resting quietly in the water that was lapping
amid the smooth, straight stems. Then he turned, paddled back to
the open and, heading toward the center of the lagoon, resumed
his interrupted breakfast.

By this time a small squadron of pintails had returned and fleets
of coots were moving out from the marginal waters until they had
practically covered the lower part of the lagoon from shore to
shore. The shoveller had no need to search the air in order to assure himself that the danger had passed. The careless confidence of
coot and pintail was a sufficient assurance and, the danger having
disappeared, the fear which it had inspired had also vanished.

Yet the surface of the lagoon bore evidence of the reality of
that danger, of how well-founded had been that fear. Twenty feet
from the reeds fringing the bank, floated the carcass of the heron
which had met death in so dramatic a fashion. The shoveller, once
he had made out what it was, never again glanced at it; but, if a
man had examined the carcass, he would have found it had been
smashed almost to a pulp by the terrific impact of that encounter
in the air. He would have noted too, that the eagle, disappointed
in his quest for choicer meat, had not fed on the heron, but had left
it contemptuously where it fell.

Such details were, however, of no interest to the crippled shoveller, or, indeed to any of the feathered denizens of the lagoon. Swiftly its population increased. From the open water where the shoveller, surrounded by squadrons of boisterous, quacking mallards and gentle, soft-voiced teal, was feeding, he could view a vast expanse of sky. Against the blue, no longer obscured by mist, he saw ducks of many kinds, not only the more abundant species feeding near, but widgeon and green-winged teal, also blue-bills, more numerous this morning, than even the mallards. Buffleheads too were there in small numbers. Lovers of the saltwater bays and inlets, they were questing inland because a winter gale was sweeping the coast.

Flock after flock shot at great speed across the field of his vision, to swerve, wheel, circle and finally settle in one of the ponds or lagoons scattered over the broad river marshes and the watery flats; yet in all that feathered concourse the shoveller drake saw not one duck of his own kind.

No hunter can tell why in some winters shovellers are common, while in other years scarcely one is to be found among the legions of ducks congregated along the Low Country rivers. This winter countless thousands of other duck fed in the freshwater marshes and the flooded rice lands, but the shovellers had chosen a different feeding ground.

At first the lone drake's search of the air had no more specific motive than a vague but persistent longing for the companionship of his own species. Of late, however, this longing had become more definite, more poignant. Although winter had still many weeks to run, he had donned his nuptial dress, and the mating instinct had awakened. When he now scanned the sky, he was not looking for a flock of shovellers, but for a female shoveller, a mate whom he might woo and win in anticipation of that joyful honeymoon journey in the spring, to the far-off northern lake where they would build their nest and rear their young.

Day after day the crippled drake had awaited the coming of that mate. Day after day his watching and waiting had been in vain. On this day, also, his search appeared doomed to failure. The sun reached and passed its zenith. The short winter afternoon faded and the night shut down. For hours the drake slept, his head resting on his back, his wide spade bill buried in his plumage. A large part of the night, however, he spent in feeding. He paddled swiftly along, his head half-submerged while he strained water and mud through the comb of his bill.

About him in the darkness he heard the voices of the feathered myriads, the hoarse or nasal tones of other ducks, the incessant, infinitely varied conversation of the coots. Dawn brought the mists of morning, and rosy sunlight melted the mists. Again the lone shoveller heard, from far across the marshes, that rolling thunder of innumerable wings which announced that the tyrant was abroad. This morning the thunder came no nearer. The big gray eagle was seeking his prey a little farther to the northward, where the flats were wider and even more populous.

The morning hours passed quietly with no hint of notable developments in store. Then, just before noon, the great event befell.

The crippled drake saw her when she was half a mile away, a mere speck against the sky, to anyone else indistinguishable from the hundreds of other ducks dotting the blue. Instantly the pupils of his eyes contracted and their golden circlets glowed like flame. Straight she came, flying almost as fast as a teal, guided by fate or chance to the one pool in that wilderness where another of her kind awaited her. Probably she saw the drake before she actually alighted, for she swerved in the air and came to rest beside him where he floated in a little open space in the midst of a great raft of coots.

Much as he had longed for her, impatiently as he had awaited her, he took her coming very calmly. With a low guttural "konk, konk," he swam slowly up to her, his head and neck held high, and for some minutes the pair swam slowly in circles. Then, without further demonstration, the shoveller drake led his demure brown sweetheart to a shallow spot near the margin where the soft, slimy mud was particularly rich in snails.

Within an hour of their meeting death came so close that they could feel the wind from his wings. The tyrant was abroad again. Straight toward their pool that ominous thunder of pinions rolled across the flats as flock after flock of ducks rose and fled from the path of the eagle. The crippled drake, remembering his narrow escape of the previous day, began swimming rapidly towards the reeds, while around him the coot fleet scattered and broke and with a hiss and roar of whirrinng pinions the duck squadrons bounded upward. Close behind the drake swam his mate, bound to him by an instinct even stronger than the terror which urged her to spread her wings and fly.

This time the eagle came more swiftly, driving through the air with powerful surging strokes which forced his big body forward at high speed. Then feet behind the two swimming shovellers, a coot gave a shrill cackling cry, opened his wings and strove to lift himself from the pool. A dead weight pulled him back, a weight that clung to his right foot and held him fast. Desperately his wings beat the water, making a mighty commotion; and the eagle, poising at that moment fifty feet above the pool, half closed his broad marbled pinions and plunged.

The female shoveller dived; the crippled drake, hampered by his broken wing, got himself under water at last. But the eagle's fierce eyes had not been fixed on either of the shovellers. His target was the struggling coot; and the latter, unable to dive or to fly because of the big terrapin which had fastened itself to its foot, was gripped and crushed in an instant by the tyrant's long curved claws. A moment the eagle's dark-gray wings .aboured mightily, their serrated tips brushing the water. Then the terrapin's hold gave way and the great bird heaved upward with his prey.

Day followed day in the long marsh-encircled lagoon beside the river: days of placid enjoyment of the lagoon's rich stores of food: days of sudden alarms and thrilling adventures. Often the two shovellers saw the gray tyrant. Three times in as many weeks the crippled drake narrowly escaped those lethal talons. His injured wing was healing. Though as yet he could not fly, he could dive more easily and he had learned to thwart the hunting eagle by disappearing promptly beneath the surface. His mate, too, understood that he could now fend for himself in his own way. Generally when the eagle appeared she took wing with the other ducks, returning after he had passed on.

The ducks had other enemies besides the eagle. Once, as the shovellers dabbled for tiny molluscs close to the reed-bordered bank between the lagoon and the river, a mink sprang at them from a clump of jocko bushes. Wildcats, raccoons and foxes walked this bank by night, and more than once the shovellers heard in the dark a shrill, tragic, choking cry which told them that some unwary coot, venturing ashore after nightfall, had met a bloody end.

When the eagle did not come, there were wide-winged haunters of the marshes who could frighten although they did not harm. The blue herons passing from time to time over the lagoon; the turkey vultures sweeping and soaring against the sky; the long-tailed marsh harriers searching the reedy plains for the small furred and feathered game on which they fed—these, as they swung over, cast swift-moving shadows on the waters, shadows which, as they might be cast by the tyrant's wings, spread sudden fright.

Gradually, almost imperceptibly, the mild Low Country winter changed to spring. Along the edges of the woods across the marshes, swamp maples flamed a brilliant red; a mist of green clothed the willows on the rice field banks; in the high air tree swallows swarmed like gnats; still higher, a speck against the sky, the first water turkey of the season drew circles between white pinnacles of cloud.

The frog choruses swelled louder; the thicket edges rang with the song of birds, golden jessamine, dogwood and Cherokee rose glowed and glimmered in the swamps. The first ospreys came, the first martins, company after company of migrating white herons. These other travellers from the lower South brought new life to the river marshes; but as these lovers of warmth increased, the duck legions diminished.

Flock after flock taking wing, returned no more. First went the hardy mallards; next the pintails, then the green-winged teal. One by one the squadrons of widgeon and bluebills began their long journey. In a single night the marsh lagoons and flooded rice lands bordering the river were almost emptied of coots. Soon, of the myriads of ducks which had spent the winter along the river flats, only small flocks of blue-winged teal, a half dozen belated widgeons or baldpates and the two shovellers remained.

The wind, which for days had blown from the east, swung to the south. Suddenly the air grew languid and warm. The lagging baldpates disappeared. Coral-billed gallinules supplanted the rearguard of the coots. An hour after the next sunrise, the last flock of teal mounted—as though at a signal, circled high, then headed away to the north. The shoveller drake and his mate watched them go; and before they disappeared in the distance, the female shoveller, without a glance at her partner or a sound of farewell, bounded upward and whirred away in pursuit.

From a dead cedar at the edge of the pineland, far across the marshes, a hawk pitched forward, opened long pointed wings, and shot northward at amazing speed—the speed of the peregrine falcon in pursuit of his prey. He passed like a winged projectile not more than a hundred yards from the lagoon of the shoveller drake. The latter did not see him, did not know that at the very outset of her journey his mate must run a race with death. All he knew was that she had left him and that she would not return—that joyously, eagerly, exultantly, she had mounted at last to the broad blue road of the sky which for weeks had beckoned her, a road which led northward and ever northward to the far-off sloughs and prairie lakes where the wild duck myriads breed.

The golden circlets rimming the crippled duck's pupils glowed a brilliant orange. Rearing his body, he stood for an instant on the surface of the water, his wings fanning the air. Not for weeks had he tried his pinions, dreading the burning agony which he had learnt to associate with every attempt to fly; but now his wings fanned faster and faster, and suddenly they lifted him. He flew for a hundred yards, then slumped abruptly, plunging with a splash into a flooded rice field which was separated by a strip of marsh from the lagoon where he had spent so many weeks.

A month passed; a month of gnawing loneliness and incessant restlessness, spent dabbling in flooded rice fields and shallow marsh ponds which he shared with noisy gallinules, long-necked water turkeys, stately milk-white egrets, herons of several kinds, and tall black and white ibises. He seldom saw the eagle, for after the departure of the duck armies, that great bird had sought a different order of prey. Day followed day uneventfully. One still sunny morning, however, as the lone drake feasted on water snails along the edge of a little peninsula of reeds, a black log, half-submerged near the margin, came suddenly to life.

As the 'gator rushed, the drake, with a hoarse, startled cry, opened his wings and launched himself into the air. On and on he flew, rising higher and higher; on and on for fifty yards, a hundred, five hundred. His wings beat evenly and strongly. No weakness or numbness assailed him. At first he flew south, the direction in which he happened to be headed when the 'gator charged him; but gradually he swung in a wide half-circle until his long bill and slender neck pointed north.

The green marshes and the shimmering blue lagoons slid past beneath. In front, a thousand miles away, a placid prairie lake, where his mate might be swimming with her little ones, beckoned and lured him on.

The eagle was taking his ease. In the frosty, windless upper air, so far above the earth that to the eyes of a man he would have appeared no larger than a gnat, he floated on outstretched wings as lightly as the wisps of cloud among which he was. This was his kingdom, his illimitable solitude; and it was there, "in those blue tracts above the thunder," that he had his throne.

Often it was peace the eagle sought when he mounted to these lofty fastnesses—the peace of boundless silence, of freedom from danger, of complete mental relaxation. Among the clouds no need for watchfulness. His senses could rest and his wide wings, motionless except for occasional slight quiverings of the flexible tips, could perform their function almost automatically. Without fatigue, almost without effort, he could remain aloft for hours, sailing in great circles or wide ellipses, keeping the same level or, if the air currents were favorable, spiralling gradually up until he approached the invisible upper frontier of his airy kingdom, beyond which even he could not soar.

This bright mid-spring morning found him drowsy. Spring was a season of plenty when his unwilling purveyors, the ospreys, being numerous and industrious, yielded him a rich tribute of fish. Although in winter he varied his fare by catching unwary coots or wounded ducks, fish was his favourite food; and, with fish plentiful and the labours of the nesting season behind, the eagle had time for rest. Shortly after sunrise, he had breakfasted on a mullet which an indignant osprey had surrendered. Then, languidly, lazily he had climbed to spend the morning circling somnolently immediately under the motionless white clouds.

For nearly two hours he had been soaring thus, more than half-asleep. Suddenly, his drowsiness fell from him. Far below to the south a black speck was moving swiftly through the air. To his far-sighted eyes this speck had the form of a duck, a duck whose wide, flat bill and slender neck identified it as a shoveller. Its course would bring it directly below the eagle; and not until it was under him did he reach a decision.

Until that moment, though he watched the oncoming duck with eyes that glowed under their beetling brows, he continued his placid soaring. Then, as if he had become suddenly aware of something unperceived until that moment, he half-closed his wings and slid downward through the hissing air.

The golden eyes of the shoveller drake, speeding north on his long delayed journey to the distant Canadian lake which all his life had been his summer home, searched the air lane ahead and the sky spaces above. Yet he had failed to see that sinister dark spot moving slowly in wide circles, a thousand feet or more above the line of his flight. He had missed it because at the moment his attention was otherwise occupied.

Half-an-hour had elapsed since he began his journey; and although at first the swiftness and evenness of his wing beats appeared to prove beyond all doubt that his injured pinion was now as serviceable as before, it was already evident that this appearance of restored strength was fictitious.

A human eye could not have detected at this stage anything abnormal in the drake's manner of flight. Nevertheless the drake, himself, knew all was not well; and the marvellous eyes of the gray eagle, looking down on the drake as it passed beneath him, perceived immediately that this was a shoveller whose powers of flight had been impaired. This discovery, determining the tyrant's course of action, had brought him shooting down like a feathered meteor.

Possibly it was sound, not sight, which first appraised the drake of his peril. He probably heard above the rush of the wind through his own pinions, a high, thin, wailing note the meaning of which he knew—the keen, wild song which the air sings when it is smitten and cleft by the hard edges of the eagle's wings as the bird plunges upon his prey. Or it may have been that the drake's golden eyes warned him of the danger.

If, until then, that distant lake where, perhaps, his mate was dabbling with her little ones, had beckoned him, the vision was instantly blotted out. Panic gripped and stabbed him; yet he did the one thing that might save him.

Directly beneath him lay a wide plain of river marsh; and not more than a quarter of a mile to his right, a loop of the river glittered in the sun. This, if he could reach it, was his haven. Instantly he wheeled in the air and, tilting his body sharply forward, drove with all the strength of his pinions towards the smooth expanse of the river. Beneath that silvery surface life awaited him. Towards that goal he ran his race with death.

It was a brave race. Until its final tenth of a second its issue was in doubt. The drake's swift maneuver, his sudden wheel to the right gained him some twenty yards. For a moment he no longer heard that thin keen wailing note behind and above him. Almost instantly, however, he heard it again, and swiftly it sharpened to a hiss which, in turn, became a loud, angry, rustling noise like the rushing of wind through bending tree-tops.

Fifteen feet above the surface of the river the race ended—ended with a savage downward thrust of widespread blue-black

talons and a smother of great gray wings furiously lashing the air.
The gray tyrant swept buoyantly onward and up, gripping in his
claws the white and russet body of the drake, the long green neck
dangling limply. Three miles away, in a tall pine on a wooded
island in the marsh, was an abandoned eagle nest which the bird
sometimes used as a storehouse for food. Toward this he set his
course.

### To the Fringed Gentian

THOU blossom bright with autumn dew,
    And colored with the heaven's own blue,
That openest when the quiet light
Succeeds the keen and frosty night,

Thou comest not when violets lean
O'er wandering brooks and springs unseen,
Or columbines, in purple dressed,
Nod o'er the ground-bird's hidden nest.

Thou waitest late and com'st alone,
When woods are bare and birds are flown,
And frosts and shortening days portend
The aged year is near his end.

Then doth thy sweet and quiet eye
Look through its fringes to the sky,
Blue—blue—as if that sky let fall
A flower from its cerulean wall.

I would that thus, when I shall see
The hour of death draw near to me,
Hope, blossoming within my heart,
May look to heaven as I depart.

                              *William Cullen Bryant*

# THE COMBAT WITH THE OCTOPUS

## Victor Hugo

*The son of a general in Napoleon's army, Victor Hugo (1802–1885) began writing poetry very early, at the age of twenty publishing a volume which brought him immediate fame. With each new book—novels, plays, essays, verse—his stature grew, so that the age-ridden French Academy admitted him into its midst when he was only thirty-eight. Hugo's most widely read novels are* Notre Dame de Paris *and* Les Misérables; *but* Toilers of the Sea *shows almost as much splendor of imagination and style, particularly in this narrative of Gilliatt's battle with the octopus. It may be noted in passing that since Hugo's day some naturalists have concluded that the undersea monster is an ineffectual fighter.*

JUST as Gilliatt was making up his mind to resign himself to sea-urchins and sea-chestnuts, a splash was made at his feet.

A huge crab, frightened by his approach, had just dropped into the water. The crab did not sink so deeply that Gilliatt lost sight of it.

Gilliatt set out on a run after the crab along the base of the reef. The crab sought to escape.

Suddenly, he was no longer in sight.

The crab had just hidden in some crevice under the rock.

Gilliatt clung to the projections of the rock, and thrust forward his head to get a look under the overhanging cliff.

There was in fact a cavity there. The crab must have taken refuge in it.

It was something more than a crevice. It was a sort of porch.

The sea entered beneath this porch, but was not deep. The bottom was visible, covered with stones. These stones were smooth and clothed with algæ, which indicated that they were never dry. They resembled the tops of children's heads covered with green hair.

Gilliatt took his knife in his teeth, climbed down with his hands and feet from the top of the cliff, and leaped into the water. It reached almost to his shoulders.

He passed under the porch. He entered a much worn corridor in the form of a rude pointed arch overhead. The walls were smooth and polished. He no longer saw the crab. He kept his foothold, and advanced through the diminishing light. He began to be unable to distinguish objects.

After about fifteen paces, the vault above him came to an end. He was out of the corridor. He had here more space, and consequently more light; and besides, the pupils of his eyes were now dilated: he saw with tolerable clearness. He had a surprise.

He was just re-entering that strange cave which he had visited a month previously.

Only he had returned to it by way of the sea.

That arch which he had then seen submerged was the one through which he had just passed. It was accessible at certain low tides.

His eyes became accustomed to the place. He saw better and better. He was astounded. He had found again that extraordinary palace of shadows, that vault, those pillars, those purple and bloodlike stains, that jewel-like vegetation, and at the end that crypt, almost a sanctuary, and that stone which was almost an altar.

He had not taken much notice of these details; but he carried the general effect in his mind, and he beheld it again.

Opposite him, at a certain height in the cliff, he saw the crevice through which he had made his entrance on the first occasion, and which, from the point where he now stood, seemed inaccessible.

He beheld again, near the pointed arch, those low and obscure grottoes, a sort of caverns within the cavern, which he had already observed from a distance. Now he was close to them. The one nearest to him was dry and easily accessible.

Still nearer than that opening he noticed a horizontal fissure in the granite above the level of the water. The crab was probably there. He thrust in his hand as far as he could and began to grope in this hole of shadows.

All at once he felt himself seized by the arm.

What he felt at that moment was indescribable horror.

Something thin, rough, flat, slimy, adhesive, and living, had just wound itself round his bare arm in the dark. It crept up towards his breast. It was like the pressure of a leather thong and the thrust of a gimlet. In less than a second an indescribable spiral form had passed around his wrist and his elbow, and reached to his shoulder. The point burrowed under his armpit.

Gilliatt threw himself backwards, but could hardly move. He was as though nailed to the spot; with his left hand, which remained free, he took his knife, which he held between his teeth, and holding the knife with his hand he braced himself against the rock, in a desperate effort to withdraw his arm. He only succeeded in disturbing the ligature a little, which resumed its pressure. It was as supple as leather, as solid as steel, as cold as night.

A second thong, narrow and pointed, issued from the crevice of the rock. It was like a tongue from the jaws of a monster. It licked Gilliatt's naked form in a terrible fashion, and suddenly stretching out, immensely long and thin, it applied itself to his skin and surrounded his whole body. At the same time, unheard-of suffering, which was comparable to nothing he had previously known, swelled Gilliatt's contracted muscles. He felt in his skin round and horrible perforations; it seemed to him that innumerable lips were fastened to his flesh and were seeking to drink his blood.

A third thong undulated outside the rock, felt of Gilliatt, and lashed his sides like a cord. It fixed itself there.

Anguish is mute when at its highest point. Gilliatt did not utter a cry. There was light enough for him to see the repulsive forms adhering to him.

A fourth ligature, this one as swift as a dart, leaped towards his belly and rolled itself around there.

Impossible either to tear or to cut away these shiny thongs which adhered closely to Gilliatt's body, and by a number of points. Each one of those points was the seat of frightful and peculiar pain. It was what would be experienced if one were being swallowed simultaneously by a throng of mouths which were too small.

A fifth prolongation leaped from the hole. It superimposed itself upon the others, and folded over Gilliatt's chest. Compression was added to horror; Gilliatt could hardly breathe.

These thongs, pointed at their extremity, spread out gradually like the blades of swords towards the hilt. All five evidently belonged to the same centre. They crept and crawled over Gilliatt.

He felt these strange points of pressure, which seemed to him to be mouths, changing their places.

Suddenly a large, round, flat, slimy mass emerged from the lower part of the crevice.

It was the centre; the five thongs were attached to it like spokes to a hub; on the opposite side of this foul disk could be distinguished the beginnings of three other tentacles, which remained under the slope of the rock. In the middle of this sliminess there were two eyes gazing.

The eyes were fixed on Gilliatt.

Gilliatt recognized the octopus (*devil-fish*).


2


To believe in the octopus, one must have seen it.

Compared with it, the hydras of old are laughable.

At certain moments one is tempted to think that the intangible forms which float through our vision encounter in the realm of the possible, certain magnetic centres to which their lineaments cling, and that from these obscure fixations of the living dream, beings spring forth. The unknown has the marvelous at its disposal, and it makes use of it to compose the monster. Orpheus, Homer, and Hesiod were only able to make the Chimæra: God made the octopus.

When God wills it, he excels in the execrable. . . .

All ideals being admitted, if terror be an object, the octopus is a masterpiece.

The whale has enormous size, the octopus is small; the hippopotamus has a cuirass, the octopus is naked; the jararoca hisses, the octopus is dumb; the rhinoceros has a horn, the octopus has no horn; the scorpion has a sting, the octopus has no sting; the buthus has claws, the octopus has no claws; the ape has a prehensile tail, the octopus has no tail; the shark has sharp fins, the octopus has no fins; the vespertilio vampire has wings armed with barbs, the octopus has no barbs; the hedgehog has quills, the octopus has no quills; the sword-fish has a sword, the octopus has no sword; the torpedo-fish has an electric shock, the octopus has none; the toad has a virus, the octopus has no virus; the viper has a venom, the octopus has no venom; the lion has claws, the octopus has no claws; the hawk has a beak, the octopus has no beak; the crocodile has jaws, the octopus has no teeth.

The octopus has no muscular organization, no menacing cry, no breastplate, no horn, no dart, no pincers, no prehensile or bruising tail, no cutting pectoral fins, no barbed wings, no quills, no sword, no electric discharge, no virus, no venom, no claws, no beak, no teeth. Of all creatures, the octopus is the most formidably armed.

What then is the octopus? It is the cupping-glass.

In open sea reefs, where the water displays and hides all its splendors, in the hollows of unvisited rocks, in the unknown caves where vegetations, crustaceans, and shell-fish abound, beneath the deep portals of the ocean,—the swimmer who hazards himself there, led on by the beauty of the place, runs the risk of an encounter. If you have this encounter, be not curious but fly. One enters there dazzled, one emerges from thence terrified.

This is the nature of the encounter always possible among rocks in the open sea.

A grayish form undulates in the water: it is as thick as a man's arm, and about half an ell long; it is a rag; its form resembles a closed umbrella without a handle. This rag gradually advances towards you, suddenly it opens: eight radii spread out abruptly around a face which has two eyes; these radii are alive; there is something of the flame in their undulation; it is a sort of wheel; unfolded, it is four or five feet in diameter. Frightful expansion. This flings itself upon you.

The hydra harpoons its victim.

This creature applies itself to its prey; covers it, and knots its long bands about it. Underneath, it is yellowish; on top, earth-colored: nothing can represent this inexplicable hue of dust; one would pronounce it a creature made of ashes, living in the water. In form it is spider-like, and like a chameleon in its coloring. When irritated it becomes violet in hue. Its most terrible quality is its softness.

Its folds strangle; its contact paralyzes.

It has an aspect of scurvy and gangrene. It is disease embodied in monstrosity.

It is not to be torn away. It adheres closely to its prey. How? By a vacuum. Its eight antennæ, large at the root, gradually taper off and end in needles. Underneath each one of them are arranged two rows of decreasing pustules, the largest near the head, the smallest ones at the tip. Each row consists of twenty-five; there are fifty pustules to each antenna, and the whole creature has four hundred of them. These pustules are cupping-glasses.

These cupping-glasses are cylindrical, horny, livid cartilages. On the large species they gradually diminish from the diameter of a five-franc piece to the size of a lentil. These fragments of tubes are thrust out from the animal and retire into it. They can be inserted into the prey for more than an inch.

This sucking apparatus has all the delicacy of a key-board. It rises, then retreats. It obeys the slightest wish of the animal. The most exquisite sensibilities cannot equal the contractibility of these suckers, always proportioned to the internal movements of the creature and to the external circumstances. This dragon is like a sensitive-plant.

This is the monster which mariners call the poulp, which science calls the cephalopod, and which legend calls the kraken. English sailors call it the "devil-fish." They also call it the "blood-sucker." In the Channel Islands it is called the *pieuvre*.

It is very rare in Guernsey, very small in Jersey, very large and quite frequent in Sark.

A print from Sonnini's edition of Buffon represents an octopus crushing a frigate. Denis Montfort thinks that the octopus of the high latitudes is really strong enough to sink a ship. Bory Saint Vincent denies this, but admits that in our latitudes it does attack man. Go to Sark and they will show you, near Brecq-Hou, the hollow in the rock where, a few years ago, an octopus seized and drowned a lobster-fisher.

Péron and Lamarck are mistaken when they doubt whether the octopus can swim, since it has no fins.

He who writes these lines has seen with his own eyes at Sark, in the cave called the Shops, an octopus swimming and chasing a bather. When killed and measured it was found to be four English feet in spread, and four hundred suckers could be counted. The dying monster thrust them out convulsively.

According to Denis Montfort, one of those observers whose strong gift of intuition causes them to descend or to ascend even to magianism, the octopus has almost the passions of a man; the octopus hates. In fact, in the absolute, to be hideous is to hate.

The misshapen struggles under a necessity of elimination, and this consequently renders it hostile.

The octopus when swimming remains, so to speak, in its sheath.

It swims with all its folds held close. Let the reader picture to himself a sewed-up sleeve with a closed fist inside of it. This fist, which is the head, pushes through the water, and advances with a vague, undulating movement. Its two eyes, though large, are not very distinct, being the color of the water.

The octopus on the chase or lying in wait, hides; it contracts, it condenses itself; it reduces itself to the simplest possible expression. It confounds itself with the shadow. It looks like a ripple of the waves. It resembles everything except something living.

The octopus is a hypocrite. When one pays no heed to it, suddenly it opens.

A glutinous mass possessed of a will—what more frightful? Glue filled with hatred.

It is in the most beautiful azure of the limpid water that this hideous, voracious star of the sea arises.

It gives no warning of its approach, which renders it more terrible. Almost always, when one sees it, one is already caught.

At night, however, and in breeding season, it is phosphorescent. This terror has its passions. It awaits the nuptial hour. It adorns itself, it lights up, it illuminates itself; and from the summit of a rock one can see it beneath, in the shadowy depths, spread out in a pallid irradiation,—a spectre sun.

It has no bones, it has no blood, it has no flesh. It is flabby. There is nothing in it. It is a skin. One can turn its eight tentacles wrong side out, like the fingers of a glove.

It has a single orifice in the centre of its radiation. Is this one hole the vent? Is it the mouth? It is both.

The same aperture fulfills both functions. The entrance is the exit.

The whole creature is cold.

The carnarius of the Mediterranean is repulsive. An odious contact has this animated gelatine, which envelops the swimmer, into which the hands sink, where the nails scratch, which one rends without killing and tears off without pulling away, a sort of flowing and tenacious being which slips between one's fingers; but no horror equals the sudden appearance of the octopus,—Medusa served by eight serpents.

No grasp equals the embrace of the cephalopod.

It is the pneumatic machine attacking you. You have to deal with a vacuum furnished with paws. Neither scratches nor bites; an indescribable scarification. A bite is formidable, but less so than a suction. A claw is nothing beside the cupping-glass. The claw means the beast entering into your flesh; the cupping-glass means yourself entering into the beast.

Your muscles swell, your fibres writhe, your skin cracks under the foul weight, your blood spurts forth and mingles frightfully with the lymph of the mollusk. The creature superimposes itself upon you by a thousand mouths; the hydra incorporates itself with the man; the man amalgamates himself with the hydra. You form but one. This dream is upon you. The tiger can only devour you; the octopus, oh horror! breathes you in. It draws you to it, and into it; and bound, ensnared, powerless, you feel yourself slowly emptied into that frightful pond, which is the monster itself.

Beyond the terrible, being devoured alive, is the inexpressible, being drunk alive. . . .

Such was the creature in whose power Gilliatt had been for several moments.

This monster was the inhabitant of that grotto. It was the frightful genius of the place. A sort of sombre demon of the water.

All these magnificences had horror for their centre.

A month previously, on the day when for the first time Gilliatt had made his way into the grotto, the dark outline, of which he had caught a glimpse in the ripples of the water, was this octopus.

This was its home.

When Gilliatt, entering that cave for the second time in pursuit of the crab, had perceived the crevices in which he thought the crab had taken refuge, the octopus was lying in wait in that hole.

Can the reader picture that lying in wait?

Not a bird would dare to brood, not an egg would dare to hatch, not a flower would dare to open, not a breast would dare to give suck, not a heart would dare to love, not a spirit would dare to take flight, if one meditated on the sinister shapes patiently lying in ambush in the abyss.

Gilliatt had thrust his arm into the hole; the octopus had seized it.

It held it.

He was the fly for this spider.

Gilliatt stood in water to his waist, his feet clinging to the slippery roundness of the stones, his right arm grasped and subdued by the flat coils of the octopus's thongs, and his body almost hidden by the folds and crossings of that horrible bandage. Of the eight arms of the octopus, three adhered to the rock while five adhered to Gilliatt. In this manner, clamped on one side to the granite, on the other to the man, it chained Gilliatt to the rock. Gilliatt had two hundred and fifty suckers upon him. A combination of anguish and disgust. To be crushed in a gigantic fist, whose elastic fingers, nearly a metre in length, are inwardly full of living pustules which ransack your flesh.

As we have said, one cannot tear one's self away from the octopus. If one attempts it, one is but the more surely bound. It only clings the closer. Its efforts increase in proportion to yours. A greater struggle produces a greater constriction.

Gilliatt had but one resource,—his knife.

He had only his left hand free; but as the reader knows, he could make powerful use of it. It might have been said of him that he had two right hands.

His open knife was in his hand.

The tentacles of an octopus cannot be cut off; they are leathery and difficult to sever, they slip away from under the blade. Moreover, the superposition is such that a cut into these thongs would attack your own flesh.

The octopus is formidable; nevertheless there is a way of getting away from it. The fishermen of Sark are acquainted with it; any one who has seen them executing abrupt movements at sea knows it. Porpoises also know it: they have a way of biting the cuttlefish which cuts off its head. Hence all the headless squids and cuttlefish which are met with on the open sea.

The octopus is in fact vulnerable only in the head.

Gilliatt was not ignorant of this fact.

He had never seen an octopus of this size. He found himself seized at the outset by one of the larger species. Any other man would have been terrified.

In the case of the octopus as in that of the bull, there is a certain moment at which to seize it: it is the instant when the bull lowers his neck, it is the instant when the octopus thrusts forward its head —a sudden movement. He who misses that juncture is lost.

All that we have related lasted but a few minutes. But Gilliatt felt the suction of the two hundred and fifty cupping-glasses increasing.

The octopus is cunning. It tries to stupefy its prey in the first place. It seizes, then waits as long as it can.

Gilliatt held his knife. The suction increased.

He gazed at the octopus, which stared at him.

All at once the creature detached its sixth tentacle from the rock, and launching it at him, attempted to seize his left arm.

At the same time it thrust its head forward swiftly. A second more and its mouth would have been applied to Gilliatt's breast. Gilliatt, wounded in the flank and with both arms pinioned, would have been a dead man.

But Gilliatt was on his guard. Being watched, he watched.

He avoided the tentacle, and at the moment when the creature was about to bite his breast, his armed fist descended on the monster.

Two convulsions in opposite directions ensued: that of Gilliatt and that of the octopus.

It was like the conflict of two flashes of lightning.

Gilliatt plunged the point of his knife into the flat, viscous mass, and with a twisting movement, similar to the flourish of a whip, describing a circle around the two eyes, he tore out the head as one wrenches out a tooth.

It was finished.

The whole creature dropped.

It resembled a sheet detaching itself. The air-pump destroyed, the vacuum no longer existed. The four hundred suckers released their hold, simultaneously, of the rock and the man.

It sank to the bottom.

Gilliatt, panting with the combat, could perceive on the rocks at his feet two shapeless, gelatinous masses, the head on one side, the rest on the other. We say "the rest," because one could not say the body.

Gilliatt, however, fearing some convulsive return of agony, retreated beyond the reach of the tentacles.

But the monster was really dead.

Gilliatt closed his knife.

It was time that Gilliatt killed the octopus. He was almost strangled; his right arm and his body were violet in hue; more than two hundred swellings were outlined upon them; the blood spurted from some of them here and there. The remedy for these wounds is salt water: Gilliatt plunged into it. At the same time he rubbed himself with the palm of his hand. The swellings subsided under this friction.

# DESERT ANIMALS

## Charles Montagu Doughty

*Arabia was, to the western world, a land unknown, a desert
filled with assassins, until Doughty (1843-1926) published his
Travels in Arabia Deserta. A student of language, geology, and
ancient ruins, he had wandered in Europe and North Africa;
in 1876 he set out with a caravan into Arabia. At the peril of his
life he observed its people and customs, its early monuments,
reaching Jidda and safety two years later. Doughty was a profound admirer of the literature of Shakespeare's day—here you
read of the animals of the desert as an Elizabethan would have
described them.*

THE short spring season is the only refreshment of the desert
year. Beasts and men swim upon this prosperous tide; the cattle
have their fill of sweet pasture, butter-milk is in the booths of the
Aarab [1]; but there was little or none in Zeyd's tent. The kids and
lambs stand all tied, each little neck in a noose, upon a ground line
which is stretched in the nomad booth. At daybreak the bleating
younglings are put under the dams, and each mother receives her
own, (it is by the scent)—she will put by every other. When the
flock is led forth to pasture, the little ones are still bound at home;
for following the dams, they would drink dry the dugs, and leave
no food for the Arabs. The worsted tent is full all day of small
hungry bleatings, until the ghrannem [2] come home at evening,
when they are loosed again, and run to drink, butting under their
mother's teats, with their wiggle tails; and in these spring weeks,
there is little rest for their feeble cries, all night in the booths of the
Aarab: the housewives draw what remains of the sweet milk after
them. The B. Wáhab tribes of these open highlands, are camel-
Beduins; the small cattle are few among them: they have new spring
milk when their hinds have calved. The yeaning camel-cow, lying

[1] Aarab—the nomad Arabs, despised by townfolk.
[2] Ghrannem—small cattle.

upon her side, is delivered without voice, the fallen calf is big as a grown man: the herdsman stretches out its legs, with all his might; and draws the calf, as dead, before the dam. She smells to her young, rises and stands upon her feet to lick it over. With a great clap of the man's palm upon that horny sole, *zôra*, (which, like a pillar, Nature has set under the camel's breast, to bear up the huge neck,) the calf revives: at three hours end, yet feeble and tottering, and after many falls, it is able to stand reaching up the long neck and feeling for the mother's teat. The next morrow this new born camel will follow to the field with the dam. The cow may be milked immediately, but that which is drawn from her, for a day or two, is purgative. The first voice of the calf is a sheep-like complaint, *bâh-bâh*, loud and well sounding. The fleece is silken soft, the head round and high; and this with a short body, borne archwise, and a leaping gait upon so long legs, makes that, a little closing the eyes, you might take them for fledglings of some colossal bird. Till twelve months be out they follow the teat; but when a few weeks old they begin, already, to crop for themselves the tops of the desert bushes: and their necks being not yet of proportionate reach, it is only betwixt the straddled fore legs, that they can feed at the ground. One evening, as I stroked the soft woolly chines of the new-born camels, 'Khalîl! said the hind (coming with a hostile face), see thou do no more so,—they will be hide-bound and not grow well; thou knowest not this!' He thought the stranger was about some maleficence; but Zeyd, whose spirit was far from all superstition, with an easy smile appeased him, and they were his own camels.

The camel calf at the birth is worth a real, and every month rises as much in value. In some 'weak' households the veal is slaughtered, where they must drink themselves all their camel milk. The bereaved dam wanders, lowing softly, and smelling for her calf; and as she mourns, you shall see her deer-like pupils, say the Arabs, 'standing full of tears.' Other ten days, and her brutish distress is gone over to forgetfulness; she will feed again full at the pasture, and yield her foster milk to the Aarab. Then three good pints may be drawn from her at morning, and as much to their supper: the udder of these huge frugal animals is not greater than I have seen the dugs of Malta goats. A milch cow with the calf is milked only at evening. Her udder has four teats, which the southern nomads divide thus: two they tie up with a worsted twine and wooden pegs, for themselves, the others they leave to the suckling. The

Aarab of the north make their camel udders sure, with a worsted bag-netting. Upon a journey, or when she is thirsting, the nâga's [3] milk is lessened to the half. All their nâgas give not milk alike. Whilst the spring milk is in, the nomads nourish themselves of little else. In poorer households it is all their victual those two months. The Beduins drink no whole-milk, save that of their camels; of their small cattle they drink but the butter-milk. The hareem [4] make butter, busily rocking the (blown) sour milk-skin upon their knees. In the plenteous northern wilderness the semîly [5] is greater; and is hanged to be rocked in the fork of a robust bearing-stake of the nomad tent. As for this milk-diet, I find it, by proof in the Beduin life, to be the best of human food. But in every nomad menzil,[6] there are some stomachs, which may never well bear it; and strong men using this sliding drink-meat feel always an hungry disease in their bodies; though they seem in never so good plight. The Beduins speak thus of the several kinds of milk: 'Goatmilk is sweet, it fattens more than strengthens the body; ewe's milk very sweet, and fattest of all, it is unwholesome to drink whole': so they say, 'it kills people,' that is, with the colic. In spite of their saws, I have many times drunk it warm from the dug, with great comfort of languishing fatigue. It is very rich in the best samn [7]; ewe butter-milk 'should be let sour somewhile in the semîly, with other milk, till all be tempered together, and then it is fit to drink.' Camel milk is they think the best of all sustenance, and that most, (as lightly purgative,) of the *bukkra*, or young nâga with her first calf, and the most sober of them add with a Beduish simplicity, 'who drinks and has a jâra [8] he would not abide an hour.' The goat and nâga milk savour of the plants where the cattle are pastured; in some cankered grounds I have found it as wormwood. One of those Allayda sheykhs called to me in the râhla,[9] 'Hast thou not some Damascus *kaak* (biscuit cakes) to give me to eat? wellah,[10] it is six weeks since I have chewed anything with the teeth; all our food is

[3] Nâga—cow-camel.
[4] Hareem—plural of *horma*, woman.
[5] Semîly—milk-bag or skin (commonly of sheep's leather; being sour, it sours fresh milk put into it and women rock it on their knees until butter comes).
[6] Menzil—camping ground of caravan or of Nomads.
[7] Samn—clarified butter.
[8] Jâra—bed.
[9] Râhla—the removing and journeying of the nomads.
[10] Wellah—verily, indeed.

now this flood of milk. Seest thou not what is the Beduins' life; they are like game scattered in all the wilderness.' Another craved of me a handful of dates; 'with this milk, only, he felt such a creeping hunger within him.' Of any dividing food with them the Beduins keep a kindly remembrance; and when they have aught will call thee heartily again.

The milk-dieted Aarab are glad to take any mouthful of small game. Besides the desert hare which is often startled in the râhlas, before other is the thób [11]; which they call here pleasantly 'Master Hamed, sheykh of wild beasts,' and say he is human, *zillamy*,[12]— this is their elvish smiling and playing—and in proof they hold up his little five-fingered hands. They eat not his palms, nor the seven latter thorny rings of sheykh Hamed's long tail, which, say they, is 'man's flesh.' His pasture is most of the sweet-smelling Nejd bush, *el-arrafej*. Sprawling wide and flat is the body, ending in a training tail of even length, where I have counted twenty-three rings. The colour is blackish and green-speckled, above the pale yellowish and dull belly: of his skin the nomads make small herdmen's milk-bottles. The manikin saurian, with the robust hands, digs his burrow under the hard gravel soil, wherein he lies all the winter, dreaming. The thób-catcher, finding the hole, and putting in his long reed armed with an iron hook, draws Hamed forth. His throat cut, they fling the carcase, whole, upon the coals; and thus baked they think it a delicate roast. His capital enemy among beasts, 'which undermines and devours him, is, they say, the *thurbàn*,' I know not whether a living or fabulous animal. The *jerboa*, or spring rat, is a small white aery creature in the wide waterless deserts, of a pitiful beauty. These lesser desert creatures lie underground in the daylight, they never drink. The hedgehog, which they call *kúnfuth*, and *abu shauk*, 'father prickles,' is eaten in these parts by Fejîr tribesmen, but by their neighbours disdained, although they be one stock with them of Annezy. Selim brought in an urchin which he had knocked on the head, he roasted Prickles in the coals and rent and distributed the morsels, to every one his part. That which fell to me I put away bye and bye to the starveling greyhound; but the dog smelling to the meat rejected it. When another day I told this tale in the next tribes, they laughed maliciously, that the Fukara should eat that which the hounds would not of. The porcupine is eaten by all the nomads, and the *wabbar*.[13]

[11] Thób—a lizard-like creature of the desert.
[12] Zillamy—a fellow, man of the people.
[13] Wabbar—a rodent animal of the desert mountains.

I have seen this thick-bodied beast as much as an heavy hare, and resembling the great Alpine rat; they go by pairs, or four, six, eight, ten, together. The wabbar is found under the border of the sandstone mountains, where tender herbs nourish him, and the gum-acacia leaves, upon which tree he climbs nimbly, holding with his pad feet without claws; the fore-paws have four toes, the hind-paws three: the flesh is fat and sweet: they are not seen to sit upon the hind quarters; the pelt is grey, and like the bear's coat.

Rarely do any nomad gunners kill the wolf, but if any fall to their shot he is eaten by the Beduins, (the wolf was eaten in mediæval Europe). The Aarab think the flesh medicinal, 'very good they say for aches in the shins,' which are so common with them that go bare-legs and bare-footed in all the seasons. Zeyd had eaten the wolf, but he allowed it to be of dog's kind, 'Eigh, billah [14] (he answered me), the wolf's mother, that is the hound's aunt.' The fox, *hosseny*, is often taken by their greyhounds, and eaten by the Fejîr; the flesh is 'sweet, and next to the hare.' They will even eat the foul hyena when they may take her, and say, 'she is good meat.' Of great desert game, but seldom slain by the shot of these pastoral and tent-dwelling people, is the bédan of the mountains (the wild goat of Scripture, *pl.* bedûn; with the Kahtân *waûl*, as in Syria). The massy horns grow to a palm-breadth, I have seen them two and a half feet long; they grow stretching back upon the chine to the haunch. The beast at need, as all hunters relate, will cast himself down headlong upon them backwards: he is nigh of kin to the stone-buck of the European Alps.

The gazelle, *ghrazel*, pl. *ghrazlán*, is of the plains; the Arabians say more often *thobby* (the N. T. Tabitha). They are white in the great sand-plains, and swart-grey upon the black *Harra* [15]; these are the roes of the Scriptures. There is yet a noble wild creature of the Arabian deserts, which was hitherto unknown among us, the *wothŷhi*, or 'wild cow' above mentioned. I saw later the male and female living at Hâyil; it is an antelope, *Beatrix*, akin to the beautiful animals of Africa. It seems that this is not the 'wild ox' of Moses: but is not this the (Hebr.) *reem*, the '*unicorn*' of the Septuagint translators?—Her horns are such slender rods as from our childhood we have seen pictured 'the horns of the unicorns.' We read in Balaam's parable, 'ÉL brought them out of Egypt; He hath as it were the strength of a *reem*': and in Moses' blessing of the tribes, 'Joseph's horns are the *two* horns of reems.' In Job especially, are

[14] Billah—verily, indeed.
[15] Harra—lava field; volcanic country.

shown the headstrong conditions of this *velox* wild creature. 'Will
the reem be willing to serve thee—canst thou bind the reem in thy
furrow?' The wounded wothŷhi is perilous to be approached; this
antelope, with a cast of her sharp horns, may strike through a man's
body; hunters await therefore the last moments to run in and cut
their quarry's throat. It was a monkish darkness in natural knowledge to ascribe a single horn to a double forehead!—and we sin not
less by addition, putting wings to the pagan images of gods and
angels; so they should have two pairs of fore-limbs! The wothŷhi
falls only to the keenest hunters: the wothŷhies accompany in the
waterless desert by troops of three and five together.

Of vermin, there are many snakes and adders; none of them
eaten by these tribes of nomads. *Felámy* is that small brown lizard
of the wilderness which starts from every footstep. Scorpions lurk
under the cool stones; I have found them in my tent, upon my
clothing, but never had any hurt. I have seen many grown persons
and children bitten, but the sting is not perilous; some wise man is
called to 'read' over them. The wounded part throbs with numbness and aching till the third day, there is not much swelling. Many
are the cities, under this desert sand, of seed-gathering ants; I have
measured some watling-street of theirs, eighty-five paces: to speed
once this length and come again, loaded as camels, is these small
busybodies' summer day's journey.

Besides, of the great predatory wild animals, most common is
the *thùbba*, hyena; then the *nimmr*, a leopard, brindled black and
brown and spotted: little common is the *fáhd*, a wild cat no bigger
than the fox; he is red and brown brindled, and spotted. In these
Beduins' memory a young fáhd was bred up amongst Bishr, which
(they are wonderfully swift footed) had been used by his nomad
master to take gazelles. In all the Arabic countries there is a strange
superstition of parents, (and this as well among the Christian sects
of Syria,) that if any child seem to be sickly, of infirm understanding, or his brethren have died before, they will put upon him a wild
beast's name, (especially, wolf, leopard, wolverine,)—that their
human fragility may take on as it were a temper of the kind of
those animals. Hawks and buzzards are often seen wheeling in the
desert sky, and *el-ágab*, which is a small black eagle, and *er-rákham*,
the small white carrion eagle,—flying in the air they resemble sea-
mews: I have not seen vultures, nor any greater eagle in the deserts
(save in Sinai). These are the most of living creatures, and there
are few besides in the wilderness of Arabia.

# THE TURTLE

## John Steinbeck

*Steinbeck is best known for his realistic stories about farmers, fruit-pickers, and ordinary laborers who live close to the soil. In* The Grapes of Wrath, *his Pulitzer Prize-winning novel about a family driven from their land in the dust bowl, he alternates chapters carrying forward the story of the Joads with chapters of a high poetic and symbolic quality; in one of these we watch an ordinary land turtle make his difficult way over a stretch of the hot Oklahoma earth.*

THE concrete highway was edged with a mat of tangled, broken, dry grass, and the grass heads were heavy with oat beards to catch on a dog's coat, and foxtails to tangle in a horse's fetlocks, and clover burrs to fasten in sheep's wool; sleeping life waiting to be spread and dispersed, every seed armed with an appliance of dispersal, twisting darts and parachutes for the wind, little spears and balls of tiny thorns, and all waiting for animals and for the wind, for a man's trouser cuff or the hem of a woman's skirt, all passive but armed with appliances of activity, still, but each possessed of the anlage of movement.

The sun lay on the grass and warmed it, and in the shade under the grass the insects moved, ants and ant lions to set traps for them, grasshoppers to jump into the air and flick their yellow wings for a second, sow bugs like little armadillos, plodding restlessly on many tender feet. And over the grass at the roadside a land turtle crawled, turning aside for nothing, dragging his high-domed shell over the grass. His hard legs and yellow-nailed feet threshed slowly through the grass, not really walking, but boosting and dragging his shell along. The barley beards slid off his shell, and the clover burrs fell on him and rolled to the ground. His horny beak was partly open, and his fierce, humorous eyes, under brows like fingernails, stared straight ahead. He came over the grass leaving a beaten trail behind

him, and the hill, which was the highway embankment, reared up
ahead of him. For a moment he stopped, his head held high. He
blinked and looked up and down. At last he started to climb the
embankment. Front clawed feet reached forward but did not
touch. The hind feet kicked his shell along, and it scraped on the
grass, and on the gravel. As the embankment grew steeper and
steeper, the more frantic were the efforts of the land turtle. Pushing
hind legs strained and slipped, boosting the shell along, and the
horny head protruded as far as the neck could stretch. Little by
little the shell slid up the embankment until at last a parapet cut
straight across its line of march, the shoulder of the road, a concrete wall four inches high. As though they worked independently
the hind legs pushed the shell against the wall. The head upraised
and peered over the wall to the broad smooth plain of cement. Now
the hands, braced on top of the wall, strained and lifted, and the
shell came slowly up and rested its front end on the wall. For a
moment the turtle rested. A red ant ran into the shell, into the soft
skin inside the shell, and suddenly head and legs snapped in, and the
armored tail clamped in sideways. The red ant was crushed between body and legs. And one head of wild oats was clamped into
the shell by a front leg. For a long moment the turtle lay still, and
then the neck crept out and the old humorous frowning eyes
looked about and the legs and tail came out. The back legs went to
work, straining like elephant legs, and the shell tipped to an angle
so that the front legs could not reach the level cement plain. But
higher and higher the hind legs boosted it, until at last the center
of balance was reached, the front tipped down, the front legs
scratched at the pavement, and it was up. But the head of wild oats
was held by its stem around the front legs.

Now the going was easy, and all the legs worked, and the shell
boosted along, waggling from side to side. A sedan driven by a
forty-year old woman approached. She saw the turtle and swung
to the right, off the highway, the wheels screamed and a cloud of
dust boiled up. Two wheels lifted for a moment and then settled.
The car skidded back onto the road, and went on, but more slowly.
The turtle had jerked into its shell, but now it hurried on, for the
highway was burning hot.

And now a light truck approached, and as it came near, the
driver saw the turtle and swerved to hit it. His front wheel struck
the edge of the shell, flipped the turtle like a tiddly-wink, spun it
like a coin, and rolled it off the highway. The truck went back to

its course along the right side. Lying on its back, the turtle was tight in its shell for a long time. But at last its legs waved in the air, reaching for something to pull it over. Its front foot caught a piece of quartz and little by little the shell pulled over and flopped upright. The wild oat head fell out and three of the spearhead seeds stuck in the ground And as the turtle crawled on down the embankment, its shell dragged dirt over the seeds. The turtle entered a dust road and jerked itself along, drawing a wavy shallow trench in the dust with its shell. The old humorous eyes looked ahead, and the horny beak opened a little. His yellow toe nails slipped a fraction in the dust.

## Work Without Hope

ALL Nature seems at work. Slugs leave their lair—
The bees are stirring—birds are on the wing—
And Winter, slumbering in the open air,
Wears on his smiling face a dream of Spring!
And I, the while, the sole unbusy thing,
Nor honey make, nor pair, nor build, nor sing.

Yet well I ken the banks where amaranths blow,
Have traced the fount whence streams of nectar flow.
Bloom, O ye amaranths! bloom for whom ye may,
For me ye bloom not! Glide, rich streams, away!
With lips unbrighten'd, wreathless brow, I stroll:
And would you learn the spells that drowse my soul?
Work without Hope draws nectar in a sieve,
And Hope without an object cannot live.

*Samuel Taylor Coleridge*

# THE MURDEROUS TIGER BAGH

## R. A. Sterndale

*In northern India, village and jungle are still close, and tigers occasionally attack cattle and men. Such an occurrence was far more common in the 1850's and 1860's, when Robert Armitage Sterndale, English traveler and author, hunted and camped in India. His book* Seonee *was one of the first to describe for the western world the dangerous and adventurous life to be found in regions where the natives knew tigers so well that they could describe the idiosyncrasies of one, the vanity of another, the reasons for a third's ferocity.*

THE sun had gone down by this time, and darkness was creeping on apace. There is but little twilight in India. However, we are wrong in saying darkness was creeping on apace, for mingling with the rays of departing day was the silvery light of the moon, now nearly at the full.

"There is a Cattle track here somewhere," remarked Fordham; "I have noticed it before. Ah! here it is; by following this we cut across the hill and come out right above our camp."

The track was a gravelly path with thick bushes on either side, with here and there a tree; it was not likely cover for anything except Nylgaie. The Pea-fowl were settling themselves to roost on the branches of the taller trees, to be well out of harm's way, and several times Fordham noticed that the loud cry of "Hank! Pa-oo! Pa-oo!" was raised. "The birds are restless tonight," he said; "some prowling Cat, or maybe a Panther, is disturbing them."

By this time they had reached the crest of the hill, and the white tents were visible in the distance as they lay embedded in the grove of mango trees. The crisp gravel cracked under their firm footsteps, and the moonbeams were glinting on the bits of quartz and mica

[ 400 ]

that lay strewn around. The twilight was nearly gone, and but a dull-red flush lingered in the western sky. Now and then a Night-jar would start up with his peculiar erratic flight from almost under their feet, as where he lay squatted close to the ground. The monotonous cry of his species resounded on all sides, resembling the oft-repeated words "Chuckoo! chuckoo! chuckoo!" Again burst forth the wild cry of a Peacock perched on a tree not far off. Fordham instinctively threw his rifle across his arm in readiness, knowing well that jungle warnings are not to be disregarded. But he said nothing to Milford, who unconsciously chatted away about the exploits of the morning. There was a slight rustle in the bushes before them, and in the next moment a magnificent Tiger, the Seonee man-eater no less, stood in the midst of the pathway, looking them full in the face.

"Steady, my boy," muttered Fordham through his teeth; "steady, my boy, flinch not a muscle."

His rifle had dropped into position to fire at once should the brute show any aggressive signs; but he knew in the night it would be folly to provoke an attack, and also that the jungle Tiger will, if met boldly, be generally the first to give way. In the bright light of the moon the eyes of the beast glared like pale emeralds, and to Milford it seemed an age of agonizing suspense. But it was only for a few seconds. Another moment and he was gone, and they heard the rustling of the branches as he bounded through the jungle.

"Thank God!" exclaimed the young fellow, with a long-drawn sigh of relief.

"Wait a bit," said his elder companion; "before we go on, send down a couple of bullets on the top of your bird shot; we must be prepared; the chances are he has made off, but there is no knowing. This is a nasty, ugly spot to meet such a brute in, and so unexpectedly too. I thought those Pea-fowl did not call for nothing. Now," continued he, seeing that the bullets were down, "you keep close to me, but with your look-out to the right and rear. I will look out left and front as we go along. Speak not a word, but keep all your senses awake. Sometimes these brutes will make a detour and come in on you again a little farther on. Now, *allons—courage!*"

It seemed a weary trudge, that little quarter of a mile down the hill and out through the belt of jungle, and right thankful were they when they stepped out once more on the open fields that lay between them and their camp.

"That was a close shave, Milford," was the first remark made by his companion.

"I'm uncommonly glad we're out of that ugly bit of jungle. If ever I felt inclined to take to my heels it was when that brute stood staring us in the face."

"The worst thing you could have done, my boy," rejoined Fordham; "he would have been down upon you like lightning. The best plan is to bear a bold front, and, though this has been your first meeting with the jungle king, it may not be your last if you stay long in these districts; so be careful never to turn your back when you come face to face with a Tiger."

Old Sheykha, a native hunter, was put on the trail of the man-eater met by our friends in the little hill near the camp, and he proceeded to make enquiries in the villages round about as to the character of the animal; for, strange though it may seem to the English reader that a Tiger should have any special character beyond the general one for cruelty and cunning, it is nevertheless a fact that each animal has certain peculiarities of temperament, which are well known to the villagers in the neighborhood. They will tell you that such a one is daring and rash; another is cunning and not to be taken in by any artifice; that one is savage and morose; another is mild and harmless.

There are few villages in the wilder parts of the Seonee and Mundla districts without an attendant Tiger, which undoubtedly does great damage in the way of destroying Cattle, but which avoids the human inhabitants of the place. So accustomed do the people get to their unwelcome visitor, that we have known the boys of a village to turn a Tiger out of quarters which were reckoned too close, and pelt him with stones; on one occasion, two of the juvenile assailants were killed by the animal they had approached too near. Herdsmen, in the same way, get callous to the danger of meddling with so dreadful a creature, and frequently rush to the rescue of their Cattle when seized. On a certain occasion, one out of a herd of Cattle was attacked close to our camp, and rescued single-handed by its owner, who laid his heavy iron-bound staff across the Tiger's back, and, on our rushing out to see what was the matter, we found the man coolly dressing the wounds of his Cow, muttering to himself, "The robber, the robber! my last Cow, and I had five of them!" He did not seem to think he had done anything wonderful, and seemed rather surprised that we should suppose that he was going to let his last Heifer go the way of all the others.

It is fortunate for these dwellers in the backwoods that but a small percentage of Tigers are man-eaters, perhaps not five per cent, otherwise village after village would be depopulated; as it is, the yearly tale of human lives lost is a heavy one.

Sheykha returned from his quest with the report that the Tiger was one of the cunning sort, and that it was no use tying out baits for him, for he would come up and walk round the lure, sharpening his claws on the ground, and then would walk off; that had been tried over and over again.

Milford was inclined to disbelieve this latter part of the story, but Fordham told him it was quite credible, for he had himself known similar cases, and had seen the marks of the Tiger's claws in the earth.

"Well, Sheykha, what do you propose? any chance with the Elephant?"

"My lord," answered the old man, "if your slave may speak, he would say, where can a hungry Tiger be found in all this long strip of jungle? Whilst you are looking for him at one end he may be at the other, and, as he is so cunning, it is likely he will flee like a Dove before a Hawk when he hears the tread of the Elephant. They tell me he has not killed for three days, so it is likely he will do so soon— this afternoon, or tomorrow perhaps; and they also say he is a heavy feeder, never returning again to the carcase, for he was once wounded over a kill by a Gond, who sat up for him in a tree. If he eats well, he will drink at the little three-cornered tank on the other side of the hill, where your honor saw him, for there is no water nearer, and he will not go far from there. Then take the Elephant."

"I am afraid we must have patience, Milford, and do as the old man advises," said Fordham to his companion, who with the impetuosity of youth could hardly brook the delay.

The old hunter keenly watched the disappointed look that came over the young man's eager face when he again spoke.

"Your slave has a petition. If the Chota Sahib will try an old shikaree's way of killing Tigers, let him come with me this afternoon, and follow the herds. For the promise of a few rupees the herdsmen will take their Cattle into the Tiger's haunts, and then if he is hungry and takes one the Sahib may by his good fortune get a shot."

"Well Milford, what do you think of his proposal? You drive a herd of Cows—not Buffaloes, mind, *they* spoil sport—slowly through the jungle, until the Tiger seizes one; the rest will bolt, and whilst he is busily engaged in struggling with his victim, you creep up to within easy shooting distance, and secure him."

"Well, that will be glorious fun! By all means let us go," eagerly replied the excited young fellow.

"I cannot go with you," replied Fordham. "Two of us would spoil sport. Let Sheykha take his matchlock, he may serve you at a pinch. The thing is not so dangerous as it looks, and is often practised by native shikarees. There are only two or three points I would impress upon you; always keep near a tree or stout bush, to dodge behind when the Cattle bolt—for there will be a regular stampede if he comes out. Again, be very careful not to expose yourself in stalking—take advantage of every bush, and, after you have fired, keep as still as a Mouse, even though he should come towards your hiding place; if you are effectually concealed, he will be quite bewildered as to where the attack comes from, and will give you a second shot if the first does not settle him. ABOVE ALL, MY DEAR BOY, KEEP YOURSELF QUITE COOL. I want you to get self-reliant, and that is one reason why I don't go with you. You couldn't have a better guide amongst natives than old Sheykha—he and Soma, the Lebhana, are the most successful practisers of this way of killing Tigers. I have tried it, but dislike the monotony of wandering about all day in the jungle after a lot of Cows, for frequently the attempt fails, and you have to go day after day before you succeed."

"When are we to start?" said Milford, looking at his watch; "it is now one o'clock."

Sheykha, on being appealed to, said that as soon as the Sahib had taken something to eat it would be time to go. Tigers often kill about 4 o'clock in the afternoon, and he had known them to wait concealed in the midst of a herd, with fat Kine wandering before their very noses, and they would not stir till about the evening, when the herd was on its way home, and then a straggling Heifer or Calf would fall a victim.

"Well, then, Milford, I advise you to make a good tiffin (lunch) before you start. Here! Koi hai! tiffin! tiffin! sharp!"

Away ran two or three men to stir up stout old Chand Khan. The Sahib wanted his tiffin at once, and was going to kill the big Tiger that nearly ate him and the Chota Sahib up the night before.

"Bah!" contemptuously replied the old fellow; "is the Sahib's gun a chowkeedar's staff that he should let a Tiger eat him? Wasn't

I with him in the Belaspore district when four Tigers came out, and didn't the Sahib knock over two of them with one gun right and left? Don't talk to me of Tigers eating the Sahib; it's the Sahib who eats the Tigers, that's what it is." And the fat old fellow, chuckling at his own conceit, stirred up a savoury curry preparatory to pouring it out into a dish.

Milford was too excited to care much about tiffin, and on this occasion we are afraid Chand Khan's culinary skill did not meet with that appreciation from the young man that it would have done had there not been a prospect of a Tiger hunt that afternoon. Sheykha had no need to complain of delay, for, barely giving himself time for a cutlet and a glass of cold water, the young sportsman appeared all ready for the encounter.

"That white hat of yours will never do, Milford," remarked Fordham; "why that Brobdignagian mushroom, though first-rate for the sun, will be as plain to the Tiger as a lighthouse on a cliff. Ride in it by all means, but take this dark-grey helmet of mine to put on when you get to your ground."

Milford acknowledged the force of his friend's remarks, for his hat was one of the largest-sized pith sunshades, a first-rate thing for howdah work, but fatal for stalking.

He accepted Fordham's offer with thanks, and then having looked to his guns, ammunition, etc., piloted by old Sheykha, the tyro in Tiger hunting went off on his expedition.

At the farthest point of the low hill, where they had met the animal the evening before, was a small village, and to this Sheykha rapidly led the way; and, on arrival, he assembled the head men for a palaver. The herds had been driven for pasturage to the open side of the village, in order to avoid the Tiger, who was known to be lurking about the edge of the jungle on the side of the hill. There was some little opposition to the plan proposed by the old shikaree, which was to drive their Cattle up the little glen between the two parallel ridges. Of course, nobody wished to lose a Cow, although all wished to have the Tiger destroyed. At last it was made clear to them that the full value of the Cow killed would be paid to the owner, and a present given to the herdsmen besides. On this there was a unanimous assent, and half the village rushed off to collect the scattered herds, and drive them up the glen. Milford got off his Pony and left it at the village, changing his mushroom hat for the grey helmet, and, shouldering one rifle (Azim Khan carrying the other), he joined Sheykha and the herdsmen in urging on the drove. After they had once entered the mouth of the glen the Cattle were allowed to spread and graze about, and Sheykha advised his temporary master to take it easy and rest under the shade of a tree.

"There is no need to hurry," said he in a low tone; "we must take time and saunter about as on ordinary occasions, otherwise he will suspect something. Allah knows he may be watching us now" ("Pleasant!" thought Milford, taking a glance round), "but even if he is not here, the lowing of the Cows and the sound of their wooden clappers will attract him. The herd is all round us just now; when they move higher up we will follow."

So saying, the old man motioned to Milford, to sit down on the turf, and then squatted down beside him. One could see, however, that with all this apparent carelessness, every sense was on the alert; his eye wandered round, and his ear caught every rustle in the bushes.

"Now, Sahib," continued he, seeing the herd that moved higher up, "we will go on a little. Make for that *rohnee* tree; there is good shade and shelter from the Cattle if they rush back."

The herdsmen kept pretty close to our friends, so a little knot of half a dozen men were formed under the tree. They spoke but little, and that in a low tone, and the greater share of the conversation fell to the old shikaree, who, with the garrulity of age, began to relate to the gaping rustics several wondrous tales connected with the kind of sport on which they were then engaged.

"I first began this way, Sahib, when I was a boy, with an old shikaree who never lifted gun to anything but Tigers. They were his enemies, and he slept neither day nor night if there was one to be killed. He was quite mad, and the people thought he had a charmed life, but his fate came at last, and he was killed. He was not of a shikaree caste, being a telee, and he never fired a gun till he was over thirty years of age; but Allah made him a shikaree to avenge the death of his wife. She was young and handsome, and he would have cut off his right hand to please her. No telee's wife was ever treated so much like a Ranee as was this woman; it used to be the joke of the village. Well, Sahib, about three coss from his village was the stronghold of a very bad man-eating Tiger; he had depopulated several villages, and had baffled all the best shikarees. He lived in a big cave at the end of a rocky ravine, and there was no getting at it except by going straight for it; at the same time the rocks were so piled about, that an animal like a Tiger could enter the ravine some hundreds of paces below, and thread his way through the boulders without being seen. All the traps that had been laid for him had proved useless, and the people said he was a *shaitan* in the form of a Tiger.

"Ah! Sahib, be ready, hush!"

The old man's quick ear had caught the angry chirrup of a small bird, which would have passed unnoticed by the others. Milford looked around in silent expectancy; all seemed still save for the sound of warbling birds, and the clatter of the wooden clappers worn round the neck by some of the Cows. They were all quietly grazing, and the young man wondered what could have attracted the old shikaree's notice. Sheykha was still attentively listening, and nodding his head. "Yes," he said, "it is, I think. Allah knows it may be a Snake, or a Mungoose, but something is disturbing that latora; it is the Tiger, I think."

At some distance off, on the topmost spray of a grislea bush, a small species of Shrike was hopping about, indignantly chattering. It might be, as Sheyka said, a Snake or a Mungoose that had aroused its puny ire, but the old man evidently thought it worthy of attention. Milford felt impatient and disappointed; the shadows were lengthening, and daylight would soon be gone. He looked up and down, but all was provokingly quiet. A lingering hope remained that Sheykha might be right about the Bird, but even it was quiet now, and had ceased its demonstrations. Nothing disturbed the stillness save the clapper-clapper of the Cattle, and a distant cry of a Pea-fowl or Partridge. He had risen to his feet, and was looking listlessly about, when, at some little distance up the glen, a yellow mass suddenly dashed out of the thicket on to the back of a white Heifer, and bore it struggling to the ground.

"*Urré! bagh! bagh!*" shouted the herdsmen, as the Cattle wildly dashed down the valley. For a few seconds nothing could be heard for the crashing of the bushes, as the terror-stricken drove madly careered through them. When they had passed the tree Sheykha whispered, "Now, Sahib, keep yon big palas bush between you and the Tiger, and run up; here, give me the other rifle, Azim Khan, and you stay here. Don't you show yourself, or you may get killed."

The palas bush was about sixty yards from them, and, running in a crouching position, they got behind it. Carefully separating the branches, the old hunter peered through, and beckoned to his young companion to do so. Milford looked through the gap thus made, and could see the poor Heifer kicking vigorously as it lay on its side, pressed down under the weight of its cruel captor, whose fangs were buried in its throat. Both Tiger and Heifer lay with their backs turned to the two men, which was favorable, for the distance was yet too great for a certain shot. Signing for Milford to follow by his side, the old man darted off at right angles, so as to bring another big bush between them and the struggling animals; up to this they ran again, crouching as they went, and again the old hunter peered through the leaves. Milford could hear the last groans of the poor Heifer, and the stertorous breathing of the Tiger, for they were now within forty yards. Old Sheykha noiselessly removed a few of the broad leaves of the palas, and Milford looking through almost started at the sight, so near did the Tiger appear. He raised his rifle, but Sheykha quietly laid a hand upon his arm, and shaking his head drummed with his fingers upon his heart, and, touching the muzzle of the weapon, tremulously shook them in the air, thus signifying in pantomime—for they were too near to allow of speech—that his nerves were not steady enough for a shot. In truth Milford's nerves were anything but steady just then; his heart panted with excitement and the exertion of running in a crouching posture, and Sheykha was wise in not allowing him to risk a shot. The old man knew there was no immediate need for hurry, and the sight was too familiar to him to cause that rapid circulation of the blood that existed at that moment in the veins of the young Englishman.

At last the Tiger shifted his position, and lay on the top of the Heifer, with one massive fore-arm stretched out, holding down one of his victim's fore-legs, whilst his jaws were still firmly fixed in its throat.

Nothing could be more favorable than the posture, exposing as it did the most vital part. So Sheykha turned to Milford, and, patting his heart once more, made signs of enquiry whether he was steady. The young man nodded assent.

Pointing in the direction of the Tiger, the shikaree placed his hand on his side, just under the arm, as a hint where to aim, and a placid smile came over his face as he saw the deadly tube levelled with a steadiness that was all that could be desired. In another moment the bright flash leapt forth, and the stricken Tiger sprang from his victim with an angry roar, and turned round and round, snapping at his side in a rage.

Sheykha pressed a firm nervous hand on Milford's arm, for at these times, reader, when life and death hang on a trifle, there is a cessation of that obsequious deference which is usually paid by the native to the European, and though Sheykha would have refrained from any interference or suggestion with such an experienced shikaree as Fordham, he knew Milford was but a novice and a boy, and he was in great measure responsible for his safety.

At last the Tiger stopped, and looked wildly round as if he were undecided where to go; he was evidently badly hit, for the blood was beginning to pour from his mouth. Milford at this moment fired again, and, just as he did so, the Beast made a bound in the direction of the bush where they were, but checked as it were in his spring, he fell flat on the ground with all four paws spread out, and was unable to rise; his hind legs were paralysed, and helplessly he writhed, roaring most horribly. His close proximity made the young Englishman almost shudder; he was not more than twenty yards away, and he fancied he could almost smell the creature's breath.

It was evident that the Tiger's spine was broken by the last shot, and his sufferings were painful to witness. In his agony he seized one of his own paws and bit it through and through, and he tore up the turf around with his claws as far as he could reach. At last, taking his second gun from Sheykha, Milford gave him the *coup de grace*. The first ball aimed at his head missed, but the second entered just behind the ear, and with a single groan the fell destroyer, the killer of a hundred men, had breathed his last.

# THE SILK WORMS OF NICE

## Tobias Smollett

*A giant among English literary giants of the eighteenth century, Smollett (1721–1771), after serving as a doctor in the Navy, set up practice in London, and started writing. His novels,* Humphry Clinker *and* Roderick Random, *are still thoroughly enjoyable today. Smollett's ceaseless literary work so affected his health that his doctor ordered him to the south of Europe. During his two years of travel, he wrote many letters, including this one from Nice, where he stayed for more than a year.*

Nice, November 10, 1764.

DEAR SIR,—I had once thoughts of writing a complete natural history of this town and county: but I found myself altogether unequal to the task. I have neither health, strength, nor opportunity, to make proper collections of the mineral, vegetable, and animal productions. I am not much conversant with these branches of natural philosophy. I have no books to direct my inquiries. I can find no person capable of giving me the least information or assistance; and I am strangely puzzled by the barbarous names they give to many different species, the descriptions of which I have read under other appellations; and which, as I have never seen them before, I cannot pretend to distinguish by the eye. You must therefore be contented with such imperfect intelligence as my opportunities can afford.

The useful arts practised at Nice, are these, gardening and agriculture, with their consequences, the making of wine; oil, and cordage; the rearing of silk-worms, with the subsequent management and manufacture of that production; and the fishing, which I have already described.

It is not many years since the Nissards learned the culture of silk-worms, of their neighbours the Piedmontese; and hitherto the progress they have made is not very considerable: the whole county of Nice produces about one hundred and thirty-three bales of three hundred pounds each, amounting in value to four hundred thousand livres.

In the beginning of April, when the mulberry-leaves begin to put forth, the eggs or grains that produce the silk-worm, are hatched. The grains are washed in wine, and those that swim on the top, are thrown away as good for nothing. The rest being deposited in small bags of linen, are worn by women in their bosoms, until the worms begin to appear: then they are placed in shallow wooden boxes, covered with a piece of white paper, cut into little holes, through which the worms ascend as they are hatched, to feed on the young mulberry-leaves, of which there is a layer above the paper. These boxes are kept for warmth between two mattrasses, and visited every day. Fresh leaves are laid in, and the worms that feed are removed successively to the other place prepared for their reception. This is an habitation, consisting of two or three stories, about twenty inches from each other, raised upon four wooden posts. The floors are made of canes, and strewed with fresh mulberry-leaves: the corner posts, and other occasional props, for sustaining the different floors, are covered with a coat of loose heath, which is twisted round the wood. The worms when hatched are laid upon the floors; and here you may see them in all the different stages of moulting or casting the slough, a change which they undergo three times successively before they begin to work.

The silk-worm is an animal of such acute and delicate sensations, that too much care cannot be taken to keep its habitation clean, and to refresh it from time to time with pure air. I have seen them languish and die in scores, in consequence of an accidental bad smell. The soiled leaves, and the filth which they necessarily produce, should be carefully shifted every day; and it would not be amiss to purify the air sometimes with fumes of vinegar, rose, or orange-flower water. These niceties, however, are but little observed. They commonly lie in heaps as thick as shrimps in a plate, some feeding on the leaves, some new hatched, some intranced in the agonies of casting their skin, some languishing, and some actually dead, with a litter of half-eaten faded leaves about them, in a close room, crouded with women and children, not at all remarkable for their cleanliness. I am assured by some persons of credit, that if they are touched, or even approached, by a woman in her catamenia, they infallibly expire. This, however, must be understood of those females whose skins have naturally a very rank flavour, which is generally heightened at such periods.

The mulberry-leaves used in this country are of the tree which bears a small white fruit not larger than a damascene. They are planted on purpose, and the leaves are sold at so much a pound. By the middle of June all the mulberry-trees are stripped; but new leaves succeed, and in a few weeks, they are cloathed again with fresh verdure. In about ten days after the last moulting, the silk-worm climbs upon the props of his house, and choosing a situation among the heath, begins to spin in a most curious manner, until he is quite inclosed, and the cocon or pod of silk, about the size of a pigeon's egg, which he has produced, remains suspended by several filaments. It is not unusual to see double cocons, spun by two worms included under a common cover.

There must be an infinite number of worms to yield any considerable quantity of silk. One ounce of eggs or grains produces four rup, or one hundred Nice pounds of cocons; and one rup, or twenty-five pounds of cocons, if they are rich, gives three pounds of raw silk; that is, twelve pounds of silk are got from one ounce of grains, which ounce of grains is produced by as many worms as are inclosed in one pound, or twelve ounces of cocons.

In preserving the cocons for breed, you must choose an equal number of males and females; and these are very easily distinguished by the shape of the cocons; that which contains the male is sharp, and the other obtuse, at the two ends. In ten or twelve days after the cocon is finished, the worm makes its way through it, in the form of a very ugly, unwieldy, aukward butterfly, and as the different sexes are placed by one another on paper or linen, they immediately engender. The female lays her eggs, which are carefully preserved; but neither she nor her mate takes any nourishment, and in eight or ten days after they quit the cocons, they generally die.

The silk of these cocons cannot be wound, because the animals in piercing through them, have destroyed the continuity of the filaments. It is therefore, first boiled, and then picked and carded like wool, and being afterwards spun, is used in the coarser stuffs of the silk manufacture. The other cocons, which yield the best silk, are managed in a different manner. Before the inclosed worm has time to penetrate, the silk is reeled off with equal care and ingenuity. A handful of the cocons are thrown away into a kettle of boiling water, which not only kills the animal, but dissolves the glutinous substance by which the fine filaments of the silk cohere or stick together, so that they are easily wound off, without breaking. Six or seven of these small filaments being joined together are passed over a kind of twisting iron, and fixed to the wheel, which one girl turns, while another, with her hands in the boiling water, disentangles the threads, joins them when they chance to break, and supplies fresh cocons with admirable dexterity and dispatch.

There is a manufacture of this kind just without one of the gates of Nice where forty or fifty of these wheels are worked together, and give employment for some weeks to double the number of young women. Those who manage the pods that float in the boiling water must be very alert, otherwise they will scald their fingers. The smell that comes from the boiling cocons is extremely offensive. Hard by the harbour, there is a very curious mill for twisting the silk, which goes by water. There is in the town of Nice, a well regulated hospital for poor orphans of both sexes, where above one hundred of them are employed in dressing, dyeing, spinning, and weaving the silk. In the villages of Provence, you see the poor women in the streets spinning raw silk upon distaves: but here the same instrument is only used for spinning hemp and flax; which last, however, is not of the growth of Nice.—But lest I should spin this letter to a tedious length, I will now wind up my bottom, and bid you heartily farewell.

### Flower in the Crannied Wall

FLOWER in the crannied wall,
I pluck you out of the crannies,
I hold you here, root and all, in my hand,
Little flower—but if I could understand
What you are, root and all, and all in all,
I should know what God and man is.

*Alfred, Lord Tennyson*

# BATTLE WITH A WHALE

## William M. Davies

*Little is known about the author of* Nimrod of the Sea, or the American Whaleman, *published in* 1874, *but William Morris Davies (c.* 1814–1890*) did go on at least one whaling trip and was present at the kill, as he tells us here. Not only did he love the excitement and adventure of the whale hunt—he was also a close student of the ways of the sea and Leviathan, its largest child. At the back of his book he even printed an exchange of correspondence between himself and "the whaling captains of New Bedford who regularly meet at the back of Kelley's watch store there," the letters serving to clear up some controversial points about right whales and sperm whales.*

SEPTEMBER 5.—It is about three weeks since we took our last whale, and we have had the greatest trial which attends the whalemen. The dulness and tedium of life on board ship at such quiet times is almost unendurable. The uninterrupted fine weather, the steady trade-wind, the daily routine of make sail, man mastheads, scrub decks; breakfast, dinner, supper; shorten sail, boat's-crew watch, and "turn in," give not a line for a journal. The men become morose and quarrelsome; we hate each other, and numerous scores are run up, and appointments made to fight them out in the first port we make. The violin fails to move, the song to enliven, and the yarn to interest us. According to custom, and as a diversion, a red-flannel shirt has been offered as a prize to him who may *raise* the first whale captured, and a pair of duck trousers have been added. Pounds of tobacco are offered by the mate, but the days pass uninterestingly. A bright gold doubloon is nailed to the mainmast, well out of reach, but in sight of all, as another reward to good eyes. Now there is more life at the masthead. Not a whitecap can show, a porpoise jump, or finback spout, but that the alarm is given, in hope that it may lead to a capture, and so obtain for the discov-

erer the pretty piece of gold glittering on the white mast. In vain!
All the whales seem to have gone to the bottom for a Rip Van Win-
kle nap. We all know they can do this, though it is contrary to the
books, which tell us that they are warm-blooded mammals: even
this is not the worst of the names the learned have given them. But
whales are uneducated, don't take the papers, and without thought
of irregularity stay down to suit their convenience an hour or a
week. Like the original Kentuckian, Nimrod Wildfire, we were
spoiling for a fight, when the captain ordered the sacrifice of a pig
to propitiate our patron saints. The offering was accepted, for the
protesting squeak of poor piggy was blended with the yell of
"There she blows!" and "Sperm whale, sir." "Where away?"
roared the officers. And in answer was heard Hinton's sweetest
song, "Four points on lee bow." We squared in the yards and kept
off, and away we ran merrily. At two miles' distance from what
seemed a good whale the boats were lowered. The activity of the
men, as they sprang barefooted into the boats and cast off the
davit-tackles; the readiness with which they handled the long,
heavy oars, and dropped them silently into the well-thrummed
thole-mats, and the ease with which they fell into the stroke, were
wonderful. Four boats were down and heading to leeward, their
course divergent, so that at two miles from the ship we peaked our
oars with a space of about one third of a mile between the boats,
thus commanding a reach of nearly two miles front.

As the boats thus ride the long, rolling swell of the sea lightly
and gracefully as an albatross (and I know nothing more graceful
than that), let us glance at the whale-boat and its fittings. It is the
fruit of a century's experience, and the sharpened sense and ingenuity of an inventive people, urged by the peril of the chase and the
value of the prize. For lightness and form; for carrying capacity, as
compared with its weight and sea-going qualities; for speed and
facility of movement at the word of command; for the placing of
the men at the best advantage in the exercise of their power; by the
nicest adaptation of the varying length of the oar to its position in
the boat; and, lastly, for a simplicity of construction which renders
repairs practicable on board the ship, the whale-boat is simply as
perfect as the combined skill of the million men who have risked
life and limb in service could make it. This paragon of a boat is
twenty-eight feet long, sharp and clean-cut as a dolphin, bow and
stern swelling amidships to six feet, with a bottom round and buoyant. The gunwale, amidships twenty-two inches above the keel,

rises with an accelerated curve to thirty-seven inches at each end, and this rise of bow and stern, with the clipper-like upper form, gives it a ducklike capacity to top the oncoming waves, so that it will dryly ride when ordinary boats would fill. The gunwales and keel, of the best timber, are her heaviest parts, and give stiffness to the whole; the timbers, sprung to shape, are a half-inch or three quarters in depth, and the planking is half-inch white cedar. Her thwarts are inch pine, supported by knees of greater strength than the other timbers. The bow-oar thwart is pierced by a three-inch hole for the mast, and is double-kneed. Through the cuddy-board projects a silk-hat shaped loggerhead, for snubbing and managing the running line; the stem of the boat is deeply grooved on top, the bottom of the groove being bushed with a block of lead, or sometimes a bronze roller, and over this the line passes from the boat. Four feet of the length of the bow is covered in by a depressed box, in which the spare line, attached to harpoons, lies in carefully adjusted coils. Immediately back of the box is a thick pine plank, in which the "clumsy cleet," or knee-brace, is cut. The gunwale is pierced at proper distances for thole-pins, of wood, and all sound of the working-oars are muffled by well-thrummed mats, kept carefully greased, so that we can steal on our prey silent as the cavalry of the poor badgered Lear. The planking is carefully smoothed with sand-paper and painted. Here we have a boat which two men may lift, and which will make ten miles an hour in dead chase by the oars alone.

The equipment of the boat consists of a line-tub, in which are coiled three hundred fathoms of hemp line, with every possible precaution against kinking in the outrun; a mast and spritsail; five oars; the harpoon and after-roar, fourteen feet; the tub and bow-oar, sixteen feet; and the midship, eighteen feet long; so placed that the two shortest and one longest pull against the two sixteen-feet oars, which arrangement preserves the balance in the encounter when the boat is worked by four oars, the harpoon oar being apeak. The boat is steered by an oar twenty-two feet long, which works through a grummet on the stern-post. The gear of the boat consists of two live harpoons, or those in use, *i.e.*, harpoons secured to the side of the boat above the thwarts, and two or three lances, secured by cords in like position, the sharp heads of all these being guarded by well fitted soft-wood sheaths. The harpoon is a barbed, triangular iron, very sharp on the edges, or it is a long, narrow piece of iron, sharpened only on one end, and affixed on the shank by a rivet, so placed that before use the cutting edge is on a line with the shank, but after penetrating the whale, and on being drawn back, the movable piece drops at right angles to the shank, and forms a square *toggle* about six inches across the narrow wound caused by its entrance. The porpoise iron is preferred among the Arctic whalemen, as, owing to the softness of the blubber, the fluked harpoon is apt to cut its way out. The upper end of a shank thirty inches long terminates in a socket, into which a heavy oak or hickory sapling pole six feet long is introduced. A short piece of the whale line, with an eye-splice at one end, is then wrapped twice around the shank below the socket, and close spliced. This line is stretched with great strain, and secured to the pole with a slight seizing of rope-yarn, intended to pay away and loose the pole in a long fight. The tub-line is secured to the eye of the short line after the boat is lowered. The lance is simply an oval-headed instrument, with a cutting edge, a shank five or six feet long, and a handle as long, with a light warp to recover it. A hatchet and a sharp knife are placed in the bow-box, convenient for cutting the line, and a water keg, fire apparatus, candles, lantern, compass, and bandages for wounds, with waif flags on poles, a fluke-spade, a boat-hook, and a "drug," or dragging float, complete the equipment of a whale-boat. Among this crowd of dangerous lines and threatening cutting-gear are six pair of legs, belonging to six skilled boatmen. Such a whale-boat is ours, as she floats two miles from the ship, each man in the crew watching under the blade of his peaked oar for the rising whale, and the captain and boat-steerer standing on the highest point, carefully sweeping the horizon with trained eye to catch the first spout, and secure the chance of "getting on."

At this moment of rest, when on the point of entering a contest in which the chances of mishap seem wonderfully provided for, I found that a green hand is apt to run back over his life with something of regret always, or forward, with a half-vow that from then and there, for ever and ever, he will be a better boy. The French-woman found goodness possible when she was well dressed. I found evil hateful when I was near a sperm whale. But how one wakes up from such moralizing as the captain lightly drops from his perch, runs out his steering-oar, and lays the boat around, with the words, "Take your oars, and spring; the whale's half a mile off!" That means that we are just four minutes from the whale, provided he is not running.

It would cheer a club man's heart to watch the movements of

the crew, the splendid stroke and time, the perfect feather of the oars, their silent dip on entering the foaming whirl of the lifted water, the ashen shaft working silently in the oiled mat, the poise of the crew, as the five trained athletes urge their perfect structure through the waves. Long and careful training under danger breeds a unity in the men. The five work as a single hand under the direction of him who is steering and throwing his whole standing force in the push on the after-oar. Every energy of my soul and body is centred in that bow-oar, and I do not differ from four others who share in the excitement. An occasional glance at my springing ash, the leaping little waves, and the resolute face of the captain, tell me to a fathom the position of the chase. His eyes are fixed on the rising and sinking whale; color has left his features; his pale lips are drawn tight, as he sways back and forth to the stroke of the oar. He, too, is straining on, and jerks out words of command, exhortation, and promise, to urge our energies to fiercer effort.

We are coming up at a killing pace. The captain, eloquent, unconscious of his words, yet with method in his frenzy, still urges us on. Now the puff of a spout joins the splash of the bow, and the old man's voice sinks to a fierce whisper as he promises all his tobacco, a share in his little farm at home, and his "lay" in the whale, as he adjures us to put him on. Human muscle cannot stand the strain much longer; the boat seems as lead; boiling foam curls and bubbles around the boat's head. The old man glances almost as low as the head of the boat; a puff is heard just under the bows; my oar-blade dips in the eddying wake of the whale's last upward stroke, and right under its blade I see the broad half-moon of his flukes as we shoot across the corner of them. Now the odor of the whale, like a bank of seaweed, comes over us. "Stand up, Ben! Pull, pull for life! Good, good! Now again! Goody Lord, give it to him!" The backward start of the boat and the upward fling of the flukes tell the rest of that story. A stroke or two astern, and we pant for breath in safety.

But lest the reader might labor under the mistake that all our prizes are secured simply by the planting of the harpoon, I shall skip from the present whale, which gave us little trouble, to another.

October 20. Lat. 5° 40' S., long. 107° 37' W.—The watch was employed in breaking-out to make stowage for one hundred and fifteen barrels of oil now on deck, the fruit of two whales taken on the 11th and 14th inst. While the decks were all a "clutter," we raised a school of sperm whales. They were erratic in their movements, and it required several hours of manœuvre to get the ship in a position for lowering the boats. But once we were down it was not long before the mate fastened to a large bull. This proved to be an ugly customer, cross-grained and bent on mischief. He ran swiftly a short distance under water, and took out considerable line; then, turning in his course, he rose to the surface and came down full speed, head far out of water, striking one boat partially with his jaw, staving in her broadside and rolling her over. Our boat hurried to the rescue, and as we pulled up the scene was stirring to our nerves, be assured. The crew of the overturned boat were swimming, and all six heads could be counted, which was a relief. The whale lay a short distance from the boat, thrashing the water madly with his flukes, and before we got on he again attacked the wreck and struck it with his jaw, cutting off about one third of her length. As we pulled past, two poor fellows who were clinging to the bottom begged for God's sake we would save them. The captain's quick eye saw that the swimming crew were well provided with means of support, and that the waist-boat was fast coming up; so he told them to hold on, and that he would coax the whale away. The poor devils had a right to be *gallied* just then, for the mad beast was coming down on them, his ugly fifteen-foot jaw at right angles with his body, and ivory gleaming about it. Watching a chance, Ben made a long dart, and struck the bull before he reached the shattered boat. This seemed to astonish the creature, and with a grand flourish of flukes he put away to windward at a tremendous pace. Evidently we had a desperate fellow to deal with. What with this continued speed, and the promiscuous manner in which he tossed his tail, it was impossible to haul line and range alongside. Resort was had to the spade. We hauled line until the head of the boat was a little astern of the spiteful flukes, and, watching his chances, the captain pitched the broad-edged tool over the flukes into the small, with the hope of severing the tendons of the tail, which here came near the surface. If this piece of surgery had proved successful the whale must have heaved to on losing control of his propeller. But it was a difficult amputation to perform on a kicking, fighting whale. He ran with undiminished speed, often rolling as he went, so as to give his flukes a side-cutting power, with the amiable intent of smashing his little antagonist.

I have already described the method of sheering the boat to one side of the whale and running parallel with him, by taking a bight of the line over the side of the boat. In this instance bow-oar had been tugging at the line for an hour, but was utterly unable to get the boat in advance of the flukes. A little line might be gained for a short time, but it would soon be torn through the clinging hands, almost taking the flesh with it. This was certainly aggravating to the excited captain. Captain B—— was a religious man, and, under his own vine and fig-tree, with none to rile or make afraid, I guess he would average well in patience line. But with our troubles on this day I believed he wished that there had been no sin in a ripping oath. He was a little hard on his bow-oarsman, and rather more than hinted at somebody's cowardice. This was too much for my hot Welsh blood, and with the aid of two others I brought the boat right up to the iron, and coolly passed a bight around the thwart and made all fast. This suggested that there would be a thundering row in the boat directly if the whale was not killed.

The captain was delighted to be held so well up to his work, and he plied his lance, thrust after thrust; but the brute seemed to bear a charmed life. He would not spout blood, and the little jets of blood which spirt from a lance wound would not bleed a whale to death in a week. Our boat buried her nose in the waves, and the bloody spray leaped over her side as we swept right royally onward.

Now our majestic race-horse grew impatient of our prodding. He milled short across our course, and we run plump against his head.

"Slack line!" roared the old man. "Starn all! Slack line and starn!"

He turned in his tracks to step aft of the bow-oar, fearing the up-cut of the jaw, when he saw that the line was fast about the thwart. "For God's sake, clear that line!" he shouted, as he sprang forward for the hatchet to cut; but the loosened bight went over the side, as the whale came up under the forward part of the boat and carried the bow clear of the water as he rounded slowly forward.

At this moment the captain and old Ben occupied the stern of the boat, and in the perilous moment I was just mad enough to enjoy the expectant look with which the two old whalemen awaited the arrival of the oncoming flukes. Fortunately for us all, the blow was delayed a moment, and when the thundering concussion came it cleared our boat by a few feet.

The other boats were out of sight, and the ship's hull was dimly seen to leeward. Yet for two hours more the whale ran and fought with redoubled energy. The captain got long darts with the lance, but to no good effect; the iron drew, and the victorious whale passed away from us. We were fagged and dead-beat; almost worn to death, and we did not reach the ship until long after nightfall. The other boats picked up the mate's crew, no one having been hurt.

On the following day the captain did handsomely by his bow-oar by remarking to me that an officer in the boat never meant half he said, and that such scolding was his habit. "But," he solemnly added, "never again, under any possible circumstances, make a line fast between the boat and a whale. Why, if that mad whale had gone down, the boat would have been a quarter of a mile under water in less than a minute, and half the crew might have been with it!" Bow-oar suggested that it was better to be under water than live under a charge of cowardice. The old man overlooked this impudence, and turned on his heel. Thus I have shown that the harpoon is to fasten to the whale, the line to keep communication with it, and the lance is the instrument by which it is killed, a spade being sometimes used to check a running whale.

## On the Sea

IT KEEPS eternal whisperings around
Desolate shores, and with its mighty swell
Gluts twice ten thousand caverns, till the spell
Of Hecate leaves them their old shadowy sound.
Often 'tis in such gentle temper found,
That scarcely will the very smallest shell
Be moved for days from whence it sometime fell,
When last the winds of heaven were unbound.
Oh ye! who have your eye-balls vexed and tired,
Feast them upon the wideness of the sea;
Oh ye! whose ears are dinned with uproar rude,
Or fed too much with cloying melody—
Sit ye near some old cavern's mouth, and brood
Until ye start, as if the sea-nymphs quired!

*John Keats*

# TAPPAN'S BURRO

## Zane Grey

*America's most popular writer of western stories, Zane Grey (1875–1939) knew the West well, and kept up his knowledge by taking long pack-trips into the wild country. As a young man, he started out to be a dentist. Had he continued in this calling, we might have missed more than sixty books from his pen.*

TAPPAN gazed down upon the newly born little burro with something of pity and consternation. It was not a vigorous offspring of the redoubtable Jennie, champion of all the numberless burros he had driven in his desert-prospecting years. He could not leave it there to die. Surely it was not strong enough to follow its mother. And to kill it was beyond him.

"Poor little devil!" soliloquized Tappan. "Reckon neither Jennie nor I wanted it to be born. . . . I'll have to hole up in this camp a few days. You can never tell what a burro will do. It might fool us an' grow strong all of a sudden."

Whereupon Tappan left Jennie and her tiny, gray lop-eared baby to themselves, and leisurely set about making permanent camp. The water at this oasis was not much to his liking, but it was drinkable, and he felt he must put up with it. For the rest the oasis was desirable enough as a camping site. Desert wanderers like Tappan favored the lonely water holes. This one was up under the bold brow of the Chocolate Mountains, where rocky wall met the desert sand, and a green patch of *palo verdes* and mesquites proved the presence of water. It had a magnificent view down a many-leagued slope of desert growths, across the dark belt of green and shining strip of red that marked the Rio Colorado, and on to the upflung Arizona land, range lifting to range until the saw-toothed peaks notched the blue sky.

Locked in the iron fastnesses of these desert mountains was gold.

[ 422 ]

Tappan, if he had any calling, was a prospector. But the lure of gold
did not bind him to this wandering life any more than the freedom
of it. He had never made a rich strike. About the best he could ever
do was to dig enough gold to grubstake himself for another prospecting trip into some remote corner of the American Desert. Tappan knew the arid Southwest from San Diego to the Pecos River
and from Picacho on the Colorado to the Tonto Basin. Few prospectors had the strength and endurance of Tappan. He was a giant
in build, and at thirty-five had never yet reached the limit of his
physical force.

With hammer and pick and magnifying glass Tappan scaled the
bare ridges. He was not an expert in testing minerals. He knew he
might easily pass by a rich vein of ore. But he did his best, sure at
least that no prospector could get more than he out of the pursuit
of gold. Tappan was more of a naturalist than a prospector, and
more of a dreamer than either. Many were the idle moments that he
sat staring down the vast reaches of the valleys, or watching some
creature of the wasteland, or marveling at the vivid hues of desert
flowers.

Tappan waited two weeks at this oasis for Jennie's baby burro
to grow strong enough to walk. And the very day that Tappan decided to break camp he found signs of gold at the head of a wash
above the oasis. Quite by chance, as he was looking for his burros,
he struck his pick into a place no different from a thousand others
there, and hit into a pocket of gold. He cleaned out the pocket
before sunset, the richer for several thousand dollars.

"You brought me luck," said Tappan, to the little gray burro
staggering around its mother. "Your name is Jenet. You're Tappan's burro, an' I reckon he'll stick to you."

Jenet belied the promise of her birth. Like a weed in fertile
ground she grew. Winter and summer Tappan patrolled the sand
beats from one trading post to another, and his burros traveled with
him. Jenet had an especially good training. Her mother had happened to be a remarkably good burro before Tappan had bought
her. And Tappan had patience; he found leisure to do things, and
he had something of pride in Jenet. Whenever he happened to drop
into Ehrenberg or Yuma, or any freighting station, some prospector
always tried to buy Jenet. She grew as large as a medium-sized
mule, and a three-hundred-pound pack was no load to discommode
her.

Tappan, in common with most lonely wanderers of the desert, talked to his burro. As the years passed this habit grew, until Tappan would talk to Jenet just to hear the sound of his voice. Perhaps that was all which kept him human.

"Jenet, you're worthy of a happier life," Tappan would say, as he unpacked her after a long day's march over the barren land. "You're a ship of the desert. Here we are, with grub an' water, a hundred miles from any camp. An' what but you could have fetched me here? No horse! No mule! No man! Nothin' but a camel, an' so I call you ship of the desert. But for you an' your kind, Jenet, there'd be no prospectors, and few gold mines. Reckon the desert would be still an unknown waste. . . . You're a great beast of burden, Jenet, an' there's no one to sing your praise."

And of a golden sunrise, when Jenet was packed and ready to face the cool, sweet fragrance of the desert, Tappan was wont to say:

"Go along with you, Jenet. The mornin's fine. Look at the mountains yonder callin' us. It's only a step down there. All purple an' violet! It's the life for us, my burro, an' Tappan's as rich as if all these sands were pearls."

But sometimes, at sunset, when the way had been long and hot and rough, Tappan would bend his shaggy head over Jenet, and talk in different mood.

"Another day gone, Jenet, another journey ended—an' Tappan is only older, wearier, sicker. There's no reward for your faithfulness. I'm only a desert rat, livin' from hole to hole. No home! No face to see. . . . Some sunset, Jenet, we'll reach the end of the trail. An' Tappan's bones will bleach in the sands. An' no one will know or care!"

When Jenet was two years old she would have taken the blue ribbon in competition with all the burros of the Southwest. She was unusually large and strong, perfectly proportioned, sound in every particular, and practically tireless. But these were not the only characteristics that made prospectors envious of Tappan. Jenet had the common virtues of all good burros magnified to an unbelievable degree. Moreover, she had sense and instinct that to Tappan bordered on the supernatural.

During these years Tappan's trail crisscrossed the mineral region of the Southwest. But, as always, the rich strike held aloof. It was like the pot of gold buried at the foot of the rainbow. Jenet knew the trails and the water holes better than Tappan. She could follow a trail obliterated by drifting sand or cut out by running water. She could scent at long distance a new spring on the desert or a strange water hole. She never wandered far from camp so that Tappan had to walk far in search of her. Wild burros, the bane of most prospectors, held no charm for Jenet. And she had never yet shown any especial liking for a tame burro. This was the strangest feature of Jenet's complex character. Burros were noted for their habit of pairing off, and forming friendships for one or more comrades. These relations were permanent. But Jenet still remained fancy free.

Tappan scarcely realized how he relied upon this big, gray, serene beast of burden. Of course, when chance threw him among men of his calling he would brag about her. But he had never really appreciated Jenet. In his way Tappan was a brooding, plodding fellow, not conscious of sentiment. When he bragged about Jenet it was her good qualities upon which he dilated. But what he really liked best about her were the little things of every day.

During the earlier years of her training Jenet had been a thief. She would pretend to be asleep for hours just to get a chance to steal something out of camp. Tappan had broken this habit in its incipiency. But he never quite trusted her. Jenet was a burro.

Jenet ate anything offered her. She could fare for herself or go without. Whatever Tappan had left from his own meals was certain to be rich dessert for Jenet. Every meal time she would stand near the camp fire, with one great long ear drooping, and the other standing erect. Her expression was one of meekness, of unending patience. She would lick a tin can until it shone resplendent. On long, hard, barren trails Jenet's deportment did not vary from that where the water holes and grassy patches were many. She did not need to have grass or grain. Brittle-bush and sage were good fare for her. She could eat greasewood, a desert plant that protected itself with a sap as sticky as varnish and far more dangerous to animals. She could eat cacti. Tappan had seen her break off leaves of the prickly pear cactus, and stamp upon them with her forefeet, mashing off the thorns, so that she could consume the succulent pulp. She liked mesquite beans, and leaves of willow, and all the trailing vines of the desert. And she could subsist in an arid waste land where a man would have died in short order.

No ascent or descent was too hard or dangerous for Jenet, provided it was possible of accomplishment. She would refuse a trail that was impassable. She seemed to have an uncanny instinct both for what she could do, and what was beyond a burro. Tappan had never known her to fail on something to which she stuck persistently. Swift streams of water, always bugbears to burros, did not stop Jenet. She hated quicksand, but could be trusted to navigate it, if that were possible. When she stepped gingerly, with little inch steps, out upon thin crust of ice or salty crust of desert sink hole, Tappan would know that it was safe, or she would turn back. Thunder and lightning, intense heat or bitter cold, the sirocco sand storm of the desert, the white dust of the alkali wastes—these were all the same to Jenet.

One August, the hottest and driest of his desert experience, Tappan found himself working a most promising claim in the lower reaches of the Panamint Mountains on the northern slope above Death Valley. It was a hard country at the most favorable season; in August it was terrible. The Panamints were infested by various small gangs of desperadoes—outlaw claim jumpers where opportunity afforded—and out-and-out robbers, even murderers where they could not get the gold any other way.

Tappan had been warned not to go into this region alone. But he never heeded any warnings. And the idea that he would ever strike a claim or dig enough gold to make himself an attractive target for outlaws seemed preposterous and not worth considering. Tappan had become a wanderer now from the unbreakable habit of it. Much to his amaze he struck a rich ledge of free gold in a canyon of the Panamints; and he worked from daylight until dark. He forgot about the claim jumpers, until one day he saw Jenet's long ears go up in the manner habitual with her when she saw strange men. Tappan watched the rest of that day, but did not catch a glimpse of any living thing. It was a desolate place, shut in, red-walled, hazy with heat, and brooding with an eternal silence.

Not long after that Tappan discovered boot tracks of several men adjacent to his camp and in an out-of-the-way spot, which persuaded him that he was being watched. Claim jumpers who were not going to jump his claim in this torrid heat, but meant to let him dig the gold and then kill him. Tappan was not the kind of man to be afraid. He grew wrathful and stubborn. He had six small canvas bags of gold and did not mean to lose them. Still, he was worried.

"Now, what's best to do?" he pondered. "I mustn't give it away that I'm wise. Reckon I'd better act natural. But I can't stay here longer. My claim's about worked out. An' these jumpers are smart enough to know it. . . . I've got to make a break at night. What to do?"

Tappan did not want to cache the gold, for in that case, of course, he would have to return for it. Still, he reluctantly admitted to himself that this was the best way to save it. Probably these robbers were watching him day and night. It would be most unwise to attempt escaping by traveling up over the Panamints.

"Reckon my only chance is goin' down into Death Valley," soliloquized Tappan, grimly.

The alternative thus presented was not to his liking. Crossing Death Valley at this season was always perilous, and never attempted in the heat of day. And at this particular time of intense torridity, when the day heat was unendurable and the midnight furnace gales were blowing, it was an enterprise from which even Tappan shrank. Added to this were the facts that he was too far west of the narrow part of the valley, and even if he did get across he would find himself in the most forbidding and desolate region of the Funeral Mountains.

Thus thinking and planning, Tappan went about his mining and camp tasks, trying his best to act natural. But he did not succeed. It was impossible, while expecting a shot at any moment, to act as if there was nothing on his mind. His camp lay at the bottom of a rocky slope. A tiny spring of water made verdure of grass and mesquite, welcome green in all that stark iron nakedness. His camp site was out in the open, on the bench near the spring. The gold claim that Tappan was working was not visible from any vantage point either below or above. It lay back at the head of a break in the rocky wall. It had two virtues—one that the sun never got to it, and the other that it was well hidden. Once there, Tappan knew he could not be seen. This, however, did not diminish his growing uneasiness. The solemn stillness was a menace. The heat of the day appeared to be augmenting to a degree beyond his experience. Every few moments Tappan would slip back through a narrow defile in the rocks and peep from his covert down at the camp. On the last of these occasions he saw Jenet out in the open. She stood motionless. Her long ears were erect. In an instant Tappan became strung with thrilling excitement. His keen eyes searched every approach to his camp. And at last in the gully below to the right he discovered two men crawling along from rock to rock. Jenet had seen them enter that gully and was now watching for them to appear. Tappan's excitement gave place to a grimmer emotion. These stealthy visitors were going to hide in ambush, and kill him as he returned to camp.

"Jenet, reckon what I owe you is a whole lot," muttered Tappan. "They'd have got me sure. . . . But now—" Tappan left his tools, and crawled out of his covert into the jumble of huge rocks toward the left of the slope. He had a six-shooter. His rifle he had left in camp. Tappan had seen only two men, but he knew there were more than that, if not actually near at hand at the moment, then surely not far away. And his chance was to worm his way like an Indian down to camp. With the rifle in his possession he would make short work of the present difficulty.

"Lucky Jenet's right in camp!" said Tappan, to himself. "It beats hell how she does things!"

Tappan was already deciding to pack and hurry away. On the moment Death Valley did not daunt him. This matter of crawling and gliding along was work unsuited to his great stature. He was too big to hide behind a little shrub or a rock. And he was not used to stepping lightly. His hobnailed boots could not be placed noiselessly upon the stones. Moreover, he could not progress without displacing little bits of weathered rock. He was sure that keen ears not too far distant could have heard him. But he kept on, making good progress around that slope to the far side of the canyon. Fortunately, he headed the gully up which his ambushers were stealing. On the other hand, this far side of the canyon afforded but little cover. The sun had gone down back of the huge red mass of the mountain. It had left the rocks so hot Tappan could not touch them with his bare hands.

He was about to stride out from his last covert and make a run for it down the rest of the slope, when, surveying the whole amphitheater below him, he espied the two men coming up out of the gully, headed toward his camp. They looked in his direction. Surely they had heard or seen him. But Tappan perceived at a glance that he was the closer to the camp. Without another moment of hesitation, he plunged from his hiding place, down the weathered slope. His giant strides set the loose rocks sliding and rattling. The men saw him. The foremost yelled to the one behind him. Then they both broke into a run. Tappan reached the level of the bench, and saw he could beat either of them into the camp. Unless he were disabled! He felt the wind of a heavy bullet before he heard it strike the rocks beyond. Then followed the boom of a Colt. One of his enemies had halted to shoot. This spurred Tappan to tremendous exertion. He flew over the rough ground, scarcely hearing the rapid shots. He could no longer see the man who was firing. But the first one was in plain sight, running hard, not yet seeing he was out of the race.

When he became aware of that he halted, and dropping on one knee, leveled his gun at the running Tappan. The distance was scarcely sixty yards. His first shot did not allow for Tappan's speed. His second kicked up the gravel in Tappan's face. Then followed three more shots in rapid succession. The man divined that Tappan had a rifle in camp. Then he steadied himself, waiting for the moment when Tappan had to slow down and halt. As Tappan reached his camp and dove for his rifle, the robber took time for his last aim, evidently hoping to get a stationary target. But Tappan did not get up from behind his camp duffel. It had been a habit of his to pile his boxes of supplies and roll of bedding together, and cover them with a canvas. He poked his rifle over the top of this and shot the robber. Then, leaping up, he ran forward to get sight of the second one. This man began to run along the edge of the gully. Tappan fired rapidly at him. The third shot knocked the fellow down. But he got up, and yelling, as if for succor, he ran off. Tappan got another shot before he disappeared.

"Ahuh!" grunted Tappan, grimly. His keen gaze came back to survey the fallen robber, and then went out over the bench, across the wide mouth of the canyon. Tappan thought he had better utilize time to pack instead of pursuing the fleeing man.

Reloading the rifle, he hurried out to find Jenet. She was coming in to camp. "Shore you're a treasure, old girl!" ejaculated Tappan.

Never in his life had he packed Jenet, or any other burro, so quickly. His last act was to drink all he could hold, fill his two canteens, and make Jenet drink. Then, rifle in hand, he drove the burro out of camp, round the corner of the red wall, to the wide gateway that opened down into Death Valley.

Tappan looked back more than he looked ahead. And he had traveled down a mile or more before he began to breathe more easily. He had escaped the claim jumpers. Even if they did show up in pursuit now, they could never catch him. Tappan believed he could travel faster and farther than any men of that ilk. But they did not appear. Perhaps the crippled one had not been able to reach his comrades in time. More likely, however, the gang had no taste for a chase in that torrid heat.

Tappan slowed his stride. He was almost as wet with sweat as if he had fallen into the spring. The great beads rolled down his face. And there seemed to be little streams of fire trickling down his breast. But despite this, and his labored panting for breath, not until he halted in the shade of a rocky wall did he realize the heat.

It was terrific. Instantly then he knew he was safe from pursuit. But he knew also that he faced a greater peril than that of robbers. He could fight evil men, but he could not fight this heat. So he rested there, regaining his breath. Already thirst was acute. Jenet stood near by, watching him. Tappan, with his habit of humanizing the burro, imagined that Jenet looked serious. A moment's thought was enough for Tappan to appreciate the gravity of his situation. He was about to go down into the upper end of Death Valley—a part of that country unfamiliar to him. He must cross it, and also the Funeral Mountains, at a season when a prospector who knew the trails and water holes would have to be forced to undertake it. Tappan had no choice.

His rifle was too hot to hold, so he stuck it in Jenet's pack; and, burdened only by a canteen of water, he set out, driving the burro ahead. Once he looked back up the wide-mouthed canyon. It appeared to smoke with red heat veils. The silence was oppressive.

Presently he turned the last corner that obstructed sight of Death Valley. Tappan had never been appalled by any aspect of the desert, but it was certain that here he halted. Back in his mountain-walled camp the sun had passed behind the high domes, but here it still held most of the valley in its blazing grip. Death Valley looked a ghastly, glaring level of white, over which a strange dull leaden haze drooped like a blanket. Ghosts of mountain peaks appeared to show dim and vague. There was no movement of anything. No wind! The valley was dead. Desolation reigned supreme. Tappan could not see far toward either end of the valley. A few miles of white glare merged at last into leaden pall. A strong odor, not unlike sulphur, seemed to add weight to the air.

Tappan strode on, mindful that Jenet had decided opinions of her own. She did not want to go straight ahead or to right or left, but back. That was the one direction impossible for Tappan. And he had to resort to a rare measure—that of beating her. But at last Jenet accepted the inevitable and headed down into the stark and naked plain. Soon Tappan reached the margin of the zone of shade cast by the mountain and was now exposed to the sun. The difference seemed tremendous. He had been hot, oppressed, weighted. It was now as if he was burned through his clothes, and walked on red-hot sands.

When Tappan ceased to sweat and his skin became dry, he drank half a canteen of water, and slowed his stride. Inured to desert hardship as he was, he could not long stand this. Jenet did not exhibit any lessening of vigor. In truth what she showed now was an increasing nervousness. It was almost as if she scented an enemy. Tappan never before had such faith in her. Jenet was equal to this task.

With that blazing sun on his back. Tappan felt he was being pursued by a furnace. He was compelled to drink the remaining half of his first canteen of water. Sunset would save him. Two more hours of such insupportable heat would lay him prostrate.

The ghastly glare of the valley took on a reddish tinge. The heat was blinding Tappan. The time came when he walked beside Jenet with a hand on her pack, for his eyes could no longer endure the furnace glare. Even with them closed he knew when the sun sank behind the Panamints. That fire no longer followed him. And the red left his eyelids.

With the sinking of the sun the world of Death Valley changed. It smoked with heat veils. But the intolerable constant burn was gone. The change was so immense that it seemed to have brought coolness.

In the twilight—strange, ghostly, somber, silent as death—Tappan followed Jenet off the sand, down upon the silt and borax level, to the crusty salt. Before dark Jenet halted at a sluggish belt of fluid —acid, it appeared to Tappan. It was not deep. And the bottom felt stable. But Jenet refused to cross. Tappan trusted her judgment more than his own. Jenet headed to the left and followed the course of the strange stream.

Night intervened. A night without stars or sky or sound, hot, breathless, charged with some intangible current! Tappan dreaded the midnight furnace winds of Death Valley. He had never encountered them. He had heard prospectors say that any man caught in Death Valley when these gales blew would never get out to tell the tale. And Jenet seemed to have something on her mind. She was no longer a leisurely, complacent burro. Tappan imagined Jenet seemed stern. Most assuredly she knew now which way she wanted to travel. It was not easy for Tappan to keep up with her, and ten paces beyond him she was out of sight.

At last Jenet headed the acid wash, and turned across the valley into a field of broken salt crust, like the roughened ice of a river that had broken and jammed, then frozen again. Impossible was it to make even a reasonable headway. It was a zone, however, that eventually gave way to Jenet's instinct for direction. Tappan had long ceased to try to keep his bearings. North, south, east, and west were all the same to him. The night was a blank—the darkness a wall —the silence a terrible menace flung at any living creature. Death Valley had endured them millions of years before living creatures had existed. It was no place for a man.

Tappan was now three hundred and more feet below sea level, in the aftermath of a day that had registered one hundred and forty-five degrees of heat. He knew, when he began to lose thought and balance—when only the primitive instincts directed his bodily machine. And he struggled with all his will power to keep hold of his sense of sight and feeling. He hoped to cross the lower level before the midnight gales began to blow.

Tappan's hope was vain. According to record, once in a long season of intense heat, there came a night when the furnace winds broke their schedule, and began early. The misfortune of Tappan was that he had struck this night.

Suddenly it seemed that the air, sodden with heat, began to move. It had weight. It moved soundlessly and ponderously. But it gathered momentum. Tappan realized what was happening. The blanket of heat generated by the day was yielding to outside pressure. Something had created a movement of the hotter air that must find its way upward, to give place for the cooler air that must find its day down.

Tappan heard the first, low, distant moan of wind and it struck terror to his heart. It did not have an earthly sound. Was that a knell for him? Nothing was surer than the fact that the desert must sooner or later claim him as a victim. Grim and strong, he rebelled against the conviction. That moan was a forerunner of others, growing louder and longer until the weird sound became continuous. Then the movement of wind was accelerated and began to carry a fine dust. Dark as the night was, it did not hide the pale sheets of dust that moved along the level plain. Tappan's feet felt the slow rise in the floor of the valley. His nose recognized the zone

of borax and alkali and niter and sulphur. He had reached the pit of
the valley at the time of the furnace winds.

The moan augmented to a roar, coming like a mighty storm
through a forest. It was hellish—like the woeful tide of Acheron. It
enveloped Tappan. And the gale bore down in tremendous volume,
like a furnace blast. Tappan seemed to feel his body penetrated by a
million needles of fire. He seemed to dry up. The blackness of night
had a spectral, whitish cast; the gloom was a whirling medium; the
valley floor was lost in a sheeted, fiercely seeping stream of silt.
Deadly fumes swept by, not lingering long enough to suffocate
Tappan. He would gasp and choke—then the poison gas was gone
on the gale. But hardest to endure was the heavy body of moving
heat. Tappan grew blind, so that he had to hold to Jenet, and stumble along. Every gasping breath was a tortured effort. He could not
bear a scarf over his face. His lungs heaved like great leather bel-
lows. His heart pumped like an engine short of fuel. This was the
supreme test for his never proven endurance. And he was all but
vanquished.

Tappan's senses of sight and smell and hearing failed him. There
was left only the sense of touch—a feeling of rope and burro and
ground—and an awful insulating pressure upon all his body. His
feet marked a change from salty plain to sandy ascent and then to
rocky slope. The pressure of wind gradually lessened: the difference in air made life possible; the feeling of being dragged endlessly
by Jenet had ceased. Tappan went his limit and fell into oblivion.

When he came to, he was suffering bodily tortures. Sight was
dim. But he saw walls of rocks, green growths of mesquite, tama-
rack, and grass. Jenet was lying down, with her pack flopped to one
side. Tappan's dead ears recovered to a strange murmuring, babbling sound. Then he realized his deliverance. Jenet had led him
across Death Valley, up into the mountain range, straight to a
spring of running water.

Tappan crawled to the edge of the water and drank guardedly,
a little at a time. He had to quell terrific craving to drink his fill.
Then he crawled to Jenet, and loosening the ropes of her pack,
freed her from its burden. Jenet got up, apparently none the worse
for her ordeal. She gazed mildly at Tappan, as if to say: "Well, I
got you out of that hole."

Tappan returned her gaze. Were they only man and beast, alone
in the desert? She seemed magnified to Tappan, no longer a plod-

ding, stupid burro. "Jenet, you—saved—my life," Tappan tried to
enunciate. "I'll never—forget."

Tappan was struck then to a realization of Jenet's service. He
was unutterably grateful. Yet the time came when he did forget.

Tappan had a weakness common to all prospectors: Any tale of
a lost gold mine would excite his interest; and well-known legends
of lost mines always obsessed him.

Peg-leg Smith's lost gold mine had lured Tappan to no less than
half a dozen trips into the terrible shifting-sand country of southern
California. There was no water near the region said to hide this
mine of fabulous wealth. Many prospectors had left their bones to
bleach white in the sun, finally to be buried by the ever blowing
sands. Upon the occasion of Tappan's last escape from this desolate
and forbidding desert, he had promised Jenet never to undertake it
again. It seemed Tappan promised the faithful burro a good many
things. It had been a habit.

When Tappan had a particularly hard experience or perilous
adventure, he always took a dislike to the immeditae country where
it had befallen him. Jenet had dragged him across Death Valley,
through incredible heat and the midnight furnace winds of that
strange place; and he had promised her he would never forget how
she had saved his life. Nor would he ever go back to Death Valley!
He made his way over the Funeral Mountains, worked down
through Nevada, and crossed the Rio Colorado above Needles, and
entered Arizona. He traveled leisurely, but he kept going, and
headed southeast toward Globe. There he cashed one of his six bags
of gold, and indulged in the luxury of a complete new outfit. Even
Jenet appreciated this fact, for the old outfit would scarcely hold
together. Tappan had the other five bags of gold in his pack; and
after hours of hesitation he decided he would not cash them and
entrust the money to a bank. He would take care of them. For him
the value of this gold amounted to a small fortune. Many plans suggested themselves to Tappan. But in the end he grew weary of
them. What did he want with a ranch, or cattle, or an outfitting
store, or any of the businesses he now had the means to buy? Towns
soon palled on Tappan. People did not long please him. Selfish interest and greed seemed paramount everywhere. Besides, if he
acquired a place to take up his time, what would become of Jenet?
That question decided him. He packed the burro and once more
took to the trails.

A dim, lofty, purple range called alluringly to Tappan. The

Superstition Mountains! Somewhere in that purple mass hid the famous treasure called the Lost Dutchman gold mine. Tappan had heard the story often. A Dutch prospector struck gold in the Superstitions. He kept the location secret. When he ran short of money, he would disappear for a few weeks, and then return with bags of gold. Wherever his strike, it assuredly was a rich one. No one ever could trail him or get a word out of him. Time passed. A few years made him old. During this time he conceived a liking for a young man, and eventually confided to him that some day he would tell him the secret of his gold mine. He had drawn a map of the landmarks adjacent to his mine. But he was careful not to put on paper directions how to get there. It chanced that he suddenly fell ill and saw his end was near. Then he summoned the young man who had been so fortunate as to win his regard. Now this individual was a ne'er-do-well, and upon this occasion he was half drunk. The dying Dutchman produced his map, and gave it with verbal directions to the young man. Then he died. When the recipient of this fortune recovered from the effects of liquor, he could not remember all the Dutchman had told him. He tortured himself to remember names and places. But the mine was up in the Superstition Mountains. He never remembered. He never found the lost mine, though he spent his life and died trying. Thus the story passed into the legend of the Lost Dutchman.

Tappan now had his try at finding it. But for him the shifting sands of the southern California desert or even the barren and desolate Death Valley were preferable to this Superstition Range. It was a harder country than the Pinacate of Sonora. Tappan hated cactus, and the Superstitions were full of it. Everywhere stood up the huge *sahuaro*, the giant cacti of the Arizona plateaus, tall like branchless trees, fluted and columnar, beautiful and fascinating to gaze upon, but obnoxious to prospector and burro.

One day from a north slope Tappan saw afar a wonderful country of black timber, above which zigzagged for many miles a yellow, winding rampart of rock. This he took to be the rim of the Mogollon Mesa, one of Arizona's freaks of nature. Something called Tappan. He was forever victim to yearnings for the unattainable. He was tired of heat, glare, dust, bare rock, and thorny cactus. The Lost Dutchman gold mine was a myth. Besides, he did not need any more gold.

Next morning Tappan packed Jenet and worked down off the north slopes of the Superstition Range. That night about sunset he made camp on the bank of a clear brook, with grass and wood in abundance—such a camp site as a prospector dreamed of but seldom found.

Before dark Jenet's long ears told of the advent of strangers. A man and a woman rode down the trail into Tappan's camp. They had poor horses, and led a pack animal that appeared too old and weak to bear up under even the meager pack he carried.

"Howdy," said the man.

Tappan rose from his task to his lofty height and returned the greeting. The man was middle-aged, swarthy, and rugged, a mountaineer, with something about him that Tappan instinctively distrusted. The woman was under thirty, comely in a full-blown way, with rich brown skin and glossy dark hair. She had wide-open black eyes that bent a curious possession-taking gaze upon Tappan.

"Care if we camp with you?" she inquired, and she smiled. That smile changed Tappan's habit and conviction of a lifetime.

"No indeed. Reckon I'd like a little company," he said.

Very probably Jenet did not understand Tappan's words, but she dropped one ear, and walked out of camp to the green bank.

"Thanks, stranger," replied the woman. "That grub shore smells good." She hesitated a moment, evidently waiting to catch her companion's eye, then she continued. "My name's Madge Beam. He's my brother Jake. . . . Who might you happen to be?"

"I'm Tappan, lone prospector, as you see," replied Tappan.

"Tappan! What's your front handle?" she queried, curiously.

"Fact is, I don't remember," replied Tappan, as he brushed a huge hand through his shaggy hair.

"Ahuh? Any name's good enough."

When she dismounted, Tappan saw that she had a tall, lithe figure, garbed in rider's overalls and boots. She unsaddled her horse with the dexterity of long practice. The saddlebags she carried over to the spot the man Jake had selected to throw the pack.

Tappan heard them talking in low tones. It struck him as strange that he did not have his usual reaction to an invasion of his privacy and solitude. Tappan had thrilled under those black eyes. And now a queer sensation of the unusual rose in him. Bending over his campfire tasks he pondered this and that, but mostly the sense of the nearness of a woman. Like most desert men, Tappan knew little of the other sex. A few that he might have been drawn to went out of his wandering life as quickly as they had entered it. This Madge Beam took possession of his thoughts. An evidence of Tappan's preoccupation was the fact that he burned his first batch of biscuits. And Tappan felt proud of his culinary ability. He was on his knees, mixing more flour and water, when the woman spoke from right behind him. "Tough luck you burned the first pan," she said. "But it's a good turn for your burro. That shore is a burro. Biggest I ever saw."

She picked up the burned biscuits and tossed them over to Jenet. Then she came back to Tappan's side, rather embarrassingly close.

"Tappan, I know how I'll eat, so I ought to ask you to let me help," she said, with a laugh.

"No, I don't need any," replied Tappan. "You sit down on my roll of beddin' there. Must be tired, aren't you?"

"Not so very," she returned. "That is, I'm not tired of ridin'." She spoke the second part of this reply in lower tone.

Tappan looked up from his task. The woman had washed her face, brushed her hair, and had put on a skirt—a singularly attractive change. Tappan thought her younger. She was the handsomest woman he had ever seen. The look of her made him clumsy. What eyes she had! They looked through him. Tappan returned to his task, wondering if he was right in his surmise that she wanted to be friendly.

"Jake an' I drove a bunch of cattle to Maricopa," she volunteered. "We sold 'em, an' Jake gambled away most of the money. I couldn't get what I wanted."

"Too bad! So you're ranchers. Once thought I'd like that. Fact is, down here at Globe a few weeks ago I came near buyin' some rancher out an' tryin' the game."

"You did?" Her query had a low, quick eagerness that somehow thrilled Tappan. But he did not look up.

"I'm a wanderer. I'd never do on a ranch."

"But if you had a woman?" Her laugh was subtle and gay.

"A woman! For me? Oh, Lord, no!" ejaculated Tappan, in confusion.

"Why not? Are you a woman-hater?"

"I can't say that," replied Tappan, soberly. "It's just—I guess—no woman would have me."

"Faint heart never won fair lady."

Tappan had no reply for that. He surely was making a mess of the second pan of biscuit dough. Manifestly the woman saw this, for with a laugh she plumped down on her knees in front of Tappan, and rolled her sleeves up over shapely brown arms.

"Poor man! Shore you need a woman. Let me show you," she said, and put her hands right down upon Tappan's. The touch gave him a strange thrill. He had to pull his hands away, and as he wiped them with his scarf he looked at her. He seemed compelled to look. She was close to him now, smiling in good nature, a little scornful of man's encroachment upon the housewifely duties of a woman. A subtle something emanated from her—a more than kindness or gayety. Tappan grasped that it was just the woman of her. And it was going to his head.

"Very well, let's see you show me," he replied, as he rose to his feet.

Just then the brother Jake strolled over, and he had a rather amused and derisive eye for his sister.

"Wal, Tappan, she's not overfond of work, but I reckon she can cook," he said.

Tappan felt greatly relieved at the approach of this brother. And he fell into conversation with him, telling something of his prospecting since leaving Globe, and listening to the man's cattle talk. By and by the woman called, "Come an' get it!" Then they sat down to eat, and, as usual with hungry wayfarers, they did not talk much until appetite was satisfied. Afterward, before the camp fire, they began to talk again, Jake being the most discursive. Tappan conceived the idea that the rancher was rather curious about him, and perhaps wanted to sell his ranch. The woman seemed more thoughtful, with her wide black eyes on the fire.

"Tappan, what way you travelin'?" finally inquired Beam.

"Can't say. I just worked down out of the Superstitions. Haven't any place in mind. Where does this road go?"

"To the Tonto Basin. Ever heard of it?"

"Yes, the name isn't new. What's in this Basin?"

The man grunted. "Tonto once was home for the Apache. It's now got a few sheep an' cattlemen, lots of rustlers. An' say, if you like to hunt bear an' deer, come along with us."

"Thanks. I don't know as I can," returned Tappan, irresolutely. He was not used to such possibilities as this suggested.

Then the woman spoke up. "It's a pretty country. Wild an' different. We live up under the rim rock. There's mineral in the canyons." Was it that about mineral which decided Tappan or the look in her eyes?

Tappan's world of thought and feeling underwent as great a

change as this Tonto Basin differed from the stark desert so long
his home. The trail to the log cabin of the Beams climbed many a
ridge and slope and foothill, all covered with manzanita, mescal,
cedar, and juniper, at last to reach the canyons of the Rim, where
lofty pines and spruces lorded it over the under forest of maples
and oaks. Though the yellow Rim towered high over the site of
the cabin, the altitude was still great, close to seven thousand feet
above sea level. Tappan had fallen in love with this wild wooded
and canyoned country. So had Jenet. It was rather funny the way
she hung around Tappan, mornings and evenings. She ate luxuriant
grass and oak leaves until her sides bulged.

There did not appear to be any flat places in this landscape.
Every bench was either up hill or down hill. The Beams had no
garden or farm or ranch that Tappan could discover. They raised
a few acres of sorghum and corn. Their log cabin was of the most
primitive kind, and outfitted poorly. Madge Beam explained that
this cabin was their winter abode, and that up on the Rim they had
a good house and ranch. Tappan did not inquire closely into anything. If he had interrogated himself, he would have found out
that the reason he did not inquire was because he feared something
might remove him from the vicinity of Madge Beam. He had
thought it strange the Beams avoided wayfarers they had met on
the trail, and had gone round a little hamlet Tappan had espied
from a hill. Madge Beam, with woman's intuition, had read his
mind, and had said: "Jake doesn't get along so well with some of
the villagers. An' I've no hankerin' for gun play." That explanation was sufficient for Tappan. He had lived long enough in his
wandering years to appreciate that people could have reasons for
being solitary.

This trip up into the Rim Rock country bade fair to become
Tappan's one and only adventure of the heart. It was not alone the
murmuring, clear brook of cold mountain water that enchanted
him, nor the stately pines, nor the beautiful silver spruces, nor the
wonder of the deep, yellow-walled canyons, so choked with verdure, and haunted by wild creatures. He dared not face his soul,
and ask why this dark-eyed woman sought him more and more.
Tappan lived in the moment.

He was aware that the few mountaineer neighbors who rode
that way rather avoided contact with him. Tappan was not so
dense that he did not perceive that the Beams preferred to keep
him from outsiders. This perhaps was owing to their desire to sell

Tappan the ranch and cattle. Jake offered to let it go at what he called a low figure. Tappan thought it just as well to go out into the forest and hide his bags of gold. He did not trust Jake Beam, and liked less the looks of the men who visited this wilderness ranch. Madge Beam might be related to a rustler, and the associate of rustlers, but that did not necessarily make her a bad woman. Tappan sensed that her attitude was changing, and she seemed to require his respect. At first, all she wanted was his admiration. Tappan's long unused deference for women returned to him, and when he saw that it was having some strange softening effect upon Madge Beam, he redoubled his attentions. They rode and climbed and hunted together. Tappan had pitched his camp not far from the cabin, on a shaded bank of the singing brook. Madge did not leave him much to himself. She was always coming up to his camp, on one pretext or another. Often she would bring two horses, and make Tappan ride with her. Some of these occasions, Tappan saw, occurred while visitors came to the cabin. In three weeks Madge Beam changed from the bold and careless woman who had ridden down into his camp that sunset, to a serious and appealing woman, growing more careful of her person and adornment, and manifestly bearing a burden on her mind.

October came. In the morning white frost glistened on the split-wood shingles of the cabin. The sun soon melted it, and grew warm. The afternoons were still and smoky, melancholy with the enchantment of Indian summer. Tappan hunted wild turkey and deer with Madge, and revived his boyish love of such pursuits. Madge appeared to be a woman of the woods, and had no mean skill with the rifle.

One day they were high on the Rim, with the great timbered basin at their feet. They had come up to hunt deer, but got no farther than the wonderful promontory where before they had lingered. "Somethin' will happen to me to-day," Madge Beam said, enigmatically.

Tappan never had been much of a talker. But he could listen. The woman unburdened herself this day. She wanted freedom, happiness, a home away from this lonely country, and all the heritage of woman. She confessed it broodingly, passionately. And Tappan recognized truth when he heard it. He was ready to do all in his power for this woman and believed she knew it. But words and acts of sentiment came hard to him.

"Are you goin' to buy Jake's ranch?" she asked.

"I don't know. Is there any hurry?" returned Tappan.

"I reckon not. But I think I'll settle that," she said, decisively.

"How so?"

"Well, Jake hasn't got any ranch," she answered. And added hastily, "No clear title, I mean. He's only homesteaded one hundred an' sixty acres, an' hasn't proved up on it yet. But don't you say I told you."

"Was Jake aimin' to be crooked?"

"I reckon. . . . An' I was willin' at first. But not now."

Tappan did not speak at once. He saw the woman was in one of her brooding moods. Besides, he wanted to weigh her words. How significant they were! To-day more than ever she had let down. Humility and simplicity seemed to abide with her. And her brooding boded a storm. Tappan's heart swelled in his broad breast. Was life going to dawn rosy and bright for the lonely prospector? He had money to make a home for this woman. What lay in the balance of the hour? Tappan waited, slowly realizing the charged atmosphere.

Madge's somber eyes gazed out over the great void. But, full of thought and passion as they were, they did not see the beauty of that scene. But Tappan saw it. And in some strange sense the color and wildness and sublimity seemed the expression of a new state of his heart. Under him sheered down the ragged and cracked cliffs of the Rim, yellow and gold and gray, full of caves and crevices, ledges for eagles and niches for lions, a thousand feet down to the upward edge of the long green slopes and canyons, and so on down and down into the abyss of forested ravine and ridge, rolling league on league away to the encompassing barrier of purple mountain ranges.

The thickets in the canyons called Tappan's eye back to linger there. How different from the scenes that used to be perpetually in his sight! What riot of color! The tips of the green pines, the crests of the silver spruces, waved about masses of vivid gold of aspen trees, and wonderful cerise and flaming red of maples, and crags of yellow rock, covered with the bronze of frostbitten sumach. Here was autumn and with it the colors of Tappan's favorite season. From below breathed up the low roar of plunging brook; an eagle screeched his wild call; an elk bugled his piercing blast. From the Rim wisps of pine needles blew away on the breeze and fell into the void. A wild country, colorful, beautiful, bountiful. Tappan imagined he could quell his wandering spirit here, with this dark-eyed woman by his side. Never before had Nature so called him. Here was not the cruelty or flinty hardness of the desert. The air was keen and sweet, cold in the shade, warm in the sun. A fragrance of balsam and spruce, spiced with pine, made his breathing a thing of difficulty and delight. How for so many years had he endured vast open spaces without such eye-soothing trees as these? Tappan's back rested against a huge pine that tipped the Rim, and had stood there, stronger than the storms, for many a hundred years. The rock of the promontory was covered with soft brown mats of pine needles. A juniper tree, with its bright green foliage and lilac-colored berries, grew near the pine, and helped to form a secluded little nook, fragrant and somehow haunting. The woman's dark head was close to Tappan, as she sat with her elbows on her knees, gazing down into the basin. Tappan saw the strained tensity of her posture, the heaving of her full bosom. He wondered, while his own emotions, so long darkened, roused to the suspense of that hour. Suddenly she flung herself into Tappan's arms. The act amazed him. It seemed to have both the passion of a woman and the shame of a girl. Before she hid her face on Tappan's breast he saw how the rich brown had paled, and then flamed. "Tappan! . . . Take me away. . . . Take me away from here—from that life down there," she cried, in smothered voice.

"Madge, you mean take you away—and marry you?" he replied.

"Oh, yes—yes—marry me, if you love me. . . . I don't see how you can—but you do, don't you?—Say you do."

"I reckon that's what ails me, Madge," he replied, simply.

"*Say* so, then," she burst out.

"All right, I do," said Tappan, with heavy breath. "Madge, words don't come easy for me. . . . But I think you're wonderful, an' I want you. I haven't dared hope for that, till now. I'm only a wanderer. But it'd be heaven to have you—my wife—an' make a home for you."

"Oh—Oh!" she returned, wildly, and lifted herself to cling round his neck, and to kiss him. "You give me joy. . . . Oh, Tappan, I love you. I never loved any man before. I know now. . . . An' I'm not wonderful—or good. But I love you."

The fire of her lips and the clasp of her arms worked havoc in Tappan. No woman had ever loved him, let alone embraced him. To awake suddenly to such rapture as this made him strong and rough in his response. Then all at once she seemed to collapse in his arms and to begin to weep. He feared he had offended or hurt her, and was clumsy in his contrition. Presently she replied:

"Pretty soon—I'll make you—beat me. It's your love—your honesty—that's shamed me. . . . Tappan, I was party to a trick to—sell you a worthless ranch. . . . I agreed to—try to make you love me—to fool you—cheat you. . . . But I've fallen in love with you.—An' my God, I care more for your love—your respect—than for my life. I can't go on with it. I've double-crossed Jake, an' all of them. . . . Now, am I worth lovin'? Am I worth havin'?"

"More than ever, dear," he said.

"You will take me away?"

"Anywhere—any time, the sooner the better."

She kissed him passionately, and then, disengaging herself from his arms, she knelt and gazed earnestly at him. "I've not told all. I will some day. But I swear now on my soul—I'll be what you think me."

"Madge, you needn't say all that. If you love me—it's enough. More than I ever dreamed of."

"You're a man. Oh, why didn't I meet you when I was eighteen instead of now—twenty-eight, an' all that between. . . . But enough. A new life begins here for me. We must plan."

"You make the plans an' I'll act on them."

For a moment she was tense and silent, head bowed, hands shut tight. Then she spoke:

"To-night we'll slip away. You make a light pack, that'll go on your saddle. I'll do the same. We'll hide the horses out near where the trail crosses the brook. An' we'll run off—ride out of the country."

Tappan in turn tried to think, but the whirl of his mind made any reason difficult. This dark-eyed, full-bosomed woman loved him, had surrendered herself, asked only his protection. The thing seemed marvelous. Yet she knelt there, those dark eyes on him, infinitely more appealing than ever, haunting with some mystery of sadness and fear he could not divine.

Suddenly Tappan remembered Jenet.

"I must take Jenet," he said.

That startled her. "Jenet— Who's she?"

"My burro."

"Your burro. You can't travel fast with that pack beast. We'll be trailed, an' we'll have to go fast. . . . You can't take the burro."

Then Tappan was startled. "What! Can't take Jenet?— Why, I—I couldn't get along without her."

"Nonsense. What's a burro? We must ride fast—do you hear?"

"Madge, I'm afraid I—I must take Jenet with me," he said, soberly.

"It's impossible. I can't go if you take her. I tell you I've got to get away. If you want *me* you'll have to leave your precious Jenet behind."

Tappan bowed his head to the inevitable. After all, Jenet was only a beast of burden. She would run wild on the ridges and soon forget him and have no need of him. Something strained in Tappan's breast. He did not see clearly here. This woman was worth more than all else to him.

"I'm stupid, dear," he said. "You see I never before ran off with a beautiful woman. . . . Of course my burro must be left behind."

Elopement, if such it could be called, was easy for them. Tappan did not understand why Madge wanted to be so secret about it. Was she not free? But then, he reflected, he did not know the circumstances she feared. Besides, he did not care. Possession of the woman was enough.

Tappan made his small pack, the weight of which was considerable owing to his bags of gold. This he tied on his saddle. It bothered him to leave most of his new outfit scattered around his camp. What would Jenet think of that? He looked for her, but for once she did not come in at meal time. Tappan thought this was singular. He could not remember when Jenet had been far from his camp at sunset. Somehow Tappan was glad.

After he had his supper, he left his utensils and supplies as they happened to be, and strode away under the trees to the trysting-place where he was to meet Madge. To his surprise she came before dark, and, unused as he was to the complexity and emotional nature of a woman, he saw that she was strangely agitated. Her face was pale. Almost a fury burned in her black eyes. When she came up to Tappan, and embraced him, almost fiercely, he felt that he was about to learn more of the nature of womankind. She thrilled him to his depths.

"Lead out the horses an' don't make any noise," she whispered.

Tappan complied, and soon he was mounted, riding behind her on the trail. It surprised him that she headed down country, and traveled fast. Moreover, she kept to a trail that continually grew rougher. They came to a road, which she crossed, and kept on through darkness and brush so thick that Tappan could not see the least sign of a trail. And at length anyone could have seen that Madge had lost her bearings. She appeared to know the direction she wanted, but traveling upon it was impossible, owing to the increasingly cut-up and brushy ground. They had to turn back, and seemed to be hours finding the road. Once Tappan fancied he heard the thud of hoofs other than those made by their own horses. Here Madge acted strangely, and where she had been obsessed by desire to hurry she now seemed to have grown weary. She turned her horse south on the road. Tappan was thus enabled to ride beside her. But they talked very little. He was satisfied with the fact of being with her on the way out of the country. Some time in the night they reached an old log shack by the roadside. Here Tappan suggested they halt, and get some sleep before dawn. The morrow would mean a long hard day.

"Yes, to-morrow will be hard," replied Madge, as she faced Tappan in the gloom. He could see her big dark eyes on him. Her tone was not one of a hopeful woman. Tappan pondered over this. But he could not understand, because he had no idea how a woman ought to act under such circumstances. Madge Beam was a creature of moods. Only the day before, on the ride down from the Rim, she had told him with a laugh that she was likely to love him madly one moment and scratch his eyes out the next. How could he know what to make of her? Still, an uneasy feeling began to stir in Tappan.

They dismounted, and unsaddled the horses. Tappan took his pack and put it aside. Something frightened the horses. They bolted down the road.

"Head them off," cried the woman, hoarsely.

Even on the instant her voice sounded strained to Tappan, as if she were choked. But, realizing the absolute necessity of catching the horses, he set off down the road on a run. And he soon succeeded in heading off the animal he had ridden. The other one, however, was contrary and cunning. When Tappan would endeavour to get ahead, it would trot briskly on. Yet it did not go so fast but what Tappan felt sure he would soon catch it. Thus walking and running, he put some distance between him and the cabin before he realized that he could not head off the wary beast. Much perturbed in mind, Tappan hurried back.

Upon reaching the cabin Tappan called to Madge. No answer! He could not see her in the gloom nor the horse he had driven back. Only silence brooded there. Tappan called again. Still no answer! Perhaps Madge had succumbed to weariness and was asleep. A search of the cabin and vicinity failed to yield any sign of her. But it disclosed the fact that Tappan's pack was gone.

Suddenly he sat down, quite overcome. He had been duped. What a fierce pang tore his heart! But it was for loss of the woman —not the gold. He was stunned, and then sick with bitter misery. Only then did Tappan realize the meaning of love and what it had done to him. The night wore on, and he sat there in the dark and cold and stillness until the gray dawn told him of the coming of day. The light showed his saddle where he had left it. Near by lay one of Madge's gloves. Tappan's keen eye sighted a bit of paper sticking out of the glove. He picked it up. It was a leaf out of a little book he had seen her carry, and upon it was written in lead pencil:

"I am Jake's wife, not his sister. I double-crossed him an' ran off with you an' would have gone to hell for you. But Jake an' his gang suspected me. They were close on our trail. I couldn't shake them. So here I chased off the horses an' sent you after them. It was the only way I could save your life."

Tappan tracked the thieves to Globe. There he learned they had gone to Phoenix—three men and one woman. Tappan had money on his person. He bought horse and saddle, and, setting out for Phoenix, he let his passion to kill grow with the miles and hours. At Phoenix he learned Beam had cashed the gold—twelve thousand dollars. So much of a fortune! Tappan's fury grew. The gang separated here. Beam and his wife took stage for Tucson. Tappan had no trouble in trailing their movements.

Gambling dives and inns and freighting posts and stage drivers told the story of the Beams and their ill-gotten gold. They went on to California, down into Tappan's country, to Yuma, and El Cajon, and San Diego. Here Tappan lost track of the woman. He could not find that she had left San Diego, nor any trace of her there. But Jake Beam had killed a Mexican in a brawl and had fled across the line.

Tappan gave up for the time being the chase of Beam, and bent his efforts to find the woman. He had no resentment toward Madge. He only loved her. All that winter he searched San Diego. He made of himself a peddler as a ruse to visit houses. But he never found

a trace of her. In the spring he wandered back to Yuma, raking over
the old clues, and so on back to Tucson and Phoenix.

This year of dream and love and passion and despair and hate
made Tappan old. His great strength and endurance were not yet
impaired, but something of his spirit had died out of him.

One day he remembered Jenet. "My burro!" he soliloquized.
"I had forgotten her. . . . Jenet!"

Then it seemed a thousand impulses merged in one drove him
to face the long road toward the Rim Rock country. To remember
Jenet was to grow doubtful. Of course she would be gone. Stolen
or dead or wandered off! But then who could tell what Jenet might
do? Tappan was both called and driven. He was a poor wanderer
again. His outfit was a pack he carried on his shoulder. But while
he could walk he would keep on until he found that last camp
where he had deserted Jenet.

October was coloring the canyon slopes when he reached the
shadow of the great wall of yellow rock. The cabin where the
Beams had lived—or had claimed they lived—was a fallen ruin,
crushed by snow. Tappan saw other signs of a severe winter and
heavy snowfall. No horse or cattle tracks showed in the trails.

To his amaze his camp was much as he had left it. The stone
fireplace, the iron pots, appeared to be in the same places. The
boxes that had held his supplies were lying here and there. And
his canvas tarpaulin, little the worse for wear of the elements, lay
on the ground under the pine where he had slept. If any man had
visited this camp in a year he had left no sign of it.

Suddenly Tappan espied a hoof track in the dust. A small track
—almost oval in shape—fresh! Tappan thrilled through all his being.

"Jenet's track, so help me God!" he murmured.

He found more of them, made that morning. And, keen now as
never before on her trail, he set out to find her. The tracks led up
the canyon. Tappan came out into a little grassy clearing, and there
stood Jenet, as he had seen her thousands of times. She had both
long ears up high. She seemed to stare out of that meek, gray face.
And then one of the long ears flopped over and drooped. Such
perhaps was the expression of her recognition.

Tappan strode up to her.

"Jenet—old girl—you hung round camp—waitin' for me, didn't
you?" he said, huskily, and his big hands fondled her long ears.
Yes, she had waited. She, too, had grown old. She was gray. The
winter of that year had been hard. What had she lived on when

the snow lay so deep? There were lion scratches on her back, and
scars on her legs. She had fought for her life.

"Jenet, a man can never always tell about a burro," said Tappan.
"I trained you to hang round camp an' wait till I came back. . . .
'Tappan's burro,' the desert rats used to say! An' they'd laugh
when I bragged how you'd stick to me where most men would
quit. But drag as I did, I never knew you, Jenet. An' I left you—an'
forgot. Jenet, it takes a human bein'—a man—a woman—to be faith-
less. An' it takes a dog or a horse or a burro to be great. . . . Beasts?
I wonder now. . . . Well, old pard, we're goin' down the trail together, an' from this day on Tappan begins to pay his debt."

Tappan never again had the old *wanderlust* for the stark and
naked desert. Something had transformed him. The green and
fragrant forests, and brown-aisled, pine-matted woodlands, the
craggy promontories and the great colored canyons, the cold
granite water springs of the Tonto seemed vastly preferable to the
heat and dust and glare and the emptiness of the waste lands. But
there was more. The ghost of his strange and only love kept pace
with his wandering steps, a spirit that hovered with him as his
shadow. Madge Beam, whatever she had been, had shown to him
the power of love to refine and ennoble. Somehow he felt closer
to her here in the cliff country where his passion had been born.
Somehow she seemed nearer to him here than in all those places
he had tracked her. So from a prospector searching for gold Tappan became a hunter, seeking only the means to keep soul and
body together. And all he cared for was his faithful burro Jenet,
and the loneliness and silence of the forest land.

He was to learn that the Tonto was a hard country in many
ways, and bitterly so in winter. Down in the brakes of the basin
it was mild in winter, the snow did not lie long, and ice seldom
formed. But up on the Rim, where Tappan always lingered as long
as possible, the storm king of the north held full sway. Fifteen feet
of snow and zero weather were the rule in dead of winter.

An old native once warned Tappan: "See hyar, friend, I reckon
you'd better not get caught up in the Rim Rock country in one of
our big storms. Fer if you do you'll never get out."

It was a way of Tappan's to follow his inclinations, regardless
of advice. He had weathered the terrible midnight storm of hot
wind in Death Valley. What were snow and cold to him? Late
autumn on the Rim was the most perfect and beautiful of seasons.

He had seen the forest land brown and darkly green one day, and the next burdened with white snow. What a transfiguration! Then when the sun loosened the white mantling on the pines, and they had shed their burdens in drifting dust of white, and rainbowed mists of melting snow, and avalanches sliding off the branches, there would be left only the wonderful white floor of the woodland. The great rugged brown tree trunks appeared mightier and statelier in the contrast; and the green of foliage, the russet of oak leaves, the gold of the aspens, turned the forest into a world enchanting to the desert-seared eyes of this wanderer.

With Tappan the years sped by. His mind grew old faster than his body. Every season saw him lonelier. He had a feeling, a vague illusive foreshadowing that his bones, instead of bleaching on the desert sands, would mingle with the pine mats and the soft fragrant moss of the forest. The idea was pleasant to Tappan.

One afternoon he was camped in Pine Canyon, a timber-sloped gorge far back from the Rim. November was well on. The fall had been singularly open and fair, with not a single storm. A few natives happening across Tappan had remarked casually that such autumns sometimes were not to be trusted.

This late afternoon was one of Indian summer beauty and warmth. The blue haze in the canyon was not all the blue smoke from Tappan's camp fire. In a narrow park of grass not far from camp Jenet grazed peacefully with elk and deer. Wild turkeys lingered there, loath to seek their winter quarters down in the basin. Gray squirrels and red squirrels barked and frisked, and dropped the pine and spruce cones, with thud and thump, on all the slopes.

Before dark a stranger strode into Tappan's camp, a big man of middle age, whose magnificent physique impressed even Tappan. He was a rugged, bearded giant, wide-eyed and of pleasant face. He had no outfit, no horse, not even a gun. "Lucky for me I smelled your smoke," he said. "Two days for me without grub."

"Howdy, stranger," was Tappan's greeting. "Are you lost?"

"Yes an' no. I could find my way out down over the Rim, but it's not healthy down there for me. So I'm hittin' north."

"Where's your horse an' pack?"

"I reckon they're with the gang thet took more of a fancy to them than me."

"Ahuh! You're welcome here, stranger," replied Tappan. "I'm Tappan."

"Ha! Heard of you. I'm Jess Blade, of anywhere. An' I'll say, Tappan, I was an honest man till I hit the Tonto." His laugh was frank, for all its note of grimness. Tappan liked the man, and sensed one who would be a good friend and bad foe.

"Come an' eat. My supplies are peterin' out, but there's plenty of meat."

Blade ate, indeed, as a man starved, and did not seem to care if Tappan's supplies were low. He did not talk. After the meal he craved a pipe and tobacco. Then he smoked in silence, in a slow realizing content. The morrow had no fears for him. The flickering ruddy light from the camp fire shone on his strong face. Tappan saw in him the drifter, the drinker, the brawler, a man with good in him, but over whom evil passion or temper dominated. Presently he smoked the pipe out, and with reluctant hand knocked out the ashes and returned it to Tappan. "I reckon I've got some news thet'd interest you," he said.

"You have?" queried Tappan.

"Yes, if you're the Tappan who tried to run off with Jake Beam's wife."

"Well, I'm that Tappan. But I'd like to say I didn't know she was married."

"Shore, I know thet. So does everybody in the Tonto. You were just meat for the Beam gang. They had played the trick before. But accordin' to what I hear thet trick was the last fer Madge Beam. She never came back to this country. An' Jake Beam, when he was drunk, owned up thet she'd left him in California. Some hint at worse. Fer Jake Beam came back a harder man. Even his gang said thet."

"Is he in the Tonto now?" queried Tappan, with a thrill of fire along his veins.

"Yep, thar fer keeps," replied Blade, grimly. "Somebody shot him."

"Ahuh!" exclaimed Tappan with a deep breath of relief. There came a sudden cooling of the heat of his blood.

After that there was a long silence. Tappan dreamed of the woman who had loved him. Blade brooded over the camp fire. The wind moaned fitfully in the lofty pines on the slope. A wolf mourned as if in hunger. The stars appeared to obscure their radiance in haze.

"Reckon thet wind sounds like storm," observed Blade, presently.

"I've heard it for weeks now," replied Tappan.

"Are you a woodsman?"

"No, I'm a desert man."

"Wal, you take my hunch an' hit the trail fer low country." This was well meant, and probably sound advice, but it alienated Tappan. He had really liked this hearty-voiced stranger. Tappan thought moodily of his slowly ingrowing mind, of the narrowness of his soul. He was past interest in his fellow men. He lived with a dream. The only living creature he loved was a lop-eared, lazy burro, growing old in contentment. Nevertheless that night Tappan shared one of his two blankets.

In the morning the gray dawn broke, and the sun rose without its brightness of gold. There was a haze over the blue sky. Thin, swift-moving clouds scudded up out of the southwest. The wind was chill, the forest shaggy and dark, the birds and squirrels were silent.

"Wal, you'll break camp to-day," asserted Blade.

"Nope. I'll stick it out yet a while," returned Tappan.

"But, man, you might get snowed in, an' up hyar thet's serious."

"Ahuh! Well, it won't bother me. An' there's nothin' holdin' you."

"Tappan, it's four days' walk down out of this woods. If a big snow set in, how'd I make it?"

"Then you'd better go out over the Rim," suggested Tappan.

"No. I'll take my chance the other way. But are you meanin' you'd rather not have me with you? Fer you can't stay hyar."

Tappan was in a quandary. Some instinct bade him tell the man to go. Not empty-handed, but to go. But this was selfish, and entirely unlike Tappan as he remembered himself of old. Finally he spoke: "You're welcome to half my outfit—go or stay."

"Thet's mighty square of you, Tappan," responded the other, feelingly. "Have you a burro you'll give me?"

"No, I've only one."

"Ha! Then I'll have to stick with you till you leave."

No more was said. They had breakfast in a strange silence. The wind brooded its secret in the tree tops. Tappan's burro strolled into camp, and caught the stranger's eye. "Wal, thet's shore a fine burro," he observed. "Never saw the like."

Tappan performed his camp tasks. And then there was nothing to do but sit around the fire. Blade evidently waited for the increasing menace of storm to rouse Tappan to decision. But the graying over of sky and the increase of wind did not affect Tappan. What did he wait for? The truth of his thoughts was that he did not like the way Jenet remained in camp. She was waiting to be packed. She knew they ought to go. Tappan yielded to a perverse devil of stubbornness. The wind brought a cold mist, then a flurry of wet snow. Tappan gathered firewood, a large quantity. Blade saw this and gave voice to earnest fears. But Tappan paid no heed. By nightfall sleet and snow began to fall steadily. The men fashioned a rude shack of spruce boughs, ate their supper, and went to bed early.

It worried Tappan that Jenet stayed right in camp. He lay awake a long time. The wind rose, and moaned through the forest. The sleet failed, and a soft, steady downfall of snow gradually set in. Tappan fell asleep. When he awoke it was to see a forest of white. The trees were mantled with blankets of wet snow, the ground covered two feet on a level. But the clouds appeared to be gone, the sky was blue, the storm over. The sun came up warm and bright.

"It'll all go in a day," said Tappan.

"If this was early October I'd agree with you," replied Blade. "But it's only makin' fer another storm. Can't you hear thet wind?"

Tappan only heard the whispers of his dreams. By now the snow was melting off the pines, and rainbows shone everywhere. Little patches of snow began to drop off the south branches of the pines and spruces, and then larger patches, until by mid-afternoon white streams and avalanches were falling everywhere. All of the snow, except in shaded places on the north sides of trees, went that day, and half of that on the ground. Next day it thinned out more, until Jenet was finding the grass and moss again. That afternoon the telltale thin clouds raced up out of the southwest and the wind moaned its menace.

"Tappan, let's pack an' hit it out of hyar," appealed Blade, anxiously. "I know this country. Mebbe I'm wrong, of course, but it feels like storm. Winter's comin' shore."

"Let her come," replied Tappan imperturbably.

"Say, do you want to get snowed in?" demanded Blade, out of patience.

"I might like a little spell of it, seein' it'd be new to me," replied Tappan.

"But man, if you ever get snowed in hyar you can't get out."

"That burro of mine could get me out."

"You're crazy. Thet burro couldn't go a hundred feet. What's more, you'd have to kill her an' eat her."

Tappan bent a strange gaze upon his companion, but made no reply. Blade began to pace up and down the small bare patch of ground before the camp fire. Manifestly, he was in a serious predicament. That day he seemed subtly to change, as did Tappan. Both answered to their peculiar instincts, Blade to that of self-preservation, and Tappan, to something like indifference. Tappan held fate in defiance. What more could happen to him?

Blade broke out again, in eloquent persuasion, giving proof of their peril, and from that he passed to amaze and then to strident anger. He cursed Tappan for a nature-loving idiot.

"An' I'll tell you what," he ended. "When mornin' comes I'll take some of your grub an' hit it out of hyar, storm or no storm."

But long before dawn broke that resolution of Blade's had become impracticable. Both men were awakened by a roar of storm through the forest, no longer a moan, but a marching roar, with now a crash and then a shriek of gale! By the light of the smoldering camp fire Tappan saw a whirling pall of snow, great flakes as large as feathers. Morning disclosed the setting in of a fierce mountain storm, with two feet of snow already on the ground, and the forest lost in a blur of white.

"I was wrong," called Tappan to his companion. "What's best to do now?"

"You damned fool!" yelled Blade. "We've got to keep from freezin' an' starvin' till the storm ends an' a crust comes on the snow."

For three days and three nights the blizzard continued, unabated in its fury. It took the men hours to keep a space cleared for their camp site, which Jenet shared with them. On the fourth day the storm ceased, the clouds broke away, the sun came out. And the temperature dropped to zero. Snow on the level just topped Tappan's lofty stature, and in drifts it was ten and fifteen feet deep. Winter had set in without compromise. The forest became a solemn, still, white world. But now Tappan had no time to dream. Dry firewood was hard to find under the snow. It was possible to cut down one of the dead trees on the slope, but impossible to pack sufficient wood to the camp. They had to burn green wood. Then the fashioning of snowshoes took much time. Tappan had no knowledge of such footgear. He could only help Blade. The men were encouraged by the piercing cold forming a crust on the snow. But just as they were about to pack and venture forth, the weather moderated, the crust refused to hold their weight, and another foot of snow fell.

"Why in hell didn't you kill an elk?" demanded Blade, sullenly. He had become darkly sinister. He knew the peril and he loved life. "Now we'll have to kill an' eat your precious Jenet. An' mebbe she won't furnish meat enough to last till this snow weather stops an' a good freeze'll make travelin' possible."

"Blade, you shut up about killin' an' eatin' my burro Jenet," returned Tappan, in a voice that silenced the other.

Thus instinctively these men became enemies. Blade thought only of himself. Tappan had forced upon him a menace to the life of his burro. For himself Tappan had not one thought.

Tappan's supplies ran low. All the bacon and coffee were gone. There was only a small haunch of venison, a bag of beans, a sack of flour, and a small quantity of salt left.

"If a crust freezes on the snow an' we can pack that flour, we'll get out alive," said Blade. "But we can't take the burro."

Another day of bright sunshine softened the snow on the southern exposures, and a night of piercing cold froze a crust that would bear a quick step of man.

"It's our only chance—an' damn slim at thet," declared Blade.

Tappan allowed Blade to choose the time and method, and supplies for the start to get out of the forest. They cooked all the beans and divided them in two sacks. Then they baked about five pounds of biscuits for each of them. Blade showed his cunning when he chose the small bag of salt for himself and let Tappan take the tobacco. This quantity of food and a blanket for each Blade declared to be all they could pack. They argued over the guns, and in the end Blade compromised on the rifle, agreeing to let Tappan carry that on a possible chance of killing a deer or elk. When this matter had been decided, Blade significantly began putting on his rude snowshoes, that had been constructed from pieces of Tappan's boxes and straps and burlap sacks.

"Reckon they won't last long," muttered Blade.

Meanwhile Tappan fed Jenet some biscuits and then began to strap a tarpaulin on her back.

"What you doin'?" queried Blade, suddenly.

"Gettin' Jenet ready," replied Tappan.

"Ready! For what?"

"Why, to go with us."

"Hell!" shouted Blade, and he threw up his hands in helpless rage.

Tappan felt a depth stirred within him. He lost his late taciturnity and silent aloofness fell away from him. Blade seemed on the moment no longer an enemy. He loomed as an aid to the saving of Jenet. Tappan burst into speech.

"I can't go without her. It'd never enter my head. Jenet's mother was a good faithful burro. I saw Jenet born way down there on the Rio Colorado. She wasn't strong. An' I had to wait for her to be able to walk. An' she grew up. Her mother died, an' Jenet an' me packed it alone. She wasn't no ordinary burro. She learned all I taught her. She was different. But I treated her same as any burro. An' she grew with the years. Desert men said there never was such a burro as Jenet. Called her Tappan's burro, an' tried to borrow an' buy an' steal her. . . . How many times in ten years Jenet has done me a good turn I can't remember. But she saved my life. She dragged me out of Death Valley. . . . An' then I forgot my debt. I ran off with a woman an' left Jenet to wait as she had been trained to wait. . . . Well, I got back in time. . . . An' now I'll not leave her here. It may be strange to you, Blade, me carin' this way. Jenet's only a burro. But I won't leave her."

"Man, you talk like that lazy lop-eared burro was a woman," declared Blade, in disgusted astonishment.

"I don't know women, but I reckon Jenet's more faithful than most of them."

"Wal, of all the stark, starin' fools I ever run into you're the worst."

"Fool or not, I know what I'll do," retorted Tappan. The softer mood left him swiftly.

"Haven't you sense enough to see thet we can't travel with your burro?" queried Blade, patiently controlling his temper. "She has little hoofs, sharp as knives. She'll cut through the crust. She'll break through in places. An' we'll have to stop to haul her out—mebbe break through ourselves. Thet would make us longer gettin' out."

"Long or short we'll take her."

Then Blade confronted Tappan as if suddenly unmasking his true meaning. His patient explanation meant nothing. Under no circumstances would he ever have consented to an attempt to take Jenet out of that snow-bound wilderness. His eyes gleamed.

"We've a hard pull to get out alive. An' hard-workin' men in winter must have meat to eat."

Tappan slowly straightened up to look at the speaker.

"What do you mean?"

For answer Blade jerked his hand backward and downward, and when it swung into sight again it held Tappan's worn and shining rifle. Then Blade, with deliberate force, that showed the nature of the man, worked the lever and threw a shell into the magazine. All the while his eyes were fastened on Tappan. His face seemed that of another man, evil, relentless, inevitable in his spirit to preserve his own life at any cost.

"I mean to kill your burro," he said, in a voice that suited his look and manner.

"No!" cried Tappan, shocked into an instant of appeal.

"Yes, I am, an' I'll bet, by God, before we get out of hyar you'll be glad to eat some of her meat!"

That roused the slow-gathering might of Tappan's wrath.

"I'd starve to death before I'd—I'd kill that burro, let alone eat her."

"Starve an' be damned!" shouted Blade, yielding to rage.

Jenet stood right behind Tappan, in her posture of contented repose, with one long ear hanging down over her gray meek face.

"You'll have to kill me first," answered Tappan, sharply.

"I'm good fer anythin'—if you push me," returned Blade, stridently.

As he stepped aside, evidently so he could have unobstructed aim at Jenet, Tappan leaped forward and knocked up the rifle as it was discharged. The bullet sped harmlessly over Jenet. Tappan heard it thud into a tree. Blade uttered a curse. And as he lowered the rifle in sudden deadly intent, Tappan grasped the barrel with his left hand. Then, clenching his right, he struck Blade a sudden blow in the face. Only Blade's hold on the rifle prevented him from falling. Blood streamed from his nose and mouth. He bellowed in hoarse fury,

"I'll kill you—fer thet!"

Tappan opened his clenched teeth: "No, Blade—you're not man enough."

Then began a terrific struggle for possession of the rifle. Tappan beat at Blade's face with his sledge-hammer fist. But the strength of the other made it imperative that he use both hands to keep his hold on the rifle. Wrestling and pulling and jerking, the men tore round the snowy camp, scattering the camp fire, knocking down the brush shelter. Blade had surrendered to a wild frenzy. He hissed his maledictions. His was the brute lust to kill an enemy that thwarted him. But Tappan was grim and terrible in his restraint. His battle was to save Jenet. Nevertheless, there mounted in him the hot physical sensations of the savage. The contact of flesh, the smell and sight of Blade's blood, the violent action, the beastly mien of his foe changed the fight to one for its own sake. To conquer this foe, to rend him and beat him down, blow on blow!

Tappan felt instinctively that he was the stronger. Suddenly he exerted all his muscular force into one tremendous wrench. The rifle broke, leaving the steel barrel in his hands, the wooden stock in Blade's. And it was the quicker-witted Blade who used his weapon first to advantage. One swift blow knocked Tappan down. As he was about to follow it up with another, Tappan kicked his opponent's feet from under him. Blade sprawled in the snow, but was up again as quickly as Tappan. They made at each other, Tappan waiting to strike, and Blade raining blows on Tappan. These were heavy blows aimed at his head, but which he contrived to receive on his arms and the rifle barrel he brandished. For a few moments Tappan stood up under a beating that would have felled a lesser man. His own blood blinded him. Then he swung his heavy weapon. The blow broke Blade's left arm. Like a wild beast, he screamed in pain; and then, without guard, rushed in, too furious for further caution. Tappan met the terrible onslaught as before, and watching his chance, again swung the rifle barrel. This time, so supreme was the force, it battered down Blade's arm and crushed his skull. He died on his feet—ghastly and horrible change!—and swaying backward, he fell into the upbanked wall of snow, and went out of sight, except for his boots, one of which still held the crude snowshoe.

Tappan stared, slowly realizing.

"Ahuh, stranger Blade!" he ejaculated, gazing at the hole in the snow bank where his foe had disappeared. "You were goin' to—kill an' eat—Tappan's burro!"

Then he sighted the bloody rifle barrel, and cast it from him. He became conscious of injuries which needed attention. But he could do little more than wash off the blood and bind up his head. Both arms and hands were badly bruised, and beginning to swell. But fortunately no bones had been broken.

Tappan finished strapping the tarpaulin upon the burro; and, taking up both his and Blade's supply of food, he called out, "Come on, Jenet."

Which way to go! Indeed, there was no more choice for him than there had been for Blade. Toward the Rim the snowdrift would be deeper and impassable. Tappan realized that the only possible chance for him was down hill. So he led Jenet out of camp without looking back once. What was it that had happened? He did not seem to be the same Tappan that had dreamily tramped into this woodland.

A deep furrow in the snow had been made by the men packing firewood into camp. At the end of this furrow the wall of snow stood higher than Tappan's head. To get out on top without breaking the crust presented a problem. He lifted Jenet up, and was relieved to see that the snow held her. But he found a different task in his own case. Returning to camp, he gathered up several of the long branches of spruce that had been part of the shelter, and carrying them out he laid them against the slant of snow he had to surmount, and by their aid he got on top. The crust held him.

Elated and with revived hope, he took up Jenet's halter and started off. Walking with his rude snowshoes was awkward. He had to go slowly, and slide them along the crust. But he progressed. Jenet's little steps kept her even with him. Now and then one of her sharp hoofs cut through, but not to hinder her particularly. Right at the start Tappan observed a singular something about Jenet. Never until now had she been dependent upon him. She knew it. Her intelligence apparently told her that if she got out of this snow-bound wilderness it would be owing to the strength and reason of her master.

Tappan kept to the north side of the canyon, where the snow crust was strongest. What he must do was to work up to the top of the canyon slope, and then keeping to the ridge travel north along it, and so down out of the forest.

Travel was slow. He soon found he had to pick his way. Jenet appeared to be absolutely unable to sense either danger or safety. Her experience had been of the rock confines and the drifting sands of the desert. She walked where Tappan led her. And it seemed to Tappan that her trust in him, her reliance upon him, were pathetic. "Well, old girl," said Tappan to her, "it's a horse of another color now—hey?"

At length he came to a wide part of the canyon, where a bench of land led to a long gradual slope, thickly studded with small pines.

This appeared to be fortunate, and turned out to be so, for when Jenet broke through the crust Tappan had trees and branches to hold to while he hauled her out. The labor of climbing that slope was such that Tappan began to appreciate Blade's absolute refusal to attempt getting Jenet out. Dusk was shadowing the white aisles of the forest when Tappan ascended to a level. He had not traveled far from camp, and the fact struck a chill upon his heart.

To go on in the dark was foolhardy. So Tappan selected a thick spruce, under which there was a considerable depression in the snow, and here made preparation to spend the night. Unstrapping the tarpaulin, he spread it on the snow. All the lower branches of this giant of the forest were dead and dry. Tappan broke off many and soon had a fire. Jenet nibbled at the moss on the trunk of the spruce tree. Tappan's meal consisted of beans, biscuits, and a ball of snow, that he held over the fire to soften. He saw to it that Jenet fared as well as he. Night soon fell, strange and weirdly white in the forest, and piercingly cold. Tappan needed the fire. Gradually it melted the snow and made a hole, down to the ground. Tappan rolled up in the tarpaulin and soon fell asleep.

In three days Tappan traveled about fifteen miles, gradually descending, until the snow crust began to fail to hold Jenet. Then whatever had been his difficulties before, they were now magnified a hundredfold. As soon as the sun was up, somewhat softening the snow, Jenet began to break through. And often when Tappan began hauling her out he broke through himself. This exertion was killing even to a man of Tappan's physical prowess. The endurance to resist heat and flying dust and dragging sand seemed another kind from that needed to toil on in this snow. The endless snow-bound forest began to be hideous to Tappan. Cold, lonely, dreary, white, mournful—the kind of ghastly and ghostly winter land that had been the terror of Tappan's boyish dreams! He loved the sun—the open. This forest had deceived him. It was a wall of ice. As he toiled on, the state of his mind gradually and subtly changed in all except the fixed and absolute will to save Jenet. In some places he carried her.

The fourth night found him dangerously near the end of his stock of food. He had been generous with Jenet. But now, considering that he had to do more work than she, he diminished her share. On the fifth day Jenet broke through the snow crust so often that Tappan realized how utterly impossible it was for her to get out of the woods by her own efforts. Therefore Tappan hit upon the plan of making her lie on the tarpaulin, so that he could drag her. The tarpaulin doubled once did not make a bad sled. All the rest of that day Tappan hauled her. And so all the rest of the next day he toiled on, hands behind him, clutching the canvas, head and shoulders bent, plodding and methodical, like a man who could not be defeated. That night he was too weary to build a fire, and too worried to eat the last of his food.

Next day Tappan was not unalive to the changing character of the forest. He had worked down out of the zone of the spruce trees; the pines had thinned out and decreased in size; oak trees began to show prominently. All these signs meant that he was getting down out of the mountain heights. But the fact, hopeful as it was, had drawbacks. The snow was still four feet deep on a level and the crust held Tappan only about half the time. Moreover, the lay of the land operated against Tappan's progress. The long, slowly descending ridge had failed. There were no more canyons, but ravines and swales were numerous. Tappan dragged on, stern, indomitable, bent to his toil. When the crust let him down, he hung his snowshoes over Jenet's back, and wallowed through, making a lane for her to follow. Two days of such heartbreaking toil, without food or fire, broke Tappan's magnificent endurance. But not his spirit! He hauled Jenet over the snow, and through the snow, down the hills and up the slopes, through the thickets, knowing that over the next ridge, perhaps was deliverance. Deer and elk tracks began to be numerous. Cedar and juniper trees now predominated. An occasional pine showed here and there. He was getting out of the forest land. Only such mighty and justifiable hope as that could have kept him on his feet.

He fell often, and it grew harder to rise and go on. The hour came when the crust failed altogether to hold Tappan and he had to abandon hauling Jenet. It was necessary to make a road for her. How weary, cold, horrible, the white reaches! Yard by yard Tappan made his way. He no longer sweat. He had no feeling in his feet or legs. Hunger ceased to gnaw at his vitals. His thirst he quenched with snow—soft snow now, that did not have to be crunched like ice. The pangs in his breast were terrible—cramps, constrictions, the piercing pains in his lungs, the dull ache of his overtaxed heart.

Tappan came to an opening in the cedar forest from which he could see afar. A long slope fronted him. It led down and down to open country. His desert eyes, keen as those of an eagle, made out flat country, sparsely covered with snow, and black dots that were cattle. The last slope! The last pull! Three feet of snow, except in drifts; down and down he plunged, making way for Jenet! All that day he toiled and fell and rolled down this league-long slope, wearing toward sunset to the end of his task, and likewise to the end of his will.

Now he seemed up and now down. There was no sense of cold or weariness. Only direction! Tappan still saw! The last of his horror at the monotony of white faded from his mind. Jenet was there, beginning to be able to travel for herself. The solemn close of endless day found Tappan arriving at the edge of the timbered country, where wind-bared patches of ground showed long, bleached grass. Jenet took to grazing.

As for Tappan, he fell with the tarpaulin, under a thick cedar, and with strengthless hands plucked and plucked at the canvas to spread it, so that he could cover himself. He looked again for Jenet. She was there, somehow a fading image, strangely blurred. But she was grazing. Tappan lay down, and stretched out, and slowly drew the tarpaulin over him.

A piercing cold night wind swept down from the snowy heights. It wailed in the edge of the cedars and moaned out toward the open country. Yet the night seemed silent. The stars shone white in a deep blue sky—passionless, cold, watchful eyes, looking down without pity or hope or censure. They were the eyes of Nature. Winter had locked the heights in its snowy grip. All night that winter wind blew down, colder and colder. Then dawn broke, steely, gray, with a flare in the east.

Jenet came back where she had left her master. Camp! As she had returned thousands of dawns in the long years of her service. She had grazed all night. Her sides that had been flat were now full. Jenet had weathered another vicissitude of her life. She stood for a while, in a doze, with one long ear down over her meek face. Jenet was waiting for Tappan.

But he did not stir from under the long roll of canvas. Jenet waited. The winter sun rose, in cold yellow flare. The snow glistened as with a crusting of diamonds. Somewhere in the distance sounded a long-drawn, discordant bray. Jenet's ears shot up. She listened. She recognized the call of one of her kind. Instinct always prompted Jenet. Sometimes she did bray. Lifting her gray head she sent forth a clarion: *"Hee-haw hee-haw-haw—hee-haw how-e-e-e!"*

That stentorian call started the echoes. They pealed down the slope and rolled out over the open country, clear as a bugle blast, yet hideous in their discordance. But this morning Tappan did not awaken.


### I Saw in Louisiana a Live-Oak Growing

I SAW in Louisiana a live-oak growing,
   All alone stood it, and the moss hung down from the branches;
Without any companion it grew there, uttering joyous leaves of dark
      green,
And its look, rude, unbending, lusty, made me think of myself;
But I wonder'd how it could utter joyous leaves, standing alone there,
      without its friend, its lover near—for I knew I could not;
And I broke off a twig with a certain number of leaves upon it, and
      twined around it a little moss,
And brought it away—and I have placed it in sight in my room;
It is not needed to remind me as of my own dear friends,
(For I believe lately I think of little else than of them:)
Yet it remains to me a curious token—it makes me think of manly love;
For all that, and though the live-oak glistens there in Louisiana,
      solitary, in a wide flat space,
Uttering joyous leaves all its life, without a friend, a lover, near,
I know very well I could not.

                                                        *Walt Whitman*

# A FURIOUS HIPPOPOTAMUS

## Sir Samuel W. Baker

*Restless, energetic Samuel Baker (1821–1893) covered half the world in his explorations and travels. In Ceylon, he founded a successful agricultural settlement, and hunted; in the Balkans, he supervised the construction of a railroad; in Africa, he discovered much about the sources of the Nile. Baker related his adventures in books of great popularity, was knighted, and commanded a military expedition to suppress the slave trade in the region of the upper Nile. His book about this trip,* Ismaila, *is filled with exciting accounts such as this one of his encounter with a raging hippopotamus.*

M Y DIAHBEEAH was in the lake waiting for the fleet to accomplish the passage. I had made an excursion one day in the dingy to examine the south end of the lake, which I found to be about eight miles in length. On returning, I was rather anxious for the small boat, as a bull hippopotamus made a hostile demonstration. The water was not more than five feet six inches deep; thus as the hippo, after having snorted and sunk, continued to approach the boat, I could distinguish the path of his advance by the slight wave raised upon the surface. He presently raised his head about twenty yards from the boat; but at the same time he received a Reilly explosive shell under the eye, which ended his worldly cares.

There were many hippopotami in this lake, and very shortly after I had killed the first I shot a second much after the same manner. I always carried a harpoon in the boat, with the rope and ambatch float. The latter was painted red, so that it could be easily observed. I therefore stuck the harpoon in the dead hippopotamus as a mark, and I hastened back to my diahbeeah for assistance, as the flesh of two hippopotami would be very welcome to the people, who had not received rations of butcher's meat for many weeks. On arrival at the diahbeeah we quickly made sail, and soon returned to the hippopotamus. By the time we had cut up this large animal and secured the flesh the sun was so low that I considered it would be better to secure the other hippo by a rope attached to the hind-legs, and tow it bodily astern of the diahbeeah. It could then be divided on the following day.

In this manner we returned to our anchorage at the tail of the lake, close to the entrance of the new channel. By the time we arrived the moon was up. The diahbeeah was close to a mud-bank covered with high grass, and about thirty yards astern of her was a shallow part of the lake about three feet deep. A light boat of zinc was full of strips of hippopotamus's flesh, and the dingy was fastened alongside.

After dinner and a pipe the usual arrangements were made for the night. There were many servants, male and female, on board; these began to suspend their mosquito-curtains to the rigging and to creep beneath; the sailors, after chatting for a considerable time, dropped off to sleep, until the sentry was the only man on board who was on the alert. I always slept on the poop-deck, which was comfortably arranged with sofas and carpets.

The night was cold, and the moon clear and bright; every one was wrapped up in warm blankets; and I was so sound asleep that I cannot describe more until I was suddenly awoke by a tremendous splashing quite close to the diahbeeah, accompanied by the hoarse, wild snorting of a furious hippopotamus. I jumped up, and immediately perceived a hippo, which was apparently about to attack the vessel. The main-deck being crowded with people sleeping beneath their thick mosquito-curtains, attached to the stairs of the poop-deck and to the rigging in all directions, rendered it impossible to descend. I at once tore away some of the ties, and awakened the sleepy people. My servant, Suleiman, was sleeping next to the cabin door. I called to him for a rifle. Before the affrighted Suleiman could bring the rifle the hippopotamus dashed at us with indescribable fury. With one blow he capsized and sank the zinc boat with its cargo of flesh. In another instant he seized the dingy in his immense jaws, and the crash of splintered wood betokened the complete destruction of my favorite boat. By this time Suleiman appeared from the cabin with an unloaded gun in his hand, and without ammunition. This was a very good man, but he was never overburdened with presence of mind; he was shaking so fearfully with nervousness that his senses had entirely abandoned him. All the people were shouting and endeavoring to scare the hippo, which attacked us without ceasing with a blind fury that I have never witnessed in any animal except a bull-dog.

By this time I had procured a rifle from the cabin, where they were always kept fixed in a row, loaded, and ready for action, with bags of breech-loading ammunition on the same shelf.

The movements of the animal were so rapid, as he charged and plunged alternately beneath the water in a cloud of foam and wave, that it was impossible to aim correctly at the small but fatal spot upon the head.

The moon was extremely bright, and presently, as he charged straight at the diahbeeah, I stopped him with a No. 8 Reilly shell. To my surprise he soon recovered, and again commenced the attack. I fired shot after shot at him without apparent effect. The diahbeeah rocked about upon the waves raised by the efforts of so large an animal; this movement rendered the aim uncertain. At length, apparently badly wounded, he retired to the high grass; there he lay by the bank, at about twenty-five yards' distance, snorting and blowing.

I could not distinguish him, as merely the head was above water, and this was concealed by the deep shadow thrown by the high grass. Thinking that he would die, I went to bed; but before this I took the precaution to arrange a white-paper sight upon the muzzle of my rifle, without which night-shooting is very uncertain.

We had fallen asleep; but in about half an hour we were awakened by another tremendous splash, and once more this mad beast came charging directly at us as though unhurt. In another instant he was at the diahbeeah; but I met him with a ball in the top of his head which sent him rolling over and over, sometimes on his back, kicking with his four legs above the surface, and again producing waves which rocked the diahbeeah. In this helpless manner he rolled for about fifty yards down the stream, and we all thought him killed.

To our amazement, he recovered, and we heard him splashing as he moved slowly along the river through the high grass by the left bank. There he remained, snorting and blowing; and as the light of the moon was of no service in the dark shadows of the high grass, we waited for a considerable time, and then went to bed, with the rifle placed in readiness on deck.

In a short time I heard louder splashing. I again got up, and I perceived him about eighty yards distant, walking slowly across the river in the shallows. Having a fair shot at the shoulder, I fired right and left with the No. 8 Reilly rifle, and I distinctly heard the bullets strike. He, nevertheless, reached the right bank, when he presently turned round and attempted to recross the shallow. This gave me a good chance at the shoulder, as his body was entirely exposed. This time he staggered forward at the shot, and fell dead in the shallow flat of the river.

He was now past recovery. It was very cold; the thermometer was 54° Fahrenheit, and the blankets were very agreeable, as once more all hands turned in to sleep.

On the following morning I made a *post-mortem* examination. He had received three shots in the flank and shoulder; four in the head, one of which had broken his lower jaw; another had passed through his nose, and, passing downward, had cut off one of his large tusks. I never witnessed such determined and unprovoked fury as was exhibited by this animal; he appeared to be raving mad. His body was a mass of frightful scars, the result of continual conflicts with bulls of his own species; some of these wounds were still unhealed. There was one scar about two feet in length, and about two inches below the level of the surface-skin, upon the flank. He was evidently a character of the worst description, but whose madness rendered him callous to all punishment. I can only suppose that the attack upon the vessels was induced by the smell of the raw hippopotamus flesh, which was hung in long strips about the rigging, and with which the zinc boat was filled. The dead hippopotamus that was floating astern, lashed to the diahbeeah, had not been molested.

# THE SHEEP-SHEARERS

## Thomas Hardy

*The author of* Jude the Obscure *and* The Return of the
Native, *Thomas Hardy* (1840–1928) *combines in his novels
studies of nature with studies of men and women. His word
pictures of the English countryside in every mood, at every
hour, are among the most beautiful and effective ever painted.
Always human beings stand in the foreground, as the Wessex
shepherds in this scene from* Far From the Madding Crowd.

IT WAS the first day of June, and the sheep-shearing season cul-
minated, the landscape, even to the leanest pasture, being all
health and colour. Every green was young, every pore was open,
and every stalk was swollen with racing currents of juice. God was
palpably present in the country, and the devil had gone with the
world to town. Flossy catkins of the later kind, fern-sprouts like
bishops' crooks, the square-headed moschatel, the odd cuckoo-
pint,—like an apoplectic saint in a niche of malachite,—clear white
ladies'-smocks, the tooth-wort, approximating to human flesh, the
enchanter's nightshade, and the black-petalled doleful-bells, were
among the quainter objects of the vegetable world in and about
Weatherbury at this teeming time; and of the animal, the meta-
morphosed figures of Mr. Jan Coggan, the master-shearer; the second and third shearers, who travelled in the exercise of their calling,
and do not require definition by name; Henery Fray the fourth
shearer, Susan Tall's husband the fifth, Joseph Poorgrass the sixth,
young Cain Ball as assistant-shearer, and Gabriel Oak as general
supervisor. None of these were clothed to any extent worth mentioning, each appearing to have hit in the matter of raiment the
decent mean between a high and low caste Hindoo. An angularity
of lineament, and a fixity of facial machinery in general, proclaimed that serious work was the order of the day.

They sheared in the great barn, called for the nonce the Shearing-barn, which on ground-plan resembled a church with transepts. It not only emulated the form of the neighbouring church of the parish, but vied with it in antiquity. Whether the barn had ever formed one of a group of conventual buildings, nobody seemed to be aware; no trace of such surroundings remained. The vast porches at the sides, lofty enough to admit a waggon laden to its highest with corn in the sheaf, were spanned by heavy-pointed arches of stone, broadly and boldly cut, whose very simplicity was the origin of a grandeur not apparent in erections where more ornament has been attempted. The dusky, filmed, chestnut roof, braced and tied in by huge collars, curves, and diagonals, was far nobler in design, because more wealthy in material, than nine-tenths of those in our modern churches. Along each side wall was a range of striding buttresses, throwing deep shadows on the spaces between them, which were perforated by lancet openings, combining in their proportions the precise requirements both of beauty and ventilation.

One could say about this barn, what could hardly be said of either the church or the castle, akin to it in age and style, that the purpose which had dictated its original erection was the same with that to which it was still applied. Unlike and superior to either of those two typical remnants of mediævalism, the old barn embodied practices which had suffered no mutilation at the hands of time. Here at least the spirit of the ancient builders was at one with the spirit of the modern beholder. Standing before this abraded pile, the eye regarded its present usage, the mind dwelt upon its past history, with a satisfied sense of functional continuity throughout—a feeling almost of gratitude, and quite of pride, at the permanence of the idea which had heaped it up. The fact that four centuries had neither proved it to be founded on a mistake, inspired any hatred of its purpose, nor given rise to any reaction that had battered it down, invested this simple grey effort of old minds with a repose, if not a grandeur, which a too curious reflection was apt to disturb in its ecclesiastical and military compeers. For once mediævalism and modernism had a common standpoint. The lanceolate windows, the time-eaten arch-stones and chamfers, the orientation of the axis, the misty chestnut work of the rafters, referred to no exploded fortifying art or worn-out religious creed. The defence and salvation of the body by daily bread is still a study, a religion, a desire.

To-day the large side doors were thrown open towards the sun to admit a bountiful light to the immediate spot of the shearers' operations, which was the wood threshing-floor in the centre, formed of thick oak, black with age and polished by the beating of flails for many generations, till it had grown as slippery and as rich in hue as the state-room floors of an Elizabethan mansion. Here the shearers knelt, the sun slanting in upon their bleached shirts, tanned arms, and the polished shears they flourished, causing them to bristle with a thousand rays strong enough to blind a weak-eyed man. Beneath them a captive sheep lay panting, quickening its pants as misgiving merged in terror, till it quivered like the hot landscape outside.

This picture of to-day with its frame of four hundred years ago did not produce that marked contrast between ancient and modern which is implied by the contrast of date. In comparison with cities Weatherbury was immutable. The citizen's *Then* is the rustic's *Now*. In London, twenty or thirty years ago are old times; in Paris ten years, or five; in Weatherbury three or four score years were included in the mere present, and nothing less than a century set a mark on its face or tone. Five decades hardly modified the cut of a gaiter, the embroidery of a smock-frock, by the breadth of a hair. Ten generations failed to alter the turn of a single phrase. In these Wessex nooks the busy out-sider's ancient times are only old; his old times are still new; his present is futurity.

So the barn was natural to the shearers, and the shearers were in harmony with the barn.

The spacious ends of the building, answering ecclesiastically to nave and chancel extremities, were fenced off with hurdles, the sheep being all collected in a crowd within these two enclosures; and in one angle a catching-pen was formed, in which three or four sheep were continuously kept ready for the shearers to seize without loss of time. In the background, mellowed by tawny shade, were the three women, Maryann Money, and Temperance and Soberness Miller, gathering up the fleeces and twisting ropes of wool with a wimble for tying them round. They were indifferently well assisted by the old maltster, who, when the malting season from October to April had passed, made himself useful upon any of the bordering farmsteads.

Behind all was Bathsheba, carefully watching the men to see that there was no cutting or wounding through carelessness, and that the animals were shorn close. Gabriel, who flitted and hovered under her bright eyes like a moth, did not shear continuously, half his time being spent in attending to the others and selecting the sheep for them. At the present moment he was engaged in handing round a mug of mild liquor, supplied from a barrel in the corner, and cut pieces of bread and cheese.

Bathsheba, after throwing a glance here, a caution there, and lecturing one of the younger operators who had allowed his last finished sheep to go off among the flock without re-stamping it with her initials, came again to Gabriel, as he put down the luncheon to drag a frightened ewe to his shear-station, flinging it over upon its back with a dexterous twist of the arm. He lopped off the tresses about its head, and opened up the neck and collar, his mistress quietly looking on.

"She blushes at the insult," murmured Bathsheba, watching the pink flush which arose and overspread the neck and shoulders of the ewe where they were left bare by the clicking shears—a flush which was enviable, for its delicacy, by many queens of coteries, and would have been creditable for its promptness, to any woman in the world.

Poor Gabriel's soul was fed with a luxury of content by having her over him, her eyes critically regarding his skilful shears, which apparently were going to gather up a piece of flesh at every close, and yet never did so. Like Guildenstern, Oak was happy in that he was not over happy. He had no wish to converse with her: that his bright lady and himself formed one group, exclusively their own, and containing no others in the world, was enough.

So the chatter was all on her side. There is a loquacity that tells nothing, which was Bathsheba's; and there is a silence which says much: that was Gabriel's. Full of this dim and temperate bliss, he went on to fling the ewe over upon her other side, covering her head with his knee, gradually running the shears line after line round the dewlap, thence about her flank and back, and finishing over the tail.

"Well done, and done quickly!" said Bathsheba, looking at her watch as the last snip resounded.

"How long, miss?" said Gabriel, wiping his brow.

"Three and twenty minutes and a half since you took the first lock from her forehead. It is the first time that I have ever seen one done in less than half-an-hour."

The clean, sleek creature arose from its fleece—how perfectly like Aphrodite rising from the foam should have been seen to be realized—looking startled and shy at the loss of its garment, which lay on the floor in one soft cloud, united throughout, the portion visible being the inner surface only, which, never before exposed, was white as snow, and without flaw or blemish of the minutest kind.

"Cain Ball!"

"Yes, Mister Oak; here I be!"

Cainy now runs forward with the tar-pot. "Be. E." is newly stamped upon the shorn skin, and away the simple dam leaps, panting, over the board into the shirtless flock outside. Then up comes Maryann; throws the loose locks into the middle of the fleece, rolls it up, and carries it into the background as three-and-a-half pounds of unadulterated warmth for the winter enjoyment of persons unknown and far away, who will, however, never experience the superlative comfort derivable from the wool as it here exists, new and pure—before the unctuousness of its nature whilst in a living state has dried, stiffened, and been washed out—rendering it just now as superior to anything *woollen* as cream is superior to milk-and-water.

For the shearing-supper a long table was placed on the grass-plot beside the house, the end of the table being thrust over the sill of the wide parlour window and a foot or two into the room. Miss Everdene sat inside the window, facing down the table. She was thus at the head without mingling with the men.

This evening Bathsheba was unusually excited, her red cheeks and lips contrasting lustrously with the mazy skeins of her shadowy hair. She seemed to expect assistance, and the seat at the bottom of the table was at her request left vacant until after they had begun the meal. She then asked Gabriel to take the place and the duties appertaining to that end, which he did with great readiness.

At this moment Mr. Boldwood came in at the gate, and crossed the green to Bathsheba at the window. He apologized for his lateness: his arrival was evidently by arrangement.

"Gabriel," said she, "will you move again, please, and let Mr. Boldwood come there?"

Oak moved in silence back to his original seat.

The gentleman-farmer was dressed in cheerful style, in a new coat and white waistcoat, quite contrasting with his usual sober suits of grey. Inwardly, too, he was blithe, and consequently chatty to an exceptional degree. So also was Bathsheba now that he had come, though the uninvited presence of Pennyways, the bailiff who had been dismissed for theft, disturbed her equanimity for a while.

Supper being ended, Coggan began on his own private account, without reference to listeners:—

> "I've lost my love, and I care not,
> I've lost my love, and I care not;
> I shall soon have another
> That's better than t'other;
> I've lost my love, and I care not."

This lyric, when concluded, was received with a silently appreciative gaze at the table, implying that the performance, like a work by those established authors who are independent of notices in the papers, was a well-known delight which required no applause.

"Now, Master Poorgrass, your song!" said Coggan.

"I be all but in liquor, and the gift is wanting in me," said Joseph, diminishing himself.

"Nonsense; wou'st never be so ungrateful, Joseph—never!" said Coggan, expressing hurt feelings by an inflection of voice. "And mistress is looking hard at ye, as much as to say, 'Sing at once, Joseph Poorgrass.'"

"Faith, so she is; well, I must suffer it! . . . Just eye my features, and see if the tell-tale blood overheats me much, neighbours?"

"No, yer blushes be quite reasonable," said Coggan.

"I always tries to keep my colours from rising when a beauty's eyes get fixed on me," said Joseph, diffidently; "but if so be 'tis willed they do, they must."

"Now, Joseph, your song, please," said Bathsheba, from the window.

"Well, really, ma'am," he replied, in a yielding tone, "I don't know what to say. It would be a poor plain ballet of my own composure."

"Hear, hear!" said the supper-party.

Poorgrass, thus assured, trilled forth a flickering yet commendable piece of sentiment, the tune of which consisted of the key-note and another, the latter being the sound chiefly dwelt upon. This was so successful that he rashly plunged into a second in the same breath, after a few false starts:—

> "I sow'-ed th'-e . . . . . . .
> I sow'-ed . . . . . . . . .
> I sow'-ed the'-e seeds' of' love',
>     I-it was' all' i'-in the'-e spring',
> I-in A'-pril', Ma'-ay, a'-nd sun'-ny' June'
>     When sma'-all bi'-irds they' do' sing."

"Well put out of hand," said Coggan, at the end of the verse. " 'They do sing,' was a very taking paragraph."

"Ay; and there was a pretty place at 'seeds of love,' and 'twas well heaved out. Though 'love' is a nasty high corner when a man's voice is getting crazed. Next verse, Master Poorgrass."

But during this rendering young Bob Coggan exhibited one of those anomalies which will afflict little people when other persons are particularly serious: in trying to check his laughter, he pushed down his throat as much of the tablecloth as he could get hold of, when, after continuing hermetically sealed for a short time, his mirth burst out through his nose. Joseph perceived it, and with hectic cheeks of indignation instantly ceased singing. Coggan boxed Bob's ears immediately.

"Go on, Joseph—go on, and never mind the young scamp," said Coggan. " 'Tis a very catching ballet. Now then again—the next bar; I'll help ye to flourish up the shrill notes where yer wind is rather wheezy:—

"Oh the wi'-il-lo'-ow tree' will' twist',
And the wil'-low tre'-ee wi'-ill twine'."

But the singer could not be set going again. Bob Coggan was sent home for his ill manners, and tranquillity was restored by Jacob Smallbury, who volunteered a ballad as inclusive and inter-minable as that with which the worthy old toper Silenus amused on a similar occasion the swains Chromis and Mnasylus, and other jolly dogs of his day.

It was still the beaming time of evening, though night was stealthily making itself visible low down upon the ground, the west-ern lines of light raking the earth without alighting upon it to any extent, or illuminating the dead levels at all. The sun had crept round the tree as a last effort before death, and then began to sink, the shearers' lower parts becoming steeped in embrowning twilight, whilst thir heads and shoulders were still enjoying day, touched with a yellow of self-sustained brilliancy that seemed rather inher-ent than acquired.

The sun went down in an ochreous mist, but they sat, and talked on, and grew as merry as the gods in Homer's heaven. Bathsheba still remained enthroned inside the window, and occupied herself in knitting, from which she sometimes looked up to view the fading scene outside. The slow twilight expanded and enveloped them completely before the signs of moving were shown.

# THE KING OF FRUITS

## Alfred Russel Wallace

*Two men on opposite sides of the world developed the theory
of evolution by survival of the fittest at the same time. One
known to all the world was the British scientist Charles Darwin. The other, afterward his friend and supporter, was Alfred Russel Wallace* (1823–1913), *a young English naturalist
in the Malay Archipelago. Wallace later expanded the ideas of
Darwinism, writing many works of scientific importance,
among them* The Malay Archipelago, *in which this appreciation of a fascinating tropical fruit appears.*

THE banks of the Saráwak River are everywhere covered with
fruit-trees, which supply the Dyaks with a great deal of their
food. The mangosteen, lansat, rambutan, jack, jambou, and blimb-
ing, are all abundant; but most abundant and most esteemed is the
durion,—a fruit about which very little is known in England, but
which both by natives and Europeans in the Malay Archipelago is
reckoned superior to all others. The old traveler Linschott, writing
in 1599, says, "It is of such an excellent taste that it surpasses in
flavor all the other fruits of the world, according to those who have
tasted it." And Doctor Paludanus adds, "This fruit is of a hot and
humid nature. To those not used to it, it seems at first to smell like
rotten onions, but immediately they have tasted it they prefer it to
all other food. The natives give it honorable titles, exalt it, and make
verses on it." When brought into a house the smell is often so offensive that some persons can never bear to taste it. This was my own
case when I first tried it in Malacca; but in Borneo I found a ripe
fruit on the ground, and eating it out of doors, I at once became a
confirmed durion eater.

The durion grows on a large and lofty forest-tree, somewhat
resembling an elm in its general character, but with a more smooth
and scaly bark. The fruit is round or slightly oval, about the size of

a large cocoanut, of a green color, and covered all over with short stout spines, the bases of which touch each other, and are consequently somewhat hexagonal, while the points are very strong and sharp. It is so completely armed that if the stalk is broken off, it is a difficult matter to lift one from the ground. The outer rind is so thick and tough that from whatever height it may fall, it is never broken. From the base to the apex five very faint lines may be traced, over which the spines arch a little; these are the sutures of the carpels, and show where the fruit may be divided with a heavy knife and a strong hand. The five cells are satiny-white within, and are each filled with an oval mass of cream-colored pulp, imbedded in which are two or three seeds about the size of chestnuts. This pulp is the eatable part, and its consistence and flavor are indescribable. A rich butter-like custard highly flavored with almonds gives the best general idea of it; but intermingled with it come wafts of flavor that call to mind cream cheese, onion sauce, brown sherry, and other incongruities. Then there is a rich glutinous smoothness in the pulp, which nothing else possesses, but which adds to its delicacy. It is neither acid, nor sweet, nor juicy, yet one feels the want of none of these qualities, for it is perfect as it is. It produces no nausea or other bad effect, and the more you eat of it the less you feel inclined to stop. In fact, to eat durions is a new sensation worth a voyage to the East to experience.

When the fruit is ripe it falls of itself; and the only way to eat durions in perfection is to get them as they fall, and the smell is then less overpowering. When unripe, it makes a very good vegetable if cooked, and it is also eaten by the Dyaks raw. In a good fruit season large quantities are preserved salted, in jars and bamboos, and kept the year round; when it acquires a most disgusting odor to Europeans, but the Dyaks appreciate it highly as a relish with their rice. There are in the forest two varieties of wild durions with much smaller fruits, one of them orange-colored inside; and these are probably the origin of the large and fine durions, which are never found wild. It would not, perhaps, be correct to say that the durion is the best of all fruits, because it cannot supply the place of the sub-acid juicy kinds, such as the orange, grape, mango, and mangosteen, whose refreshing and cooling qualities are so wholesome and grateful; but as producing a food of the most exquisite flavor it is unsurpassed. If I had to fix on two only as representing the perfection of the two classes, I should certainly choose the durion and the orange as the king and queen of fruits.

The durion is however sometimes dangerous. When the fruit begins to ripen, it falls daily and almost hourly, and accidents not unfrequently happen to persons walking or working under the trees. When the durion strikes a man in its fall, it produces a dreadful wound, the strong spines tearing open the flesh, while the blow itself is very heavy; but from this very circumstance death rarely ensues, the copious effusion of blood preventing the inflammation which might otherwise take place. A Dyak chief informed me that he had been struck down by a durion falling on his head, which he thought would certainly have caused his death, yet he recovered in a very short time.

Poets and moralists, judging from our English trees and fruits, have thought that small fruits always grew on lofty trees, so that their fall should be harmless to man, while the large ones trailed on the ground. Two of the largest and heaviest fruits known, however, —the Brazil-nut fruit (Bertholletia) and durion,—grow on lofty forest-trees, from which they fall as soon as they are ripe, and often wound or kill the native inhabitants. From this we may learn two things: first, not to draw general conclusions from a very partial view of nature; and secondly, that trees and fruits, no less than the varied productions of the animal kingdom, do not appear to be organized with exclusive reference to the use and convenience of man.

### God Made the Country

God made the country, and man made the town.
What wonder then that health and virtue, gifts
That can alone make sweet the bitter draught
That life holds out to all, should most abound
And least be threatened in the fields and groves?

*William Cowper*

# LAKE TAHOE

## Mark Twain

*Samuel Langhorne Clemens (1835–1910), after serving as a printer's apprentice, a steamboat pilot on the Mississippi, and a soldier in the Civil War, set out for the Nevada Territory. There, he joined the staff of a Virginia City newspaper and began writing under the name of Mark Twain. In* Roughing It *he told the story of his first western trip, during which he visited the isolated wilderness lake now one of our most famous resorts.*

I<sup>T</sup> was the end of August, and the skies were cloudless and the weather superb. In two or three weeks I had grown wonderfully fascinated with the curious new country, and concluded to put off my return to "the States" awhile. I had grown well accustomed to wearing a damaged slouch hat, blue woolen shirt, and pants crammed into boot-tops, and gloried in the absence of coat, vest, and braces. I felt rowdyish and "bully" (as the historian Josephus phrases it, in his fine chapter upon the destruction of the Temple). It seemed to me that nothing could be so fine and so romantic. I had become an officer of the government, but that was for mere sublimity. The office was an unique sinecure. I had nothing to do and no salary. I was private secretary to his majesty the Secretary, and there was not yet writing enough for two of us. So Johnny K—— and I devoted our time to amusement. He was the young son of an Ohio nabob and was out there for recreation. He got it. We had heard a world of talk about the marvelous beauty of Lake Tahoe, and finally curiosity drove us thither to see it. Three or four members of the Brigade had been there and located some timber-lands on its shores and stored up a quantity of provisions in their camp. We strapped a couple of blankets on our shoulders and took an ax apiece and started—for we intended to take up a wood ranch or so ourselves and become wealthy. We

were on foot. The reader will find it advantageous to go horseback. We were told that the distance was eleven miles. We tramped
a long time on level ground, and then toiled laboriously up a
mountain about a thousand miles high and looked over. No lake
there. We descended on the other side, crossed the valley and
toiled up another mountain three or four thousand miles high,
apparently, and looked over again. No lake yet. We sat down tired
and perspiring, and hired a couple of Chinamen to curse those
people who had beguiled us. Thus refreshed, we presently resumed the march with renewed vigor and determination. We
plodded on, two or three hours longer, and at last the lake burst
upon us—a noble sheet of blue water lifted six thousand three
hundred feet above the level of the sea, and walled in by a rim
of snow-clad mountain peaks that towered aloft full three thousand feet higher still! It was a vast oval, and one would have to
use up eighty or a hundred good miles in traveling around it. As
it lay there with the shadows of the mountains brilliantly photo-
graphed upon its still surface I thought it must surely be the fairest
picture the whole earth affords.

We found the small skiff belonging to the Brigade boys, and
without loss of time set out across a deep bend of the lake toward
the landmarks that signified the locality of the camp. I got Johnny
to row—not because I mind exertion myself, but because it makes
me sick to ride backward when I am at work. But I steered. A
three-mile pull brought us to the camp just as the night fell, and
we stepped ashore very tired and wolfishly hungry. In a "cache"
among the rocks we found the provisions and the cooking-
utensils, and then, all fatigued as I was, I sat down on a boulder
and superintended while Johnny gathered wood and cooked supper. Many a man who had gone through what I had, would have
wanted to rest.

It was a delicious supper—hot bread, fried bacon, and black
coffee. It was a delicious solitude we were in, too. Three miles
away was a sawmill and some workmen, but there were not fifteen
other human beings throughout the wide circumference of the
lake. As the darkness closed down and the stars came out and
spangled the great mirror with jewels, we smoked meditatively
in the solemn hush and forgot our troubles and our pains. In due
time we spread our blankets in the warm sand between two large
boulders and soon fell asleep, careless of the procession of ants
that passed in through rents in our clothing and explored our per-

sons. Nothing could disturb the sleep that fettered us, for it had been fairly earned, and if our consciences had any sins on them they had to adjourn court for that night, anyway. The wind rose just as we were losing consciousness, and we were lulled to sleep by the beating of the surf upon the shore.

It is always very cold on that lake-shore in the night, but we had plenty of blankets and were warm enough. We never moved a muscle all night, but waked at early dawn in the original positions, and got up at once, thoroughly refreshed, free from soreness, and brim full of friskiness. There is no end of wholesome medicine in such an experience. That morning we could have whipped ten such people as we were the day before—sick ones at any rate. But the world is slow, and people will go to "water cures" and "movement cures" and to foreign lands for health. Three months of camp life on Lake Tahoe would restore an Egyptian mummy to his pristine vigor, and give him an appetite like an alligator. I do not mean the oldest and driest mummies, of course, but the fresher ones. The air up there in the clouds is very pure and fine, bracing and delicious. And why shouldn't it be?—it is the same the angels breathe. I think that hardly any amount of fatigue can be gathered together that a man cannot sleep off in one night on the sand by its side. Not under a roof, but under the sky; it seldom or never rains there in the summer-time. I know a man who went there to die. But he made a failure of it. He was a skeleton when he came, and could barely stand. He had no appetite, and did nothing but read tracts and reflect on the future. Three months later he was sleeping out-of-doors regularly, eating all he could hold, three times a day, and chasing game over mountains three thousand feet high for recreation. And he was a skeleton no longer, but weighed part of a ton. This is no fancy sketch, but the truth. His disease was consumption. I confidently commend his experience to other skeletons.

I superintended again, and as soon as we had eaten breakfast we got in the boat and skirted along the lake-shore about three miles and disembarked. We liked the appearance of the place, and so we claimed some three hundred acres of it and stuck our "notices" on a tree. It was yellow-pine timber-land—a dense forest of trees a hundred feet high and from one to five feet through at the butt. It was necessary to fence our property or we could not hold it. That is to say, it was necessary to cut down trees here and there and make them fall in such a way as to form a sort of in-

closure (with pretty wide gaps in it). We cut down three trees
apiece, and found it such heartbreaking work that we decided to
"rest our case" on those; if they held the property, well and good;
if they didn't, let the property spill out through the gaps and go;
it was no use to work ourselves to death merely to save a few
acres of land. Next day we came back to build a house—for a house
was also necessary, in order to hold the property. We decided to
build a substantial log house and excite the envy of the Brigade
boys; but by the time we had cut and trimmed the first log it
seemed unnecessary to be so elaborate, and so we concluded to
build it of saplings. However, two saplings, duly cut and trimmed,
compelled recognition of the fact that a still modester architecture
would satisfy the law, and so we concluded to build a "brush"
house. We devoted the next day to this work, but we did so much
"sitting around" and discussing, that by the middle of the afternoon we had achieved only a half-way sort of affair which one of
us had to watch while the other cut brush, lest if both turned our
backs we might not be able to find it again, it had such a strong
family resemblance to the surrounding vegetation. But we were
satisfied with it.

We were landowners now, duly seized and possessed, and
within the protection of the law. Therefore we decided to take up
our residence on our own domain and enjoy that large sense of
independence which only such an experience can bring. Late the
next afternoon, after a good long rest, we sailed away from the
Brigade camp with all the provisions and cooking-utensils we
could carry off—borrow is the more accurate word—and just as
the night was falling we beached the boat at our own landing.

If there is any life that is happier than the life we led on our
timber ranch for the next two or three weeks, it must be a sort of
life which I have not read of in books or experienced in person.
We did not see a human being but ourselves during the time, or
hear any sounds but those that were made by the wind and the
waves, the sighing of the pines, and now and then the far-off
thunder of an avalanche. The forest about us was dense and cool,
the sky above us was cloudless and brilliant with sunshine, the
broad lake before us was glassy and clear, or rippled and breezy,
or black and storm-tossed, according to Nature's mood; and its
circling border of mountain domes, clothed with forests, scarred
with landslides, cloven by cañons and valleys, and helmeted with

glittering snow, fitly framed and finished the noble picture. The view was always fascinating, bewitching, entrancing. The eye was never tired of gazing, night or day, in calm or storm; it suffered but one grief, and that was that it could not look always, but must close sometimes in sleep.

We slept in the sand close to the water's edge, between two protecting boulders, which took care of the stormy night winds for us. We never took any paregoric to make us sleep. At the first break of dawn we were always up and running foot-races to tone down excess of physical vigor and exuberance of spirits. That is, Johnny was—but I held his hat. While smoking the pipe of peace after breakfast we watched the sentinel peaks put on the glory of the sun, and followed the conquering light as it swept down among the shadows, and set the captive crags and forests free. We watched the tinted pictures grow and brighten upon the water till every little detail of forest, precipice, and pinnacle was wrought in and finished, and the miracle of the enchanter complete. Then to "business."

That is, drifting around in the boat. We were on the north shore. There, the rocks on the bottom are sometimes gray, sometimes white. This gives the marvelous transparency of the water a fuller advantage than it has elsewhere on the lake. We usually pushed out a hundred yards or so from the shore, and then lay down on the thwarts in the sun, and let the boat drift by the hour whither it would. We seldom talked. It interrupted the Sabbath stillness, and marred the dreams the luxurious rest and indolence brought. The shore all along was indented with deep, curved bays and coves, bordered by narrow sand-beaches; and where the sand ended, the steep mountainsides rose right up aloft into space—rose up like a vast wall a little out of the perpendicular, and thickly wooded with tall pines.

So singularly clear was the water, that where it was only twenty or thirty feet deep the bottom was so perfectly distinct that the boat seemed floating in the air! Yes, where it was even *eighty* feet deep. Every little pebble was distinct, every speckled trout, every hand's breadth of sand. Often, as we lay on our faces, a granite boulder, as large as a village church, would start out of the bottom apparently, and seem climbing up rapidly to the surface, till presently it threatened to touch our faces, and we could not resist the impulse to seize an oar and avert the danger. But the boat would float on, and the boulder descend again, and then we could see that when we had been exactly above it, it must still have been twenty or thirty feet below the surface. Down through the transparency of these great depths, the water was not *merely* transparent, but dazzlingly, brilliantly so. All objects seen through it had a bright, strong vividness, not only of outline, but of every minute detail, which they would not have had when seen simply through the same depth of atmosphere. So empty and airy did all spaces seem below us, and so strong was the sense of floating high aloft in mid-nothingness, that we called these boat excursions "balloon voyages."

We fished a good deal, but we did not average one fish a week. We could see trout by the thousand winging about in the emptiness under us, or sleeping in shoals on the bottom, but they would not bite—they could see the line too plainly, perhaps. We frequently selected the trout we wanted, and rested the bait patiently and persistently on the end of his nose at a depth of eighty feet, but he would only shake it off with an annoyed manner, and shift his position.

We bathed occasionally, but the water was rather chilly, for all it looked so sunny. Sometimes we rowed out to the "blue water," a mile or two from shore. It was as dead blue as indigo there, because of the immense depth. By official measurement, the lake in its center is one thousand five hundred and twenty-five feet deep!

Sometimes, on lazy afternoons, we lolled on the sand in camp, and smoked pipes and read some old well-worn novels. At night, by the camp-fire, we played euchre and seven-up to strengthen the mind—and played them with cards so greasy and defaced that only a whole summer's acquaintance with them could enable the student to tell the ace of clubs from the jack of diamonds.

We never slept in our "house." It never occurred to us, for one thing; and besides, it was built to hold ground, and that was enough. We did not wish to strain it.

By and by our provisions began to run short, and we went back to the old camp and laid in a new supply. We were gone all day, and reached home again about nightfall, pretty tired and hungry. While Johnny was carrying the main bulk of the provisions up to our "house" for future use, I took the loaf of bread, some slices of bacon, and the coffee-pot, ashore, set them down by a tree, lit a fire, and went back to the boat to get the frying-pan. While I was at this, I heard a shout from Johnny, and looking up I saw that my fire was galloping all over the premises!

Johnny was on the other side of it. He had to run through the flames to get to the lake-shore, and then we stood helpless and watched the devastation.

The ground was deeply carpeted with dry pine-needles, and the fire touched them off as if they were gunpowder. It was wonderful to see with what fierce speed the tall sheet of flame traveled! My coffeepot was gone, and everything with it. In a minute and a half the fire seized upon a dense growth of dry manzanita chaparral six or eight feet high, and then the roaring and popping and crackling was something terrific. We were driven to the boat by the intense heat, and there we remained, spellbound.

Within half an hour all before us was a tossing, blinding tempest of flame! It went surging up adjacent ridges—surmounted them and disappeared in the cañons beyond—burst into view upon higher and farther ridges, presently—shed a grander illumination abroad, and dove again—flamed out again, directly, higher and still higher up the mountainside—threw out skirmishing parties of fire here and there, and sent them trailing their crimson spirals away among remote ramparts and ribs and gorges, till as far as the eye could reach the lofty mountain-fronts were webbed as it were with a tangled network of red lava streams. Away across the water the crags and domes were lit with a ruddy glare, and the firmament above was a reflected hell!

Every feature of the spectacle was repeated in the glowing mirror of the lake! Both pictures were sublime, both were beautiful; but that in the lake had a bewildering richness about it that enchanted the eye and held it with the stronger fascination.

We sat absorbed and motionless through four long hours. We never thought of supper, and never felt fatigue. But at eleven o'clock the conflagration had traveled beyond our range of vision, and then darkness stole down upon the landscape again.

Hunger asserted itself now, but there was nothing to eat. The provisions were all cooked, no doubt, but we did not go to see. We were homeless wanderers again, without any property. Our fence was gone, our house burned down; no insurance. Our pine forest was well scorched, the dead trees all burned up, and our broad acres of manzanita swept away. Our blankets were on our usual sand-bed, however, and so we lay down and went to sleep. The next morning we started back to the old camp, but while out a long way from shore, so great a storm came up that we dared not try to land. So I bailed out the seas we shipped, and Johnny

pulled heavily through the billows till we had reached a point three
or four miles beyond the camp. The storm was increasing, and it
became evident that it was better to take the hazard of beaching
the boat than go down in a hundred fathoms of water; so we ran
in, with tall white-caps following, and I sat down in the stern-
sheets and pointed her head-on to the shore. The instant the bow
struck, a wave came over the stern that washed crew and cargo
ashore, and saved a deal of trouble. We shivered in the lee of a
boulder all the rest of the day, and froze all the night through.
In the morning the tempest had gone down, and we paddled down
to the camp without any unnecessary delay. We were so starved
that we ate up the rest of the Brigade's provisions, and then set
out to Carson to tell them about it and ask their forgiveness. It was
accorded, upon payment of damages.

We made many trips to the lake after that, and had many a
hair-breadth escape and blood-curdling adventure which will
never be recorded of any history.

## A Fish Answers

AMAZING monster! that, for aught I know,
    With the first sight of thee didst make our race
For ever stare! O flat and shocking face,
Grimly divided from the breast below!
Thou that on dry land horribly dost go
With a split body and most ridiculous pace,
Prong after prong, disgracer of all grace,
Long-useless-finned, haired, upright, unwet, slow!
O breather of the unbreathable, sword-sharp air,
How canst exist? How bear thyself, thou dry
And dreary sloth? What particle canst share
Of the only blessed life, the watery?
I sometimes see of ye an actual pair
Go by! linked fin by fin! most odiously.

*Leigh Hunt*

# INITIATION

## Joseph Conrad

*One of the greatest modern English writers did not learn the language until he was almost twenty years old. Josef Conrad Korzeniowski (1856-1924), who afterward called himself Joseph Conrad, was born in Poland, served on French ships in his teens, and later became a master in the British merchant fleet. His adventures at sea and in many lands provided a background for a great number of memorable tales. The tropics and, above all, the sea have rarely been described as effectively as in this selection from* The Mirror of the Sea.

I FELT its dread for the first time in mid-Atlantic one day, many years ago, when we took off the crew of a Danish brig homeward bound from the West Indies. A thin, silvery mist softened the calm and majestic splendour of light without shadows—seemed to render the sky less remote and the ocean less immense. It was one of the days, when the might of the sea appears indeed lovable, like the nature of a strong man in moments of quiet intimacy. At sunrise we had made out a black speck to the westward, apparently suspended high up in the void behind a stirring, shimmering veil of silvery blue gauze that seemed at times to stir and float in the breeze that fanned us slowly along. The peace of that enchanting forenoon was so profound, so untroubled, that it seemed that every word pronounced loudly on our deck would penetrate to the very heart of that infinite mystery born from the conjunction of water and sky. We did not raise our voices. 'A water-logged derelict, I think, sir,' said the second officer quietly, coming down from aloft with the binoculars in their case slung across his shoulders; and our captain, without a word, signed to the helmsman to steer for the black speck. Presently we made out a low, jagged stump sticking up forward—all that remained of her departed masts.

The captain was expatiating in a low conversational tone to the

chief mate upon the danger of these derelicts, and upon his dread
of coming upon them at night, when suddenly a man forward
screamed out, 'There's people on board of her, sir! I see them!' in
a most extraordinary voice—a voice never heard before in our ship;
the amazing voice of a stranger. It gave the signal for a sudden
tumult of shouts. The watch below ran up the forecastle head in a
body, the cook dashed out of the galley. Everybody saw the poor
fellows now. They were there! And all at once our ship, which had
the well-earned name of being without a rival for speed in light
winds, seemed to us to have lost the power of motion, as if the sea,
becoming viscous, had clung to her sides. And yet she moved. Immensity, the inseparable companion of a ship's life, chose that day
to breathe upon her as gently as a sleeping child. The clamour of
our excitement had died out, and our living ship, famous for never
losing steerage way as long as there was air enough to float a
feather, stole, without a ripple, silent and white as a ghost, towards
her mutilated and wounded sister, come upon at the point of death
in the sunlit haze of a calm day at sea.

With the binoculars glued to his eyes, the captain said in a
quavering tone: 'They are waving to us with something aft there.'
He put down the glasses on the skylight brusquely, and began to
walk about the poop. 'A shirt or a flag,' he ejaculated irritably.
'Can't make it out. . . . Some damn rag or other!' He took a few
more turns on the poop, glancing down over the rail now and then
to see how fast we were moving. His nervous footsteps rang sharply
in the quiet of the ship, where the other men, all looking the same
way, had forgotten themselves in a staring immobility. 'This will
never do!' he cried out suddenly. 'Lower the boats at once! Down
with them!'

Before I jumped into mine he took me aside, as being an inexperienced junior, for a word of warning:

'You look out as you come alongside that she doesn't take you
down with her. You understand?'

He murmured this confidentially, so that none of the men at
the falls should overhear, and I was shocked. 'Heavens! as if in such
an emergency one stopped to think of danger!' I exclaimed to myself mentally, in scorn of such cold-blooded caution.

It takes many lessons to make a real seaman, and I got my rebuke
at once. My experienced commander seemed in one searching
glance to read my thoughts on my ingenuous face.

'What you're going for is to save life, not to drown your boat's crew for nothing,' he growled severely in my ear. But as we shoved off he leaned over and cried out: 'It all rests on the power of your arms, men. Give way for life!'

We made a race of it, and I would never have believed that a common boat's crew of a merchantman could keep up so much determined fierceness in the regular swing of their stroke. What our captain had clearly perceived before we left had become plain to all of us since. The issue of our enterprise hung on a hair above that abyss of waters which will not give up its dead till the Day of Judgment. It was a race of two ship's boats matched against Death for a prize of nine men's lives, and Death had a long start. We saw the crew of the brig from afar working at the pumps—still pumping on that wreck, which already had settled so far down that the gentle, low swell, over which our boats rose and fell easily without a check to their speed, welling up almost level with her head-rails, plucked at the ends of broken gear swinging desolately under her naked bowsprit.

We could not, in all conscience, have picked out a better day for our regatta had we had the free choice of all the days that ever dawned upon the lonely struggles and solitary agonies of ships since the Norse rovers first steered to the westward against the run of Atlantic waves. It was a very good race. At the finish there was not an oar's length between the first and second boat, with Death coming in a good third on the top of the very next smooth swell, for all one knew to the contrary. The scuppers of the brig gurgled softly all together when the waters rising against her sides subsided sleepily with a low wash, as if playing about an immovable rock. Her bulwarks were gone fore and aft, and one saw her bare deck low-lying like a raft and swept clean of boats, spars, houses—of everything except the ring-bolts and the heads of the pumps. I had one dismal glimpse of it as I braced myself up to receive upon my breast the last man to leave her, the captain, who literally let himself fall into my arms.

It had been a weirdly silent rescue—a rescue without a hail, without a single uttered word, without a gesture or a sign, without a conscious exchange of glances. Up to the very last moment those on board stuck to their pumps, which spouted two clear streams of water upon their bare feet. Their brown skin showed through the rents of their shirts; and the two small bunches of half-naked, tattered men went on bowing from the waist to each other in their back-breaking labour, up and down, absorbed, with no time for a glance over the shoulder at the help that was coming to them. As we dashed, unregarded, alongside a voice let out one, only one hoarse howl of command, and then, just as they stood, without caps, with the salt drying grey in the wrinkles and folds of their hairy, haggard faces, blinking stupidly at us their red eyelids, they made a bolt away from the handles, tottering and jostling against each other, and positively flung themselves over upon our very heads. The clatter they made tumbling into the boats had an extraordinarily destructive effect upon the illusion of tragic dignity our self-esteem had thrown over the contests of mankind with the sea. On that exquisite day of gently breathing peace and veiled sunshine perished my romantic love of what men's imagination had proclaimed the most august aspect of nature. The cynical indifference of the sea to the merits of human suffering and courage, laid bare in this ridiculous, panic-tainted performance extorted from the dire extremity of nine good and honourable seamen, revolted me. I saw the duplicity of the sea's most tender mood. It was so because it could not help itself, but the awed aspect of the early days was gone. I felt ready to smile bitterly at its enchanting charm and glare viciously at its furies. In a moment, before we shoved off, I had looked coolly at the life of my choice. Its illusions were gone, but its fascination remained. I had become a seaman at last.

We pulled hard for a quarter of an hour, then laid on our oars waiting for our ship. She was delicately tall and exquisitely noble through the mist. The captain of the brig, who sat in the stern sheets by my side with his face in his hands, raised his head and began to speak with a sort of sombre volubility. They had lost their masts and sprung a leak in a hurricane; drifted for weeks, always at the pumps, met more bad weather; the ships they sighted failed to make them out, the leak gained upon them slowly, and the seas had left them nothing to make a raft of. It was very hard to see ship after ship pass by at a distance, 'as if everybody had agreed that we must be left to drown,' he added. But they went on trying to keep the brig afloat as long as possible, and working the pumps constantly on insufficient food, mostly raw, till 'yesterday evening,' he continued monotonously, 'just as the sun went down, the men's hearts broke.'

He made an almost imperceptible pause here, and went on again with exactly the same intonation:

'They told me the brig could not be saved, and they thought they had done enough for themselves. I said nothing to that. It was true. It was no mutiny. I had nothing to say to them. They lay about aft all night, as still as so many dead men. I did not lie down. I kept a look-out. When the first light came I saw your ship at once. I waited for more light; the breeze began to fail on my face. Then I shouted out as loud as I was able: "Look at that ship!" but only two men got up very slowly and came to me. At first only we three stood alone, for a long time, watching you coming down to us, and feeling the breeze drop to a calm almost; but afterwards others, too, rose, one after another, and by and by I had all my crew behind me. I turned round and said to them that they could see the ship was coming our way, but in this small breeze she might come too late after all, unless we turned to and tried to keep the brig afloat long enough to give you time to save us all. I spoke like that to them, and then I gave the command to man the pumps.'

He gave the command, and gave the example, too, by going himself to the handles, but it seems that these men did actually hang back for a moment, looking at each other dubiously before they followed him. 'He! he! he!' He broke out into a most unexpected, imbecile, pathetic, nervous little giggle. 'Their hearts were broken so! They had been played with too long,' he explained apologetically, lowering his eyes, and became silent.

Twenty-five years is a long time—a quarter of a century is a dim and distant past; but to this day I remember the dark-brown feet, hands, and faces of two of these men whose hearts had been broken by the sea. They were lying very still on their sides on the bottom boards between the thwarts, curled up like dogs. My boat's crew, leaning over the looms of their oars, stared and listened as if at the play. The master of the brig looked up suddenly to ask me what day it was.

They had lost the date. When I told him it was Sunday, the 22nd, he frowned, making some mental calculation, then nodded twice sadly to himself, staring at nothing.

His aspect was miserably unkempt and wildly sorrowful. Had it not been for the unquenchable candour of his blue eyes, whose unhappy, tired glance every moment sought his abandoned, sinking brig, as if it could find rest nowhere else, he would have appeared mad. But he was too simple to go mad, too simple with that manly simplicity which alone can bear men unscathed in mind and body through an encounter with the deadly playfulness of the sea or with its less abominable fury.

Neither angry, nor playful, nor smiling, it enveloped our distant ship growing bigger as she neared us, our boats with the rescued men and the dismantled hull of the brig we were leaving behind, in the large and placid embrace of its quietness, half lost in the fair haze, as if in a dream of infinite and tender clemency. There was no frown, no wrinkle on its face, not a ripple. And the run of the slight swell was so smooth that it resembled the graceful undulation of a piece of shimmering grey silk shot with gleams of green. We pulled an easy stroke; but when the master of the brig, after a glance over his shoulder, stood up with a low exclamation, my men feathered their oars instinctively, without an order, and the boat lost her way.

He was steadying himself on my shoulder with a strong grip, while his other arm, flung up rigidly, pointed a denunciatory finger at the immense tranquillity of the ocean. After his first exclamation, which stopped the swing of our oars, he made no sound, but his whole attitude seemed to cry out an indignant 'Behold!' . . . I could not imagine what vision of evil had come to him. I was startled, and the amazing energy of his immobilized gesture made my heart beat faster with the anticipation of something monstrous and unsuspected. The stillness around us became crushing.

For a moment the succession of silky undulations ran on innocently. I saw each of them swell up the misty line of the horizon, far, far away beyond the derelict brig, and the next moment, with a slight friendly toss of our boat, it had passed under us and was gone. The lulling cadence of the rise and fall, the invariable gentleness of this irresistible force, the great charm of the deep waters, warmed my breast deliciously, like the subtle poison of a lovepotion. But all this lasted only a few soothing seconds before I jumped up too, making the boat roll like the veriest land-lubber.

Something startling, mysterious, hastily confused, was taking place. I watched it with incredulous and fascinated awe; as one watches the confused, swift movements of some deed of violence done in the dark. As if at a given signal, the run of the smooth undulations seemed checked suddenly around the brig. By a strange optical delusion the whole sea appeared to rise upon her in one overwhelming heave of its silky surface, where in one spot a smother of foam broke out ferociously. And then the effort subsided. It was all over, and the smooth swell ran on as before from the horizon in uninterrupted cadence of motion, passing under us with a slight friendly toss of our boat. Far away, where the brig had been, an angry white stain undulating on the surface of steely-grey waters, shot with gleams of green, diminished swiftly, without a hiss, like a patch of pure snow melting in the sun. And the great stillness after this initiation into the seas' implacable hate seemed full of dread thoughts and shadows of disaster.

'Gone!' ejaculated from the depths of his chest my bowman in a final tone. He spat in his hands, and took a better grip on his oar. The captain of the brig lowered his rigid arm slowly, and looked at our faces in a solemnly conscious silence, which called upon us to share in his simple-minded, marvelling awe. All at once he sat down by my side, and leaned forward earnestly at my boat's crew, who, swinging together in a long, easy stroke, kept their eyes fixed upon him faithfully.

'No ship could have done so well,' he addressed them firmly, after a moment of strained silence, during which he seemed with trembling lips to seek for words fit to bear such high testimony. 'She was small, but she was good. I had no anxiety. She was strong. Last voyage I had my wife and two children in her. No other ship could have stood so long the weather she had to live through for days and days before we got dismasted a fortnight ago. She was fairly worn out, and that's all. You may believe me. She lasted under us for days and days, but she could not last for ever. It was long enough. I am glad it is over. No better ship was ever left to sink at sea on such a day as this.'

He was competent to pronounce the funeral oration of a ship, this son of ancient sea-folk, whose rational existence, so little stained by the excesses of manly virtues, had demanded nothing but the merest foothold from the earth. By the merits of his sea-wise fore-fathers and by the artlessness of his heart, he was made fit to deliver this excellent discourse. There was nothing wanting in its orderly arrangement—neither piety nor faith, nor the tribute of praise due to the worthy dead, with the edifying recital of their achievement. She had lived, he had loved her; she had suffered, and he was glad she was at rest. It was an excellent discourse. And it was orthodox, too, in its fidelity to the cardinal article of a seaman's faith, of which it was a single-minded confession. 'Ships are all right.' They are. They who live with the sea have got to hold by that creed first and last; and it came to me, as I glanced at him sideways, that some men were not altogether unworthy in honour and conscience to pro-nounce the funeral eulogium of a ship's constancy in life and death.

After this, sitting by my side with his loosely clasped hands hanging between his knees, he uttered no word, made no movement till the shadow of our ship's sails fell on the boat, when, at the loud cheer greeting the return of the victors with their prize, he lifted up his troubled face with a faint smile of pathetic indulgence. This smile of the worthy descendant of the most ancient sea-folk whose audacity and hardihood had left no trace of greatness and glory upon the waters, completed the cycle of my initiation. There was an infinite depth of hereditary wisdom in its pitying sadness. It made the hearty bursts of cheering sound like a childish noise of triumph. Our crew shouted with immense confidence—honest souls! As if anybody could ever make sure of having prevailed against the sea, which has betrayed so many ships of great 'name', so many proud men, so many towering ambitions of fame, power, wealth, greatness!

As I brought the boat under the falls my captain, in high good-humour, leaned over, spreading his red and freckled elbows on the rail, and called down to me sarcastically, out of the depths of his cynic philosopher's beard:

'So you have brought the boat back after all, have you?'

Sarcasm was 'his way', and the most that can be said for it is that it was natural. This did not make it lovable. But it is decorous and expedient to fall in with one's commander's way. 'Yes. I brought the boat back all right, sir,' I answered. And the good man believed me. It was not for him to discern upon me the marks of my recent initiation. And yet I was not exactly the same youngster who had taken the boat away—all impatience for a race against Death, with the pride of nine men's lives at the end.

Already I looked with other eyes upon the sea. I knew it capable of betraying the generous ardour of youth as implacably as, in-different to evil and good, it would have betrayed the basest greed or the noblest heroism. My conception of its magnanimous great-ness was gone. And I looked upon the true sea—the sea that plays with men till their hearts are broken, and wears stout ships to death. Nothing can touch the brooding bitterness of its soul. Open to all and faithful to none, it exercises its fascination for the undoing of the best. To love it is not well. It knows no bond of plighted troth, no fidelity to misfortune, to long companionship, to long devotion. The promise it holds out perpetually is very great; but the only secret of its possession is strength, strength—the jealous, sleepless strength of a man guarding a coveted treasure within his gates.

# ADVENTURES IN POLYNESIA

## Herman Melville

*At eighteen, Herman Melville (1819–1891) shipped as a cabin boy on a sailing craft bound for Liverpool. He later tried teaching, but the sea called him again—he sailed on a whaler for the South Seas. Jumping ship in the Marquesas, Melville lived pleasantly as a captive of the natives, finally escaping on an Australian trader, the* Julia. *Together with his friend, Dr. Long Ghost, he left the ship at Tahiti. Melville's book* Omoo *tells how they explored the near-by islands, going first to Imeeo, where they knew there were two white planters.*

### The Valley of Martair

WE WENT up through groves to an open space, where we heard voices, and a light was seen glimmering from out a bamboo dwelling. It was the planters' retreat; and in their absence, several girls were keeping house, assisted by an old native, who, wrapped up in tappa, lay in the corner, smoking.

A hasty meal was prepared, and after it we essayed a nap; but, alas! a plague, little anticipated, prevented. Unknown in Tahiti, the mosquitoes here fairly eddied round us. But more of them anon.

We were up betimes, and strolled out to view the country. We were in the valley of Martair; shut in, on both sides, by lofty hills. Here and there, were steep cliffs, gay with flowering shrubs, or hung with pendulous vines, swinging blossoms in the air. Of considerable width at the sea, the vale contracts as it runs inland; terminating, at the distance of several miles, in a range of the most grotesque elevations, which seem embattled with turrets and towers, grown over with verdure, and waving with trees. The valley itself, is a wilderness of woodland; with links of streams flashing through, and narrow pathways, fairly tunnelled through masses of foliage.

[ 493 ]

All alone, in this wild place, was the abode of the planters; the only one back from the beach—their sole neighbours, the few fishermen and their families, dwelling in a small grove of coco-nut trees, whose roots were washed by the sea.

The cleared tract which they occupied, comprised some thirty acres, level as a prairie, part of which was under cultivation; the whole being fenced in by a stout palisade of trunks and boughs of trees, staked firmly in the ground. This was necessary, as a defence against the wild cattle and hogs overrunning the island.

Thus far, Tombez potatoes were the principal crop raised; a ready sale for them being obtained among the shipping touching at Papeetee. There was a small patch of the *taro*, or Indian turnip, also; another of yams; and, in one corner, a thrifty growth of the sugarcane, just ripening.

On the side of the enclosure, next the sea, was the house; newly built of bamboos, in the native style. The furniture consisted of a couple of sea-chests, an old box, a few cooking utensils, and agricultural tools; together with three fowling-pieces, hanging from a rafter; and two enormous hammocks, swinging in opposite corners, and composed of dried bullocks' hides, stretched out with poles.

The whole plantation was shut in by a dense forest; and, close by the house, a dwarfed "Aoa," or species of banian-tree, had purposely been left twisting over the palisade, in the most grotesque manner, and thus made a pleasant shade. The branches of this curious tree afforded low perches, upon which the natives frequently squatted, after the fashion of their race, and smoked and gossiped by the hour.

We had a good breakfast of fish—speared by the natives, before sunrise, on the reef—pudding of Indian turnip, fried bananas, and roasted breadfruit.

During the repast, our new friends were quite sociable and communicative. It seems that, like nearly all uneducated foreigners, residing in Polynesia, they had, some time previous, deserted from a ship; and, having heard a good deal about the money to be made by raising supplies for whaling-vessels, they determined upon embarking in the business. Strolling about, with this intention, they, at last, came to Martair; and, thinking the soil would suit, set themselves to work. They began, by finding out the owner of the particular spot coveted, and then making a "tayo" of him.

He turned out to be Tonoi, the chief of the fishermen; who, one day, when exhilarated with brandy, tore his meagre tappa from his

loins, and gave me to know, that he was allied by blood with Pomaree herself; and that his mother came from the illustrious race of
pontiffs, who, in old times, swayed their bamboo crosier over all the
pagans of Imeeo. A regal and right reverend lineage! But, at the time
I speak of, the dusky noble was in decayed circumstances, and
therefore, by no means unwilling to alienate a few useless acres. As
an equivalent, he received from the strangers two or three rheumatic old muskets, several red woollen shirts, and a promise to be
provided for in his old age: he was always to find a home with the
planters.

Desirous of living on the cosy footing of a father-in-law, he
frankly offered his two daughters for wives; but as such, they were
politely declined; the adventurers, though not averse to courting,
being unwilling to entangle themselves in a matrimonial alliance,
however splendid in point of family.

Tonoi's men, the fishermen of the grove, were a sad set. Secluded, in a great measure, from the ministrations of the mission-
aries, they gave themselves up to all manner of lazy wickedness.
Strolling among the trees of a morning, you came upon them napping on the shady side of a canoe hauled up among the bushes; lying
under a tree smoking; or, more frequently still, gambling with
pebbles; though, a little tobacco excepted, what they gambled for
at their outlandish games, it would be hard to tell. Other idle diversions they had also, in which they seemed to take great delight. As
for fishing, it employed but a small part of their time. Upon the
whole, they were a merry, indigent, godless race.

Tonoi, the old sinner, leaning against the fallen trunk of a coco-
nut tree, invariably squandered his mornings at pebbles; a grey-
headed rook of a native regularly plucking him of every other stick
of tobacco obtained from his friends, the planters. Toward afternoon, he strolled back to their abode; where he tarried till the next
morning, smoking and snoozing, and, at times, prating about the
hapless fortunes of the House of Tonoi. But like any other easy-
going old dotard, he seemed for the most part perfectly content
with cheerful board and lodging.

On the whole, the valley of Martair was the quietest place
imaginable. Could the mosquitoes be induced to emigrate, one
might spend the month of August there quite pleasantly. But this
was not the case with the luckless Long Ghost and myself; as will
presently be seen.

*Farming in Polynesia*

The planters were both whole-souled fellows; but in other respects, as unlike as possible.

One was a tall, robust Yankee, born in the backwoods of Maine, sallow, and with a long face;—the other was a short little Cockney, who had first clapped his eyes on the Monument.

The voice of Zeke, the Yankee, had a twang like a cracked viol; and Shorty (as his comrade called him), clipped the aspirate from every word beginning with one. The latter, though not the tallest man in the world, was a good-looking young fellow of twenty-five. His cheeks were dyed with the fine Saxon red, burned deeper from his roving life; his blue eye opened well, and a profusion of fair hair curled over a well shaped head.

But Zeke was no beauty. A strong, ugly man, he was well adapted for manual labour; and that was all. His eyes were made to see with, and not for ogling. Compared with the Cockney, he was grave, and rather taciturn; but there was a deal of good old humour bottled up in him, after all. For the rest, he was frank, good-hearted, shrewd, and resolute; and like Shorty, quite illiterate.

Though a curious conjunction, the pair got along together famously. But, as no two men were ever united in any enterprise, without one getting the upper hand of the other; so, in most matters, Zeke had his own way. Shorty, too, had imbibed from him a spirit of invincible industry; and Heaven only knows what ideas of making a fortune on their plantation.

We were much concerned at this; for the prospect of their setting us in their own persons an example of downright hard labour, was anything but agreeable. But it was now too late to repent what we had done.

The first day—thank fortune—we did nothing. Having treated us as guests thus far, they no doubt thought it would be wanting in delicacy, to set us to work before the compliments of the occasion were well over. The next morning, however, they both looked business-like, and we were put to.

"Wall, b'ys" (boys), said Zeke, knocking the ashes out of his pipe, after breakfast—"we must get at it. Shorty, give Peter there (the doctor), the big hoe, and Paul the other, and let's be off." Going to a corner, Shorty brought forth three of the implements; and distributing them impartially, trudged on after his partner, who took the lead with something in the shape of an axe.

For a moment left alone in the house, we looked at each other, quaking. We were each equipped with a great, clumsy piece of a tree, armed at one end with a heavy, flat mass of iron.

The cutlery part—especially adapted to a primitive soil—was an importation from Sydney; the handles must have been of domestic manufacture. "Hoes"—so called—we had heard of, and seen; but they were harmless, in comparison with the tools in our hands.

"What's to be done with them?" inquired I of Peter.

"Lift them up and down," he replied; "or put them in motion, some way or other. Paul, we are in a scrape—but hark; they are calling;" and shouldering the hoes, off we marched.

Our destination was the farther side of the plantation, where the ground, cleared in part, had not yet been broken up; but they were now setting about it. Upon halting, I asked why a plough was not used: some of the young wild steers might be caught, and trained for draught.

Zeke replied, that, for such a purpose, no cattle, to his knowledge, had ever been used in any part of Polynesia. As for the soil of Martair, so obstructed was it with roots, crossing and recrossing each other at all points, that no kind of a plough could be used to advantage. The heavy Sydney hoes were the only thing for such land.

Our work was now before us; but, previous to commencing operations, I endeavoured to engage the Yankee in a little further friendly chat, concerning the nature of virgin soils in general, and that of the valley of Martair in particular. So masterly a stratagem made Long Ghost brighten up; and he stood by ready to join in. But what our friend had to say about agriculture, all referred to the particular part of his plantation upon which we stood; and having communicated enough on this head to enable us to set to work to the best advantage, he fell to, himself; and Shorty, who had been looking on, followed suit.

The surface, here and there, presented closely amputated branches of what had once ben a dense thicket. They seemed purposely left projecting, as if to furnish a handle whereby to drag out the roots beneath. After loosening the hard soil, by dint of much thumping and pounding, the Yankee jerked one of the roots this way and that, twisting it round and round, and then tugging at it horizontally.

"Come! lend us a hand!" he cried, at last; and, running, up we all four strained away in concert. The tough obstacle convulsed the surface with throes and spasms; but stuck fast, notwithstanding.

"Dumn it!" cried Zeke, "we'll have to get a rope; run to the house, Shorty, and fetch one."

The end of this being attached, we took plenty of room, and strained away once more.

"Give us a song, Shorty," said the doctor; who was rather sociable, on a short acquaintance. Where the work to be accomplished is any way difficult, this mode of enlivening toil is quite efficacious among sailors. So, willing to make everything as cheerful as possible, Shorty struck up, "Were you ever in Dumbarton?" a marvellously inspiring, but somewhat indecorous windlass chorus.

At last, the Yankee cast a damper on his enthusiasm, by exclaiming, in a pet, "Oh! dumn your singing! keep quiet, and pull away!" This we now did, in the most uninteresting silence; until, with a jerk, that made every elbow hum, the root dragged out; and, most inelegantly, we all landed upon the ground. The doctor, quite exhausted, stayed there; and, deluded into believing, that, after so doughty a performance, we would be allowed a cessation of toil, took off his hat, and fanned himself.

"Rayther a hard customer, that, Peter," observed the Yankee, going up to him: "but it's no use for any on 'em to hang back; for, I'm dumned if they hain't got to come out, whether or not. Hurrah! let's get at it agin!"

"Mercy!" ejaculated the doctor, rising slowly, and turning round. "He'll be the death of us!"

Falling to with our hoes again, we worked singly, or together, as occasion required, until "Nooning Time" came.

The period, so called by the planters, embraced about three hours in the middle of the day; during which it was so excessively hot, in this still, brooding valley, shut out from the Trades, and only open toward the leeward side of the island, that labour in the sun was out of the question. To use a hyperbolical phrase of Shorty's, "It was 'ot enough to melt the nose h'off a brass monkey."

Returning to the house, Shorty, assisted by old Tonoi, cooked the dinner; and, after we had all partaken thereof, both the Cockney and Zeke threw themselves into one of the hammocks, inviting us to occupy the other. Thinking it no bad idea, we did so; and, after skirmishing with the mosquitoes, managed to fall into a doze. As for the planters, more accustomed to "Nooning," they, at once, presented a nuptial back to each other; and were soon snoring away at a great rate. Tonoi snoozed on a mat, in one corner.

At last, we were roused by Zeke's crying out, "Up! b'ys; up! rise, and shine; time to get at it agin!"

Looking at the doctor, I perceived, very plainly, that he had decided upon something.

In a languid voice, he told Zeke, that he was not very well: indeed, that he had not been himself for some time past; though a little rest, no doubt, would recruit him. The Yankee, thinking, from this, that our valuable services might be lost to him altogether, were he too hard upon us at the outset, at once begged us both to consult our own feelings, and not exert ourselves for the present, unless we felt like it. Then—without recognizing the fact, that my comrade claimed to be actually unwell—he simply suggested, that, since he was so *tired*, he had better, perhaps, swing in his hammock for the rest of the day. If agreeable, however, I myself might accompany him upon a little bullock hunting excursion, in the neighbouring hills. In this proposition, I gladly acquiesced; though Peter, who was a great sportsman, put on a long face. The muskets and ammunition were forthwith got down from overhead; and, everything being then ready, Zeke cried out, "Tonoi! come; aramai! (get up) we want you for pilot. Shorty, my lad, look arter things, you know; and, if you likes, why, there's them roots in the field yonder."

Having thus arranged his domestic affairs to please himself, though little to Shorty's satisfaction, I thought; he slung his powder-horn over his shoulder, and we started. Tonoi was, at once, sent on in advance; and, leaving the plantation, he struck into a path, which led towards the mountains.

After hurrying through the thickets for some time, we came out into the sunlight, in an open glade, just under the shadow of the hills. Here, Zeke pointed aloft, to a beetling crag, far distant; where a bullock, with horns thrown back, stood like a statue.

## A Hunting Ramble with Zeke

At the foot of the mountain, a steep path went up among rocks and clefts, mantled with verdure. Here and there were green gulfs, down which it made one giddy to peep. At last we gained an overhanging, wooded shelf of land which crowned the heights; and along this, the path, well shaded, ran like a gallery.

In every direction, the scenery was enchanting. There was a low, rustling breeze; and below, in the vale, the leaves were quivering; the sea lay, blue and serene, in the distance; and inland the surface swelled up, ridge after ridge, and peak upon peak, all bathed in the Indian haze of the Tropics, and dreamy to look upon. Still valleys, leagues away, reposed in the deep shadows of the mountains; and here and there, waterfalls lifted up their voices in the solitude. High above all, and central, the "Marling-spike" lifted its finger. Upon the hillsides, small groups of bullocks were seen; some quietly browsing; other slowly winding into the valleys.

We went on, directing our course for a slope of the hills, a mile or two farther, where the nearest bullocks were seen.

We were cautious in keeping to windward of them; their sense of smell and hearing being, like those of all wild creatures, exceedingly acute.

As there was no knowing that we might not surprise some other kind of game in the coverts through which we were passing, we crept along warily.

The wild hogs of the island are uncommonly fierce; and as they often attack the natives, I could not help following Tonoi's example of once in a while peeping in under the foliage. Frequent retrospective glances also served to assure me that our retreat was not cut off.

As we rounded a clump of bushes, a noise behind them, like the crackling of dry branches, broke the stillness. In an instant, Tonoi's hand was on a bough, ready for a spring, and Zeke's finger touched the trigger of his piece. Again the stillness was broken; and thinking it high time to get ready, I brought my musket to my shoulder.

"Look sharp!" cried the Yankee; and dropping on one knee, he brushed the twigs aside. Presently, off went his piece; and with a wild snort, a black, bristly boar—his cherry red lip curled up by two glittering tusks—dashed, unharmed, across the path, and crashed through the opposite thicket. I saluted him with a charge as he disappeared; but not the slightest notice was taken of the civility.

By this time, Tonoi, the illustrious descendant of the Bishops of Imeeo, was twenty feet from the ground. "Aramai! come down, you old fool!" cried the Yankee; "the pesky critter's on t'other side of the island afore this."

"I rayther guess," he continued, as we began reloading, "that we've spoiled sport by firing at that 'ere 'tarnal hog. Them bullocks heard the racket, and is flinging their tails about now on the keen jump. Quick, Paul, and let's climb that rock yonder, and see if so be there's any in sight."

But none were to be seen, except at such a distance that they looked like ants.

As evening was now at hand, my companion proposed our returning home forthwith; and then, after a sound night's rest, starting in the morning upon a good day's hunt with the whole force of the plantation.

Following another path, in descending into the valley, we passed through some nobly wooded land on the face of the mountain.

One variety of tree particularly attracted my attention. The dark mossy stem, over seventy feet high, was perfectly branchless for many feet above the ground, when it shot out in broad boughs laden with lustrous leaves of the deepest green. And all round the lower part of the trunk, thin, slab-like buttresses of bark, perfectly smooth, and radiating from a common centre projected along the ground for at least two yards. From below, these natural props tapered upward until gradually blended with the trunk itself. There were signs of the wild cattle having sheltered themselves behind them. Zeke called this the canoe-tree; as in old times it supplied the navies of the Kings of Tahiti. For canoe-building, the wood is still used. Being extremely dense, and impervious to worms, it is very durable.

Emerging from the forest, when half-way down the hillside, we came upon an open space, covered with ferns and grass, over which a few lonely trees were casting long shadows in the setting sun. Here, a piece of ground some hundred feet square, covered with weeds and brambles, and sounding hollow to the tread, was enclosed by a ruinous wall of stones. Tonoi said it was an almost forgotten burial-place, of great antiquity, where no one had been interred since the islanders had been Christians. Sealed up in dry, deep vaults, many a dead heathen was lying here.

Curious to prove the old man's statement, I was anxious to get a peep at the catacombs; but hermetically overgrown with vegetation, as they were, no aperture was visible.

Before gaining the level of the valley, we passed by the site of a village, near a water-course, long deserted. There was nothing but stone walls, and rude dismantled foundations of houses, constructed of the same material. Large trees and brush-wood were growing rankly among them.

I asked Tonoi how long it was since any one had lived here. "Me, *tammaree* (boy)—plenty *kannaker* (men) Martair," he replied. "Now, only poor *pehe kannaka* (fishermen) left—me born here."

Going down the valley, vegetation of every kind presented a different aspect from that of the high land.

Chief among the trees of the plain on this island, is the "*Ati*," large and lofty, with a massive trunk, and broad, laurel-shaped leaves. The wood is splendid. In Tahiti, I was shown a narrow, polished plank, fit to make a cabinet for a king. Taken from the heart of the tree, it was of a deep, rich scarlet, traced with yellow veins, and in some places clouded with hazel.

In the same grove with the regal "*Ati*," you may see the beautiful flowering "*Hotoo*"; its pyramid of shining leaves diversified with numberless small, white blossoms.

Planted with trees as the valley is, almost throughout its entire length, I was astonished to observe so very few which were useful to the natives: not one in a hundred was a coco-nut or breadfruit tree.

But here Tonoi again enlightened me. In the sanguinary religious hostilities which ensued upon the conversion to Christianity of the first Pomaree, a war party from Tahiti destroyed (by "girdling" the bark) entire groves of these invaluable trees. For some time afterward, they stood stark and leafless in the sun; sad monuments of the fate which befell the inhabitants of the valley.

## The Second Hunt in the Mountains

Fair dawned, over the hills of Martair, the jocund morning of our hunt.

Everything had been prepared for it overnight; and, when we arrived at the house, a good breakfast was spread by Shorty: and old Tonoi was bustling about like an innkeeper. Several of his men, also, were in attendance, to accompany us with calabashes of food; and, in case we met with any success, to officiate as bearers of burdens, on our return.

Apprised, the evening previous, of the meditated sport, the doctor had announced his willingness to take part therein.

Now, subsequent events made us regard this expedition as a shrewd device of the Yankee's. Once get us off on a pleasure trip, and with what face could we afterward refuse to work? Besides, he enjoyed all the credit of giving us a holiday. Nor did he omit assuring us, that, work or play, our wages were all the while running on.

A dilapidated old musket of Tonoi's was borrowed for the doctor. It was exceedingly short and heavy, with a clumsy lock, which required a strong finger to pull the trigger. On trying the piece, by firing at a mark, Long Ghost was satisfied that it could not fail of doing execution: the charge went one way, and he the other.

Upon this, he endeavoured to negotiate an exchange of muskets with Shorty; but the Cockney was proof against his blandishments; at last he entrusted his weapon to one of the natives to carry for him.

Marshalling our forces, we started for the head of the valley; near which, a path ascended to a range of high land, said to be a favourite resort of the cattle.

Shortly after gaining the heights, a small herd, some way off, was perceived entering a wood. We hurried on; and, dividing our party, went in after them, at four different points; each white man followed by several natives.

I soon found myself in a dense covert; and, after looking round, was just emerging into a clear space, when I heard a report, and a bullet knocked the bark from a tree near by. The same instant, there was a trampling and crashing; and five bullocks, nearly abreast, broke into view across the opening, and plunged right toward the spot where myself and three of the islanders were standing.

They were small, black, vicious-looking creatures; with short, sharp horns, red nostrils, and eyes like coals of fire. On they came— their dark woolly heads hanging down.

By this time, my island backers were roosting among the trees. Glancing round, for an instant, to discover a retreat in case of emergency, I raised my piece, when a voice cried out, from the wood, "Right between the 'orns, Paul! right between the 'orns!" Down went my barrel, in range with a small white tuft on the forehead of the headmost one; and, letting him have it, I darted to one side. As I turned again, the five bullocks shot by like a blast, making the air eddy in their wake.

The Yankee now burst into view, and saluted them in flank. Whereupon, the fierce little bull with the tufted forehead, flirted his long tail over his buttocks; kicked out with his hind feet, and shot forward a full length. It was nothing but a graze; and, in an instant, they were out of sight, the thicket into which they broke rocking overhead, and marking their progress.

The action over, the heavy artillery came up, in the person of the Long Doctor, with his blunderbuss.

"Where are they?" he cried, out of breath.

"A mile or two h'off, by this time," replied the Cockney. "Lord, Paul! you ought to've sent an 'ail stone into that little black 'un."

While excusing my want of skill, as well as I could, Zeke, rushing forward, suddenly exclaimed, "Creation! what are you 'bout there, Peter?"

Peter, incensed at our ill luck, and ignorantly imputing it to the cowardice of our native auxiliaries, was bringing his piece to bear upon his trembling squire—the musket carrier—now descending a tree.

Pulling trigger, the bullet went high over his head; and, hopping to the ground, bellowing like a calf, the fellow ran away as fast as his heels could carry him. The rest followed us, after this, with fear and trembling.

After forming our line of march anew, we went on for several hours, without catching a glimpse of the game; the reports of the muskets having been heard at a great distance. At last, we mounted a craggy height, to obtain a wide view of the country. From this place, we beheld three cattle; quietly browsing in a green opening of a wood below; the trees shutting them in all round.

A general re-examination of the muskets now took place, followed by a hasty lunch from the calabashes: we then started. As we descended the mountainside, the cattle were in plain sight, until we entered the forest, when we lost sight of them for a moment; but only to see them again, as we crept close up to the spot where they grazed.

They were a bull, a cow, and a calf. The cow was lying down in the shade, by the edge of the wood; the calf, sprawling out before her in the grass, licking her lips; while old Taurus himself stood close by, casting a paternal glance at this domestic little scene, and conjugally elevating his nose in the air.

"Now then," said Zeke, in a whisper, "let's take the poor creeturs, while they are huddled together. Crawl along, b'ys; crawl along. Fire together, mind; and not 'till I say the word."

We crept up to the very edge of the open ground, and knelt behind a clump of bushes; resting our levelled barrels among the branches. The slight rustling was heard. Taurus turned round, dropped his head to the ground, and sent forth a low, sullen bellow; then snuffed the air. The cow rose on her fore knees, pitched forward alarmedly, and stood upon her legs; while the calf, with ears pricked, got right underneath her. All three were now grouped, and, in an instant would be off.

"I take the bull," cried our leader; "fire!"

The calf fell like a clod; its dam uttered a cry, and thrust her head into the thicket; but she turned, and came moaning up to the lifeless calf, going round and round it, snuffing fiercely with her bleeding nostrils. A crashing in the wood, and a loud roar, announced the flying bull.

Soon, another shot was fired, and the cow fell. Leaving some of the natives to look after the dead cattle, the rest of us hurried on after the bull; his dreadful bellowings guiding us to the spot where he lay. Wounded in the shoulder, in his fright and agony he had bounded into the wood; but when we came up to him, he had sunk to the earth in a green hollow, thrusting his black muzzle into a pool of his own blood, and tossing it over his hide in clots.

The Yankee brought his piece to a rest; and, the next instant, the wild brute sprang into the air, and with his fore legs crouching under him, fell dead.

Our island friends were now in high spirits; all courage and alacrity. Old Tonoi thought nothing of taking poor Taurus himself by the horns, and peering into his glazed eyes.

Our ship knives were at once in request; and, skinning the cattle, we hung them high up by cords of bark from the boughs of a tree. Withdrawing into a covert, we there waited for the wild hogs; which, according to Zeke, would soon make their appearance, lured by the smell of blood. Presently, we heard them coming, in two or three different directions; and, in a moment, they were tearing the offal to pieces.

As only one shot at these creatures could be relied on, we intended firing simultaneously; but, somehow or other, the doctor's piece went off by itself, and one of the hogs dropped. The others then breaking into the thicket, the rest of us sprang after them; resolved to have another shot at all hazards.

The Cockney darted among some bushes; and, a few moments after, we heard the report of his musket followed by a quick cry. On running up, we saw our comrade doing battle with a young devil of a boar, as black as night, whose snout had been partly torn away. Firing when the game was in full career, and coming directly toward him, Shorty had been assailed by the enraged brute; it was now crunching the breech of the musket, with which he had tried to club it; Shorty holding fast to the barrel, and fingering his waist for a knife. Being in advance of the others, I clapped my gun to the boar's head, and so put an end to the contest.

Evening now coming on, we set to work loading our carriers. The cattle were so small, that a stout native could walk off with an entire quarter; brushing through thickets, and descending rocks without an apparent effort: though, to tell the truth, no white man present could have done the thing with any ease. As for the wild hogs, none of the islanders could be induced to carry Shorty's; some invincible superstition being connected with its black colour. We were, therefore, obliged to leave it. The other, a spotted one, being slung by green thongs to a pole, was marched off with by two young natives.

With our bearers of burdens ahead, we then commenced our return down the valley. Half-way home, darkness overtook us in the woods; and torches became necessary. We stopped, and made them of dry palm branches; and then, sending two lads on in advance, for the purpose of gathering fuel to feed the flambeaux, we continued our journey.

It was a wild sight. The torches, waved aloft, flashed through the forest; and, where the ground admitted, the islanders went along on a brisk trot, notwithstanding they bent forward under their loads.

Their naked backs were stained with blood; and occasionally, running by each other, they raised wild cries, which startled the hillsides.

### The Hunting-Feast; and a Visit to Afrehitoo

Two bullocks and a boar! No bad trophies of our day's sport. So by torchlight we marched into the plantation, the wild hog rocking from its pole, and the doctor singing an old hunting-song —Tallyho! the chorus of which swelled high above the yells of the natives.

We resolved to make a night of it. Kindling a great fire just outside the dwelling, and hanging one of the heifer's quarters from a limb of the banian-tree, every one was at liberty to cut and broil for himself. Baskets of roasted breadfruit, and plenty of taro pudding; bunches of bananas, and young coco-nuts, had also been provided by the natives against our return.

The fire burned bravely, keeping off the mosquitoes, and making every man's face glow like a beaker of Port. The meat had the true wild-game flavour, not at all impaired by our famous appetites, and a couple of flasks of white brandy, which Zeke, producing from his secret store, circulated freely.

There was no end to my long comrade's spirits. After telling his stories, and singing his songs, he sprang to his feet, clasped a young damsel of the grove round the waist, and waltzed over the grass with her. But there's no telling all the pranks he played that night. The natives, who delight in a wag, emphatically pronounced him "maitai."

It was long after midnight ere we broke up; but when the rest had retired, Zeke, with the true thrift of a Yankee, salted down what was left of the meat.

The next day was Sunday; and at my request, Shorty accompanied me to Afrehitoo—a neighbouring bay, and the seat of a mission, almost directly opposite Papeetee. In Afrehitoo is a large church and schoolhouse, both quite dilapidated; and planted amid shrubbery on a fine knoll, stands a very tasteful cottage, commanding a view across the channel. In passing, I caught sight of a graceful calico skirt disappearing from the piazza through a doorway. The place was the residence of the missionary.

A trim little sail-boat was dancing out at her moorings, a few yards from the beach.

Straggling over the lowlands in the vicinity were several native huts—untidy enough—but much better every way, than most of those in Tahiti.

We attended service at the church, where we found but a small congregation; and after what I had seen in Papeetee, nothing very interesting took place. But the audience had a curious, fidgety look, which I knew not how to account for, until we ascertained that a sermon with the eighth commandment for a text was being preached.

It seemed that there lived an Englishman in the district, who, like our friends, the planters, was cultivating Tombez potatoes for the Papeetee market.

In spite of all his precautions, the natives were in the habit of making nocturnal forays into his enclosure, and carrying off the potatoes. One night he fired a fowling-piece, charged with pepper and salt, at several shadows which he discovered stealing across his premises. They fled. But it was like seasoning anything else: the knaves stole again with a greater relish than ever; and the very next night, he caught a party in the act of roasting a basket full of potatoes under his own cooking-shed. At last, he stated his grievances to the missionary; who, for the benefit of his congregation, preached the sermon we heard.

Now, there were no thieves in Martair; but then, the people of the valley were bribed to be honest. It was a regular business transaction between them and the planters. In consideration of so many potatoes "to them in hand, duly paid," they were to abstain from all depredations upon the plantation. Another security against roguery, was the permanent resident upon the premises, of their chief, Tonoi.

On our return to Martair, in the afternoon, we found the doctor and Zeke making themselves comfortable. The latter was reclining on the ground, pipe in mouth, watching the doctor, who, sitting like a Turk, before a large iron kettle, was slicing potatoes and Indian turnip, and now and then shattering splinters from a bone; all of which, by turns, were thrown into the pot. He was making what he called "Bullock broth."

In gastronomic affairs, my friend was something of an artist; and by way of improving his knowledge, did nothing the rest of the day but practise in what might be called Experimental Cookery: broiling and grilling, and devilling slices of meat, and subjecting them to all sorts of igneous operations. It was the first fresh beef that either of us had tasted in more than a year.

"Oh, ye'll pick up arter a while, Peter," observed Zeke toward night, as Long Ghost was turning a great rib over the coals— "what d'ye think, Paul?"

"He'll get along, I dare say," replied I; "he only wants to get those cheeks of his tanned." To tell the truth, I was not a little pleased to see the doctor's reputation as an invalid fading away so fast; especially, as on the strength of his being one, he had promised to have such easy times of it, and very likely, too, at my expense.

## What They Thought of Us in Martair

Several quiet days now passed away, during which, we just worked sufficiently to sharpen our appetites; the planters leniently exempting us from any severe toil.

Their desire to retain us became more and more evident; which was not to be wondered at; for, besides esteeming us from the beginning a couple of civil, good-natured fellows, who would soon become quite at home with them, they were not slow in perceiving that we were far different from the common run of rovers; and that our society was both entertaining and instructive to a couple of solitary, illiterate men, like themselves.

In a literary point of view, indeed, they soon regarded us with emotions of envy and wonder; and the doctor was considered nothing short of a prodigy. The Cockney found out, that he (the doctor) could read a book upside down, without even so much as spelling the big words beforehand; and the Yankee, in the twinkling of an eye, received from him the sum total of several arithmetical items, stated aloud, with the view of testing the extent of his mathematical lore.

Then, frequently, in discoursing upon men and things, my long comrade employed such imposing phrases, that, upon one occasion, they actually remained uncovered while he talked.

In short, their favourable opinion of Long Ghost in particular, rose higher and higher every day; and they began to indulge in all manner of dreams concerning the advantages to be derived from employing so learned a labourer. Among other projects revealed, was that of building a small craft of some forty tons, for the purpose of trading among the neighbouring islands. With a native crew, we would then take turns cruising over the tranquil Pacific; touching here and there, as caprice suggested, and collecting romantic articles of commerce;—bêche-de-mer, the pearl-oyster, arrow-root, ambergris, sandalwood, coco-nut oil, and edible birds'-nests.

This South Sea yachting was delightful to think of; and straightway, the doctor announced his willingness to navigate the future schooner clear of all shoals and reefs whatsoever. His impudence was audacious. He enlarged upon the science of navigation; treated us to a dissertation on Mercator's Sailing and the Azimuth compass; and went into an inexplicable explanation of the Lord only knows what plan of his, for infallibly settling the longitude.

Whenever my comrade thus gave the reins to his fine fancy, it was a treat to listen, and therefore I never interfered; but, with the planters, sat in mute admiration before him. This apparent self-abasement on my part, must have been considered as truly indicative of our respective merits; for, to my no small concern, I quickly perceived that, in the estimate formed of us, Long Ghost began to be rated far above myself. For aught I knew, indeed, he might have privately thrown out a hint concerning the difference in our respective stations aboard the *Julia;* or else, the planters must have considered him some illustrious individual, for certain inscrutable reasons, going incog. With this idea of him, his undisguised disinclination for work became venial; and, entertaining such views of extending their business, they counted more upon his ultimate value to them as a man of science, than as a mere ditcher.

Nor did the humorous doctor forbear to foster an opinion every way so advantageous to himself; at times, for the sake of the joke, assuming airs of superiority over myself, which, though laughable enough, were sometimes annoying.

To tell the plain truth, things at last came to such a pass, that I told him, up and down, that I had no notion to put up with his pretensions; if he were going to play the gentleman, I was going to follow suit; and then, there would quickly be an explosion.

At this he laughed heartily; and after some mirthful chat, we resolved upon leaving the valley, as soon as we could do so with a proper regard to politeness.

At supper, therefore, the same evening, the doctor hinted at our intention.

Though much surprised, and vexed, Zeke moved not a muscle. "Peter," said he at last—very gravely—and after mature deliberation, "would you like to do the *cooking?* It's easy work; and you needn't do anything else. Paul's heartier; he can work in the field when it suits him; and before long, we'll have ye at something more agreeable:—won't we, Shorty?"

Shorty assented.

Doubtless, the proposed arrangement was a snug one; especially the sinecure for the doctor; but I by no means relished the functions allotted to myself—they were too indefinite. Nothing final, however, was agreed upon;—our intention to leave was revealed, and that was enough for the present. But, as we said nothing further about going, the Yankee must have concluded that we might yet be induced to remain. He redoubled his endeavours to make us contented.

It was during this state of affairs, that one morning, before breakfast, we were set to weeding in a potato-patch; and the planters being engaged at the house, we were left to ourselves.

Now, though the pulling of weeds was considered by our employers an easy occupation (for which reason they had assigned it to us), and although as a garden recreation, it may be pleasant enough for those who like it—still, long persisted in, the business becomes excessively irksome.

Nevertheless, we toiled away for some time, until the doctor, who, from his height, was obliged to stoop at a very acute angle, suddenly sprang upright; and, with one hand propping his spinal column, exclaimed, "Oh, that one's joints were but provided with holes to drop a little oil through!"

Vain as the aspiration was for this proposed improvement upon our species, I cordially responded thereto; for every vertebra in my spine was articulating its sympathy.

Presently, the sun rose over the mountains, inducing that deadly morning languor, so fatal to early exertion in a warm climate. We could stand it no longer; but, shouldering our hoes, moved on to the house, resolved to impose no more upon the good nature of the planters, by continuing one moment longer in an occupation so extremely uncongenial.

We freely told them so. Zeke was exceedingly hurt, and said everything he could think of to alter our determination; but finding all unavailing, he very hospitably urged us not to be in any hurry about leaving; for we might stay with him as guests until we had time to decide upon our future movements.

We thanked him sincerely; but replied, that the following morning, we must turn our backs upon the hills of Martair.

### Preparing for the Journey

During the remainder of the day we loitered about, talking over our plans.

The doctor was all eagerness to visit Tamai, a solitary inland village, standing upon the banks of a considerable lake of the same name, and embosomed among groves. From Afrehitoo you went to this place by a lonely pathway, leading through the wildest scenery in the world. Much, too, we had heard concerning the lake itself, which abounded in such delicious fish, that, in former times, angling parties occasionally came over to it, from Papeetee.

Upon its banks, moreover, grew the finest fruit of the islands, and in their greatest perfection. The "Ve," or Brazilian plum, here attained the size of an orange; and the gorgeous "Arheea," or red apple of Tahiti, blushed with deeper dyes than in any of the seaward valleys.

Besides all this, in Tamai dwelt the most beautiful and un-sophisticated women in the entire Society group. In short, the village was so remote from the coast, and had been so much less affected by recent changes than other places that, in most things, Tahitian life was here seen, as formerly existing in the days of young Otoo, the boy-king, in Cook's time.

After obtaining from the planters all the information which was needed, we decided upon penetrating to the village; and after a temporary sojourn there, to strike the beach again, and journey round to Taloo, a harbour on the opposite side of the island.

We at once put ourselves in travelling trim. Just previous to leaving Tahiti, having found my wardrobe reduced to two suits (frock and trousers, both much the worse for wear), I had quilted them together for mutual preservation (after a fashion peculiar to sailors); engrafting a red frock upon a blue one, and producing thereby a choice variety in the way of clothing. This was the extent of my wardrobe. Nor was the doctor by any means better off. His improvidence had at last driven him to don the nautical garb; but by this time, his frock—a light cotton one—had almost given out, and he had nothing to replace it. Shorty very generously offered him one which was a little less ragged; but the alms was proudly refused; Long Ghost preferring to assume the ancient costume of Tahiti—the "*Roora.*"

This garment, once worn as a festival dress, is now seldom met with; but Captain Bob had often shown us one which he kept as an heirloom. It was a cloak, or mantle of yellow tappa, precisely similar to the "*poncho,*" worn by the South-American Spaniards. The head being slipped through a slit in the middle, the robe hangs about the person in ample drapery. Tonoi obtained sufficient coarse brown tappa to make a short mantle of this description; and in five minutes the doctor was equipped. Zeke, eyeing his *toga* critically, reminded its proprietor that there were many streams to ford, and precipices to scale, between Martair and Tamai; and if he travelled in petticoats, he had better hold them up.

Besides other deficiencies, we were utterly shoeless. In the free and easy Pacific, sailors seldom wear shoes; mine had been tossed overboard the day we met the Trades; and except in one or two tramps ashore, I had never worn any since. In Martair, they would have been desirable; but none were to be had. For the expedition we meditated, however, they were indispensable. Zeke, being the owner of a pair of huge, dilapidated boots, hanging from a rafter like saddle-bags, the doctor succeeded in exchanging for them a case-knife, the last valuable article in his possession. For myself, I made sandals from a bullock's hide, such as are worn by the Indians in California. They are made in a minute; the sole, rudely fashioned to the foot, being confined across the instep by three straps of leather.

Our headgear deserves a passing word. My comrade's was a brave old Panama hat, made of grass, almost as fine as threads of silk; and so elastic, that upon rolling it up, it sprang into perfect shape again. Set off by the jaunty slouch of this Spanish sombrero, Doctor Long Ghost, in this and his Roora, looked like a mendicant grandee.

Nor was my own appearance in an Eastern turban less distinguished. The way I came to wear it was this. My hat having been knocked overboard, a few days before reaching Papeetee, I was obliged to mount an abominable wad of parti-coloured worsted—what sailors call a Scotch cap. Every one knows the elasticity of knit wool; and this Caledonian headdress crowned my temples so effectually, that the confined atmosphere engendered was prejudicial to my curls. In vain I tried to ventilate the cap: every gash made, seemed to heal whole in no time. Then such a continual chafing as it kept up in a hot sun.

Seeing my dislike to the thing, Kooloo, my worthy friend, prevailed upon me to bestow it upon him. I did so; hinting that a good boiling might restore the original brilliancy of the colours.

It was then that I mounted the turban. Taking a new Regatta frock of the doctor's, which was of a gay calico, and winding it round my head in folds, I allowed the sleeves to droop behind—thus forming a good defence against the sun, though in a shower it was best off. The pendent sleeves adding much to the effect, the doctor always called me the Bashaw with Two Tails.

Thus arrayed, we were ready for Tamai; in whose green saloons we counted upon creating no small sensation.

### Tamai

Long before sunrise the next morning, my sandals were laced on, and the doctor had vaulted into Zeke's boots.

Expecting to see us again before we went to Taloo, the planters wished us a pleasant journey; and, on parting, very generously presented us with a pound or two of what sailors call "plug" tobacco; telling us to cut it up into small change; the Virginian weed being the principal circulating medium on the island.

Tamai, we were told, was not more than three or four leagues distant; so making allowances for a wild road, a few hours to rest at noon, and our determination to take the journey leisurely, we counted upon reaching the shores of the lake some time in the flush of the evening.

For several hours we went on slowly through wood and ravine, and over hill and precipice, seeing nothing but occasional herds of wild cattle, and often resting; until we found ourselves, about noon, in the very heart of the island.

It was a green, cool hollow among the mountains, into which we at last descended with a bound. The place was gushing with a hundred springs, and shaded over with great solemn trees, on whose mossy boles the moisture stood in beads. Strange to say, no traces of the bullocks ever having been here were revealed. Nor was there a sound to be heard, nor a bird to be seen, nor any breath of wind stirring the leaves. The utter solitude and silence were oppressive; and after peering about under the shades, and seeing nothing but ranks of dark, motionless trunks, we hurried across the hollow, and ascended a steep mountain opposite.

Midway up, we rested where the earth had gathered about the roots of three palms, and thus formed a pleasant lounge, from which we looked down upon the hollow, now one dark-green tuft of woodland at our feet. Here we brought forth a small calabash of "*poee*," a parting present from Tonoi. After eating heartily, we obtained fire by two sticks, and throwing ourselves back, puffed forth our fatigue in wreaths of smoke. At last we fell asleep; nor did we waken till the sun had sunk so low that its rays darted in upon us under the foliage.

Starting up, we then continued our journey; and as we gained the mountain top—there, to our surprise, lay the lake and village of Tamai. We had thought it a good league off. Where we stood, the yellow sunset was still lingering; but over the valley below, long shadows were stealing—the rippling green lake reflecting the houses and trees, just as they stood along its banks. Several small canoes, moored here and there to posts in the water, were dancing upon the waves; and one solitary fisherman was paddling over to a grassy point. In front of the houses, groups of natives were seen; some thrown at full length upon the ground, and others indolently leaning against the bamboos.

With whoop and halloo, we ran down the hills, the villagers soon hurrying forth to see who were coming. As we drew near, they gathered round, all curiosity to know what brought the "karhowries" into their quiet country. The doctor contriving to make them understand the purely social object of our visit, they gave us a true Tahitian welcome; pointing into their dwellings, and saying they were ours as long as we chose to remain.

We were struck by the appearance of these people, both men and women; so much more healthful than the inhabitants of the bays. As for the young girls, they were more retiring and modest, more tidy in their dress, and far fresher and more beautiful than the damsels of the coast. A thousand pities, thought I, that they should bury their charms in this nook of a valley.

That night we abode in the house of Rartoo, a hospitable old chief. It was right on the shore of the lake; and at supper, we looked out through a rustling screen of foliage upon the surface of the starlit water.

The next day we rambled about, and found a happy little community, comparatively free from many deplorable evils to which the rest of their countrymen are subject. Their time, too, was more occupied. To my surprise, the manufacture of tappa was going on in several buildings. European calicoes were seldom seen, and not many articles of foreign origin of any description.

The people of Tamai were nominally Christians; but being so remote from ecclesiastical jurisdiction, their religion sat lightly upon them. We had been told, even, that many heathenish games and dances still secretly lingered in their valley.

Now the prospect of seeing an old-fashioned "hevar," or Tahitian reel, was one of the inducements which brought us here; and so, finding Rartoo rather liberal in his religious ideas, we disclosed our desire. At first, he demurred; and shrugging his shoulders like a Frenchman, declared it could not be brought about—was a dangerous matter to attempt, and might bring all concerned into trouble. But we overcame all this, convinced him that the thing could be done, and a "hevar," a genuine pagan fandango, was arranged for that very night.

### A Dance in the Valley

There were some ill-natured people—tell-tales—it seemed, in Tamai; and hence there was a deal of mystery about getting up the dance.

An hour or two before midnight, Rartoo entered the house, and, throwing robes of tappa over us, bade us follow at a distance behind him; and, until out of the village, hood our faces. Keenly alive to the adventure, we obeyed. At last, after taking a wide circuit, we came out upon the farthest shore of the lake. It was a wide, dewy space; lighted up by a full moon, and carpeted with a minute species of fern, growing closely together. It swept right down to the water, showing the village opposite, glistening among the groves.

Near the trees, on one side of the clear space, was a ruinous pile of stones, many rods in extent; upon which had formerly stood a temple of Oro. At present, there was nothing but a rude hut, planted on the lowermost terrace. It seemed to have been used as a "*tappa herree*"; or house for making the native cloth.

Here, we saw lights gleaming from between the bamboos, and casting long, rod-like shadows upon the ground without. Voices also were heard. We went up, and had a peep at the dancers; who were getting ready for the ballet. They were some twenty in number; waited upon by hideous old crones, who might have been duennas. Long Ghost proposed to send the latter packing; but Rartoo said it would never do, and so they were permitted to remain.

We tried to effect an entrance at the door, which was fastened; but, after a noisy discussion with one of the old witches within, our guide became fidgety, and, at last, told us to desist, or we would spoil all. He then led us off to a distance, to await the performance; as the girls, he said, did not wish to be recognized. He, furthermore, made us promise to remain where we were, until all was over, and the dancers had retired.

We waited impatiently; and, at last, they came forth. They were arrayed in short tunics of white tappa; with garlands of flowers on their heads. Following them, were the duennas, who remained clustering about the house, while the girls advanced a few paces; and, in an instant, two of them, taller than their companions, were standing, side by side, in the middle of a ring, formed by the clasped hands of the rest. This movement was made in perfect silence.

Presently, the two girls joined hands overhead; and, crying out, "Ahloo! ahloo!" wave them to and fro. Upon which, the ring begins to circle slowly; the dancers moving sideways, with their arms a little drooping. Soon they quicken their pace; and, at last, fly round and round: bosoms heaving, hair streaming, flowers dropping, and every sparkling eye circling in what seemed a line of light.

Meanwhile, the pair within are passing and repassing each other incessantly. Inclining sideways, so that their long hair falls far over, they glide this way and that; one foot continually in the air, and their fingers thrown forth, and twirling in the moonbeams.

"Ahloo! ahloo!" again cry the dance queens; and, coming together in the middle of the ring, they once more lift up the arch, and stand motionless.

"Ahloo! ahloo!" Every link of the circle is broken; and the girls, deeply breathing, stand perfectly still. They pant hard and fast, a moment or two; and then, just as the deep flush is dying away from their faces, slowly recede, all round; thus enlarging the ring.

Again the two leaders wave their hands, when the rest pause; and now, far apart, stand in the still moonlight, like a circle of fairies. Presently, raising a strange chant, they softly sway themselves, gradually quickening the movement, until, at length, for a few passionate moments, with throbbing bosoms and glowing cheeks, they abandon themselves to all the spirit of the dance, apparently lost to everything around. But soon subsiding again into the same languid measure, as before, they become motionless; and then, reeling forward on all sides, their eyes swimming in their heads, join in one wild chorus, and sink into each other's arms.

Such is the Lory-Lory, I think they call it; the dance of the backsliding girls of Tamai.

While it was going on, we had as much as we could do to keep the doctor from rushing forward and seizing a partner.

They would give us no more "hevars," that night; and Rartoo fairly dragged us away to a canoe, hauled up on the lake shore; when we reluctantly embarked, and, paddling over to the village, arrived there in time for a good nap before sunrise.

The next day, the doctor went about, trying to hunt up the overnight dancers. He thought to detect them by their late rising; but never was man more mistaken; for, on first sallying out, the whole village was asleep, waking up in concert about an hour after. But, in the course of the day, he came across several, whom he at once charged with taking part in the "hevar." There were some prim-looking fellows standing by (visiting elders from Afrehitoo, perhaps), and the girls looked embarrassed; but parried the charge most skilfully.

Though soft as doves, in general, the ladies of Tamai are, nevertheless, flavoured with a slight tincture of what we queerly enough call the *"devil"*; and they showed it on the present occasion. For when the doctor pressed one rather hard, she all at once turned round upon him, and giving him a box on the ear, told him to "hanree perrar!" (be off with himself).

### Mysterious

There was a little old man, of a most hideous aspect, living in Tamai, who, in a coarse mantle of tappa, went about the village, dancing, and singing, and making faces. He followed us about, wherever we went; and, when unobserved by others, plucked at our garments, making frightful signs for us to go along with him somewhere, and see something.

It was in vain that we tried to get rid of him. Kicks and cuffs, even, were at last resorted to; but, though he howled like one possessed, he would not go away, but still haunted us. At last, we conjured the natives to rid us of him; but they only laughed; so, we were forced to endure the dispensation as well as we could.

On the fourth night of our visit, returning home late from paying a few calls through the village, we turned a dark corner of trees, and came full upon our goblin friend; as usual, chattering, and motioning with his hands. The doctor, venting a curse, hurried forward; but, from some impulse or other, I stood my ground, resolved to find out what this unaccountable object wanted of us. Seeing me pause, he crept close up to me, peered into my face, and then retreated, beckoning me to follow; which I did.

In a few moments the village was behind us; and with my guide in advance, I found myself in the shadow of the heights overlooking the farther side of the valley. Here my guide paused until I came up with him; when, side by side, and without speaking, we ascended the hill.

Presently, we came to a wretched hut, barely distinguishable in the shade cast by the neighbouring trees. Pushing aside a rude, sliding door, held together with thongs, the goblin signed me to enter. Within, it looked dark as pitch; so, I gave him to understand that he must strike a light, and go in before me. Without replying, he disappeared in the darkness; and, after groping about, I heard two sticks rubbing together, and directly saw a spark. A native taper was then lighted, and I stooped, and entered.

It was a mere kennel. Foul old mats, and broken coco-nut shells, and calabashes were strewn about the floor of earth; and overhead,

I caught glimpses of the stars through chinks in the roof. Here and there, the thatch had fallen through, and hung down in wisps.

I now told him to set about what he was going to do, or produce whatever he had to show without delay. Looking round fearfully, as if dreading a surprise, he commenced turning over and over the rubbish in one corner. At last, he clutched a calabash, stained black, and with the neck broken off; on one side of it was a large hole. Something seemed to be stuffed away in the vessel; and after a deal of poking at the aperture, a musty old pair of sailor trousers was drawn forth; and, holding them up eagerly, he inquired how many pieces of tobacco I would give for them.

Without replying, I hurried away; the old man chasing me, and shouting as I ran, until I gained the village. Here, I dodged him, and made my way home, resolved never to disclose so inglorious an adventure.

To no purpose, the next morning, my comrade besought me to enlighten him: I preserved a mysterious silence.

The occurrence served me a good turn, however, so long as we abode in Tamai; for the old clothesman never afterward troubled me; but for ever haunted the doctor, who, in vain, supplicated Heaven to be delivered from him.

### The Hegira, or Flight

"I say, doctor," cried I, a few days after my adventure with the goblin, as, in the absence of our host, we were one morning lounging upon the matting in his dwelling, smoking our reed pipes, "Tamai's a thriving place; why not settle down?"

"Faith!" said he, "not a bad idea, Paul. But do you fancy they'll let us stay, though?"

"Why, certainly: they would be overjoyed to have a couple of karhowrees for townsmen."

"Gad! you're right, my pleasant fellow. Ha! ha! I'll put up a banana leaf as physician from London—deliver lectures on Polynesian antiquities—teach English in five lessons, of one hour each—establish power-looms for the manufacture of tappa—lay out a public park in the middle of the village, and found a festival in honour of Captain Cook!"

"But, surely, not without stopping to take breath," observed I.

The doctor's projects, to be sure, were of a rather visionary cast; but we seriously thought, nevertheless, of prolonging our stay in the valley for an indefinite period; and, with this understanding, we were turning over various plans for spending our time pleasantly, when several women came running into the house, and hurriedly besought us to *heree! heree!* (make our escape), crying out something about the *mickonarees*.

Thinking that we were about to be taken up under the act for the suppression of vagrancy, we flew out of the house, sprang into a canoe before the door, and paddled with might and main over to the opposite side of the lake.

Approaching Rartoo's dwelling, was a great crowd, among which we perceived several natives, who, from their partly European dress, we were certain did not reside in Tamai.

Plunging into the groves, we thanked our stars that we had thus narrowly escaped being apprehended as runaway seamen, and marched off to the beach. This, at least, was what we thought we had escaped.

Having fled the village, we could not think of prowling about its vicinity, and then returning; in doing so, we might be risking our liberty again. We therefore determined upon journeying back to Martair; and setting our faces thitherward, we reached the planters' house about nightfall. They gave us a cordial reception, and a hearty supper; and we sat up talking until a late hour.

We now prepared to go round to Taloo, a place from which we were not far off when at Tamai; but wishing to see as much of the island as we could, we preferred returning to Martair, and then going round by way of the beach.

Taloo, the only frequented harbour of Imeeo, lies on the western side of the island, almost directly over against Martair. Upon one shore of the bay stands the village of Partoowye, a missionary station. In its vicinity is an extensive sugar plantation—the best in the South Seas, perhaps—worked by a person from Sydney.

The patrimonial property of the husband of Pomaree, and every way a delightful retreat, Partoowye was one of the occasional residences of the court. But at the time I write of, it was permanently fixed there, the queen having fled thither from Tahiti.

Partoowye, they told us, was, by no means, the place Papeetee was. Ships seldom touched, and very few foreigners were living ashore. A solitary whaler, however, was reported to be lying in the harbour, wooding and watering, and said to be in want of men.

All things considered, I could not help looking upon Taloo as offering "a splendid opening" for us adventurers. To say nothing of the facilities presented for going to sea in the whaler, or hiring ourselves out as day labourers in the sugar plantation, there were hopes to be entertained of being promoted to some office of high trust and emolument, about the person of her majesty, the queen.

Nor was this expectation altogether Quixotic. In the train of many Polynesian princes, roving whites are frequently found: gentlemen pensioners of state, basking in the tropical sunshine of the court, and leading the pleasantest lives in the world. Upon islands little visited by foreigners, the first seaman that settles down is generally domesticated in the family of the head chief or king; where he frequently discharges the functions of various offices elsewhere filled by as many different individuals. As historiographer, for instance, he gives the natives some account of distant countries; as commissioner of the arts and sciences, he instructs them in the use of the jack-knife, and the best way of shaping bits of iron hoop into spearheads; and as interpreter to his majesty, he facilitates intercourse with strangers; besides instructing the people generally in the uses of the most common English phrases, civil and profane; but oftener the latter.

These men generally marry well; often—like Hardy of Hannamanoo—into the blood royal.

Sometimes they officiate as personal attendant, or First Lord in Waiting, to the king. At Amboi, one of the Tonga Islands, a vagabond Welshman bends his knee as cupbearer to his cannibal majesty. He mixes his morning cup of "arva," and, with profound genuflections, presents it in a coco-nut bowl, richly carved. Upon another island of the same group, where it is customary to bestow no small pains in dressing the hair—frizzing it out by a curious process, into an enormous Pope's-head—an old man-of-war's-man fills the post of barber to the king. And as his majesty is not very neat, his mop is exceedingly populous; so that, when Jack is not engaged in dressing the head entrusted to his charge, he busies himself in gently titillating it—a sort of skewer being actually worn about in the patient's hair for that special purpose.

Even upon the Sandwich Islands, a low rabble of foreigners is kept about the person of Tammahammaha, for the purpose of ministering to his ease or enjoyment.

Billy Loon, a jolly little Negro, tricked out in a soiled blue jacket, studded all over with rusty bell-buttons, and garnished with shabby gold lace, is the royal drummer and pounder of the tambourine. Joe, a wooden-legged Portuguese, who lost his leg by a whale, is

violinist; and Mordecai, as he is called, a villainous-looking scamp,
going about with his cups and balls in a side pocket, diverts the
court with his jugglery. These idle rascals receive no fixed salary,
being altogether dependent upon the casual bounty of their master.
Now and then they run up a score at the Dance Houses in Hono-
lulu, where the illustrious Tammahammaha III afterward calls and
settles the bill.

A few years since, an auctioneer to his majesty came near being
added to the retinue of state. It seems that he was the first man who
had practised his vocation on the Sandwich Islands; and delighted
with the sport of bidding upon his wares, the king was one of his
best customers. At last he besought the man to leave all and follow
him, and he should be handsomely provided for at court. But the
auctioneer refused; and so the ivory hammer lost the chance of
being borne before him on a velvet cushion, when the next king
went to be crowned.

But it was not as strolling players, nor as footmen out of employ, that the doctor and myself looked forward to our approaching introduction to the court of the Queen of Tahiti. On the contrary, as before hinted, we expected to swell the appropriations of
breadfruit and coco-nuts on the Civil List, by filling some honourable office in her gift.

We were told, that to resist the usurpation of the French, the
queen was rallying about her person all the foreigners she could.
Her partiality for the English and Americans was well known; and
this was an additional ground for our anticipating a favourable
reception. Zeke had informed us, moreover, that by the queen's
counsellors at Partoowye, a war of aggression against the invaders
at Papeetee had been seriously thought of. Should this prove true,
a surgeon's commission for the doctor, and a lieutenancy for myself, were certainly counted upon in our sanguine expectations.

Such, then, were our views, and such our hopes in projecting
a trip to Taloo. But in our most lofty aspirations, we by no means
lost sight of any minor matters which might help us to promotion.
The doctor had informed me that he excelled in playing the fiddle.
I now suggested, that as soon as we arrived at Partoowye, we should
endeavour to borrow a violin for him; or if this could not be done,
that he should manufacture some kind of a substitute, and thus
equipped, apply for an audience of the queen. Her well-known
passion for music would at once secure his admittance; and so, un-

der the most favourable auspices, bring about our introduction to her notice.

"And who knows," said my waggish comrade, throwing his head back, and performing an imaginary air by briskly drawing one arm across the other, "who knows, that I may not fiddle myself into her majesty's good graces, so as to become a sort of Rizzio to the Tahitian princess."

### How We Were to Get to Taloo

The inglorious circumstances of our somewhat premature departure from Tamai, filled the sagacious doctor, and myself, with sundry misgivings for the future.

Under Zeke's protection, we were secure from all impertinent interference in our concerns, on the part of the natives. But as friendless wanderers over the island, we ran the risk of being apprehended as runaways, and as such, sent back to Tahiti. The truth is, that the rewards constantly offered for the apprehension of deserters from ships, induce some of the natives to eye all strangers suspiciously.

A passport was therefore desirable; but such a thing had never been heard of in Imeeo. At last, Long Ghost suggested, that as the Yankee was well known, and much respected all over the island, we should endeavour to obtain from him some sort of paper, not only certifying to our having been in his employ, but also to our not being highwaymen, kidnappers, nor yet runaway seamen. Even written in English, a paper like this would answer every purpose; for the unlettered natives, standing in great awe of the document, would not dare to molest us until acquainted with its purport. Then, if it came to the worst, we might repair to the nearest missionary, and have the passport explained.

Upon informing Zeke of these matters, he seemed highly flattered with the opinion we entertained of his reputation abroad; and he agreed to oblige us. The doctor at once offered to furnish him with a draft of the paper; but he refused, saying he would write it himself. With a rooster's quill, therefore, a bit of soiled paper, and a stout heart, he set to work. Evidently, he was not accustomed to composition; for his literary throes were so violent, that the doctor suggested that some sort of a Cæsarian operation might be necessary.

The precious paper was at last finished; and a great curiosity it was. We were much diverted with his reasons for not dating it.

"In this here dumned climate," he ordered, "a feller can't keep the run of the months, nohow; cause there's no seasons; no summer and winter, to go by. One's etarnally thinkin' it's always July, it's so pesky hot."

A passport provided, we cast about for some means of getting to Taloo.

The island of Imeeo is very nearly surrounded by a regular breakwater of coral, extending within a mile or less of the shore. The smooth canal within, furnishes the best means of communication with the different settlements; all of which, with the exception of Tamai, are right upon the water. And so indolent are the Imeeose, that they think nothing of going twenty or thirty miles round the island in a canoe, in order to reach a place not a quarter of that distance by land. But as hinted before, the fear of the bullocks has something to do with this.

The idea of journeying in a canoe struck our fancy quite pleasantly; and we at once set about chartering one, if possible. But none could we obtain. For not only did we have nothing to pay for hiring one, but we could not expect to have it loaned; inasmuch as the good-natured owner would, in all probability, have to walk along the beach as we paddled, in order to bring back his property when we had no further use for it.

At last, it was decided to commence our journey on foot; trusting that we would soon fall in with a canoe going our way, in which we might take passage.

The planters said we would find no beaten path:—all we had to do was to follow the beach; and however inviting it might look inland, on no account must we stray from it. In short, the longest way round was the nearest way to Taloo. At intervals, there were little hamlets along the shore, besides lonely fishermen's huts here and there, where we could get plenty to eat without pay; so there was no necessity to lay in any store.

Intending to be off before sunrise the next morning, so as to have the benefit of the coolest part of the day, we bade our kind hosts farewell, overnight; and then, repairing to the beach, we launched our floating pallet, and slept away merrily till dawn.

### The Journey Round the Beach

It was on the fourth day of the first month of the Hegira, or Flight from Tamai (we now reckoned our time thus), that, rising bright and early, we were up and away out of the valley of Martair, before the fishermen even were stirring.

It was the earliest dawn. The morning only showed itself along the lower edge of a bank of purple clouds, pierced by the misty peaks of Tahiti. The tropical day seemed too languid to rise. Sometimes, starting fitfully, it decked the clouds with faint edgings of pink and grey, which, fading away, left all dim again. Anon, it threw out thin, pale rays, growing lighter and lighter, until at last, the golden morning sprang out of the East with a bound—darting its bright beams hither and thither, higher and higher, and sending them, broadcast, over the face of the heavens.

All balmy from the groves of Tahiti, came an indolent air, cooled by its transit over the waters; and grateful under foot was the damp and slightly yielding beach, from which the waves seemed just retired.

The doctor was in famous spirits; removing his Roora, he went splashing into the sea; and, after swimming a few yards, waded ashore, hopping, skipping, and jumping along the beach; but very careful to cut all his capers in the direction of our journey.

Say what they will of the glowing independence one feels in the saddle, give me the first morning flush of your cheery pedestrian!

Thus exhilarated, we went on, as light-hearted and care-free, as we could wish.

And here, I cannot refrain from lauding the very superior inducements which most intertropical countries afford, not only to mere rovers like ourselves, but to penniless people, generally. In these genial regions, one's wants are naturally diminished; and those which remain are easily gratified: fuel, house-shelter, and, if you please, clothing, may be entirely dispensed with.

How different, our hard northern latitudes! Alas! the lot of a "poor devil," twenty degrees north of the tropic of Cancer, is indeed pitiable.

At last, the beach contracted to hardly a yard's width, and the dense thicket almost dipped into the sea. In place of the smooth sand, too, we had sharp fragments of broken coral, which made travelling exceedingly unpleasant. "Lord! my foot!" roared the doctor, fetching it up for inspection, with a galvanic fling of the limb. A sharp splinter had thrust itself into the flesh, through a hole in his boot. My sandals were worse yet; their soles taking a sort of fossil impression of everything trod upon.

Turning round a bold sweep of the beach, we came upon a

piece of fine, open ground, with a fisherman's dwelling in the distance, crowning a knoll which rolled off into the water.

The hut proved to be a low, rude erection, very recently thrown up; for the bamboos were still green as grass, and the thatching, fresh and fragrant as meadow hay. It was open upon three sides; so that, upon drawing near, the domestic arrangements within were in plain sight. No one was stirring; and nothing was to be seen but a clumsy old chest of native workmanship, a few calabashes, and bundles of tappa hanging against a post; and a heap of something, we knew not what, in a dark corner. Upon close inspection, the doctor discovered it to be a loving old couple, locked in each other's arms, and rolled together in a tappa mantle.

"Halloa! Darby!" he cried, shaking the one with a beard. But Darby heeded him not; though Joan, a wrinkled old body, started up in affright, and yelled aloud. Neither of us attempting to gag her, she presently became quiet; and after staring hard, and asking some unintelligible questions, she proceeded to rouse her still slumbering mate.

What ailed him, we could not tell; but there was no waking him. Equally in vain were all his dear spouse's cuffs, pinches, and other endearments; he lay like a log, face up, and snoring away like a cavalry trumpeter.

"Here, my good woman," said Long Ghost, "just let *me* try;" and, taking the patient right by his nose, he so lifted him bodily, into a sitting position, and held him there until his eyes opened. When this event came to pass, Darby looked round like one stupefied; and then, springing to his feet, backed away into a corner, from which place we became the objects of his earnest and respectful attention.

"Permit me, my dear Darby, to introduce to you my esteemed friend and comrade, Paul," said the doctor, gallanting me up with all the grimace and flourish imaginable. Upon this, Darby began to recover his faculties, and surprised us not a little, by talking a few words of English. So far as could be understood, they were expressive of his having been aware, that there were two "karhowrees" in the neighbourhood; that he was glad to see us, and would have something for us to eat in no time.

How he came by his English, was explained to us before we left. Some time previous, he had been a denizen of Papeetee, where the native language is broidered over with the most classic sailor phrases. He seemed to be quite proud of his residence there; and alluded to it in the same significant way in which a provincial informs you, that in his time he has resided in the capital. The old fellow was disposed to be garrulous; but being sharp-set, we told him to get breakfast; after which we would hear his anecdotes. While employed among the calabashes, the strange, antiquated fondness between these old semi-savages was really amusing. I made no doubt, that they were saying to each other, "yes, my love" —"no, my life," just in the same way that some young couples do, at home.

They gave us a hearty meal; and while we were discussing its merits, they assured us, over and over again, that they expected nothing in return for their attentions; more: we were at liberty to stay as long as we pleased; and as long as we *did* stay, their house and everything they had, was no longer theirs, but ours; still more: they themselves were our slaves—the old lady, to a degree that was altogether superfluous. This, now, is Tahitian hospitality! Self-immolation upon one's own hearthstone for the benefit of the guest.

The Polynesians carry their hospitality to an amazing extent. Let a native of Waiurar, the westernmost part of Tahiti, make his appearance as a traveller at Partoowye, the most easterly village of Imeeo; though a perfect stranger, the inhabitants on all sides accost him at their doorways, inviting him to enter, and make himself at home. But the traveller passes on, examining every house attentively; until at last, he pauses before one which suits him, and then exclaiming, "ah, ena maita" (this one will do, I think), he steps in, and makes himself perfectly at ease; flinging himself upon the mats, and very probably calling for a nice young coco-nut, and a piece of toasted breadfruit, sliced thin, and done brown.

Curious to relate, however, should a stranger carrying it thus bravely, be afterward discovered to be without a house of his own, why he may thenceforth go a-begging for his lodgings. The "karhowrees," or white men, are exceptions to this rule. Thus is it precisely as in civilized countries; where those who have houses and lands are incessantly bored to death with invitations to come and live in other people's houses; while many a poor gentleman who inks the seams of his coat, and to whom the like invitation would be really acceptable, may go and sue for it. But to the credit of the ancient Tahitians, it should here be observed, that this blemish upon their hospitality is only of recent origin, and was wholly unknown in old times. So told me, Captain Bob.

In Polynesia, it is esteemed "a great hit," if a man succeed in marrying into a family to which the best part of the community is related (Heaven knows it is otherwise with us). The reason is, that when he goes a-travelling, the greater number of houses are the more completely at his service.

Receiving a paternal benediction from old Darby and Joan, we continued our journey; resolved to stop at the very next place of attraction which offered.

Nor did we long stroll for it. A fine walk along a beach of shells, and we came to a spot, where, with trees here and there, the land was all meadow, sloping away to the water, which stirred a sedgy growth of reeds bordering its margin. Close by, was a little cove, walled in with coral, where a fleet of canoes was dancing up and down. A few paces distant, on a natural terrace overlooking the sea, were several native dwellings, newly thatched, and peeping into view out of the foliage, like summer-houses.

As we drew near, forth came a burst of voices; and presently, three gay girls, overflowing with life, health, and youth; and full of spirits and mischief. One was arrayed in a flaunting robe of calico; and her long black hair was braided behind in two immense tresses, joined together at the ends, and wreathed with the green tendrils of a vine. From her self-possessed and forward air, I fancied she might be some young lady from Papeetee, on a visit to her country relations. Her companions wore mere slips of cotton cloth; their hair was dishevelled; and though very pretty, they betrayed the reserve and embarrassment characteristic of the provinces.

The little gipsy first mentioned, ran up to me with great cordiality; and giving the Tahitian salutation, opened upon me such a fire of questions, that there was no understanding, much less answering them. But our hearty welcome to Loohooloo, as she called the hamlet, was made plain enough. Meanwhile, Doctor Long Ghost gallantly presented an arm to each of the other young ladies; which, at first, they knew not what to make of; but at last, taking it for some kind of joke, accepted the civility.

The names of these three damsels were at once made known by themselves; and being so exceedingly romantic, I cannot forbear particularizing them. Upon my comrade's arms, then, were hanging Night and Morning, in the persons of Farnowar, or the Day-Born, and Farnoopoo, or the Night-Born. She with the tresses, was very appropriately styled Marhar-Rarrar, the Wakeful, or Bright-Eyed.

By this time, the houses were emptied of the rest of their inmates —a few old men and women, and several strapping young fellows rubbing their eyes and yawning. All crowded round, putting questions as to whence we came. Upon being informed of our acquaintance with Zeke, they were delighted; and one of them recognized the boots worn by the doctor. "Keehee (Zeke) maitai," they cried, "nuee nuee hanna hanna portarto"—(Makes plenty of potatoes).

There was now a little friendly altercation, as to who should have the honour of entertaining the strangers. At last, a tall old gentleman, by name Marharvai, with a bald head and white beard, took us each by the hand, and led us into his dwelling. Once inside, Marharvai, pointing about with his staff, was so obsequious in assuring us that his house was ours, that Long Ghost suggested he might as well hand over the deed.

It was drawing near noon; so after a light lunch of roasted bread-fruit, a few whiffs of a pipe, and some lively chatting, our host admonished the company to lie down, and take the everlasting siesta. We complied; and had a social nap all round.

## A Dinner-Party in Imeeo

It was just in the middle of the merry, mellow afternoon, that they ushered us to dinner, underneath a green shelter of palm boughs; open all round, and so low at the eaves that we stooped to enter.

Within, the ground was strewn over with aromatic ferns—called "nahee"—freshly gathered; which, stirred under foot, diffused the sweetest odour. On one side was a row of yellow mats, inwrought with fibres of bark, stained a bright red. Here, seated after the fashion of the Turk, we looked out, over a verdant bank, upon the mild, blue, endless Pacific. So far round had we skirted the island, that the view of Tahiti was now intercepted.

Upon the ferns before us, were laid several layers of broad, thick "pooroo" leaves; lapping over, one upon the other. And upon these were placed, side by side, newly plucked banana leaves, at least two yards in length, and very wide; the stalks were withdrawn, so as to make them lie flat. This green cloth was set out and garnished, in the manner following:—

First, a number of "pooroo" leaves, by way of plates, were ranged along on one side; and by each was a rustic nut-bowl, half-filled with sea-water, and a Tahitian roll, or small breadfruit, roasted brown. An immense flat calabash, placed in the centre, was heaped up with numberless small packages of moist, steaming leaves: in each was a small fish, baked in the earth, and done to a turn. This pyramid of a dish was flanked on either side by an ornamental calabash. One was brimming with the golden-hued "poee," or pudding, made from the red plantain of the mountains: the other was stacked up with cakes of the Indian turnip, previously macerated in a mortar, kneaded with the milk of the coco-nut, and then baked. In the spaces between the three dishes, were piled young coco-nuts, stripped of their husks. Their eyes had been opened and enlarged; so that each was a ready-charged goblet.

There was a sort of side-cloth in one corner, upon which, in bright, buff jackets, lay the fattest of bananas; "avees," red-ripe; guavas, with the shadows of their crimson pulp flushing through a transparent skin, and almost coming and going there like blushes; oranges, tinged, here and there, berry-brown; and great, jolly melons, which rolled about in very portliness. Such a heap! All ruddy, ripe, and round—bursting with the good cheer of the tropical soil, from which they sprang!

"A land of orchards!" cried the doctor, in a rapture; and he snatched a morsel from a sort of fruit of which gentlemen of the sanguine temperament are remarkably fond; namely, the ripe cherry lips of Miss Day-Born, who stood looking on.

Marharvai allotted seats to his guests; and the meal began. Thinking that his hospitality needed some acknowledgment, I rose, and pledged him in the vegetable wine of the coco-nut; merely repeating the ordinary salutation, "Yar onor boyoee." Sensible that some compliment, after the fashion of white men, was paid him, with a smile, and a courteous flourish of the hand, he bade me be seated. No people, however refined, are more easy and graceful in their manners than the Imeeose.

The doctor, sitting next our host, now came under his special protection. Laying before his guest one of the packages of fish, Marharvai opened it; and commended its contents to his particular regards. But my comrade was one of those, who, on convivial occasions, can always take care of themselves. He ate an indefinite number of "Peehee Lee Lees" (small fish), his own and next neighbour's breadfruit; and helped himself, to right and left, with all the ease of an accomplished diner-out.

"Paul," said he, as last, "you don't seem to be getting along; why don't you try the pepper sauce?" and, by way of example, he steeped a morsel of food into his nutful of sea-water. On following suit, I found it quite piquant, though rather bitter; but, on the whole, a capital substitute for salt. The Imeeose invariably use sea-water in this way, deeming it quite a treat; and considering that their country is surrounded by an ocean of catsup, the luxury cannot be deemed an expensive one.

The fish were delicious; the manner of cooking them in the ground, preserving all the juices, and rendering them exceedingly sweet and tender. The plantain pudding was almost cloying; the cakes of Indian turnip, quite palatable; and the roasted breadfruit, crisp as toast.

During the meal, a native lad walked round and round the party; carrying a long staff of bamboo. This he occasionally tapped upon the cloth, before each guest; when a white clotted substance dropped forth, with a savour not unlike that of a curd. This proved to be "Lownee," an excellent relish, prepared from the grated meat of ripe coco-nuts, moistened with coco-nut milk and salt water, and kept perfectly tight, until a little past the saccharine stage of fermentation.

Throughout the repast there was much lively chatting among the islanders, in which their conversational powers quite exceeded ours. The young ladies, too, showed themselves very expert in the use of their tongues, and contributed much to the gaiety which prevailed.

Nor did these lively nymphs suffer the meal to languish; for upon the doctor's throwing himself back, with an air of much satisfaction, they sprang to their feet, and pelted him with oranges and guavas. This, at last, put an end to the entertainment.

By a hundred whimsical oddities, my long friend became a great favourite with these people; and they bestowed upon him a long comical title, expressive of his lank figure and Roora combined. The latter, by the by, never failed to excite the remark of everybody we encountered.

The giving of nicknames is quite a passion with the people of Tahiti and Imeeo. No one, with any peculiarity, whether of person or temper, is exempt; not even strangers.

A pompous captain of a man-of-war, visiting Tahiti for the second time, discovered that, among the natives, he went by the dignified title of "Atee Poee"—literally, Poee Head, or Pudding Head. Nor is the highest rank among themselves any protection. The first husband of the present queen was commonly known in the court circles as "Pot Belly." He carried the greater part of his person before him, to be sure; and so did the gentlemanly George IV—but what a title for a king consort!

Even "Pomaree" itself, the royal patronymic, was, originally, a mere nickname; and literally signifies, one talking through his nose. The first monarch of that name, being on a war party, and sleeping overnight among the mountains, awoke one morning with a cold in his head; and some wag of a courtier, had no more manners than to vulgarize him thus.

How different from the volatile Polynesian in this, as in all other respects, is our grave and decorous North American Indian. While the former bestows a name in accordance with some humorous or ignoble trait, the latter seizes upon what is deemed the most exalted or warlike: and hence, among the red tribes, we have the truly patrician appellations of "White Eagles," "Young Oaks," "Fiery Eyes," and "Bended Bows."

### The Coco-Palm

While the doctor and the natives were taking a digestive nap after dinner, I strolled forth to have a peep at the country, which could produce so generous a meal.

To my surprise, a fine strip of land in the vicinity of the hamlet, and protected seaward by a grove of coco-nut and breadfruit trees, was under high cultivation. Sweet potatoes, Indian turnips, and yams were growing; also melons, a few pine-apples, and other fruits. Still more pleasing was the sight of young breadfruit and coco-nut trees set out with great care, as if, for once, the improvident Polynesian had thought of his posterity. But this was the only instance of native thrift which ever came under my observation. For, in all my rambles over Tahiti and Imeeo, nothing so much struck me as the comparative scarcity of these trees in many places where they ought to abound. Entire valleys, like Martair, of inexhaustible fertility, are abandoned to all the rankness of untamed vegetation. Alluvial flats bordering the sea, and watered by streams from the mountains, are overgrown with a wild, scrub guava-bush, introduced by foreigners, and which spreads with such fatal rapidity, that the natives, standing still while it grows, anticipate its covering the entire island. Even tracts of clear land, which, with so little pains, might be made to wave with orchards, lie wholly neglected.

When I considered their unequalled soil and climate, thus unaccountably slighted, I often turned in amazement upon the natives about Papeetee; some of whom all but starve in their gardens run to waste. Upon other islands which I have visited, of similar fertility, and wholly unreclaimed from their first discovered condition, no spectacle of this sort was presented.

The high estimation in which many of their fruit-trees are held by the Tahitians and Imeeose—their beauty in the landscape—their manifold uses, and the facility with which they are propagated, are considerations which render the remissness alluded to still more unaccountable. The coco-palm is an example; a tree by far the most important production of Nature in the Tropics. To the Polynesian, it is emphatically the Tree of Life; transcending even the breadfruit in the multifarious uses to which it is applied.

Its very aspect is imposing. Asserting its supremacy by an erect and lofty bearing, it may be said to compare with other trees as man with inferior creatures.

The blessings it confers are incalculable. Year after year, the islander reposes beneath its shade, both eating and drinking of its fruit; he thatches his hut with its boughs, and weaves them into baskets to carry his food; he cools himself with a fan plaited from the young leaflets, and shields his head from the sun by a bonnet of the leaves; sometimes he clothes himself with the cloth-like substance which wraps round the base of the stalks, whose elastic rods, strung with filberts, are used as a taper; the larger nuts, thinned and polished, furnish him with a beautiful goblet: the smaller ones, with bowls for his pipes; the dry husks kindle his fires; their fibres are twisted into fishing-lines and cords for his canoes; he heals his wounds with a balsam compounded from the juice of the nut; and with the oil extracted from its meat, embalms the bodies of the dead.

The noble trunk itself is far from being valueless. Sawn into posts, it upholds the islander's dwelling; converted into charcoal, it cooks his food; and supported on blocks of stone, rails in his lands. He impels his canoe through the water with a paddle of the wood, and goes to battle with clubs and spears of the same hard material.

In pagan Tahiti a coco-nut branch was the symbol of regal authority. Laid upon the sacrifice in the temple, it made the offering sacred; and with it, the priests chastised and put to flight the evil spirits which assailed them. The supreme majesty of Oro, the great god of their mythology, was declared in the coco-nut log from which his image was rudely carved. Upon one of the Tonga Islands, there stands a living tree, revered itself as a deity. Even upon the Sandwich Islands, the coco-palm retains all its ancient reputation; the people there having thought of adopting it as the national emblem.

The coco-nut is planted as follows: Selecting a suitable place, you drop into the ground a fully ripe nut, and leave it. In a few days, a thin, lance-like shoot forces itself through a minute hole in the shell, pierces the husk, and soon unfolds three pale-green leaves in the air; while, originating in the same soft white sponge which now completely fills the nut, a pair of fibrous roots, pushing away the stoppers which close two holes in an opposite direction, penetrate the shell, and strike vertically into the ground. A day or two more, and the shell and husk, which, in the last and germinating stage of the nut, are so hard that a knife will scarcely make any impression, spontaneously burst by some force within; and, henceforth, the hardy young plant thrives apace; and needing no culture, pruning, or attention of any sort, rapidly advances to maturity. In four or five years it bears; in twice as many more, it begins to lift its head among the groves, where, waxing strong, it flourishes for near a century.

Thus, as some voyager has said, the man who but drops one of these nuts into the ground, may be said to confer a greater and more certain benefit upon himself and posterity, than many a life's toil in less genial climes.

The fruitfulness of the tree is remarkable. As long as it lives, it bears; and without intermission. Two hundred nuts, besides innumerable white blossoms of others, may be seen upon it at one time; and though a whole year is required to bring any one of them to the germinating point, no two, perhaps, are at one time in precisely the same stage of growth.

The tree delights in a maritime situation. In its greatest perfection, it is perhaps found right on the sea-shore, where its roots are actually washed. But such instances are only met with upon islands where the swell of the sea is prevented from breaking on the beach by an encircling reef. No saline flavour is perceptible in the nut produced in such a place. Although it bears in any soil, whether upland or bottom, it does not flourish vigorously inland; and I have frequently observed, that when met with far up the valleys, its tall stem inclines seaward, as if pining after a more genial region.

It is a curious fact, that if you deprive the coco-nut tree of the verdant tuft at its head, it dies at once; and if allowed to stand thus, the trunk, which, when alive, is encased in so hard a bark, as to be almost impervious to a bullet, moulders away, and, in an incredibly short period, becomes dust. This is, perhaps, partly owing to the peculiar constitution of the trunk, a mere cylinder of minute hollow reeds, closely packed, and very hard; but when exposed at top, peculiarly fitted to convey moisture and decay through the entire stem.

The finest orchard of coco-palms I know, and the only plantation of them I ever saw at the islands, is one that stands right upon the southern shore of Papeetee Bay. They were set out by the first Pomaree, almost half-a-century ago; and the soil being especially adapted to their growth, the noble trees now form a magnificent grove, nearly a mile in extent. No other plant, scarcely a bush, is to be seen within its precincts. The Broom Road passes through its entire length.

At noonday, this grove is one of the most beautiful, serene, witching places that ever was seen. High overhead, are ranges of green rustling arches; through which the sun's rays come down to you in sparkles. You seem to be wandering through illimitable halls of pillars; everywhere you catch glimpses of stately aisles, intersecting each other at all points. A strange silence, too, reigns far and near; the air flushed with the mellow stillness of a sunset.

But after the long morning calms, the sea-breeze comes in; and creeping over the tops of these thousand trees, they nod their plumes. Soon the breeze freshens; and you hear the branches brushing against each other; and the flexible trunks begin to sway. Toward evening, the whole grove is rocking to and fro; and the traveller on the Broom Road is startled by the frequent falling of the nuts, snapped from their brittle stems. They come flying through the air, ringing like jugglers' balls; and often bound along the ground for many rods.

### Life at Loohooloo

Finding the society at Loohooloo very pleasant, the young ladies, in particular, being extremely sociable; and, moreover, in love with the famous good cheer of old Marharvai, we acquiesced in an invitation of his, to tarry a few days longer. We might then, he said, join a small canoe party, which was going to a place a league or two distant. So averse to all exertion are these people, that they really thought the prospect of thus getting rid of a few miles' walking, would prevail with us, even if there were no other inducement.

The people of the hamlet, as we soon discovered, formed a snug little community of cousins; of which our host seemed the head. Marharvai, in truth, was a petty chief, who owned the neighbouring lands. And as the wealthy, in most cases, rejoice in a numerous kindred, the family footing upon which everybody visited him, was, perhaps, ascribable to the fact of his being the lord of the manor. Like Captain Bob, he was, in some things, a gentleman of the old school—a stickler for the customs of a past and pagan age.

Nowhere else, except in Tamai, did we find the manners of the natives less vitiated by recent changes. The old-fashioned Tahitian dinner they gave us on the day of our arrival was a fair sample of their general mode of living.

Our time passed delightfully. The doctor went his way, and I mine. With a pleasant companion, he was for ever strolling inland, ostensibly to collect botanical specimens; while I, for the most part, kept near the sea; sometimes taking the girls an aquatic excursion in a canoe.

Often we went fishing; not dozing over stupid hooks and lines, but leaping right into the water, and chasing our prey over the coral rocks, spear in hand.

Spearing fish is glorious sport. The Imeeose, all round the island, catch them in no other way. The smooth shallows between the reef and the shore, and, at low water, the reef itself, being admirably adapted to this mode of capturing them. At almost any time of the day—save ever the sacred hour of noon—you may see the fish-hunters pursuing their sport; with loud halloos, brandishing their spears, and splashing through the water in all directions. Sometimes a solitary native is seen, far out upon a lonely shallow, wading slowly along, with eye intent and poised spear.

But the best sport of all, is going out upon the great reef itself, by torch-light. The natives follow this recreation with as much spirit as a gentleman of England does the chase; and take full as much delight in it.

The torch is nothing more than a bunch of dry reeds, bound firmly together: the spear, a long, light pole, with an iron head, on one side barbed.

I shall never forget the night that old Marhavai and the rest of us, paddling off to the reef, leaped at midnight upon the coral ledges with waving torches and spears. We were more than a mile from the land; the sullen ocean, thundering upon the outside of the rocks, dashed the spray in our faces, almost extinguishing the flambeaux; and, far as the eye could reach, the darkness of sky and water was streaked with a long, misty line of foam, marking the course of the coral barrier. The wild fishermen, flourishing their weapons, and yelling like so many demons to scare their prey, sprang from ledge to ledge, and sometimes darted their spears in the very midst of the breakers.

But fish-spearing was not the only sport we had at Loohooloo. Right on the beach was a mighty old coco-nut tree, the roots of which had been under-washed by the waves, so that the trunk inclined far over its base. From the tuft of the tree, a stout cord of bark depended, the end of which swept the water several yards from the shore. This was a Tahitian swing. A native lad seizes hold of the cord, and, after swinging to and fro quite leisurely, all at once sends himself fifty or sixty feet from the water, rushing through the air like a rocket. I doubt whether any of our rope-dancers would attempt the feat. For my own part, I had neither head nor heart for it; so, after sending a lad aloft with an additional cord; by way of security, I constructed a large basket of green boughs, in which I and some particular friends of mine, used to swing over sea and land by the hour.

## We Start for Taloo

Bright was the morning, and brighter still the smiles of the young ladies who accompanied us, when we sprang into a sort of family canoe—wide and roomy—and bade adieu to the hospitable Marharvai and his tenantry. As we paddled away, they stood upon the beach, waving their hands, and crying out, "Aroha! aroha!" (farewell! farewell!) as long as we were within hearing.

Very sad at parting with them, we endeavoured, nevertheless, to console ourselves in the society of our fellow-passengers. Among these were two old ladies; but as they said nothing to us, we will say nothing about them; nor anything about the old men who managed the canoe. But of the three mischievous, dark-eyed young witches, who lounged in the stern of that comfortable old island gondola, I have a great deal to say.

In the first place, one of them was Marhar-Rarrar, the Bright-Eyed; and, in the second place, neither she nor the romps, her companions, ever dreamed of taking the voyage, until the doctor and myself announced our intention; their going along was nothing more than a madcap frolic; in short, they were a parcel of wicked hoydens, bent on mischief, who laughed in your face when you looked sentimental, and only tolerated your company when making merry at your expense.

Something or other about us was perpetually awaking their mirth. Attributing this to his own remarkable figure, the doctor increased their enjoyment, by assuming the part of a Merry Andrew. Yet his cap and bells never jingled but to some tune; and while playing the Tom-fool, I more than suspected that he was trying to play the rake. At home, it is deemed auspicious to go a-wooing in epaulets; but among the Polynesians, your best dress in courting is motley.

A fresh breeze springing up, we set our sail of matting, and glided along as tranquilly as if floating upon an inland stream; the white reef on one hand, and the green shore on the other.

Soon, as we turned a headland, we encountered another canoe, paddling with might and main in an opposite direction; the strangers shouting to each other, and a tall fellow, in the bow, dancing up and down like a crazy man. They shot by us like an arrow, though our fellow-voyagers shouted again and again, for them to cease paddling.

According to the natives, this was a kind of royal mail-canoe, carrying a message from the queen to her friends in a distant part of the island.

Passing several shady bowers, which looked quite inviting, we proposed touching, and diversifying the monotony of a sea-voyage by a stroll ashore. So, forcing our canoe among the bushes, behind a decayed palm, lying partly in the water, we left the old folks to take a nap in the shade, and gallanted the others among the trees, which were here trellised with vines and creeping shrubs.

In the early part of the afternoon, we drew near the place to which the party were going. It was a solitary house, inhabited by four or five old women, who, when we entered, were gathered in a circle about the mats, eating *poee* from a cracked calabash. They seemed delighted at seeing our companions, but rather drew up when introduced to ourselves. Eyeing us distrustfully, they whispered to know who we were. The answers they received were not satisfactory; for they treated us with marked coolness and reserve, and seemed desirous of breaking off our acquaintance with the girls.

Unwilling, therefore, to stay where our company was disagreeable, we resolved to depart, without even eating a meal.

Informed of this, Marhar-Rarrar and her companions evinced the most lively concern; and equally unmindful of their former spirits, and the remonstrances of the old ladies, broke forth into sobs and lamentations, which were not to be withstood. We agreed, therefore, to tarry until they left for home; which would be at the "Aheharar," or Falling of the Sun; in other words, at sunset.

When the hour arrived, after much leave-taking, we saw them safely embarked. As the canoe turned a bluff, they seized the paddles from the hands of the old men, and waved them silently in the air. This was meant for a touching farewell, as the paddle is only waved thus, when the parties separating never more expect to meet.

We now continued our journey; and following the beach, soon came to a level and lofty overhanging bank, which, planted here and there with trees, took a broad sweep round a considerable part of the island. A fine pathway skirted the edge of the bank; and often we paused to admire the scenery. The evening was still and fair, even for so heavenly a climate; and all round, far as the eye could reach, was the blending blue sky and ocean.

As we went on, the reef-belt still accompanied us; turning as we turned, and thundering its distant bass upon the ear, like the unbroken roar of a cataract. Dashing for ever against their coral rampart, the breakers looked, in the distance, like a line of rearing white chargers, reined in, tossing their white manes, and bridling with foam.

These great natural breakwaters are admirably designed for the protection of the land. Nearly all the Society Islands are defended by them. Were the vast swells of the Pacific to break against the soft alluvial bottoms which in many places border the sea, the soil would soon be washed away, and the natives be thus deprived of their most productive lands. As it is, the banks of no rivulet are firmer.

But the coral barriers answer another purpose. They form all the harbours of this group, including the twenty-four round about the shores of Tahiti. Curiously enough, the openings in the reefs, by which alone vessels enter to their anchorage, are invariably opposite the mouths of running streams: an advantage fully appreciated by the mariner who touches for the purpose of watering his ship.

It is said, that the fresh water of the land, mixing with the salts held in solution by the sea, so acts upon the latter, as to resist the formation of the coral; and hence the breaks. Here and there, these openings are sentinelled, as it were, by little fairy islets, green as emerald, and waving with palms. Strangely and beautifully diversifying the long line of breakers, no objects can strike the fancy more vividly. Pomaree II, with a taste in watering-place truly Tahitian, selected one of them as a royal retreat. We passed it on our journey.

### Let Me Go Where'er I Will

Let me go where'er I will,
  I hear a sky-born music still;
It sounds from all things old,
It sounds from all things young,
From all that's fair, from all that's foul,
Peals out a cheerful song.
It is not only in the rose,
It is not only in the bird,
Not only where the rainbow glows,
Nor in the song of woman heard,
But in the darkest, meanest things
There alway, alway something sings.
'T is not in the high stars alone,
Nor in the cups of budding flowers,
Nor in the red-breast's mellow tone,
Nor in the bow that smiles in showers,
But in the mud and scum of things
There alway, alway something sings.

*Ralph Waldo Emerson*

# THE BARBADOS

## Charles Kingsley

*Though nowadays we know him mostly as a poet and novelist,
Kingsley (1819–1875) was many other things—chaplain to
Queen Victoria, professor of modern history at Cambridge,
and an enthusiastic student of natural history and geology.
His* Westward Ho!, *still one of the most widely read of English adventure stories, tells of the search of Amyas Leigh for
his sweetheart on many seas and shores. When he disembarks
at the Barbados, we recognize the accents of Kingsley the
nature-lover over those of his Elizabethan voyagers.*

Land! land! land! Yes, there it was, far away to the south and
west, beside the setting sun, a long blue bar between the crimson sea and golden sky. Land at last, with fresh streams and cooling
fruits, and free room for cramped and scurvy-weakened limbs.
And there, too, might be gold, and gems, and all the wealth of Ind.
Who knew? Why not? The old world of fact and prose lay thousands of miles behind them, and before them and around them was
the realm of wonder and fable, of boundless hope and possibility.
Sick men crawled up out of their stifling hammocks; strong men
fell on their knees and gave God thanks; and all eyes and hands
were stretched eagerly toward the far blue cloud, fading as the sun
sank down, yet rising higher and broader as the ship rushed on before the rich trade-wind, which whispered lovingly round brow
and sail, "I am the faithful friend of those who dare!" "Blow
freshly, freshlier yet, thou good trade-wind, of whom it is written
that He makes the winds His angels, ministering breaths to the heirs
of His salvation. Blow freshlier yet, and save, if not me from death,
yet her from worse than death. Blow on, and land me at her feet,
to call the lost lamb home, and die!"

So murmured Frank to himself, as with straining eyes he gazed
upon that first outline of the New World which held his all. His

cheeks were thin and wasted, and the hectic spot on each glowed crimson in the crimson light of the setting sun. A few minutes more, and the rainbows of the West were gone; emerald and topaz, amethyst and ruby, had faded into silver-grey; and overhead, through the dark sapphire depths, the Moon and Venus reigned above the sea.

"That should be Barbados, your worship," said Drew, the master; "unless my reckoning is far out, which, Heaven knows, it has no right to be, after such a passage, and God be praised."

"Barbados? I never heard of it."

"Very like, sir; but Yeo and I were here with Captain Drake, and I was here after, too, with poor Captain Barlow; and there is good harbourage to the south and west of it, I remember."

"And neither Spaniard, cannibal, or other evil beast," said Yeo. "A very garden of the Lord, sir, hid away in the seas, for an inheritance to those who love Him. I heard Captain Drake talk of planting it, if ever he had a chance."

"I recollect now," said Amyas, "some talk between him and poor Sir Humphrey about an island here. Would God he had gone thither instead of to Newfoundland!"

"Nay, then," said Yeo, "he is in bliss now with the Lord; and you would not have kept him from that, sir?"

"He would have waited as willingly as he went, if he could have served his Queen thereby. But what say you, my masters? How can we do better than to spend a few days here, to get our sick round, before we make the Main, and set to our work?"

All approved the counsel except Frank, who was silent.

"Come, fellow-adventurer," said Cary, "we must have your voice too."

"To my impatience, Will," said he, aside in a low voice, "there is but one place on earth, and I am all day longing for wings to fly thither: but the counsel is right. I approve it."

So the verdict was announced, and received with a hearty cheer by the crew; and long before morning they had run along the southern shore of the island, and were feeling their way into the bay where Bridgetown now stands. All eyes were eagerly fixed on the low wooded hills which slept in the moonlight, spangled by fire-flies with a million dancing stars; all nostrils drank greedily the fragrant air, which swept from the land, laden with the scent of a thousand flowers; all ears welcomed, as a grateful change from the monotonous whisper and lap of the water, the hum of insects, the snore of the tree-toads, the plaintive notes of the shore-fowl, which fill a tropic night with noisy life.

At last she stopped; at last the cable rattled through the hawse-hole; and then, careless of the chance of lurking Spaniard or Carib, an instinctive cheer burst from every throat. Poor fellows! Amyas had much ado to prevent them going on shore at once, dark as it was, by reminding them that it wanted but two hours of day.

"Never were two such long hours," said one young lad, fidgeting up and down.

"You never were in the Inquisition," said Yeo, "or you'd know better how slow time can run. Stand you still, and give God thanks you're where you are."

"I say, Gunner, be there goold to that island?"

"Never heard of none; and so much the better for it," said Yeo, drily.

"But, I say, Gunner," said a poor scurvy-stricken cripple, licking his lips, "be there oranges and limmons there?"

"Not of my seeing; but plenty of good fruit down to the beach, thank the Lord. There comes the dawn at last."

Up flushed the rose, up rushed the sun, and the level rays glittered on the smooth stems of the palm-trees, and threw rainbows across the foam upon the coral-reefs, and gilded lonely uplands far away, where now stands many a stately country-seat and busy engine-house. Long lines of pelicans went clanging out to sea; the hum of the insects hushed, and a thousand birds burst into jubilant song; a thin blue mist crept upward toward the inner downs, and vanished, leaving them to quiver in the burning glare; the land-breeze, which had blown fresh out to sea all night, died away into glassy calm, and the tropic day was begun.

The sick were lifted over the side, and landed boat-load after boat-load on the beach, to stretch themselves in the shade of the palms; and in half-an-hour the whole crew were scattered on the shore, except some dozen worthy men, who had volunteered to keep watch and ward on board till noon.

And now the first instinctive cry of nature was for fruit! fruit! fruit! The poor lame wretches crawled from place to place plucking greedily the violet grapes of the creeping shore vine, and staining their mouths and blistering their lips with the prickly pears, in spite of Yeo's entreaties and warnings against the thorns. Some of the healthy began hewing down cocoa-nut trees to get at the nuts, doing little thereby but blunt their hatchets; till Yeo and Drew,

having mustered half-a-dozen reasonable men, went off inland, and
returned in an hour laden with the dainties of that primeval orchard
—with acid junipa-apples, luscious guavas, and crowned ananas,
queen of all the fruits which they had found by hundreds on
the broiling ledges of the low tufa-cliffs; and then all, sitting on
the sandy turf, defiant of galliwasps and jackspaniards, and all the
weapons of the insect host, partook of the equal banquet, while old
blue land-crabs sat in their house-doors and brandished their fists
in defiance at the invaders, and solemn cranes stood in the water on
the shoals with their heads on one side, and meditated how long it
was since they had seen bipeds without feathers breaking the solitude of their isle.

And Frank wandered up and down, silent, but rather in wonder
than in sadness, while great Amyas walked after him, his mouth full
of junipa-apples, and enacted the part of showman, with a sort of
patronising air, as one who had seen the wonders already, and was
above being astonished at them.

"New, new; everything new!" said Frank, meditatively. "Oh,
awful feeling! All things changed around us, even to the tiniest fly
and flower; yet we the same; the same for ever!"

Amyas, to whom such utterances were altogether sibylline and
unintelligible, answered by—

"Look, Frank, that's a colibri. You've heard of colibris?"

Frank looked at the living gem, which hung, loud humming,
over some fantastic bloom, and then dashed away, seemingly to
call its mate, and whirred and danced with it round and round the
flower-starred bushes, flashing fresh rainbows at every shifting of
the lights.

Frank watched solemnly awhile, and then—

"*Qualis Natura formatrix, si talis formata?* Oh, my God, how
fair must be Thy real world, if even Thy phantoms are so fair!"

"Phantoms?" asked Amyas, uneasily. "That's no ghost, Frank,
but a jolly little honey-sucker, with a wee wife, and children no
bigger than peas, but yet solid greedy little fellows enough, I'll
warrant."

"Not phantoms in thy sense, good fellow, but in the sense of
those who know the worthlessness of all below."

"I'll tell you what, brother Frank, you are a great deal wiser
than me, I know; but I can't abide to see you turn up your nose as it
were at God's good earth. See now, God made all these things; and
never a man, perhaps, set eyes on them till fifty years agone; and

yet they were as pretty as they are now, ever since the making of the world. And why do you think God could have put them here, then, but to please Himself"—and Amyas took off his hat—"with the sight of them? Now, I say, brother Frank, what's good enough to please God, is good enough to please you and me."

"Your rebuke is just, dear old simple-hearted fellow; and God forgive me, if with all my learning, which has brought me no profit, and my longings, which have brought me no peace, I presume at moments, sinner that I am, to be more dainty than the Lord Himself. He walked in Paradise among the trees of the garden, Amyas; and so will we, and be content with what He sends. Why should we long for the next world, before we are fit even for this one?"

"And in the meanwhile," said Amyas, "this earth's quite good enough, at least here in Barbados."

"Do you believe," asked Frank, trying to turn his own thoughts, "in those tales of the Spaniards, that the Sirens and Tritons are heard singing in these seas?"

"I can't tell. There's more fish in the water than ever came out of it, and more wonders in the world, I'll warrant, than we ever dreamt of; but I was never in these parts before; and in the South Sea, I must say, I never came across any, though Yeo says he has heard fair music at night up in the Gulf, far away from land."

"The Spaniards report, that at certain seasons choirs of these nymphs assemble in the sea, and with ravishing music sing their watery loves. It may be so. For Nature, which has peopled the land with rational souls, may not have left the sea altogether barren of them; above all, when we remember that the ocean is as it were the very fount of all fertility, and its slime (as the most learned hold with Thales of Miletus) that *prima materia* out of which all things were one by one concocted. Therefore, the ancients feigned wisely that Venus, the mother of all living things, whereby they designed the plastic force of nature, was born of the sea-foam, and rising from the deep, floated ashore upon the isles of Greece."

"I don't know what plastic force is; but I wish I had had the luck to be by when the pretty poppet came up: however, the nearest thing I ever saw to that was maidens swimming alongside us when we were in the South Seas, and would have come aboard, too; but Drake sent them all off again for a lot of naughty packs, and I verily believe they were no better. Look at the butterflies, now! Don't you wish you were a boy again, and not too proud to go catching them in your cap?"

And so the two wandered on together through the glorious tropic woods, and then returned to the beach to find the sick already grown cheerful, and many who that morning could not stir from their hammocks, pacing up and down, and gaining strength with every step.

"Well done, lads!" cried Amyas, "keep a cheerful mind. We will have the music ashore after dinner, for want of mermaids to sing to us, and those that can dance may."

And so those four days were spent; and the men, like schoolboys on a holiday, gave themselves up to simple merriment, not forgetting, however, to wash the clothes, take in fresh water, and store up a good supply of such fruit as seemed likely to keep; until, tired with fruitless rambles after gold, which they expected to find in every bush, in spite of Yeo's warnings that none had been heard of on the island, they were fain to lounge about, full-grown babies, picking up shells and sea-fans to take home to their sweethearts, smoking agoutis out of the hollow trees, with shout and laughter, and tormenting every living thing they could come near, till not a land-crab dare look out of his hole, or an armadillo unroll himself, till they were safe out of the bay, and off again to the westward, unconscious pioneers of all the wealth, and commerce, and beauty, and science, which has in later centuries made that lovely isle the richest gem of all the tropic seas.

### *Stanza from* Auguries of Innocence

To SEE a World in a grain of sand,
    And a Heaven in a wild flower;
Hold Infinity in the palm of your hand,
    And eternity in an hour.

*William Blake*

# A FALL ON THE MATTER-HORN

## Edward Whymper

*A wood-engraver of great ability, Whymper (1840–1911), when he was only twenty, was commissioned to do a series of sketches of an attempt to climb Mont Pelvoux in the Alps. The attempt failed. The following year Whymper returned as climber himself, as well as artist, and succeeded. Later he scaled many peaks never before conquered, his greatest achievement being the ascent of the Matterhorn. Four men died on the way down. The whole dramatic story he relates in this selection from his* Scrambles Among the Alps.

THREE times I had assayed ascent of this mountain, and on each occasion had failed ignominiously. I had not advanced a yard beyond my predecessors. Up to the height of nearly thirteen thousand feet there were no extraordinary difficulties; the way so far might even become "a matter of amusement." Only eighteen hundred feet remained; but they were as yet untrodden, and might present the most formidable obstacles. No man could expect to climb them by himself. A morsel of rock only seven feet high might at any time defeat him if it were perpendicular. Such a place might be possible to two, or a bagatelle to three men. It was evident that a party should consist of three men at least. But where could the other two men be obtained? Carrel was the only man who exhibited any enthusiasm in the matter; and he, in 1861, absolutely refused to go unless the party consisted of at least four persons. Want of men made the difficulty, not the mountain. The weather became bad again, so I went to Zermatt on the chance of picking up a man, and remained there during a week of storms. Not one of the good men, however, could be induced to come, and I returned to Breil on the 17th, 1862, hoping to combine the skill of Carrel with the willingness of Meynet on a new attempt by the same route as before; for the Hörnli ridge, which I had examined in the meantime, seemed to be entirely impracticable. Both men were inclined to go, but their ordinary occupations prevented them from starting at once.

My tent had been left rolled up at the second platform, and while waiting for the men it occurred to me that it might have been blown away during the late stormy weather; so I started off on the 18th to see if this were so or not. The way was by this time familiar, and I mounted rapidly, astonishing the friendly herdsmen—who nodded recognition as I flitted past them and the cows—for I was alone, because no man was available. But more deliberation was necessary when the pastures were passed and climbing began, for it was needful to mark each step, in case of mist or surprise by night.

The tent was safe, although snowed up, and I turned to contemplate the view, which, when seen alone and undisturbed, had all the strength and charm of complete novelty.

Time sped away unregarded, and the little birds which had built their nests on the neighboring cliffs had begun to chirp their evening hymn before I thought of returning. Half mechanically I turned to the tent, unrolled it, and set it up; it contained food enough for several days, and I resolved to stay over the night. I had started from Breil without provisions or telling Favre—the innkeeper, who was accustomed to my erratic ways—where I was going. I returned to the view. The sun was setting, and its rosy rays, blending with the snowy blue, had thrown a pale, pure violet far as the eye could see; the valleys were drowned in a purple gloom, while the summits shone with unnatural brightness; and as I sat in the door of the tent, and watched the twilight change to darkness, the earth seemed to become less earthy and almost sublime; the world seemed dead, and I its sole inhabitant. By and by the moon, as it rose, brought the hills again into sight, and by a judicious repression of detail rendered the view yet more magnificent. Something in the south hung like a great glow-worm in the air; it was too large for a star, and too steady for a meteor, and it was long before I could realize the incredible fact that it was the moonlight glittering on the great snow-slope on the north side of Monte Viso, at a distance, as the crow flies, of ninety-eight miles. Shivering, at last I entered the tent and made my coffee. The night was passed comfortably, and the next morning, tempted by the brilliancy of the weather, I proceeded yet higher up in search of another place for a platform.

The rocks of the southwest ridge are by no means difficult for some distance above the Col du Lion. This is true of the rocks up to the level of the Chimney, but they steepen when that is passed, and, remaining smooth and with but few fractures, and continuing to dip outwards, present some steps of a very uncertain kind, particularly when they are glazed with ice. At this point (just above the Chimney) the climber is obliged to follow the southern (or Breil) side of the ridge, but, in a few feet more, one must turn over to the northern (or Z'Mutt) side, where, in most years, nature kindly provides a snow-slope. When this is surmounted one can again return to the crest of the ridge, and follow it by easy rocks to the foot of the Great Tower. This was the highest point attained by Mr. Hawkins in 1860, and it was also our highest on the 9th of July.

This Great Tower is one of the most striking features of the ridge. It stands out like a turret at the angle of a castle. Behind it a battlemented wall leads upward to the citadel. Seen from the Theodule pass it looks only an insignificant pinnacle, but as one approaches it (on the ridge) so it seems to rise, and when one is at its base it completely conceals the upper parts of the mountain. I found here a suitable place for the tent; which, although not so well protected as the second platform, possessed the advantage of being three hundred feet higher up; and, fascinated by the wildness of the cliffs and enticed by the perfection of the weather, I went on to see what was behind.

The first step was a difficult one; the ridge became diminished to the least possible width—it was hard to keep one's balance—and just where it was narrowest a more than perpendicular mass barred the way. Nothing fairly within arm's reach could be laid hold of; it was necessary to spring up, and then to haul one's self over the sharp edge by sheer strength. Progression directly upward was then impossible. Enormous and appalling precipices plunged down to the Tiefenmatten glacier on the left, but round the right-hand side it was just possible to go. One hinderance then succeeded another, and much time was consumed in seeking the way. I have a vivid recollection of a gully of more than usual perplexity at the side of the Great Tower, with minute ledges and steep walls; of the ledges dwindling down and at last ceasing; and of finding myself, with arms and legs divergent, fixed as if crucified, pressing against the rock, and feeling each rise and fall of my chest as I breathed; of screwing my head round to look for hold and not seeing any, and of jumping sideways on to the other side.

This long digression has been caused by an innocent gully which I feared the reader might think was dangerous. It was an un-trodden vestibule which led to a scene so wild that even the most sober description of it must seem an exaggeration. There was a change in the quantity of the rock, and there was a change in the appearance of the ridge. The rocks (talcose gneiss) below this spot were singularly firm; it was rarely necessary to test one's hold; the way led over the living rock, and not up rent-off fragments. But here all was decay and ruin. The crest of the ridge was shattered and cleft, and the feet sank in the chips which had drifted down; while above, huge blocks, hacked and carved by the hand of time, nodded to the sky, looking like the gravestones of giants. Out of curiosity I wandered to a notch in the ridge, between two tottering piles of immense masses, which seemed to need but a few pounds on one or the other side to make them fall; so nicely poised that they would literally have rocked in the wind, for they were put in motion by a touch; and based on support so frail that I wondered they did not collapse before my eyes. In the whole range of my Alpine experience I have seen nothing more striking than this deso-late, ruined, and shattered ridge at the back of the Great Tower. I have seen stranger shapes—rocks which mimic the human form, with monstrous leering faces—and isolated pinnacles, sharper and greater than any here; but I have never seen exhibited so impres-sively the tremendous effects which may be produced by frost and the long-continued action of forces whose individual effects are imperceptible.

It is needless to say that it is impossible to climb by the crest of the ridge at this part; still one is compelled to keep near to it, for there is no other way. Generally speaking the angles on the Matter-horn are too steep to allow the formation of considerable beds of snow, but here there is a corner which permits it to accumulate, and it is turned to gratefully, for by its assistance one can ascend four times as rapidly as upon the rocks.

The Tower was now almost out of sight, and I looked over the central Pennine Alps to the Grand Combin and to the chain of Mont Blanc. My neighbor, the Dent d'Hérens, still rose above me, although but slightly, and the height which had been attained could be measured by its help. So far I had no doubts about my capacity to descend that which had been ascended; but in a short time, on looking ahead, I saw that the cliffs steepened, and I turned back (without pushing on to them, and getting into inextricable difficulties), exulting in the thought that I had already, without assistance, got nearly to the height of the Dent d'Hérens, and considerably higher than any one had been before. My exultation was a little premature.

About five P.M. I left the tent again, and thought myself as good as at Breil. The friendly rope and claw had done good service, and had smoothed all the difficulties. I lowered myself through the Chimney, however, by making a fixture of the rope, which I then cut off and left behind, as there was enough and to spare. My axe had proved a great nuisance in coming down, and I left it in the tent. It was not attached to the bâton, but was a separate affair—an old navy boarding-axe. While cutting up the different snow-beds on the ascent the bâton trailed behind fastened to the rope; and when climbing, the axe was carried behind, run through the rope tied round my waist, and was sufficiently out of the way; but in descending, when coming down face outward (as is always the best where it is possible), the head or the handle of the weapon caught frequently against the rocks, and several times nearly upset me. So, out of laziness if you will, it was left in the tent. I dearly paid for the imprudence.

The Col du Lion was passed, and fifty yards more would have placed me on the "Great Staircase," down which one can run. But on arriving at an angle of the cliffs of the Tête du Lion, while skirting the upper edge of the snow which abuts against them, I found that the heat of the two past days had nearly obliterated the steps which had been cut when coming up. The rocks happened to be impracticable just at this corner, so nothing could be done except make the steps afresh. The snow was too hard to beat or tread down, and at the angle it was all but ice; half a dozen steps only were required, and then the ledges could be followed again. So I held to the rock with my right hand, and prodded at the snow with the point of my stick until a good step was made, and then, leaning round the angle, did the same for the other side. So far well, but in attempting to pass the corner (to the present moment I cannot tell how it happened) I slipped and fell.

The slope was steep on which this took place, and was at the top of a gully that led down through two subordinate buttresses towards the Glacier du Lion, which was just seen, a thousand feet below. The gully narrowed and narrowed, until there was a mere thread of snow lying between two walls of rock, which came to an abrupt termination at the top of a precipice that intervened beteen it and the glacier. Imagine a funnel cut in half through its length, placed at an angle of forty-five degrees, with its point below and its concave side uppermost, and you will have a fair idea of the place.

The knapsack brought my head down first, and I pitched into some rocks about a dozen feet below; they caught something and tumbled me off the edge, head over heels, into the gully; the bâton was dashed from my hands, and I whirled downward in a series of bounds, each longer than the last, now over ice, now into rocks, striking my head four or five times, each time with increased force. The last bound sent me spinning through the air in a leap of fifty or sixty feet from one side of the gully to the other, and I struck the rocks, luckily, with the whole of my left side. They caught my clothes for a moment, and I fell on to the snow with motion arrested; my head, fortunately, came the right side up, and a few frantic catches brought me to a halt in the neck of the gully and on the verge of the precipice. Bâton, hat, and veil skimmed by and disappeared, and the crash of the rocks, which I had started, as they fell on the glacier, told how narrow had been the escape from utter destruction. As it was, I fell nearly two hundred feet in seven or eight bounds. Ten feet more would have taken me, in one gigantic leap of eight hundred feet, on to the glacier below.

The situation was still sufficiently serious. The rocks could not be left go for a moment, and the blood was spurting out of more than twenty cuts. The most serious ones were in the head, and I vainly tried to close them with one hand while holding on with the other. It was useless; the blood jerked out in blinding jets at every pulsation. At last, in a moment of inspiration, I kicked out a big lump of snow, and stuck it as a plaster on my head. The idea was a happy one, and the flow of blood diminished; then, scrambling up, I got, not a moment too soon, to a place of safety and fainted away. The sun was setting when consciousness returned, and it was pitch dark before the Great Staircase was descended; but, by a combination of luck and care, the whole four thousand eight hundred feet of descent to Breil was accomplished without a slip, or once missing the way. I slunk past the cabin of the cowherds, who were talking and laughing inside, utterly ashamed of the state to which I had been brought by my imbecility, and entered the inn stealthily, wishing to escape to my room unnoticed. But Favre met me in the passage, demanded, "Who is it?" screamed with fright when he got a light, and aroused the household. Two dozen heads then held solemn council over mine, with more talk than action. The natives were unanimous in recommending that hot wine (syn. vinegar), mixed with salt, should be rubbed into the cuts. I protested, but they insisted. It was all the doctoring they received. Whether their rapid healing was to be attributed to that simple remedy, or to a good state of health, is a question; they closed up remarkably quickly, and in a few days I was able to move again.

As it seldom happens that one survives such a fall, it may be interesting to record what my sensations were during its occurrence. I was perfectly conscious of what was happening, and felt each blow; but, like a patient under chloroform, experienced no pain. Each blow was, naturally, more severe than that which preceded it, and I distinctly remember thinking "Well, if the next is harder still, that will be the end!" Like persons who have been rescued from drowning, I remember that the recollection of a multitude of things rushed through my head, many of them trivialities or absurdities, which had been forgotten long before; and, more remarkable, this bounding through space did not feel disagreeable. But I think that in no very great distance more, consciousness as well as sensation would have been lost, and upon that I base my belief, improbable as it seems, that death by a fall from a great height is as painless an end as can be experienced.

The battering was very rough, yet no bones were broken. The most severe cuts were one of four inches long on the top of the head and another of three inches on the right temple: this latter bled frightfully. There was a formidable-looking cut, of about the same size as the last, on the palm of the left hand, and every limb was grazed or cut, more or less seriously. The tips of the ears were taken off, and a sharp rock cut a circular bit out of the side of the left boot, sock, and ankle at one stroke. The loss of blood, although so great, did not seem to be permanently injurious. The only serious effect has been the reduction of a naturally retentive memory to a very commonplace one; and although my recollections of more distant occurrences remain unshaken, the events of that particular day would be clean gone but for the few notes which were written down before the accident.

On Wednesday morning, the 12th of July, Lord Francis Douglas and myself crossed the Col Théodule, to seek guides at Zermatt. After quitting the snow on the northern side we rounded the foot of the glacier, crossing the Furgge Glacier, and left my tent, ropes, and other matters in the little chapel at the Lac Noir. We then descended to Zermatt, engaged Peter Taugwalder, and gave him permission to choose another guide. In the course of the evening, the Rev. Charles Hudson came into our hotel with a friend, Mr. Hadow; and they, in answer to some inquiries, announced their intention of starting to attempt the Matterhorn on the following morning. Lord Francis Douglas agreed with me that it was undesirable that two independent parties should be on the mountain at the same time, and with the same object. Mr. Hudson was therefore invited to join us, and he accepted our proposal. Before admitting Mr. Hadow I took the precaution to inquire what he had done in the Alps, and, as well as I can remember, Mr. Hudson's reply was, "Mr. Hadow has done the Mont Blanc in less time than most men." He then mentioned several other excursions that were then unknown to me, and added, in answer to a further question, "I consider he is a sufficiently good man to go with us." This was an excellent certificate, given as it was by a first-rate mountaineer, and Mr. Hadow was admitted without any further question.

We started from Zermatt on the 13th of July, at half-past five, on a brilliant and perfectly cloudless morning. We were eight in number—Croz, old Peter and his two sons, Lord F. Douglas, Hadow, Hudson, and I. To insure steady motion, one tourist and one native walked together. The youngest Taugwalder fell to my share, and the lad marched well, proud to be on the expedition, and happy to show his powers. The wine-bags also fell to my lot to carry, and throughout the day, after each drink, I replenished them secretly with water, so that at the next halt they were found fuller than before! This was considered a good omen, and little short of miraculous.

On the first day we did not intend to ascend to any great height, and we mounted, accordingly, very leisurely; picked up the things which were left in the chapel at the Schwarzsee at 8.20, and proceeded thence along the ridge connecting the Hörnli with the Matterhorn. At half-past eleven we arrived at the base of the actual peak; then quitted the ridge, and clambered round some ledges on to the eastern face. We were now fairly upon the mountain, and were astonished to find that places which from the Riffel, or even from the Furggengletscher, looked entirely impracticable, were so easy that we could *run about*.

Before twelve o'clock we had found a good position for the tent, at a height of 11,000 feet. Croz and young Peter went on to see what was above, in order to save time on the following morning. At length, just before three P.M., we saw them coming down, evidently much excited. "What are they saying, Peter?" "Gentlemen, they say it is no good." But when they came near we heard a different story. "Nothing but what was good; not a difficulty, not a single difficulty! We could have gone to the summit and returned to-day easily!"

We passed the remaining hours of daylight—some basking in the sunshine, some sketching or collecting; and when the sun went down, giving, as it departed, a glorious promise for the morrow, we returned to the tent to arrange for the night. Hudson made tea, I coffee, and we then retired each one to his blanket-bag; the Taugwalders, Lord Francis Douglas, and myself occupying the tent, the others remaining, by preference, outside. Long after dusk the cliffs above echoed with our laughter and with the songs of the guides, for we were happy that night in camp, and feared no evil.

We assembled together outside the tent before dawn on the morning of the 14th, and started directly it was light enough to move. Young Peter came on with us as a guide, and his brother returned to Zermatt. We followed the route which had been taken on the previous day, and in a few minutes turned the rib which had intercepted the view of the eastern face from our tent platform. The whole of this great slope was now revealed, rising for 3000 feet like a huge natural staircase. Some parts were more and others were less easy; but we were not once brought to a halt by any serious impediment, for when an obstruction was met in front it could always be turned to the right or to the left. For the greater part of the way there was, indeed, no occasion for the rope, and sometimes Hudson led, sometimes myself. At 6.20 we had attained a height of 12,800 feet, and halted for half an hour; we then continued the ascent without a break until 9.55, when we stopped for fifty minutes, at a height of 14,000 feet. Twice we struck the northeast ridge, and followed it for some little distance—to no advantage, for it was usually more rotten and steep, and always more difficult than the face. Still, we kept near to it, lest stones perchance might fall.

We had now arrived at the foot of that part which, from the Riffelberg or from Zermatt, seems perpendicular or overhanging, and could no longer continue upon the eastern side. For a little distance we ascended by snow upon the arête—that is, the ridge—descending towards Zermatt, and then, by common consent, turned over to the right, or to the northern side. Before doing so we made a change in the order of ascent. Croz went first, I followed, Hudson came third; Hadow and old Peter were last. "Now," said Croz, as he led off, "now for something altogether different." The work became difficult, and required caution. In some places there was little to hold, and it was desirable that those should be in front who were least likely to slip. The general slope of the mountain at this part was *less* than 40°, and snow had accumulated in, and had filled up the interstices of, the rock-face, leaving only occasional fragments projecting here and there. These were at times covered with a thin film of ice produced from the melting and refreezing of the snow. It was a place over which any fair mountaineer might pass in safety, and Mr. Hudson ascended this part, and, as far as I know, the entire mountain, without having the slightest assistance rendered to him upon any occasion. Sometimes after I had taken a hand from Croz, or received a pull, I turned to offer the same to Hudson; but he invariably declined, saying that it was not necessary. Mr. Hadow, however, was not accustomed to this kind of work, and required continual assistance. It is only fair to say that the difficulty which he found at this part arose simply and entirely from want of experience.

This solitary difficult part was of no great extent. We bore away over it at first nearly horizontally for a distance of about four hundred feet; then ascended directly towards the summit for about sixty feet; and then doubled back to the ridge which descends towards Zermatt. A long stride round a rather awkward corner brought us to snow once more. The last doubt vanished! The Matterhorn was ours! Nothing but two hundred feet of easy snow remained to be surmounted. The slope eased off, at length we could be detached, and Croz and I, dashing away, ran a neck-and-neck race, which ended in a dead heat. At 1.40 P.M. the world was at our feet, and the Matterhorn was conquered. Hurrah! Not a footstep could be seen.

It was not yet certain that we had not been beaten. The summit of the Matterhorn was formed of a rudely level ridge about three hundred and fifty feet long, and the Italians might have been at its farther extremity. I hastened to the southern end, scanning the snow to the right and left eagerly. Hurrah! again; it was untrodden. Croz now took the tent-pole, and planted it in the highest snow. "Yes," we said, "there is the flag-staff, but where is the flag?" "Here it is," he answered, pulling off his blouse and fixing it to the stick. It made a poor flag, and there was no wind to float it out, yet it was seen all around. They saw it at Zermatt, at the Riffel, in the Val Tournanche.

We returned to the southern end of the ridge to build a cairn, and then paid homage to the view. The day was one of those super-latively calm and clear ones which usually precede bad weather. The atmosphere was perfectly still, and free from all clouds or vapors. Mountains fifty—nay, a hundred—miles off, looked sharp and near. All their details, ridge and crag, snow and glacier, stood out with faultless definition. Pleasant thoughts of happy days in bygone years came up unbidden, as we recognized the old familiar forms. All were revealed; not one of the principal peaks of the Alps was hidden. Ten thousand feet beneath us were the green fields of Zermatt, dotted with chalets, from which blue smoke rose lazily. Eight thousands feet below, on the other side, were the pastures of Breil. There were forests black and gloomy, and meadows bright and lively; bounding waterfalls and tranquil lakes; fertile lands and savage wastes; sunny plains and frigid plateaux. There were the most rugged forms, the most graceful outlines—bold, perpendicular cliffs, and gentle, undulating slopes; rocky mountains and snowy mountains, sombre and solemn, or glittering and white, with walls, turrets, pinnacles, pyramids, domes, cones, and spires. There was every combination that the world can give, and every contrast the heart could desire.

We remained on the summit for one hour,

"One crowded hour of glorious life."

It passed away too quickly, and we began to prepare for the de-scent.

Hudson and I again consulted as to the best and safest arrange-ment of the party. We agreed that it would be best for Croz to go first, and Hadow second; Hudson, who was almost equal to a guide in sureness of foot, wished to be third; Lord F. Douglas was placed next, and old Peter, the strongest of the remainder, after him. I sug-gested to Hudson that we should attach a rope to the rocks on our arrival at the difficult bit, and hold it as we descended, as an additional protection. He approved the idea, but it was not definitely settled that it should be done. The party was being arranged in the above order while I was sketching the summit, and they had finished, and were waiting for me to be tied in line, when some one remembered that our names had not been left in a bottle. They requested me to write them down, and moved off while it was being done.

A few minutes afterwards I tied myself to young Peter, ran down after the others, and caught them just as they were commencing the descent of the difficult part. Great care was being taken. Only one man was moving at a time; when he was firmly planted the next advanced, and so on. They had not, however, attached the additional rope to the rocks, and nothing was said about it. The suggestion was not made for my own sake, and I am not sure that it ever occurred to me again. For some little distance we two followed the others, detached from them, and should have continued so had not Lord F. Douglas asked me, about three P.M., to tie on to old Peter, as he feared, he said, that Taugwalder would not be able to hold his ground if a slip occurred.

A few minutes later, a sharp-eyed lad ran into the Monte Rosa hotel, to Seiler, saying that he had seen an avalanche fall from the summit of the Matterhorn on to the Matterhorngletscher. The boy was reproved for telling idle stories; he was right, nevertheless, and this was what he saw.

Michel Croz had laid aside his axe, and, in order to give Mr. Hadow greater security, was taking hold of his legs, and putting his feet, one by one, into their proper positions. As far as I know, no one was actually descending. I cannot speak with certainty, because the two leading men were partially hidden from my sight by an intervening mass of rock, but it is my belief, from the movements of their shoulders, that Croz, having done as I have said, was in the act of turning round to go down a step or two himself; at this moment Mr. Hadow slipped, fell against him, and knocked him over. I heard one startled exclamation from Croz, then saw him and Mr. Hadow flying downward; in another moment Hudson was dragged from his steps, and Lord F. Douglas immediately after him. All this was the work of a moment. Immediately we heard Croz's exclamation, old Peter and I planted ourselves as firmly as the rocks would permit; the rope was taut between us, and the jerk came on us both as on one man. We held; but the rope broke midway between Taugwalder and Lord Francis Douglas. For a few seconds we saw our unfortunate companions sliding downward on their backs, and spreading out their hands, endeavoring to save themselves. They passed from our sight uninjured, disappeared one by one, and fell from precipice to precipice on to the Matterhorngletscher below, a distance of nearly four thousand feet in height. From the moment the rope broke it was impossible to help them.

So perished our comrades! For the space of half an hour we remained on the spot without moving a single step. The two men, paralyzed by terror, cried like infants, and trembled in such a manner as to threaten us with the fate of the others. Old Peter rent the air with exclamations of "Chamounix! Oh, what will Chamounix say?" He meant, Who would believe that Croz could fall? The young man did nothing but scream or sob, "We are lost! we are lost!" Fixed between the two, I could neither move up nor down. I begged young Peter to descend, but he dared not. Old Peter became alive to the danger, and swelled the cry, "We are lost! we are lost!" The father's fear was natural—he trembled for his son; the young man's fear was cowardly—he thought of self alone. At last old Peter summoned up courage and changed his position to a rock to which he could fix the rope; the young man then descended, and we all stood together. Immediately we did so I asked for the rope which had given way, and found, to my surprise—indeed, to my horror—that it was the weakest of the three ropes. It was not brought, and should not have been employed, for the purpose for which it was used. It was old rope, and, compared with the others, was feeble. It was intended as a reserve, in case we had to leave much rope behind, attached to rocks. I saw at once that a serious question was involved, and made him give me the end. It had broken in mid-air, and it did not appear to have sustained previous injury.

For more than two hours afterwards I thought almost every moment that the next would be my last; for the Taugwalders, utterly unnerved, were not only incapable of giving assistance, but were in such a state that a slip might have been expected from them at any moment. After a time we were able to do that which should have been done at first, and fixed rope to firm rocks, in addition to being tied together. These ropes were cut from time to time, and were left behind. Even with their assurance the men were afraid to proceed, and several times old Peter turned with ashy face and faltering limbs, and said, with terrible emphasis, "*I cannot!*"

About six P.M. we arrived at the snow upon the ridge descend-

ing towards Zermatt, and all peril was over. We frequently looked,
but in vain, for traces of our unfortunate companions; we bent over
the ridge and cried to them, but no sound returned. Convinced at
last that they were neither within sight nor hearing, we ceased from
our useless efforts; and, too cast down for speech, silently gathered
up our things, and the little effects of those who were lost, preparatory to continuing the descent.

Night fell; and for an hour the descent was continued in the
darkness. At half-past nine a resting-place was found, and upon a
wretched slab, barely large enough to hold the three, we passed six
miserable hours. At daybreak the descent was resumed, and from
the Hörnli ridge we ran down to the chalets of Buhl, and on to
Zermatt. Seiler met me at his door, and followed in silence to my
room. "What is the matter?" "The Taugwalders and I have returned." He did not need more, and burst into tears; but lost no
time in useless lamentations, and set to work to arouse the village.
Ere long a score of men had started to ascend the Hohlicht heights,
above Kalbermatt and Z'Mutt, which commanded the plateau of
the Matterhorngletscher. They returned after six hours, and re-
ported that they had seen the bodies lying motionless on the snow.
This was on Saturday; and they proposed that we should leave on
Sunday evening, so as to arrive upon the plateau at daybreak on
Monday.

We started at two A.M. on Sunday the 16th, and followed the
route that we had taken on the previous Thursday as far as the
Hörnli. From thence we went down to the right of the ridge, and
mounted through the *séracs* of the Matterhorngletscher. By 8.30
we had got to the plateau at the top of the glacier, and within sight
of the corner in which we knew my companions must be. As we
saw one weather-beaten man after another raise the telescope, turn
deadly pale, and pass it on without a word to the next, we knew that
all hope was gone. We approached. They had fallen below as they
had fallen above—Croz a little in advance, Hadow near him, and
Hudson some distance behind; but of Lord F. Douglas we could see
nothing. We left them where they fell; buried in snow at the base of
the grandest cliff of the most majestic mountain of the Alps.

All those who had fallen had been tied with the manilla, or with
the second and equally strong rope, and, consequently, there had
been only one link—that between old Peter and Lord F. Douglas—
where the weaker rope had been used. This had a very ugly look for
Taugwalder, for it was not possible to suppose that the others

would have sanctioned the employment of a rope so greatly inferior in strength when there were more than two hundred and fifty feet of the better qualities still remaining out of use. For the sake of the old guide (who bore a good reputation), and upon all other accounts, it was desirable that this matter should be cleared up; and after my examination before the court of inquiry which was instituted by the government was over, I handed in a number of questions which were framed so as to afford old Peter an opportunity of exculpating himself from the grave suspicions which at once fell upon him. The questions, I was told, were put and answered; but the answers, although promised, have never reached me.

Meanwhile the administration sent strict injunctions to recover the bodies, and upon the 19th of July twenty-one men of Zermatt accomplished that sad and dangerous task. Of the body of Lord Francis Douglas, they, too, saw nothing; it is probably still arrested on the rocks above. The remains of Hudson and Hadow were interred upon the north side of the Zermatt church, in the presence of a reverent crowd of sympathizing friends. The body of Michel Croz lies upon the other side, under a simpler tomb, whose inscription bears honorable testimony to his rectitude, to his courage, and to his devotion.

### Rain

Is it raining, little flower?—
  Be glad of rain!
Too much sun would wither thee;
  'Twill shine again.

The sky is very black, 'tis true;
But just behind it shines the blue.

God watches; and thou wilt have sun,
When clouds their perfect work have done.

*Lucy Larcom*

# THE MYSTERIOUS FOREST

## W. H. Hudson

*An American born in Argentina, Hudson (1841–1922), at twenty-nine, went to England, living and writing there for the rest of his life. Most of his books, however, deal with his early experiences in South America. He called himself an old-fashioned naturalist, one interested in watching and understanding animals in their natural state. His novel* Green Mansions *tells of Mr. Abel wandering farther and farther into the jungles east of Venezuela. Staying with an Indian tribe, he decides to explore a forest they dread.*

THREE weeks had passed by not unpleasantly when, one morning, I took it into my head to walk by myself across that somewhat sterile savannah west of the village and stream, which ended, as I have said, in a long, low, stony ridge. From the village there was nothing to attract the eye in that direction; but I wished to get a better view of that great solitary hill or mountain of Ytaioa, and of the cloud-like summits beyond it in the distance. From the stream the ground rose in a gradual slope, and the highest part of the ridge for which I made was about two miles from the starting-point—a parched brown plain, with nothing growing on it but scattered tussocks of sere hair-like grass.

When I reached the top and could see the country beyond, I was agreeably disappointed at the discovery that the sterile ground extended only about a mile and a quarter on the further side, and was succeeded by a forest—a very inviting patch of woodland covering five or six square miles, occupying a kind of oblong basin, extending from the foot of Ytaioa on the north to a low range of rocky hills on the south. From the wooded basin long narrow strips of forest ran out in various directions like the arms of an octopus, one pair embracing the slopes of Ytaioa, another much broader belt extending along a valley which cut through the ridge of hills on the south side at right angles, and was lost to sight beyond; far away in the west and south and north distant mountains appeared, not in regular ranges, but in groups or singly, or looking like blue banked-up clouds on the horizon.

Glad at having discovered the existence of this forest so near at home, and wondering why my Indian friends had never taken me to it, or ever went out on that side, I set forth with a light heart to explore it for myself, regretting only that I was without a proper weapon for procuring game. The walk from the ridge over the savannah was easy, as the barren, stony ground sloped downward the whole way. The outer part of the wood on my side was very open, composed in most part of dwarf trees that grow on stony soil, and scattered thorny bushes bearing a yellow pea-shaped blossom. Presently I came to thicker wood, where the trees were much taller and in greater variety; and after this came another sterile strip, like that on the edge of the wood, where stone cropped out from the ground and nothing grew except the yellow-flowered thorn bushes. Passing this sterile ribbon, which seemed to extend to a considerable distance north and south, and was fifty to a hundred yards wide, the forest again became dense and the trees large, with much undergrowth in places obstructing the view and making progress difficult.

I spent several hours in this wild paradise, which was so much more delightful than the extensive gloomier forests I had so often penetrated in Guayana: for here, if the trees did not attain to such majestic proportions, the variety of vegetable forms was even greater; as far as I went it was nowhere dark under the trees, and the number of lovely parasites everywhere illustrated the kindly influence of light and air. Even where the trees were largest the sunshine penetrated, subdued by the foliage to exquisite greenish-golden tints, filling the wide lower spaces with tender half-lights, and faint blue-and-grey shadows. Lying on my back and gazing up, I felt reluctant to rise and renew my ramble. For what a roof was that above my head! Roof I call it, just as the poets in their poverty sometimes describe the infinite ethereal sky by that word; but it was no more roof-like and hindering to the soaring spirit than the higher clouds that float in changing forms and tints, and like the foliage chasten the intolerable noonday beams. How far above me seemed that leafy cloudland into which I gazed! Nature, we know, first taught the architect to produce by long colonnades the illusion of distance; but the light-excluding roof prevents him from getting

the same effect above. Here Nature is unapproachable with her
green, airy canopy, a sun-impregnated cloud—cloud above cloud;
and though the highest may be unreached by the eye, the beams yet
filter through, illuming the wide spaces beneath—chamber succeeded by chamber, each with its own special lights and shadows.
Far above me, but not nearly so far as it seemed, the tender gloom
of one such chamber or space is traversed now by a golden shaft of
light falling through some break in the upper foliage, giving a
strange glory to everything it touches—projecting leaves, and
beard-like tuft of moss, and snaky bush-rope. And in the most open
part of that most open space, suspended on nothing to the eye, the
shaft reveals a tangle of shining silver threads—the web of some
large tree-spider. These seemingly distant, yet distinctly visible
threads, serve to remind me that the human artist is only able to get
his horizontal distance by a monotonous reduplication of pillar and
arch, placed at regular intervals, and that the least departure from
this order would destroy the effect. But Nature produces her
effects at random, and seems only to increase the beautiful illusion
by that infinite variety of decoration in which she revels, binding
tree to tree in a tangle of anaconda-like lianas, and dwindling down
from these huge cables to airy webs and hair-like fibres that vibrate
to the wind of the passing insect's wing.

　　Thus in idleness, with such thoughts for company, I spent my
time, glad that no human being, savage or civilised, was with me. It
was better to be alone to listen to the monkeys that chattered without offending; to watch them occupied with the unserious business
of their lives. With that luxuriant tropical nature, its green clouds
and illusive aerial spaces, full of mystery, they harmonised well in
language, appearance and motions;—mountebank angels, living
their fantastic lives far above earth in a half-way heaven of their
own.

　　I saw more monkeys on that morning than I usually saw in the
course of a week's rambling. And other animals were seen; I particularly remember two accouries I startled, that after rushing away
a few yards stopped and stood peering back at me as if not knowing
whether to regard me as friend or enemy. Birds, too, were strangely
abundant; and altogether this struck me as being the richest
hunting-ground I had seen, and it astonished me to think that the
Indians of the village did not appear to visit it.

　　On my return in the afternoon I gave an enthusiastic account of
my day's ramble, speaking not of the things that had moved my

soul, but only of those which move the Guayana Indian's soul—the animal food he craves, and which, one would imagine, Nature would prefer him to do without, so hard he finds it to wrest a sufficiency from her. To my surprise they shook their heads and looked troubled at what I said; and finally, my host informed me that the wood I had been in was a dangerous place; that if they went there to hunt a great injury would be done to them; and he finished by advising me not to visit it again.

I began to understand from their looks and the old man's vague words that their fear of the wood was superstitious. If dangerous creatures had existed there—tigers, or camoodis, or solitary murderous savages—they would have said so; but when I pressed them with questions they could only repeat that "something bad" existed in the place, that animals were abundant there because no Indian who valued his life dared venture into it. I replied that unless they gave me some more definite information I should certainly go again, and put myself in the way of the danger they feared.

My reckless courage, as they considered it, surprised them; but they had already begun to find out that their superstitions had no effect on me, that I listened to them as to stories invented to amuse a child, and for the moment they made no further attempt to dissuade me.

Next day I returned to the forest of evil report, which had now a new and even greater charm—the fascination of the unknown and the mysterious; still, the warning I had received made me distrustful and cautious at first, for I could not help thinking about it. When we consider how much of their life is passed in the woods, which become as familiar to them as the streets of our native town to us, it seems almost incredible that these savages have a superstitious fear of all forests, fearing them as much, even in the bright light of day, as a nervous child with memory filled with ghost-stories fears a dark room. But, like the child in the dark room, they fear the forest only when alone in it, and for this reason always hunt in couples or parties. What, then, prevented them from visiting this particular wood, which offered so tempting a harvest? The question troubled me not a little; at the same time I was ashamed of the feeling, and fought against it; and in the end I made my way to the same sequestered spot where I had rested so long on my previous visit.

In this place I witnessed a new thing, and had a strange experience. Sitting on the ground in the shade of a large tree, I began to

hear a confused noise as of a coming tempest of wind mixed with
shrill calls and cries. Nearer and nearer it came, and at last a multitude of birds of many kinds, but mostly small, appeared in sight
swarming through the trees, some running on the trunks and larger
branches, others flitting through the foliage, and many keeping on
the wing, now hovering and now darting this way or that. They
were all busily searching for and pursuing the insects, moving on
at the same time, and in a very few minutes they had finished examining the trees near me, and were gone; but not satisfied with what
I had witnessed, I jumped up and rushed after the flock to keep it in
sight. All my caution and all recollection of what the Indians had
said was now forgot, so great was my interest in this bird-army;
but as they moved on without pause they quickly left me behind,
and presently my career was stopped by an impenetrable tangle of
bushes, vines, and roots of large trees extending like huge cables
along the ground. In the midst of this leafy labyrinth I sat down on
a projecting root to cool my blood before attempting to make my
way back to my former position. After that tempest of motion and
confused noises the silence of the forest seemed very profound; but
before I had been resting many moments it was broken by a low
strain of exquisite bird-melody, wonderfully pure and expressive,
unlike any musical sound I had ever heard before. It seemed to issue
from a thick cluster of broad leaves of a creeper only a few yards
from where I sat. With my eyes fixed on this green hiding-place I
waited with suspended breath for its repetition, wondering whether
any civilised being had ever listened to such a strain before. Surely
not, I thought, else the fame of so divine a melody would long ago
have been noised abroad. I thought of the rialejo, the celebrated
organ-bird or flute-bird, and of the various ways in which hearers
are affected by it. To some its warbling is like the sound of a beautiful mysterious instrument, while to others it seems like the singing
of a blithe-hearted child with a highly melodious voice. I had often
heard and listened with delight to the singing of the rialejo in the
Guayana forests, but this song, or musical phrase, was utterly unlike
it in character. It was pure, more expressive, softer—so low that at
a distance of forty yards I could hardly have heard it. But its greatest charm was its resemblance to the human voice—a voice purified
and brightened to something almost angelic. Imagine, then, my impatience as I sat there straining my sense, my deep disappointment
when it was not repeated! I rose at length very reluctantly and
slowly began making my way back; but when I had progressed

about thirty yards, again the sweet voice sounded just behind me, and turning quickly I stood still and waited. The same voice, but not the same song—not the same phrase; the notes were different, more varied and rapidly enunciated, as if the singer had been more excited. The blood rushed to my heart as I listened; my nerves tingled with a strange new delight, the rapture produced by such music heigthened by a sense of mystery. Before many moments I heard it again, not rapid now, but a soft warbling, lower than at first, infinitely sweet and tender, sinking to lisping sounds that soon ceased to be audible; the whole having lasted as long as it would take me to repeat a sentence of a dozen words. This seemed the singer's farewell to me, for I waited and listened in vain to hear it repeated; and after getting back to the starting-point I sat for upwards of an hour, still hoping to hear it once more!

The westering sun at length compelled me to quit the wood, but not before I had resolved to return the next morning and seek for the spot where I had met with so enchanting an experience. After crossing the sterile belt I have mentioned within the wood, and just before I came to the open outer edge where the stunted trees and bushes die away on the border of the savannah, what was my delight and astonishment at hearing the mysterious melody once more! It seemed to issue from a clump of bushes close by; but by this time I had come to the conclusion that there was a ventriloquism in this woodland voice which made it impossible for me to determine its exact direction. Of one thing I was, however, now quite convinced, and that was that the singer had been following me all the time. Again and again as I stood there listening it sounded, now so faint and apparently far off as to be scarcely audible; then all at once it would ring out bright and clear within a few yards of me, as if the shy little thing had suddenly grown bold; but, far or near, the vocalist remained invisible, and at length the tantalising melody ceased altogether.

I was not disappointed on my next visit to the forest, nor on several succeeding visits; and this seemed to show that if I was right in believing that these strange, melodious utterances proceeded from one individual, then the bird or being, although still refusing to show itself, was always on the watch for my appearance, and followed me wherever I went. This thought only served to increase my curiosity; I was constantly pondering over the subject, and at last concluded that it would be best to induce one of the

Indians to go with me to the wood on the chance of his being able to explain the mystery.

One of the treasures I had managed to preserve in my sojourn with these children of nature, who were always anxious to become possessors of my belongings, was a small prettily fashioned metal match-box, opening with a spring. Remembering that Kua-kó, among others, had looked at this trifle with covetous eyes—the covetous way in which they all looked at it had given it a fictitious value in my own—I tried to bribe him with the offer of it to accompany me to my favourite haunt. The brave young hunter refused again and again; but on each occasion he offered to perform some other service or to give me something in exchange for the box. At last I told him that I would give it to the first person who should accompany me, and fearing that someone would be found valiant enough to win the prize, he at length plucked up a spirit, and on the next day, seeing me going out for a walk, he all at once offered to go with me. He cunningly tried to get the box before starting— his cunning, poor youth! was not very deep. I told him that the forest we were about to visit abounded with plants and birds un- like any I had seen elsewhere, that I wished to learn their names, and everything about them, and that when I had got the required information the box would be his—not sooner. Finally we started, he, as usual, armed with his zabatana, with which, I imagined, he would procure more game than usually fell to his little poisoned arrows. When we reached the wood I could see that he was ill at ease: nothing would persuade him to go into the deeper part; and even where it was very open and light he was constantly gazing into bushes and shadowy places, as if expecting to see some fright- ful creature lying in wait for him. This behaviour might have had a disquieting effect on me had I not been thoroughly convinced that his fears were purely superstitious, and that there could be no dangerous animal in a spot I was accustomed to walk in every day. My plan was to ramble about with an unconcerned air, occasionally pointing out an uncommon tree or shrub or vine, or calling his attention to a distant bird cry and asking the bird's name, in the hope that the mysterious voice would make itself heard, and that he would be able to give me some explanation of it. But for upwards of two hours we moved about, hearing nothing except the usual bird-voices, and during all that time he never stirred a yard from my side nor made an attempt to capture anything. At length we sat down under a tree, in an open spot close to the border of the wood. He sat down very reluctantly, and seemed more troubled in his mind than ever, keeping his eyes continuously roving about, while he listened intently to every sound. The sounds were not few, owing to the abundance of animal and especially of bird life in this favoured spot. I began to question my companion as to some of the cries we heard. There were notes and cries familiar to me as the crowing of the cock—parrot screams and yelping of toucans, the distant wailing calls of maam and duraquara; and shrill laughter-like notes of the large tree-climber as it passed from tree to tree; the quick whistle of cotingas; and strange throbbing and thrilling sounds, as of pigmies beating on metallic drums, of the skulking pitta-thrushes; and with these mingled other notes less well known. One came from the treetops, where it was perpetually wandering amid the foliage—a low note, repeated at intervals of a few seconds, so thin and mournful and full of mystery, that I half expected to hear that it proceeded from the restless ghost of some dead bird. But no; he only said it was uttered by a "little bird"—too little presumably to have a name. From the foliage of a neighbouring tree came a few tinkling chirps, as of a small mandolin, two or three strings of which had been carelessly struck by the player. He said that it came from a small green frog that lived in trees; and in this way my rude Indian—vexed perhaps at being asked such trivial questions—brushed away the pretty fantasies my mind had woven in the woodland solitude. For I often listened to this tinkling music, and it had suggested the idea that the place was frequented by a tribe of fairy-like troubadour monkeys, and that if I could only be quick-sighted enough I might one day be able to detect the minstrel sitting, in a green tunic perhaps, cross-legged on some high, swaying bough, carelessly touching his mandolin suspended from his neck by a yellow ribbon.

By-and-by a bird came with low, swift flight, its great tail spread open fan-wise, and perched itself on an exposed bough not thirty yards from us. It was all of a chestnut-red colour, long-bodied, in size like a big pigeon: its actions showed that its curiosity had been greatly excited, for it jerked from side to side, eyeing us first with one eye, then the other, while its long tail rose and fell in a measured way.

"Look, Kua-kó," I said in a whisper, "there is a bird for you to kill."

But he only shook his head, still watchful.

"Give me the blow-pipe, then," I said, with a laugh, putting out my hand to take it. But he refused to let me take it, knowing that it would only be an arrow wasted if I attempted to shoot anything.

As I persisted in telling him to kill the bird, he at last bent his lips near me and said in a half-whisper, as if fearful of being over-heard, "I can kill nothing here. If I shot at the bird the daughter of the Didi would catch the dart in her hand and throw it back and hit me here," touching his breast just over his heart.

I laughed again, saying to myself, with some amusement, that Kua-kó was not such a bad companion after all—that he was not without imagination. But in spite of my laughter his words roused my interest, and suggested the idea that the voice I was curious about had been heard by the Indians, and was as great a mystery to them as to me; since not being like that of any creature known to them, it would be attributed by their superstitious minds to one of the numerous demons or semi-human monsters inhabiting every forest, stream, and mountain; and fear of it would drive them from the wood. In this case, judging from my companion's words, they had varied the form of the superstition somewhat, inventing a daughter of a water-spirit to be afraid of. My thought was that if their keen, practised eyes had never been able to see this flitting woodland creature with a musical soul, it was not likely that I would succeed in my quest.

I began to question him, but he now appeared less inclined to talk and more frightened than ever, and each time I attempted to speak he imposed silence, with a quick gesture of alarm, while he continued to stare about him with dilated eyes. All at once he sprang to his feet as if overcome with terror, and started running at full speed. His fear infected me, and, springing up, I followed as fast as I could, but he was far ahead of me, running for dear life; and before I had gone forty yards my feet were caught in a creeper trailing along the surface, and I measured my length on the ground. The sudden, violent shock almost took away my senses for a moment, but when I jumped up and stared round to see no unspeakable monster—Curupitá or other—rushing on to slay and devour me there and then, I began to feel ashamed of my cowardice; and in the end I turned and walked back to the spot I had just quitted and sat down once more. I even tried to hum a tune, just to prove to myself that I had completely recovered from the panic caught from the miserable Indian; but it is never possible in such cases to get back one's serenity immediately, and a vague suspicion continued to trouble me for a time. After sitting there for half an hour or so, listening to distant bird sounds, I began to recover my old confidence, and even to feel inclined to penetrate further into the wood. All at once, making me almost jump, so sudden it was, so much nearer and louder than I had ever heard it before, the mysterious melody began. Unmistakably it was uttered by the same being heard on former occasions; but to-day it was different in character. The utterance was far more rapid, with fewer silent intervals, and it had none of the usual tenderness in it, nor ever once sunk to that low, whisper-like talking, which had seemed to me as if the spirit of the wind had breathed its low sighs in syllables and speech. Now it was not only loud, rapid, and continuous, but, while still musical, there was an incisiveness in it, a sharp ring as of resentment, which made it strike painfully on the sense.

The impression of an intelligent unhuman being addressing me in anger took so firm a hold on my mind that the old fear returned, and, rising, I began to walk rapidly away, intending to escape from the wood. The voice continued violently rating me, as it seemed to my mind, moving with me, which caused me to accelerate my steps; and very soon I would have broken into a run, when its character began to change again. There were pauses now, intervals of silence, long or short, and after each one the voice came to my ear with a more subdued and dulcet sound—more of that melting, flute-like quality it had possessed at other times; and this softness of tone, coupled with the talking-like form of utterance, gave me the idea of a being no longer incensed, addressing me now in a peaceable spirit, reasoning away my unworthy tremors, and imploring me to remain with it in the wood. Strange as this voice without a body was, and always productive of a slightly uncomfortable feeling on account of its mystery, it seemed impossible to doubt that it came to me now in a spirit of pure friendliness; and when I had recovered my composure I found a new delight in listening to it—all the greater because of the fear so lately experienced, and of its seeming intelligence. For the third time I reseated myself on the same spot, and at intervals the voice talked to me there for some time, and to my fancy expressed satisfaction and pleasure at my presence. But later, without losing its friendly tone, it changed again. It seemed to move away and to be thrown back from a considerable distance; and, at long intervals, it would approach me again with a new sound, which I began to interpret as of command, or entreaty. Was it, I asked myself, inviting me to follow? And if I obeyed, to what delightful discoveries or fright-

ful dangers might it lead? My curiosity, together with the belief
that the being—I called it being, not bird, now—was friendly to me,
overcame all timidity, and I rose and walked at random towards
the interior of the wood. Very soon I had no doubt left that the
being had desired me to follow; for there was now a new note of
gladness in its voice, and it continued near me as I walked, at intervals approaching me so closely as to set me staring into the surrounding shadowy places like poor scared Kua-kó.

On this occasion, too, I began to have a new fancy, for fancy
or illusion I was determined to regard it, that some swift-footed
being was treading the ground near me; that I occasionally caught
the faint rustle of a light footstep, and detected a motion in leaves
and fronds and thread-like stems of creepers hanging near the
surface, as if some passing body had touched and made them tremble; and once or twice that I even had a glimpse of a grey, misty
object moving at no great distance in the deeper shadows.

Led by this wandering tricksy being, I came to a spot where
the trees were very large and the damp dark ground almost free
from undergrowth; and here the voice ceased to be heard. After
patiently waiting and listening for some time I began to look about
me with a slight feeling of apprehension. It was still about two
hours before sunset; only in this place the shade of the vast trees
made a perpetual twilight: moreover, it was strangely silent here,
the few bird cries that reached me coming from a long distance.
I had flattered myself that the voice had become to some extent
intelligible to me; its outburst of anger caused no doubt by my
cowardly flight after the Indian; then its recovered friendliness
which had induced me to return; and, finally, its desire to be followed. Now that it had led me to this place of shadow and profound
silence, and had ceased to speak and to lead, I could not help thinking that this was my goal, that I had been brought to this spot with
a purpose, that in this wild and solitary retreat some tremendous
adventure was about to befall me.

As the silence continued unbroken there was time to dwell on
this thought. I gazed before me and listened intently, scarcely
breathing, until the suspense became painful—too painful at last,
and I turned and took a step with the idea of going back to the
border of the wood, when close by, clear as a silver bell, sounded
the voice once more, but only for a moment—two or three syllables
in response to my movement, then it was silent again.

Once more I was standing still, as if in obedience to a command, in the same state of suspense; and whether the change was real or only imagined I know not, but the silence every minute grew more profound and the gloom deeper. Imaginary terrors began to assail me. Ancient fables of men allured by beautiful forms and melodious voices to destruction all at once acquired a fearful significance. I recalled some of the Indian beliefs, especially that of the misshapen, man-devouring monster who is said to beguile his victims into the dark forest by mimicking the human voice—the voice sometimes of a woman in distress—or by singing some strange and beautiful melody. I grew almost afraid to look round lest I should catch sight of him stealing towards me on his huge feet with toes pointing backwards, his mouth snarling horribly to display his great green fangs. It was distressing to have such fancies in this wild, solitary spot—hateful to feel their power over me when I knew that they were nothing but fancies and creations of the savage mind. But if these supernatural beings had no existence, there were other monsters, only too real, in these woods which it would be dreadful to encounter alone and unarmed, since against such adversaries a revolver would be as ineffectual as a popgun. Some huge camoodi, able to crush my bones like brittle twigs in its constricting coils, might lurk in these shadows, and approach me stealthily, unseen in its dark colour on the dark ground. Or some jaguar or black tiger might steal towards me, masked by a bush or tree-trunk, to spring upon me unawares. Or worse still, this way might suddenly come a pack of those swift-footed, unspeakably terrible hunting-leopards, from which every living thing in the forest flies with shrieks of consternation or else falls paralysed in their path to be instantly torn to pieces and devoured.

A slight rustling sound in the foliage above me made me start and cast up my eyes. High up, where a pale gleam of tempered sunlight fell through the leaves, a grotesque human-like face, black as ebony and adorned with a great red beard, appeared staring down upon me. In another moment it was gone. It was only a large araguato, or howling monkey, but I was so unnerved that I could not get rid of the idea that it was something more than a monkey. Once more I moved, and again, the instant I moved my foot, clear, and keen, and imperative, sounded the voice! It was no longer possible to doubt its meaning. It commanded me to stand still—to wait—to watch—to listen! Had it cried "Listen! Do not move!" I could not have understood it better. Trying as the suspense was, I now felt powerless to escape. Something very terrible, I felt con-

vinced, was about to happen, either to destroy or to release me
from the spell that held me.

And while I stood thus rooted to the ground, the sweat standing
in large drops on my forehead, all at once close to me sounded a
cry, fine and clear at first, and rising at the end to a shriek so loud,
piercing, and unearthly in character that the blood seemed to freeze
in my veins, and a despairing cry to heaven escaped my lips; then,
before that long shriek expired, a mighty chorus of thunderous
voices burst forth around me; and in this awful tempest of sound I
trembled like a leaf; and the leaves on the trees were agitated as if
by a high wind, and the earth itself seemed to shake beneath my
feet. Indescribably horrible were my sensations at that moment;
I was deafened, and would possibly have been maddened had I not,
as by a miracle, chanced to see a large araguato on a branch overhead, roaring with open mouth and inflated throat and chest.

It was simply a concert of howling monkeys which had so terrified me! But my extreme fear was not strange in the circumstances;
since everything that had led up to the display, the gloom and silence, the period of suspense and my heated imagination, had raised
my mind to the highest degree of excitement and expectancy.
I had rightly conjectured, no doubt, that my unseen guide had led
me to that spot for a purpose; and the purpose had been to set me
in the midst of a congregation of araguatos to enable me for the first
time fully to appreciate their unparalleled vocal powers. I had always heard them at a distance: here they were gathered in scores,
possibly hundreds—the whole araguato population of the forest, I
should think—close to me; and it may give some faint conception
of the tremendous power and awful character of the sound thus
produced by their combined voices when I say that this animal—
miscalled "howler" in English—would outroar the mightiest lion
that ever woke the echoes of an African wilderness.

This roaring concert, which lasted three or four minutes, having ended, I lingered a few minutes longer on the spot, and not
hearing the voice again, went back to the edge of the wood, and
then started on my way back to the village.

# THE BATTLE OF THE MARTEN
# AND THE PORCUPINE

## Mayne Reid

*Through his more than ninety books, Mayne Reid (1818–1883) told millions of readers about the American Southwest and prairie country. Exciting romances, these books also presented highly accurate reports on the animals of the region. Reid, born in Ireland, came to the United States as a youth, and was a storekeeper, journalist, teacher, actor, Indian fighter, and army captain. He was fascinated by the continual battle for survival in nature. Two exciting struggles to the death are described in these selections from* The Desert Home.

IT WAS in the middle of the winter. A light snow had fallen upon the ground—just enough to enable us to follow the trail of any animal we might light upon. Of course, the snow filled us with the idea of hunting; and Harry and I started out upon the tracks of a brace of Elk that had passed through our opening during the night. The tracks were very fresh-looking; and it was evident that the animals had passed in the morning, just before we were up. We concluded, therefore, that they had not gone far off; and we hoped soon to come up with them.

The trail led us along the side of the lake, and then up the left bank of the stream. Castor and Pollux were with us; but in our hunting excursions we usually led them on a leash, so that they might not frighten the game by running ahead of us.

When about half a mile from the house, we found that the Elk had crossed to the right bank of the stream. We were about to follow, when all at once our eyes fell upon a most singular track or tracks that led off into the woods. They were *the tracks of human feet—the feet of children!*

So thought we, at first sight of them; and you may fancy the surprise into which we were suddenly thrown. They were about five inches in length, and exactly such as would have been made by a barefooted urchin of six years old. There appeared to be two sets of them, as if two children had passed, following one another, on the same trail. What could it mean? After all, were there human beings in the valley besides ourselves? Could these be the footprints of two young Indians?

All at once, I thought of the Diggers—the *Yamparicos*—the root eaters—who are found in almost every hole and corner of the American Desert. Could it be possible that a family of these wretched creatures existed in the valley? "Quite possible," thought I, when I reflected upon their habits. Living upon roots, insects, and reptiles, burrowing in holes and caves like the wild animals around them, a family or more might have been living all this time in some unexplored corner of the valley, without our having encountered any traces of them. Was this really so? and were the tracks before us the footmarks of a brace of young Diggers who had been passing from point to point?

Of course, our Elk hunt was given up until this mystery should be solved; and we turned off from the trail of the latter to follow that of the children.

In coming out to an open place, where the snow lay smoothly, and the foot-prints appeared well defined, I stooped down to examine them more minutely, in order to be satisfied that they were the tracks of human feet. Sure enough, there were the heels, the regular widening of the foot near the toes, and the toes themselves, all plainly stamped upon the snow. Here, however, arose another mystery. On counting the toes, I found that in some of the tracks there were five,—as there should have been,—while in others there were only four! This led me to examine the print of the toes more carefully; and I now saw that each of them was armed with a claw, which on account of some hairy covering, had made but a very indefinite impression in the snow. The tracks, then, were *not* the footmarks of children, but those of some animal with claws.

Notwithstanding that we had come to this conclusion, we still continued to follow the trail. We were curious to see what sort of a creature had made it. Perhaps it might be some animal unknown to naturalists—some new species; and we might one day have the merit of being the first to describe it. We had not far to go: a hundred yards or so brought us in sight of a grove of young cottonwoods; and these we saw at a glance were "barked" by a Porcupine.

The whole mystery was cleared up—we had been following in the trail of this animal.

I now remembered that the Porcupine was one of the *planti-grade* family, with five toes on his hind feet, and only four on the fore ones. The tracks were undoubtedly his.

My companion and I were somewhat chagrined at being thus drawn away from our hunt by such an insignificant object; and we vowed to take vengeance upon the Porcupine, as soon as we should set our eyes upon him. We were not long in doing this; for, as we stole quietly forward, we caught sight of a shaggy animal moving among the branches of a tree about fifty yards ahead of us. It was he, of course. At the same moment, however, another animal "hove in sight," in appearance as different from the Porcupine as a Bull from a bluebottle.

This creature—tail and all—was not less than a yard and a quarter in length, and yet its body was not thicker than the upper part of a man's arm. Its head was broad and somewhat flattened, with short erect ears and pointed nose. It was bearded like a Cat, although the face had more of the Dog in its expression. Its legs were short and strong; and both legs and body denoted the possession of agility and strength. It was of a reddish brown color, with a white mark on the breast, and darker along the back and on the legs, feet, nose, and tail. Its whole appearance reminded one of a gigantic Weasel,—which in fact it was,—the great Marten of America, generally though improperly, called the "Fisher." When we first saw it, it was crouching along a high log that ran directly towards the tree, upon which was the Porcupine. Its eyes were fixed intently upon the latter; and it was evidently meditating an attack. We stopped to watch it.

The Porcupine had not yet perceived his enemy, as he was busily engaged in splitting the bark from the cottonwood. The Marten, after reconnoitring him for some moments, sprang off from the log, and came running towards the tree. The other now saw him, and at the same instant uttered a sort of shrill, querulous cry, and appeared to be greatly affrighted. To our astonishment, however, instead of remaining where it was, it suddenly dropped to the ground, almost at the very nose of its adversary! I could not, at first, understand the policy of this strange tactic on the part of the Porcupine; but a moment's reflection convinced me it was sound policy. The Marten would have been as much at home on the tree as himself; and had he remained among the branches—

which were slender ones,—his throat and the under part of his body
—both of which are soft, and without quills—would have been exposed to the teeth of his adversary. This, then, was why he had let
himself down so unexpectedly; and we noticed that the instant he
touched the ground, he rolled himself into a round clew, presenting on all sides the formidable *chevaux-de-frise* of his quills.

The Marten now ran around him, doubling his long, vermiform
body with great activity—at intervals showing his teeth, erecting
his back, and snarling like a Cat. We expected every moment to
see him spring forward upon his victim; but he did not do so. He
evidently understood the peril of such an act; and appeared for a
moment puzzled as to how he should proceed. All this while, the
Porcupine lay quiet—except the tail. This was, in fact, the only
"feature" of the animal that could be seen, as the head and feet
were completely hidden under the body. The tail, however, was
kept constantly in motion—jerked from side to side, and flirted
occasionally upwards.

What would the Marten do? There was not an inch of the
other's body that was not defended by the sharp and barbed quills—
not a spot where he could insert the tip of his nose. Would he
abandon the contest? So thought we, for a while; but we were
soon convinced of our error.

After running around several times, as we have described, he
at length posted himself near the hind quarters of the Porcupine,
and with his nose a few inches from the tail of the latter. In this
position, he stood for some moments, apparently watching the tail,
which still continued to oscillate rapidly. He stood in perfect
silence, and without making a movement.

The Porcupine, not being able to see him, and perhaps thinking
that he was gone, now waved his tail more slowly, and then suffered
it to drop motionless.

This was what the other was waiting for; and, the next moment,
he had seized the tail in his teeth. We saw that he held it by the tip,
where it is destitute of the thorny spines.

What would he do next? Was he going to bite off the end of the
Porcupine's tail? No such thing. He had a different game from that
to play as we soon witnessed.

The moment he caught the tail, the Porcupine uttered its querulous cries; but the Marten, heeding not these, commenced walking
backward, dragging the other after him. Where was he dragging
it to? We soon saw. He was pulling it to a tree close by, with low

branches, that forked out near the ground. "But for what purpose?" thought we. We wondered as we watched.

The Porcupine could offer no resistance. Its feet gave way, and slipped along the snowy ground; for the Marten was evidently the much stronger animal.

In a short time, the latter had reached the tree, dragging the other after him to its foot. He now commenced ascending, still holding the Porcupine's tail in his teeth, and taking precious care not to brush too closely to the quills. "Surely," thought we, "he cannot climb up, carrying a body almost as big as himself, in that manner!" It was not his intention to climb up,—only to one of the lowermost branches,—and the next moment, he had reached it, stretching his long body out on the limb, and clutching it firmly with his Cat-like claws. He still held fast hold of the Porcupine's tail, which animal was now lifted into such a position that only its fore quarters rested on the ground, and it appeared to stand upon its head, all the while uttering its pitiful cries.

For the life of us, we could not guess what the Marten meant by all this manoeuvring. *He* knew well enough, as he gave proof the moment after. When he had got the other, as it were, on a balance, he suddenly sprang back to the ground, in such a direction that the impetus of his leap jerked the Porcupine upon its back. Before the clumsy creature was able to turn over and "clew" itself, the active Weasel had pounced upon its belly, and buried his claws in the soft flesh, while, at the same time, his teeth were made fast in the throat!

In vain the Porcupine struggled. The other rode him with such agility, that he was unable to get right side up again; and in a few moments the struggle would have ended by the Porcupine's throat being cut; but we saw that it was time for us to interfere; and, slipping Castor and Pollux from the leash, we ran forward.

The Dogs soon drove the Marten from his victim, but he did not run from them. On the contrary, he turned round upon them, keeping them at bay with his sharp teeth and fierce snarling. In truth, they would have had a very tough job of it, had we not been near; but, on seeing us approach, the animal took to a tree, running up it like a Squirrel. A rifle bullet soon brought him down again; and his long body lay stretched out on the earth, emitting a strong odor of musk, that was quite disagreeable.

On returning to the Porcupine, which our Dogs took care not to meddle with—we found the animal already better than half dead.

The blood was running from its throat, which the Marten had torn open. Of course, we put the creature out of pain, by killing it outright; and taking the Marten along with us for the purpose of skinning it, we returned homeward, leaving the Elk hunt for another day.

### To Daffodils

FAIR daffodils, we weep to see
   You haste away so soon;
As yet the early rising sun
   Has not attained his noon.
     Stay, stay,
Until the hasting day
   Has run
But to the even-song;
And, having prayed together, we
   Will go with you along.

We have short time to stay as you,
   We have as short a spring;
As quick as growth to meet decay,
   As you, or anything.
     We die,
As your hours do, and dry
   Away,
Like to the summer's rain,
Or as the pearls of morning's dew,
   Ne'er to be found again.

*Robert Herrick*

# THE BATTLE OF THE SNAKES

## Mayne Reid

ALL at once, we were interrupted by a series of curious incidents which took place within sight of our fire. Our attention was first drawn to them by hearing loud screams at a short distance from us, which we all recognized as the voice of the Blue Jay. There is nothing unusual in hearing this bird screaming half the day—for it is, perhaps, more easily excited than any other feathered creature. But, if you have ever noticed, it utters a very peculiar cry when there is something unusual in the wind. When some much-dreaded enemy is at hand, its note becomes extremely shrill and disagreeable. So it was then; and for that reason, it drew my attention, as well as that of my companions.

We looked towards the spot whence the cry came. We could see the branches of a low tree in motion, and the beautiful sky-blue wings of the bird closing and spreading again as it fluttered through them. We could see nothing else upon the tree,—that is, no enemy of the bird,—nor on any of the trees near it. On lowering our eyes to the ground, however, we perceived at once what had set the Jay to scolding. Slowly drawing itself along the earth, gliding through the grass and over the dry leaves, without causing even the driest of them to rustle, went a hideous Reptile—a Snake. Its yellowish body, dappled with black blotches, glittered as the sun glanced from its lubricated scales, while it rose and fell in wavy undulations as it moved. It moved slowly—by vertical sinuosities, almost in a direct line, with its head slightly raised from the grass. At intervals, it stopped, elevated its neck, lowered its flat, coffin-shaped head, like a feeding Swan, gently oscillated it in a horizontal direction, touched the crisp leaves with its red tongue,—as though it was *feeling for a trail*,—and then moved on again. In its frequent pauses, as it lay stretched along the ground, it appeared cylindrical, as long as the tallest man, and, as thick as a man's forearm. Its tail ended in a horny appendage, about a foot in length, and resembling a string of large, yellowish, ill-shaped beads, or a portion of its own vertebræ stripped of the flesh. This peculiarity told us its species. We saw before us the dreaded Rattlesnake—the *Crotalus horridus.*

My companions were eager to rush forward and at once attack the monster. I restrained them, Dogs and all. I had heard—who has not?—of the power of fascination which these Reptiles possess. I knew not whether to believe or disbelieve it. Here was an opportunity to test its truth. Would it charm the Bird? We should see. One and all of us remained motionless and silent. The Snake crawled on.

The Bird followed overhead, pitching itself from branch to branch, from tree to tree, screaming with open throat. Neither of them noticed us, as we were partially concealed where we sat.

On reaching the foot of a tall magnolia, the Rattlesnake—after going once round the tree, and apparently smelling the bark—slowly and carefully wound itself into a spiral coil, close into the trunk. Its body now presented the appearance of a speckled and glittering cable, as they are usually coiled on the deck of a ship. The tail, with its horny appendage, protruded beneath, and the flat head peeped over above, resting upon the uppermost ring of the body. The nictitating membrane was drawn over its eyes. It appeared to sleep. This I thought strange, as I had heard that the fascinating power of these creatures lay in the eyes. It soon became evident, however, that the Bird was not its object; for the latter, on seeing that the Snake lay still, ceased its chattering, and flew off into the woods.

Believing that the interest of the scene was now over, I was about raising my rifle to take aim at the Snake, when a motion on its part convinced me that it was not asleep, but watching. Watching for what? A Squirrel, perhaps, for this is its favorite prey. It looked up into the tree. It had all the appearance of being what is termed a "Squirrel tree"—that is, a tree in which Squirrels have their hole and nest. Ha! just as I expected: there was a hole in the trunk, high up; and around its orifice the bark was slightly discolored, evidently by the paws of the Squirrels passing in and out. Moreover, on looking to the ground again, I perceived that a little beaten path, like a Rat track, led off through the grass. A ridge-like protuberance that projected from the foot of the tree—marking the direction of one of its great roots—ran right into this path; and, from the discoloration of the bark above it, it was evident that the

Squirrels usually climbed up or descended along this ridge. The Rattlesnake was coiled beside it—so close, that no animal could pass in that way without coming within his reach. I felt certain, then, that he was waiting for the descent of the Squirrel; and, desirous to see what should happen, I muttered some words of caution to my companions, who remained silent as before.

We sat watching the hole, expecting every moment to see the Squirrel come forth. At length, the little Rat-shaped head peeped cautiously out; but in this position the animal remained, and did not seem inclined to trust itself beyond the mouth of its den. It was evidently observing us,—which it could easily do, from its elevated position,—and was not intending to come down.

We were about giving up all hopes of witnessing a "scene," when our attention was drawn to a rustling among the dead leaves in the woods beyond. We looked in that direction. A Squirrel was running towards the tree. It was running at full speed,—now along the fallen logs, now through the grass and dry leaves,—apparently pursued. It *was* pursued; for almost at the same instant its pursuer came in sight—an animal with a long, slender body, twice the length of the Squirrel itself, and of a bright, yellow color. It was the *Pine Weasel*. There were not twenty feet between them as they ran, and both were doing their best.

I cast a glance at the Rattlesnake. He knew what was coming. His jaws were extended,—the lower one drawn back until it touched his throat,—his poisoned fangs were naked and visible; his tongue was protruded forward; his eyes glanced like diamonds; and his whole body rose, and fell, as with a quick respiration. He seemed to have dilated himself to twice his natural size.

The Squirrel, looking only behind, ran for the tree; and, like a streak of light, passed along the ridge and upward. We saw the Snake launch out his head, as the other passed him; but so quick had been the action, that it did not seem that he had even touched it.

"Good!" thought we, as we saw the Squirrel sweep up the trunk, and fancied that it was safe. Before it had reached the first fork, however, we observed that it climbed more slowly—then faltered—then stopped altogether. Its hind feet slipped from the bark; its body oscillated a moment, hanging by the fore claws, and then dropped heavily back into the very jaws of the Serpent!

The Weasel, on seeing the Snake, had suddenly stopped a few feet from it, and now ran around, doubling its long, worm-like body, and occasionally standing erect—all the while spitting and

snarling, like an angry Cat. It was evidently furious at being robbed
of its prey; and we thought for a while it was going to give battle
to the Snake. The latter had recoiled himself on seeing this enemy,
and lay with open jaws, awaiting the attack. The body of the
Squirrel, now quite dead, was close up to his coil, so that the other
could not snatch it without coming within reach of his dangerous
fangs.

On seeing this, and evidently afraid to encounter such a terrible
antagonist, the Weasel after a while ceased its hostile demonstrations; and, turning to one side, bounded off into the woods.

The Reptile now leisurely uncoiled the upper half of his body;
and, stretching out his neck towards the Squirrel, prepared to
swallow it. He drew the latter out to its full length along the
ground, so that its head lay towards him. This he purposed to swallow first,—in order to take the animal "with the grain," and he now
commenced lubricating it with the saliva that ran from his forked
tongue.

While we sat watching this curious operation, our attention
was attracted to a movement in the leaves above the spot where
the Snake lay. Directly over him, at a height of twenty or more
feet, a huge *liana*, of the trumpet species, stretched across from tree
to tree. It was full as thick as a man's arm, and covered with green
leaves, and large, crimson, cuneiform blossoms, such as belonged
to itself. There were other blossoms mingling with these, for still
other parasites—smaller ones—were twined around it, and we could
distinguish the beautiful, starlike flowers of the cypress vine.
Among these, an object was in motion,—a living object, a body,—
the body of a great Snake, nearly as thick as the *liana* itself.

Another Rattlesnake! No; the Rattlesnake is *not a tree climber*—
it could not be that. Besides, the color of the one upon the vine was
entirely different. It was of a uniform black all over—smooth and
glittering. It was the Black Snake, then—the "Constrictor" of the
North.

When we first noticed it, it was wound upon the *liana* in spiral
rings, like the worm of a gigantic screw. We saw that it was slowly
gliding downward—for the vine tended diagonally from tree to
tree, and its lowest end impinged upon the trunk of the magnolia,
about twenty feet from the ground.

On reaching this point, the Snake gradually drew its rings closer
together, until they appeared to touch each other, lapping the
*liana*. It then commenced unwinding itself by the head, which was

slowly circled backward around the vine—still, however, creasing
closely along it. After a sufficient number of evolutions, the rings
had completely disappeared,—with the exception of one or two
near the tail,—and the Reptile lay doubled along the *liana*. These
manœuvres it had executed silently and with great caution; and it
now seemed to pause, and survey what was going on below.

During all this while, the Rattlesnake had been busily engaged
with the Squirrel, and thought of nothing else. After licking the
latter to his satisfaction, he extended his purple jaws, drew in the
head of his victim, and, stretching his long body to its full extent,
proceeded to swallow it, tail and all. In a few seconds, the head
and shoulders of the Squirrel had disappeared.

But the glutton was suddenly interrupted in his meal, for, at this
moment, we observed the Black Snake gradually lower himself
from the *liana*, until nothing remained upon the tree but a single
loop of his prehensile tail; and his long body, stretching downwards, hung directly over the other.

"Surely," thought we, "he is not going to encounter the Rattlesnake—the most terrible of all Reptiles." But the Constrictor understood *one* chapter of herpetology better than we—for the next moment we saw him drop to the ground; and almost as quick as
thought, he appeared, lapped in sable folds around the speckled
body of the Crotalus!

It was a singular sight to see these two creatures writhing and
wriggling over the grass and it was some time before we could tell
how they battled with each other. There was no great difference
between them, in point of size. The Black Snake was longer,—by a
foot or so,—but much more slender in the body than his antagonist.
He possessed, however, an advantage that soon made itself apparent—his activity, which was ten times that of the Rattlesnake. We
saw that he could easily evolve or wind himself at pleasure around
the body of the latter, each time compressing him with those muscular powers which have entitled him to his name—"Constrictor."
At each fresh embrace, the body of the Crotalus appeared to writhe
and contract under the crushing influence of his sable adversary.

The Rattlesnake had but one weapon which he could have employed with effect—his fangs. These were already locked in the
body of the Squirrel, and he could not use them on his adversary.
He could not get rid of that hairy morsel, that, like a barbed arrow,
now stuck in his throat. We could see that the Squirrel still remained there, for, as the two Reptiles struggled over the grass, its

bushy tail was seen waving in the midst of their tortuous contest.

At length the battle began to flag. The motions of both combatants waxed slower and slower. We could now see *how* they fought. We could see—strange as it appeared to us—that instead of battling head to head,—face to face,—the fangs of the Constrictor were buried in the rattles of the Crotalus! Stranger still, the tail of the former rose and fell with a muscular and powerful impetus, whipping the latter to death!

The contest was soon ended. The Rattlesnake lay stretched at full length, evidently dead; while the Black Constrictor still continued to hug the speckled body, as though it was an object to be loved. This lasted for a moment or so; and then, slowly unwinding itself, the conqueror turned round, crept through the grass, and proceeded to appropriate the prey. The "scene" was over, and we all leaped to our feet to enact the *finale*.

I should have spared the Constrictor, after the good service he had done in destroying the Rattlesnake; but Cudjo, who hated all sorts of creeping things, was ahead of me; and, before I could come up I beheld the victor suspended upon his spear!

### Down in a Valley

Down in a valley, by a forest's side,
    Near where the crystal Thames rolls on her waves,
I saw a mushroom stand in haughty pride,
As if the lilies grew to be his slaves.
The gentle daisy, with her silver crown,
Worn in the breast of many a shepherd's lass;
The humble violet, that lowly down
Salutes the gay nymphs as they trimly pass;
These with a many more, methought, complained
That nature should those needless things produce,
Which not alone, the sun from others gained,
But turn it wholly to their proper use.
I could not choose but grieve that nature made
So glorious flowers to live in such a shade.

*William Browne*

# THE STORY OF MY CATS

## Jean Henri Fabre

*As a boy, Fabre (1823–1915) lived in great poverty in southern France. One of his earliest chores was to drive a few ducks to a pond close by and watch over them. He often came home with pockets bulging with grasshoppers, frogs, and beetles; his peasant parents thought him a bit crazy. Many years later, he gave this early "craziness" full rein, so that we have from him some of the most scientific observations ever made and some of the most delightful reading of any kind.*

To what extent does the Cat deserve his reputation of being able to return to the beloved home, to the scenes of his amorous exploits, on the tiles and in the hay-lofts? The most curious facts are told of his instinct; children's books on natural history abound with feats that do the greatest credit to his prowess as a pilgrim. I do not attach much importance to these stories: they come from casual observers, uncritical folk given to exaggeration. It is not everybody who can talk about animals correctly. When some one not of the craft gets on the subject and says to me, "Such or such an animal is black," I begin by finding out if it does not happen to be white; and many a time the truth is discovered in the converse proposition. Men come to me and sing the praises of the Cat as a travelling expert. Well and good: we will now look upon the Cat as a poor traveller. And that would be the extent of my knowledge if I had only the evidence of books and of people unaccustomed to the scruples of scientific examination. Fortunately, I am acquainted with a few incidents that will stand the test of my incredulity. The Cat really deserves his reputation as a discerning pilgrim. Let us relate these incidents.

One day—it was at Avignon—there appeared upon the garden-wall a wretched-looking Cat, with matted coat and protruding ribs; so thin that his back was a jagged ridge. He was mewing with hunger. My children, at that time very young, took pity on his misery. Bread soaked in milk was offered him at the end of a reed. He took it. And the mouthfuls succeeded one another to such good purpose that he was sated and went off, heedless of the "Puss! Puss!" of his compassionate friends. Hunger returned; and the starveling reappeared in his wall-top refectory. He received the same fare of bread soaked in milk, the same soft words. He allowed himself to be tempted. He came down from the wall. The children were able to stroke his back. Goodness, how thin he was!

It was the great topic of conversation. We discussed it at table: we would tame the vagabond, we would keep him, we would make him a bed of hay. It was a most important matter: I can see to this day, I shall always see the council of rattleheads deliberating on the Cat's fate. They were not satisfied until the savage animal remained. Soon he grew into a magnificent Tom. His large round head, his muscular legs, his reddish fur, flecked with darker patches, reminded one of a little jaguar. He was christened Ginger because of his tawny hue. A mate joined him later, picked up in almost similar circumstances. Such was the origin of my series of Gingers, which I have retained for little short of twenty years through the vicissitudes of my various removals.

The first of these removals took place in 1870. A little earlier, a minister who has left a lasting memory in the University, that fine man, Victor Duruy, had instituted classes for the secondary education of girls. This was the beginning, as far as was then possible, of the burning question of to-day. I very gladly lent my humble aid to this labour of light. I was put to teach physical and natural science. I had faith and was not sparing of work, with the result that I rarely faced a more attentive or interested audience. The days on which the lessons fell were red-letter days, especially when the lesson was botany and the table disappeared from view under the treasures of the neighbouring conservatories.

That was going too far. In fact, you can see how heinous my crime was: I taught those young persons what air and water are; whence the lightning comes and the thunder; by what device our thoughts are transmitted across the seas and continents by means of a metal wire; why fire burns and why we breathe; how a seed puts forth shoots and how a flower blossoms: all eminently hateful things in the eyes of some people, whose feeble eyes are dazzled by the light of day.

The little lamp must be put out as quickly as possible and measures taken to get rid of the officious person who strove to keep it alight. The scheme was darkly plotted with the old maids who owned my house and who saw the abomination of desolation in these new educational methods. I had no written agreement to protect me. The bailiff appeared with a notice on stamped paper. It baldly informed me that I must move out within four weeks from date, failing which the law would turn my goods and chattels into the street. I had hurriedly to provide myself with a dwelling. The first house which we found happened to be at Orange. Thus was my exodus from Avignon effected.

We were somewhat anxious about the moving of the Cats. We were all of us attached to them and should have thought it nothing short of criminal to abandon the poor creatures, whom we had so often petted, to distress and probably to thoughtless persecution. The shes and the kittens would travel without any trouble: all you have to do is to put them in a basket; they will keep quiet on the journey. But the old Tom-cats were a serious problem. I had two: the head of the family, the patriarch; and one of his descendants, as strong as himself. We decided to take the grandsire, if he consented to come, and to leave the grandson behind, after finding him a home.

My friend Dr. Loriol offered to take charge of the forsaken one. The animal was carried to him at nightfall in a closed hamper. Hardly were we seated at the evening-meal, talking of the good fortune of our Tom-cat, when we saw a dripping mass jump through the window. The shapeless bundle came and rubbed itself against our legs, purring with happiness. It was the Cat.

I learnt his story next day. On arriving at Dr. Loriol's, he was locked up in a bedroom. The moment he saw himself a prisoner in the unfamiliar room, he began to jump about wildly on the furniture, against the window-panes, among the ornaments on the mantelpiece, threatening to make short work of everything. Mme. Loriol was frightened by the little lunatic; she hastened to open the window; and the Cat leapt out among the passers-by. A few minutes later, he was back at home. And it was no easy matter: he had to cross the town almost from end to end; he had to make his way through a long labyrinth of crowded streets, amid a thousand dangers, including first boys and next dogs; lastly—and this perhaps was an even more serious obstacle—he had to pass over the Sorgue, a river running through Avignon. There were bridges at hand, many, in fact; but the animal, taking the shortest cut, had used none of them, bravely jumping into the water, as its streaming fur showed. I had pity on the poor Cat, so faithful to his home. We agreed to do our utmost to take him with us. We were spared the worry: a few days later, he was found lying stiff and stark under a shrub in the garden. The plucky animal had fallen a victim to some stupid act of spite. Some one had poisoned him for me. Who? It is not likely that it was a friend!

There remained the old Cat. He was not indoors when we started; he was prowling round the hay-lofts of the neighbourhood. The carrier was promised an extra ten francs if he brought the Cat to Orange with one of the loads which he had still to convey. On his last journey he brought him stowed away under the driver's seat. I scarcely knew my old Tom when we opened the moving prison in which he had been confined since the day before. He came out looking a most alarming beast, scratching and spitting, with bristling hair, bloodshot eyes, lips white with foam. I thought him mad and watched him closely for a time. I was wrong: it was merely the fright of a bewildered animal. Had there been trouble with the carrier when he was caught? Did he have a bad time on the journey? History is silent on both points. What I do know is that the very nature of the Cat seemed changed: there was no more friendly purring, no more rubbing against our legs; nothing but a wild expression and the deepest gloom. Kind treatment could not soothe him. For a few weeks longer, he dragged his wretched existence from corner to corner; then, one day, I found him lying dead in the ashes on the hearth. Grief, with the help of old age, had killed him. Would he have gone back to Avignon, had he had the strength? I would not venture to affirm it. But, at least, I think it very remarkable that an animal should let itself die of homesickness because the infirmities of age prevent it from returning to its old haunts.

What the patriarch could not attempt, we shall see another do, over a much shorter distance, I admit. A fresh move is resolved upon, to give me, at long length, the peace and quiet essential to my work. This time, I hope that it will be the last. I leave Orange for Sérignan.

The family of Gingers has been renewed: the old ones have passed away, new ones have come, including a full-grown Tom, worthy in all respects of his ancestors. He alone will give us some difficulty; the others, the babies and the mothers, can be removed without trouble. We put them into baskets. The Tom has one to himself, so that the peace may be kept. The journey is made by carriage, in company with my family. Nothing striking happens before our arrival. Released from their hampers, the females inspect the new home, explore the rooms one by one; with their pink noses they recognize the furniture: they find their own seats, their own tables, their own arm-chairs; but the surroundings are different. They give little surprised miaows and questioning glances. A few caresses and a saucer of milk allay all their apprehensions; and, by the next day, the mother Cats are acclimatized.

It is a different matter with the Tom. We house him in the attics, where he will find ample room for his capers; we keep him company, to relieve the weariness of captivity; we take him a double portion of plates to lick; from time to time, we place him in touch with some of his family, to show him that he is not alone in the house; we pay him a host of attentions, in the hope of making him forget Orange. He appears, in fact, to forget it: he is gentle under the hand that pets him, he comes when called, purrs, arches his back. It is well: a week of seclusion and kindly treatment have banished all notions of returning. Let us give him his liberty. He goes down to the kitchen, stands by the table like the others, goes out into the garden, under the watchful eye of Aglaé, who does not lose sight of him; he prowls all around with the most innocent air. He comes back. Victory! The Tom-cat will not run away.

Next morning:

"Puss! Puss!"

Not a sign of him! We hunt, we call. Nothing. Oh, the hypocrite, the hypocrite! How he has tricked us! He has gone, he is at Orange. None of those about me can believe in this venturesome pilgrimage. I declare that the deserter is at this moment at Orange mewing outside the empty house.

Aglaé and Claire went to Orange. They found the Cat, as I said they would, and brought him back in a hamper. His paws and belly were covered with red clay; and yet the weather was dry, there was no mud. The Cat, therefore, must have got wet crossing the Aygues torrent; and the moist fur had kept the red earth of the fields through which he had passed. The distance from Sérignan to Orange, in a straight line, is four and a half miles. There are two bridges over the Aygues, one above and one below that line, some distance away. The Cat took neither the one nor the other: his instinct told him the shortest road and he followed that road, as his belly, covered with red mud, proved. He crossed the torrent in May, at a time when the rivers run high; he overcame his repugnance to water in order to return to his beloved home. The Avignon Tom did the same when crossing the Sorgue.

The deserter was reinstated in his attic at Sérignan. He stayed there for a fortnight; and at last we let him out. Twenty-four hours had not elapsed before he was back at Orange. We had to abandon him to his unhappy fate. A neighbour living out in the country, near my former house, told me that he saw him one day hiding behind a hedge with a rabbit in his mouth. Once no longer provided with food, he, accustomed to all the sweets of a Cat's existence, turned poacher, taking toll of the farm-yards round about my old home. I heard no more of him. He came to a bad end, no doubt: he had become a robber and must have met with a robber's fate.

The experiment has been made and here is the conclusion, twice proved. Full-grown Cats can find their way home, in spite of the distance and their complete ignorance of the intervening ground. They have, in their own fashion, the instinct of my Mason-bees. A second point remains to be cleared up, that of the swinging motion in the bag. Are they thrown out of their latitude by this stratagem, or are they not? I was thinking of making some experiments, when more precise information arrived and taught me that it was not necessary. The first who acquainted me with the method of the revolving bag was telling the story told him by a second person, who repeated the story of a third, a story related on the authority of a fourth; and so on. None had tried it, none had seen it for himself. It is a tradition of the country-side. One and all extol it as an infallible method, without, for the most part, having attempted it. And the reason which they give for its success is, in their eyes, conclusive. If, say they, we ourselves are blindfolded and then spin round for a few seconds, we no longer know where we are. Even so with the Cat carried off in the darkness of the swinging bag. They argue from man to the animal, just as others argue from the animal to man: a faulty method in either case, if there really be two distinct psychic worlds.

The belief would not be so deep-rooted in the peasant's mind, if facts had not from time to time confirmed it. But we may assume that, in successful cases, the Cats made to lose their bearings were young and unemancipated animals. With those neophytes, a drop of milk is enough to dispel the grief of exile. They do not return home, whether they have been whirled in a bag or not. People have thought it as well to subject them to the whirling operation by way of an additional precaution; and the method has received the credit of a success that has nothing to do with it. In order to test the method properly, it should have been tried on a full-grown Cat, a genuine Tom.

I did in the end get the evidence which I wanted on this point. Intelligent and thrustworthy people, not given to jumping to conclusions, have told me that they have tried the trick of the swinging bag to keep Cats from returning to their homes. None of them succeeded when the animal was full-grown. Though carried to a great distance, into another house, and subjected to a conscientious series of revolutions, the Cat always came back. I have in mind, more particularly a destroyer of the Gold-fish in a fountain, who, when transported from Sérignan to Piolenc, according to the time-honoured method, returned to his fish; who, when carried into the mountain and left in the woods, returned once more. The bag and the swinging round proved of no avail; and the miscreant had to be put to death. I have verified a fair number of similar instances, all under most favourable conditions. The evidence is unanimous: the revolving motion never keeps the adult Cat from returning home. The popular belief, which I found so seductive at first, is a country prejudice, based upon imperfect observation. We must, therefore, abandon Darwin's idea when trying to explain the homing of the Cat as well as of the Mason-bee.

### Pippa's Song

THE year's at the spring,
 And day's at the morn;
Morning's at seven;
The hill-side's dew-pearled.
The lark's on the wing;
The snail's on the thorn;
God's in his heaven—
All's right with the world!

*Robert Browning*

# THE CARE OF HOUNDS

## Scrutator

*"Scrutator"—K. W. Horlock—was the author of dozens of books on hunting and similar subjects which appeared during the middle of the nineteenth century. Unlike many professional English sportsmen, he had a sentimental attachment to animals, even when they had outlived their usefulness in the hunt. In this anecdote about his old hound, Pilgrim, from* Letters on Hunting, *he shows to what lengths he would go to make an old dog happy—though he scarcely considered the happiness of the fox involved.*

THIS hound, so long a favourite, never quitted my kennels; and I must here plead guilty to an impeachment which has often been laid to my charge, of being over-soft (as my friends used to term it) towards animals in my possession. I never parted with an old favourite, whether horse or hound; many of the latter, when worn out by hard service, were continually about the premises. They had a warm house to go into at night, next the boiling-house, and plenty to eat, and I have no doubt they enjoyed their *'otium cum dignitate'* as much as any old pensioners in Greenwich Hospital. With good living and no work, they certainly did become most extraordinary-looking figures, very much resembling aldermen in appearance, and their very looks gave a flat contradiction to the recommendation of my friends, to put those 'wretched old animals out of their *misery*.' Having spent the best of their days in my service, and done their utmost to afford me pleasure, I always considered it at least my duty to afford them that protection and refuge in their old age which they so well deserved; and, notwithstanding the taunts often received from other friendly masters of hounds, nothing ever induced me to alter that fixed principle—at my hand, or by my orders, their lives were never required. Upon hunting days, during the season, these old hounds were always shut up, to prevent their following the pack; but in the cub-hunting they could always do as they liked, and they generally honoured us with their company upon these occasions.

An old hound I had, called Pilgrim, showed most extraordinary sagacity one day, which may be considered rather too romantic to be true, but I vouch for the fact. He was out with us in the early part of the season, when we brought a fox to our home coverts, and ran him to ground there in a large rabbit pipe. As we tried on for another fox, the earth was stopped up, but not finding again, I returned home and fed the hounds. Old Pilgrim was with us then, and the terriers, which, after feeding, were, as usual, let run about. This was about 2 o'clock in the day. At 4 o'clock I went down to see the hounds again, and, not finding either the terriers or old Pilgrim in their usual sleeping apartment, I made enquiries where they were. No one could tell; but the feeder had seen them, about an hour previously, in the yard together. We searched and looked everywhere for them, but in vain. It being a fine afternoon, and having nothing to do, I walked across to the covert where we had run the fox to ground in the morning, to see if he had scratched his way out again, as some loose stones only had been thrown into the earth. Great, indeed, was my surprise, when I discovered Old Pilgrim lying at the mouth of the pipe, having removed all the stones, and dug a hole nearly large enough to hold himself; greater still was my surprise, when, upon listening at the earth. I heard the two terriers inside at the fox! The old dog wagged his tail, and gave me a knowing look, as much as to say, 'that will do, we shall soon have him out,' and I was so much pleased with his cunning, that I resolved he should not be disappointed. I accordingly hallooed to a man I saw at work, and sent him home for the whipper-in and a spade. We soon dug the fox out, and carried him home in a sack. Nothing could exceed the delight of the old hound, when he saw the fox safely bagged—he danced and jumped about, and led the way in high glee, as much as to say, 'Here he comes! this is my doing.' Having deposited the fox in a safe place, the old hound appeared quite satisfied; but when it became dark, we turned him loose again.

There is nothing extraordinary in the hound going again to visit the place where he had seen the fox run to ground, but the mystery is how he prevailed upon the terriers, which had not been out that day, to go with him. Instinct, in dogs, is very nearly allied to reason, and this dog must have considered that he could not get the fox out without the assistance of the terriers; and, but for my appearance on the scene, I have no doubt they would have succeeded in their object, as the pipe was not deep, and the soil sandy.

# ELEPHANT

## Carl Akeley

*One of our most famous portrayers of African wild life—in impressive sculpture, paintings, and books—started out as a lad with the desire to be a taxidermist. That desire led Carl Akeley (1864–1926) from familiar American birds and animals to trailing the fearsome lords of the jungle with camera and gun in their native habitat. His name is commemorated in the great African Hall of New York's Museum of Natural History.*

HUGE gray shadows are creeping through the forest but there is not even an echo of a footfall. The feathery foliage is stirring overhead. But there is no sound. You are only dimly conscious that something is happening in the great mysterious jungle. Something is living, breathing, moving vaguely, in the awesome gloom. A faint whisper—"Tembo!" The black gun boy has seen! His eyes are a hundred times keener than a white man's will ever be. Cold steel—your heavy gun barrel—is slipping through your cold fingers. They shake a little as you grasp your rifle and bring it to your shoulder. Suddenly you are face to face with the greatest mammal in the world. The elephant! Free and fearless, quick and powerful almost beyond comprehension, he fixes his small wicked-looking eyes upon those who have dared to cross his trail. With ease and grace his long, prehensile trunk, so near and so menacing, may reach out and smite, finishing an earthly career forever. The herd has been disturbed; it stands tensely silent, while the scales of life and death balance and a coin spins at the feet of the gods.

Now, with scarcely a murmur, the great elephant herd shifts and ebbs and flows. It has seen you, but the dawn breeze has been favorable. Tembo has not smelled you. He glides noiselessly into the inner recesses of the great dark forest. The lord of the land has spoken and his word is "peace."

The sun breaks through a piled up cloud, its rays filtering

through the tree tops to the trail beneath. A tiny bird twitters—bursts into song high up on a moss-draped bough. The silence is shattered. Something relaxes the whole length and breadth of your nervous system. Tembo has retreated to the remote feeding grounds of his jungle home.

The elephant always may be trusted to provide the hunter with plenty of excitement. His great size, colossal strength and magnificent courage are qualities that make him stand out as one of the most interesting as well as one of the most dangerous of beasts. Often he appears when least expected and frequently does the totally unexpected. Walking unprepared into his presence is like stepping out of a quiet home into No Man's Land—it may be perfectly safe but the odds are considerably against it.

One day in Uganda we followed the trail of two old bull elephants for five hours. We were in a big feeding ground and the elephant tracks crossed, intermingled and circled in a bewildering maze. I had told Bill, my faithful Kikuyu gun bearer, to follow the trail, more to test his ability than in the hope that he would succeed in bringing me to the herd. But I underrated Bill. Suddenly the boy stopped short and held up his cane as a signal for caution. Not more than twenty feet from us stood the two old bulls. They had not heard our approach nor had they caught our scent, but as I studied them from the shelter of a dense bush I realized that we were in a very dangerous position.

I had no desire to kill an elephant, except one for my museum group—and that meant only an unusually fine specimen; but I had even less desire to be killed by an elephant. So, with two of them as close to me as if we had been in the same room, and with nothing between us but a flimsy screen of bushes, I could take no chances. I hesitated, trying to convince myself that the tusks were fine enough to justify a shot. Then, without warning, my decision was made for me. A great gray trunk was thrust inquiringly forward—forward until it nearly touched my gun barrel. The movement may have been an attempt to catch my scent. I do not know. I had one glimpse of angry eyes set in a solid wall-like head—and I fired. The animal, wounded in the neck, swung around and bolted. I could not watch him nor gauge the effect of my shot, as his companion was right in front of me. He paused for a moment; then, apparently familiar with the deadly language of the rifle, he made a quick retreat.

Bill and I followed for about a hundred yards. The wounded bull scented us, turned and charged. I took aim, but there was no need to press the trigger, for the giant had made his last stand. His column-like legs swayed, crumpled beneath his weight, and the tremendous body lay outstretched on the ground. My bullet had pierced the jugular vein—a quick death. It had been a chance shot but, fired from such a short distance, it was much more effective than such shots usually are.

I had luck that day. Not, however, until some years later, when I talked with other hunters in Nairobi, did I realize how good my luck really was. I talked with men there who had had experiences similar to my own but who had not had my good fortune in escaping without injury. Great hunters who had been tossed and trampled—and lived to tell the tale.

Outram by keeping cool in a great emergency saved himself from a most unpleasant death. He had shot an elephant and the beast had fallen. Believing it finished, Outram approached. "Suddenly," he said, "to my surprise and horror the *dead* elephant rose and rushed at me. He caught me with his trunk and I went spinning through the air. I don't know whether in that brief flight I thought at all, but by the time I landed rather hard in the grass, amazement had given way to fear and I was sure that something had to be done and done quickly.

"I could see the elephant coming after me to trample me into the ground. Fortunately he paused for a second to crush my helmet, which had fallen off during the attack. That second saved me. I got under the beast's tail and there I clung while he wheeled and circled in a vicious attempt to get me in reach of trunk or tusks or feet. After a few moments of this sport, my injuries began to tell on me. The unequal contest could not have lasted much longer. Fortunately at the crucial moment my companion arrived and killed the elephant."

Hutchinson's story was similar to Outram's. An elephant caught him in the same way, wiped up the ground with him and then threw him into the trampled vegetation; but he had presence of mind enough to mix himself up in the animal's legs until his gun boy could fire.

The angry beast that caught Alan Black more nearly carried his charge to a finish. The method of attack was the same; but when the elephant discarded him, Black landed in a bush that broke his fall. The elephant followed and stepped on him, returning two or three times to step on him again, but the bush into which Black had fallen served as a cushion and saved his life.

The elephant's trunk is the most remarkable organ any animal possesses. The arm of a man is notable because it may be swung about at any angle from the shoulder, but the elephant's trunk may be twisted and turned in any direction and at any point in its entire length. It is just as powerful in one position as in another. It is without bone—a great flexible cable of muscles and sinew, so tough that the sharpest knife will scarcely cut it. It is so delicate that the elephant may pluck the tenderest blade of grass, yet so strong that he may lift a tree weighing a ton and toss it about easily. With his great height and short, thick neck, the elephant would find it difficult indeed to feed if it were not for his trunk. However it enables him to secure the choicest morsels on the ground or in the tree tops and to strip a whole forest of bark and branches, if he feels like it. With his trunk he has a most extraordinary ability to detect the faintest scent and to punish or kill an enemy.

Since the elephant has something like a fair chance, elephant hunting, unlike a good deal of the shooting that is done in the name of sport, always seems to me a legitimate game. This splendid animal wields a pair of heavy weapons—his mighty tusks—each one of which may weigh as much as the average man; and they are backed by several tons of brute strength. With an agility and a sagacity not to be rivaled by any other beast of his size today, he is a worthy opponent for any sportsman. Elephant hunting is always a game full of interest and excitement, because the elephant is such a wise old fellow that the hunter never learns all of his tricks.

Swifty and surely the white man and the white man's rifles are getting the better of old Tembo. Everywhere is he compelled to retreat before the advance of civilization. But occasionally the African elephant has his innings; and when he does, he winds up the episode with a dramatic flourish of trunk and tusks that the most spectacular handling of a gun cannot rival.

Every elephant hunter has known moments of nerve-torturing suspense—moments when his wits, his courage and his skill with a gun have stood between him and an open grave. His opponent is adroit, fearless, resourceful, and possessed of tremendous strength. Of course, no one can put himself in the elephant's place and imagine the animal's feeling when it faces a rifle, but I am convinced that this great beast's attitude is one of supreme confidence. A man is handicapped, when he confronts a charging elephant, by his own state of mind. He knows he has "picked the fight." He knows he is the intruder. And he has a guilty feeling that creates in him a demoralizing fear that could never affect one who enters a contest with an absolute conviction of right.

"Here's something about half as big as one of my legs," says Tembo to himself. "A dwarfed thing equally objectionable to my eyes and nose. He's trying to frighten me with that little stick he's carrying but I'll trample the runt and gore him and perhaps sit on him afterwards."

Then, when the "stick" emits a roar and a flash, if death is not instantaneous, the elephant is thoroughly angered and becomes more dangerous than before. To the hunter it is a different story. He is not overconfident, through ignorance of his antagonist's power. Instead, he is handicapped by the knowledge that if his gun or his wits or his nerves fail him he will be quickly finished by the charging beast.

If the man keeps his head, he has slightly more than half a chance in any combat with elephants; but if the elephant gets his man, it is fairly certain that there will be no need for the services of a doctor. There are exceptions to this rule—once in a while the victim survives—as I can testify.

I had been on a collecting expedition for the museum, and had obtained all the necessary specimens, when an old bull who tried the quiet waiting game "got" me. Descending from the ice fields of Mount Kenya, that snow-capped peak on the equator, we had made a temporary camp, intending to rest until our base camp could be portered to us. The interlude gave me an opportunity to make some pictures of the typical elephant country all about us. With a party of fifteen, including gun boys and a few porters, I went back up the mountain to an elevation of nine thousand feet at the edge of the dense bamboo forest.

Probably all would have gone well, and I might have obtained some valuable photographs, had we not run across the spoor of three large bulls. It was an old trail and I knew it would take time to follow it, but the tracks were so unusual in size that I could not resist the temptation. There was always the chance that the trail might be crossed by a fresher one made as the bulls circled about feeding, but instead it led us on from noon until sundown without bringing us to any new sign.

The night on the mountain was so bitterly cold that we were glad to be up and on the move again at daybreak. There was frost

in the air and the morning was still misty when we entered a great
elephant feeding ground. It was an open space where the rank
growth attained eight or ten feet in height and where the animals
milled about eating the vegetation and trampling it down until
there was very little left. The place itself was a labyrinth of trails,
and from it, as the spokes of a wheel radiate from a hub, were the
clear and definite tracks of the departing elephants. Soon after we
left this feeding ground I came upon the fresh tracks of my three
old bulls, so fresh that they must have been in that very spot an
hour before.

But the network of paths led nowhere. For some time we wandered about in an attempt to follow the elephants; then, growing
impatient, I left the clearing, intending to circle about it in the hope
of finding on its outskirts the trail which the tuskers had taken. I
had gone but a short distance when I found more fresh tracks.
I stopped to examine them, and, as I did so, the crackling of bamboo
not two hundred yards ahead caught my attention. The bulls were
almost within rifle shot and were giving me the signal for the final
stalk.

I waited while one of my trackers ran silently along the trail to
a point about fifty yards away where it made an abrupt turn. He
indicated the direction the animals had taken. Then I turned my
attention to the porters, watching them select a place to lay down
their loads in a clump of trees where they would be somewhat protected in case of a stampede. The second gun boy presented his rifle
for inspection. I examined it, found everything in order, and sent
the boy to a safe distance with the porters. The first gun boy
presented his gun; I took it, handing him the rifle I had already
examined. The second gun was now ready. I leaned it against my
body and stood, my back to the wall of the forest, blowing upon
my hands numbed by the cold and chafing them in order to have at
a moment's notice a supple trigger finger. At the same time the first
gun boy was taking the cartridges from his bandolier and holding
them up so that I could be sure that each was a full steel-jacketed
bullet—the only kind that will penetrate an elephant's head. There
was no reason to suppose that the animals suspected our presence,
and I prepared for the stalk with my customary caution and with
more than my usual deliberation.

I was standing with my gun leaning against my hip, still warming my hands and still looking at the cartridges one after another.
In a flash, one of the calmest moments of my hunting experience

changed to the most profoundly intense moment of my entire life. I suddenly *knew* that an elephant was right behind me. Something must have warned me, but I have no idea what it was. I grabbed my gun, and as I wheeled around I tried to shove the safety catch forward. It would not budge. I wanted desperately to look at it, but there was no time. I remember thinking that I must pull the trigger hard enough to fire. Then something struck me a staggering blow. I saw the point of a tusk right at my chest. Instinctively I seized it in my left hand, reached out for the other tusk with my right, and went to the ground between them as the great body bore down upon me. One merciless little eye gleamed savagely above me as the elephant drove his tusks into the ground on either side of me, his rolled-up trunk against my chest. I heard a wheezy grunt as the great bull plunged forward, and I realized vaguely that I was being crushed beneath him. Then the light went out.

It was evening before I recovered consciousness, in a dazed sort of way. I was dimly aware of seeing a fire. I was lying where the old bull had left me, in a cold mountain rain, while my superstitious black boys, believing that I was dead, refused to touch me. I tried to shout, and I must have succeeded after a fashion, for a little later I felt myself being carried away by my legs and shoulders.

Later I had another lucid interval, in which I realized that I was in one of the porters' tents. Then I tried to piece together the events that had led to my accident. I supposed that my back was broken because I could not move. I felt no pain. I was miserably cold and numb, and that reminded me of a bottle of brandy, carried for emergencies. I ordered the boys to bring it to me and pour it down my throat. I also had them prepare for me some hot bovril, and gradually the numbness left me. Then I discovered that I could move my arm a little. I tried the same experiment with my leg and was successful. Though the effort brought pain, it told me that I had at least a chance for recovery.

When morning came, my mind was clear enough to inquire for my white companions at the camp below, and the boys told me that soon after the elephant knelt on me they had dispatched a messenger asking for help. At that rate, assistance should have been close at hand. Fearing that the rescue party was lost on the mountain, I ordered my heavy gun to be fired every fifteen minutes, and within an hour my boys heard an answering shot from a smaller rifle.

When relief arrived I was a sorry looking spectacle. The blow from the elephant's trunk which had stunned me had also skinned my forehead, blackened and closed an eye, broken my nose and torn open one cheek so that my teeth were exposed. Several of my ribs were broken and my lungs were punctured. I was covered with mud and splashed with blood. But apparently it was my face that was the awful sight.

Just why I was not crushed completely, I shall never know. Beneath the old bull's weight, or even under the pressure of his enormous trunk, my body would have offered about as much resistance as a soda cracker. My only explanation—and I think it is the correct one—is that a root or rock under the surface of the ground must have stopped his tusks, and that seeing me unconscious he must have thought he had killed me. He had then left me and had charged about the clearing after the black boys.

My experience is just one more illustration of my idea that a combat between a man and an elephant is still a fairly equal contest. Even the express rifles of the twentieth century have not given the hunter an overwhelming advantage over this mighty beast.

### *To One Who Has Been Long in City Pent*

To one who has been long in city pent
'Tis very sweet to look into the fair
And open face of heaven—to breathe a prayer
Full in the smile of the blue firmament.
Who is more happy, when, with heart's content,
Fatigued he sinks into some pleasant lair
Of wavy grass, and reads a debonair
And gentle tale of love and languishment?
Returning home at evening, with an ear
Catching the notes of Philomel—an eye
Watching the sailing cloudlet's bright career,
He mourns that day so soon has glided by:
E'en like the passage of an angel's tear
That falls through the clear ether silently.

*John Keats*

# ON THE ADVISABLENESS OF IMPROVING NATURAL KNOWLEDGE

## T. H. Huxley

*Huxley (1825–1895), for years the dean of the world's scientific men, himself had almost no formal education. He was the great agnostic of his day, a champion of Darwinism, and an active worker for social improvement. This is one of his "lay sermons"—talks he delivered frequently to the general public, which loved them for their clarity, vigor, and color. After considering the assertion that pure science is valuable for its contributions to material civilization, like the spinning jenny and steam pump, Huxley describes here the profounder, more abiding values that make the pursuit of natural knowledge worth while.*

BUT spinning jenny and steam pump are, after all, but toys, possessing an accidental value; and natural knowledge creates multitudes of more subtle contrivances, the praises of which do not happen to be sung because they are not directly convertible into instruments for creating wealth. When I contemplate natural knowledge squandering such gifts among men, the only appropriate comparison I can find for her is, to liken her to such a peasant woman as one sees in the Alps, striding ever upward, heavily burdened, and with mind bent only on her home; but yet, without effort and without thought, knitting for her children. Now stockings are good and comfortable things, and the children will undoubtedly be much the better for them; but surely it would be short-sighted, to say the least of it, to depreciate this toiling mother as a mere stocking-machine—a mere provider of physical comforts?

However, there are blind leaders of the blind, and not a few of them, who take this view of natural knowledge, and can see nothing in the bountiful mother of humanity but a sort of comfort-grinding machine. According to them, the improvement of natural knowledge always has been, and always must be, synonymous with no more than the improvement of the material resources and the increase of the gratifications of men.

Natural knowledge is, in their eyes, no real mother of mankind, bringing them up with kindness, and, if need be, with sternness, in the way they should go, and instructing them in all things needful for their welfare; but a sort of fairy god-mother, ready to furnish her pets with shoes of swiftness, swords of sharpness, and omnipotent Aladdin's lamps, so that they may have telegraphs to Saturn, and see the other side of the moon, and thank God they are better than their benighted ancestors.

If this talk were true, I, for one, should not greatly care to toil in the service of natural knowledge. I think I would just as soon be quietly chipping my own flint axe, after the manner of my forefathers a few thousand years back, as be troubled with the endless malady of thought which now infests us all, for such reward. But I venture to say that such views are contrary alike to reason and to fact. Those who discourse in such fashion seem to me to be so intent upon trying to see what is above nature, or what is behind her, that they are blind to what stares them in the face, in her.

I should not venture to speak thus strongly if my justification were not to be found in the simplest and most obvious facts,—if it needed more than an appeal to the most notorious truths to justify my assertion, that the improvement of natural knowledge, whatever direction it has taken, and however low the aims of those who may have commenced it—has not only conferred practical benefits on men, but, in so doing, has effected a revolution in their conceptions of the universe and of themselves, and has profoundly altered their modes of thinking and their views of right and wrong. I say that natural knowledge, seeking to satisfy natural wants, has found the ideas which can alone still spiritual cravings. I say that natural knowledge, in desiring to ascertain the laws of comfort, has been driven to discover those of conduct, and to lay the foundations of a new morality.

Let us take these points separately; and, first, what great ideas has natural knowledge introduced into men's minds?

I cannot but think that the foundations of all natural knowledge were laid when the reason of man first came face to face with the facts of nature; when the savage first learned that the fingers of one hand are fewer than those of both; that it is shorter to cross a stream than to head it; that a stone stops where it is unless it be moved, and that it drops from the hand which lets it go; that light and heat come and go with the sun; that sticks burn away in a fire; that plants and animals grow and die; that if he struck his fellow savage a blow he would make him angry, and perhaps get a blow in return; while if he offered him a fruit he would please him, and perhaps receive a fish in exchange. When men had acquired this much knowledge, the outlines, rude though they were, of mathematics, of physics, of chemistry, of biology, of moral, economical, and political science, were sketched. Nor did the germ of religion fail when science began to bud. Listen to words which, though new, are yet three thousand years old:—

> ". . . When in heaven the stars about the moon
> Look beautiful, when all the winds are laid,
> And every height comes out, and jutting peak
> And valley, and the immeasurable heavens
> Break open to their highest, and all the stars
> Shine, and the shepherd gladdens in his heart."

But if the half-savage Greek could share our feelings thus far, it is irrational to doubt that he went further, to find, as we do, that upon that brief gladness there follows a certain sorrow,—the little light of awakened human intelligence shines so mere a spark amidst the abyss of the unknown and unknowable; seems so insufficient to do more than illuminate the imperfections that cannot be remedied, the aspirations that cannot be realised, of man's own nature. But in this sadness, this consciousness of the limitation of man, this sense of an open secret which he cannot penetrate, lies the essence of all religion; and the attempt to embody it in the forms furnished by the intellect is the origin of the higher theologies.

Thus it seems impossible to imagine but that the foundations of all knowledge—secular or sacred—were laid when intelligence dawned, though the superstructure remained for long ages so slight and feeble as to be compatible with the existence of almost any general view respecting the mode of governance of the universe. No doubt, from the first, there were certain phænomena which, to the rudest mind, presented a constancy of occurrence, and suggested that a fixed order ruled, among them at any rate. I doubt if the grossest of Fetish worshippers ever imagined that a stone must have a god within it to make it fall, or that a fruit had a god within it to make it taste sweet. With regard to such matters as these, it is hardly questionable that mankind from the first took strictly positive and scientific views.

But, with respect to all the less familiar occurrences which present themselves, uncultured man, no doubt, has always taken himself as the standard of comparison, as the centre and measure of the world; nor could he well avoid doing so. And finding that his apparently uncaused will has a powerful effect in giving rise to many occurrences, he naturally enough ascribed other and greater events to other and greater volitions, and came to look upon the world and all that therein is, as the product of the volitions of persons like himself, but stronger, and capable of being appeased or angered, as he himself might be soothed or irritated. Through such conceptions of the plan and working of the universe all mankind have passed, or are passing. And we may now consider what has been the effect of the improvement of natural knowledge on the views of men who have reached this stage, and who have begun to cultivate natural knowledge with no desire but that of "increasing God's honour and bettering man's estate."

For example: what could seem wiser, from a mere material point of view, more innocent from a theological one, to an ancient people, than that they should learn the exact succession of the seasons, as warnings for their husbandmen; or the position of the stars, as guides to their rude navigators? But what has grown out of this search for natural knowledge of so merely useful a character? You all know the reply. Astronomy,—which of all sciences has filled men's minds with general ideas of a character most foreign to their daily experience, and has, more than any other, rendered it impossible for them to accept the beliefs of their fathers. Astronomy,—which tells them that this so vast and seemingly solid earth is but an atom among atoms, whirling, no man knows whither, through illimitable space; which demonstrates that what we call the peaceful heaven above us, is but that space, filled by an infinitely subtle matter whose particles are seething and surging, like the waves of an angry sea; which opens up to us infinite regions where nothing is known, or ever seems to have been known, but matter and force, operating according to rigid rules; which leads us to contemplate phænomena the very nature of which demonstrates that they must have had a beginning, and that they must have an end, but the very nature of which also proves that the beginning

was, to our conceptions of time, infinitely remote, and that the end
is as immeasurably distant.

But it is not alone those who pursue astronomy who ask for
bread and receive ideas. What more harmless than the attempt to
lift and distribute water by pumping it; what more absolutely and
grossly utilitarian? But out of pumps grew the discussions about
nature's abhorrence of a vacuum; and then it was discovered that
nature does not abhor a vacuum, but that air has weight; and that
notion paved the way for the doctrine that all matter has weight,
and that the force which produces weight is co-extensive with the
universe,—in short, to the theory of universal gravitation and endless force. And learning how to handle gases led to the discovery
of oxygen and to modern chemistry, and to the notion of the indestructibility of matter.

Again, what simpler, or more absolutely practical, than the
attempt to keep the axle of a wheel from heating when the wheel
turns round very fast? How useful for carters and gig drivers to
know something about this; and how good were it, if any ingenious
person would find out the cause of such phænomena, and thence
educe a general remedy for them. Such an ingenious person was
Count Rumford; and he and his successors have landed us in the
theory of the persistence or indestructibility of force. And in the
infinitely minute, as in the infinitely great, the seekers after natural
knowledge of the kinds called physical and chemical, have everywhere found a definite order and succession of events which seem
never to be infringed.

And how has it fared with "Physick" and Anatomy? Have the
anatomist, the physiologist, or the physician, whose business it has
been to devote themselves assiduously to that eminently practical
and direct end, the alleviation of the sufferings of mankind,—have
they been able to confine their vision more absolutely to the strictly
useful? I fear they are the worst offenders of all. For if the astronomer has set before us the infinite magnitude of space, and the
practical eternity of the duration of the universe; if the physical
and chemical philosophers have demonstrated the infinite minuteness of its constituent parts, and the practical eternity of matter
and of force; and if both have alike proclaimed the universality of
a definite and predicable order and succession of events, the workers in biology have not only accepted all these, but have added more
startling theses of their own. For, as the astronomers discover in the

earth no centre of the universe, but an eccentric speck, so the naturalists find man to be no centre of the living world, but one amidst endless modifications of life; and as the astronomer observes the mark of practically endless time set upon the arrangements of the solar system, so the student of life finds the records of ancient forms of existence peopling the world for ages, which, in relation to human experience, are infinite.

Furthermore, the physiologist finds life to be as dependent for its manifestation on particular molecular arrangements as any physical or chemical phenomenon; and, wherever he extends his researches, fixed order and unchanging causation reveal themselves, as plainly as in the rest of nature.

Nor can I find that any other fate has awaited the germ of Religion. Arising, like all other kinds of knowledge, out of the action and interaction of man's mind, with that which is not man's mind, it has taken the intellectual coverings of Fetishism or Polytheism; of Theism or Atheism; of Superstition or Rationalism. With these, and their relative merits and demerits, I have nothing to do; but this it is needful for my purpose to say, that if the religion of the present differs from that of the past, it is because the theology of the present has become more scientific than that of the past; because it has not only renounced idols of wood and idols of stone, but begins to see the necessity of breaking in pieces the idols built up of books and traditions and fine-spun ecclesiastical cobwebs: and of cherishing the noblest and most human of man's emotions, by worship "for the most part of the silent sort" at the altar of the Unknown and Unknowable.

Such are a few of the new conceptions implanted in our minds by the improvement of natural knowledge. Men have acquired the ideas of the practically infinite extent of the universe and of its practical eternity; they are familiar with the conception that our earth is but an infinitesimal fragment of that part of the universe which can be seen; and that, nevertheless, its duration is, as compared with our standards of time, infinite. They have further acquired the idea that man is but one of innumerable forms of life now existing on the globe, and that the present existences are but the last of an immeasurable series of predecessors. Furthermore, every step they have made in natural knowledge has tended to extend and rivet in their minds the conception of a definite order of the universe—which is embodied in what are called, by an unhappy metaphor, the laws of nature—and to narrow the range and loosen the force of men's belief in spontaneity, or in changes other than such as arise out of that definite order itself.

Whether these ideas are well or ill founded is not the question. No one can deny that they exist, and have been the inevitable outgrowth of the improvement of natural knowledge. And if so, it cannot be doubted that they are changing the form of men's most cherished and most important convictions.

And as regards the second point—the extent to which the improvement of natural knowledge has remodelled and altered what may be termed the intellectual ethics of men—what are among the moral convictions most fondly held by barbarous and semi-barbarous people.

They are the convictions that authority is the soundest basis of belief; that merit attaches to a readiness to believe; that the doubting disposition is a bad one, and scepticism a sin; that when good authority has pronounced what is to be believed, and faith has accepted it, reason has no further duty. There are many excellent persons who yet hold by these principles, and it is not my present business, or intention, to discuss their views. All I wish to bring clearly before your minds is the unquestionable fact that the improvement of natural knowledge is effected by methods which directly give the lie to all these convictions, and assume the exact reverse of each to be true.

The improver of natural knowledge absolutely refuses to acknowledge authority, as such. For him, scepticism is the highest of duties; blind faith the one unpardonable sin. And it cannot be otherwise, for every great advance in natural knowledge has involved the absolute rejection of authority, the cherishing of the keenest scepticism, the annihilation of the spirit of blind faith; and the most ardent votary of science holds his firmest convictions, not because the men he most venerates hold them; not because their verity is testified by portents and wonders; but because his experience teaches him that whenever he chooses to bring these convictions into contact with their primary source, nature—whenever he thinks fit to test them by appealing to experiment and to observation—nature will confirm them. The man of science has learned to believe in justification, not by faith, but by verification.

Thus, without for a moment pretending to despise the practical results of the improvement of natural knowledge, and its beneficial influence on material civilisation, it must, I think, be admitted that the great ideas, some of which I have indicated, and the ethical spirit which I have endeavoured to sketch, in the few moments which remained at my disposal, constitute the real and permanent significance of natural knowledge.

If these ideas be destined, as I believe they are, to be more and more firmly established as the world grows older; if that spirit be fated, as I believe it is, to extend itself into all departments of human thought, and to become co-extensive with the range of knowledge; if, as our race approaches its maturity, it discovers, as I believe it will, that there is but one kind of knowledge and but one method of acquiring it; then we, who are still children, may justly feel it our highest duty to recognise the advisableness of improving natural knowledge, and so to aid ourselves and our successors in our course towards the noble goal which lies before mankind.

## To the Evening Star

THOU fair-haired angel of the evening,
　Now, whilst the sun rests on the mountain, light
Thy brilliant torch of love; thy radiant crown
Put on, and smile upon our evening bed!
Smile on our loves; and whilst thou drawest round
The curtains of the sky, scatter thy dew
On every flower that closes its sweet eyes
In timely sleep. Let thy west wind sleep on
The lake; speak silence with thy glimmering eyes,
And wash the dusk with silver. Soon, full soon
Dost thou withdraw; then the wolf rages wide,
And then the lion glares through the dun forest.
The fleeces of our rocks are covered with
Thy sacred dew: protect them with thine influence.

*William Blake*

# A DRIVE THROUGH THE FOREST

## Ivan Turgenev

*Turgenev (1818–1883), one of the first to write with sympathy and realism of the wretched life of the lower classes of Russia, was himself an aristocrat. In 1852 appeared his first important work,* The Papers of a Sportsman *(from which this selection is taken). Here the author of* Fathers and Sons *shows as great a sensitivity to the beauties of nature as he does to the plight of his fellow-men.*

ANOTHER time you order the racing droshky to be got out, and set off to the forest to shoot wood-cock. It is pleasant making your way along the narrow path between two high walls of rye. The ears softly strike you in the face; the cornflowers cling round your legs; the quails call around; the horse moves along at a lazy trot. And here is the forest, all shade and silence. Graceful aspens rustle high above you; the long-hanging branches of the birches scarcely stir; a mighty oak stands like a champion beside a lovely lime-tree. You go along the green path, streaked with shade; great yellow flies stay suspended, motionless, in the sunny air, and suddenly dart away; midges hover in a cloud, bright in the shade, dark in the sun; the birds are singing peacefully; the golden little voice of the warbler sings of innocent, babbling joyousness, in sweet accord with the scent of the lilies of the valley. Further, further, deeper into the forest . . . the forest grows more dense. . . . An unutterable stillness falls upon the soul within; without, too, all is still and dreamy. But now a wind has sprung up, and the tree-tops are booming like falling waves. Here and there, through last year's brown leaves, grow tall grasses; funguses stand apart under their wide-brimmed hats. All at once a hare skips out; the dog scurries after it with a resounding bark. . . .

And how fair is this same forest in late autumn, when the snipe are on the wing! They do not keep in the heart of the forest; one must look for them along the outskirts. There is no wind, and no sun; no light, no shade, no movement, no sound: the autumn perfume, like the perfume of wine, is diffused in the soft air; a delicate haze hangs over the yellow fields in the distance. The still sky is a peacefully untroubled white through the bare brown branches; in parts, on the limes, hang the last golden leaves. The damp earth is elastic under your feet; the high dry blades of grass do not stir; long threads lie shining on the blanched turf, white with dew. You breathe tranquilly; but there is a strange tremor in the soul. You walk along the forest's edge, look after your dog, and meanwhile loved forms, loved faces dead and living, come to your mind; long, long slumbering impressions unexpectedly awaken; the fancy darts off and soars like a bird; and all moves so clearly and stands out before your eyes. The heart at one time throbs and beats, plunging passionately forward; at another it is drowned beyond recall in memories. Your whole life, as it were, unrolls lightly and rapidly before you: a man at such times possesses all his past, all his feelings and his powers—all his soul; and there is nothing around to hinder him—no sun, no wind, no sound. . . .

And a clear, rather cold autumn day, with a frost in the morning, when the birch, all golden like some tree in a fairy tale, stands out picturesquely against the pale blue sky; when the sun, standing low in the sky, does not warm, but shines more brightly than in summer; the small aspen copse is all a-sparkle through and through, as though it were glad and at ease in its nakedness; the hoar-frost is still white at the bottom of the hollows; while a fresh wind softly stirs up and drives before it the falling, crumpled leaves; when blue ripples whisk gladly along the river, lifting rhythmically the heedless geese and ducks; in the distance the mill creaks, half-hidden by the willows; and with changing colours in the clear air the pigeons wheel in swift circles above it. . . .

Sweet, too, are dull days in summer, though the sportsmen do not like them. On such days one can't shoot the bird that flutters up from under your very feet, and vanishes at once in the whitish dark of the hanging fog. But how peaceful, how unutterably peaceful it is everywhere! Everything is awake, and everything is hushed. You pass by a tree: it does not stir a leaf; it is musing in repose. Through the thin steamy mist, evenly diffused in the air, there is a long streak of black before you. You take it for a neighbouring copse close at hand; you go up—the copse is transformed into a high row of wormwood in the boundary-ditch. Above you, around you, on all sides—mist. . . . But now a breeze is faintly astir; a patch of pale-blue sky peeps dimly out; through the thinning, as it were, smoky mist, a ray of golden yellow sunshine breaks out suddenly, flows in a long stream, strikes on the fields and in the copse—and now everything is overcast again. For long this struggle is drawn out, but how unutterably brilliant and magnificent the day becomes when at last light triumphs and the last waves of the warmed mist here unroll and are drawn out over the plains, there wind away and vanish into the deep, tenderly shining heights. . . .

Again you set off into outlying country, to the steppe. For some ten miles you make your way over cross-roads, and here at last is the high-road. Past endless trains of wagons, past wayside taverns with the hissing samovar under a shed, wide-open gates and a well, from one hamlet to another; across endless fields, alongside green hempfields, a long, long time you drive. The magpies flutter from willow to willow; peasant women with long rakes in their hands wander in the fields; a man in a threadbare nankin overcoat, with a wicker pannier over his shoulder, trudges along with weary step; a heavy country coach, harnessed with six tall, broken-winded horses, rolls to meet you. The corner of a cushion is sticking out of a window, and on a sack up behind, hanging on to a string, perches a groom in a fur-cloak, splashed with mud to his very eyebrows. And here is the little district town with its crooked little wooden houses, its endless fences, its empty stone shops, its old-fashioned bridge over a deep ravine. . . . On, on! . . . The steppe country is reached at last. You look from a hilltop; what a view! Round low hills, tilled and sown to their very tops, are seen in broad undulations; ravines, overgrown with bushes, wind coiling among them; small copses are scattered like oblong islands; from village to village run narrow paths; churches stand out white; between willow-bushes glimmers a little river, in four places dammed up by dykes; far off, in a field, in a line, an old manor-house, with its outhouses, fruit-garden, and threshing-floor, huddles close up to a small lake. But on, on you go. The hills are smaller and ever smaller; there is scarcely a tree to be seen. Here it is at last—the boundless, untrodden steppe!

And on a winter day to walk over the high snowdrifts after hares; to breathe the keen frosty air, while half-closing the eyes involuntarily at the fine blinding sparkle of the soft snow; to ad-

mire the emerald sky above the reddish forest! ... And the first
spring day when everything is shining, and breaking up, when
across the heavy streams, from the melting snow, there is already
the scent of the thawing earth; when on the bare thawed places,
under the slanting sunshine, the larks are singing confidingly, and,
with glad splash and roar, the torrents roll from ravine to ravine....

### The Nile

IT FLOWS through old hushed Egypt and its sands,
   Like some grave mighty thought threading a dream,
And times and things, as in that vision, seem
Keeping along in their eternal sands,—
Caves, pillars, pyramids, the shepherd bands
That roamed through the young world, the glory extreme
Of high Sesostris, and that southern beam,
The laughing queen that caught the world's great hands.
Then comes a mightier silence, stern and strong,
As of a world left empty of its throng,
And the void weighs on us; and then we wake,
And hear the fruitful stream lapsing along
'Twixt villages, and think how we shall take
Our own calm journey on for human sake.

*Leigh Hunt*

# NIGHT ON THE GREAT BEACH

## Henry Beston

*The man on the shore can know the sea, its moods and its crea-
tures almost as well as the sailor. In his book* The Outermost
House, *Henry Beston tells of a year he spent in a shack, the
Fo'castle, at the point where Cape Cod juts farthest into the
Atlantic, close by the Nauset Coast Guard Station; here, on the
fringes of the ocean, he discovered a world of wonders that
the casual passer-by seldom sees.*

OUR fantastic civilization has fallen out of touch with many
aspects of nature, and with none more completely than with
night. Primitive folk, gathered at a cave mouth round a fire, do not
fear night; they fear, rather, the energies and creatures to whom
night gives power; we of the age of the machines, having delivered
ourselves of nocturnal enemies, now have a dislike of night itself.
With lights and ever more lights, we drive the holiness and beauty
of night back to the forests and the sea; the little village, the cross-
roads even, will have none of it. Are modern folk, perhaps, afraid
of night? Do they fear that vast serenity, the mystery of infinite
space, the austerity of stars? Having made themselves at home in a
civilization obsessed with power, which explains its whole world
in terms of energy, do they fear at night for their dull acquiescence
and the pattern of their beliefs? Be the answer what it will, today's
civilization is full of people who have not the slightest notion of
the character or the poetry of the night, who have never even
seen night. Yet to live thus, to know only artificial night, is as absurd and evil as to know only artificial day.

Night is very beautiful on this great beach. It is the true other
half of the day's tremendous wheel; no lights without meaning
stab or trouble it; it is beauty, it is fulfillment, it is rest. Thin clouds
float in these heavens, islands of obscurity in a splendor of space
and stars: the Milky Way bridges earth and ocean; the beach re-

solves itself into a unity of form, its summer lagoons, its slopes and uplands merging; against the western sky and the falling bow of sun rise the silent and superb undulations of the dunes.

My nights are at their darkest when a dense fog streams in from the sea under a black, unbroken floor of cloud. Such nights are rare, but are most to be expected when fog gathers off the coast in early summer; this last Wednesday night was the darkest I have known. Between ten o'clock and two in the morning three vessels stranded on the outer beach—a fisherman, a four-masted schooner, and a beam trawler. The fisherman and the schooner have been towed off, but the trawler, they say, is still ashore.

I went down to the beach that night just after ten o'clock. So utterly black, pitch dark it was, and so thick with moisture and trailing showers, that there was no sign whatever of the beam of Nauset; the sea was only a sound, and when I reached the edge of the surf the dunes themselves had disappeared behind. I stood as isolate in that immensity of rain and night as I might have stood in interplanetary space. The sea was troubled and noisy, and when I opened the darkness with an outlined cone of light from my electric torch I saw that the waves were washing up green coils of sea grass, all coldly wet and bright in the motionless and unnatural radiance. Far off a single ship was groaning its way along the shoals. The fog was compact of the finest moisture; passing by, it spun itself into my lens of light like a kind of strange, aerial, and liquid silk. Effin Chalke, the new coast guard, passed me going north and told me that he had had news at the halfway house of the schooner at Cahoon's.

It was dark, pitch dark to my eye, yet complete darkness, I imagine, is exceedingly rare, perhaps unknown in outer nature. The nearest natural approximation to it is probably the gloom of forest country buried in night and cloud. Dark as the night was here, there was still light on the surface of the planet. Standing on the shelving beach, with the surf breaking at my feet, I could see the endless wild upbrush, slide, and withdrawal of the sea's white rim of foam. The men at Nauset tell me that on such nights they follow along this vague crawl of whiteness, trusting to habit and a sixth sense to warn them of their approach to the halfway house.

Animals descend by starlight to the beach. North, beyond the dunes, muskrats forsake the cliff and nose about in the driftwood and weed, leaving intricate trails and figure eights to be obliterated by the day; the lesser folk—the mice, the occasional small sand-colored toads, the burrowing moles—keep to the upper beach and leave their tiny footprints under the overhanging wall. In autumn skunks, beset by a shrinking larder, go beachcombing early in the night. The animal is by preference a clean feeder and turns up his nose at rankness. I almost stepped on a big fellow one night as I was walking north to meet the first man south from Nauset. There was a scamper, and the creature ran up the beach from under my feet; alarmed he certainly was, yet was he contained and continent. Deer are frequently seen, especially north of the light. I find their tracks upon the summer dunes.

Years ago, while camping on this beach north of Nauset, I went for a stroll along the top of the cliff at break of dawn. Though the path followed close enough along the edge, the beach below was often hidden, and I looked directly from the height to the flush of sunrise at sea. Presently the path, turning, approached the brink of the earth precipice, and on the beach below, in the cool, wet rosiness of dawn, I saw three deer playing. They frolicked, rose on their hind legs, scampered off, and returned again, and were merry. Just before sunrise they trotted off north together down the beach toward a hollow in the cliff and the path that climbs it.

Occasionally a sea creature visits the shore at night. Lone coast guardsmen, trudging the sand at some deserted hour, have been startled by seals. One man fell flat on a creature's back, and it drew away from under him, flippering toward the sea, with a sound "halfway between a squeal and a bark." I myself once had rather a start. It was long after sundown, the light dying and uncertain, and I was walking home on the top level of the beach and close along the slope descending to the ebbing tide. A little more than halfway to the Fo'castle a huge unexpected something suddenly writhed horribly in the darkness under my bare foot. I had stepped on a skate left stranded by some recent crest of surf, and my weight had momentarily annoyed it back to life.

Facing north, the beam of Nauset becomes part of the dune night. As I walk toward it, I see the lantern, now as a star of light which waxes and wanes three mathematic times, now as a lovely pale flare of light behind the rounded summits of the dunes. The changes in the atmosphere change the color of the beam; it is now whitish, now flame golden, now golden red; it changes its form as well, from a star to a blare of light, from a blare of light to a cone of radiance sweeping a circumference of fog. To the west of Nauset I often see the apocalyptic flash of the great light at the

Highland reflected on the clouds or even on the moisture in the starlit air, and, seeing it, I often think of the pleasant hours I have spent there when George and Mary Smith were at the light and I had the good fortune to visit as their guest. Instead of going to sleep in the room under the eaves, I would lie awake, looking out of a window to the great spokes of light revolving as solemnly as a part of the universe.

All night long the lights of coastwise vessels pass at sea, green lights going south, red lights moving north. Fishing schooners and flounder draggers anchor two or three miles out and keep a bright riding light burning on the mast. I see them come to anchor at sundown, but I rarely see them go, for they are off at dawn. When busy at night, these fishermen illumine their decks with a scatter of oil flares. From shore, the ships might be thought afire. I have watched the scene through a night glass. I could see no smoke, only the waving flares, the reddish radiance on sail and rigging, an edge of reflection overside, and the enormous night and sea beyond.

One July night, as I returned at three o'clock from an expedition north, the whole night, in one strange, burning instant, turned into a phantom day. I stopped and, questioning, stared about. An enormous meteor, the largest I have ever seen, was consuming itself in an effulgence of light west of the zenith. Beach and dune and ocean appeared out of nothing, shadowless and motionless, a landscape whose every tremor and vibration were stilled, a landscape in a dream.

The beach at night has a voice all its own, a sound in fullest harmony with its spirit and mood—with its little, dry noise of sand forever moving, with its solemn, overspilling, rhythmic seas, with its eternity of stars that sometimes seem to hang down like lamps from the high heavens—and that sound the piping of a bird. As I walk the beach in early summer my solitary coming disturbs it on its nest, and it flies away, troubled, invisible, piping its sweet, plaintive cry. The bird I write of is the piping plover, *Charadrius melodus*, sometimes called the beach plover or the mourning bird. Its note is a whistled syllable, the loveliest musical note, I think, sounded by any North Atlantic bird.

Now that summer is here I often cook myself a camp supper on the beach. Beyond the crackling, salt-yellow driftwood flame, over the pyramid of barrel staves, broken boards, and old sticks all atwist with climbing fire, the unseen ocean thunders and booms, the breaker sounding hollow as it falls. The wall of the sand cliff be-

hind, with its rim of grass and withering roots, its sandy crumblings
and erosions, stands gilded with flame; wind cries over it; a covey of
sandpipers pass between the ocean and the fire. There are stars, and
to the south Scorpio hangs curving down the sky with ringed
Saturn shining in his claw.

Learn to reverence night and to put away the vulgar fear of it,
for, with the banishment of night from the experience of man, there
vanishes as well a religious emotion, a poetic mood, which gives
depth to the adventure of humanity. By day, space is one with the
earth and with man—it is his sun that is shining, his clouds that are
floating past; at night, space is his no more. When the great earth,
abandoning day, rolls up the deeps of the heavens and the universe,
a new door opens for the human spirit, and there are few so clown-
ish that some awareness of the mystery of being does not touch
them as they gaze. For a moment of night we have a glimpse of ourselves and of our world islanded in its stream of stars—pilgrims of
mortality, voyaging between horizons across eternal seas of space
and time. Fugitive though the instant be, the spirit of man is, during
it, ennobled by a genuine moment of emotional dignity, and poetry
makes its own both the human spirit and experience.

At intervals during the summer, often enough when the tides
are high and the moon is near the full, the surf along the beach turns
from a churn of empty moonlit water to a mass of panic life. Driven
in by schools of larger fish, swarms of little fish enter the tumble of
the surf, the eaters follow them, the surf catches them both up and
throws them, mauled and confused, ashore.

Under a sailing moon the whole churn of sea close off the beach
vibrates with a primeval ferocity and intensity of life; yet is this war
of rushing mouth and living food without a sound save for the
breaking of the seas. But let me tell of such a night.

I had spent an afternoon ashore with friends, and they had
driven me to Nauset Station just after nine o'clock. The moon, two
days from the full, was very lovely on the moors and on the channels and flat, moon-green isles of the lagoon; the wind was southerly
and light. Moved by its own enormous rhythms, the surf that night
was a stately incoming of high, serried waves, the last wave alone
breaking. This inmost wave broke heavily in a smother and rebound
of sandy foam, and thin sheets of seethe, racing before it up the
beach, vanished endlessly into the endless thirst of the sands. As I
neared the surf rim to begin my walk to the southward, I saw that

the beach close along the breakers, as far as the eye would reach, was curiously atwinkle in the moonlight with the convulsive dance of myriads of tiny fish. The breakers were spilling them on the sands; it was indeed, for the time being, a surf of life. And this surf of life was breaking for miles along the Cape.

Little herring or mackerel? Sand eels? I picked a dancer out of the tide and held him up to the moon. It was the familiar sand eel or sand launce, *Ammodytes americanus*, of the waters between Hatteras and Labrador. This is no kin of the true eels, though he rather resembles one in general appearance, for his body is slender, eel-like, and round. Instead of ending bluntly, however, this "eel" has a large, well-forked tail. The fish in the surf were two and three inches long.

Homeward that night I walked barefooted in the surf, watching the convulsive, twinkling dance, now and then feeling the squirm of a fish across my toes. Presently something occurred which made me keep to the thinnest edge of the foam. Some ten feet ahead, an enormous dogfish was suddenly borne up the beach on the rim of a slide of foam; he moved with it unresisting while it carried him; the slide withdrawing and drying up, it rolled him twice over seaward; he then twisted heavily and another minor slide carried him back again to shore. The fish was about three feet long, a real junior shark, purplish black in the increasing light—for the moon was moving west across the long axis of the breakers—and his dark, important bulk seemed strange in the bright dance of the smaller fish about him.

It was then that I began to look carefully at the width of gathering seas. Here were the greater fish, the mouths, the eaters who had driven the "eels" ashore to the edge of their world and into ours. The surf was alive with dogfish, aswarm with them, with the rush, the cold bellies, the twist and tear of their wolfish violence of life. Yet there was but little sign of it in the waters—a rare fin slicing past, and once the odd and instant glimpse of a fish embedded like a fly in amber in the bright, overturning volute of a wave.

Too far in, the dogfish were now in the grip of the surf, and presently began to come ashore. As I walked the next half mile every other breaker seemed to leave behind its ebb a mauled and stranded sharklet feebly sculling with his tail. I kicked many back into the seas, risking a toe, perhaps; some I caught by the tails and flung, for I did not want them corrupting on the beach. The next morning, in the mile and three quarters between the Fo'castle and the station, I counted seventy-one dogfish lying dead on the upper beach. There were also a dozen or two skates—the skate is really a kind of shark—which had stranded the same night. Skates follow in many things, and are forever being flung upon these sands.

I sat up late that night, at the Fo'castle, often putting down the book I read to return to the beach.

A little after eleven came Bill Eldredge to the door, with a grin on his face and one hand held behind his back. "Have you ordered tomorrow's dinner yet?" said he. "No." "Well, here it is," and Bill produced a fine cod from behind his back. "Just found him right in front of your door, alive and flopping. Yes, yes, haddock and cod often chase these sand eels in with the bigger fish; often find them on the beach about this time of the year. Got any place to keep him? Let me have a piece of string and I'll hang him on your clothesline. He'll keep all right." With a deft unforking of two fingers, Bill drew the line through the gills, and as he did so the heavy fish flopped noisily. No fear about him being dead. Make a nice chowder. Bill stepped outside; I heard him at the clothesline. Afterward we talked till it was time for him to shoulder his clock and Coston case again, pick up his watch cap, whistle in his little black dog, and go down over the dune to the beach and Nauset Station.

There were nights in June when there was phosphorescence in the surf and on the beach, and one such night I think I shall remember as the most strange and beautiful of all the year.

Early this summer the middle beach moulded itself into a bar, and between it and the dunes are long, shallow runnels into which the ocean spills over at high tide. On the night I write of, the first quarter of the moon hung in the west, and its light on the sheets of incoming tide coursing then across the bar was very beautiful to see. Just after sundown I walked to Nauset with friends who had been with me during the afternoon; the tide was still rising and a current running in the pools. I lingered at the station with my friends till the last of sunset had died and the light upon the planet, which had been moonlight mingled with sunset pink, had cleared to pure cold moon.

Southward, then, I turned, and because the flooded runnels were deep close by the station, I could not cross them and had to walk their inner shores. The tide had fallen half a foot, perhaps, but the breakers were still leaping up against the bar as against a wall, the greater ones still spilling over sheets of vanishing foam.

It grew darker with the westing of the moon. There was light on the western tops of the dunes, a fainter light on the lower beach and the breakers; the face of the dunes was a unity of dusk.

The tide had ebbed in the pools, and their edges were wet and dark. There was a strange contrast between the still levels of the pool and the seethe of the sea. I kept close to the land edge of the lagoons, and as I advanced my boots kicked wet spatters of sand ahead as they might have kicked particles of snow. Every spatter was a crumb of phosphorescence; I walked in a dust of stars. Behind me, in my footprints, luminous patches burned. With the double-ebb moonlight and tide, the deepening brims of the pools took shape in smouldering wet fire. So strangely did the luminous speckles smoulder and die and glow that it seemed as if some wind were passing, by whose breath they were kindled and extinguished. Occasional whole breakers of phosphorescence rolled in out of the vague sea—the whole wave one ghostly motion, one creamy light—and, breaking against the bar, flung up pale sprays of fire.

A strange thing happens here during these luminous tides. The phosphorescence is itself a mass of life, sometimes protozoan its origin, sometimes bacteria, the phosphorescence I write of being probably the latter. Once this living light has seeped into the beach, colonies of it speedily invade the tissues of the ten thousand thousand sand fleas which are forever hopping on this edge of ocean. Within an hour the grey bodies of these swarming amphipods, these useful, ever hungry sea scavengers (*Orchestia agilis; Talorchestia megalophthalma*) show phosphorescent pinpoints, and these points grow and unite till the whole creature is luminous. The attack is really a disease, an infection of light. The process had already begun when I arrived on the beach on the night of which I am writing, and the luminous fleas hopping off before my boots were an extraordinary sight. It was curious to see them hop from the pool rims to the upper beach, paling as they reached the width of peaceful moonlight lying landward of the strange, crawling beauty of the pools. This infection kills them, I think; at least, I have often found one of the larger creatures lying dead on the fringe of the beach, his huge porcelain eyes and water-grey body one core of living fire. Round and about him, disregarding, ten thousand kinsmen, carrying on life and the plan of life, ate the bounty of the tide.

All winter long I slept on a couch in my larger room, but with the coming of warm weather I have put my bedroom in order—I used it as a kind of storage space during the cold season—and returned to my old and rather rusty iron cot. Every once in a while, however, moved by some obscure mood, I lift off the bed-clothing and make up the couch again for a few nights. I like the seven windows of the larger room, and the sense one may have there of being almost out-of-doors. My couch stands alongside the two front windows, and from my pillow I can look out to sea and watch the passing lights, the stars rising over ocean, the swaying lanterns of the anchored fishermen, and the white spill of the surf whose long sound fills the quiet of the dunes.

Ever since my coming I have wanted to see a thunderstorm bear down upon this elemental coast. A thunderstorm is a "tempest" on the Cape. The quoted word, as Shakespeare used it, means lightning and thunder, and it is in this old and beautiful Elizabethan sense that the word is used in Eastham. When a schoolboy in the Orleans or the Wellfleet High reads the Shakespearean play, its title means to him exactly what it meant to the man from Stratford; elsewhere in America, the term seems to mean anything from a tornado to a blizzard. I imagine that this old significance of the word is now to be found only in certain parts of England and Cape Cod.

On the night of the June tempest, I was sleeping in my larger room, the windows were open, and the first low roll of thunder opened my eyes. It had been very still when I went to bed, but now a wind from the west-nor'west was blowing through the windows in a strong and steady current, and as I closed them there was lightning to the west and far away. I looked at my watch; it was just after one o'clock. Then came a time of waiting in the darkness, long minutes broken by more thunder, and intervals of quiet in which I heard a faintest sound of light surf upon the beach. Suddenly the heavens cracked open in an immense instant of pinkish-violet lightning. My seven windows filled with the violent, inhuman light, and I had a glimpse of the great, solitary dunes staringly empty of familiar shadows; a tremendous crash then mingled with the withdrawal of the light, and echoes of thunder rumbled away and grew faint in a returning rush of darkness. A moment after, rain began to fall gently as if someone had just released its flow, a blessed sound on a roof of wooden shingles, and one I have loved ever since I was a child. From a gentle patter the sound of the rain grew swiftly to a drumming roar, and with the rain came the chuckling of water from the eaves. The tempest was crossing the Cape, striking at the ancient land on its way to the heavens above the sea.

Now came flash after stabbing flash amid a roaring of rain, and heavy thunder that rolled on till its last echoes were swallowed up in vast detonations which jarred the walls. Houses were struck that night in Eastham village. My lonely world, full of lightning and rain, was strange to look upon. I do not share the usual fear of lightning, but that night there came over me, for the first and last time of all my solitary year, a sense of isolation and remoteness from my kind. I remember that I stood up, watching, in the middle of the room. On the great marshes the lightning surfaced the winding channels with a metallic splendor and arrest of motion, all very strange through windows blurred by rain. Under the violences of light the great dunes took on a kind of elemental passivity, the quiet of earth enchanted into stone, and as I watched them appear and plunge back into a darkness that had an intensity of its own I felt, as never before, a sense of the vast time, of the thousands of cyclic and uncounted years which had passed since these giants had risen from the dark ocean at their feet and given themselves to the wind and the bright day.

Fantastic things were visible at sea. Beaten down by the rain, and sheltered by the Cape itself from the river of west wind, the off-shore brim of ocean remained unusually calm. The tide was about halfway up the beach, and rising, and long parallels of low waves, forming close inshore, were curling over and breaking placidly along the lonely, rain-drenched miles. The intense crackling flares and quiverings of the storm, moving out to sea, illumined every inch of the beach and the plain of the Atlantic, all save the hollow bellies of the little breakers, which were shielded from the light by their overcurling crests. The effect was dramatic and strangely beautiful, for what one saw was a bright ocean rimmed with parallel bands of blackest advancing darkness, each one melting back to light as the wave toppled down upon the beach in foam.

Stars came out after the storm, and when I woke again before sunrise I found the heavens and the earth rainwashed, cool, and clear. Saturn and the Scorpion were setting, but Jupiter was riding the zenith and paling on his throne. The tide was low in the marsh channels; the gulls had scarcely stirred upon their gravel banks and bars. Suddenly, thus wandering about, I disturbed a song sparrow on her nest. She flew to the roof of my house, grasped the ridgepole, and turned about, apprehensive, inquiring . . . '*tsiped* her monosyllable of alarm. Then back toward her nest she flew, alighted in a plum bush, and, reassured at last, trilled out a morning song.

# IGUANA

## James M. Cain

*The author of* The Postman Always Rings Twice *and other
novels of the "hard-boiled school" would not suggest himself
to most readers as a nature writer. But some of the best pieces
about animals, or about storms, or dramatic aspects of nature
are often buried in books of quite a different nature. In*
Serenade, *an American and a Mexican girl take refuge in a deserted church. Hungry, they look about for food and find—
iguana.*

THE afternoon of the second day it let up for about a half hour,
and we slid down in the mud to have a look at the arroyo. It was
a torrent. No chance of making Acapulco that night. We went up
the hill and the sun came out plenty hot. When we got to the
church the rocks back of it were alive with lizards. There was every
size lizard you could think of, from little ones that were transparent
like shrimps, to big ones three feet long. They were a kind of blue
gray, and moved so fast you could hardly follow them with your
eyes. They leveled out with their tail, somehow, so they went over
the rocks in a straight line, and almost seemed to fly. Looking at
them you could believe it all right, that they turned into birds just
by letting their scales grow into feathers. You could almost believe
it that they were half bird already.

We climbed down and stood looking at them, when all of a
sudden she began to scream. "Iguana! Iguana! Look, look, big
iguana!"

I looked, and couldn't see anything. Then, still as the rock it
was laying on, and just about the color of it, I saw the evilest-
looking thing I ever laid eyes on. It looked like some prehistoric
monster you see in the encyclopedia, between two and three feet
long, with a scruff of spines that started at its head and went clear
down its back, and a look in its eye like something in a nightmare.

[ 626 ]

She had grabbed up a little tree that had washed out by the roots, and was closing in on him. "What are you doing? Let that goddam thing alone!"

When I spoke he shot out for the next rock like something on springs, but she made a swipe and caught him in mid-air. He landed about ten feet away, with his yellow belly showing and all four legs churning him around in circles. She scrambled over, hit him again, and then she grabbed him. "Machete! Quick, bring machete!"

"Machete, hell, let him go I tell you!"

"Is iguana! We cook! We eat!"

"*Eat!*—that thing?"

"The machete, the machete!"

He was scratching her by that time, and if she wouldn't let him go I wasn't letting him make hash out of her. I dove in the church for the machete. But then some memory of this animal caught me. I don't know whether it was something I had read in Cortés, or Diaz, or Martyr, or somebody, about how they cooked it when the Aztecs still ran Mexico, or some instinct I had brought away from Paris, or what. All I knew was that if we ever cut his head off he was going to be dead, and maybe that wouldn't be right. I didn't grab a machete. I grabbed a basket, with a top on it, and dug out there with it. "The machete! The machete, give me machete!"

He had come to by now, and was fighting all he knew, but I grabbed him. The only place to grab him was in the belly, on account of those spines on his back, and that put his claws right up your arm. She was bleeding up to her elbows, and now it was my turn. Never mind how he felt and how he stunk. It was enough to turn your stomach. But I gave him the squeeze, shoved him head-down in the basket, and clapped the top on. Then I held it tight with both hands.

"Get some twine."

"But the machete! Why you no bring—"

"Never mind. I'm doing this. Twine—string—that the things were tied with."

I carried him in, and she got some twine, and I tied the top on, tight. Then I set him down and tried to think. She didn't make any sense out of it, but she let me alone. In a minute I fed up the fire, took the pot out and filled it with water. It had started to rain again. I came in and put the pot on to heat. It took a long while. Inside the basket those claws were ripping at the wicker, and I wondered if it would hold.

At last I got a simmer, and then I took the pot off and got another basket-top ready. I picked him up, held him way above my head, and dropped him to the floor. I remember what shock did to him the first time, and I hoped it would work again. It didn't. When I cut the string and grabbed, I got teeth, but I held on and socked him in the pot. I whipped the basket-top on and held it with my knee. For three seconds it was like I had dropped an electric fan in there, but then it stopped. I took the top off and fished him out. He was dead, or as dead as a reptile ever gets. Then I found out why it was that something had told me to put him in the pot alive, and not cook him dead, with his head cut off, like she wanted to do. When he hit that scalding water he let go. He purged, and that meant he was clean inside as a whistle.

I went out, emptied the pot, heated a little more water, and scrubbed it clean with cornhusks, from the eggs. Then I scrubbed him off. Then I filled the pot, or about two thirds filled it, with clean water, and put it on the fire. When it began to smoke I dropped him in. "But is very fonny. Mamma no cook that way."

"Is fonny, but inspiration has hit me. Never mind how Mamma does it. This is how I do it, and I think it's going to be good."

I fed up the fire, and pretty soon it boiled. I cut it down to a simmer, and this smell began to come off it. It was a stink, and yet it smelled right, like I knew it was going to smell. I let it cook along, and every now and then I'd fish him up and pull one of his claws. When a claw pulled out I figured he was done. I took him out and put him in a bowl. She reached for the pot to go out and empty it. I almost fainted. "Let that water alone. Leave it there, right where it is."

I cut off his head, opened his belly, and cleaned him. I saved his liver, and was plenty careful how I dissected off the gall bladder. Then I skinned him and took off the meat. The best of it was along the back and down the tail, but I carved the legs too, so as not to miss anything. The meat and liver I stowed in a little bowl. The guts I threw out. The bones I put back in the pot and fed up the fire again, so it began to simmer. "You better make yourself comfortable. It's a long time before dinner."

I aimed to boil about half that water away. It began to get dark and we lit the candles and watched and smelled. I washed off three eggs and dropped them in. When they were hard I fished them out, peeled them, and laid them in a bowl with the meat. She pounded up some coffee. After a long time that soup was almost done. Then something popped into my mind. "Listen, we got any paprika?"

"No, no paprika."

"Gee, we ought to have paprika."

"Pepper, salt, yes. No paprika."

"Go out there to the car and have a look. This stuff needs paprika, and it would be a shame not to have it just because we didn't look."

"I go, but is no paprika."

She took a candle and went back to the car. I didn't need any paprika. But I wanted to get rid of her so I could pull off something without any more talk about the *sacrilegio*. I took a candle and a machete and went back of the altar. There were four or five closets back there, and a couple of them were locked. I slipped the machete blade into one and snapped the lock. It was full of firecrackers for high mass and stuff for the Christmas crèche. I broke into another one. There it was, what I was looking for, six or eight bottles of sacramental wine. I grabbed a bottle, closed the closets, and came back. I dug the cork out with my knife and tasted it. It was A-1 sherry. I socked about a pint in the pot and hid the bottle. As soon as it heated up a little I lifted the pot off, dropped the meat in, sliced up the eggs, and put them in. I sprinkled in some salt and a little pepper.

She came back. "Is no paprika."

"It's all right. We won't need it. Dinner's ready."

We dug in.

Well, brother, you can have your Terrapin Maryland. It's a noble dish, but it's not Iguana John Howard Sharp. The meat is a little like chicken, a little like frog-legs, and a little like muskrat, but it's tenderer than any of them. The soup is one of the great soups of the world, and I've eaten Marseilles bouillabaisse, New Orleans crayfish bisque, clear green turtle, thick green turtle, and all kinds of other turtle there are. I think it was still better that we had to drink it out of bowls, and fish the meat out with a knife.

# HARE-HUNTING

## Robert Smith Surtees

*His hobby gained the upper hand when the English lawyer
Surtees (1803–1864) founded and became editor of the* New
Sporting Magazine. *A few years later he published his first
novel,* Jorrock's Jaunts and Jollities, *featuring the sporting
Cockney grocer, Mr. Jorrocks; this, not long afterward, sug-
gested an even more famous book to an author named Charles
Dickens—Pickwick Papers. Surtees wrote more successful sto-
ries, some about the immortal Mr. Jorrocks, and one called*
Hawbuck Grange, *about the hare-hunting sportsmen who
ride below.*

THEY were now upon the moors, with nothing to fear but bogs
and holes and ruts, things that did not seem to be included in
the list of casualties of the Goose and Dumpling Hunt, for all the
members began charging abreast instead of following in the goose
fashion they had been pursuing before.

The hounds were long out of sight; indeed, they had run up a
ravine, from which the *détour* by Bewdley Bridge had interposed
a hill; but the fatties saw by the staring of the sheep the line they
had taken, and the field jogged on in high exultation at the splendour of the run, and delighted at the idea of astonishing the
stranger.

Presently they got within sight of where sheep were still running, or rather wheeling about, and then a shepherd's hat on the
sky-line of a far-off hill announced where they were.

The riding was only awkward, the heather hiding both stones
and holes, and the turf on the bare places, particularly on the hillside, being extremely slippery. Nevertheless they clattered on,
trusting entirely to their horses for safety.

Presently they heard the cry of hounds.

"Hold hard!" exclaimed Mr. Trumper, "they are coming

towards us. Hark!" exclaimed he (pulling up short, and holding up his hand)—"now, Mr. Scott, if you'll come here, I'll show you the hare," said he.

Accordingly, Scott followed him through a narrow defile to the left, and, looking over a hollow in the rocky hill upon the country below, he saw poor puss dribbling along in a listening sort of canter.

The field followed to partake of the treat.

"Oh, she's a fine-un!" exclaimed Mr. Trumper, his eyes sparkling as he spoke; "but she's pretty well beat," added he; "she'll most likely begin to play some of her tricks: these things have far more cunning nor foxes," added he. "Now this is the time," continued he, addressing himself seriously to Scott, "that you wild fox-hunters would take advantage of, for the purpose of cutting short the diversion, by mobbing, and shouting, and taking every advantage of him; but we do the thing differently. *We* let our hounds hunt; and if they can't kill a hare fairly, why they lose her."

The hounds had now descended from the hills and turned the corner of the last angle that shut them out from view. They were working a middling scent, which they caught and lost and lost and caught alternately.

Puss heard them, and regulated her pace by theirs.

Presently she began the tricks Mr. Trumper anticipated. Having got into a small fallow, she dribbled up a furrow above which her back was scarcely visible, and having run the length of it, she deliberately returned the same way, and with a mighty spring landed in a thick hedge-row.

"That'll puzzle them," said Mr. Trumper, "for the scent is but cold at best, and the wet of yon furrow won't improve what little there is."

"But you'll let them hunt it, of course?" observed Scott, thinking Mr. Trumper was paving the way to a little assistance.

"*Undoubtedly*," replied Trumper, with a deep side-way inclination of the head—"undoubtedly," repeated Trumper. "*We'd scorn to take an unfair advantage* of her. But look how they hunt!" added he. "Did you ever see hounds work better? No babblers, no skirters, no do-nothing gentlemen here; twelve couple and all workers; *we* keep no cats that don't catch mice, Mr. Scott. Oh, but they're beauties!" added he in ecstasy, as they came hunting her as true as an arrow.

When they got upon the fallow it certainly was not propitious.

There wasn't a hound that could speak to the scent, and Twister and Towler alone guided them on the line.

"Those hounds are worth two hundred thousand pounds a-piece to Prince Albert, or any of the royal family who really know what hunting is," whispered Mr. Trumper. "See what confidence they all have in them. Hark! Cottager threw his tongue. That's the first time he's spoke since he came into the field, but he's had the scent the whole way. Oh! hare-hunting is beautiful sport, the most delightful amusement under the sun," added he. "There's nothing to compare to it. Is there, Beaney?" continued he, who with the rest of the field were now clustered behind in ardent admiration of their darlings.

"*Nothing! nothing! nothing!*" was vociferated by all.

The hounds had now got to the end of the double, and several of the young ones dashed beyond. Not so Twister and Towler, who cast a small semi-circle in advance, and then returned to the spot.

"*That's hunting now!*" exclaimed Mr. Trumper, "your wild fox-dogs would have been half over the next parish by this time, but those hounds won't move an inch without a scent. See how they hunt it back. That's something like now. Far better than getting a hold of them and pretending to tell *them* what you keep them to tell you, *which way the hare went.*"

"Ah, that's all very well," observed Scott, "with the hare sitting in the hedge-row; but a fox, you know, keeps travelling on. There's no time for dawdling with him."

"You don't know but that hare may be in Jollyrise township by this time," snapped Mr. Trumper; "it doesn't follow because she took the hedge-row, that she's there still. But we are in no hurry. Fair-play's the universal motto of hare-hunters. We even have it on our buttons," added he, turning up a great pewter-plate-looking thing with a hare and the words "Fair Play" underneath.

"The gentleman doesn't seem to understand much about the thing, I think," observed Michael Hobbletrot, who had got dribbled up from his *détour* by Maddingly Common, after a most enjoyable ride of the line.

"Fox-hunters seldom do," rejoined Simon Driblet.

# A VOYAGE UP THE TAPAJOS

## H. W. Bates

*In the Golden Age of English naturalists, when Darwin, Huxley, and Wallace were revolutionizing the world's ideas about nature, Bates (1825–1892) was a less famous but equally brilliant investigator. He spent eleven years in Brazil and came home with specimens representing 14,712 species—about eight thousand of these had never been known to science. Bates, exploring the Amazon and its tributaries, met many perils with great courage. His ascent of the tortuous Tapajos River (he tells of it in* The Naturalist on the Amazons) *would have been much harder but for the aid and companionship of a loyal native called José.*

I WAS obliged, this time, to travel in a vessel of my own; partly because trading canoes large enough to accommodate a Naturalist very seldom pass between Santarem and the thinly-peopled settlements on the river, and partly because I wished to explore districts at my ease, far out of the ordinary track of traders. I soon found a suitable canoe; a two-masted cuberta, of about six tons' burthen, strongly built of Itaüba or stonewood, a timber of which all the best vessels in the Amazons country are constructed, and said to be more durable than teak. This I hired of a merchant at the cheap rate of 500 reis, or about one shilling and twopence per day. I fitted up the cabin, which, as usual in canoes of this class, was a square structure with its floor above the water-line, as my sleeping and working apartment. My chests, filled with store-boxes and trays for specimens, were arranged on each side, and above them were shelves and pegs to hold my little stock of useful books, guns, and game bags, boards and materials for skinning and preserving animals, botanical press and papers, drying cages for insects and birds and so forth. A rush mat was spread on the floor, and my rolled-up hammock, to be used only when sleeping ashore, served

for a pillow. The arched covering over the hold in the fore part of
the vessel contained, besides a sleeping place for the crew, my heavy
chests, stock of salt provisions and groceries, and an assortment of
goods wherewith to pay my way amongst the half-civilised or
savage inhabitants of the interior. The goods consisted of cashaça,
powder and shot, a few pieces of coarse checked-cotton cloth and
prints, fish-hooks, axes, large knives, harpoons, arrow-heads,
looking-glasses, beads, and other small wares. José and myself were
busy for many days arranging these matters. We had to salt the
meat and grind a supply of coffee ourselves. Cooking utensils,
crockery, water-jars, a set of useful carpenter's tools, and many
other things had to be provided. We put all the groceries and other
perishable articles in tin canisters and boxes, having found that this
was the only way of preserving them from damp and insects in this
climate. When all was done, our canoe looked like a little floating
workshop.

I could get little information about the river, except vague
accounts of the difficulty of the navigation, and the famito or hunger which reigned on its banks. As I have before mentioned, it is
about 1000 miles in length, and flows from south to north; in magnitude it stands the sixth amongst the tributaries of the Amazons. It is
navigable, however, by sailing vessels only for about 160 miles
above Santarem. The hiring of men to navigate the vessel was our
greatest trouble. José was to be my helmsman, and we thought three
other hands would be the fewest with which we could venture. But
all our endeavours to procure these were fruitless. Santarem is
worse provided with Indian canoemen than any other town on the
river. I found on applying to the tradesmen to whom I had brought
letters of introduction and to the Brazilian authorities, that almost
any favour would be sooner granted than the loan of hands. A
stranger, however, is obliged to depend on them; for it is impossible
to find an Indian or half-caste whom some one or other of the head-
men do not claim as owing him money or labour. I was afraid at one
time I should have been forced to abandon my project on this account. At length, after many rebuffs and disappointments, José
contrived to engage one man, a mulatto, named Pinto, a native of
the mining country of Interior Brazil, who knew the river well;
and with these two I resolved to start, hoping to meet with others
at the first village on the road.

We left Santarem on the 8th of June. The waters were then at
their highest point, and my canoe had been anchored close to the

back door of our house. The morning was cool and a brisk wind blew, with which we sped rapidly past the whitewashed houses and thatched Indian huts of the suburbs. The charming little bay of Mapirí was soon left behind; we then doubled Point Maria Josepha, a headland formed of high cliffs of Tabatinga clay, capped with forest. This forms the limit of the river view from Santarem, and here we had our last glimpse, at a distance of seven or eight miles, of the city, a bright line of tiny white buildings resting on the dark water. A stretch of wild, rocky, uninhabited coast was before us, and we were fairly within the Tapajos.

Our course lay due west for about twenty miles. The wind increased as we neared Point Cururú, where the river bends from its northern course. A vast expanse of water here stretches to the west and south, and the waves, with a strong breeze, run very high. As we were doubling the Point, the cable which held our montaria in tow astern, parted, and in endeavouring to recover the boat, without which we knew it would be difficult to get ashore on many parts of the coast, we were very near capsizing. We tried to tack down the river; a vain attempt with a strong breeze and no current. Our ropes snapped, the sails flew to rags, and the vessel, which we now found was deficient in ballast, heeled over frightfully. Contrary to José's advice, I ran the cuberta into a little bay, thinking to cast anchor there and wait for the boat coming up with the wind; but the anchor dragged on the smooth sandy bottom, and the vessel went broadside on to the rocky beach. With a little dexterous management, but not until after we had sustained some severe bumps, we managed to get out of this difficulty, clearing the rocky point at a close shave with our jib-sail. Soon after, we drifted into the smooth water of a sheltered bay which leads to the charmingly situated village of Altar do Chao; and we were obliged to give up our attempt to recover the montaria.

The little settlement, Altar do Chao (altar of the ground, or Earth altar), owes its singular name to the existence at the entrance to the harbour of one of those strange flat-topped hills which are so common in this part of the Amazons country, shaped like the high altar in Roman Catholic churches. It is an isolated one, and much lower in height than the similarly truncated hills and ridges near Almeyrim, being elevated probably not more than 300 feet above the level of the river. It is bare of trees, but covered in place with a species of fern. At the head of the bay is an inner harbour, which communicates by a channel with a series of lakes lying in the valleys between hills, and stretching far into the interior of the land. The village is peopled almost entirely by semi-civilised Indians, to the number of sixty or seventy families; and the scattered houses are arranged in broad streets on a strip of greensward, at the foot of a high, gloriously-wooded ridge.

I was so much pleased with the situation of this settlement, and the number of rare birds and insects which tenanted the forest, that I revisited it in the following year, and spent four months making collections. The village itself is a neglected, poverty-stricken place: the governor (Captain of Trabalhadores, or Indian workmen) being an old, apathetic, half-breed, who had spent all his life here. The priest was a most profligate character; I seldom saw him sober; he was a white, however, and a man of good ability. I may as well mention here, that a moral and zealous priest is a great rarity in this province: the only ministers of religion in the whole country who appeared sincere in their calling being the Bishop of Pará and the Vicars of Ega on the Upper Amazons and Obydos. The houses in the village swarmed with vermin; bats in the thatch; fire-ants (formiga de fogo) under the floors; cockroaches and spiders on the walls. Very few of them had wooden doors and locks. Altar do Chao was originally a settlement of the aborigines, and was called Burarí. The Indians were always hostile to the Portuguese, and during the disorders of 1835–6 joined the rebels in their attack on Santarem. Few of them escaped the subsequent slaughter, and for this reason there is now scarcely an old or middle-aged man in the place. As in all the semi-civilised villages, where the original orderly and industrious habits of the Indian have been lost without anything being learnt from the whites to make amends, the inhabitants live in the greatest poverty. The scarcity of fish in the clear waters and rocky bays of the neighbourhood is no doubt partly the cause of the poverty and perennial hunger which reign here. When we arrived in the port our canoe was crowded with the half-naked villagers—men, women, and children, who came to beg each a piece of salt pirarucu "for the love of God." They are not quite so badly off in the dry season. The shallow lakes and bays then contain plenty of fish, and the boys and women go out at night to spear them by torchlight; the torches being made of thin strips of green bark from the leaf-stalks of palms, tied in bundles. Many excellent kinds of fish are thus obtained; amongst them the Pescada, whose white and flaky flesh, when boiled, has the appearance and flavour of cod-fish;

and the Tucunaré (Cichla temensis), a handsome species, with a large prettily-coloured, eye-like spot on its tail. Many small Salmonidæ are also met with, and a kind of sole, called Aramassá, which moves along the clear sandy bottom of the bay. At these times a species of sting-ray is common on the sloping beach, and bathers are frequently stung most severely by it. The weapon of this fish is a strong blade with jagged edges, about three inches long, growing from the side of the long fleshy tail. I once saw a woman wounded by it whilst bathing; she shrieked frightfully, and was obliged to be carried to her hammock, where she lay for a week in great pain; I have known strong men to be lamed for many months by the sting.

There was a mode of taking fish here which I had not before seen employed, but found afterwards to be very common on the Tapajos. This is by using a poisonous liana called Timbó (Paullinia pinnata). It will act only in the still waters of creeks and pools. A few rods, a yard in length, are mashed and soaked in the water, which quickly becomes discoloured with the milky deleterious juice of the plant. In about half an hour all the smaller fishes, over a rather wide space around the spot, rise to the surface floating on their sides, and with the gills wide open. The poison acts evidently by suffocating the fishes; it spreads slowly in the water, and a very slight mixture seems sufficient to stupefy them. I was surprised, on beating the water in places where no fishes were visible in the clear depths for many yards round, to find, sooner or later, sometimes twenty-four hours afterwards, a considerable number floating dead on the surface.

The people occupy themselves the greater part of the year with their small plantations of mandioca. All the heavy work, such as felling and burning the timber, planting and weeding, is done in the plantation of each family by a congregation of neighbours, which they call a "pucherum"—a similar custom to the "bee" in the backwood settlements of North America. They make quite a holiday of each pucherum. When the invitation is issued, the family prepares a great quantity of fermented drink, called in this part Tarobá, from soaked mandioca cakes, and porridge of Manicueira. This latter is a kind of sweet mandioca, very different from the Yuca of the Peruvians and Macasheira of the Brazilians (Manihot Aypi), having oblong juicy roots, which become very sweet a few days after they are gathered. With these simple provisions they regale their helpers.

The work is certainly done, but after a very rude fashion; all become soddened with Tarobá, and the day finishes often in a drunken brawl.

The climate is rather more humid than that of Santarem. I suppose this is to be attributed to the neighbouring country being densely wooded, instead of an open campo. In no part of the country did I enjoy more the moonlit nights than here, in the dry season. After the day's work was done, I used to go down to the shores of the bay, and lie at full length on the cool sand for two or three hours before bed-time. The soft pale light, resting on broad sandy beaches and palm-thatched huts, reproduced the effect of a midwinter scene in the cold north when a coating of snow lies on the landscape. A heavy shower falls about once a week, and the shrubby vegetation never becomes parched up as at Santarem. Between the rains the heat and dryness increase from day to day: the weather on the first day after the rain is gleamy, with intervals of melting sunshine and passing clouds; the next day is rather drier, and the east wind begins to blow; then follow days of cloudless sky, with gradually increasing strength of breeze. When this has continued about a week, a light mistiness begins to gather about the horizon; clouds are formed; grumbling thunder is heard, and then, generally in the night-time, down falls the refreshing rain. The sudden chill caused by the rains produces colds, which are accompanied by the same symptoms as in our own climate; with this exception the place is very healthy.

*June 17th.*—The two young men returned without meeting with my montaria, and I found it impossible here to buy a new one. Captain Thomás could find me only one hand. This was a bluntspoken but willing young Indian, named Manoel. He came on board this morning at eight o'clock, and we then got up our anchor and resumed our voyage.

The wind was light and variable all day, and we made only about fifteen miles by seven o'clock in the evening. The coast formed a succession of long, shallow bays with sandy beaches, on which the waves broke in a long line of surf. Ten miles above Altar do Chao is a conspicuous headland, called Point Cajetúba. During a lull of the wind, towards midday, we ran the cuberta aground in shallow water and waded ashore, but the woods were scarcely penetrable, and not a bird was to be seen. The only thing observed worthy of note, was the quantity of drowned winged ants along the beach; they were all of one species, the terrible formiga de fogo (Myrmica sævissima); the dead, or half-dead bodies of which were heaped up in a line an inch or two in height and breadth, the line continuing without interruption for miles at the edge of the water. The countless thousands had been doubtless cast into the river whilst flying during a sudden squall the night before, and afterwards cast ashore by the waves. We found ourselves at seven o'clock near the mouth of a creek leading to a small lake, called Aramána-í, and the wind having died away, we anchored, guided by the lights ashore, near the house of a settler, named Jeronymo, whom I knew, and who, soon after, showed us a snug little harbour, where we could remain in safety for the night. The river here cannot be less than ten miles broad; it is quite clear of islands and free from shoals at this season of the year. The opposite coast appeared in the daytime as a long thin line of forest, with dim grey hills in the background.

To-day (19th) we had a good wind, which carried us to the mouth of a creek, called Paquiatúba, where the "inspector" of the district lived, Senhor Cypriano, for whom I had brought an order from Captain Thomás to supply me with another hand. We had great difficulty in finding a place to land. The coast in this part was a tract of level, densely-wooded country, through which flowed the winding rivulet, or creek, which gives its name to a small scattered settlement hidden in the wilderness; the hills here receding two or three miles towards the interior. A large portion of the forest was flooded, the trunks of the very high trees near the mouth of the creek standing eighteen feet deep in water. We lost two hours working our way with poles through the inundated woods in search of the port. Every inlet we tried ended in a labyrinth choked up with bushes, but we were at length guided to the right place by the crowing of cocks. On shouting for a montaria an Indian boy made his appearance, guiding one through the gloomy thickets; but he was so alarmed, I suppose at the apparition of a strange-looking white man in spectacles bawling from the prow of the vessel, that he shot back quickly into the bushes. He returned when Manoel spoke, and we went ashore: the montaria winding along a gloomy overshadowed water-path, made by cutting away the lower branches and underwood. The foot-road to the houses was a narrow, sandy alley, bordered by trees of stupendous height, overrun with creepers, and having an unusual number of long air-roots dangling from the epiphytes on their branches.

After passing one low smoky little hut, half-buried in foliage, the path branched off in various directions, and the boy having left us, we took the wrong turn. We were brought to a stand soon after by the barking of dogs; and on shouting, as is customary on approaching a dwelling, "O da casa!" (Oh of the house!) a dark-skinned native, a Cafuzo, with a most unpleasant expression of countenance, came forth through the tangled maze of bushes, armed with a long knife, with which he pretended to be whittling a stick. He directed us to the house of Cypriano, which was about a mile distant along another forest road. The circumstance of the Cafuzo coming out armed to receive visitors very much astonished my companions, who talked it over at every place we visited for several days afterwards; the freest and most unsuspecting welcome in these retired places being always counted upon by strangers. But, as Manoel remarked, the fellow may have been one of the unpardoned rebel leaders who had settled here after the recapture of Santarem in 1836, and lived in fear of being inquired for by the authorities of Santarem. After all our troubles we found Cypriano absent from home. His house was a large one, and full of people, old and young, women and children, all of whom were Indians or mamelucos. Several smaller huts surrounded the large dwelling, besides extensive open sheds containing mandioca ovens and rude wooden mills for grinding sugar-cane to make molasses. All the buildings were embosomed in trees: it would be scarcely possible to find a more retired nook, and an air of contentment was spread over the whole establishment. Cypriano's wife, a good-looking mameluco girl, was superintending the packing of farinha. Two or three old women, seated on mats, were making baskets with narrow strips of bark from the leaf-stalks of palms, whilst others were occupied lining them with the broad leaves of a species of maranta, and filling them afterwards with farinha, which was previously measured in a rude square vessel. It appeared that Senhor Cypriano was a large producer of the article, selling 300 baskets (sixty pounds' weight each) annually to Santarem traders. I was sorry we were unable to see him, but it was useless waiting, as we were told all the men were at present occupied in "pucherums," and he would be unable to give me the assistance I required. We returned to the canoe in the evening, and, after moving out into the river, anchored and slept.

*June 20th.*—We had a light, baffling wind off shore all day on the 20th, and made but fourteen or fifteen miles by six P.M.; when, the wind failing us, we anchored at the mouth of a narrow channel, called Tapaiúna, which runs between a large island and the mainland. About three o'clock we passed in front of Boim, a village on the opposite (western) coast. The breadth of the river is here six or seven miles: a confused patch of white on the high land opposite was all we saw of the village, the separate houses being undistinguishable on account of the distance. The coast along which we sailed to-day is a continuation of the low and flooded land of Paquiatúba.

*June 21st.*—The next morning we sailed along the Tapaiúna channel, which is from 400 to 600 yards in breadth. We advanced but slowly, as the wind was generally dead against us, and stopped frequently to ramble ashore. Wherever the landing-place was sandy it was impossible to walk about, on account of the swarms of the terrible fire-ant, whose sting is likened by the Brazilians to the puncture of a red-hot needle. There was scarcely a square inch of ground free from them. About three P.M. we glided into a quiet, shady creek, on whose banks an industrious white settler had located himself. I resolved to pass the rest of the day and night here, and endeavour to obtain a fresh supply of provisions, our stock of salt beef being now nearly exhausted. The situation of the house was beautiful; the little harbour being gay with water plants, Pontederiæ, now full of purple blossom, from which flocks of stilt-legged water-fowl started up screaming as we entered. The owner sent a boy with my men to show them the best place for fish up the creek, and in the course of the evening sold me a number of fowls, besides baskets of beans and farinha. The result of the fishing was a good supply of Jandiá, a handsome spotted Siluride fish, and Piránha, a kind of Salmon. Piránhas are of several kinds, many of which abound in the waters of the Tapajos. They are caught with almost any kind of bait, for their taste is indiscriminate and their appetite most ravenous. They often attack the legs of bathers near the shore, inflicting severe wounds with their strong triangular teeth. At Paquiatúba and this place I added about twenty species of small fishes to my collection; caught by hook and line, or with the hand in shallow pools under the shade of the forest.

*June 23rd.*—The wind freshened at ten o'clock in the morning of the 23rd. A thick black cloud then began to spread itself over the sky a long way down the river; the storm which it portended, however, did not reach us, as the dark threatening mass crossed from east to west, and the only effect it had was to impel a column of cold air up river, creating a breeze with which we bounded rapidly forward. The wind in the afternoon strengthened to a gale; we carried on with one foresail only, two of the men holding on to the boom to prevent the whole thing from flying to pieces. The rocky coast continued for about twelve miles above Itá-puáma: then succeeded a tract of low marshy land, which had evidently been once an island whose channel of separation from the mainland had become silted up. The island of Capitarí and another group of islets succeeding it, called Jacaré, on the opposite side, helped also to contract at this point the breadth of the river, which was now not more than about three miles. The little cuberta almost flew along this coast, there being no perceptible current, past extensive swamps, margined with thick floating grasses. At length, on rounding a low point, higher land again appeared on the right bank of the river, and the village of Aveyros hove in sight, in the port of which we cast anchor late in the afternoon.

Little happened worth narrating during my forty days' stay at Aveyros. The time was spent in the quiet, regular pursuit of Natural History: every morning I had my long ramble in the forest, which extended to the back-doors of the houses, and the afternoons were occupied in preserving and studying the objects collected. The priest was a lively old man, but rather a bore from being able to talk of scarcely anything except homœopathy, having been smitten with the mania during a recent visit to Santarem. He had a Portuguese Homœopathic Dictionary, and a little leather case containing glass tubes filled with globules, with which he was doctoring the whole village.

The weather, during the month of July, was uninterruptedly fine; not a drop of rain fell, and the river sank rapidly. The mornings, for two hours after sunrise, were very cold; we were glad to wrap ourselves in blankets on turning out of our hammocks, and walk about at a quick pace in the early sunshine. But in the afternoons the heat was sickening; for the glowing sun then shone full on the front of the row of whitewashed houses, and there was seldom any wind to moderate its effects. I began now to understand why the branch rivers of the Amazons were so unhealthy, whilst the main stream was pretty nearly free from diseases arising from malaria. The cause lies, without doubt, in the slack currents of the tributaries in the dry season, and the absence of the cooling Amazonian trade-wind, which purifies the air along the banks of the main river. The trade-wind does not deviate from its nearly straight westerly course, so that the branch streams, which run generally at right angles to the Amazons, and have a slack current for a long distance from their mouths, are left to the horrors of nearly stagnant air and water.

Aveyros may be called the head-quarters of the fire-ant, which might be fittingly termed the scourge of this fine river. The Tapajos is nearly free from the insect pests of other parts, mosquitoes, sandflies, Motúcas and piums; but the formiga de fogo is perhaps a greater plague than all the others put together. It is found only on sandy soils in open places, and seems to thrive most in the neighbourhood of houses and weedy villages, such as Aveyros: it does not occur at all in the shades of the forest. I noticed it in most places on the banks of the Amazons, but the species is not very common on the main river, and its presence is there scarcely noticed, because it does not attack man, and the sting is not so virulent as it is in the same species on the banks of the Tapajos. Aveyros was deserted a few years before my visit on account of this little tormentor, and the inhabitants had only recently returned to their houses, thinking its numbers had decreased. It is a small species, of a shining reddish colour, not greatly differing from the common red stinging ant of our own country (Myrmica rubra), except that the pain and irritation caused by its sting are much greater. The soil of the whole village is undermined by it: the ground is perforated with the entrances to their subterranean galleries, and a little sandy dome occurs here and there, where the insects bring their young to receive warmth near the surface. The houses are overrun with them; they dispute every fragment of food with the inhabitants, and destroy clothing for the sake of the starch. All eatables are obliged to be suspended in baskets from the rafters, and the cords well soaked with copaüba balsam, which is the only means known of preventing them from climbing. They seem to attack persons out of sheer malice: if we stood for a few moments in the street, even at a distance from their nests, we were sure to be overrun and severely punished, for the moment an ant touched the flesh, he secured himself with his jaws, doubled in his tail, and stung with all his might. When we were seated on chairs in the evenings in front of the house to enjoy a chat with our neighbours, we had stools to support our feet, the legs of which as well as those of the chairs, were well anointed with the balsam. The cords of hammocks are obliged to be smeared in the same way to prevent the ants from paying sleepers a visit.

The inhabitants declare that the fire-ant was unknown on the Tapajos before the disorders of 1835–6, and believe that the hosts sprang up from the blood of the slaughtered Cabanas or rebels. They have, doubtless, increased since that time, but the cause lies in the depopulation of the villages and the rank growth of weeds in the previously cleared, well-kept spaces. I have already described the line of sediment formed on the sandy shores lower down the river by the dead bodies of the winged individuals of this species. The exodus from their nests of the males and females takes place at the end of the rainy season (June), when the swarms are blown into the river by squalls of wind, and subsequently cast ashore by the waves, I was told that this wholesale destruction of ant-life takes place annually, and that the same compact heap of dead bodies which I saw only in part, extends along the banks of the river for twelve or fifteen miles.

The forest behind Aveyros yielded me little except insects, but in these it was very rich. It is not too dense, and broad sunny paths skirted by luxuriant beds of Lycopodiums, which form attractive sporting places for insects, extend from the village to a swampy hollow or ygapó, which lies about a mile inland. Of butterflies alone I enumerated fully 300 species, captured or seen in the course of forty days within a half-hour's walk of the village. This is a greater number than is found in the whole of Europe. The only monkey I observed was the Callithrix moloch—one of the kinds called by the Indians Whaiápu-saí. It is a moderate-sized species, clothed with long brown hair, and having hands of a whitish hue. Although nearly allied to the Cebi it has none of their restless vivacity, but is a dull listless animal. It goes in small flocks of five or six individuals, running along the main boughs of the trees. One of the specimens which I obtained here was caught on a low fruit-tree at the back of our house at sunrise one morning. This was the only instance of a monkey being captured in such a position that I ever heard of. As the tree was isolated it must have descended to the ground from the neighbouring forest and walked some distance to get at it. The species is sometimes kept in a tame state by the natives: it does not make a very amusing pet, and survives captivity only a short time.

I heard that the white Cebus, the Caiarára branca, a kind of monkey I had not yet seen, and wished very much to obtain, inhabited the forests on the opposite side of the river; so one day, on an opportunity being afforded by our host going over in a large boat, I crossed to go in search of it. We were about twenty persons in all, and the boat was an old rickety affair with the gaping seams rudely stuffed with tow and pitch. In addition to the human freight we took three sheep with us, which Captain Antonio had just received from Santarem and was going to add to his new cattle farm on the other side. Ten Indian paddlers carried us quickly across. The breadth of the river could not be less than three miles, and the current was scarcely perceptible. When a boat has to cross the main Amazons, it is obliged to ascend along the banks for half a mile or more to allow for drifting by the current; in this lower part of the Tapajos this is not necessary. When about halfway, the sheep, in moving about, kicked a hole in the bottom of the boat. The passengers took the matter very coolly, although the water spouted up alarmingly, and I thought we should inevitably be swamped. Captain Antonio took off his socks to stop the leak, inviting me and the Juiz de Paz, who was one of the party, to do the same, whilst two Indians baled out the water with large cuyas. We thus managed to keep afloat until we reached our destination, when the men patched up the leak for our return journey.

The landing-place lay a short distance within the mouth of a shady inlet, on whose banks, hidden amongst the dense woods, were the houses of a few Indian and mameluco settlers. The path to the cattle farm led first through a tract of swampy forest; it then ascended a slope and emerged on a fine sweep of prairie, varied with patches of timber. The wooded portion occupied the hollows where the soil was of a rich chocolate-brown colour, and of a peaty nature. The higher grassy, undulating parts of the campo had a lighter and more sandy soil. Leaving our friends, I and José took our guns and dived into the woods in search of the monkeys. As we walked rapidly along I was very near treading on a rattlesnake, which lay stretched out nearly in a straight line on the bare sandy pathway. It made no movement to get out of the way, and I escaped the danger by a timely and sudden leap, being unable to check my steps in the hurried walk. We tried to excite the sluggish reptile by throwing handsfull of sand and sticks at it, but the only notice it took was to raise its ugly horny tail and shake its rattle. At length it began to move rather nimbly, when we despatched it by a blow on the head with a pole, not wishing to fire on account of alarming our game.

We saw nothing of the white Caiarára; we met, however, with

a flock of the common light-brown allied species (Cebus albi-frons?), and killed one as a specimen. A resident on this side of the river told us that the white kind was found further to the south, beyond Santa Cruz. The light-brown Caiarára is pretty generally distributed over the forests of the level country. I saw it very frequently on the banks of the Upper Amazons, where it was always a treat to watch a flock leaping amongst the trees, for it is the most wonderful performer in this line of the whole tribe. The troops consist of thirty or more individuals, which travel in single file. When the foremost of the flock reaches the outermost branch of an unusually lofty tree, he springs forth into the air without a moment's hesitation and alights on the dome of yielding foliage belonging to the neighbouring tree, maybe fifty feet beneath; all the rest following the example. They grasp, on falling, with hands and tail, right themselves in a moment, and then away they go along branch and bough to the next tree. The Caiarára owes its name in the Tupí language, macaw or large-headed (Acain, head, and Arára, macaw), to the disproportionate size of the head compared with the rest of the body. It is very frequently kept as a pet in houses of natives. I kept one myself for about a year, which accompanied me in my voyages and became very familiar, coming to me always on wet nights to share my blanket. It is a most restless creature, but is not playful like most of the American monkeys; the restlessness of its disposition seeming to arise from great nervous irritability and discontent. The anxious, painful, and changeable expression of its countenance, and the want of purpose in its movements, betray this. Its actions are like those of a wayward child; it does not seem happy even when it has plenty of its favourite food, bananas; but will leave its own meal to snatch the morsels out of the hands of its companions. It differs in these mental traits from its nearest kindred, for another common Cebus, found in the same parts of the forest, the Prego monkey (Cebus cirrhifer?), is a much quieter and better-tempered animal; it is full of tricks, but these are generally of a playful character.

The Caiarára keeps the house in a perpetual uproar where it is kept: when alarmed, or hungry, or excited by envy, it screams piteously; it is always, however, making some noise or other, often screwing up its mouth and uttering a succession of loud notes resembling a whistle. My little pet, when loose, used to run after me, supporting itself for some distance on its hind legs, without, however, having been taught to do it. He offended me greatly, one day, by killing, in one of his jealous fits, another and much choicer pet—the nocturnal owl-faced monkey (Nyctipithecus trivirgatus). Some one had given this a fruit, which the other coveted, so the two got to quarrelling. The Nyctipithecus fought only with its paws, clawing out and hissing like a cat; the other soon obtained the mastery, and before I could interfere, finished his rival by cracking its skull with his teeth. Upon this I got rid of him.

On recrossing the river to Aveyros in the evening, a pretty little parrot fell from a great height headlong into the water near the boat; having dropped from a flock which seemed to be fighting in the air. One of the Indians secured it for me, and I was surprised to find the bird uninjured. There had probably been a quarrel about mates, resulting in our little stranger being temporarily stunned by a blow on the head from the beak of a jealous comrade. The species was the Conurus guianensis, called by the natives Maracaná; the plumage green, with a patch of scarlet under the wings. I wished to keep the bird alive and tame it, but all our efforts to reconcile it to captivity were vain; it refused food, bit every one who went near it, and damaged its plumage in its exertions to free itself. My friends in Aveyros said that this kind of parrot never became domesticated. After trying nearly a week I was recommended to lend the intractable creature to an old Indian woman, living in the village, who was said to be a skilful bird-tamer. In two days she brought it back almost as tame as the familiar love-birds of our aviaries. I kept my little pet for upwards of two years; it learned to talk pretty well, and was considered quite a wonder as being a bird usually so difficult of domestication. I do not know what arts the old woman used: Captain Antonio said she fed it with her saliva. The chief reason why almost all animals become so wonderfully tame in the houses of the natives is, I believe, their being treated with uniform gentleness, and allowed to run at large about the rooms. Our Maracaná used to accompany us sometimes in our rambles, one of the lads carrying it on his head. One day, in the middle of a long forest road, it was missed, having clung probably to an overhanging bough and escaped into the thicket without the boy perceiving it. Three hours afterwards, on our return by the same path, a voice greeted us in a colloquial tone as we passed "Maracaná!" We looked about for some time, but could not see anything, until the word was repeated with emphasis "Mara-

caná-á!" when we espied the little truant half concealed in the
foliage of a tree. He came down and delivered himself up, evidently
as much rejoiced at the meeting as we were.

After I had obtained the two men promised, stout young
Indians, seventeen or eighteen years of age, one named Ricardo
and the other Alberto, I paid a second visit to the western side of
the river in my own canoe; being determined, if possible, to obtain
specimens of the White Cebus. We crossed over first to the mission
village, Santa Cruz, which consists of thirty or forty wretched-
looking mud huts, closely built together in three straight ugly rows
on a high gravelly bank. The place was deserted, with the exception
of two or three old men and women and a few children. A narrow
belt of wood runs behind the village; beyond this is an elevated
barren campo, with a clayey and gravelly soil. To the south, the
coast country is of a similar description; a succession of scantily-
wooded hills, bare grassy spaces, and richly-timbered hollows. We
traversed forest and campo in various directions during three days
without meeting monkeys, or indeed with anything that repaid
us the time and trouble. The soil of the district appeared too dry;
at this season of the year I had noticed, in other parts of the country, that mammals and birds resorted to the more humid areas of
forest; we therefore proceeded to explore carefully the low and
partly swampy tract along the coast to the north of Santa Cruz.
We spent two days in this way, landing at many places, and penetrating a good distance in the interior. Although unsuccessful with
regard to the White Cebus, the time was not wholly lost, as I added
several small birds of species new to my collection. On the second
evening we surprised a large flock, composed of about fifty individuals, of a curious eagle with a very long and slender hooked
beak, the Rostrhamus hamatus. They were perched on the bushes
which surrounded a shallow lagoon, separated from the river by a
belt of floating grass: my men said they fed on toads and lizards
found at the margins of pools. They formed a beautiful sight as
they flew up and wheeled about at a great height in the air. We obtained only one specimen.

Before returning to Aveyros, we paid another visit to the Jacaré
inlet, leading to Captain Antonio's cattle farm, for the sake of se-
curing further specimens of the many rare and handsome insects
found there; landing at the port of one of the settlers. The owner
of the house was not at home, and the wife, a buxom young woman,
a dark mameluca, with clear though dark complexion and fine rosy

cheeks, was preparing, in company with another stout-built Amazon, her rod and lines to go out fishing for the day's dinner. It was now the season for Tucunarés, and Senhora Joaquina showed us the fly baits used to take this kind of fish, which she had made with her own hands of parrots' feathers. The rods used are slender bamboos, and the lines made from the fibres of pine-apple leaves. It is not very common for the Indian and half-caste women to provide for themselves in the way these spirited dames were doing, although they are all expert paddlers, and very frequently cross wide rivers in their frail boats without the aid of men. It is possible that parties of Indian women, seen travelling alone in this manner, may have given rise to the fable of a nation of Amazons, invented by the first Spanish explorers of the country. Senhora Joaquina invited me and José to a Tucunaré dinner for the afternoon, and then shouldering their paddles and tucking up their skirts, the two dusky fisherwomen marched down to their canoe. We sent the two Indians into the woods to cut palm-leaves to mend the thatch of our cuberta, whilst I and José rambled through the woods which skirted the campo. On our return, we found a most bountiful spread in the house of our hostess. A spotless white cloth was laid on the mat, with a plate for each guest and a pile of fragrant newly-made farinha by the side of it. The boiled Tucunarés were soon taken from the kettles and set before us. I thought the men must be happy husbands who owned such wives as these. The Indian and memeluco women certainly do make excellent managers; they are more industrious than the men, and most of them manufacture farinha for sale on their own account, their credit always standing higher with the traders on the river than that of their male connections. I was quite surprised at the quantity of fish they had taken; there being sufficient for the whole party, including several children, two old men from a neighbouring hut, and my Indians. I made our good-natured entertainers a small present of needles and sewing-cotton, articles very much prized, and soon after we re-embarked, and again crossed the river to Aveyros.

*August 2nd.*—Left Aveyros; having resolved to ascend a branch river, the Cuparí, which enters the Tapajos about eight miles above this village, instead of going forward along the main stream.

We entered the mouth of the Cuparí on the evening of the following day (August 3rd). It was not more than a hundred yards wide, but very deep: we found no bottom in the middle with a line of eight fathoms. The banks were gloriously wooded; the familiar foliage of the cacao growing abundantly amongst the mass of other trees, reminding me of the forests of the main Amazons. We rowed for five or six miles, generally in a southeasterly direction, although the river had many abrupt bends, and stopped for the night at a settler's house, situated on a high bank, and accessible only by a flight of rude wooden steps fixed in the clayey slope. The owners were two brothers, half-breeds, who with their families shared the large roomy dwelling; one of them was a blacksmith, and we found him working with two Indian lads at his forge, in an open shed under the shade of mango trees. They were the sons of a Portuguese immigrant, who had settled here forty years previously, and married a Mundurucú woman. He must have been a far more industrious man than the majority of his countrymen who emigrate to Brazil nowadays, for there were signs of former extensive cultivation at the back of the house in groves of orange, lemon, and coffee trees, and a large plantation of cacao occupied the lower grounds.

The next morning one of the brothers brought me a beautiful opossum, which had been caught in the fowl-house a little before sunrise. It was not so large as a rat, and had soft brown fur, paler beneath and on the face, with a black stripe on each cheek. This made the third species of marsupial rat I had so far obtained: but the number of these animals is very considerable in Brazil, where they take the place of the shrews of Europe, shrew mice and, indeed, the whole of the insectivorous order of mammals, being entirely absent from Tropical America. One kind of these rat-like opossums is aquatic, and has webbed feet. The terrestrial species are nocturnal in their habits, sleeping during the day in hollow trees, and coming forth at night to prey on birds in their roosting places. It is very difficult to rear poultry in this country on account of these small opossums, scarcely a night passing, in some parts, in which the fowls are not attacked by them.

*August 5th.*—The river reminds me of some parts of the Jaburú channel, being hemmed in by two walls of forest, rising to the height of at least a hundred feet, and the outlines of the trees being concealed throughout by a dense curtain of leafy creepers. The impression of vegetable profusion and overwhelming luxuriance increases at every step. The deep and narrow valley of the Cuparí has a moister climate than the banks of the Tapajos. We have now frequent showers, whereas we left everything parched up by the sun at Aveyros.

After leaving the last sitio we advanced about eight miles, and then stopped at the house of Senhor Antonio Malagueita, a mameluco settler, whom we had been recommended to visit. His house and outbuildings were extensive, the grounds well weeded, and the whole wore an air of comfort and well-being which is very uncommon in this country. A bank of indurated white clay sloped gently up from the tree-shaded port to the house, and beds of kitchen-herbs extended on each side, with (rare sight!) rose and jasmine trees in full bloom. Senhor Antonio, a rather tall middle-aged man, with a countenance beaming with good nature, came down to the port as soon as we anchored. I was quite a stranger to him, but he had heard of my coming, and seemed to have made preparations. I never met with a heartier welcome. On entering the house, the wife, who had more of the Indian tint and features than her husband, was equally warm and frank in her greeting. Senhor Antonio had spent his younger days at Pará, and had acquired a profound respect for Englishmen. I stayed here two days. My host accompanied me in my excursions; in fact, his attentions, with those of his wife, and the host of relatives of all degrees who constituted his household, were quite troublesome, as they left me not a moment's privacy from morning till night.

We had, together, several long and successful rambles along a narrow pathway which extended several miles into the forest. I here met with a new insect pest, one which the natives may be thankful is not spread more widely over the country: it was a large brown fly of the Tabanidæ family (genus Pangonia), with a proboscis half an inch long and sharper than the finest needle. It settled on our backs by twos and threes at a time, and pricked us through our thick cotton shirts, making us start and cry out with the sudden pain. I secured a dozen or two as specimens. As an instance of the extremely confined ranges of certain species it may be mentioned that I did not find this insect in any other part of the country except along half a mile or so of this gloomy forest road.

We were amused at the excessive and almost absurd tameness of a fine Mutum or Curassow turkey, that ran about the house. It was a large glossy-black species (the Mitu tuberosa), having an orange-coloured beak, surmounted by a bean-shaped excrescence of the same hue. It seemed to consider itself as one of the family: attended at all the meals, passing from one person to another round the mat to be fed, and rubbing the sides of its head in a coaxing way against their cheeks or shoulders. At night it went to roost on a chest in a sleeping-room beside the hammock of one of the little girls, to whom it seemed particularly attached, following her wherever she went about the grounds. I found this kind of Curassow bird was very common in the forest of the Cuparí; but it is rare on the Upper Amazons, where an allied species, which has a round instead of a bean-shaped waxen excrescence on the beak (Crax globicera), is the prevailing kind. These birds in their natural state never descend from the tops of the loftiest trees, where they live in small flocks and build their nests. The Mitu tuberosa lays two rough-shelled, white eggs; it is fully as large a bird as the common turkey, but the flesh when cooked is drier and not so well flavoured. It is difficult to find the reason why these superb birds have not been reduced to domestication by the Indians, seeing that they so readily become tame. The obstacle offered by their not breeding in confinement, which is probably owing to their arboreal habits, might perhaps be overcome by repeated experiment; but for this the Indians probably had not sufficient patience or intelligence. The reason cannot lie in their insensibility to the value of such birds, for the common turkey, which has been introduced into the country, is much prized by them.

We had an unwelcome visitor whilst at anchor in the port of Antonio Malagueita. I was awoke a little after midnight, as I lay in my little cabin, by a heavy blow struck at the sides of the canoe close to my head, which was succeeded by the sound of a weighty body plunging in the water. I got up; but all was again quiet, except the cackle of fowls in our hen-coop, which hung over the side of the vessel about three feet from the cabin door. I could find no explanation of the circumstance, and, my men being all ashore, I turned in again and slept till morning. I then found my poultry loose about the canoe, and a large rent in the bottom of the hen-coop, which was about two feet from the surface of the water: a couple of fowls were missing. Senhor Antonio said the depredator was a Sucurujú (the Indian name for the Anaconda, or great water serpent—Eunectes murinus), which had for months past been haunting this part of the river, and had carried off many ducks and fowls from the ports of various houses. I was inclined to doubt the fact of a serpent striking at its prey from the water, and thought an alligator more likely to be the culprit, although we had not yet met with alligators in the river. Some days afterwards the young men belonging to the different sitios agreed together to go in search of the serpent. They began in a systematic manner, forming two parties, each embarked in three or four canoes, and starting from points several miles apart, whence they gradually approximated, searching all the little inlets on both sides the river. The reptile was found at last, sunning itself on a log at the mouth of a muddy rivulet, and despatched with harpoons. I saw it the day after it was killed: it was not a very large specimen, measuring only eighteen feet nine inches in length, and sixteen inches in circumference at the widest part of the body. I measured skins of the Anaconda afterwards, twenty-one feet in length and two feet in girth. The reptile has a most hideous appearance, owing to its being very broad in the middle and tapering abruptly at both ends. It is very abundant in some parts of the country; nowhere more so than in the Lago Grande, near Santarem, where it is often seen coiled up in the corners of farm-yards, and is detested for its habit of carrying off poultry, young calves, or whatever animal it can get within reach of.

At Ega, a large Anaconda was once near making a meal of a young lad about ten years of age, belonging to one of my neighbours. The father and his son went, as was their custom, a few miles up the Teffé to gather wild fruit; landing on a sloping sandy shore, where the boy was left to mind the canoe whilst the man entered the forest. The beaches of the Teffé form groves of wild guava and myrtle trees, and during most months of the year are partly overflown by the river. Whilst the boy was playing in the water under the shade of these trees, a huge reptile of this species stealthily wound its coils around him, unperceived until it was too late to escape. His cries brought the father quickly to the rescue; who rushed forward, and seizing the Anaconda boldly by the head, tore his jaws asunder. There appears to be no doubt that this formidable serpent grows to an enormous bulk, and lives to a great age, for I heard of specimens having been killed which measured forty-two feet in length, or double the size of the largest I had an opportunity of examining. The natives of the Amazons country universally believe in the existence of a monster water-serpent, said to be many score fathoms in length, which appears successively in different parts of the river. They call it the Mai d'agoa—the mother, or spirit, of the water. This fable, which was doubtless suggested by the occasional appearance of Sucurujús of unusually large size, takes a great variety of forms, and the wild legends form the subject of conversation amongst old and young, over the wood fires in lonely settlements.

*August 6th and 7th.*—On leaving the sitio of Antonio Malagueita we continued our way along the windings of the river, generally in a south-east and south-south-east direction, but sometimes due north, for about fifteen miles, when we stopped at the house of one Paulo Christo, a mameluco whose acquaintance I had made at Aveyros. Here we spent the night and part of the next day; doing in the morning a good five hours' work in the forest, accompanied by the owner of the place. In the afternoon of the 7th we were again under way: the river makes a bend to the east-north-east for a short distance above Paulo Christo's establishment, it then turns abruptly to the south-west, running from that direction about four miles. The hilly country of the interior then commences: the first token of it being a magnificently-wooded bluff, rising nearly straight from the water to a height of about 250 feet. The breadth of the stream hereabout was not more than sixty yards, and the forest assumed a new appearance from the abundance of the Uru-curí palm, a species which has a noble crown of broad fronds, with symmetrical rigid leaflets.

We reached, in the evening, the house of the last civilised settler on the river, Senhor Joao (John) Aracú, a wiry, active fellow and capital hunter, whom I wished to make a friend of and persuade to accompany me to the Mundurucú village and the falls of the Cuparí, some forty miles further up the river.

I stayed at the sitio of John Aracú until the 19th, and again, in descending, spent fourteen days at the same place. The situation was most favourable for collecting the natural products of the district. The forest was not crowded with underwood, and pathways led through it for many miles and in various directions. I could make no use here of our two men as hunters, so, to keep them employed whilst José and I worked daily in the woods, I set them to make a montaria under John Aracú's directions. The first day a suitable tree was found for the shell of the boat, of the kind called Itaüba amarello, the yellow variety of the stone-wood. They felled it, and shaped out of the trunk a log nineteen feet in length: this they dragged from the forest, with the help of my host's men, over a road they had previously made with cylindrical pieces of wood to act as rollers. The distance was about half a mile, and the ropes used for drawing the heavy load were tough lianas cut from the surrounding trees. This part of the work occupied about a week: the log had then to be hollowed out, which was done with strong chisels through a slit made down the whole length. The heavy portion of the task being then completed, nothing remained but to widen the opening, fit two planks for the sides and the same number of semicircular boards for the ends, make the benches, and caulk the seams.

The expanding of the log thus hollowed out is a critical operation, and not always successful, many a good shell being spoilt by its splitting or expanding irregularly. It is first reared on tressels, with the slit downwards, over a large fire, which is kept up for seven or eight hours, the process requiring unremitting attention to avoid cracks and make the plank bend with the proper dip at the two ends. Wooden straddlers, made by cleaving pieces of tough elastic wood and fixing them with wedges, are inserted into the opening, their compass being altered gradually as the work goes on, but in different degree according to the part of the boat operated upon. Our casca turned out a good one: it took a long time to cool, and was kept in shape whilst it did so by means of wooden cross-pieces. When the boat was finished it was launched with great merriment by the men, who hoisted coloured handkerchiefs for flags, and paddled it up and down the stream to try its capabilities. My people had suffered as much inconvenience from the want of a montaria as myself, so this was a day of rejoicing to all of us.

I was very successful at this place with regard to the objects of my journey. About twenty new species of fishes and a considerable number of small reptiles were added to my collection; but very few birds were met with worth preserving. A great number of the most conspicuous insects of the locality were new to me, and turned out to be species peculiar to this part of the Amazons valley. The most interesting acquisition was a large and handsome monkey, of a species I had not before met with—the white-whiskered Coaitá, or spider-monkey (Ateles marginatus). I saw a pair one day in the forest moving slowly along the branches of a lofty tree, and shot one of them; the next day John Aracú brought down another, possibly the companion. The species is of about the same size as the common black kind, of which I have given an account in a former chapter, and has a similar lean body, with limbs clothed with coarse black hair; but it differs in having the whiskers and a triangular patch on the crown of the head of a white colour. I thought the meat the best flavoured I had ever tasted. It resembled beef, but had a richer and sweeter taste. During the time of our stay in this part of the Cuparí, we could get scarcely anything but fish to eat, and as this diet ill agreed with me, three successive days of it reducing me to a state of great weakness, I was obliged to make the most of our Coaitá meat. We smoke-dried the joints instead of salting them; placing them for several hours on a framework of sticks arranged over a fire, a plan adopted by the natives to preserve fish when they have no salt, and which they call "muquiar." Meat putrefies in this climate in less than twenty-four hours, and salting is of no use, unless the pieces are cut in thin slices and dried immediately in the sun. My monkeys lasted me about a fortnight, the last joint being an arm with the clenched fist, which I used with great economy, hanging it in the intervals between my frugal meals on a nail in the cabin. Nothing but the hardest necessity could have driven me so near to cannibalism as this, but we had the greatest difficulty in obtaining here a sufficient supply of animal food. About every three days the work on the montaria had to be suspended, and all hands turned out for the day to hunt and fish, in which they were often unsuccessful, for although there was plenty of game in the forest, it was too widely scattered to be available. Ricardo and Alberto occasionally brought in a tortoise or ant-eater, which served us for one day's consumption. We made acquaintance here with many strange dishes, amongst them Iguana eggs; these are of oblong form, about an inch in length, and covered with a flexible shell. The lizard lays about two score of them in the hollows of trees. They have an oily taste; the men ate them raw, beaten up with farinha, mixing a pinch of salt in the mess; I could only do with them when mixed with Tucupí sauce, of which we had a large jar full always ready to temper unsavoury morsels.

One day as I was entomologising alone and unarmed, in a dry Ygapó, where the trees were rather wide apart and the ground coated to the depth of eight or ten inches with dead leaves, I was near coming into collision with a boa constrictor. I had just entered a little thicket to capture an insect, and whilst pinning it was rather startled by a rushing noise in the vicinity. I looked up to the sky, thinking a squall was coming on, but not a breath of wind stirred in the tree-tops. On stepping out of the bushes I met face to face a huge serpent coming down a slope, and making the dry twigs crack and fly with his weight as he moved over them. I had very frequently met with a smaller boa, the Cutim-boia, in a similar way, and knew from the habits of the family that there was no danger, so I stood my ground. On seeing me the reptile suddenly turned, and glided at an accelerated pace down the path. Wishing to take a note of his probable size and the colours and markings of his skin, I set off after him; but he increased his speed, and I was unable to get near enough for the purpose. There was very little of the serpentine movement in his course. The rapidly moving and shining body looked like a stream of brown liquid flowing over the thick bed of fallen leaves, rather than a serpent with skin of varied colours. He descended towards the lower and moister parts of the Ygapó. The huge trunk of an uprooted tree here lay across the road; this he glided over in his undeviating course, and soon after penetrated a dense swampy thicket, where of course I did not choose to follow him.

A small creek traversed the forest behind John Aracú's house, and entered the river a few yards from our anchoring place; I used to cross it twice a day, on going and returning from my hunting ground. One day early in September, I noticed that the water was two or three inches higher in the afternoon than it had been in the morning. This phenomenon was repeated the next day, and in fact daily, until the creek became dry with the continued subsidence of the Cuparí, the time of rising shifting a little from day to day. I pointed out the circumstance to John Aracú, who had not noticed it before (it was only his second year of residence in the locality), but agreed with me that it must be the "maré." Yes, the tide! the throb of the great oceanic pulse felt in this remote corner, 530 miles distant from the place where it first strikes the body of fresh water at the mouth of the Amazons. I hesitated at first at this conclusion, but on reflecting that the tide was known to be perceptible at Obydos, more than 400 miles from the sea; that at high water in the dry season a large flood from the Amazons enters the mouth of the Tapajos, and that there is but a very small difference of level between that point and the Cuparí, a fact shown by the absence of current in the dry season; I could have no doubt that this conclusion was a correct one.

The fact of the tide being felt 530 miles up the Amazons, passing from the main stream to one of its affluents 380 miles from its mouth, and thence to a branch in the third degree, is a proof of the extreme flatness of the land which forms the lower part of the Amazonian valley. This uniformity of level is shown also in the broad lake-like expanses of water formed near their mouths by the principal affluents which cross the valley to join the main river.

# TO BUILD A FIRE

## Jack London

*Jack London (1876–1916) probably lived more adventures than he ever wrote about. He was an oyster pirate with his own boat when he was sixteen years old. At seventeen he served before the mast. At twenty-one the Klondike gold fever caught him and he headed north. The vagabond eventually became a well-known foreign correspondent and author.* The Call of the Wild, White Fang, *and many short stories came out of his Alaska days—none more powerful than this one, which shows man's futile battle against the terrifying forces of nature.*

D AY had broken cold and gray, exceedingly cold and gray, when the man turned aside from the main Yukon trail and climbed the high earth-bank, where a dim and little-travelled trail led eastward through the fat spruce timberland. It was a steep bank, and he paused for breath at the top, excusing the act to himself by looking at his watch. It was nine o'clock. There was no sun nor hint of sun, though there was not a cloud in the sky. It was a clear day, and yet there seemed an intangible pall over the face of things, a subtle gloom that made the day dark, and that was due to the absence of sun. This fact did not worry the man. He was used to the lack of sun. It had been days since he had seen the sun, and he knew that a few more days must pass before that cheerful orb, due south, would just peep above the sky-line and dip immediately from view.

The man flung a look back along the way he had come. The Yukon lay a mile wide and hidden under three feet of ice. On top of this ice were as many feet of snow. It was all pure white, rolling in gentle undulations where the ice-jams of the freeze-up had formed. North and south, as far as his eye could see, it was unbroken white, save for a dark hair-line that curved and twisted from around the spruce-covered island to the south, and that curved and twisted away into the north, where it disappeared behind another spruce-covered island. This dark hair-line was the trail—the main trail—that led south five hundred miles to the Chilcoot Pass, Dyea, and salt water; and that led north seventy miles to Dawson, and still on to the north a thousand miles to Nulato, and finally to St. Michael on Bering Sea, a thousand miles and half a thousand more.

But all this—the mysterious, far-reaching hair-line trail, the absence of sun from the sky, the tremendous cold, and the strangeness and weirdness of it all—made no impression on the man. It was not because he was long used to it. He was a newcomer in the land, a *chechaquo*, and this was his first winter. The trouble with him was that he was without imagination. He was quick and alert in the things of life, but only in the things, and not in the significances. Fifty degrees below zero meant eighty-odd degrees of frost. Such fact impressed him as being cold and uncomfortable, and that was all. It did not lead him to meditate upon his frailty as a creature of temperature, and upon man's frailty in general, able only to live within certain narrow limits of heat and cold; and from there on it did not lead him to the conjectural field of immortality and man's place in the universe. Fifty degrees below zero stood for a bite of frost that hurt and that must be guarded against by the use of mittens, ear-flaps, warm moccasins, and thick socks. Fifty degrees below zero was to him just precisely fifty degrees below zero. That there should be anything more to it than that was a thought that never entered his head.

As he turned to go on, he spat speculatively. There was a sharp, explosive crackle that startled him. He spat again. And again, in the air, before it could fall to the snow, the spittle crackled. He knew that at fifty below spittle crackled on the snow, but this spittle had crackled in the air. Undoubtedly it was colder than fifty below—how much colder he did not know. But the temperature did not matter. He was bound for the old claim on the left fork of Henderson Creek, where the boys were already. They had come over across the divide from the Indian Creek country, while he had come the roundabout way to take a look at the possibilities of getting out logs in the spring from the islands in the Yukon. He would be in to camp by six o'clock; a bit after dark, it was true, but the boys would be there, a fire would be going, and a hot supper would be ready. As for lunch, he pressed his hand against the protruding bundle under his jacket. It was also under his shirt, wrapped up in a handkerchief and lying against the naked skin. It was the only way to keep the biscuits from freezing. He smiled agreeably to himself as he thought of those biscuits, each cut open and sopped in bacon grease, and each enclosing a generous slice of fried bacon.

He plunged in among the big spruce trees. The trail was faint. A foot of snow had fallen since the last sled had passed over, and he was glad he was without a sled, travelling light. In fact, he carried nothing but the lunch wrapped in the handkerchief. He was surprised, however, at the cold. It certainly was cold, he concluded, as he rubbed his numb nose and cheek-bones with his mittened hand. He was a warm-whiskered man, but the hair on his face did not protect the high cheek-bones and the eager nose that thrust itself aggressively into the frosty air.

At the man's heels trotted a dog, a big native husky, the proper wolf-dog, gray-coated and without any visible or temperamental difference from its brother, the wild wolf. The animal was depressed by the tremendous cold. It knew that it was no time for travelling. Its instinct told it a truer tale than was told to the man by the man's judgment. In reality, it was not merely colder than fifty below zero; it was colder than sixty below, than seventy below. It was seventy-five below zero. Since the freezing-point is thirty-two above zero, it meant that one hundred and seven degrees of frost obtained. The dog did not know anything about thermometers. Possibly in its brain there was no sharp consciousness of a condition of very cold such as was in the man's brain. But the brute had its instinct. It experienced a vague but menacing apprehension that subdued it and made it slink along at the man's heels, and that made it question eagerly every unwonted movement of the man as if expecting him to go into camp or to seek shelter somewhere and build a fire. The dog had learned fire, and it wanted fire, or else to burrow under the snow and cuddle its warmth away from the air.

The frozen moisture of its breathing had settled on its fur in a fine powder of frost, and especially were its jowls, muzzle, and eyelashes whitened by its crystalled breath. The man's red beard and mustache were likewise frosted, but more solidly, the deposit taking the form of ice and increasing with every warm, moist breath he exhaled. Also, the man was chewing tobacco, and the muzzle of ice held his lips so rigidly that he was unable to clear his chin when he expelled the juice. The result was that a crystal beard of the color and solidity of amber was increasing its length on his chin. If he fell down it would shatter itself, like glass, into brittle fragments. But he did not mind the appendage. It was the penalty all tobacco-chewers paid in that country, and he had been out before in two cold snaps. They had not been so cold as this, he knew, but by the spirit thermometer at Sixty Mile he knew they had been registered at fifty below and at fifty-five.

He held on through the level stretch of woods for several miles, crossed a wide flat of nigger-heads, and dropped down a bank to the frozen bed of a small stream. This was Henderson Creek, and he knew he was ten miles from the forks. He looked at his watch. It was ten o'clock. He was making four miles an hour, and he calculated that he would arrive at the forks at half-past twelve. He decided to celebrate that event by eating his lunch there.

The dog dropped in again at his heels, with a tail drooping discouragement, as the man swung along the creek-bed. The furrow of the old sled-trail was plainly visible, but a dozen inches of snow covered the marks of the last runners. In a month no man had come up or down that silent creek. The man held steadily on. He was not much given to thinking, and just then particularly he had nothing to think about save that he would eat lunch at the forks and that at six o'clock he would be in camp with the boys. There was nobody to talk to; and, had there been, speech would have been impossible because of the ice-muzzle on his mouth. So he continued monotonously to chew tobacco and to increase the length of his amber beard.

Once in a while the thought reiterated itself that it was very cold and that he had never experienced such cold. As he walked along he rubbed his cheek-bones and nose with the back of his mittened hand. He did this automatically, now and again changing hands. But rub as he would, the instant he stopped his cheek-bones went numb, and the following instant the end of his nose went numb. He was sure to frost his cheeks; he knew that, and experienced a pang of regret that he had not devised a nose-strap of the sort Bud wore in cold snaps. Such a strap passed across the cheeks, as well, and saved them. But it didn't matter much, after all. What were frosted cheeks? A bit painful, that was all; they were never serious.

Empty as the man's mind was of thoughts, he was keenly observant, and he noticed the changes in the creek, the curves and bends and timber-jams, and always he sharply noted where he placed his feet. Once, coming around a bend, he shied abruptly, like a startled horse, curved away from the place where he had been

walking, and retreated several paces back along the trail. The
creek he knew was frozen clear to the bottom,—no creek could
contain water in that arctic winter,—but he knew also that there
were springs that bubbled out from the hillsides and ran along
under the snow and on top the ice of the creek. He knew that the
coldest snaps never froze these springs, and he knew likewise their
danger. They were traps. They hid pools of water under the snow
that might be three inches deep, or three feet. Sometimes a skin of
ice half an inch thick covered them, and in turn was covered by
the snow. Sometimes there were alternate layers of water and ice-
skin, so that when one broke through he kept on breaking through
for a while, sometimes wetting himself to the waist.

That was why he had shied in such panic. He had felt the give
under his feet and heard the crackle of a snow-hidden ice-skin. And
to get his feet wet in such a temperature meant trouble and danger.
At the very least it meant delay, for he would be forced to stop
and build a fire, and under its protection to bare his feet while he
dried his socks and moccasins. He stood and studied the creek-bed
and its banks, and decided that the flow of water came from the
right. He reflected awhile, rubbing his nose and cheeks, then skirted
to the left, stepping gingerly and testing the footing for each step.
Once clear of the danger, he took a fresh chew of tobacco and
swung along at his four-mile gait.

In the course of the next two hours he came upon several similar
traps. Usually the snow above the hidden pools had a sunken, can-
died appearance that advertised the danger. Once again, however,
he had a close call; and once, suspecting danger, he compelled the
dog to go on in front. The dog did not want to go. It hung back
until the man shoved it forward, and then it went quickly across
the white, unbroken surface. Suddenly it broke through, floundered to one side, and got away to firmer footing. It had wet its
forefeet and legs, and almost immediately the water that clung to it
turned to ice. It made quick efforts to lick the ice off its legs, then
dropped down in the snow and began to bite out the ice that had
formed between the toes. This was a matter of instinct. To permit
the ice to remain would mean sore feet. It did not know this. It
merely obeyed the mysterious prompting that arose from the deep
crypts of its being. But the man knew, having achieved a judgment on the subject, and he removed the mitten from his right
hand and helped tear out the ice-particles. He did not expose his
fingers more than a minute, and was astonished at the swift numb-

ness that smote them. It certainly was cold. He pulled on the mitten hastily, and beat the hand savagely across his chest.

At twelve o'clock the day was at its brightest. Yet the sun was too far south on its winter journey to clear the horizon. The bulge of the earth intervened between it and Henderson Creek, where the man walked under a clear sky at noon and cast no shadow. At half-past twelve, to the minute, he arrived at the forks of the creek. He was pleased at the speed he had made. If he kept it up, he would certainly be with the boys by six. He unbuttoned his jacket and shirt and drew forth his lunch. The action consumed no more than a quarter of a minute, yet in that brief moment the numbness laid hold of the exposed fingers. He did not put the mitten on, but, instead, struck the fingers a dozen sharp smashes against his leg. Then he sat down on a snow-covered log to eat. The sting that followed upon the striking of his fingers against his leg ceased so quickly that he was startled. He had had no chance to take a bite of biscuit. He struck the fingers repeatedly and returned them to the mitten, baring the other hand for the purpose of eating. He tried to take a mouthful, but the ice-muzzle prevented. He had forgotten to build a fire and thaw out. He chuckled at his foolishness, and as he chuckled he noted the numbness creeping into the exposed fingers. Also, he noted that the stinging which had first come to his toes when he sat down was already passing away. He wondered whether the toes were warm or numb. He moved them inside the moccasins and decided that they were numb.

He pulled the mitten on hurriedly and stood up. He was a bit frightened. He stamped up and down until the stinging returned into the feet. It certainly was cold, was his thought. That man from Sulphur Creek had spoken the truth when telling how cold it sometimes got in the country. And he had laughed at him at the time! That showed one must not be too sure of things. There was no mistake about it, it *was* cold. He strode up and down, stamping his feet and threshing his arms, until reassured by the returning warmth. Then he got out matches and proceeded to make a fire. From the undergrowth, where high water of the previous spring had lodged a supply of seasoned twigs, he got his fire-wood. Working carefully from a small beginning, he soon had a roaring fire, over which he thawed the ice from his face and in the protection of which he ate his biscuits. For the moment the cold of space was outwitted. The dog took satisfaction in the fire, stretching out close enough for warmth and far enough away to escape being singed.

When the man had finished, he filled his pipe and took his comfortable time over a smoke. Then he pulled on his mittens, settled the ear-flaps of his cap firmly about his ears, and took the creek trail up the left fork. The dog was disappointed and yearned back toward the fire. This man did not know cold. Possibly all the generations of his ancestry had been ignorant of cold, of real cold, of cold one hundred and seven degrees below freezing-point. But the dog knew; all its ancestry knew, and it had inherited the knowledge. And it knew that it was not good to walk abroad in such fearful cold. It was the time to lie snug in a hole in the snow and wait for a curtain of cloud to be drawn across the face of outer space whence this cold came. On the other hand, there was no keen intimacy between the dog and the man. The one was the toil-slave of the other, and the only caresses it had ever received were the caresses of the whip-lash and of harsh and menacing throat-sounds that threatened the whip-lash. So the dog made no effort to communicate its apprehension to the man. It was not concerned in the welfare of the man; it was for its own sake that it yearned back toward the fire. But the man whistled, and spoke to it with the sound of whip-lashes, and the dog swung in at the man's heels and followed after.

The man took a chew of tobacco and proceeded to start a new amber beard. Also, his moist breath quickly powdered with white his mustache, eyebrows, and lashes. There did not seem to be so many springs on the left fork of the Henderson, and for half an hour the man saw no signs of any. And then it happened. At a place where there were no signs, where the soft, unbroken snow seemed to advertise solidity beneath, the man broke through. It was not deep. He wet himself halfway to the knees before he floundered out to the firm crust.

He was angry, and cursed his luck aloud. He had hoped to get into camp with the boys at six o'clock, and this would delay him an hour, for he would have to build a fire and dry out his foot-gear. This was imperative at that low temperature—he knew that much; and he turned aside to the bank, which he climbed. On top, tangled in the underbrush about the trunks of several small spruce trees, was a high-water deposit of dry fire-wood—sticks and twigs, principally, but also larger portions of seasoned branches and fine, dry, last-year's grasses. He threw down several large pieces on top of the snow. This served for a foundation and prevented the young flame from drowning itself in the snow it otherwise would melt.

The flame he got by touching a match to a small shred of birch-bark that he took from his pocket. This burned even more readily than paper. Placing it on the foundation, he fed the young flame with wisps of dry grass and with the tiniest dry twigs.

He worked slowly and carefully, keenly aware of his danger. Gradually, as the flame grew stronger, he increased the size of the twigs with which he fed it. He squatted in the snow, pulling the twigs out from their entanglement in the brush and feeding directly to the flame. He knew there must be no failure. When it is seventy-five below zero, a man must not fail in his first attempt to build a fire—that is, if his feet are wet. If his feet are dry, and he fails, he can run along the trail for half a mile and restore his circulation. But the circulation of wet and freezing feet cannot be restored by running when it is seventy-five below. No matter how fast he runs, the wet feet will freeze the harder.

All this the man knew. The old-timer on Sulphur Creek had told him about it the previous fall, and now he was appreciating the advice. Already all sensation had gone out of his feet. To build the fire he had been forced to remove his mittens, and the fingers had quickly gone numb. His pace of four miles an hour had kept his heart pumping blood to the surface of his body and to all the ex-tremities. But the instant he stopped, the action of the pump eased down. The cold of space smote the unprotected tip of the planet, and he, being on that unprotected tip, received the full force of the blow. The blood of his body recoiled before it. The blood was alive, like the dog, and like the dog it wanted to hide away and cover itself up from the fearful cold. So long as he walked four miles an hour, he pumped that blood, willy-nilly, to the surface; but now it ebbed away and sank down into the recesses of his body. The extremities were the first to feel its absence. His wet feet froze the faster, and his exposed fingers numbed the faster, though they had not yet begun to freeze. Nose and cheeks were already freez-ing, while the skin of all his body chilled as it lost its blood.

But he was safe. Toes and nose and cheeks would be only touched by the frost, for the fire was beginning to burn with strength. He was feeding it with twigs the size of his finger. In another minute he would be able to feed it with branches the size of his wrist, and then he could remove his wet foot-gear, and, while it dried, he could keep his naked feet warm by the fire, rubbing them at first, of course, with snow. The fire was a success. He was safe. He remembered the advice of the old-timer on Sulphur Creek,

and smiled. The old-timer had been very serious in laying down
the law that no man must travel alone in the Klondike after fifty
below. Well, here he was; he had had the accident; he was alone;
and he had saved himself. Those old-timers were rather womanish,
some of them, he thought. All a man had to do was to keep his
head, and he was all right. Any man who was a man could travel
alone. But it was surprising, the rapidity with which his cheeks
and nose were freezing. And he had not thought his fingers could
go lifeless in so short a time. Lifeless they were, for he could
scarcely make them move together to grip a twig, and they seemed
remote from his body and from him. When he touched a twig, he
had to look and see whether or not he had hold of it. The wires
were pretty well down between him and his finger-ends.

All of which counted for little. There was the fire, snapping
and crackling and promising life with every dancing flame. He
started to untie his moccasins. They were coated with ice; the thick
German socks were like sheaths of iron halfway to the knees; and
the moccasin strings were like rods of steel all twisted and knotted
as by some conflagration. For a moment he tugged with his numb
fingers, then, realizing the folly of it, he drew his sheath-knife.

But before he could cut the strings, it happened. It was his own
fault or, rather, his mistake. He should not have built the fire under
the spruce tree. He should have built it in the open. But it had been
easier to pull the twigs from the brush and drop them directly on
the fire. Now the tree under which he had done this carried a
weight of snow on its boughs. No wind had blown for weeks, and
each bough was fully freighted. Each time he had pulled a twig he
had communicated a slight agitation to the tree—an imperceptible
agitation, so far as he was concerned, but an agitation sufficient to
bring about the disaster. High up in the tree one bough capsized its
load of snow. This fell on the boughs beneath, capsizing them. This
process continued, spreading out and involving the whole tree. It
grew like an avalanche, and it descended without warning upon
the man and the fire, and the fire was blotted out! Where it had
burned was a mantle of fresh and disordered snow.

The man was shocked. It was as though he had just heard his
own sentence of death. For a moment he sat and stared at the spot
where the fire had been. Then he grew very calm. Perhaps the old-
timer on Sulphur Creek was right. If he had only had a trail-mate
he would have been in no danger now. The trail-mate could have
built the fire. Well, it was up to him to build the fire over again,

and this second time there must be no failure. Even if he succeeded, he would most likely lose some toes. His feet must be
badly frozen by now, and there would be some time before the
second fire was ready.

Such were his thoughts, but he did not sit and think them. He
was busy all the time they were passing through his mind. He made
a new foundation for a fire, this time in the open, where no
treacherous tree could blot it out. Next, he gathered dry grasses
and tiny twigs from the high-water flotsam. He could not bring his
fingers together to pull them out, but he was able to gather them
by the handful. In this way he got many rotten twigs and bits of
green moss that were undesirable, but it was the best he could do.
He worked methodically, even collecting an armful of the larger
branches to be used later when the fire gathered strength. And all
the while the dog sat and watched him, a certain yearning wistful-
ness in its eyes, for it looked upon him as the fire-provider, and
the fire was slow in coming.

When all was ready, the man reached in his pocket for a second
piece of birch-bark. He knew the bark was there, and, though he
could not feel it with his fingers, he could hear its crisp rustling as
he fumbled for it. Try as he would, he could not clutch hold of it.
And all the time, in his consciousness, was the knowledge that each
instant his feet were freezing. This thought tended to put him in a
panic, but he fought against it and kept calm. He pulled on his
mittens with his teeth, and threshed his arms back and forth, beating his hands with all his might against his sides. He did this sitting
down, and he stood up to do it; and all the while the dog sat in the
snow, its wolf-brush of a tail curled around warmly over its forefeet, its sharp wolf-ears pricked forward intently as it watched the
man. And the man, as he beat and threshed with his arms and hands,
felt a great surge of envy as he regarded the creature that was warm
and secure in its natural covering.

After a time he was aware of the first far-away signals of sensation in his beaten fingers. The faint tingling grew stronger till it
evolved into a stinging ache that was excruciating, but which the
man hailed with satisfaction. He stripped the mitten from his right
hand and fetched forth the birch-bark. The exposed fingers were
quickly going numb again. Next he brought out his bunch of sulphur matches. But the tremendous cold had already driven the life
out of his fingers. In his effort to separate one match from the
others, the whole bunch fell in the snow. He tried to pick it out of

the snow, but failed. The dead fingers could neither touch nor clutch. He was very careful. He drove the thought of his freezing feet, and nose, and cheeks, out of his mind, devoting his whole soul to the matches. He watched, using the sense of vision in place of that of touch, and when he saw his fingers on each side the bunch, he closed them—that is, he willed to close them, for the wires were down, and the fingers did not obey. He pulled the mitten on the right hand, and beat it fiercely against his knee. Then, with both mittened hands, he scooped the bunch of matches, along with much snow, into his lap. Yet he was no better off.

After some manipulation he managed to get the bunch between the heels of his mittened hands. In this fashion he carried it to his mouth. The ice crackled and snapped when by a violent effort he opened his mouth. He drew the lower jaw in, curled the upper lip out of the way, and scraped the bunch with his upper teeth in order to separate a match. He succeeded in getting one, which he dropped on his lap. He was no better off. He could not pick it up. Then he devised a way. He picked it up in his teeth and scratched it on his leg. Twenty times he scratched before he succeeded in lighting it. As it flamed he held it with his teeth to the birch-bark. But the burning brimstone went up his nostrils and into his lungs, causing him to cough spasmodically. The match fell into the snow and went out.

The old-timer on Sulphur Creek was right, he thought in the moment of controlled despair that ensued: after fifty below, a man should travel with a partner. He beat his hands, but failed in exciting any sensation. Suddenly he bared both hands, removing the mittens with his teeth. He caught the whole bunch between the heels of his hands. His arm-muscles not being frozen enabled him to press the hand-heels tightly against the matches. Then he scratched the bunch along his leg. It flared into flame, seventy sulphur matches at once! There was no wind to blow them out. He kept his head to one side to escape the strangling fumes, and held the blazing bunch to the birch-bark. As he so held it, he became aware of sensation in his hand. His flesh was burning. He could smell it. Deep down below the surface he could feel it. The sensation developed into pain that grew acute. And still he endured it, holding the flame of the matches clumsily to the bark that would not light readily because his own burning hands were in the way, absorbing most of the flame.

At last, when he could endure no more, he jerked his hands

apart. The blazing matches fell sizzling into the snow, but the birch-bark was alight. He began laying dry grasses and the tiniest twigs on the flame. He could not pick and choose, for he had to lift the fuel between the heels of his hands. Small pieces of rotten wood and green moss clung to the twigs, and he bit them off as well as he could with his teeth. He cherished the flame carefully and awkwardly. It meant life, and it must not perish. The withdrawal of blood from the surface of his body now made him begin to shiver, and he grew more awkward. A large piece of green moss fell squarely on the little fire. He tried to poke it out with his fingers, but his shivering frame made him poke too far, and he disrupted the nucleus of the little fire, the burning grasses and tiny twigs separating and scattering. He tried to poke them together again, but in spite of the tenseness of the effort, his shivering got away with him, and the twigs were hopelessly scattered. Each twig gushed a puff of smoke and went out. The fire-provider had failed. As he looked apathetically about him, his eyes chanced on the dog, sitting across the ruins of the fire from him, in the snow, making restless, hunching movements, slightly lifting one forefoot and then the other, shifting its weight back and forth on them with wistful eagerness.

The sight of the dog put a wild idea into his head. He remembered the tale of the man, caught in a blizzard, who killed a steer and crawled inside the carcass, and so was saved. He would kill the dog and bury his hands in the warm body until the numbness went out of them. Then he could build another fire. He spoke to the dog, calling it to him; but in his voice was a strange note of fear that frightened the animal, who had never known the man to speak in such way before. Something was the matter, and its suspicious nature sensed danger—it knew not what danger, but somewhere, somehow, in its brain arose an apprehension of the man. It flattened its ears down at the sound of the man's voice, and its restless, hunching movements and the liftings and shiftings of its forefeet became more pronounced; but it would not come to the man. He got on his hands and knees and crawled toward the dog. This unusual posture again excited suspicion, and the animal sidled mincingly away.

The man sat up in the snow for a moment and struggled for calmness. Then he pulled on his mittens, by means of his teeth, and got upon his feet. He glanced down at first in order to assure himself that he was really standing up, for the absence of sensation in his feet left him unrelated to the earth. His erect position in itself started to drive the webs of suspicion from the dog's mind; and when he spoke peremptorily, with the sound of whip-lashes in his voice, the dog rendered its customary allegiance and came to him. As it came within reaching distance, the man lost his control. His arms flashed out to the dog, and he experienced genuine surprise when he discovered that his hands could not clutch, that there was neither bend nor feeling in the fingers. He had forgotten for the moment that they were frozen and that they were freezing more and more. All this happened quickly, and before the animal could get away, he encircled its body with his arms. He sat down in the snow, and in this fashion held the dog, while it snarled and whined and struggled.

But it was all he could do, hold its body encircled in his arms and sit there. He realized that he could not kill the dog. There was no way to do it. With his helpless hands he could neither draw nor hold his sheath-knife nor throttle the animal. He released it, and it plunged wildly away, with tail between its legs, and still snarling. It halted forty feet away and surveyed him curiously, with ears sharply pricked forward. The man looked down at his hands in order to locate them, and found them hanging on the ends of his arms. It struck him as curious that one should have to use his eyes in order to find out where his hands were. He began threshing his arms back and forth, beating the mittened hands against his sides. He did this for five minutes, violently, and his heart pumped enough blood up to the surface to put a stop to his shivering. But no sensation was aroused in the hands. He had an impression that they hung like weights on the ends of his arms, but when he tried to run the impression down, he could not find it.

A certain fear of death, dull and oppressive, came to him. This fear quickly became poignant as he realized that it was no longer a mere matter of freezing his fingers and toes, or of losing his hands and feet, but that it was a matter of life and death with the chances against him. This threw him into a panic, and he turned and ran up the creek-bed along the old, dim trail. The dog joined in behind and kept up with him. He ran blindly, without intention, in fear such as he had never known in his life. Slowly, as he ploughed and floundered through the snow, he began to see things again,—the banks of the creek, the old timber-jams, the leafless aspens, and the sky. The running made him feel better. He did not shiver. Maybe, if he ran on, his feet would thaw out; and, anyway, if he ran far enough, he would reach camp and the boys. Without doubt he would lose some fingers and toes and some of his face; but the boys would take care of him, and save the rest of him when he got there. And at the same time there was another thought in his mind that said he would never get to the camp and the boys; that it was too many miles away, that the freezing had too great a start on him, and that he would soon be stiff and dead. This thought he kept in the background and refused to consider. Sometimes it pushed itself forward and demanded to be heard, but he thrust it back and strove to think of other things.

It struck him as curious that he could run at all on feet so frozen that he could not feel them when they struck the earth and took the weight of his body. He seemed to himself to skim along above the surface, and to have no connection with the earth. Somewhere he had once seen a winged Mercury, and he wondered if Mercury felt as he felt when skimming over the earth.

His theory of running until he reached camp and the boys had one flaw in it: he lacked the endurance. Several times he stumbled, and finally he tottered, crumpled up, and fell. When he tried to rise, he failed. He must sit and rest, he decided, and next time he would merely walk and keep on going. As he sat and regained his breath, he noted that he was feeling quite warm and comfortable. He was not shivering, and it even seemed that a warm glow had come to his chest and trunk. And yet, when he touched his nose or cheeks, there was no sensation. Running would not thaw them out. Nor would it thaw out his hands and feet. Then the thought came to him that the frozen portions of his body must be extending. He tried to keep this thought down, to forget it, to think of something else; he was aware of the panicky feeling that it caused, and he was afraid of the panic. But the thought asserted itself, and persisted, until it produced a vision of his body totally frozen. This was too much, and he made another wild run along the trail. Once he slowed down to a walk, but the thought of the freezing extending itself made him run again.

And all the time the dog ran with him, at his heels. When he fell down a second time, it curled its tail over its forefeet and sat in front of him, facing him, curiously eager and intent. The warmth and security of the animal angered him, and he cursed it till it flattened down its ears appeasingly. This time the shivering came more quickly upon the man. He was losing in his battle with the frost. It was creeping into his body from all sides. The thought of it drove him on, but he ran no more than a hundred feet, when he staggered and pitched headlong. It was his last panic. When he had recovered his breath and control, he sat up and entertained in his mind the conception of meeting death with dignity. However, the conception did not come to him in such terms. His idea of it was that he had been making a fool of himself, running around like a chicken with its head cut off—such was the simile that occurred to him. Well, he was bound to freeze anyway, and he might as well take it decently. With this new-found peace of mind came the first glimmerings of drowsiness. A good idea, he thought, to sleep off to death. It was like taking an anæsthetic. Freezing was not so bad as people thought. There were lots worse ways to die.

He pictured the boys finding his body next day. Suddenly he found himself with them, coming along the trail and looking for himself. And, still with them, he came around a turn in the trail and found himself lying in the snow. He did not belong with himself any more, for even then he was out of himself, standing with the boys and looking at himself in the snow. It certainly was cold, was his thought. When he got back to the States he could tell the folks what real cold was. He drifted on from this to a vision of the old-timer on Sulphur Creek. He could see him quite clearly, warm and comfortable, and smoking a pipe.

"You were right, old hoss; you were right," the man mumbled to the old-timer of Sulphur Creek.

The the man drowsed off into what seemed to him the most comfortable and satisfying sleep he had ever known. The dog sat facing him and waiting. The brief day drew to a close in a long, slow twilight. There were no signs of a fire to be made, and, besides, never in the dog's experience had it known a man to sit like that in the snow and make no fire. As the twilight drew on, its eager yearning for the fire mastered it, and with a great lifting and shifting of forefeet, it whined softly, then flattened its ears down in anticipation of being chidden by the man. But the man remained silent. Later, the dog whined loudly. And still later it crept close to the man and caught the scent of death. This made the animal bristle and back away. A little longer it delayed, howling under the stars that leaped and danced and shone brightly in the cold sky. Then it turned and trotted up the trail in the direction of the camp it knew, where were the other food-providers and fire-providers.

# HOUSE-MARTINS

## Gilbert White

*Gilbert White* (1720–1793) *so loved his birthplace at Selborne, in Hampshire, England, that he refused numerous posts that would have taken him away from there. He spent his life as curate in the small town, recording every aspect of it and the country roundabout in* The Natural History and Antiquities of Selborne, *one of the classics of nature-writing, from which these two short pieces on birds are chosen.*

A FEW house-martins begin to appear about April 16th; usually some few days later than the swallow. For some time after they appear the hirundines in general pay no attention to the business of nidification, but play and sport about either to recruit from the fatigue of their journey, if they do migrate at all, or else that their blood may recover its true tone and texture after it has been so long benumbed by the severities of winter. About the middle of May, if the weather be fine, the martin begins to think in earnest of providing a mansion for its family. The crust or shell of this nest seems to be formed of such dirt or loam as comes most readily to hand, and is tempered and wrought together with little bits of broken straws to render it tough and tenacious. As this bird often builds against a perpendicular wall without any projecting ledge under, it requires its utmost efforts to get the first foundation firmly fixed, so that it may safely carry the superstructure. On this occasion the bird not only clings with its claws, but partly supports itself by strongly inclining its tail against the wall, making that a fulcrum; and thus steadied it works and plasters the materials into the face of the brick or stone. But then, that this work may not, while it is soft and green, pull itself down by its own weight, the provident architect has prudence and forbearance enough not to advance her work too fast; but by building only in the morning, and by dedicating the rest of the day to food and amusement, gives it sufficient time to dry and

[ 673 ]

harden. About half an inch seems to be a sufficient layer for a day. Thus careful workmen when they build mud-walls (informed at first perhaps by this little bird) raise but a moderate layer at a time, and then desist, lest the work should become top-heavy, and so be ruined by its own weight. By this method in about ten or twelve days is formed an hemispheric nest with a small aperture towards the top, strong, compact, and warm; and perfectly fitted for all the purposes for which it was intended. But then nothing is more common than for the house-sparrow, as soon as the shell is finished, to seize on it as its own, to eject the owner, and to line it after its own manner.

After so much labour is bestowed in erecting a mansion, as nature seldom works in vain, martins will breed on for several years together in the same nest, where it happens to be well sheltered and secure from the injuries of weather. The shell or crust of the nest is a sort of rustic work full of knobs and protuberances on the outside; nor is the inside of those that I have examined smoothed with any exactness at all; but is rendered soft and warm and fit for incubation, by a lining of small straws, grasses, and feathers; and sometimes by a bed of moss interwoven with wool. In this nest they tread, or engender frequently during the time of building; and the hen lays from three to five white eggs.

At first, when the young are hatched, and are in a naked and helpless condition, the parent birds, with tender assiduity carry out what comes away from their young. Was it not for this affectionate cleanliness the nestlings would soon be burnt up, and destroyed in so deep and hollow a nest, by their own caustic excrement. In the quadruped creation the same neat precaution is made use of; particularly among dogs and cats, where the dams lick away what proceeds from their young. But in birds there seems to be a particular provision, that the dung of nestlings is enveloped into a tough kind of jelly, and therefore is the easier conveyed off without soiling or daubing. Yet, as nature is cleanly in all her ways, the young perform this office for themselves in a little time by thrusting their tails out at the aperture of their nest. As the young of small birds presently arrive at their full growth, they soon become impatient of confinement, and sit all day with their heads out at the orifice, where the dams, by clinging to the nest, supply them with food from morning to night. For a time the young are fed on the wing by their parents; but the feat is done by so quick and almost imperceptible a sleight, that a person must have attended very exactly to their motions before he would be able to perceive it. As soon as the young are able to shift for themselves, the dams immediately turn their thoughts to the business of another brood: while the first flight, shaken off and rejected by their nurses, congregate in great flocks, and are the birds that are seen clustering and hovering on sunny mornings and evenings round towers and steeples, and on the roofs of churches and houses. These congregatings usually begin to take place about the first week in August; therefore we may conclude that by that time the first flight is pretty well over. The young of this species do not quit their abodes all together; but the more forward birds get abroad some days before the rest. These approaching the eaves of buildings, and playing about before them, make people think that several old ones attend one nest. They are often capricious in fixing on a nesting place, beginning many edifices, and leaving them unfinished; but when once a nest is completed in a sheltered place, it serves for several seasons. Those which breed in a ready finished house get the start in hatching of those that build new by ten days or a fortnight. These industrious artificers are at their labours in the long days before four in the morning: when they fix their materials they plaster them on with their chins, moving their heads with a quick vibratory motion. They dip and wash as they fly sometimes in very hot weather, but not so frequently as swallows. It has been observed that martins usually build to a north-east or north-west aspect, that the heat of the sun may not crack and destroy their nests: but instances are also remembered where they bred for many years in vast abundance in a hot stifled inn-yard, against a wall facing to the south.

Birds in general are wise in their choice of situation: but in this neighbourhood every summer is seen a strong proof to the contrary at an house without eaves in an exposed district, where some martins build year by year in the corners of the windows. But, as the corners of these windows (which face to the south-east and south-west) are too shallow, the nests are washed down every hard rain; and yet these birds drudge on to no purpose from summer to summer, without changing their aspect or house. It is a piteous sight to see them labouring when half their nest is washed away and bringing dirt . . . 'generis lapsi sarcire ruinas'. Thus is instinct a most wonderful unequal faculty; in some instances so much above reason, in other respects so far below it! Martins love to frequent towns, especially if there are great lakes and rivers at hand; nay, they even affect the close air of London. And I have not only seen them nesting in the Borough, but even in the Strand and Fleet Street; but then it was obvious from the dinginess of their aspect that their feathers partook of the filth of that sooty atmosphere. Martins are by far the least agile of the four species; their wings and tails are short, and therefore they are not capable of such surprising turns and quick and glancing evolutions as the swallow. Accordingly they make use of a placid easy motion in a middle region of the air, seldom mounting to any great height, and never sweeping long together over the surface of the ground or water. They do not wander far for food, but affect sheltered districts, over some lake, or under some hanging wood, or in some hollow vale, especially in windy weather. They breed the latest of all the swallow kind; in 1772 they had nestlings on to October the 21st, and are never without unfledged young as late as Michaelmas.

As the summer declines the congregating flocks increase in numbers daily by the constant accession of the second broods; till at last they swarm in myriads upon myriads round the villages on the Thames, darkening the face of the sky as they frequent the aits of that river, where they roost. They retire, the bulk of them I mean, in vast flocks together about the beginning of October: but have appeared of late years in a considerable flight in this neighbourhood, for one day or two, as late as November the 3rd and 6th, after they were supposed to have been gone for more than a fortnight. They therefore withdraw with us the latest of any species. Unless these birds are very short-lived indeed, or unless they do not return to the district where they are bred, they must undergo vast devastation somehow, and somewhere; for the birds that return yearly bear no manner of proportion to the birds that retire.

House-martins are distinguished from their congeners by having their legs covered with soft downy feathers down to their toes. They are no songsters; but twitter in a pretty inward soft manner in their nests. During the time of breeding they are often greatly molested with fleas.

# SWIFTS

## Gilbert White

As the swift or black-martin is the largest of the British hirundines, so is it undoubtedly the latest comer. For I remember but one instance of its appearing before the last week in April: and in some of our late frosty, harsh springs, it has not been seen till the beginning of May. This species usually arrives in pairs.

The swift, like the sand-martin, is very defective in architecture, making no crust, or shell, for its nest; but forming it of dry grasses and feathers, very crudely and inartificially put together. With all my attention to these birds, I have never been able once to discover one in the act of collecting or carrying in materials: so that I have suspected (since their nests are exactly the same) that they sometimes usurp upon the house-sparrows, and expel them, as sparrows do the house- and sand-martin; well remembering that I have seen them squabbling together at the entrance of their holes; and the sparrows up in arms, and much disconcerted at these intruders. And yet I am assured, by a nice observer in such matters, that they do collect feathers for their nests in Andalusia; and that he has shot them with such materials in their mouths.

Swifts, like sand-martins, carry on the business of nidification quite in the dark, in crannies of castles, and towers, and steeples, and upon the tops of the walls of churches under the roof; and therefore cannot be so narrowly watched as those species that build more openly: but, from what I could ever observe, they begin nesting about the middle of May; and I have remarked, from eggs taken, that they have sat hard by June 9th. In general they haunt tall buildings, churches, and steeples, and breed only in such: yet in this village some pairs frequent the lowest and meanest cottages, and educate their young under those thatched roofs. We remember but one instance where they breed out of buildings; and that is in the sides of a deep chalk-pit near the town of Odiham, in this county, where we have seen many pairs entering the crevices, and skimming and squeaking round the precipices.

As I have regarded these amusive birds with no small attention, if I should advance something new and peculiar with respect to them, and different from all other birds, I might perhaps be credited; especially as my assertion is the result of many years' exact observation. The fact that I would advance is, that swifts tread, or copulate, on the wing; and I would wish any nice observer, that is startled at this supposition, to use his own eyes, and I think he will soon be convinced. In another class of animals, viz., the insect, nothing is so common as to see the different species of many genera in conjunction as they fly. The swift is almost continually on the wing; and as it never settles on the ground, on trees, or roofs, would seldom find opportunity for amorous rites, was it not enabled to indulge them in the air. If any person would watch these birds of a fine morning in May, as they are sailing round at a great height from the ground, he would see, every now and then, one drop on the back of another, and both of them sink down together for many fathoms with a loud piercing shriek. This I take to be the juncture when the business of generation is carrying on.

As the swift eats, drinks, collects materials for its nest, and, as it seems, propagates on the wing; it appears to live more in the air than any other bird, and to perform all functions there save those of sleeping and incubation.

This hirundo differs widely from its congeners in laying invariably but two eggs at a time, which are milk-white, long, and peaked at the small end; whereas the other species lay at each brood from four to six. It is a most alert bird, rising very early, and retiring to roost very late; and is on the wing in the height of summer at least sixteen hours. In the longest days it does not withdraw to rest till a quarter before nine in the evening, being the latest of all day birds. Just before they retire whole groups of them assemble high in the air, and squeak, and shoot about with wonderful rapidity. But this bird is never so much alive as in sultry thundery weather, when it expresses great alacrity, and calls forth all its powers. In hot mornings several, getting together in little parties, dash round the steeples and churches, squeaking as they go in a very clamorous manner; these, by nice observers, are supposed to be males, serenading their sitting hens; and not without reason, since they seldom squeak till they come close to the walls or eaves, and since those within utter at the same time a little inward note of complacency.

When the hen has sat hard all day, she rushes forth just as it is almost dark, and stretches and relieves her weary limbs, and snatches a scanty meal for a few minutes, and then returns to her duty of incubation. Swifts, when wantonly and cruelly shot while they have young, discover a little lump of insects in their mouths, which they pouch and hold under their tongue. In general they feed in a much higher district than the other species; a proof that gnats and other insects do also abound to a considerable height in the air; they also range to vast distances; since locomotion is no labour to them who are endowed with such wonderful powers of wing. Their powers seem to be in proportion to their levers; and their wings are longer in proportion than those of almost any other bird. When they mute, or ease themselves in flight, they raise their wings, and make them meet over their backs.

### The Young Dandelion

I AM a bold fellow
  As ever was seen,
With my shield of yellow,
  In the grass green.

You may uproot me
  From field and from lane,
Trample me, cull me—
  I spring up again.

I never flinch, sir,
  Wherever I dwell,
Give me an inch, sir,
  I'll soon take an ell.

Drive me from garden,
  In anger and pride,
I'll thrive and harden
  By the roadside.

                *Dinah Mulock Craik*

# THE GREAT RUN

## John Coulson Tregarthen

*The huntsman has told his story many times—not so the*
*hunted. But here we see the chase through the eyes of the fox.*
*Cornwall, where Tregarthen was born in 1854, remained the*
*wildest part of England for many years—deer, fox, otter, and*
*badger were hunted there. With his sympathetic understand-*
*ing of animals and gift for story-telling, it was natural for Tre-*
*garthen to write of such things, but from the animal's view-*
*point. In* The Life Story of a Fox, *which includes "The Great*
*Run," he lets the fox tell his own tale.*

THE hunting season next but one after the death of the Hound is
memorable because of the new huntsman, whose energy,
knowledge and perseverance were a revelation to us. Between him
and his predecessor there was a difference as great as that between
the brindled Hound and old Shep. Whilst Yoicks the First was with
us we used to look on him as a terror, and it was only after he was
gone that we learnt to appreciate how gentle a persecutor he really
was. It was his custom to sit his Horse on the outskirts of the cover,
whilst the Hounds idled the time away inside or chivied the Rabbits.
As a rule, a few of them would dawdle behind in each cover, and do
a little hunting on their own account; so that by the end of the day
Yoicks would find himself ever so many couples short. To collect
the loiterers, he used to stand on the tor and blow his horn for an
hour at a stretch; but it was of little good, and he generally went his
way without them. I have seen Hounds going home at all hours of
the night. Naturally they stumbled on us sometimes, and I am far
from saying that when scent was breast-high they could not swing
along and account for the best of us; but these occasions were rare,
and on poor scenting days, they did not seem to try at all.

We soon discovered what a friend we had lost when Yoicks the
Second took over the horn, and put a term to the good old days.

Instead of yelling to the Hounds from the outskirts, he would enter the brake afoot, and have them all round him. The difference this made was amazing. With an occasional word to cheer them, the Hounds kept on searching as if they meant to find us; and find us they did, and nimble we had to be to get out of the cover alive. Then, too, there was no stealing away unobserved by the new whippers-in, no hanging back on the part of the Hounds. The scream that told a Fox had gone away, brought every Hound on his line; and then with the improved dash they showed, only the fleetest and staunchest of us could live before them. I cannot say how many Foxes they killed before the year was out, but it must have been a large number; and to my grief, my little mate was among them.

Had the chase been left absolutely between us and the Hounds, as for the sake of fair play I think it ought to be, we should have beaten them again and again by ruses known to ourselves; but it was not. When Hounds were at fault, the huntsman was generally on the spot to assist them, and seldom without success, for the wide casts he made would have caused old Yoicks to stand agape. To do the new huntsman justice, I must say that I do not think he interfered until the Hounds had done all they knew to help themselves.

I believe it was so the day they found me on the hill, and followed close on my heels to the dunes. There I turned short along a trough between the sand-hills, hoping they would overrun my line, and so they did. The huntsman was with them, but as I heard neither the horn nor his voice between their losing the scent and the renewal of the full cry, I have always thought they put themselves right without his assistance. Later in the run, I gave them the slip in the fen; and not on that occasion only, but twice subsequently. Twenty couple of Hounds were no match for me in the maze of overgrown waterways near the mere, to which I always led them. It was no easy matter, however, to shake them off in the open country away from the fen, as I discovered later in the same season.

One morning I lay on the moor, and Hounds found me by working up to my kennel along the line by which I had reached it. Fortunately I heard them coming, and was up and away with a good start, though not before I was viewed. My first thought was to try and reach the fen; and for a while I headed that way, but a southerly gale, impossible to face, swept the moor and compelled me to turn and run before it. Nothing short of dire necessity would have induced me to do this, as there was not an earth or a clitter of rocks on the miles of undulating waste that stretched between me and the cliffs. Nevertheless, I did not doubt that my fleetness and endurance would be more than a match for my pursuers, formidable as they had become.

For a long time my confidence in my powers did not waver, but I began to have misgivings on seeing the pack sweep up the wide slope beyond the jagged ridge at such a pace that it seemed as if the terrible burst of speed at which we had crossed the miles of heather had made no difference to them. Whether it really was so, I cannot, of course, say; but I was conscious of failing strength, and greatly feared I might be pulled down before I could reach the cliffs. When yet a mile separated me from them, the Hounds had got danger- ously near, and, despite my utmost efforts, were gaining foot by foot as the rocky pinnacles ahead grew nearer. Though the boulders strewing the sward were in my favor, the leading Hound was nearly as clever in threading them as I was, and nothing apparently could save me from his jaws. At last he was so close to my brush that I had no time to choose a way down the cliff, and but for a narrow ledge which happened to be within reach, I must have fallen head- long into the sea. The ledge gained, I immediately dropped to that beneath, and so to the last one, below which the cliff fell sheer to the foam. There I remained out of sight of the maddened Hounds on the brink of the cliff, and, as I hoped, safe from further molestation.

Presently, however, a stone fell on my shelf, and then another; and, looking up, I saw a madcap of a Terrier leaping from one ledge to the next, from the intense eagerness in his face, evidently deter- mined to reach me. Seeing that to remain where I was would mean death to both, I sprang at great risk across a wide chasm to the only shelf within my reach. The crumbling edge gave as I alighted on it, and I was nearly gone, but after a life-and-death scramble I man- aged to save myself from falling and to gain a lodgment. Whilst I had been struggling to get foothold here, the Terrier had reached the ledge I had quitted; and though he could not come at me on account of the width of the chasm, he stood there trembling in every limb, yapping as well as he could for shortness of breath, until I felt sick of the sound of his voice.

This went on, as it seemed, for hours—so long, indeed, that I began to fear we should spend the night there facing one another; but at last I saw a man being lowered by a rope down the face of the cliff. Down, down he came, very quietly until he reached the ledge where the Terrier was; and then he shouted "Hold hard!" It was Yoicks himself. Scarcely were his feet at rest before he saw me. The instant he did so he shook his fist at me, and in a voice that made me hug the rock, stuttered: "This is the third or fourth time you've beaten me, Mr. Fox, but look to yourself, for I mean to have that fine brush of yours before the season is over." Then he picked up the Terrier with one hand, and holding the rope with the other, was hauled up out of sight.

I was truly glad to be rid of this terrible man, but my position was not an enviable one. If my shelf was difficult to gain, the ledge from which I had reached it was much more difficult to regain. Not a circumstance was in my favor. The take-off was bad: the ledge opposite was higher than the shelf where I stood; and my muscles, stiff from the chase, were getting more rigid as I grew colder. For this reason, it would be wiser to make the attempt the moment the huntsman was out of sight, instead of deferring it until the sun had set. To tell the truth, it was not the approach of night I awaited. I shrank from the ordeal, though I knew it had to be faced. At last I braced my self for the spring, only to hesitate again before the desperate leap. Once more I gathered myself on the brink of the shelf; and, putting forth all my strength, so far cleared the chasm as to get my forepaws over the margin of the ledge. Even then I feared the waves would have me, but the roughness of the rock enabled me by a frantic effort to drag my dangling body into a position of safety. There I stayed awhile to steady myself for the ascent, which, full of difficulties though it was, I made without mishap. On gaining the summit, I set out for the earth as fast as my tired limbs would carry me, and found its safe shelter very welcome after the dangers I had passed.

I have dwelt on this incident because I have seldom been driven to such straits; and yet the peril to which I was then exposed was less deadly than that which threatened me in what I consider to be the run of my life. This I will now endeavor to describe; but for a proper understanding of it, I must first speak a little of the long ramble on the February night that preceded it.

It was the pairing season, and I was in quest of a new mate. Too impatient to await the dusk, I left my kennel whilst the clump of firs on our hill looked black against the crimson west, and travelled so fast that soon after the stars were fully out, I was breasting the hill that had hitherto marked the limit of my wanderings. From its crest I overlooked a valley divided by walls into small fields, and dotted with the lights of three homesteads. A Dog barked in a farm-

yard that I skirted; but I kept straight on, and, crossing the silent
meads, struck and followed a track that rains had zigzagged on the
flank of the opposite hill. It led me to a craggy ridge, where I called
and listened and called again, but the only response was the mocking echo of my own voice.

On and on I journeyed, traversing at one place a lonely beach,
noisy with the roar of the troubled sea, at another a sheltered woodland, where dead leaves crackled underfoot; nor did I check my
pace until from a lofty hilltop far beyond, a most unfamiliar spectacle met my gaze. For a while it made me forget the object of my
journey.

On more than one dark night I had seen a brake sparkling with
glowworms, but what were their pale fires or the twinklings of the
frosty stars to the array of brilliant lights below me? At first I was
lost in wonderment, but gradually I became aware that I was looking down upon the haunts of men. It seemed incredible that they
should be crowded together as closely as the cells of a wasps' comb;
but so they were. What I had mistaken for a mist arising from the
wide creek was the smoke from a thousand chimneys, and the subdued uproar that jarred with the murmur of the waves was the
hubbub of a multitude.

In disgust I turned my brush on this human hive with its swarm
of occupants; and, keeping to the ridge of a wooded slope that ran
down to an estuary, I regained the unfrequented country-side, and
resumed my quest. But why recount the stages of my bootless search
through the long night? As the hours passed, I wearied more and
more of wandering and calling; and at the approach of dawn, disappointed and forlorn, I gave it up and began to look about me for
a kennel to spend the day in. But every break and coppice seemed
uninviting. One by one I passed them by, and in the end, bent my
steps towards a solitary peak that had the sickle moon above it. Two
slopes rose between, and before I reached the base of the hill beyond
the darkness had paled. In the gray light I hurried up the grassy
steep, till, threading the furze above, I gained the bare rocks of the
wind-swept summit.

Presently a faint flush suffused the eastern sky, and, spreading,
touched the clouds with rose, and awoke the slumbering color of
the hills. Then the glowing rim of the sun showed above the sea,
grew and grew until the whole disc showed like a ball of fire on
the horizon.

Turning, I searched the gilded crags for some known landmark, and there in the distance my eyes lit on the unmistakable crest of the old tor. With a clear knowledge of my whereabouts—without which no Fox betakes himself in content to a strange kennel—I sought and found a sheltered spot amongst the rocks in the full sunlight. There I lay and licked my pads, my glossy coat, and my beautiful ruffle; for I was in full courting attire. This done, I curled up on the heather and tried to forget my disappointment.

Sleep was long in coming, as, indeed, it always is when ten or a dozen miles separate me from my own country; but by degrees I became less and less conscious of the light and of the wind whistling about the column of rock above me. How long I slept I cannot say, but I awoke with a fearful start, wondering where I was, and what I had heard. Only some wild gust about the peak or scream of passing bird, thought I, as I stretched myself on the edge of the furze hard by my couch. I was about to give my coat a shake and lie down again, when the crack of a whip broke the stillness, followed, to my horror, by the cries with which the huntsman sends the Hounds into cover. The situation was disconcerting, but I had not an instant to lose if I was to get away alive. Already, if my ears did not deceive me, the Hounds were in the brake and my escape imperilled. With the utmost caution I made my way down, halting now and again to let a Hound cross in front of me; and near the bottom, I actually followed in the wake of another until he turned aside from my path.

When I had reached the edge of the cover I stopped to reconnoitre, despite the clamor behind me; and then, believing the coast clear, took to the open grassy slope leading to the valley. I had gone perhaps a hundred yards when there was a shrill scream that must have startled the whole countryside. You would have thought I had been shot had you seen me spring from the ground, but the next instant I steadied myself and settled into my stride, conscious that nerve and muscle must be husbanded for the run before me.

From near the crest of the opposing slope I looked back at my pursuers. The leading Hounds were crossing the stream just in front of the main body of the pack; a crowd of red-coats was thundering down the hill, but the only man I heeded among them all was the lean, wiry huntsman there in his usual place between the "field" and the hindmost Hounds. The speed at which they were coming on confirmed my fear that I was leaving a burning scent; but there was no help for it; my only hope, until I had passed out of this strange country, was in my pace. My way led across the heart of a level moor, but the wind blew in my teeth and caused me to swerve to the left from the line I should otherwise have taken.

The heathery waste now fell away before me to a sudden valley, where a ploughman stopped his team to mock me, but I kept straight towards the corner I was heading for, regardless of his shouting. As I left the field—and it was not a very big one—a couple of Hounds showed at the gap where I had entered it. They were much too close behind me; but though I led my pursuers over mile after mile of undulating country as fast as I could gallop, I did not add to my lead, and they were not more than a couple of gunshots behind when I passed a roofless linhay on a barren upland.

There, through a depression in the ground, I caught a glimpse of the sea—my last, thought I, with a pang; but there was no moment for pause or regret.

I kept on towards the cliffs, looking eagerly about me for some earth in which I might take refuge. Not one did I see; and, strange as it may seem, it was an obstacle that finally befriended me, for in the next valley I came on a long, high wall which I must surmount or be taken. At the first attempt I fell back, and thought I was lost; but at the second, by a sidelong leap, and with the help of my brush, I just managed to reach the top, dragging myself up before the Hounds could seize me and pull me back. They did not follow, and I kept wondering why, until I realized they could not climb the wall. I heard their maddened cries as I sped over a wide, wide field, dotted with groups of tall trees, nor did I lose them until I had crossed a broad stream, which I know now to be the lower reach of our salmon river.

Issuing from a thicket of evergreens on the further bank, I passed under a spreading cedar, and came upon a lawn in front of a mansion. The place seemed deserted, but a Peacock which flew in affright to the top of a stone gateway filled my ears with its harsh cries as I threaded a perfect maze of yew-bordered paths, and at length reached a boundary-wall even higher than the first. Seeing that it was beyond my powers to climb, I ran along its base until I came to a big gate, through which I passed, in spite of the sour-visaged crone at the lodge who shook her apron at me and tried to drive me back.

With the chart of the country still clear in my brain, I went on and on, and had succeeded in reaching the springy sward that slopes gently to the cliffs when, to my dismay, I again heard the Hounds coming after me. I say dismay, not surprise, because, though I had begun to hope that I had shaken them off, I was well aware that nothing but night would make that terrible huntsman desist from the pursuit of a sinking Fox which had beaten him thrice before. He it was who had put them afresh on my line, and now he was once more up with them, for I caught a glimpse of him and of his white Horse just before I dropped over the edge of the cliff. Down its steep face I leapt from rock to rock, until I gained the strip of turf on the edge of the lower cliff. I sped along this as fast as my failing strength would permit; and after a time passing the old drinking-place amongst the reeds, I came on the little playground where I had gambolled as a cub. What happy nights I had spent on the little green across which I was now laboring, a bedraggled fugitive, with the clamor of the Hounds ever louder and louder in my ears! Though I glanced at the cobwebbed mouth of the hole where I was littered, I knew I should find no safe refuge in such a shallow earth; and, distressed as I was, I preferred to struggle on and take my chance.

Deem me a coward if you will, but I own to a great fear then in my heart; yet my brain was hard at work to discover some means of baffling my pursuers. Nothing but a ruse put into instant execution could save me, and it was but a stroke of the good luck I have always enjoyed that with the need should come the opportunity.

I can see now the rude path athwart the face of the cliff along which I hurried and doubled, so that I might gain a lower, hidden track before the Hounds could intercept me. As soon as I had leapt to this second path, they came on. It was an anxious moment when the leading Hounds reached the parting of the ways, for in my despair I had resolved on a desperate step. Had but a single Hound followed me, I should have dropped over the dizzy edge into the surging sea below. Luckily for me, they all took the upper track and, as I expected, on overrunning the scent, ceased their excited clamor.

In the silence that ensued, I kept stealing along the shelf, fearful the while of being viewed by the riders on the edge of the upper cliff. At every exposed place I had to pass, closely as I hugged the furze, I dreaded to hear that awful scream that would announce my discovery; but nothing reached my ears except the voice of the huntsman, who had now come to the help of the Hounds.

Abreast of the headland, I left the sea, and made my way along the bed of a little stream; but at what a pace! A Hedgehog might travel wellnigh as fast. On my left lay the fen; but I was too distressed to seek it. Across the reedy plain was the sett which had been my point when I left my kennel on the peak; but though it was almost within sight, I felt that I had not the strength to reach it. I might, however, gain the screes, and for this I headed. What a time I was in reaching the wood! and what a weary way it was through it to the rocks!

At length I passed under the last of the pines, and came within sight of my goal, only, however, to find that I had been forestalled. A couple of red-coats seated on the boulders sprang to their feet on viewing me, and yelled at the top of their voices. I never in all my life heard such a row as they made. Whether their shouts reached the ears of the huntsman or not I do not know; I was too much exhausted, however, to face the hullabaloo, and turned off towards the sett. I had not a doubt that it would be open; was it in my power to reach it? I dragged myself over the upper part of the fen, too far gone greatly to heed the Hounds, whom I thought I could hear at times. Past the old trysting-place I crawled to the river. I scarce can tell how I managed to swim the swollen water; but I did, and, what is more, I wormed myself along and along until at last I reached the sett.

Stopped! For a moment my heart failed me, and I lay down before the fresh-tainted faggots to await my fate. Yet, terrible as my extremity was, I could not remain there when I still had strength to struggle a little farther. Even then, life was too sweet to surrender whilst stiffening muscles were not too rigid to obey the will. So I staggered to the edge of the furze; and, catching the whimper of Hounds as I neared a big boulder, summoned all my little remaining force, till by a desperate effort, I succeeded in scrambling to the top. It was there the vixen used to sit and watch the cubs at play. The hollow crown held a little water, which I lapped before crouching as low as my arched back would let me, and thus refreshed, I prepared to face my fate.

I watched the pack as it crossed the marsh, and saw it take to the water followed by the Horse of the huntsman, who swam by its side. There was no scent—at least, the Hounds did not own to any—but the huntsman knew I should make for home, and he was aware that I had been stopped out. On reaching the earth he stopped, took a hurried glance at the faggots, and then led his Horse past me up the hill. "Wind him, my boys!" he kept shouting to the weary Hounds as he brushed through the furze. His voice grew fainter and fainter, but whether he went over the crest of the hill I do not know, because I could not turn my head to see. At least, he went so far that I felt sure he would not return. He did; what is more, he and his Horse came and stood abreast the rock that befriended me. Presently the Horse's pricked ears and fixed gaze betrayed my forlorn refuge. The huntsman turned his head, and I was discovered.

My relentless pursuer looked at me, and I met his eye unflinchingly to try and fathom his intent. I could not. Mercy I did not expect; yet man had given me my life once, and might again. But my former friend was a kind-hearted man, willing himself to suffer rather than ill-treat a helpless creature; while this was a merciless wretch who had cried "Whoo-whoop!" over my little mate, who had hounded many another Fox to death, and who would certainly not forego the crowning success of this great run. So I expected every moment to hear him shout, to hear him cheer the hungry Hounds on their helpless victim. He was silent, however—silent through what seemed to me a lifetime of despair and dawning hope, and when at last his lips did move, he simply muttered, "Poor devil!"

Then he went to the earth, pulled out the faggots, and rode slowly away, leaving me alone with the night.

### The Trees

Time is never wasted listening to the trees;
  If to heaven so grandly we arose as these,
Holding toward each other half their kindly grace,
Haply we were worthier of our human place.

Bending down to meet you on the hillside path,
Birch and oak and maple each his welcome hath;
Each his own fine cadence, his familiar word,
By the ear accustomed, always plainly heard.

Every tree gives answer to some different mood,
This one helps you climbing; that for rest is good;
Beckoning friends, companions, sentinels they are;
Good to live and die with, good to greet afar.

*Lucy Larcom*

# A DAY AMONG THE SÉRACS

## John Tyndall

*One of the most versatile and inspiring of British scientific
men, Tyndall (1820–1893) wrestled with poverty for many
years until his brilliant research in the field of magnetism won
him the professorship of natural history at the Royal Institu-
tion, and many honors. Visiting Switzerland to study the motion of glaciers, he became the first man to ascend the Alpine
peak, the Weisshorn. In this piece about the ice-towers of a
glacier, he shows plainly his delight in combining mountain-
climbing with scientific research.*

HAVING fixed my headquarters at the Pavilion of the Montanvert, I was engaged for nearly six weeks during the summer
of 1857 in making observations on the Mer de Glace and its tributaries. Throughout this time I had the advantage of the able and
unremitting assistance of my friend, Dr. Thomas Hirst, who kindly
undertook, in most cases, the measurement of the motion of the
glacier. My permanent guide, Edouard Simond, an intelligent and
trustworthy man, was assistant on these occasions, and having
arranged with Dr. Hirst the measurements required to be made, it
was my custom to leave the execution of them to him, and to spend
much of my time alone upon the glaciers. Days have thus been
occupied amid the confusion of the Glacier du Géant, at the base
of the great icefall of La Noire, in trying to connect the veined
structure of the glacier with the stratification of its *névé;* and often,
after wandering almost unconsciously from peak to peak and from
hollow to hollow, I have found myself, as the day was waning, in
places from which it required a sound axe and a vigorous stroke to
set me free.

This practice gradually developed my powers of dealing with
the difficulties of the glacier. On some occasions, however, I found
the assistance of a companion necessary, and at such times it was

my habit to take with me a hardy boy named Balmat, who was attached at the time to the hotel at the Montanvert. He could climb like a cat, and one of our first expeditions together was to a point above Trelaporte, from which a magnificent view of the entire glacier is obtained. This point lies to the left of a remarkable cleft in the mountain side, beneath the Aiguille de Charmoz, which is sure to attract the traveller's attention on looking upwards from the Montanvert. We reached the place through a precipitous *couloir* on the Montanvert side of the mountain, and while two chamois watched us from the crags above, we made our observations, and ended our survey by pledging the health of Forbes and other explorers of the Alps.

We descended from the eminence by a different route, and during both ascent and descent I had occasion to admire the courage and caution of my young companion, and the extraordinary cohesive force by which he clung to the rock. I ought perhaps to mention his *firmness* also. He evidently felt himself responsible for my safety, and once when I asserted my independence so far as to attempt descending a kind of "chimney," which, though rather dangerous looking, I considered to be practicable, he sprang to my side, and, with outstretched arm and ringing voice, exclaimed, *"Monsieur, je vous défends de passer par là!"*

Anxious to avoid the inconvenience which the rules of the Chamouni guides were calculated to impose upon me, my aim, from the first, was to render myself as far as possible independent of their assistance. Wishing to explore the slopes of the Col du Géant, not for the purpose of crossing into Piedmont, but to examine the fine ice sections which it exhibits, and to trace amid its chasms the gradual conversion of the snow into ice, I at first thought of attempting the ascent of the col alone; but "le petit Balmat," as my host at the Montanvert always named him, acquitted himself so well on the occasion referred to, that I thought he would make a suitable companion. On naming the project to him he eagerly embraced my proposal; in fact, he said he was willing to try Mont Blanc with me if I desired it.

On the morning of Friday, July the 24th, we accordingly set off for the Tacul, I making, as we ascended, such few observations as lay in our way. The sun shone gloriously upon the mountains, and gleamed by reflection from the surface of the glacier. Looked at through a pair of very dark spectacles, the scene was exceedingly striking and instructive. Terraces of snow clung to the moun-

tains, exposing, here and there, high vertical sections, which cast
dense shadows upon the adjacent plateaux. The glacier was thrown
into heaps and "hummocks," with their tops glistening with white,
silvery light, and their sides intensely shaded. When the lateral light
was quite shut out, and all that reached the eyes had to pass through
the spectacles, the contrast between light and shade was much
stronger than when the glacier was viewed by the broad light of
day. In fact, the shadows were no longer grey merely, but black; a
similar augmentation of contrast towards the close of day explains
the fact that the "Dirt Bands" of the Mer de Glace are best seen by
twilight.

A gentleman had started in the morning to cross the col, accompanied by two strong guides. We met a man returning from the
Jardin, who told us that he had seen the party that preceded us;
that they had been detained a long time amid the séracs, and that
our ascending without ladders was quite out of the question. As we
approached the Tacul, my lynx-eyed little companion thought he
could see the travellers; but on looking through the telescope, he
found that he was mistaken. However, he continued to range with
the glass over the snowy slopes of the col, and at length exclaimed,
"*Je les vois, tous les trois!*"—the *Monsieur* in the middle, and a guide
before and behind. They seemed like three black specks upon the
shoulders of the Giant; below them was the vast ice-cascade, resembling the foam of ten Niagaras placed end to end and stiffened
into rest, while the travellers seemed to walk upon a floor as smooth
as polished Carrara marble. Here and there, however, its uniformity
was broken by vertical faults, exposing precipices of the strati-
fied *névé*. On pointing my opera-glass downwards and looking
obliquely through it at the pass and mountains, every spike of rock
became a pointed flame, every snow patch resting on the brown
rock, every rock protruding from the white snow, had its fringe
of glory which no artist could imitate. If beauty of colouring, instead of sharpness of outline, were the thing desired, nothing could
be more magnificent than this resolution of the solar light by the
virtual prisms formed by the lenses of the opera-glass.

On an old moraine near the Tacul, piled up centuries ago by
the Glacier de Léchaud, immense masses of granite are thrown
confusedly together; and one enormous slab is so cast over a number of others as to form a kind of sheltered grotto, which we proposed to make our resting-place for the night. Having deposited
our loads here, I proceeded to the icefall of the Talèfre, while my

companion set out towards the Couvercle in search of firewood. I walked round the base of the cascade, and climbed up among its riven pinnacles, examining the structure as I ascended. The hollow rumble of the rocks as they fell into the crevasses was incessant. From holes in the ice-cliffs clear cataracts gushed, coming I knew not whence, and going I knew not whither. Sometimes the deep gurgle of sub-glacial water was heard, far down in the ice. The resonance of the water as it fell into shafts struck me suddenly at intervals on turning corners, and seemed, in each case, as if a new torrent had bounded into life. Streams flowed through deep channels which they themselves had worn, revealing beautifully the "ribboned structure." At the further side of the Glacier de Léchaud the Capucin Rock stood, like a preacher; and below him a fantastic group of granite pinnacles suggested the idea of a congregation. The outlines of some of the ice-cliffs were also very singular; and it needed but a slight effort of the imagination to people the place with natural sculpture.

At six o'clock, the shrill whistle of my companion announced that our time of meeting was come. He had found some wood— dry twigs of rhododendrons, and a couple of heavy stumps of juniper. I shouldered the largest of the latter, while he strapped his twigs on his back, and led the way to the Tacul. The sun shot his oblique rays against us over the heights of Charmoz, and cast our shadows far up the glacier. It was a pleasant time. Ministering thus to our own wants, we felt all the strength of independence as we strode over the ice. With body and mind in perfect order, the conscious vigour of existence was itself a sufficient joy. We filled our saucepan, which Balmat named "a machine," with the clear water of the glacier, and bore it to our cavern, where the fire was soon crackling under the machine. I was assailed by the smoke, which set my eyes dripping tears; but this cleared away when the fire brightened, and we boiled our chocolate and made a comfortable evening meal. I afterwards clambered up the moraine to watch the tints which the setting sun threw upon the mountains; clouds floated round the Aiguille de Charmoz, and were changed from grey to red, and from red to grey, as the density of the masses varied. The shadows of the isolated peaks and pinnacles were drawn, at times, in black bands across the clouds; and the Aiguille du Moine smiled and frowned alternately, as sunshine and shade fell upon its crags. One high snow-peak alone enjoyed the unaltered radiance of the sinking day: the sunshine never forsook it,

but glowed there, like the steady light of love, while a kind of co-
quetry was carried on between the atmosphere and the surrounding
mountains. The notched summits of the Grande and Petite Jorasse
leaned peacefully against the blue firmament. The highest mountain
crags were cleft, in some cases, into fantastic forms; single pillars
stood out from all else, like lonely watchers, over the mountain
scene; while little red clouds playfully embraced them at intervals,
and converted them into pillars of fire. The sun at length departed,
and all became cold and grey upon the mountains; but a brief
secondary glow came afterwards, and warmed up the brown cliffs
once more. I descended the moraine, the smell of the smoke guiding
me towards the rock under which I was to pass the night. I stood
in front of it; and, had I been a painter, I had a capital subject. A fire
was burning at the mouth of the grotto, reddening with its glare
the darkness of the interior; beside the fire sat my little companion,
with a tall, conical, red night-cap drawn completely over his ears;
our saucepan was bubbling on the fire; he watched it meditatively,
adding at times a twig, which sprang immediately into flame, and
strengthened the glow upon his countenance; he looked, in fact,
more like a demon of the ice world than a being of ordinary flesh
and blood. I had been recommended to take a bit of a tallow candle
with me to rub my face with, as a protection against the sun; by
the light of this we spread our rugs, lay down upon them, and
wrapped them round us.

The countless noises heard upon the glacier during the day were
now stilled, and dead silence ruled the ice world; the roar of an
occasional avalanche, however, shooting down the flanks of Mont
Mallet broke upon us with startling energy. I did not sleep till towards four o'clock in the morning, when I dozed, and dreamed,
and mingled my actual condition with my dream. I thought I was
in company with a clergyman, for whom I entertained a strong
affection when a boy, and that he wished me to go home with him.
I wished to decline, as I felt weary and sleepy through some unexplained cause. I went, however, but on entering the door found
that the house was full of company. The weight upon my brain
became doubly manifest: "This will never do," I said, "I must return." The effort to do this brought me to my senses, and I found
my head weary enough upon the clay of the old moraine, my ribs
pressed closely against a block of granite, and my feet amid sundry
fragments of the same material. It was nearly five o'clock on Saturday the 25th when I arose; my companion quickly followed my

example. He also had slept but little, and once or twice during the night I fancied I could feel him shiver. We were, however, well protected from the cold. The high moraine of the Glacier de Léchaud was on one side, that of the Glacier du Géant on the other, while the cliffs of Mont Tacul formed the third side of a triangle, which completely sheltered us from the sharper action of the wind. At times the calm was perfect, and I felt almost too warm; then again a searching wind would enter the grotto, and cause the skin to shrink on all exposed parts of the body. It had frozen hard, and to obtain water for washing I had to break through a sheet of ice which coated one of the pools upon the glacier.

In a few minutes our juniper fire was flaming and crackling briskly and cheerily; we made our chocolate and breakfasted. My companion emptied the contents of a small brandy bottle into my flask, which, however, was too small to hold it all, and on the principle, I suppose, of avoiding waste, he drank what remained. It was not much, but sufficient to muddle his brain, and to make him sluggish and drowsy for a time. We put the necessary food in our knapsacks and faced our task; first ascending the Glacier du Tacul along its eastern side, until we came to the base of the séracs. The vast mass of snow collected on the plateau of the Col du Géant, and compressed to ice by its own weight, reaches the throat of the valley, which stretches from the rocks called Le Rognon to the promontory of the Aiguille Noire. Through this defile it is forced, falling steeply, and forming one of the grandest ice-cascades in the Alps. At the summit it is broken into transverse chasms of enormous width and depth; the ridges between these break across again, and form those castellated masses to which the name of *séracs* has been applied. In descending the cascade the ice is crushed and riven; ruined towers, which have tumbled from the summit, cumber the slope, and smooth vertical precipices of ice rise in succession out of the ruins. At the base of the fall the broken masses are again squeezed together, but the confusion is still great, and the glacier is here tossed into billowy shapes, scooped into caverns, and cut into gorges by torrents which expand here and there into deep green lakes.

Across this portion of the glacier we proceeded westward, purposing to attempt the ascent at the Rognon side. Our work soon commenced in earnest, and perils and difficulties thickened round us as we advanced. The confusion of ice-pinnacles, crags, and chasms, amid which we hewed our way, was very bewildering.

Plates of ice jutted from the glacier like enormous fins, along the edges of which we had to walk; and often, while perched upon these eminences, we were flanked right and left by crevasses, the depth of which might be inferred from their impenetrable gloom. At some places forces of extreme complexity had acted on the mass; the ridges were broken into columns, and some of these were twisted half round, as if with a vortical motion; while the chasms were cut up into shafts which resembled gigantic honeycombs, round the edges of which we crept tortuously. Our work was very difficult, sometimes disheartening; nevertheless, our inspiration was, that what man has done man may do, and we accordingly persevered. My fellow-traveller was silent for a time: the brandy had its effect upon him, and he confessed it; but I know that a contact with the cold ice would soon cause this to disappear, and I resolved that when restored to his normal condition I would not influence his judgment in the least.

Looking now to the right, I suddenly became aware that high above us, a multitude of crags and leaning columns of ice, on the stability of which we could not for an instant calculate, covered the precipitous incline. We were not long without an illustration of the peril of our situation. We had reached a position where massive ice cliffs protected us on one side, while in front of us was a space more open than any we had yet passed; the reason being that the ice avalanches had chosen it for their principal path. We had just stepped upon this space when a peal above us brought us to a stand. Crash! crash! crash! nearer and nearer, the sound becoming more continuous and confused as the descending masses broke into smaller blocks. Onward they came! boulders half a ton and more in weight, leaping down with a kind of maniacal fury, as if their sole mission was to crush the séracs to powder. Some of them on striking the ice rebounded like elastic balls, described parabolas through the air, again madly smote the ice, and scattered its dust like clouds in the atmosphere. Some blocks were deflected by the collision with the glacier, and were carried past us within a few yards of the spot where we stood. I had never before witnessed an exhibition of force at all comparable to this, and its proximity rendered that fearful which at a little distance would have been sublime.

My companion held his breath for a time, and then exclaimed, "*C'est terrible! il faut retourner.*" In fact, while the avalanche continued we could not at all calculate upon our safety. When we heard the first peal we had instinctively retreated to the shelter of the ice bastions; but what if one of these missiles struck the tower beside us! would it be able to withstand the shock? We knew not. In reply to the proposal of my companion, I simply said, "By all means, if you desire it; but let us wait a little." I felt that fear was just as bad a counsellor as rashness, and thought it but fair to wait until my companion's terror had subsided. We waited accordingly, and he seemed to gather courage and assurance. I scanned the heights and saw that a little more effort in an upward direction would place us in a much less perilous position, as far as the avalanches were concerned. I pointed this out to my companion, and we went forward. Once indeed, for a minute or two, I felt anxious. We had to cross in the shadow of a tower of ice, of a loose and threatening character, which quite overhung our track. The freshly broken masses at its base, and at some distance below it, showed that it must have partially given way some hours before. "Don't speak, or make any noise," said my companion; and, although rather sceptical as to the influence of speech in such a case, I held my tongue and escaped from the dangerous vicinity as fast as my legs and alpenstock could carry me.

Unbroken spaces, covered with snow, now began to spread between the crevasses; these latter, however, became larger, and were generally placed end to end *en échelon*. When, therefore, we arrived at the edge of a chasm, by walking along it we usually soon reached a point where a second one joined on it. The extremities of the chasms ran parallel to each other for some distance, one being separated from the other, throughout this distance, by a wall of incipient ice, coped at the top by snow. At other places, however, the lower portion of the partition between the fissures had melted away, leaving the chasm spanned by a bridge of snow, the capacity of which to bear us was often a matter of delicate experiment. Over these bridges we stepped as lightly as possible: "*Allez doucement ici,*" was the perpetual admonition of my companion, "*et il faut toujours sonder.*" In many cases, indeed, we could not at all guess at the state of matters underneath the covering of snow. We had picked up a few hints upon this subject, but neither of us was at this time sufficiently experienced to make practical use of them. The "sounding" too was rather weary work, as, to make it of any value, the bâton must be driven into the snow with considerable force. Further up in the *névé* the fissures became less frequent, but some of them were of great depth and width. On those silent heights there is something peculiarly solemn in the aspect of the crevasses, yawning gloomily day and night, as if with a never-satisfied hunger. We stumbled on the skeleton of a chamois, which had probably met its death by falling into a chasm, and been disgorged lower down. But a thousand chamois between these cavernous jaws would not make a mouthful. I scarcely knew which to choose—these pitfalls of the *névé*, or the avalanches. The latter are terrible, but they are grand, outspoken things; the ice crags proclaim from their heights, "Do not trust us, we are momentary and merciless." They wear the aspect of hostility undisguised; but these chasms of the *névé* are typified by the treachery of the moral world; they hide themselves under shining coverlets of snow, and compass their ends by dissimulation.

After some time we alighted on the trace of those who had crossed the day before. The danger was over when we made the discovery, but it saved us some exploring amid the crevasses which still remained. We at length got quite clear of the fissures, and mounted zigzag to the summit of the col. Clouds drove up against us from the valley of Courmayeur, but they made no way over the col. At the summit they encountered a stratum of drier air, mixing with which they were reduced, as fast as they came, to a state of invisible vapour. Upon the very top of the col I spread my plaid, and with the appetites of hungry eagles we attacked our chicken and mutton. I examined the snow, and made some experiments on sound; but little Balmat's feet were so cold that he feared being frostbitten, and at his entreaty we started on our descent again as soon as possible.

To the top of the séracs we retraced the course by which we had ascended, but here we lost the track, and had to strike out a new path for our return to the foot of the ice-cascade. A new lesson was now before us: a fresh discipline in courage, caution, and perseverance. We kept nearer to the centre of the glacier than when we ascended, thereby escaping the avalanches, but getting into ice more riven and dislocated. We were often utterly at a loss how to proceed. My companion made several attempts to regain the morning's track, preferring to risk the avalanches rather than be blocked and ditched up in an ice prison from which we saw no means of escape. Wherever we turned peril stared us in the face; but the recurrence of danger had rendered us callous to it, and this indifference gave a mechanical surety to the step in places where such surety was the only means of avoiding destruction. Once or twice, while standing on the summit of a peak of ice, and looking at the pits and chasms beneath me, at the distance through which we had hewn our way, and at the work still to be accomplished, I experienced an incipient flush of terror. But this was immediately drowned in action. Indeed the case was so bad, the necessity for exertion so paramount, that the will acquired an energy almost desperate, and crushed all terrors in the bud. We proceeded, however, with the most steady watchfulness. When we arrived at a difficulty which seemed insuperable, we calmly inspected it, looking at it on all sides; and though we had often to retrace our steps amid cliffs and chasms, to seek an outlet elsewhere, still formidable obstacles often disappeared before our cool and searching examination. We made no haste, we took no rest, but ever tended downwards. With all our instincts of self-preservation awake, we crossed places which, without the spur of necessity to drive us, we should have deemed impassable.

The closest approach which I made to destruction was in the following way. We had walked for some distance along the edge of a high wedge of ice, and had to descend its left face in order to cross a crevasse. The ice was of that loose granular character which causes it to resemble an aggregate of little polyhedrons jointed together more than a coherent solid. I was not aware that the substance was so utterly disintegrated as it proved to be. I endeavoured to plant my foot securely on the edge of the crevasse, and to help me to do so, I laid hold of a projecting corner of the ice. It crumbled to pieces in my hand; I tottered for a moment in the effort to regain my balance, my footing gave way, and down I went into the chasm. A wild scream burst from my companion, "*O! mon Dieu, il est perdu!*" but I escaped unhurt. A ledge about two feet wide jutted from the side of the crevasse, and to this I clung; my fall not amounting to more than three or four feet. A block of ice which partially jammed up the chasm concealed me from my companion. I called to him, and he responded by another exclamation, "*O! mon Dieu, comme j'ai peur!*" He helped me up, and looking anxiously in my face, demanded, "*N'avez-vous pas peur?*" The fear, however, was soon forgotten in further effort. Sometimes cheered by success, we congratulated ourselves upon reaching easier ground; but such ground often led us to the brink of precipices, which compelled us to retrace our steps and to seek escape in some other direction. Thus was our progress, as I suppose all progress is, a mixture of success and defeat. What matter, if in the final summing up of things the ending be success? It was so in our case. The difficulties lessened by degrees, and we began to gladden ourselves by mutual expressions of "content" with what we had accomplished. We reached the base of the séracs; ordinary crevasses were trivial in comparison with those from which we had escaped, so we hastened along the glacier, without halting, to the Tacul.

Here a paltry piece of treacherous snow caused me more damage than all the dangers of the day. I was passing a rock, the snow beside it seemed firm, and I placed my bâton upon it, leaning trustfully upon the staff. Through the warmth of the rock, or some other cause, the mass had been rendered hollow underneath; it yielded, I fell forward, and although a cat-like capacity of helping myself in such cases saved me from serious hurt, it did not prevent my knee from being urged with all my weight against an edge of granite. I rested for half an hour in our grotto at the Tacul, and afterwards struggled lamely along the Mer de Glace home to the Montanvert. Bloodshot eyes, burnt cheeks, and blistered lips were the result of the journey, but these soon disappeared, and fresh strength was gained for future action.

The above account was written on the day following the ascent, and while all its incidents were fresh in my memory. Last September, guided by the tracks of previous travellers, I ascended nearly to the summit of the icefall, along its eastern side, and to those acquainted only with such dangers as I then experienced the account which I have just given must appear exaggerated. I can only say that the track which I pursued in 1858 bore no resemblance in point of difficulty to that which I followed in 1857. The reason probably is, that in my first expedition neither myself nor my companion knew anything of the route, and we were totally destitute of the adjuncts which guides commonly use in crossing the "Grand Col."

# SEAL HUNTING

## Vilhjalmur Stefansson

*An outstanding authority on the Arctic regions, Stefansson was born in Canada of Icelandic parents. After studying in the United States, he took part in two archaeological voyages to Iceland. But it is chiefly for his many intrepid expeditions to the unexplored Arctic that he will be remembered. There he has wandered for months on moving ice, discovered new lands, and lived as a brother with the Eskimos. This account of native seal-hunting is taken from his book* My Life with the Eskimos.

IT WAS at this time that I first became familiar with the psychology of seals. Arctic explorers of some experience have said in print that a white man may learn to hunt caribou as well as an Eskimo, but no white man can ever learn to hunt seals successfully on top of the Arctic spring ice. This is so far from being true in my experience that I should say it is much easier to stalk seals than it is to stalk caribou. All you have to know is one or two elementary facts about the seal's habits and mental processes. One day Dr. Anderson and I were out on the sea ice and happened to notice a seal basking in the sun. As a matter of scientific interest one of us watched him through the field glasses, while the other held a watch in one hand and a pencil in the other, and noted down the length of the naps the seal was taking between his short periods of wakefulness. Like other seals at this time of year, he was lying beside his hole, enjoying the warm sun. After each short nap he would raise his head about twelve inches above the level of the ice, take a survey of the horizon, and drop to sleep again. From his movements we took down the following series of observations:

| Awake | Asleep | | Awake | Asleep |
|-------|--------|---|-------|--------|
| 5 seconds | 70 seconds | | 4 seconds | 20 seconds |
| 2 " | 10 " | | 5 " | 30 " |
| 10 " | 10 " | | 2 " | 5 " |
| 1 " | 30 " | | 3 " | 18 " |
| 8 " | 2 " | | 5 " | 90 " |
| 7 " | 7 " | | 2 " | 60 " |
| 8 " | 48 " | | 3 " | 4 " |
| 2 " | 15 " | | 4 " | 48 " |
| 6 " | 45 " | | | |

From this we deduced the interesting fact that the ratio of the lengths of his periods of wakefulness to those of his periods of sleep was as 1:6.6, and further, that the average length of his periods of wakefulness was 4.5 seconds, and the average length of his naps was 30.1 seconds.

Another day, watching another seal, we got the following results:

| Awake | Asleep | | Awake | Asleep |
|-------|--------|---|-------|--------|
| 8 seconds | 60 seconds | | 7 seconds | 50 seconds |
| 8 " | 22 " | | 3 " | 25 " |
| 4 " | 100 " | | 4 " | 18 " |
| 6 " | 14 " | | 4 " | 20 " |

This seal was evidently somewhat more somnolent than the first, for his sleeping time was to his waking as 1:7.02. He was awake on an average 5.5 seconds at a time and his naps averaged 35.6 seconds each.

The whole principle of successfully stalking a seal is just in realizing from the first that he is bound to see you and that your only hope is in pretending that you also are a seal. If you act and look so as to convince him from the first that you are a brother seal, he will regard you with unconcern. To simulate a seal well enough to deceive a seal is not difficult, for, to begin with, we know from experience that his eye-sight is poor. You can walk up without taking any special precautions until, under ordinary conditions of light, you are within two hundred and fifty or three hundred yards. Then you have to begin to be more careful. You move ahead while he is asleep, and when he wakes up you stop motionless. You can safely proceed on all fours until within something less than two hundred yards, but after that you will have to play seal more faithfully. Your method of locomotion will then have to be that of the seal, which does not differ very materially from that of a snake, and which therefore has its disadvantages at a season of the year when the surface of the ice is covered with puddles of water anywhere from an inch to twenty inches in depth, as it is in spring and early summer. You must not only crawl ahead, seal-fashion, but you must be careful to always present a side view of your body to the seal, for a man coming head-on does not look particularly like a seal.

Until you are within a hundred yards or so the seal is not likely to notice you, but somewhere between the hundred yard and the seventy-five yard mark his attention will suddenly be attracted to you, and instead of going to sleep at the end of his ordinary short period of wakefulness, he will remain awake and stare at you steadily. The seal knows, exactly as well as the seal hunter knows, that no seal in this world will sleep continuously for as much as four minutes at a time. If you lie still that long, he will know you are no seal, and up will go his tail and down he will slide into the water in the twinkling of an eye. When the seal, therefore, has been watching you carefully for twenty or thirty seconds, you must raise your head twelve or fifteen inches above the ice, look around seal-fashion, so that your eyes will sweep the whole circle of the horizon, and drop your head again upon the ice. By the time he has seen you repeat this process two or three times in the space of five or six minutes he will be convinced that you are a seal, and all his worries will be gone. From then on you can proceed more rapidly, crawling ahead while he sleeps and stopping while he remains awake, never doing anything unbecoming a seal. In this way you can crawl within five or ten yards of him if you like, and as a matter of fact I have known of expert seal hunters who under emergencies would go after a seal without any ordinary weapon and crawl so near him that they could seize him by a flipper, pull him away from his hole, and club or stab him. My Eskimo companions generally used to crawl within about fifteen or twenty yards; but I have found under ordinary circumstances that fifty yards is close enough for a man with a rifle. The animal lies on a slippery incline beside his hole, so that the shot that kills him must kill him instantly. It must shatter the brain or break the spinal cord of the neck; the slightest quiver of a muscle will send him sliding into the water and all your work will have been to no purpose.

Seals were not common in this locality, and although we got a few we were anxious also to get some caribou. The second day after our enforced halt Natkusiak and I accordingly went off in different directions looking for caribou. It was a long hunt for both of us. I returned in about eighteen hours with a young fawn for a back-load, which was one of two animals I had seen, while Natkusiak returned six or eight hours later with the story of having killed two caribou out of three that he saw. Evidently this was no paradise for big game. Ducks, however, were very abundant.

As our main food supply at this time was waterfowl, we expected our dogs as well as ourselves to live on ducks, but this did not suit them very well at first. Our experience with dogs shows that their food prejudices are very much like those of men. It is the common opinion of those who keep hotels and boarding schools that they can tell much about a man's bringing up from the things he objects to eating. The son of wealthy parents who is used to eating fifty different articles of food in a week will take readily to the fifty-first; but a farmer's son who from one year's end to another has lived on nothing but fat pork, potatoes, bread, and tea, is likely to be so wedded to the idea that nothing but pork and potatoes is fit to eat that when he meets with a new dish, the fifth or sixth one of his experience, it strikes him as an unheard-of thing and unfit for food. It is common knowledge among guides in such out of the way places as Iceland that the wealthy travelers who visit the country will readily and with enjoyment adapt themselves to the food of the peasant, while the servants who accompany their wealthy masters have to be specially looked after by the guides and insist on being fed on provisions such as they are used to having in their own country.

The same principle applies to our house dogs, which are used to eating all the varied things that we eat. They are used to so many different flavors that they take readily to one more that happens to be strange. The white man's dog that comes to the Arctic is likely to eat seal meat or any other meat of local growth the first time it is offered him, but take an Indian's dog, that has been brought up inland on nothing but caribou meat, and bring him to the coast, and he will starve for a week before he is willing to swallow the first mouthful of seal. Similarly, I have known Eskimo dogs brought up on seal meat, which when taken inland would have to be starved for a week or more before they would eat the first mouthful of caribou.

We now had with us dogs which we had brought from the Mackenzie River and which it had taken several days of starvation to teach to eat seal; we also had with us dogs of Eskimo bringing up which had similarly been forced to eat caribou meat, but now all of these were simultaneously brought face to face with a new diet (ducks), and it took long periods of abstinence from food to enable them to get up an appetite for the new dish. An interesting observation in this connection is that we have invariably found the conservatism of the females to be greater than that of the males. Out of any pack of dogs that are compelled to learn to eat a new kind of food, the last to give in are the female dogs.

Numerous travelers have pointed out that dogs will not eat dog meat, and have considered this a proof that dogs have an inherent aversion to cannibalism. We have seen nothing to substantiate this view, for a dog that has been brought up on seal meat will eat dog meat quite as readily as he will caribou, and a dog brought up on caribou meat will learn to eat dog meat quite as readily as he will learn to eat seal or duck. There is prejudice against the new but no disinclination to cannibalism.

In the summer season eggs usually form some part of our diet, and this year we got the first on June 16th, for Natkusiak found the nest of a willow ptarmigan. Although we have spent four summers in a country frequented by ptarmigan in large numbers, we have not found over a dozen nests all together, for the male continually stands guard on some eminence near the nest and gives ample warning to the female of the approach of danger, so that the spot where the female flies up is never an indication of the location of the nest. But if for some reason the male be unable to give warning in season the female will remain on the nest without stirring until you are about to step on it. The protective coloration both of the bird itself and the eggs is so nearly perfect that to discover them is almost impossible. A very different matter is the swan's nest, of which we found some in the Colville delta, although they are not nearly so numerous there as in certain other districts such as the vicinity of Cape Parry. You cannot see the ptarmigan until you are about to step on them, but a swan sitting on a nest is the most conspicuous thing in the animal life of the North, for the nest is on the barren shore of some lake and consists of a dun-colored heap of straw the size of a bushel basket, upon the top of which the snow-white bird can be seen much farther than either the caribou or the grizzly bear. From the point of view of food supply a swan's nest is a find of some importance, for there are as many as six eggs, and each of them is double the size of a goose egg.

In saying that the ptarmigan eggs of June 16th were the first of the season, I am refraining from an encroachment upon Dr. Anderson's special field as an ornithologist. Of course, he had found nests of snow buntings, Lapland long-spurs, sandpipers and other small fry of that kind much earlier in the season.

On June 23d we launched the umiak, loaded all our gear into it, and paddled away eastward along the coast, through the narrow lane of open water between the land and the as yet immovable sea ice. On the 24th the first mosquito of the year appeared. We saw only a single one that day, but three days later we had them in millions. The 25th we entered the western edge of the Colville delta proper and the day after that we fell in with a camp of the Colville Eskimo, consisting of three families. They told us that during the winter all of them had starved more or less, but none to death, although they had lost a good many dogs. Now the main body of the people were camping at the trading site of Nirlik, about six miles to the east, where they would wait for the arrival of the Point Barrow traders.

Rare caribou tracks were to be seen here and there in the delta, but none of the Eskimo had killed any so far. On the evening of the 28th I happened to see a small black dot on the landscape and pointed it out to one of the Eskimo, who said it was undoubtedly a mound of earth. I let it go at that, for I appreciated the social value of being in a position to give away meat rather than to receive it from others; and accordingly Dr. Anderson, Natkusiak, and I set out, when the others were not looking, toward this object, which my glasses had shown to be a deer. There turned out to be three of them—all very restless on account of the plague of mosquitoes. Dr. Anderson and Natkusiak therefore approached them from one side, and myself from the other. Apparently they must have either seen or winded them for they came running toward me. They turned out to be all skin poor, as was to be expected on account of the season of the year, for in June no caribou except the oldest bulls have any traces of fat on them whatever in this district. The Colville Eskimo consider themselves the greatest caribou hunters in the country and to them venison is the one palatable and satisfactory article of diet. It was something therefore to be able to show our prowess greater than theirs, and to feed them in their own country on caribou meat, of which they had not had a taste for several months.

July 31st we arrived at Nirlik and found thirty-eight people there. They were catching numbers of fish in nets set in the river, and were sun-drying some of them. A party of eighteen, we were told, had gone to the southeastern edge of the Colville delta near Oliktok, where they were hunting seal to get skins for their water boots for the summer, and oil for their lamps for the coming winter.

### Where Lies the Land?

WHERE lies the land to which the ship would go?
　　Far, far ahead, is all her seamen know.
And where the land she travels from? Away,
Far, far behind, is all that they can say.

On sunny noons upon the deck's smooth face,
Linked arm in arm, how pleasant here to pace;
Or, o'er the stern reclining, watch below
The foaming wake far widening as we go.

On stormy nights when wild northwesters rave,
How proud a thing to fight with wind and wave!
The dripping sailor on the reeling mast
Exults to bear, and scorns to wish it past.

Where lies the land to which the ship would go?
Far, far ahead, is all her seamen know.
And where the land she travels from? Away,
Far, far behind, is all that they can say.

*Arthur Hugh Clough*

# THE THOUSAND-AND-SECOND
# TALE OF SCHEHERAZADE

## Edgar Allan Poe

*The unusual and startling things in life fascinated Poe (1809–1849). The child of wandering actors, he was orphaned early and adopted by a Richmond family named Allan; for a while he studied at the University of Virginia and West Point. In his brief forty years, he wrote many stories and poems of great beauty and power, and edited some of the leading periodicals of his day. A master of the macabre, he could also be a humorist, as in this narrative of Sinbad's encounters with some oddities of Nature.*

Truth is stranger than fiction.—*Old Saying.*

HAVING had occasion, lately, in the course of some oriental investigations, to consult the *Tellmenow Isitsoörnot*,[1] a work which (like the Zohar of Simeon Jochaides) is scarcely known at all, even in Europe, and which has never been quoted to my knowledge, by any American—if we except, perhaps, the author of the "Curiosities of American Literature";—having had occasion, I say, to turn over some pages of the first-mentioned very remarkable work, I was not a little astonished to discover that the literary world has hitherto been strangely in error respecting the fate of the vizier's daughter, Scheherazade, as that fate is depicted in the "Arabian Nights," and that the *dénouement* there given, if not altogether inaccurate, as far as it goes, is at least to blame in not having gone very much farther.

For full information on this interesting topic, I must refer the inquisitive reader to the "Isitsoörnot" itself: but, in the mean time, I shall be pardoned for giving a summary of what I there discovered.

[1] Tell me now, Is it so or not?

[ 708 ]

It will be remembered that, in the usual version of the tales, a certain monarch, having good cause to be jealous of his queen, not only puts her to death, but makes a vow by his beard and the prophet, to espouse each night the most beautiful maiden in his dominions, and the next morning to deliver her up to the executioner.

Having fulfilled this vow for many years to the letter, and with a religious punctuality and method that conferred great credit upon him as a man of devout feelings and excellent sense, he was interrupted one afternoon (no doubt at his prayers) by a visit from his grand vizier, to whose daughter, it appears, there had occurred an idea.

Her name was Scheherazade, and her idea was, that she would either redeem the land from the depopulating tax upon its beauty, or perish, after the approved fashion of all heroines, in the attempt.

Accordingly, and although we do not find it to be leap-year (which makes the sacrifice more meritorious), she deputes her father, the grand vizier, to make an offer to the king of her hand. This hand the king eagerly accepts—(he had intended to take it at all events, and had put off the matter from day to day, only through fear of the vizier)—but, in accepting it now, he gives all parties very distinctly to understand that, grand vizier or no grand vizier, he has not the slightest design of giving up one iota of his vow or of his privileges. When, therefore, the fair Scheherazade insisted upon marrying the king, and did actually marry him despite her father's excellent advice not to do anything of the kind—when she would and did marry him, I say, will I nill I, it was with her beautiful black eyes as thoroughly open as the nature of the case would allow.

It seems, however, that this politic damsel (who had been reading Machiavelli, beyond doubt) had a very ingenious little plot in her mind. On the night of the wedding she contrived, upon I forget what specious pretence, to have her sister occupy a couch sufficiently near that of the royal pair to admit of easy conversation from bed to bed; and, a little before cock-crowing, she took care to awaken the good monarch, her husband (who bore her none the worse will because he intended to wring her neck on the morrow); —she managed to awaken him, I say (although, on account of a capital conscience and an easy digestion, he slept well), by the profound interest of a story (about a rat and a black cat, I think) which she was narrating (all in an undertone, of course,) to her sister. When the day broke, it so happened that this history was not altogether finished, and that Scheherazade, in the nature of things, could not finish it just then, since it was high time for her to get up and be bowstrung—a thing very little more pleasant than hanging, only a trifle more genteel.

The king's curiosity, however, prevailing, I am sorry to say, even over his sound religious principles, induced him for this once to postpone the fulfilment of his vow until next morning, for the purpose and with the hope of hearing that night how it fared in the end with the black cat (a black cat I think it was) and the rat.

The night having arrived, however, the Lady Scheherazade not only put the finishing stroke to the black cat and the rat (the rat was blue), but before she well knew what she was about, found herself deep in the intricacies of a narration, having reference (if I am not altogether mistaken) to a pink horse (with green wings) that went, in a violent manner, by clock-work, and was wound up with an indigo key. With this history the king was even more profoundly interested than with the other, and as the day broke before its conclusion (notwithstanding all the queen's endeavours to get through with it in time for the bowstringing), there was again no resource but to postpone that ceremony as before, for twenty-four hours. The next night there happened a similar accident with a similar result; and then the next—and then again the next; so that, in the end, the good monarch, having been unavoidably deprived of all opportunity to keep his vow during a period of no less than one thousand and one nights, either forgets it altogether by the expiration of this time or gets himself absolved of it in the regular way, or (what is more probable) breaks it outright as well as the head of his father confessor. At all events, Scheherazade, who, being lineally descended from Eve, fell heir, perhaps, to the whole seven baskets of talk which the latter lady, we all know, picked up from under the trees in the garden of Eden—Scheherazade, I say, finally triumphed, and the tariff upon beauty was repealed.

Now, this conclusion (which is that of the story as we have it upon record) is, no doubt, excessively proper and pleasant—but, alas! like a great many pleasant things, is more pleasant than true; and I am indebted altogether to the "Isitsoörnot" for the means of correcting the error. "*Le mieux*," says a French proverb, "*est l'ennemi du bien*," and, in mentioning that Scheherazade had inherited the seven baskets of talk, I should have added that she put them out at compound interest until they amounted to seventy-seven.

"My dear sister," said she, on the thousand-and-second night [I quote the language of the "Isitsoörnot," at this point, *verbatim*,], "my dear sister," said she, "now that all this little difficulty about the bowstring has blown over, and that this odious tax is so happily repealed, I feel that I have been guilty of great indiscretion in withholding from you and the King (who, I am sorry to say, snores—a thing no gentleman would do) the full conclusion of the history of Sinbad the sailor. This person went through numerous other and more interesting adventures than those which I related; but the truth is, I felt sleepy on the particular night of their narration, and so was seduced into cutting them short—a grievous piece of misconduct, for which I only trust that Allah will forgive me. But even yet it is not too late to remedy my great neglect, and as soon as I have given the King a pinch or two in order to wake him up so far that he may stop making that horrible noise, I will forthwith entertain you (and him if he pleases) with the sequel of this very remarkable story."

Hereupon the sister of Scheherazade, as I have it from the "Isitsoörnot," expressed no very particular intensity of gratification; but the king having been sufficiently pinched, at length ceased snoring, and finally said "hum!" and then "hoo!" when the queen understanding these words (which are no doubt Arabic) to signify that he was all attention, and would do his best not to snore any more,—the queen, I say, having arranged these matters to her satisfaction, re-entered thus, at once, into the history of Sinbad the sailor.

" 'At length in my old age,' [these are the words of Sinbad himself, as retailed by Scheherazade]—'at length, in my old age, and after enjoying many years of tranquillity at home, I became once more possessed with a desire of visiting foreign countries; and one day, without acquainting any of my family with my design, I packed up some bundles of such merchandise as was most precious and least bulky, and, engaging a porter to carry them, went with him down to the seashore, to await the arrival of any chance vessel that might convey me out of the kingdom into some region which I had not as yet explored.

" 'Having deposited the packages upon the sands, we sat down beneath some trees and looked out into the ocean in the hope of perceiving a ship, but during several hours we saw none whatever.

At length I fancied that I could hear a singular buzzing or humming sound, and the porter, after listening awhile, declared that he also could distinguish it. Presently it grew louder, and then still louder, so that we could have no doubt that the object which caused it was approaching us. At length, on the edge of the horizon, we discovered a black speck, which rapidly increased in size until we made it out to be a vast monster, swimming with a great part of its body above the surface of the sea. It came towards us with inconceivable swiftness, throwing up huge waves of foam around its breast, and illuminating all that part of the sea through which it passed, with a long line of fire that extended far off into the distance.

" 'As the thing drew near we saw it very distinctly. Its length was equal to that of three of the loftiest trees that grow, and it was as wide as the great hall of audience in your palace, O most sublime and munificent of the Caliphs. Its body, which was unlike that of ordinary fishes, was as solid as a rock, and of a jetty blackness throughout all that portion of it which floated above the water, with the exception of a narrow blood-red streak that completely begirdled it. The belly, which floated beneath the surface, and of which we could get only a glimpse now and then as the monster rose and fell with the billows, was entirely covered with metallic scales, of a colour like that of the moon in misty weather. The back was flat and nearly white, and from it there extended upwards six spines, about half the length of the whole body.

" 'This horrible creature had no mouth that we could perceive; but, as if to make up for this deficiency, it was provided with at least four score of eyes, that protruded from their sockets like those of the green dragonfly, and were arranged all around the body in two rows, one above the other, and parallel to the blood-red streak, which seemed to answer the purpose of an eyebrow. Two or three of these dreadful eyes were much larger than the others, and had the appearance of solid gold.

" 'Although this beast approached us, as I have before said, with the greatest rapidity, it must have been moved altogether by necromancy—for it had neither fins like a fish, nor web-feet like a duck, nor wings like the sea-shell which is blown along in the manner of a vessel; nor yet did it writhe itself forward as do the eels. Its head and its tail were shaped precisely alike, only, not far from the latter, were two small holes that served for nostrils, and through which the monster puffed out its thick breath with prodigious violence, and with a shrieking disagreeable noise.

" 'Our terror at beholding this hideous thing was very great; but it was even surpassed by our astonishment when, upon getting a nearer look, we perceived upon the creature's back a vast number of animals about the size and shape of men, and altogether much resembling them, except that they wore no garments (as men do), being supplied (by nature no doubt) with an ugly, uncomfortable covering, a good deal like cloth, but fitting so tight to the skin as to render the poor wretches laughably awkward and put them apparently to severe pain. On the very tips of their heads were certain square-looking boxes, which, at first sight, I thought might have been intended to answer as turbans, but I soon discovered that they were excessively heavy and solid, and I therefore concluded they were contrivances designed, by their great weight, to keep the heads of the animals steady and safe upon their shoulders. Around the necks of the creatures were fastened black collars (badges of servitude, no doubt), such as we keep on our dogs, only much wider and infinitely stiffer, so that it was quite impossible for these poor victims to move their heads in any direction without moving the body at the same time; and thus they were doomed to perpetual contemplation of their noses—a view puggish and snubby in a wonderful, if not positively in an awful degree.

" 'When the monster had nearly reached the shore where we stood, it suddenly pushed out one of its eyes to a great extent, and emitted from it a terrible flash of fire, accompanied by a dense cloud of smoke and a noise that I can compare to nothing but thunder. As the smoke cleared away, we saw one of the odd man-animals standing near the head of the large beast with a trumpet in his hand, through which (putting it to his mouth) he presently addressed us in loud, harsh and disagreeable accents, that, perhaps, we should have mistaken for language had they not come altogether through the nose.

" 'Being thus evidently spoken to, I was at a loss how to reply, as I could in no manner understand what was said; and in this difficulty I turned to the porter, who was near swooning through affright, and demanded of him his opinion as to what species of monster it was, what it wanted, and what kind of creatures those were that so swarmed upon its back. To this the porter replied, as well as he could for trepidation, that he had once before heard of this sea-beast; that it was a cruel demon, with bowels of sulphur and blood of fire, created by evil genii as the means of inflicting misery upon mankind; that the things upon its back were vermin, such as sometimes infest cats and dogs, only a little larger and more savage; and that these vermin had their uses, however evil—for, through the torture they caused the beast by their nibblings and stingings, it was goaded into that degree of wrath which was requisite to make it roar and commit ill, and so fulfil the vengeful and malicious designs of the wicked genii.

" 'This account determined me to take to my heels, and, without once even looking behind me, I ran at full speed up into the hills, while the porter ran equally fast, although nearly in an opposite direction, so that, by these means, he finally made his escape with my bundles, of which I have no doubt he took excellent care—although this is a point I cannot determine, as I do not remember that I ever beheld him again.

" 'For myself, I was so hotly pursued by a swarm of the men-vermin (who had come to the shore in boats) that I was very soon overtaken, bound hand and foot, and conveyed to the beast, which immediately swam out again into the middle of the sea.

" 'I now bitterly repented my folly in quitting a comfortable home to peril my life in such adventures as this; but regret being useless, I made the best of my condition and exerted myself to secure the good-will of the man-animal that owned the trumpet, and who appeared to exercise authority over his fellows. I succeeded so well in this endeavour that, in a few days, the creature bestowed upon me various tokens of its favour, and, in the end, even went to the trouble of teaching me the rudiments of what it was vain enough to denominate its language; so that, at length, I was enabled to converse with it readily, and came to make it comprehend the ardent desire I had of seeing the world.

" ' "*Washish squashish squeak, Sinbad, hey-diddle diddle, grunt unt grumble, hiss, fiss, whiss,*" said he to me, one day after dinner—but I beg a thousand pardons, I had forgotten that your majesty is not conversant with the dialect of the Cock-neighs (so the man-animals were called; I presume because their language formed the connecting link between that of the horse and that of the rooster). With your permission, I will translate. "*Washish squashish,*" and so forth:—that is to say, "I am happy to find, my dear Sinbad, that you are really a very excellent fellow; we are now about doing a thing which is called circumnavigating the globe; and since you are so desirous of seeing the world, I will strain a point and give you a free passage upon the back of the beast." ' "

When the Lady Scheherazade had proceeded thus far, relates the "Isitsoörnot," the king turned over from his left side to his right, and said—

"It is, in fact, *very* surprising, my dear queen, that you omitted, hitherto, these latter adventures of Sinbad. Do you know I think them exceedingly entertaining and strange?"

The king having thus expressed himself, we are told, the fair Scheherazade resumed her history in the following words:—

"Sinbad went on in this manner, with his narrative to the Caliph —'I thanked the man-animal for its kindness, and soon found myself very much at home on the beast, which swam at a prodigious rate through the ocean; although the surface of the latter is, in that part of the world, by no means flat, but round like a pomegranate, so that we went—so to say—either up hill or down hill all the time.' "

"That, I think, was very singular," interrupted the king.

"Nevertheless, it is quite true," replied Scheherazade.

"I have my doubts," rejoined the king; "but, pray, be so good as to go on with the story."

"I will," said the queen. " 'The beast,' continued Sinbad to the Caliph, 'swam, as I have related, up hill and down hill, until, at length, we arrived at an island, many hundreds of miles in circumference, but which, nevertheless, had been built in the middle of the sea by a colony of little things like caterpillars.' " [1]

"Hum!" said the king.

" 'Leaving this island,' said Sinbad—(for Scheherazade, it must be understood, took no notice of her husband's ill-mannered ejaculation)—'leaving this island, we came to another where the forests were of solid stone, and so hard that they shivered to pieces the finest-tempered axes with which we endeavoured to cut them down.' " [2]

---

[1] The corallites.

[2] "One of the most remarkable natural curiosities in Texas is a petrified forest, near the head of Pasigno river. It consists of several hundred trees, in an erect position, all turned to stone. Some trees, now growing, are partly petrified. This is a startling fact for natural philosophers, and must cause them to modify the existing theory of petrifaction."—KENNEDY. [*Texas*, I. p. 120.]

This account, at first discredited, has since been corroborated by the discovery of a completely petrified forest, near the head waters of the Chayenne, or Chienne river, which has its source in the Black Hills of the Rocky chain. There is scarcely, perhaps, a spectacle on the surface of the globe more re-

"Hum!" said the king, again; but Scheherazade, paying him no attention, continued in the language of Sinbad.

" 'Passing beyond this last island, we reached a country where there was a cave that ran to the distance of thirty or forty miles within the bowels of the earth, and that contained a greater number of far more spacious and more magnificent palaces than are to be found in all Damascus and Bagdad. From the roofs of these palaces there hung myriads of gems, like diamonds, but larger than men; and in among the streets of towers and pyramids and temples, there flowed immense rivers as black as ebony and swarming with fish that had no eyes.' " [1]

"Hum!" said the king.

" 'We then swam into a region of the sea where we found a lofty mountain, down whose sides there streamed torrents of melted metal, some of which were twelve miles wide and sixty miles long; [2] while from an abyss on the summit, issued so vast a quantity of ashes that the sun was entirely blotted out from the heavens, and it became darker than the darkest midnight; so that, when we

markable, either in a geological or picturesque point of view, than that presented by the petrified forest, near Cairo. The traveller, having passed the tombs of the caliphs, just beyond the gates of the city, proceeds to the southward, nearly at right angles to the road across the desert to Suez, and after having travelled some ten miles up a low barren valley, covered with sand, gravel, and sea-shells, fresh as if the tide had retired but yesterday, crosses a low range of sandhills, which has for some distance run parallel to his path. The scene now presented to him is beyond conception singular and desolate. A mass of fragments of trees, all converted into stone, and when struck by his horse's hoof ringing like cast iron, is seen to extend itself for miles and miles around him, in the form of a decayed and prostrate forest. The wood is of a dark brown hue, but retains its form in perfection, the pieces being from one to fifteen feet in length, and from half a foot to three feet in thickness, strewed so closely together, as far as the eye can reach, that an Egyptian donkey can scarcely thread its way through amongst them, and so natural that, were it in Scotland or Ireland, it might pass without remark for some enormous drained bog, on which the exhumed trees lay rotting in the sun. The roots and rudiments of the branches are, in many cases, nearly perfect, and in some the worm-holes eaten under the bark are readily recognizable. The most delicate of the sap vessels, and all the finer portions of the centre of the wood, are perfectly entire, and bear to be examined with the strongest magnifiers. The whole are so thoroughly silicified as to scratch glass and be capable of receiving the highest polish.—*Asiatic Magazine*. [Vol. III. p. 359: Third Series.]

[1] The Mammoth Cave of Kentucky.

[2] In Iceland, 1783.

were even at the distance of a hundred and fifty miles from the mountain, it was impossible to see the whitest object, however close we held it to our eyes.' " [1]

"Hum!" said the king.

" 'After quitting this coast, the beast continued his voyage until we met with a land in which the nature of things seemed reversed— for we here saw a great lake, at the bottom of which, more than a hundred feet beneath the surface of the water, there flourished in full leaf a forest of tall and luxuriant trees.' " [2]

"Hoo!" said the king.

" 'Some hundred miles farther on brought us to a climate where the atmosphere was so dense as to sustain iron or steel, just as our own does feathers.' " [3]

"Fiddle de dee," said the king.

" 'Proceeding still in the same direction, we presently arrived at the most magnificent region in the whole world. Through it there meandered a glorious river for several thousands of miles. This river was of unspeakable depth, and of a transparency richer than that of amber. It was from three to six miles in width; and its banks, which arose on either side to twelve hundred feet in perpendicular height, were crowned with ever-blossoming trees and perpetual sweet-scented flowers that made the whole territory one gorgeous garden; but the name of this luxuriant land was the kingdom of Horror, and to enter it was inevitable death.' " [4]

[1] "During the eruption of Hecla, in 1766, clouds of this kind produced such a degree of darkness that, at Glaumba, which is more than fifty leagues from the mountain, people could only find their way by groping. During the eruption of Vesuvius, in 1794, at Caserta, four leagues distant, people could only walk by the light of torches. On the first of May, 1812, a cloud of volcanic ashes and sand, coming from a volcano in the island of St. Vincent, covered the whole of Barbadoes, spreading over it so intense a darkness that, at mid-day, in the open air, one could not perceive the trees or other objects near him, or even a white handkerchief placed at the distance of six inches from the eye."—MURRAY, p. 215, *Phil. edit.* [I. Encyclopædia of Geography.]

[2] "In the year 1790, in the Caraccas, during an earthquake, a portion of the granite soil sank and left a lake eight hundred yards in diameter, and from eighty to a hundred feet deep. It was a part of the Forest of Aripao which sank, and the trees remained green for several months under the water."—MURRAY, p. 221. [Encyc. of Geog.]

[3] The hardest steel ever manufactured may, under the action of a blowpipe, be reduced to an impalpable powder, which will float readily in the atmospheric air.

[4] The region of the Niger. See SIMOND's *Colonial Magazine.*

"Humph!" said the king.

" 'We left this kingdom in great haste, and, after some days, came to another, where we were astonished to perceive myriads of monstrous animals with horns resembling scythes upon their heads. These hideous beasts dig for themselves vast caverns in the soil, of a funnel shape, and line the sides of them with rocks, so disposed one upon the other that they fall instantly, when trodden upon by other animals, thus precipitating them into the monsters' dens, where their blood is immediately sucked, and their carcasses afterwards hurled contemptuously out to an immense distance from the caverns of death.' " [1]

"Pooh!" said the king.

" 'Continuing our progress, we perceived a district abounding with vegetables that grew not upon any soil but in the air.[2] There were others that sprang from the substance of other vegetables; [3] others that derived their sustenance from the bodies of living animals; [4] and then, again, there were others that glowed all over with intense fire; [5] others that moved from place to place at pleasure,[6] and what is still more wonderful, we discovered flowers that lived and breathed and moved their limbs at will, and had, moreover, the detestable passion of mankind for enslaving other crea-

---

[1] The *Myrmeleon*—lion-ant. The term "monster" is equally applicable to small abnormal things and to great, while such epithets as "vast" are merely comparative. The cavern of the myrmeleon is *vast* in comparison with the hole of the common red ant. A grain of silex is, also, a "rock."

[2] The *Epidendron, Flos Aeris*, of the family of the *Orchideæ*, grows with merely the surface of its roots attached to a tree or other object, from which it derives no nutriment—subsisting altogether upon air.

[3] The *Parasites*, such as the wonderful *rafflesia Arnoldi*.

[4] Schouw advocates a class of plants that grow upon living animals—the *plantæ Epizoæ*. Of this class are the *Fuci* and *Algæ*.

Mr. J. B. Williams, of Salem, Mass., presented the "National Institute," with an insect from New Zealand, with the following description:—" 'The Hotte,' a decided caterpillar, or worm, is found growing at the foot of the *Rata* tree, with a plant growing out of its head. This most peculiar and most extraordinary insect travels up both the *Rata* and *Puriri* trees, and entering into the top, eats its way, perforating the trunk of the tree until it reaches the root; it then comes out of the root, and dies, or remains dormant, and the plant propagates out of its head; the body remains perfect and entire, of a harder substance than when alive. From this insect the natives make a colouring for tattooing."

[5] In mines and natural caves we find a species of cryptogamous *fungus* that emits an intense phosphorescence.

[6] The *orchis, scabius* and *vallisneria*.

tures, and confining them in horrid and solitary prisons until the fulfilment of appointed tasks.' " [1]

"Pshaw!" said the king.

" 'Quitting this land, we soon arrived at another in which the bees and the birds are mathematicians of such genius and erudition, that they give daily instructions in the science of geometry to the wise men of the empire. The king of the place having offered a reward for the solution of two very difficult problems, they were solved upon the spot—the one by the bees, and the other by the birds; but the king keeping their solutions a secret, it was only after the most profound researches and labour, and the writing of an infinity of big books, during a long series of years, that the men-mathematicians at length arrived at the identical solutions which had been given upon the spot by the bees and by the birds.' " [2]

[1] "The corolla of this flower (*Aristolochia Clematitis*), which is tubular, but terminating upwards in a ligulate limb, is inflated into a globular figure at the base. The tubular part is internally beset with stiff hairs, pointing downwards. The globular part contains the pistil, which consists merely of a germen and stigma, together with the surrounding stamens. But the stamens, being shorter than even the germen, cannot discharge the pollen so as to throw it upon the stigma, as the flower stands always upright till after impregnation. And hence, without some additional and peculiar aid, the pollen must necessarily fall down to the bottom of the flower. Now, the aid that Nature has furnished in this case, is that of the *Tipula Pennicornis*, a small insect, which entering the tube of the corolla in quest of honey, descends to the bottom, and rummages about till it becomes quite covered with pollen; but, not being able to force its way out again, owing to the downward position of the hairs, which converge to a point like the wires of a mouse-trap, and being somewhat impatient of its confinement, it brushes backwards and forwards, trying every corner, till, after repeatedly traversing the stigma, it covers it with pollen sufficient for its impregnation, in consequence of which the flower soon begins to droop and the hairs to shrink to the side of the tube, effecting an easy passage for the escape of the insect."—REV. P. KEITH, *System of Physiological Botany*.

[2] The bees—ever since bees were—have been constructing their cells with just such sides, in just such number, and at just such inclinations, as it has been demonstrated (in a problem involving the profoundest mathematical principles) are the very sides, in the very number, and at the very angles which will afford the creatures the most room that is compatible with the greatest stability of structure.

During the latter part of the last century, the question arose among mathematicians—"to determine the best form that can be given to the sails of a windmill, according to their varying distances from the revolving vanes, and likewise from the centres of revolution." This is an excessively complex problem; for it is, in other words, to find the best possible position at an infinity of varied distances, and at an infinity of points on the arm. There were a thou-

"Oh my!" said the king.

" 'We had scarcely lost sight of this empire when we found ourselves close upon another, from whose shores there flew over our heads a flock of fowls a mile in breadth and two hundred and forty miles long; so that, although they flew a mile during every minute, it required no less than four hours for the whole flock to pass over us—in which there were several millions of millions of fowls.' " [1]

"Oh fy!" said the king.

" 'No sooner had we got rid of these birds, which occasioned us great annoyance, than we were terrified by the appearance of a fowl of another kind, and infinitely larger than even the rocs which I met in my former voyages; for it was bigger than the biggest of the domes upon your seraglio, oh, most Munificent of Caliphs. This terrible fowl had no head that we could perceive, but was fashioned entirely of belly, which was of a prodigious fatness and roundness, of a soft-looking substance, smooth, shining and striped with various colours. In its talons, the monster was bearing away to his eyrie in the heavens, a house from which it had knocked off the roof, and in the interior of which we distinctly saw human beings, who, beyond doubt, were in a state of frightful despair at the horrible fate which awaited them. We shouted with all our might, in the hope of frightening the bird into letting go of its prey; but it merely gave a snort or puff, as if of rage, and then let fall upon our heads a heavy sack which proved to be filled with sand.' "

"Stuff!" said the king.

" 'It was just after this adventure that we encountered a continent of immense extent and of prodigious solidity, but which, nevertheless, was supported entirely upon the back of a sky-blue cow that had no fewer than four hundred horns.' " [2]

"*That*, now, I believe," said the king, "because I have read something of the kind before, in a book."

---

sand futile attempts to answer the query on the part of the most illustrious mathematicians; and when, at length, an undeniable solution was discovered, men found that the wings of a bird had given it with absolute precision, ever since the first bird had traversed the air.

[1] He observed a flock of pigeons passing betwixt Frankfort and the Indiana territory, one mile at least in breadth; it took up four hours in passing; which, at the rate of one mile per minute, gives a length of 240 miles; and, supposing three pigeons to each square yard, gives 2,230,272,000 pigeons. *Travels in Canada and the United States*, by LIEUT. F. HALL.

[2] "The earth is upheld by a cow of a blue colour, having horns four hundred in number."—SALE's *Koran*.

" 'We passed immediately beneath this continent (swimming in between the legs of the cow), and, after some hours, found ourselves in a wonderful country indeed, which, I was informed by the man-animal, was his own native land, inhabited by things of his own species. This elevated the man-animal very much in my esteem; and in fact, I now began to feel ashamed of the contemptuous familiarity with which I had treated him; for I found that the man-animals in general were a nation of the most powerful magicians, who lived with worms in their brains,[1] which, no doubt, served to stimulate them by their painful writhings and wrigglings to the most miraculous efforts of imagination.' "

"Nonsense!" said the king.

" 'Among the magicians, were domesticated several animals of very singular kinds; for example, there was a huge horse whose bones were iron and whose blood was boiling water. In place of corn, he had black stones for his usual food; and yet, in spite of so hard a diet, he was so strong and swift that he would drag a load more weighty than the grandest temple in this city, at a rate surpassing that of the flight of most birds.' "[2]

"Twattle!" said the king.

" 'I saw, also, among these people a hen without feathers, but bigger than a camel; instead of flesh and bone she had iron and brick; her blood, like that of the horse (to whom in fact she was nearly related), was boiling water; and like him she ate nothing but wood or black stones. This hen brought forth very frequently, a hundred chickens in the day; and, after birth, they took up their residence for several weeks within the stomach of their mother.' "[3]

"Fal lal!" said the king.

" 'One of this nation of mighty conjurors created a man out of brass and wood, and leather, and endowed him with such ingenuity that he would have beaten at chess, all the race of mankind with the exception of the great Caliph, Haroun Alraschid.[4] Another of these magi constructed (of like material) a creature that put to shame even the genius of him who made it; for so great were its reasoning powers that, in a second, it performed calculations of so

[1] "The *Entozoa*, or intestinal worms, have repeatedly been observed in the muscles, and in the cerebral substance of men." See WYATT's *Physiology*, p. 143.

[2] On the great Western Railway, between London and Exeter, a speed of 71 miles per hour has been attained. A train weighing 90 tons was whirled from Paddington to Didcot (53 miles) in 51 minutes.

[3] The *Eccaleobion*.

[4] Maelzel's Automaton Chess-player.

vast an extent that they would have required the united labour of
fifty thousand fleshly men for a year.[1] But a still more wonderful
conjuror fashioned for himself a mighty thing that was neither man
nor beast, but which had brains of lead intermixed with a black
matter like pitch, and fingers that it employed with such incredible
speed and dexterity that it would have had no trouble in writing
out twenty thousand copies of the Koran in an hour; and this with
so exquisite a precision, that in all the copies there should not be
found one to vary from another by the breadth of the finest hair.
This thing was of prodigious strength, so that it erected or over-
threw the mightiest empires at a breath; but its power was exercised
equally for evil and for good.' "

"Ridiculous!" said the king.

" 'Among this nation of necromancers there was also one who
had in his veins the blood of the salamanders; for he made no scruple
of sitting down to smoke his chibouque in a red-hot oven until his
dinner was thoroughly roasted upon its floor.[2] Another had the
faculty of converting the common metals into gold, without even
looking at them during the process.[3] Another had such delicacy
of touch that he made a wire so fine as to be invisible.[4] Another had
such quickness of perception that he counted all the separate motions of an elastic body, while it was springing backwards and forwards at the rate of nine hundred millions of times in a second.' " [5]

"Absurd!" said the king.

" 'Another of these magicians, by means of a fluid that nobody
ever yet saw, could make the corpses of his friends brandish their
arms, kick out their legs, fight, or even get up and dance at his
will.[6] Another had cultivated his voice to so great an extent that
he could have made himself heard from one end of the earth to the
other.[7] Another had so long an arm that he could sit down in
Damascus and indite a letter at Bagdad—or indeed at any distance

[1] Babbage's Calculating Machine.

[2] Chabert, and since him, a hundred others.

[3] The Electrotype [Electroplate?].

[4] Wollaston made of platinum for the field of views in a telescope a wire
one eighteen-thousandth part of an inch in thickness. It could be seen only
by means of the microscope.

[5] Newton demonstrated that the retina beneath the influence of the violet
ray of the spectrum, vibrated 900,000,000 of times in a second.

[6] The Voltaic pile.

[7] The Electro Telegraph transmits intelligence instantaneously—at least
so far as regards any distance upon the earth.

whatsoever.[1] Another commanded the lightning to come down to him out of the heavens, and it came at his call; and served him for a plaything when it came. Another took two loud sounds and out of them made a silence. Another constructed a deep darkness out of two brilliant lights.[2] Another made ice in a red-hot furnace.[3] Another directed the sun to paint his portrait, and the sun did.[4] Another took this luminary with the moon and the planets, and having first weighed them with scrupulous accuracy, probed into their depths and found out the solidity of the substance of which they are made. But the whole nation is, indeed, of so surprising a necromantic ability, that not even their infants, nor their commonest cats and dogs have any difficulty in seeing objects that do not exist at all, or that for twenty thousand years before the birth of the nation itself, had been blotted out from the face of creation.' " [5]

[1] The Electro Telegraph Printing Apparatus.

[2] Common experiments in Natural Philosophy. If two red rays from two luminous points be admitted into a dark chamber so as to fall on a white surface, and differ in their length by 0.0000258 of an inch, their intensity is doubled. So also if the difference in length be any whole-number multiple of that fraction. A multiple by 2¼, 3¼, etc., gives an intensity equal to one ray only; but a multiple by 2½, 3½, etc., gives the result of total darkness. In violet rays similar effects arise when the difference in length is 0.000157 of an inch; and with all other rays the results are the same—the difference varying with a uniform increase from the violet to the red.
Analogous experiments in respect to sound produce analogous results.

[3] Place a platina crucible over a spirit lamp, and keep it a red heat; pour in some sulphuric acid, which, though the most volatile of bodies at a common temperature, will be found to become completely fixed in a hot crucible, and not a drop evaporates—being surrounded by an atmosphere of its own, it does not, in fact, touch the sides. A few drops of water are now introduced, when the acid immediately coming in contact with the heated sides of the crucible, flies off in sulphurous acid vapour, and so rapid is its progress, that the caloric of the water passes off with it, which falls a lump of ice to the bottom; by taking advantage of the moment before it is allowed to re-melt, it may be turned out a lump of ice from a red-hot vessel.

[4] The Daguerreotype.

[5] Although light travels 200,000 miles in a second, the distance of what we suppose to be the nearest fixed star (Sirius) is so inconceivably great, that its rays would require *at least* three years to reach the earth. For stars beyond this 20—or even 1000 years—would be a moderate estimate. Thus, if they had been annihilated 20 or 1000 years ago, we might still see them today, by the light which *started* from their surfaces, 20 or 1000 years in the past time. That many which we see daily are really extinct, is not impossible—not even improbable. [Broadway Journal Note.]

The elder Herschel maintains that the light of the faintest nebulæ seen through his great telescope, must have taken 3,000,000 years in reaching the earth. Some, made visible by Lord Ross's instrument must, then, have required at least 20,000,000. [Griswold Note.]

"Preposterous!" said the king.

" 'The wives and daughters of these incomparably great and wise magi,' " continued Scheherazade, without being in any manner disturbed by these frequent and most ungentlemanly interruptions on the part of her husband—" 'the wives and daughters of these eminent conjurors are everything that is accomplished and refined; and would be everything that is interesting and beautiful, but for an unhappy fatality that besets them, and from which not even the miraculous power of their husbands and fathers has, hitherto, been adequate to save them. Some fatalities come in certain shapes, and some in others—but this of which I speak, has come in the shape of a crotchet.' "

"A what?" said the king.

" 'A crotchet,' said Scheherazade. " 'One of the evil genii who are perpetually upon the watch to inflict ill, has put it into the heads of these accomplished ladies that the thing which we describe as personal beauty, consists altogether in the protuberance of the region which lies not very far below the small of the back.—Perfection of loveliness, they say, is in the direct ratio of the extent of this hump. Having been long possessed of this idea, and bolsters being cheap in that country, the days have long gone by since it was possible to distinguish a woman from a dromedary—' "

"Stop!" said the king,—"I can't stand that, and I won't. You have already given me a dreadful headache with your lies. The day, too, I perceive, is beginning to break. How long have we been married?—my conscience is getting to be troublesome again. And then that dromedary touch—do you take me for a fool? Upon the whole you might as well get up and be throttled."

These words, as I learn from the "Isitsoörnot," both grieved and astonished Scheherazade; but, as she knew the king to be a man of scrupulous integrity, and quite unlikely to forfeit his word, she submitted to her fate with a good grace. She derived, however, great consolation (during the tightening of the bow-string), from the reflection that much of the history remained still untold, and that the petulance of her brute of a husband had reaped for him a most righteous reward, in depriving him of many inconceivable adventures.

# A DRY GALE

## Richard Henry Dana, Jr.

*Hoping to restore his failing health, a Harvard student, in 1834, shipped as a common seaman on a sailing vessel bound round the Horn to California. When he returned, he wrote the story of his adventures—hardships, work, fun, daily doings on ship, storms, friendships, punishments at the hands of a cruel captain. That story,* Two Years Before the Mast, *not only has influenced all literature about the sea since that time, but did much to improve the lot of sailors throughout the world. For the rest of his life, Dana (1815–1882) was a successful lawyer.*

W<small>E HAD</small> been below but a short time before we had the usual premonitions of a coming gale,—seas washing over the whole forward part of the vessel, and her bows beating against them with a force and sound like the driving of piles. The watch, too, seemed very busy trampling about decks and singing out at the ropes. A sailor can tell by the sound what sail is coming in; and in a short time we heard the top-gallant-sails come in, one after another, and then the flying jib. This seemed to ease her a good deal, and we were fast going off to the land of Nod, when—bang, bang, bang on the scuttle, and "All hands, reef topsails, ahoy!" started us out of our berths, and it not being very cold weather, we had nothing extra to put on, and were soon on deck.

I shall never forget the fineness of the sight. It was a clear and rather a chilly night; the stars were twinkling with an intense brightness, and as far as the eye could reach there was not a cloud to be seen. The horizon met the sea in a defined line. A painter could not have painted so clear a sky. There was not a speck upon it. Yet it was blowing great guns from the northwest. When you can see a cloud to windward, you feel that there is a place for the wind to come from; but here it seemed to come from nowhere. No person could have told from the heavens, by their eyesight alone, that it was not a still summer's night.

One reef after another we took in the topsails, and before we could get them hoisted up we heard a sound like a short quick rattling of thunder, and the jib was blown to atoms out of the bolt-rope. We got the topsails set, and the fragments of the jib stowed away, and the foretopmast staysail set in its place, when the great mainsail gaped open, and the sail ripped from head to foot.

"Lay up on that main yard and furl the sail, before it blows to tatters!" shouted the captain; and in a moment we were up, gathering the remains of it upon the yard. We got it wrapped round the yard, and passed gaskets over it as snugly as possible, and were just on deck again, when with another loud rent, which was heard throughout the ship, the foretopsail, which had been double-reefed, split in two athwartships, just below the reef-band, from earing to earing. Here again it was—down yard, haul out reef-tackles, and lay out upon the yard for reefing. By hauling the reef-tackles chock-a-block we took the strain from the other earings, and passing the close-reef earing, and knotting the points carefully, we succeeded in setting the sail, close reefed.

We had but just got the rigging coiled up and were waiting to hear "Go below the watch!" when the main royal worked loose from the gaskets, and blew directly out to leeward, flapping and shaking the mast like a wand. Here was a job for somebody. The royal must come in or be cut adrift, or the mast would be snapped short off. All the light hands in the starboard watch were sent up one after another, but they could do nothing with it. At length John, the tall Frenchman, the head of the starboard watch (and a better sailor never stepped upon a deck), sprang aloft, and by the help of his long arms and legs succeeded after a hard struggle,—the sail blowing over the yard-arm to leeward, and the skysail adrift directly over his head,—in smothering it and frapping it with long pieces of sinnet.

He came very near being blown or shaken from the yard several times, but he was a true sailor, every finger a fish-hook. Having made the sail snug, he prepared to send the yard down, which was a long and difficult job; for frequently he was obliged to stop and hold on with all his might for several minutes, the ship pitching so as to make it impossible to do anything else at that height. The yard at length came down safe, and after it the fore and mizzen royal yards were sent down. All hands were then sent aloft, and for an hour or two we were hard at work, making the booms well fast, un-reeving the studding sail and royal and skysail gear, getting rolling-ropes on the yard, setting up the weather breast-backstays, and making other preparations for a storm. It was a fine night for a gale, just cool and bracing enough for quick work, without being cold, and as bright as day. It was sport to have a gale in such weather as this. Yet it blew like a hurricane. The wind seemed to come with a spite, an edge to it, which threatened to scrape us off the yards. The force of the wind was greater than I had ever felt it before; but darkness, cold, and wet are the worst parts of a storm to a sailor.

Having got on deck again, we looked round to see what time of night it was, and whose watch. In a few minutes the man at the wheel struck four bells, and we found that the other watch was out and our own half out. Accordingly the starboard watch went be-low, and left the ship to us for a couple of hours, yet with orders to stand by for a call.

Hardly had they got below before away went the foretopmast staysail, blown to ribands. This was a small sail, which we could manage in the watch, so that we were not obliged to call up the other watch. We laid upon the bowsprit, where we were under water half the time, and took in the fragments of the sail; and as she must have some headsail on her, prepared to bend another stay-sail. We got the new one out into the nettings; seized on the tack, sheets, and halyards, and the hanks; manned the halyards, cut adrift the frapping-lines, and hoisted away; but before it was half-way up the stay it was blown all to pieces. When we belayed the hal-yards, there was nothing left but the bolt-rope. Now large eyes began to show themselves in the foresail; and knowing that it must soon go, the mate ordered us upon the yard to furl it. Being un-willing to call up the watch, who had been on deck all night, he roused out the carpenter, sailmaker, cook, and steward, and with their help we manned the foreyard, and after nearly half an hour's struggle, mastered the sail and got it well furled round the yard.

The force of the wind had never been greater than at this mo-ment. In going up the rigging it seemed absolutely to pin us down to the shrouds; and on the yard there was no such thing as turning a face to windward. Yet there was no driving sleet and darkness and wet and cold as off Cape Horn; and instead of stiff oilcloth suits, southwester caps, and thick boots, we had on hats, round jackets, duck trousers, light shoes, and everything light and easy. These things make a great difference to a sailor.

When we got on deck the man at the wheel struck eight bells (four o'clock in the morning), and "All starbowlines, ahoy!"

brought the other watch up, but there was no going below for us. The gale was now at its height, "blowing like scissors and thumb-screws"; the captain was on deck; the ship, which was light, rolling and pitching as though she would shake the long sticks out of her, and the sails were gaping open and splitting in every direction. The mizzen-topsail, which was a comparatively new sail and close reefed, split from head to foot in the bunt; the foretopsail went in one rent from clew to earing, and was blowing to tatters; one of the chain bobstays parted; the spritsailyard sprung in the slings, the martingale had slued away off to leeward; and owing to the long dry weather the lee rigging hung in large bights at every lurch. One of the main-topgallant shrouds had parted; and to crown all, the galley had got adrift and gone over to leeward, and the anchor on the lee bow had worked loose and was thumping the side. Here was work enough for all hands for half a day. Our gang laid out on the mizzen-topsailyard, and after more than half an hour's hard work furled the sail, though it bellied out over our heads, and again, by a slat of the wind, blew in under the yard with a fearful jerk and almost threw us off from the foot-ropes.

Double gaskets were passed round the yards, rolling tackles and other gear bowsed taut, and everything made as secure as it could be. Coming down, we found the rest of the crew just coming down the fore rigging, having furled the tattered topsail, or rather, swathed it round the yard, which looked like a broken limb bandaged. There was no sail now on the ship but the spanker and the close-reefed main-topsail, which still held good. But this was too much after-sail, and order was given to furl the spanker. The brails were hauled up, and all the light hands in the starboard watch sent out on the gaff to pass the gaskets; but they could do nothing with it. The second mate swore at them for a parcel of "sogers," and sent up a couple of the best men; but they could do no better, and the gaff was lowered down. All hands were now employed in setting up the lee rigging, fishing the spritsail yard, lashing the galley, and getting tackles upon the martingale, to bowse it to windward. Being in the larboard watch, my duty was forward, to assist in setting up the martingale. Three of us were out on the martingale guys and back-ropes for more than half an hour, carrying out, hooking, and unhooking the tackles, several times buried in the seas, until the mate ordered us in from fear of our being washed off. The anchors were then to be taken up on the rail, which kept all hands on the forecastle for an hour, though every now and then the seas broke over it, washing the rigging off to leeward, filling the lee scuppers breast-high, and washing chock aft to the taffrail.

Having got everything secure again, we were promising ourselves some breakfast, for it was now nearly nine o'clock in the forenoon, when the main-topsail showed evident signs of giving way. Some sail must be kept on the ship, and the captain ordered the fore and main spencer gaffs to be lowered down, and the two spencers (which were storm sails, brand-new, small, and made of the strongest canvas) to be got up and bent; leaving the main-topsail to blow away, with a blessing on it, if it would only last until we could set the spencers. These we bent on very carefully, with strong robands and seizings, and making tackles fast to the clews, bowsed them down to the water-ways. By this time the main-topsail was among the things that have been, and we went aloft to stow away the remnant of the last sail of all those which were on the ship twenty-four hours before. The spencers were now the only whole sails on the ship, and being strong and small, and near the deck, presenting but little surface to the wind above the rail, promised to hold out well. Hove-to under these, and eased by having no sail above the tops, the ship rose and fell, and drifted off to leeward like a line-of-battle ship.

It was now eleven o'clock, and the watch was sent below to get breakfast, and at eight bells (noon), as everything was snug, although the gale had not in the least abated, the watch was set and the other watch and idlers sent below. For three days and three nights the gale continued with unabated fury, and with singular regularity. There were no lulls, and very little variation in its fierceness. Our ship, being light, rolled so as almost to send the fore yard-arm under water, and drifted off bodily to leeward. All this time there was not a cloud to be seen in the sky, day or night; no, not so large as a man's hand. Every morning the sun rose cloudless from the sea, and set again at night in the sea in a flood of light. The stars, too, came out of the blue one after another, night after night, unobscured, and twinkled as clear as on a still frosty night at home, until the day came upon them. All this time the sea was rolling in immense surges, white with foam, as far as the eye could reach, on every side; for we were now leagues and leagues from shore.

# WINTER ORCHARD

## Josephine Johnson

*Here is the quiet, simple story of what happened in an orchard during a severe ice-storm—to the trees, the birds and animals, and the fish in the near-by pond. Josephine Johnson, a Missouri author whose novel* Now in November *won the Pulitzer Prize in 1934, is a poet as well, even in her prose.*

THE HILLS are mild but high, long-sloping and yet not austere. They rise gradually, one after another, and on the second hill is the orchard where knotty fruit still hangs, red and wizened ghoul apples and brown peachstones like cocoons. Not even the young terrific winds of March can loosen these old shrivels, though in October the young fruit fell like plummets even in the moving of a mist.

In the winter of the ice storm, when nothing was left unsheathed or open to the air, all the trees were seen as through glass, so that the sun clashed and burned in their branches, but without heat; and every bud dripped small and glittering icicles. The ground was frozen over with four layers of snow and ice, and had a crust like white, undented iron. The rabbits starved, and skittered over its surface to gnaw the apple boles. The gashes of their teeth stretched two feet high above the ground, yellow and alive in all the frozen cold. They gnawed the stems of snowberries, and the low vines were peeled white. In the saw of the north wind we scattered corn under the trees to fill the rabbits' shrunken pelts, but they stripped the bark in increasing circles and died because they had not strength to escape the hawks and hunters, or the beagle hounds that skidded noisily over the ice fields, shattering the frozen aster stalks and stems of sorrel. Torn tufts of rabbit fur blew in the buck-brush clump, and their hawk-picked bones were scattered on the fallen sycamore. Those that lived gnawed frozen apples, and starved until the spring.

[ 730 ]

It was beautiful, though, in its white and awful indifference. The north wind rattled the elm branches together, and the brittle goldenrod shot across the ice ground, broken from its stem. It was hard to walk upright even on the level places, and the slopes were impossible to climb. We slid down hills and crawled up on our hands and knees, or pounded out each step to make some foothold in the steel. The air came icedown, cold like mountain water, in the lungs. There was no food for the woodpeckers. Each branch was bound in a solid coat of glass, and in the bitter wind the crows and jays disappeared, so that the orchard was empty of all sound except the thin branches thrown against each other. Wherever they could break through the icy sheath, the titmice tore open the orchard-moth cocoons and ate the fat pupa cases there, so that few moths lived to the spring. But those that the titmice could not break were among the few things that had no suffering or starvation in this iron winter, and lay senseless in the dark quiet of their shells.

At sunset the orchard reflected the sky-like water, and the west light changed to shell and orchid when it struck the ice, and ran like cold sap along the glassy twigs. It was somehow terrible, walking between the frozen boles in the clear light—for it was bitterly clear in those days, and the sun without heat—to think of them bound unmoving in the hard ground, unable to stir or to escape the wind. All night in the poured moon-air and in the coldest hours near dawn they would have to stand there, fastened by their own iron gyves into the earth. The nights had a bitter intensity, and when the wind died it was like a world in which trees and shadows and the light were frozen in the air, which itself was solid ice, and through it the stars were seen, magnified and enormous.

The trees were planted within a road's space of the pond, and in the spring rains the water spread out until the apple trees along the edge stood inch-deep in sloppy pools. But in the ice winter the pond was frozen a foot deep, and the marsh grasses along the rim were bent over in a glassy mesh. The only air that the fish could get came from the broken holes when ice was cut, and these froze over in an hour's time. The willows had a gaunt, twisted look, and their roots were level with the ice, submerged all winter in the frozen water. It was queer to think that the pond had ever shrunk till its bare mud rim stretched out on every side and the willows were a long way off, as though they had moved themselves away.

Quail lived, through that winter, where the corn was scattered under a brush pile near the orchard, and once the dogs sent up a

hawk with the bloody body of one in its claws, while the covey
flew off with a queer crying sound, more sad than frightened. Blood
spots were on the snow, and small breast feathers blown and tangled
in the rusty vines. When the snow fell at night, adding layer after
layer to the already smothered earth, the tracks of field mice were
stitched across its surface in the morning, and the brush marks of
wings that had come near for an instant to the snow, then were
carried up in heavy flight. There was something, neither mouse nor
mole, which made its tunnel under the spot where the corn was
scattered. It was dark-furred, with small round ears, and one saw it
only either coming or going, never quite in view. But it fed well,
having made its home under the very table of its food.

The long freezing came slowly to a close, and late in February
the first inches of the icy shell softened and spread in pools along
the ice beneath. There were days of cold rain and fog in which the
tired ice slid and shattered to the pitmarked earth. Slowly the
earth showed through the ragged southern banks, and at last there
came an hour in which a redness flowed along the apple branches—
a redness which was not sun on ice, but the warm magenta stain
of birth.

## Mist

Low anchored cloud,
 Newfoundland air,
Fountain-head and source of rivers,
Dew-cloth, dream drapery,
And napkins spread by fays;
Drifting meadow of the air,
Where bloom the daisied banks and violets,
And in whose fenny labyrinth
The bittern booms and heron wades;
Spirit of lakes and seas and rivers,—
Bear only perfumes and the scent
Of healing herbs to just men's fields.

*Henry David Thoreau*

# HIGH-WATER MARK

## Bret Harte

*One of the first great literary figures from the Far West, Harte (1836–1902) was born in Albany, New York. He was eighteen when he went to California. After eight years and many jobs, mining among them, he founded* The Overland Monthly; *for it he wrote "The Luck of Roaring Camp," "The Outcasts of Poker Flat," and many other stories that made him famous. As few others, Harte knew the hard-bitten folk of the frontier and the forces of nature confronting them, like the flood in this story.*

WHEN the tide was out on the Dedlow Marsh, its extended dreariness was patent. Its spongy, low-lying surface, sluggish, inky pools, and tortuous sloughs, twisting their slimy way, eel-like, toward the open bay, were all hard facts. So were the few green tussocks, with their scant blades, their amphibious flavor, and unpleasant dampness. And if you choose to indulge your fancy,—although the flat monotony of the Dedlow Marsh was not inspiring,—the wavy line of scattered drift gave an unpleasant consciousness of the spent waters, and made the dead certainty of the returning tide a gloomy reflection, which no present sunshine could dissipate. The greener meadowland seemed oppressed with this idea, and made no positive attempt at vegetation until the work of reclamation should be complete. In the bitter fruit of the low cranberry-bushes one might fancy he detected a naturally sweet disposition curdled and soured by an injudicious course of too much regular cold water.

The vocal expression of the Dedlow Marsh was also melancholy and depressing. The sepulchral boom of the bittern, the shriek of the curlew, the scream of passing brent, the wrangling of quarrelsome teal, the sharp, querulous protest of the startled crane, and syllabled complaint of the "killdeer" plover were beyond the power of written expression. Nor was the aspect of these mournful fowls at all cheerful and inspiring. Certainly not the blue heron standing midleg deep in the water, obviously catching cold in a reckless disregard of wet feet and consequences; nor the mournful curlew, the dejected plover, or the low-spirited snipe, who saw fit to join him in his suicidal contemplation; nor the impassive king-fisher—an ornithological Marius—reviewing the desolate expanse; nor the black raven that went to and fro over the face of the marsh continually, but evidently couldn't make up his mind whether the waters had subsided, and felt low-spirited in the reflection that, after all this trouble, he wouldn't be able to give a definite answer. On the contrary, it was evident at a glance that the dreary expanse of Dedlow Marsh told unpleasantly on the birds, and that the season of migration was looked forward to with a feeling of relief and satisfaction by the full-grown, and of extravagant anticipation by the callow, brood. But if Dedlow Marsh was cheerless at the slack of the low tide, you should have seen it when the tide was strong and full. When the damp air blew chilly over the cold, glittering expanse, and came to the faces of those who looked sea-ward like another tide; when a steel-like glint marked the low hollows and the sinuous line of slough; when the great shell-incrusted trunks of fallen trees arose again, and went forth on their dreary, purposeless wanderings, drifting hither and thither, but getting no farther toward any goal at the falling tide or the day's decline than the cursed Hebrew in the legend; when the glossy ducks swung silently, making neither ripple nor furrow on the shimmering surface; when the fog came in with the tide and shut out the blue above, even as the green below had been obliter-ated; when boatmen, lost in that fog, paddling about in a hopeless way, started at what seemed the brushing of mermen's fingers on the boat's keel, or shrank from the tufts of grass spreading around like the floating hair of a corpse, and knew by these signs that they were lost upon Dedlow Marsh, and must make a night of it, and a gloomy one at that,—then you might know something of Dedlow Marsh at high water.

Let me recall a story connected with this latter view which never failed to recur to my mind in my long gunning excursions upon Dedlow Marsh. Although the event was briefly recorded in the county paper, I had the story, in all its eloquent detail, from the lips of the principal actor. I cannot hope to catch the varying emphasis and peculiar coloring of feminine delineation, for my narrator was a woman; but I'll try to give at least its substance.

She lived midway of the great slough of Dedlow Marsh and a good-sized river, which debouched four miles beyond into an estuary formed by the Pacific Ocean, on the long sandy peninsula which constituted the southwestern boundary of a noble bay. The house in which she lived was a small frame cabin raised from the marsh a few feet by stout piles, and was three miles distant from the settlements upon the river. Her husband was a logger,—a profitable business in a country where the principal occupation was the manufacture of lumber.

It was the season of early spring, when her husband left on the ebb of a high tide, with a raft of logs for the usual transportation to the lower end of the bay. As she stood by the door of the little cabin when the voyagers departed she noticed a cold look in the southeastern sky, and she remembered hearing her husband say to his companions that they must endeavor to complete their voyage before the coming of the southwesterly gale which he saw brewing. And that night it began to storm and blow harder than she had ever before experienced, and some great trees fell in the forest by the river, and the house rocked like her baby's cradle.

But however the storm might roar about the little cabin, she knew that one she trusted had driven bolt and bar with his own strong hand, and that had he feared for her he would not have left her. This, and her domestic duties, and the care of her little sickly baby, helped to keep her mind from dwelling on the weather, except, of course, to hope that he was safely harbored with the logs at Utopia in the dreary distance. But she noticed that day, when she went out to feed the chickens and look after the cow, that the tide was up to the little fence of their garden-patch, and the roar of the surf on the south beach, though miles away, she could hear distinctly. And she began to think that she would like to have some one to talk with about matters, and she believed that if it had not been so far and so stormy, and the trail so impassable, she would have taken the baby and have gone over to Ryckman's, her nearest neighbor. But then, you see, he might have returned in the storm, all wet, with no one to see to him; and it was a long exposure for baby, who was croupy and ailing.

But that night, she never could tell why, she didn't feel like sleeping or even lying down. The storm had somewhat abated, but she still "sat and sat," and even tried to read. I don't know whether it was a Bible or some profane magazine that this poor woman read, but most probably the latter, for the words all ran together and made such sad nonsense that she was forced at last to put the book down and turn to that dearer volume which lay before her in the cradle, with its white initial leaf as yet unsoiled, and try to look forward to its mysterious future. And, rocking the cradle, she thought of everything and everybody, but still was wide awake as ever.

It was nearly twelve o'clock when she at last laid down in her clothes. How long she slept she could not remember, but she awoke with a dreadful choking in her throat, and found herself standing, trembling all over, in the middle of the room, with her baby clasped to her breast, and she was "saying something." The baby cried and sobbed, and she walked up and down trying to hush it, when she heard a scratching at the door. She opened it fearfully, and was glad to see it was only old Pete, their dog, who crawled, dripping with water, into the room. She would like to have looked out, not in the faint hope of her husband's coming, but to see how things looked; but the wind shook the door so savagely that she could hardly hold it. Then she sat down a little while, and then walked up and down a little while, and then she lay down again a little while. Lying close by the wall of the little cabin, she thought she heard once or twice something scrape slowly against the clapboards, like the scraping of branches. Then there was a little gurgling sound, "like the baby made when it was swallowing"; then something went "click-click" and "cluck-cluck," so that she sat up in bed. When she did so she was attracted by something else that seemed creeping from the back door towards the centre of the room. It wasn't much wider than her little finger, but soon it swelled to the width of her hand, and began spreading all over the floor. It was water.

She ran to the front door and threw it wide open, and saw nothing but water. She ran to the back door and threw it open, and saw nothing but water. She ran to the side window, and, throwing that open, she saw nothing but water. Then she remembered hearing her husband once say that there was no danger in the tide, for that fell regularly, and people could calculate on it, and that he would rather live near the bay than the river, whose banks might overflow at any time. But was it the tide? So she ran again to the back door, and threw out a stick of wood. It drifted away towards the bay. She scooped up some of the water and put it eagerly to her lips. It was fresh and sweet. It was the river, and not the tide!

It was then—O, God be praised for his goodness! she did neither faint nor fall; it was then—blessed be the Saviour for it was his merciful hand that touched and strengthened her in this awful moment—that fear dropped from her like a garment, and her trembling ceased. It was then and thereafter that she never lost her self-command, through all the trials of that gloomy night.

She drew the bedstead towards the middle of the room, and placed a table upon it and on that she put the cradle. The water on the floor was already over her ankles, and the house once or twice moved so perceptibly, and seemed to be racked so, that the closet doors all flew open. Then she heard the same rasping and thumping against the wall, and, looking out, saw that a large uprooted tree, which had lain near the road at the upper end of the pasture, had floated down to the house. Luckily its long roots dragged in the soil and kept it from moving as rapidly as the current, for had it struck the house in its full career, even the strong nails and bolts in the piles could not have withstood the shock. The hound had leaped upon its knotty surface, and crouched near the roots shivering and whining. A ray of hope flashed across her mind. She drew a heavy blanket from the bed, and, wrapping it about the babe, waded in the deepening waters to the door. As the tree swung again, broadside on, making the little cabin creak and tremble, she leaped on to its trunk. By God's mercy she succeeded in obtaining a footing on its slippery surface, and, twining an arm about its roots, she held in the other her moaning child. Then something cracked near the front porch, and the whole front of the house she had just quitted fell forward,—just as cattle fall on their knees before they lie down, —and at the same moment the great redwood-tree swung round and drifted away with its living cargo into the black night.

For all the excitement and danger, for all her soothing of her crying babe, for all the whistling of the wind, for all the uncertainty of her situation, she still turned to look at the deserted and water-swept cabin. She remembered even then, and she wondered how foolish she was to think of it at that time, that she wished she had put on another dress and the baby's best clothes; and she kept praying that the house would be spared so that he, when he returned, would have something to come to, and it wouldn't be quite so desolate, and—how could he ever know what had become of her and baby? And at the thought she grew sick and faint. But she had something else to do besides worrying, for whenever the long roots of her ark struck an obstacle, the whole trunk made half a revolution, and twice dipped her in the black water. The hound, who kept distracting her by running up and down the tree and howling, at last fell off at one of these collisions. He swam for some time beside her, and she tried to get the poor beast upon the tree, but he "acted silly" and wild, and at last she lost sight of him forever. Then she and her baby were left alone. The light which had burned for a few minutes in the deserted cabin was quenched suddenly. She could not then tell whither she was drifting. The outline of the white dunes on the peninsula showed dimly ahead, and she judged the tree was moving in a line with the river. It must be about slack water, and she had probably reached the eddy formed by the confluence of the tide and the overflowing waters of the river. Unless the tide fell soon, there was present danger of her drifting to its channel, and being carried out to sea or crushed in the floating drift. That peril averted, if she were carried out on the ebb toward the bay, she might hope to strike one of the wooded promontories of the peninsula, and rest till daylight. Sometimes she thought she heard voices and shouts from the river, and the bellowing of cattle and bleating of sheep. Then again it was only the ringing in her ears and throbbing of her heart. She found at about this time that she was so chilled and stiffened in her cramped position that she could scarcely move, and the baby cried so when she put it to her breast that she noticed the milk refused to flow; and she was so frightened at that, that she put her head under her shawl, and for the first time cried bitterly.

When she raised her head again, the boom of the surf was behind her, and she knew that her ark had again swung round. She dipped up the water to cool her parched throat, and found that it was salt as her tears. There was a relief, though, for by this sign she knew that she was drifting with the tide. It was then the wind went down, and the great and awful silence oppressed her. There was scarcely a ripple against the furrowed sides of the great trunk on which she rested, and around her all was black gloom and quiet. She spoke to the baby just to hear herself speak, and to know that she had not lost her voice. She thought then,—it was queer, but she could not help thinking it,—how awful must have been the night when the great ship swung over the Asiatic peak, and the sounds of creation were blotted out from the world. She thought, too, of mariners clinging to spars, and of poor women who were lashed to rafts, and beaten to death by the cruel sea. She tried to thank God that she was thus spared, and lifted her eyes from the baby who had fallen into a fretful sleep. Suddenly, away to the south-ward, a great light lifted itself out of the gloom, and flashed and flickered, and flickered and flashed again. Her heart fluttered quickly against the baby's cold cheek. It was the lighthouse at the entrance of the bay. As she was yet wondering, the tree suddenly rolled a little, dragged a little, and then seemed to lie quiet and still. She put out her hand and the current gurgled against it. The tree was aground, and, by the position of the light and the noise of the surf, aground upon the Dedlow Marsh.

Had it not been for her baby, who was ailing and croupy, had it not been for the sudden drying up of that sensitive fountain, she would have felt safe and relieved. Perhaps it was this which tended to make all her impressions mournful and gloomy. As the tide rapidly fell, a great flock of black brent fluttered by her, screaming and crying. Then the plover flew up and piped mournfully, as they wheeled around the trunk, and at last fearlessly lit upon it like a gray cloud. Then the heron flew over and around her, shrieking and protesting, and at last dropped its gaunt legs only a few yards from her. But, strangest of all, a pretty white bird, larger than a dove,—like a pelican, but not a pelican,—circled around and around her. At last it lit upon a rootlet of the tree, quite over her shoulder. She put out her hand and stroked its beautiful white neck, and it never appeared to move. It stayed there so long that she thought she would lift up the baby to see it, and try to attract her attention. But when she did so, the child was so chilled and cold, and had such a blue look under the little lashes which it didn't raise at all, that she screamed aloud, and the bird flew away, and she fainted.

Well, that was the worst of it, and perhaps it was not so much, after all, to any but herself. For when she recovered her senses it was bright sunlight, and dead low water. There was a confused noise of guttural voices about her, and an old squaw, singing an Indian "hushaby," and rocking herself from side to side before a fire built on the marsh, before which she, the recovered wife and mother, lay weak and weary. Her first thought was for her baby, and she was about to speak, when a young squaw, who must have been a mother herself, fathomed her thought and brought her the "mowitch," pale but living, in such a queer little willow cradle all bound up, just like the squaw's own young one, that she laughed and cried together, and the young squaw and the old squaw showed their big white teeth and glinted their black eyes and said, "Plenty get well, skeena mowitch," "wagee man come plenty soon," and she could have kissed their brown faces in her joy. And then she found that they had been gathering berries on the marsh in their queer, comical baskets, and saw the skirt of her gown fluttering on the tree from afar, and the old squaw couldn't resist the temptation of procuring a new garment, and came down and discovered the "wagee" woman and child. And of course she gave the garment to the old squaw, as you may imagine, and when *he* came at last and rushed up to her, looking about ten years older in anxiety, she felt so faint again that they had to carry her to the canoe. For, you see, he knew nothing about the flood until he met the Indians at Utopia, and knew by the signs that the poor woman was his wife. And at the next high-tide he towed the tree away back home, although it wasn't worth the trouble, and built another house, using the old tree for the foundation and props, and called it after her, "Mary's Ark!" But you may guess the next house was built above High-Water Mark. And that's all.

Not much, perhaps, considering the malevolent capacity of the Dedlow Marsh. But you must tramp over it at low water, or paddle over it at high tide, or get lost upon it once or twice in the fog, as I have, to understand properly Mary's adventure, or to appreciate duly the blessings of living beyond High-Water Mark.

### The Sick Rose

O Rose, thou art sick!
    The invisible worm,
That flies in the night,
    In the howling storm,

Has found out thy bed
    Of crimson joy;
And his dark secret love
    Does thy life destroy.

*William Blake*

# WILDERNESS ORPHAN

## Dorothy Cottrell

*Here is an unusual story of animal adventure—a full-length
novelette about a wild creature reared by men and then almost
destroyed by them. Chut, the kangaroo, and his world "down
under" come vividly alive in this moving tale by a well-known
novelist and short-story writer.*

THE big moon poked up through the dead trees at the head of
the backwash of Tom Henton's Dam; its golden face reflected
in the still waters. The moon was immense, dramatic, and as it rose
the landscape took on pale colors; grey and silver, lilac and faint
green; a splendid, silver shining that paled the stars.

A group of teal stirred in the growing radiance. A heron on a
high tree changed from one leg to the other. The innumerable elephant moths in quest of honey became grey, darting and pausing
velvet blurs—instead of merely unseen, humming, brushing bodies.
The thin-petalled, wild white spider lilies all along the semi-arid,
sloping bank of the water-way shone as brighter star-reflections
on the dry earth; their scent filling the night like some invisible,
still tide; through which the three men crept down to the shelter
of a pile of weather-bleached mulga logs. There were several faint
clicks as the hunters threw up the cartridges in their rifles and set
the safety catches. . . . Then silence again.

And, presently, down a little dusty pad through the bleached
silver grass of the bank-top came a kangaroo family on its way to
water, moving with tranquil undulation upon hoppers and hands.

The "old man" of the mob came first—an immense red warrior,
velvet-furred in pale chestnut across back and thighs, tawny cream
on chest and belly; weighing three hundred pounds, and standing
seven feet when he rose upright upon toes and tail to face an enemy.
In his train, sixteen wives and several small, fat joeys followed de-
corously; the does much smaller than their lord, and, with the ex-

ception of one who was a beautiful dove-blue, all furred in brownish mouse-color. Their ears against the moon-paled stars were large and quivering, and sensitive as weather-vanes; their eyes immense and liquidly dark, deer-like and seeming deeply sad. Yet in reality they were most happy creatures.

Seeking for shoots or seeds beside the pad, they chitted conversationally and caught with little dark hands at each other's heavy muscular tails where these dragged in the dust. . . .

Then they had come out upon the open sward by the dam, tasted the green picking, and moved to the margin to drink, taking a long time about it and flicking their ears.

And here, as the drink was finished, Chut took his first good look at the world. From this it must not be gathered that he was doing anything as exciting as being born. On the contrary he had lived in his mother's pouch for a long time, changing there from the semblance of a rather undressed pink mouse to a plump, small, ten-pound creature of an exquisitely delicate loveliness. He was confiding, velvety, trembling-eared, with huge dark eyes and little, dark, clutching hands.

Tonight, for the first time, he was dissatisfied with the warm musky security of the pouch. His tiny legs, with their two polished ebony toenails, rebelled at being neatly tucked above his head.

"*Chut!*" he called sharply. "Chut! *Chut!*"

His mother, the little blue doe, answered with a reproving "*Chit!*" and drew shut her pouch-mouth with matronly severity. But Chut had glimpsed a world of magic brightness and keen new scents. He wanted to get out! He kicked, he clawed, making strange commotions beneath his mother's cream-velvet pinafore.

She opened the pouch-mouth with her horny-palmed little hands and spoke sternly to him, whereat he reached up his own small arms and caught her nose, touching his to it as if with a kiss; thereby reducing her to doting adulation.

Had she been older she would never have trusted him to the moonlit dam bank while he was still so little; but she was a very young doe and he was her first baby. Tucking her hands down beside him, she lifted him out and set him on the grass. He staggered clumsily, the moonlight glinting on the silken velvet cowslick in the middle of his plump back, and shining in pinkish-coral through his quivering, veined ears. He clutched at his mother's skirts, tried to steady himself upon his slender hoppers, wobbled—and fell onto his back, his legs sticking up absurdly.

In this attitude the earth felt more secure. After a moment he tentatively grasped at one of his hoppers, as a baby might at its foot. He stretched out to his full length, feeling the unfamiliar thrill of free muscular movement. He grasped his toes again, and looked about him with bright, knowing eyes.

The little doe became less agitated. She too was experiencing for the first time in many weeks the sense of freedom from the warm, nestling burden in her pouch. She sat up to her full height, like a girl-mother pleased by her recovered slenderness. She grasped playfully at a passing elephant moth. And then she too lay down and rolled in the sand and across the short, pungent carpet of herbage. Another doe came and rolled beside her. They grappled, they turned and twisted like any playful children. They leaped up and played tag through the trees.

And then the blue doe found herself at the edge of the lily patch, where the "old man" was pulling up a lily stalk with six white blossoms at its crown—and the young blue doe took it away from him!

Fifty yards up the bank, one of the hunters rested his rifle across the fallen mulga heads. The moon gleamed coldly on the barrel. . . . And the frivolous little doe with the lily was the first to see it!

She drew herself up, holding her hands as a little dog does in begging, her body rigid and backward-curving, her ears fluted in interrogation. Her snicker of danger brought every animal to its feet. For a heart-beat, they poised tensely, lily petals caught in many of their lips: uncertain where to fly—one mother with her hand clutching her baby's ear.

One of the men looked along the luminous sights, steadied for the slow squeeze of the trigger. . . . He wanted the "old man" for a specimen skin.

The shot rent the night—a jarring agony of sound, sending the teal bursting up like shrapnel from their log, sending the heron floating away with harsh cries: shaking the grey moths from the ice-white lilies.

The "old man" staggered, reared high upon magnificent toes and arching lower tail. Up! As he had stood in a hundred fights.

Then he was quiveringly convulsed and fell crashing into the dead twigs behind him.

The frivolous doe dropped her coquettish lily, and fled chitting towards Chut. Other mothers scooped small fat babies into their pouches, boxed larger babies into bouncing flight. Then the mob

was off, twenty, thirty feet at a bound, away through the moonlit
bush.

Only the very young mother was left, because she could not
get Chut back into the pouch. He was frightened out of his baby
wits by the shot, by the panic about him, by the keen smell of
blood.

He grabbed at his mother's fur, trying to find the pouch-mouth
where it was not, refusing to let her guide him.

The men were running up. The mother made a last frantic
effort to get the joey into her pouch. He missed it and slipped, chitting, to the ground. Terror got the better of her, and she bolted—
only to halt fifty yards away in a patch of shadow and call loudly
for Chut. But Chut was too little to come. He called back: "Chut!
*Chut*-chut!"

The men were bending over the old 'roo.

The doe began to come back, hesitating, trembling. Chut made
a wobbling dash for her, and she grabbed him up, and this time he
found the pouch-mouth and was back in its musky security.

One of the men shouted: "Jove! There's another!"

The doe cleared the bar of fallen timber in a terrific leap, and
was away. Chut, crouching trembling in her pouch, felt the flying
surge of the leaps, the strong urge of her muscles as she landed and
took off again.

Then there was a paralyzing shock. Accompanied by a duller
repetition of the sound that had started all the trouble. Instead of
coming to ground with a lithe-cushioned, elastic ease, they came
down with a crushing, crashing fall.

Then the doe was up again, on again, with a wild, erratic,
stumbling flight. The men's voices died out behind them.

Chut could feel the trembling shock of the doe's heart. Then
her speed slackened, faltered.

He felt that danger was over and began to re-settle himself in
the pouch preparatory to his evening meal. To his surprise the doe
gave a shrill cry of pain and clutched him out to the earth. Even
as she did so, she fell. He saw that all her side was strangely dark
and wet. He was frightened and held to her fur, but she made no
effort to caress him. Instead, her hands clutched at her side. She
rolled as if playing, but he knew that she was not playing.

Then she became quite still. Chut was frightened by the silence.
He wanted to go back into the despised pouch. He wanted food.

He called and called, protesting at her callousness. Presently he even nubbled at her nose, and as he did so something told him that she was no longer there. He had no definite thought for it, but he knew that this was ending of warm softness and warm food, of nubbled noses, and mutual chitting.

A weak, small, furry thing, with great deer's eyes and quivering ears, he sat up, holding his little hands as a small dog does when it begs.

He had no knowledge of the world in which he sat, but something told him that it was as well to show a brave face towards it. He chittered with all the energy of his minute voice.

"Chut-chit! *Chut!*"

Repeatedly he rose to the full of his twenty-inch height and scolded the great grey-and-black bowl of the earth and the cold whiteness of the now high-risen moon. Then, feeling a little reassured, and because it is the nature of babies to sleep, he slept, holding tightly to the fur of his dead mother. . . .

He woke with an overwhelming shock of panic. Light such as he had never known was beating upon and blinding him. He tried futilely to hide from it, but there was no escape. Light gleamed upon the silver of the dead grass, upon the red dust, still damp with dew, light hammered from the vast blue sky.

Last night he had been safe in the warm darkness of his mother's pouch, where, after the manner of the kangaroos, she would have carried him for many weeks to come. In the dark he would have slept there, warm and a little stuffy and very secure: been fed abundantly with sweet, thick milk from long leathery maternal teats: peeped at the varied world; withdrawn again. As he had grown stronger he would have come out for moonlit games by the dam—somersaulted back into the pouch. In the daylight he would have felt the warmth and the amber glow of the sun striking through the delicate, furred membranes of the pouch-wall. As he grew older still he would have followed his mother with little dainty hoppings along the sunny trails through the grass: but always she would have been there.

A rifle shot in the moonlight had ended all that. His mother lay stiff and still in the early light. For Chut there was neither shelter nor food. And his long legs were still wobbly with babyhood, his little quick, black hands infantinely uncertain of their movements.

As he sat, unhappy and shelterless in the flood of light, a great shadow swept across the dust as a big wedge-tailed eagle passed overhead.

Chut called to it tentatively—it was at least life. For a moment the great bird hung almost motionless in the pervading, incredible blue. Its black wing feathers quivering and bending a little beneath the burden of its weight, its eyes sharply golden, its burnished neck feathers sweeping down to the small, cruel, black head with its curved, polished beak.

The little kangaroo looked back at the bird of prey without fear: apart from the shock and fright of the shot last night, Chut had found the world wholly kind.

The big bird half closed its wings, so that its whole form became that of a wedge, at the same moment it altered its angle to the earth so that it tilted forward, poised, and then shot with the hurtling velocity of a missile towards the furred baby at the edge of the grass. As the missile neared its mark the great taloned legs shot from their feathered sheathes and extended, tensely clutching for the small, fat back beneath the velvet fur.

Had Chut been a day older, he would have been the eagle's prey in that first swoop, for he would have tried to escape by hopping flight, and been grasped up at the first hop. As it was he tried to hop, lost his balance, and fell ignominiously straddled, upon his stomach.

The eagle's wings opened, he clutched at Chut, leaving a knife-like cut across the russet fur, missed his hold, and rocketed up again with his own momentum. Chut quivered; amazed by pain. The eagle's every wing feather sang in sharp sibilance as he wheeled and plunged again at the terrified joey, and as he did so another eagle, who had come up unobserved, struck him with a ridged wing with a force of a five hundred foot plunge behind it!

Both birds were thrown off their balance and smote the air with heavy floppings, giving harsh calls of rage. Once upset in this way it took them some moments to recover the even sureness of their flight.

Before they did so, another eagle settled upon the carcass of the dead doe. The two first arrivals were outraged. For a moment they wheeled between the dead mother and the living baby—then laziness and greed got the better of them. Like a pair of greedy, flapping old hens they lighted on the earth near the body, and flopped and hopped grotesquely towards it. Chut fled wobblingly into the grass. He had learned one lesson—to place no unobservant trust in the sky.

For a while he sat trembling in the tall grass, then an idea began to take shape. He believed that if he could find the dam again he would be all right.

He had been happy there last night, and, more important, there had been many moon-silvered forms like his mother's feeding amongst the lilies on the bank. . . . With many hesitations, he set out, guided by a blind, inherent sense of direction.

The grass tripped him up, and the barbed leaf-edges cut his tender velvet skin across the hocks and thighs. The twigs poked him ignominiously in the furry expanse of his little stomach. He jumped at shadows, twittered with fear at the sounds of the wind. Then he stumbled upon a little dusty pad through the grass. It smelled of kangaroos! Here juicy crowfoot had been crushed. Here seed-heads scattered. Something told him that the pad led to the dam, and he moved along it, the while his legs were becoming a trifle more sure of themselves. He felt better on the pad. The amber wall of the kangaroo grass towered up upon either side of him, the golden ears screening away the fearful sky.

He travelled on and on—farther than he had known there was—making absurdly small hopper-marks in the dust as he went.

At last he had come perhaps some five hundred yards; and he believed that he was not so far from the dam. He was exhausted now, but hunger and fright drove him forward. Then, from ahead, there came a terrifying sound! A pattering, moving sound of many bodies crowding round the bend of the path. Chut sat up. His ears fanned forward, listening: his chubby little body bending backward with surprise.

And then a huge, woolly creature came round the turn: stopped, looked at him, and stamped its terrible hoof!

Behind it were more huge creatures of the same kind.

Chut was not to know that the old ewe was quite as alarmed as he was, and that her stamps were her one inadequate defense against a marauding world.

To the little kangaroo she appeared to have the proportions of a dinosaur and a forehead of thunder.

Stumbling, bleeding and weak, Chut turned and fled back the way he had come.

The day burned through its fierce noon, and faded through the long, golden afternoon. And dusk had almost come before he got within scent of the dam again, and his sides were pinched with thirst and his fur dust-draggled from falls. But he hung on to his purpose.

And then the earth began to slope towards the glimmer of evening-pinkened water, and he smelled the overpowering scent of the lilies. The cool short herbage was grateful to his small bruised feet, and led by some obscure instinct, he, who had never tasted water, hurried on hands and hoppers towards the water.

But at the margin he did not know what to do. He was terribly thirsty but he had never drunk anything but milk, and to do this he had wriggled upon his back in the pouch and grasped one of his mother's teats in his little hands.

Now, something told him that the water might soothe the torture of his thirst, but he never dreamed of *stooping* his lips to it. Instead, after looking warily about, he placed his little hands on the sod, lowered his head between them and turned a quite dexterous somersault! Once on his back his hands reached up hopefully— but there was no kind source of food and drink awaiting them.

He called, but there was silence and emptiness.

Far up, little pink curdled clouds moved over an amber-green sky. Then from down the dam a shrieking cloud of rose-breasted galah parrots went home to bed, and the noise sent Chut scuttling beneath a bush.

But he was so hungry now that he soon came out again. And then he saw the shadowy, insolently graceful forms of kangaroos coming down to the water through the warm dusk.

For a minute he was so excited that he sat still, with his heart beating so that it shook his little body. Then he chitted and darted out towards them, moving swiftly, hop, hop, hop, his little hands held out as if he was reaching for something.

He was so driven by his desperate urgency, so haunted by the frights of the day, that he simply rushed to the nearest one of the shadowy forms which his instinct told him was a mother. Here was shelter, warm food, small touches in the dark!

He clutched at her fur, nubbling it with his little nose, clinging, and chitting sibilantly. The doe, whose own joey was in her pouch, looked down for a moment in astonishment. Then, with a loud scolding of rage, she fell upon the intruder, catching his ears in her hands, shaking him to and fro, scratching him, and finally kicking him in the stomach with the unwomanly dexterity of a French boxer.

Chut fell upon his little round back into the tangle of fleshy wild-lily leaves, too astonished for further protest.

Then he crept weakly away into the shadows, twittering with bewilderment. And as he did so the night was split and shattered by fire and sound!

The young male who had been leading the mob fell dead. The young female who had scuffed Chut so ruthlessly, also fell. There was thudding flight, confusion, and then the three men ran up.

They made sure that the fallen kangaroos were dead, then laughed, and set to work at their skinning. Just as they were finish-ing, one dropped his knife. Flashing his torch to find it—the beams illumined Chut.

"Jove!" said the man. "There's a little fellow!"

He pounced upon Chut, who simply shrank into himself and waited for the last spasm of the terror which was death.

"He's a little beauty," said the man. "I'm going to take him home to my wife." He held Chut up ridiculously by the scruff of the neck and poked him with his finger. Then the man looked puzzled. "He's all scratched and he's been cut across the back—looks like an eagle's had him. . . . Say, I guess, he must have belonged to the doe that got away last night! Poor little nipper!" The other two men pressed round.

"Let's take him and give him a drink!" Gathering up the skins, they moved off round the head of the dam, Chut hanging limp and hopeless under the big man's arm.

At the camp, back over the ridge, there was discussion as to how the baby should be fed and some facetious suggestions of sending for Dr. Holt's *Book on Infant Feeding*. Then the first man said: "He won't drink unless he's upside down. . . ."

So they got an old pair of trousers and tied a knot in one leg at the knee, and hung the trousers to a tree limb by the back-strap.

Then they held Chut up before it. He looked at it in confusion.

"Better let him get in himself," said the big man. He gave Chut a friendly pinch. It worked. Instinctively Chut grasped the edge of the trousers, lowered his head, and bracing his hoppers against the big man's stomach, turned his dexterous somersault into the warm depths of the leg!

Once again he was swinging as a little kangaroo should swing. He was enclosed; safe. He gave a feeble, twittering chitter.

One of the other men stepped forward and presented him with

the end of a bit of insulating rubber, from which the wire had been withdrawn, and whose other end was in a tin of milk.

Chut sucked, sucked again. Milk was in his mouth. He gave little ticking sounds of bliss, and, still drinking, he fell asleep in the maternal embrace of the trouser leg.

Chut's wound healed. The men were good to him. He learned the new smells of fire-smoke, and potatoes roasting in ashes; the mellow smell of coffee and the sharp tang of tea, the odors of frizzling bacon and grilling chops; of tobacco smoke by a camp fire under stars; and the sneeziness of raw flour, and the smell of men. He learned that fire was hot, and kerosene nasty. His ears attuned themselves to new sounds, for the men were as noisy as the wilderness was silent. Clatter of plates, loud jests and louder laughter, galloping of horses and clanging music of horse-bells, ceased to appall him.

When, after a month's work on the lower run, the big man returned to his selection house, Chut went with him—swinging securely in one leg of a pair of old trousers attached to the man's saddle. Only when the horse's trotting caused the trouser leg to bounce did he chirrup in protest. Arrived at the small, tree-set homestead, the man was met by his young wife; and Chut observing the meeting through a cigarette hole in the trouser leg, sensed that it was affectionate.

"I've brought you home a baby!" the big man said.

As his wife stared at him between laughter-crinkled eyelids, he untied the old trousers from the pommel of the saddle, and extended them towards her—one of the legs showing plumply bulged. She took the garments hesitatingly, peered into the top, perceived Chut where he waited in bright-eyed, velvet-furred minuteness, and exclaimed: "Oh, the darling, sweet, tiny thing!"

The man dismounted, and stepped up to her.

"He is *so little!*" she said.

"And *so soft* . . ."

"And *so fat* . . ."

At that the man took her in his arms.

"What," she said, "will we call him?"

But, squeezed between the big man and his wife, Chut was very uncomfortable. He gave a surprisingly loud and indignant cry of protest.

"Chut! Chut! *Chut-ch-ch-ch-ch!*"

So he was called "Chut" which prior to this time had simply been his staple of conversation and announcement of his presence.

During the day he followed the girl about like a little dog. At night he slept in the trousers which swung by the big, outside fire-place—these habiliments coming to be known as "Chut's pants."

He would come when the woman called him, and somersault neatly into her lap as she sat on the steps. There, lying on his back, he took his supper to the accompaniment of small kicks of pleasure. He was also promoted to all the dignity of a real baby's bottle instead of the bit of insulating tube fastened to a condensed milk tin with which the men had nourished him in camp. The selection dogs were introduced to him one by one, it being forcefully explained to them that he was taboo.

There was soft green grass in which he might roll, and many trailing pepper trees beneath which to play small solitary games. In short, his world was eminently satisfactory—save for one thing.

There was at the homestead a ridiculously fat, excessively bumptious lamb, by name William Mutton. To William had belonged the baby's bottle before Chut took it over, and William harbored a dark and bitter resentment at the loss of his bottle.

He was an incredibly greedy lamb. And, although fed to repletion, he was forever sucking at the woman's fingers, at her apron strings, at the tassels of blinds—anything. A moment after having eaten until he could eat no more, he called pitifully of his semi-starvation. To see anyone else eat appeared to cause him pain.

"That lamb," said the big man, "is not, I fear, of a generous turn of mind. He might even be described as a little grasping."

At least, to see Chut being nourished appeared to sear the very soul of William Mutton.

Chut had been eager to be friendly. Upon one of the first occasions when he had ventured on a little walk by himself, he had come upon the lamb around a trailing pepper branch. The baleful gleam in William Mutton's eye meant nothing to him. All he saw was a creature of approximately his own size who might possibly want to sport a little.

Chut drew himself up to his now twenty-five-inch height, and standing poised upon the arch of his lower tail and the tips of his toes he gave a few stiff, bouncing, little side-hops—the kangaroo's invitation to play.

"Chut!" he remarked affably. "Chut! Ch-ch!"

William's head dropped lower. He focused evilly upon the

cream-velvet rotundity of Chut's stomach. Then, with a malevolent "Baa," he charged upon the little kangaroo.

His round woolly head met Chut's silk-furred stomach with a resonant *plop*. Chut grunted and fell, kicking, while William strolled triumphantly about his business without even deigning to look back.

After that he took especial pains to make the little kangaroo's life wretched. He specialized in knocking Chut down from different directions and in varying localities. He learned his victim's weaknesses and played upon them.

For instance, if Chut was asleep in the sun by the kitchen door, it was only necessary for William Mutton to sneak up upon him and give a loud "Baa" to bring Chut to his feet in the most convenient position to be butted into the ash pit.

He was also fond of waiting beneath the pepper trees for the little kangaroo to go hopping past in one of his games—and then charging out and catching him in mid-hop. Still the original "stomach-butt" remained his favorite; perhaps because it had the nicest, ploppiest sound.

Persistent persecution will, of course, develop wariness in the most confiding creature, and as Chut grew older he became harder to catch. On the other hand, if William's butts became less frequent, they became harder: for William was a particularly hefty young sheep and in addition he was growing horns—only nubby buds as yet, but distinctly uncomfortable when applied to Chut's person.

Then, about the time that, greatly to his own surprise, Chut outgrew his trouser leg, the big man, whose name Chut now knew was Tom Henton, brought in two little does who were just a shade smaller than Chut had been at the time of his capture.

And the woman whom everyone but Tom Henton called Mrs. Henton christened them Zodie and Blue Baby, and Chut promptly adopted them both. He would sit for twenty minutes at a time chitting and whispering into the mouths of their sleeping bags. He nosed them, and pulled in a manly, masterful way at their ears.

When they were old enough to come out to play, he romped with them, and at times put his little arms round both their necks so that the three small heads were drawn close together. Then he led them upon little gallops beneath the trees.

Of the two little does, Blue Baby was his darling. For as gentlemen allegedly prefer blondes, so male kangaroos seem melted by a blue tone in a lady's fur: experienced old kangaroo hunters having often noticed that amongst all the mouse-hued harem an "old man" will make a pet of a blue doe.

And Blue Baby was furred in an exquisite shade of smoke-blue, brighter than the bluest of squirrel fur, and her stomach and chest were clear, cream-velvet. Her slender little tail, hoppers and hands, were dark, her eyes dark and dewy-soft. But for some reason she was slightly lame.

She could travel all right on her hoppers and hands, but when she attempted to hop in an upright position she stumbled and fell. Hence she was always left behind in the races. And Chut would always circle back for her, and pass and repass her—as though he did not want her to be left out.

When she too outgrew the trousers, he slept with one little arm about her neck, their attitudes touchingly like those of sleeping children.

As an evil shadow on the sunshine of young romance hovered the malevolent-eyed Mutton, always ready to charge upon the unguarded Chut and knock the wind out of him.

But Chut was growing miraculously fast now. His chubbiness had gone from him, likewise the legginess of youth that followed it. He was nowhere near his full growth—would not reach it for a long time yet—but he was strong-boned, erect, with the muscles swelling deeply beneath the skin of his forearms and back. When he drew himself up, he was almost as tall as Mrs. Henton. But at her call his great body still somersaulted innocently into her lap, and, when he could inveigle her into giving it to him, he still adored his bottle. He still lay on his back in the sun and played with his toes, and he still had an infantile attachment for the pair of trousers which had been his foster-mother.

After the manner of kangaroos he was consumingly curious. He wanted to see everything. He tasted everything, and loved bread and sugar.

Gentle and awkward on the slippery oilcloth, the three kangaroos would come begging about the dinner table for pieces of sugared bread, which they had been taught to carry outside before eating—although they often fell to temptation and snatched little bites as they went.

One day they had just got their precious sweetened bread, and carried it out beneath the big pepper tree, when the marauding Mutton bore down upon them.

Chut and Zodie hopped out of the way, still holding their crusts, but Blue Baby was clumsy and in her agitation she dropped her bread.

Had William Mutton contented himself with merely taking the bread, it is doubtful if Chut would have noticed, but William, who in the past had always confined his attacks to Chut, suddenly decided that Blue Baby would do as well. And, with an evil "Baa," he charged her—sending her sprawling to the grass with little chittering exclamations of fright.

Chut looked up. Blue Baby chittered more alarmedly.

Chut dropped his bread and drew himself up onto toes and lower tail-arch, and made a few little bouncing dancing steps: a kangaroo's invitation to play or fight.

William Mutton had seized Blue Baby's bit of bread. Blue Baby still lay on her back in the grass too astonished and frightened to rise.

Chut danced up to the sheep, his arms hanging out from his sides like a belligerent man's, his ribs expanded.

"*Chut!*" he cried harshly. "Chut! Chut! *Chut!*"

"*Ba-a!*" said William Mutton, contemptuously masticating. Next moment he was grabbed by the backwool, and one of Chut's long hind toes kicked him dexterously in the side, tearing out a hunk of wool as it ripped downward.

Like most bullies, William was an arrant coward. He bleated and leapt for safety. Chut clawed for his fat rump as he went, and pulled out more wool. William gathered pulsing momentum of baa-punctuated bounds. And Chut followed him, trying vainly for another kick—for anything as low as a sheep is a most awkward thing for a kangaroo to fight.

William fled wildly, crying for undeserved help. The swimming pool lay before them. At its edge William, who dreaded water, tried to wheel, and at the same moment gave a foolish, prancing rear!

This was fatal. A kangaroo cannot kick well unless it can embrace the thing it is kicking. William's semi-leap brought him to the perfect height for Chut's best attentions. Chut's hands clutched the miserable sheep's neck, his strong-muscled arms tightened like virgin rubber as he clasped the writhing form of Mutton to his chest. With "chuts" and nickers of rage he delivered a whirlwind of kicks to his victim's stomach.

They were his first fighting kicks, and poorly directed—which was as well for William—but they drew bleats and wool at each application.

Then Chut lost his balance, released his hold for a moment, and William Mutton made a frantic leap for safety—into the pool.

Tom Henton, who had been an amused and astonished spectator of the fight, fished him out again. He emerged a sadder and wiser sheep, to whom a kangaroo's stomach was forever after invisible.

But Chut had tasted the hot wine of his own strength. He wanted someone to wrestle with! During the next days he hopped pompously about the garden enclosure, with his arms swinging a little out from his sides, his chest expanded and his spine curving backward with his erectness. He stood in front of Tom Henton as he came in of an evening, and made little sparring, sideward hops on the extreme tips of his toes and the ridged arch of his lower-tail.

One night the man laughed, saying: "All right then!" and put on boxing gloves to spar with the great young kangaroo. Mrs. Henton had viewed the proceeding with alarm, for a kangaroo can disembowel a man or dog with a single scythe-rip of his hooked foot. But it was soon obvious that Chut fully understood the playful nature of the battle. He would no more have thought of letting his strength go than the man would have dreamed of putting his full weight behind a blow to Chut's jaw.

They clinched and swayed, they sparred and side-stepped, until Tom leapt back to wipe the sweat from his streaming face, and Chut panted, and cooled his arms by licking them to the semblance of dark rubber.

After this they wrestled almost every evening, and so "boxing" was added to Chut's tricks. At the end of a match, if he had "played" well, he got his little bit of bread and sugar—which he held in both hands and smeared disgustingly about his face.

It happened that the summer had been a very busy one for Tom Henton, and so he had engaged a "yardman" to look after the cows, and the wood-chopping, and the home vegetable garden. The youth who performed these duties was not prepossessing, his manner alternating between over-familiarity and sullenness, while his progress was exasperatingly deliberate. A seemingly permanent cigarette drooped from his lower lip, and he did not remove it as he spoke.

Still, labor was hard to get, and Tom Henton decided to keep the man until after the shearing.

William Mutton, who had no decent pride, would follow the

yardman about in the hope of sneaking something from the fowls'
bucket, but Chut ignored the youth's existence.

At least he ignored it until the shearing-time came.

The shearing shed and the sheep yards were some  half-mile
from the house, but dust clouds stirred up from the drafting pens
and came to Chut's nostrils with exciting scents of heat and sheep
trailing from them. He caught far, murmurous bleatings, stockwhip
cracks, distant shoutings. . . .

And Chut wanted to go and see the shearing! He plainly indicated as much as Tom Henton was riding out of a morning: placing one horny, confiding hand upon the man's stirrup in hint that
he was coming too. When, in spite of this, he was left behind, he
hopped up and down inside the enclosure fence, thumping his
twenty-pound tail deliberately and loudly upon the ground as an
intimation of his extreme displeasure and agitation.

Tom Henton had given very definite instructions that the big
kangaroo was not to be let out during shearing. He didn't want
any tricks played upon Chut, and shearer-men have an odd sense
of humor. Also there was always the chance of a sudden fright
temporarily stampeding the kangaroo into the bush, and there he
might be shot in mistake for a wild 'roo.

"Keep the gates shut," said Tom to the yardman. "And be
dead sure they're fastened!" The youth spat and said "O.K.," but
he had already resolved to take Chut down to th  shed and stage
a demonstration fight for a shilling-a-man admission.

To do this he waited until a Sunday afternoon, when Tom
Henton was away bringing in sheep for Monday's "run," and
Mrs. Henton was lying down asleep.

Chut was also dozing under a pepper tree, with his legs sticking absurdly skyward, when the yardman whispered his name and
enticed him with bread. But he took no notice until he saw the
man open the gate. Then he followed, and continued following all
the way to the shed: hopping behind the yardman's pony. At the
shed he was embarrassed by the numbers of people about and by
the great wool-smelling iron rooms.

And because the yardman was at least familiar, Chut followed
him more closely still.

The yardman collected his shillings, and then led the big, puzzled kangaroo into the wool room, while the audience seated itself
upon the stacked bales of wool.

The yardman fastened on Chut's gloves and put on gloves himself: then he stepped out in a fighting attitude, saying:

"Come on, Boy!"

Chut didn't want to come on, however. He was rather frightened by the laughter, the voices, and the smoke haze. Also he was particular about the people with whom he fought. His boxing was a love-game that he played with Tom Henton.

"Put 'em up!" said the yardman, tapping Chut lightly upon the cheek. Chut sat far back on his haunches and chutted offendedly: a small sound in appealing contrast to his size. The man danced up and down before him and poked him in the ribs. Chut protested with dignity, but made no attempt to fight.

Grumbling began amongst the members of the audience.

"Hey, where's my shilling?" "Aw, I'm going home." "This is a dead show!" "That the best he can do?"

The yardman began to lose his temper. The fool beast fought quick enough when he wanted to! He was going to fight now! He hit Chut rather ungently in the lower ribs. Chut grunted and looked about with great soft eyes—appealing for fair play! He was not hurting this man, and the man was getting rough with him!

Still he obviously had no intention of sparring. He was a picture of gentle, slightly pompous, and much-offended courtesy. He looked about for Tom or Mrs. Henton. . . .

"Garn! He ain't no fighter!" yelled the men. "Where's them shillin's?"

The yardman was hot, nervous and exasperated. His audience was threatening to walk out on him. Unnoticed by any of the spectators, he brushed the live cigarette from his lips, and holding it hidden in his glove he pressed the glowing tip upon Chut's sensitive nose. Pressed it hard, twisted it.

The sequel happened so quickly that no one was sure of just how Chut got the silly gloves off. But next second he was holding the screaming yardman in his powerful hug, and, having torn the youth's trousers off, was operating on his shirt-tail to the accompaniment of a ripping, rag-bag sort of sound!

As the shirt vanished, Chut's great-toe plied artistically for a hold upon the yardman's abdomen. With his forehands he clawed out the yardman's hair. His eyes had a new, murderous light. He shook and bent the man in his embrace.

Then half the men in the shed were on him. Beating at him with rails, prodding him with wool hooks.

He dropped the frantic and badly clawed yardman, and wheeled—to receive a bewildering rain of blows.

His swift anger was already over. All he wanted was to go home. He burst through the threatening circle and hopped majestically out of the wool-room door: gathering momentum as he went, and moving homeward, not with the frantic thirty-feet-at-a-bound of a frightened doe, but ponderously and rhythmically covering a steady fifteen feet at a hop. One man fired after him, but the shots went wide.

It was at this stage that Tom Henton rode up to the shed, to be horrified at the tale of Chut's ferocity and the spectacle of the bleeding man. With relief he found that no vital injury had been done, but it was with a heavy heart that he at last rode home. The shearers, none of whom had observed the cigarette outrage, had assured him that the yardman had simply been inviting Chut to a friendly sparring bout!

If Chut was going to make unprovoked attacks like that, he was not safe. . . .

Mrs. Henton was likewise shocked at the account of the yardman's injuries. But she refused to believe that Chut's anger had been unprovoked.

"We simply couldn't shoot him!" she cried. "Why, if he could tell us what happened, he could very likely explain everything! Oh Tom, he is so dear and funny!"

"We can't get his side of it," said the man. "And the fact remains that if he hadn't been beaten off he might have killed someone."

"*You can't shoot him!*"

"I can't see how we can keep him. . . . I'd be afraid for you, honey. Afraid to have him lose around—and I'd sooner shoot him than cage him."

"I *know* he wouldn't hurt anyone unless they hurt him!" she cried. But Tom looked away with troubled face.

"You know how we would feel if there was an accident," he said.

"Well, don't do it yet—after dinner—not yet."

The evening meal passed in heavy silence. They were both thinking about what would have to be done. As they rose from the table the woman began to cry. She said: "Oh, Tom, you *can't!*"

"I'll have to," said the man, still looking away from her. Suddenly she took his arm.

"Come and see him, before we make up our minds!"

They passed along the veranda to the old outside fireplace. Chut was lying on his back beside the faded and shredded remains of the trousers that had mothered him. His eyes were soft and sad with dreams.

As the man and woman looked down at him, he reached up great arms to catch at his great toe.

With tears and laughter mingling in her voice, the woman said: "Oh Tom, he *can't* be dangerous! Look at him!"

"He doesn't look it," said the man, tears gleaming in his own eyes.

Just then the girl fell swiftly to her knees, her fingers searching the velvet fur just above the kangaroo's quivering nose. "Look!" she cried. "*Look!*"

The man held the lamp down. On Chut's nose there was a small, deep, raw pit, eaten into the flesh. About the edges of the rawness the hair was singed and burnt.

"Couldn't that have been done by a cigarette?" she questioned.

"You bet it was!" he replied.

"Well," she said, "that's *his* side of the story for you, Tom!" Then she reached down and clasped her arms about Chut's neck. "Oh I am so glad! So glad!"

They stood up.

"I," said the man, "am sorry. . . ."

"What do you mean?" questioned the girl.

"I'm sorry Chut's done such a good job with the yardman that he hasn't left me a chance!" said Tom Henton, his fingers lingering about the swell of his biceps.

Later the girl slipped back and gave Chut a whole half-loaf of bread with melted sugar. He ate it placidly and blissfully, with small tickings of pleasure. Sugar ran down his chin and got into his fur. He was soon perfectly horrible with sugar and covered with crumbs. Nevertheless his mistress stooped and kissed him.

By the time that he was three years old Chut was magnificent. A creature of strength and grace, ponderous force and lamb-like gentleness. His weight was a good three hundred pounds. He could stand almost seven feet when he drew himself up onto the lower-arch of his great tail and the tips of his hopper-toes. His forearms swelled like those of a man, and the muscles rippled and rolled and melted beneath his fur at each movement.

His ears were veined and tremulous, his eyes dark and soft
as a deer's. His coat toned from vivid chestnut on the back to warm
buff and cream across the chest and belly, and in almost any part
of this coat he could run down a flea with surprising dexterity,
while he could scratch out his ear with his hind foot with a dreamy,
rotating motion, truly fine.

Those who did not know him were afraid of his strength. Tom
Henton and his wife knew the big kangaroo as a creature of most
docile tractability, with a touching, childish passion for bread and
sugar; a giant who, given the chance, would still drink innocently
from the baby's bottle from which he had been fed as a joey!

Old kangaroo hunters said that he was the finest red 'roo they
had ever seen. Young women from the cities said that he was "a
great brute." His mistress laughed at both these statements, and
said that he was a darling.

Tom Henton, coming home of an evening, would call:
"Where's my boxing pardner?" For through many games with
Tom, Chut could box as no other kangaroo had ever been able
to box. And Chut would come to the enclosure gate and make little
dancing movements on the tips of toes and tail, and throw out his
chest and "chut" with eagerness. And then he would get in Tom
Henton's way, as the man walked to the grassy stretch by the well
where they wrestled. And there they swayed and hugged, and
pushed and reeled, and sparred for wind, until the man broke up
the game to go for his shower.

While Tom bathed, Chut would stretch his great length in the
grass and lick his forearms to the semblance of dark rubber, or hop
majestically about the enclosure thudding his tail upon the ground
as a warning to other old men kangaroos that he was ready for
them.

"Chut!" he would exclaim. "Chut-ch-ch!" All of which very
much impressed his two does.

But for some reason the big kangaroo had never mated. He
played with Zodie and Blue Baby, was ready to defend them from
strange dogs, and slept often with one arm twined about Blue
Baby's neck. Yet, perhaps because he had grown up with them instead of meeting them after the hot stir of some wilderness encounter, he never paid court to them.

His days passed in long dreamy hours under the big pepper
trees, in games of tag with Zodie, in fur-nubbling play with Blue
Baby, who still had a lameness which, while it did not now show

when she hopped slowly, prevented her from racing with the other two. At meal times he came solemnly into the dining room, a little embarrassed by the slippery oilcloth, but very eager for a taste of bread and sugar—and when he received a scrap he carried it outside as obediently as a great dog.

The first time that Shorty Magee, the owner of a second-rate buckjump show, offered to buy Chut, Tom Henton laughed at him.

"You couldn't buy that 'roo for any money!" he said. Shorty reviewed the possibilities of stealing Chut, decided that this was unfortunately impossible, and spat and went away.

But because Chut could, by this time, box as no other kangaroo had ever been able to box, Shorty did not forget. And not long afterwards drought settled upon the West.

Even Chut noticed that the country beyond the artificial green of the irrigations was bleached and withered, while the red dust fanned up from it under the hot winds. But he did not feel any pinch of drought—until Tom Henton began to come in too tired and worried to play with him. So tired that he would not play even when Chut hopped beside him all the way to the bathroom, explaining that Tom had forgotten their game!

"I'm sorry old boy," said Tom Henton, pulling Chut's ears. "But God knows how much longer I'll be here at all—if this goes on!"

And then Tom and his wife would sit down to a meal at which they would try to avoid thinking of growing debts and dying stock.

For a while the stock were fed by cutting scrub—but at last the scrub lost its leaves and became withered twigs. Then Tom bought lucerne for feed, at ever-rising prices—until there was no lucerne left to buy.

By this time the sheep had eaten more than they were worth; but, apart from the fact that a man doesn't like to sit down and see his flock starve about him, it was necessary to send good money after bad—in the hope of rain. So Tom bought corn, and began a still more costly feeding.

About the time that rain seemed very near, his credit gave out. For months on end he had been working eighteen hours a day, and he was exhausted.

"I guess this is the finish," he said. Then he sat down with his head between his hands and wept.

It was then that Shorty Magee came back. He stood by the veranda and pointed over his shoulder with a dirty thumb.

"I'll give you three hundred pounds for them two 'roos—the purty blue one an' the fightin' red one," he said. He added: "I'll take care of 'em like a pair of babies, I will."

All that night Tom and his wife talked it out. But they had known what their answer must be from the beginning—for here was succor for the starving sheep—new hope—and another chance.

In the morning Chut came in for his breakfast, slipping comically on the oilcloth, and being careful not to drop crumbs. And they fed him much more than was good for him, but did not look at him—and their own breakfasts stood untouched.

When Magee brought up the empty pony van, Chut went out to see it, as he always went to see any new or strange thing.

It was only when Magee and his men tried to drive him in, that he rebelled, drawing himself up to his magnificent height and chutting with offended dignity.

"We must rope and throw him," said Shorty Magee. At that Tom Henton's wife came forward, crying: "Oh, *no!*"

And with tears streaming down her young and pretty face, she climbed into the van, and called. And with scrambling obedience, and perfect trust. Chut followed her.

Then she slipped out, and as they shut the door on him, she ran away, with her hands over her ears, whispering:

"He will always think I meant to do it! He will always think that I wanted to do it to him. . . . Oh, Chut!"

Little fat Zodie was left to play alone in the enclosure—because she was a common mouse-colored little kangaroo of no special beauty. During the days that followed she tried many things to bring the others back; racing and calling, going to all the old, known places, darting provocatively under trailing branches—but they never came.

The sheep were fed, however, and not long afterwards came rain, in grey, life-giving sheets; rain roaring on the iron roofs, streaming from the eaves, foaming in yellow rivers along the roads, and waking a thousand forgotten scents from the bush.

Chut was surprised when the van doors closed upon him, surprised when Blue Baby was lifted into the forward compartment; but he had implicit confidence in his people, and did not doubt that he would soon be released.

When the cart began to move, he was startled. This was a

motion which he had never known. He called loudly: "Chut! Chut! Chut! *Ch-ch!*" But even then he was more puzzled than alarmed.

Blue Baby, however, was terrified. She had always been timid, and she clutched at the dividing bars with dark and frantic little hands, and at intervals, when the lurching of the cart threw Chut towards her, she plucked agitatedly at his fur. Presently he gave a reassuring "Chut," and moved a bit closer. She stretched her little arm through the bars and clutched it about his mightly shoulder. "Chut!" he said. "Chut!" It was a tender admonition that all would be well; he personally would attend to it.

They clung together far into the rocking, jolting night. At last Blue Baby's hand began to drop away with sleep. Her ears drooped as she sat, and then she swayed and lost her balance. At last she lay down to sleep, close against the bars.

Chut remained on guard all night, ticking occasionally with self-importance.

Shorty did not bother with his captives, apart from feeding and watering them, until they were established in winter quarters in Sydney. There he rented an old freight shed and went to "work."

His motto was: "Animal training ain't hard. You just got to get them *scared* enough—and the rest's easy."

Of course promiscuous fright would not do. It was necessary to have certain definite sounds which meant "danger." Shorty's little buckjump ponies trembled and made foolish efforts to hide behind each other when he gave a long low whistle.

He began to teach the significance of this same whistle to Chut and Blue Baby. It was very simple. He had chained them—Chut with stout trace-chain, and Blue Baby with a dog chain—each chain having been fastened at one end to a ring in the floor, and being held in place upon the captive by much the same sort of harness that bulldogs wear.

Then he took his heavy, plaited whip and stepped up, just beyond the reach of the chains: then whistled and brought down the whip.

At first they were stupidly confused, frantic. They struggled, and stumbled, and fell—Chut in his efforts to get at his tormentor, Blue Baby in her attempts to fly. But Shorty was in no hurry, and he was careful not to do them any damage. Long, ridged weals rose beneath velvet fur, but he didn't, to use his own words, "flick any hide." He wasn't going to leave scars which would excite otherwise-entertained old ladies! He was also careful not to give them too much "training" at a time: wild animals are more easily rendered broken-hearted than are dogs and horses, who have learned endurance from long centuries with men.

After half an hour of "instruction" he would leave them alone, to tremble and pull at the unyielding chains, and roll their great eyes, and at last cease trembling, and begin to chit nervously to each other, and still later begin to eat their ration of lucerne and bran. He always kept his animals "in condition": a starved-looking animal had a bad effect on audiences.

After a few days the kangaroos began to get the significance of the whistle. They no longer struggled, but Chut would rear up and growl as soon as he heard it, and Blue Baby would cower, ducking her head between her little trembling forepaws or trying to hide behind some inadequate object such as her drinking saucer.

If Chut was near, she would make a dart for him, and hold out her arms to him, calling for help.

Shorty saw the possibility of quite an appealing trick in that. . . .

By the end of a week they had learned the first lesson—fear. Now they must learn the second—obedience. With additional ropes, and one of his assistants, Shorty began to teach them to "Come." Going over and over it until they understood his will. Then impressing upon them with his heavy whip that his will was to be done. And always he preluded a blow with his low whistle.

At last he brought them to the point where they understood what he wanted, but would not do it without feeling a pull on the ropes. Then they would do it without the ropes, but not until they had tasted the whip.

At last they would come when he commanded it—and simply followed his command with his low whistle.

For days they rehearsed this until it was seldom necessary for him even to repeat a command.

Then he began to offer a reward for obedience. When they came without being whipped, he would proffer them a little bit of bread and sugar.

Chut refused to touch the sweet, but Blue Baby would chitter with timid pleasure at this unexpected treat amidst so much unexpected pain. Her ears trembled almost continuously, now, and she was nervous even in her sleep. But she ate the sugared bread with eager haste, hoping to have it finished before some fresh punishment overtook her. She was servile to Magee, terribly eager to please.

After having learned to "Come," they learned to "Jump," to "Lie down," to drink from a bottle and to pretend to sleep. For although they had done all these tricks for Tom Henton and his wife, they had done them as love-tricks, which they could do if they wished or leave undone while they hunted fleas if they were feeling impertinent. Shorty Magee's definition of knowing a trick was not a sentimental or amateurish one.

When the animals' joint education was finished Shorty taught Blue Baby to "Go to Chut" and hold his fur, and also to jump through a hoop, a trick which she would sometimes fail at from old lameness.

Then he began Chut's specialized education: starting the rehearsing of the act for which he had bought the furred giant.

First he cut Chut's toenails down to the quick, and on the big kangaroo's forehands fastened special gloves, which, while properly fastened, could not be torn free. Then Shorty went in to "box" with Chut. And for this there was no teaching: Chut had learned hatred in the last months, and he tried to kill his tyrant. But, because of shorn nails and hampering gloves, he was helpless, and his exhibition of white rage must seem to an audience no more than hilariously funny.

His efforts to hold Shorty Magee—as a kangaroo must hold to get in the full power of his fatal kick—had the semblance of clumsy blows. Blows which for all their futility never lost their energy. He had boxed for love with Tom Henton. Now he boxed for hate.

He tried all the tricks of his boxing repertoire: but they were useless. For Shorty was quick, and if ever Chut threatened damage, as occasionally he did even with clipped reaping-hook toes and muffled hands, Shorty knocked him off his balance and they had to go into a clinch.

"Watch out for that fellow—if he ever grows his nails and gets the gloves off!" warned Shorty's assistant.

"He won't never," said Shorty, and spat.

So Chut "wrestled" every day, with a red, shining light in his great eyes, and with his great body trembling with futile fury. But still the wrestling matches were good for him. They kept him in condition, and they burned up a lot of the agony of helpless resentment which might otherwise have sent him "queer," as captive wild things sometimes go.

He still slept soundly—which was unusual for one of Shorty's animals—and he retained his weight and glossy coat.

By spring Shorty was ready to take his new show on the road.

It was an instant success. The program began with the animals "coming" to him for their bread and sugar: progressed through a performance of their mutual tricks. Tricks which now included Blue Baby's jump through a burning hoop; a spectacular trick that the audience liked, as they liked the way Shorty had to whistle to encourage her to do it! Being comfortably removed from the sawdust ring they could not see the pounding of her heart which shook her ribs for an hour afterwards.

After the "tricks" were done, Chut and Shorty boxed: with "seconds" in their respective corners, and wet sponges, and fanning towels and a bell. And the audience roared itself hilarious with laughter!

Then, as the pretty finale, Shorty would say: "Well, that's all for today, children." And then give his long, hissing whistle, and Blue Baby would dart to Chut and cling to his fur, looking back over her shoulder. It was very pretty indeed.

Wherever they went, pictures of that last little embrace got into the illustrated papers. Inserts of Shorty smiling and saying: "Well I guess it's kindness and patience!" and inserts of Chut with the gloves on.

Altogether they were a great success. And Chut was accorded the title of the Champion of All Boxing Kangaroos.

The press nicknamed him "Step Right Up," because of the comical way he danced up to Shorty on rigid toes and tail.

Once Tom Henton, looking rather awkward in his town clothes, came and asked to talk to Shorty outside the tent.

"I've come," he said, "to buy back those two 'roos." He lit his pipe to hide his eagerness.

Shorty laughed: "Nothing doing," he said. "You couldn't buy those 'roos for any money."

"I'll give you double what you gave," said the bushman slowly.

"Nope," said Shorty.

Tom looked full in the showman's face: "Maybe I shouldn't have offered my top price for a start—"

"It don't make no difference."

"But what I want you to get is that it *is* my top. It's just about twice what I can afford to give. Taken us a year to scrape it up."

"Nix."

"I have it right here, in cash," said the bushman.

Shorty moved his head once from left to right and back to center.

He added: "Would you like to see 'em?"

"Not since you won't sell—I guess I'd rather not." He turned away, looking so disconsolate that Shorty laughed outright and wondered if he had been thinking of a show of his own.

When Tom was almost swallowed by the dusk he stopped and called: "You won't change your mind?"

But Shorty had told the truth. He would not have sold Chut for anything less than a small fortune. With the big kangaroo's aid he was making more money than he had ever made before.

As a result he drank more. It never stopped him from putting on a show: simply making him the more red-faced, roaring and genial while before his public.

He was a born showman, and an even better showman when drunk. But on the following mornings Chut and Blue Baby paid bitterly for his "night befores."

One morning when he was coaching Blue Baby in her burning-hoop jump her old lameness caught her and she missed her spring, and could not make it again.

"Jump," roared Shorty. Twice she tried and failed—singeing her fur. Her ears shook with fright. With pathetic, placating haste she went through all her other tricks, hoping through their excellence to escape punishment for the trick she could not do. But they chained her up and Shorty swore and rained blows upon her.

At that she broke. She called shrilly. She scrambled on the floor, trying to escape: gathering herself up she hurled herself to the concrete, while Chut fought at his chain and frothed at the lips. The man continued to rain punishment until one of his assistants caught his arm, crying: "Hey, you ought to be able to see she *can't!*"

But with some frantic effort of her small strength Blue Baby had broken her dog-chain. Blind with fear, she leapt down the long shed, gathering wild speed as she went, dashing with all her strength for liberty—and straight into the concrete wall at the shed's end. It smashed her to the ground in a twisted heap, and when they picked her up she was quite docile again, only her great, mild eyes were filled with wonder about what had happened.

She lived for three more days, trying to start up now and then from fitful sleep—and falling back to the straw. At times she called for Chut, and he strained constantly to reach her, but his chain would not permit it. As she grew weaker he called more and more loudly to her, as if he feared that she was going away. But she did not hear him towards the end. Instead she lifted her head feebly but hopefully, and chittered, and held up her hands as though for a bit of bread and sugar.

Then she was racked with trembling and grew still. Next morning they dragged her away, and Chut thrashed and struggled at his chain until the assistant was afraid. . . .

After that Chut became the whole show, and Shorty worked him harder than ever. And because, after Blue Baby's death, Chut had developed a growing intractability, the big kangaroo's punishments become more savage.

And the show was less successful. For one thing Blue Baby's startling prettiness had given it appeal. For another, they had covered most of the remunerative towns, and all the cities, and the show did not stand too frequent "repeats." Further, Shorty was drinking so heavily now that he sometimes lost his feet in a wrestling match or showed that he was drunk during a performance. Also he no longer employed assistants, and that meant that, when Shorty was drunk, Chut was not well fed or watered, and began to lose the gloss of his beauty, and that made him less attractive to the public.

It would have been good business for Shorty to have sold Chut to Tom now, but he had developed a drunken hatred of the captive whom he could not break. He was not going to let Chut go.

"You don't get away from me, my boy!" said Shorty, lifting to unshaven lips the bottle which seldom left his hand.

Chut tried to get at him.

Through the fiery heat of midsummer they bumped down towards a little town of New South Wales.

Shorty drove the Ford truck which had supplanted the pony wagon. Chut lay imprisoned in the stuffy box of the truck body: the heat was frightful, and he licked his great arms in the vain effort to keep cool.

He panted, and at times rose and went to his empty water tin. Then he would come back and lie down to suffer out another hour. His one comfort was that his toenails were growing again—Shorty having been too drunk to bother trimming them. At times Chut lay upon his back and thoughtfully examined them, and then rolled and stretched his still mighty, if emaciated, muscles.

At long intervals, they stopped at some wayside shanty, and he heard voices. But he was never given water.

As the day passed his thirst became maddening, a terrible ceaseless misery. He moved restlessly from side to side of his prison. He called.

By night his one thought was water. His life was burning out, shrivelling within him—for water! He was in torment.

But when Shorty opened the truck doors it was only to lead Chut into a hot show tent and to a glaring sawdust ring.

Water! Water! Chut looked about for it, in dumb anguish. He hardly noticed when Shorty fastened the gloves on his forepaws.

*Water!* . . . Then he smelled it. Outside the tent, across the dry, burr-patched expanse of the town common, a little bore drain flowed, gleaming in the twilight! Chut moved to go to it, and Shorty stood before him. . . . Water, running between narrow borders of purple couch grass as the water had run in the house enclosure at Tom Henton's selection when the world was sweet!

Chut moved sideways, and went to pass. He could easily jump the ropes of the ring, and then be out there in the cool night air. . . . In the twilight wherein he used to play with Blue Baby and Zodie! He was a little confused and thought he might find them there, somehow.

As he moved, Shorty hit him viciously in the stomach.

And suddenly all the suppressed and futile rage, all the pain of the last years, burned in him like molten scalding metal, searing his brain, trebling his strength. He knew that this man had taken him away from all the sweet things of twilight and running water. He knew that he would not find Blue Baby—this man had killed Blue Baby. This man had beaten and humiliated him, Chut! This man stood now in Chut's way, stopping him from reaching water for which he died.

He ripped off the ill-fastened gloves. He clutched at Shorty Magee's shoulders; hugging with his forepaws; ripping, tearing with new-grown toenails. Madly he rent and slashed the shrieking thing before him!

He chutted with rage. His fur, his claws, were wet and red— and the excitement of the scent of blood was in his nostrils!

And then the crowd was on him; beating him with bits of plank; with prodding battens; plucking with many hands.

He turned and saw a gap through the crowd—and beyond it the twilight sky!

He bore no malice to the crowd. The thing was still and dead that had wronged him so; his reckoning was paid.

He twisted free. He gathered his mighty strength, and rose over the rope railings, and the nearer benches. Descended lightly and majestically: and in hopping, deliberate flight he was gone, hot and bruised and sore—but triumphant!—into the night.

As soon as he was far enough from the tent for sense of safety, he turned to the little stream and drank with long rapture. And with the touch of the clear-running water, and the strange artesian odor of it, something stirred in him! Up through the red mist of long hatreds and long suffering and loneliness—he increasingly remembered. Many things: lilies by the still water of a sleeping dam. Grey moth-wings in the moonlight. Dusty paths through the tall, bleached-silver of the Queensland grass. . . . He wanted southwest Queensland!

He was too deeply hurt, too deeply wronged, to want men, even Tom Henton or Tom Henton's wife. He was too weary to want his own kind. Since the loss of Blue Baby he had ceased even to call at night.

*But he wanted the West, the place where he had been born.*

Away across the burr-patched common a crimson streak marked the last of sunset. Surely and deliberately, Chut turned towards it—a little north of it! Deliberately and solemnly he thudded on all through the night.

He was five hundred miles from home. There were fences and rivers and innumerable deadly perils between. But he did not doubt that he would see the dam again, where the moon rose in deep gold immensity amongst the dead trees and the teal ducks slept on the half-rotted logs. . . .

The newspaper headlines screamed "Savage Kangaroo Mutilates Trainer." "Man-killing 'Roo at Large."

But there was really nothing sinister about the worn traveler who was going home to find the dam where the white spider lilies grew up the banks and there was starry silence.

Chut was free—but there was a price upon his head. He did not know of this latter fact; his only realizations being that he was free, and that he was going home.

Shorty Magee had beaten Chut many times. In drunken cruelty he had beaten and killed Blue Baby, who had been Chut's playmate. So, when, at the last, Shorty had failed to clip Chut's toenails or

securely fasten on Chut's muffling gloves before he took him out
to "box," Chut, by nature gentlest of creatures, had killed Shorty
in the silly saw-dust ring.

He did not know that because of this the hand of every man
was against him, or that his gleaming brass collar must be a damning
identification mark. Instead, he simply knew that he was *free*.

He was no longer "Step Right Up, the Boxing Kangaroo Marvel." He could lie down, or hop this way or that, or dexterously
scratch out his ear with his hind foot—using a rotating motion and
taking all the time he liked—and it was nobody's business.

But his life with Shorty Magee had left marks upon him: not
only in the weals beneath his red-velvet fur, but upon his inmost
makeup. In the last mad hour of vengeance he had thrown Shorty
Magee screaming and bloody upon the show-tent floor—but Shorty
Magee had, very effectively, taken the gladness out of Chut.

He was pleased to be free; pleased with the blue silence of
radiant noon, beating down upon a dry swamp that smelled of hay,
wherein he could lie in the feathery shade of the cane grass. He was
pleased with the abundance of sweet, sun-dried fodder: pleased
with the running, whispering, artesian drains, where he could drink
with interminable deliberation in the twilight. But he was only
pleased with all these things as contrast to the sideshow: not pleased
with the foolish and almost inextinguishable gladness of mere living
which is a wild thing's birthright.

With his liberty his coat returned to its soft, bright beauty. His
eyes again were darkly limpid. His muscles re-rounded to their
swelling, deep-curved grace. But there was little corresponding
healing of the spirit. He never played: and when a kangaroo will
not play—either by small, solitary leapings back and forth across
some bore drain, or rolling upon its back and reaching up at a
dancing leaf, or grasping at its own toes—then there is something
very wrong indeed.

Nor was this wrongness born of a loneliness for his own kind.
He had several times, since his escape, come upon the signs of kangaroos beside a stream, or the forms where the "old men" had
been sleeping in the heat at the foot of some great box tree—and
he had shown no slightest interest.

Then one night the warm young wind brought him a scent of
white spider lilies. And because all kangaroos like the honey-filled
flowers of the lilies, Chut hopped slowly up the wind, until he came
out upon a little lily patch amongst the dead, grey trees.

There were many kangaroos feeding in the glade: does and joeys, and, over to the farther side, a young buck.

Chut was not interested in the shadowy forms. He had known only two of his kind with intimacy. One of them, little fat Zodie, with whom he had romped in the long ago at Tom Henton's selection, and who had been lost in the great unexplained blankness that had taken so many things when the showman had bought Chut. The other, Blue Baby, who had shared his miseries in the sideshow, and who had been so frightened of Shorty Magee that her ears had begun to shake whenever the man appeared: Blue Baby who had worked so hard at her tricks trying to please Shorty Magee—and had been killed at last because she failed to please . . .

Neither Zodie nor Blue Baby was in the lily patch, and so Chut took no notice of the nibbling, gossiping does.

But he did very much want some lily flowers.

He hopped, majestic and immense, into the midst of the patch. And the little does sat up to look at him: their delicate ears trembling: their great eyes innocent as those of fawns—but none the less all quite ready for flirtation with the superb and thrilling stranger!

"Chit! Chit-ch-ch-ch!" they said.

The young buck, their lord, apparently knew them to be as fickle as fair. He kicked the wife nearest to him and smacked her ears vehemently, and then advanced upon Chut with the hesitance born of a sinking heart.

He did not want to advance at all—but with the eyes of eleven wives upon him, he had to do something about the matter. And as a preliminary indication of his displeasure he hopped across the glade immediately before Chut, thumping his tail loudly upon the ground.

Chut appeared to be both blind and deaf to the intimations that he was unwelcome. His intentions were, in fact, so completely innocent that he never dreamed of the wrath he was occasioning.

The young buck hopped back again, thumping more loudly still. Chut continued deliberately to pluck and eat the honeyed, frost-white buds.

The young buck hopped almost within touching distance, and, after a perfectly reverberating bang of his tail, he made a few sparring, dancing steps upon rigid toes! Then, gathering all his courage, he made a clawing smack at Chut's shoulder, and launched an ill-directed kick to the stomach. At that Chut reared up to the full of his superb height, spine curving backward, chest swelled, arms hanging out from his sides as a fighter's do. Offended and immense he towered above the young buck—who was so appalled at the sight that he became hysterical, and grasping the mountain about his abdomen, delivered a really vicious kick which he fully expected to be his last.

Then the miracle happened! The monster shook himself free: waggled his ears, and, slowly turning, more in sorrow than in anger, hopped away into the night.

The young buck was left as astonished possessor of the field and of his velvet harem, and was at once filled with an opinion of his own powers so over-rated that it must speedily lead him into serious trouble: but, none the less, tasting one of life's great moments as his does came up to congratulate him—and he chitted prolonged defiance at starry night and sleeping bush.

Chut was hurt, and more annoyed. He had interfered with no one and had been treated with gross rudeness!

After this he avoided the sweetness of the lily patches. He was too tired to fight. Or, rather, he had nothing for which it seemed worth while to fight. Solitary and dignified, he worked ahead— always north and west.

Sometimes he would stay for a month in some place where the blue grass was good, or where he discovered a salt-lick on a dry creek's bank. . . . But always the thought of the section where he had been born came back to him.

He crossed the west of New South Wales: worming his way through the wire fences and jumping the rabbit-nettings: sometimes, perhaps, stopped for days by some seven-foot dog fence. But he had always gotten through the barrier at last; either by finding some place where the nettings had been crushed beneath a fallen tree, or discovering a hole torn by some of his own kind in an interstation fight. For if two "old men" happen to arrive at once upon the opposite sides of a netting fence, one will invariably make a playful gesture at the other—and get his arm ripped in the wire or his toenail wrenched by its unyielding mesh. He promptly tells his neighbor what he thinks of a man who would do that sort of thing to another man who was out for a little fun—and the neighbor slaps him back. And then, between them, they tear a section of the fence to the semblance of a patent dish-washer—before honor is satisfied, and they go away to tell their wives of how brave they have been.

It never occurred to Chut to tear a hole for himself, although he could easily have done so. . . .

In the late summer, he came to the boundary of Willdoon, near the Queensland border. The manager's pride was his dog fence. It was perhaps the trimmest, stoutest fence in New South Wales. It was strained and braced and tied to resist the most energetic fighting kangaroo. The trees were cleared back upon either side so that it would not be crushed should any tree blow down. In addition it was "ridden" at least once a week by stalwart men in Ford cars.

Chut travelled along that fence for fifty miles—and found no break. He came back—and found it in slightly better order than before, as, in the interval, the manager had made a personal inspection.

Gates are unintelligible things to a wild kangaroo. But Chut knew all about them, and he knew that his only chance of getting through that fence was by way of the great gates on the stock route to the West.

He tried to open them himself, but the fastenings defied his efforts: so, after he had struggled with them until he lost his temper, he settled down to wait for a man to come along. For, although he had feared Shorty, he was not afraid of the common run of men, and he knew nothing about the meaning of firearms—the shot that had killed his mother and sent him into captivity having been long forgotten.

Thus he waited by the gate with far more pomposity and self-assurance than his circumstances justified—and had no realization of his good fortune when a drover, who was about to shoot him, happened to see his brass collar.

As the rest of the droving plant clattered up, the man shouted: "Hey! Here's a pet 'roo!"

And as they had not heard of the fate of Shorty Magee, they adopted Chut as a member of the camp. And he went with them because they were going in the direction that he wished to go, and because he knew that gates presented no difficulties to men. Also these were the men he liked, rough and burned Western men, such as he had seen years before about Tom Henton's run.

He permitted them no familiarities, and would not allow them to lay their hands upon him, but otherwise he moved deliberately about the camp and accepted with much dignity the scraps they gave him. During the day he hopped tirelessly behind the cook's wagon, for although the cook did not like him, he dared not show his dislike, and the cook's assistant doted upon anything furred, haired, or feathered. . . . And something in Chut began to heal a little. Men were kind again. His memory of Shorty began to blur a trifle.

There came a time when he let the cook's assistant poke him in the stomach and scratch his ears out for him.

As the days passed in sun-flooded monotony of rumbling, dusty progress, he began to feel inclined to play a little—queer, awkward, small games, stiff with unfamiliarity.

But luck was still against him. As the plant began to roll its dusty way through southwest Queensland, the cook received a box of eatables from his wife, all of which were rolled in old newspapers.

Literature is scarce in the West. The cook read a divorce greasily wrapped about a ham, then he read some sticky politics off the marmalade, and some sports items from around a pound cake.

As the evening meal was ending, he burst, stammering with excitement, upon the eating men.

"Listen to this, here!" he cried. "What did I tell you about that 'roo?"

Men laid down their knives to listen, and Chut sat peacefully at the edge of the firelight, licking his great arms and tidying his left ear. The cook read shrilly from the discolored paper: "Savage Kangaroo Assaults Trainer. 'Step Right Up,' the Boxing Marvel, Kills Shorty Magee. Murderous Attack Occurs While Show in Progress . . ." "An' here's his description," cried the cook, more shrilly still. "Step Right Up, or Chut, as he is sometimes called, is a giant red kangaroo with pronounced cream underbody, and he is wearing a wide brass collar with his name, 'Chut,' inscribed upon it. . . . The trainer died almost instantly." There was an astonished murmur of voices, and Chut glanced up for a moment, and then, having got his ear into good order, he began to operate upon the burrs in his stomach-fur.

Men talked all together. Above the general commotion rose the voice of the cook.

"He ain't fit to be loose a minute! What did I always say?"

"Well," said the bearded drover, "I don't like doing it, but I guess it's got to be done!" He rose and went to the wagon for his rifle.

"I wouldn't shoot him," said the cook's helper, eagerly. "We don't know what that Shorty bloke may have done to him! He's a real friendly cuss if he's treated right!"

But he was unheeded. The drover slowly loaded the rifle. Chut, holding the creamy fur of his belly apart preparatory to burr extraction, looked up as the breach closed.

"Aw! *Give* him a chance!" said the cook's assistant.

"He ain't fit to be loose," said the cook. The cook's assistant grasped a stone. Then, as the drover raised the rifle, the assistant gave a whoop that might raise the dead, and let fly his stone! It caught Chut full in the chest, staggering him. As he rose, chutting with rage, the assistant ran at him flapping a bit of tent!

Chut would have faced most things. But the apparition of the ghost-white tent, on top of the unexpected blow, was too much for him. With a great bound, he was gone into the dark.

"He's going to have a chance anyway!" said the assistant, through his teeth.

Men shouted and got in each other's way.

"I'm going to get Monty's hound dogs!" shrieked the cook. "Monty's over to Blister with a broken leg, but he'll lend the dogs."

Bruised and angry and hurt, Chut held on through the night. He had liked the drover-men! He had been so well behaved—never once raiding the tempting tucker box! And this was the way that they had treated him.

With a soft-cushioned thudding of boundless, rhythmic strength, he moved surely through the dark. . . . And as he went something told him that he was at last near the place of his desire! That somewhere, not many miles away, was a long winding dam with lily-set banks and little trails running down to it through the high grey grass. Men were hostile. His own kind were hostile. There remained only "place."

He had no reasoning for it, but he believed that "there" was solace for the many hurts that he had borne: the many indignities meted out to him by life.

He had no definite expectation of anything except rest in the tall grass: cool water to drink, and lily buds, sweet with honey to the moon. But he travelled all that night.

Dawn came in a thin wash of strange silver up the sky; then red, and the songs of birds. Chut was travelling faster now, for he knew that his "place" was near.

It was about mid-morning when he heard the sounds of dogs, far away behind him. He halted and listened, and, although he had never been hunted by dogs, he knew that these dogs were following him.

He resumed his motion, but at intervals he listened to the cries of the pack. They were coming closer! He had never feared dogs, but there was a rhythmical menace in the cry of these hounds; a oneness of purpose which was disconcerting.

Chut increased his pace, so that instead of covering ten feet at a bound he covered fifteen. At that the cries of the dogs no longer crept up on him—but at the same time he could not shake them off. As the hours passed he began to grow hot and angry. Then he halted to lick his arms and breathe—and at once the dog-voices came closer. The musical, unnerving "Boo-oo-oo" of hounds on a strong scent. He went on with his arms half-licked.

Sometimes he would gain so that he no longer heard his pursuers, and then he would snatch a little dry picking, or a drink, if a drain was near. And then, away at the end of hearing, he would catch a far, thin sound, which gathered distinctness, and became again the musical menace of the pack.

All day he heard them, and all day he heard the silent whisper telling him that home, home, home, was near! For five hundred miles he had followed the blind sense of place that led him north and west. Now, as surely as he had known where home was, he knew that it was almost reached.

At sunset he came down to a wide, shallow swamp, its still, muddy water mirroring the sky. He crossed it—and threw the dogs off his trail so that they ran whimpering and wagging amongst the puddles and ash-grey cane grass tufts. A narrow stream they would have crossed at once, but the great swamp puzzled them.

The men came up and tried to urge the dogs across, but without their owner's familiar commands they were confused, and turned back to pick up the lost scent.

Finally the men swore and gave up the chase—being already weary—and the dogs snuffed and whimpered alone.

Then the leader, coasting a little farther into the swamp, picked up a scent on a mud-bar—and gave tongue! A moment, and another dog had found a whisp of Chut's fur on a wild fuchsia bush. At last convinced their quarry had crossed, they chorused and swept on.

At midnight Chut awoke from a brief rest, to hear them belling. He scrambled to his feet with panic-pitching heart: then shook his ears and chutted with hot rage. But he went on; faster than ever now: although he was feeling the strain of his all-night-and-all-day-and-half-a-new-night of travelling.

In spite of his wrath his ears drooped a little, and his course was less unswervingly direct. Hop, hop, hop—not a disjointed gait such as the word hop suggests, but rather flight with a pulse to it—fifteen feet at a rhythmic bound, great tail balancing him, great feet descending lightly—amazingly lightly for his weight—then spurning the earth so that his three-hundred-pound body sailed up and forward in another mighty, rhythmic arc.

As a new dawn broke he was still forging forward.

But his chest was heaving desperately now, and he was not judging his distances quite so well, so that he bruised his feet upon the tangled mulga heads. And the pack was coming closer!

"Boo-oo-oo! Boo-oo-oo!" "Overtake and kill!" the one thought mirrored in a musical and multiple cry.

All across the morning the savage music sounded, and hunter and hunted held to their positions.

Through the glare of noon they came out upon a long, silver-grassed glade amongst the dead mulga trees. Chut's ears were hanging far down now, his body had lost its spring. He was coming down heavily at the end of each leap. As he reached the farther end of the glade he now looked back, and for the first time saw the dogs, as they burst from the distant timber. There were twelve of them, big, heavy, half-bred hounds, their tongues lolling, their eyes glazed with the ecstasy of pursuit and the strain of exhaustion.

At sight of their quarry they broke into a new note, and increased their reeling speed. Running low, huddled together, they came down the glade, all the force of their heredity and their training impelling them to drag down this thing which fled before them.

"BOO-oo-OO-ii-ii-ii!" Chut turned to go on, but he stumbled ignominiously. Then he wheeled—with his back to a forked tree: drew himself up to his regal height, and waited.

The dogs closed in with a rush, their jaws working, their eyes malevolent with the impersonal fury of the chase.

The leader, a length ahead of the rest, sprang straight for Chut's throat. The big kangaroo caught the dog in his embrace, brought up his reaping-hook toe, and hurled the hound away—ripped and bleeding—to die on the ground. But another dog had him by the flank, white teeth tearing through fur and hide. Another was springing for his shoulder, and the others surged yapping and snapping about him; more cautious now, but still sure of the end: still ecstatically frenzied for his life.

Chut struck left and right, clutching, kicking. He tore off the dog on his flank—and another slashed his forearm open, so that a red gush of blood leapt out! He disembowelled another of his tormentors, and another bounding liver-and-white body struck him from the side and snapping jaws ripped his ear to the base.

As fast as he repelled one attacker, another was upon him, and their noise, and their surging insistence, confused him. He was surrounded by leaping, slavering, frantic dogs. The sheer weight of numbers was overbearing him.

It seemed only a matter of moments now until he must be borne to the ground, buried in a seething mass of dogs, suffocated under hot bodies, his life ripped out by the white fangs!

He was weak from long effort and loss of blood. His ears drooped. He repelled the dogs less strongly—and then the sense of his nearness to all that he had sought came to him again. Home!

He shook himself free for a moment. He gathered himself in a great leap above the snapping and startled hounds. With the last of his mighty strength he sought to leave them behind. Twenty, thirty feet at a bound he moved, taking the fallen timber in his leap, seeming barely to touch the ground, but rather to wing in undulant flight! But the dogs too had been seized by a new frenzy of energy.

They had tasted blood. They were hot, and quivering, and mad to kill. They followed, a leap behind; too eager even to give tongue now, and the more deadly for their silence.

And then, before pursuers and pursued, there rose to view a seven-foot, barb-topped fence. Chut saw it and increased his speed, exhibiting one of the marvels of motion; the supreme flight of a hunted kangaroo.

Straight for the fence he went. Measured it, gathered momentum, braced his vast body, and twenty feet from the barrier he hurled himself into the air, up! up! Gathering his legs under him and a little sideways, as a jumping pony will to clear the rails. Up! And OVER the fence-top! And down twenty feet upon its inner side! Then on to safety, as the dogs reared, raging and thwarted, without.

Several of the hounds climbed halfway up the netting, only to fall back. One reached the top, only to be defeated by the barbs.

Chut stumbled into the tall, amber kangaroo grass—on until he could no longer hear the dogs—then curled to sleep.

He slept almost uninterruptedly for days, going down to a little artesian stream to drink in the evenings and pick for a few moments at the rich green couch grass along the drain edge, then sleeping again.

At last, fully rested, he began to travel once more. But he travelled more slowly now. For the something was whispering to him that he had reached the "there" for which he so long had hungered.

He moved aimlessly: casting about for familiar things: and one evening, under a rosy sky, he came out upon a little wandering path running down to the long waters of a dam . . . and suddenly he knew that it was the dam where his mother had lifted him from the pouch for the first time.

In the close, sharp-scented herbage along the banks the broad, green leaves and thin-petalled white flowers of the lilies poked up.

A grey heron was roosting on a high, dead limb. Teal were settling for the night on the half-submerged logs. . . . This was his place. This was what he had sought.

He moved down to the water, travelling deliberately upon hoppers and hands. The water was cool, and brown with the stain of dead leaves, and very sweet.

But presently he found that it was not all as satisfying as he had expected it to be. He was lonely. Through all the hundreds of miles of his journey there had always been this objective before him. Now the objective was attained—and he was lonely. He wanted another of his kind. He wanted a mate.

He sat up and called shrilly—a small sound, of remarkable carrying power. He hopped back and forth along the dam edge, thudding his tail to prove his size and worth. . . . And as the gold edge of the moon began to poke up, he heard a modest answer. Out of the shadows came a sturdy, plump, mouse-colored kangaroo-doe. Glossy of coat, with great limpid eyes upon which the moon struck. He went to her—and suddenly he knew her. It was Zodie.

They twittered and chitted with joy at seeing each other. They touched their noses over each other's fur. They chutted and chitted more loudly. But to him she was not simply the playmate of his babyhood, she was a female of his kind, the satisfaction of the hunger of loneliness growing within him.

He was utterly delighted with her, but, as he wooed, she grew more coy. She retreated, she fled; doubling in and out of the trees: pausing until he almost touched her, and then fleeing tantalizingly.

It was a game such as they had played a thousand times in the past. Yet it was different—as, in his eyes, little fat Zodie was different. The moon lost the gold of its first rising and sailed slowly up in white, still splendor.

The lilies poured out their scent—and the game went on and on!

And then the little doe doubled into an angle formed by some fallen trees. She might perhaps have jumped them, but she pretended that this was impossible. And so he caught her, at last.

Some months later Tom Henton and his wife were camped by the dam, and in the dusk a little fat kangaroo came up to chit at the tent door—followed by a red-furred giant with a brass collar gleaming upon his neck.

Tom Henton whispered between his teeth: "Chut! By all that's marvelous! And with *Zodie!*"

"Oh," said the girl, "I *knew* he would come home! I always knew it! When I asked you to make this place a kangaroo sanctuary, I was wanting it to be safe when *he* came back! I knew he would come back to where he had been born—even if he wouldn't forgive men enough to come back to us at the house. When I turned little Zodie loose, it was because I thought they might find each other! Oh, Tom, it's a romance!"

They were interrupted by a peevish, resentful chitting issuing from a little doe—who apparently wished she had run faster, and farther. Sitting protestingly before them, Zodie held open her pouch with indignant little hands, thus displaying a fat, bright-eyed joey. Complaining bitterly, she lifted him out. And revealed the fact that through some misadventure he had gotten into the bindee-eye burrs—which in turn had gotten in large quantity into Zodie's outraged pocket!

. . . And now, each still evening, just at dusk, a great red kangaroo leads his ever-growing harem down to water: and amongst the does are many, many little, vivid red joeys.

But sometimes the "old man" will exhibit a strange impatience and break away from all his flock, and go ranging and calling alone through the bush.

Tom Henton's wife believes that he is looking for Blue Baby.

# CORAL REEFS

## Jean Louis Rodolphe Agassiz

*One of the great American naturalists, Agassiz (1807–1873)
was born in Switzerland, worked for many years in France,
and was already a famous man when he came to the United
States. Huge audiences attended his lectures at Harvard, where
he worked for the rest of his life. Attacking vigorously the
study of nature through dead classics, he urged careful observation and experimentation instead. These qualities are
shown clearly in this selection about the tiny sea creatures
which build whole islands and reefs by themselves.*

For a long time it was supposed that the reef-builders inhabited
very deep waters; for they were sometimes brought up upon
sounding-lines from a depth of many hundreds or even thousands
of feet, and it was taken for granted that they must have had their
home where they were found: but the facts recently ascertained
respecting the subsidence of ocean-bottoms have shown that the
foundation of a coral-wall may have sunk far below the place where
it was laid. And it is now proved, beyond a doubt, that no reef-
building coral can thrive at a depth of more than fifteen fathoms,
though corals of other kinds occur far lower, and that the dead
reef-corals, sometimes brought to the surface from much greater
depths, are only broken fragments of some reef that has subsided
with the bottom on which it was growing. But though fifteen
fathoms is the maximum depth at which any reef-builder can pros-
per, there are many which will not sustain even that degree of pressure; and this fact has, as we shall see, an important influence on the
structure of the reef.

Imagine now a sloping shore on some tropical coast descending
gradually below the surface of the sea. Upon that slope, at a depth
of from ten to twelve or fifteen fathoms, and two or three or more
miles from the mainland, according to the shelving of the shore, we

will suppose that one of those little coral animals, to whom a home in such deep waters is congenial, has established itself. How it happens that such a being, which we know is immovably attached to the ground, and forms the foundation of a solid wall, was ever able to swim freely about in the water till it found a suitable resting-place, I shall explain hereafter, when I say something of the mode of reproduction of these animals. Accept, for the moment, my unsustained assertion, and plant our little coral on this sloping shore, some twelve or fifteen fathoms below the surface of the sea.

The internal structure of such a coral corresponds to that of the sea-anemone. The body is divided by vertical partitions from top to bottom, leaving open chambers between; while in the centre hangs the digestive cavity, connected by an opening in the bottom with all these chambers. At the top is an aperture serving as a mouth, surrounded by a wreath of hollow tentacles, each one of which connects at its base with one of the chambers, so that all parts of the animal communicate freely with each other. But though the structure of the coral is identical in all its parts with the sea-anemone, it nevertheless presents one important difference. The body of the sea-anemone is soft, while that of the coral is hard.

It is well known that all animals and plants have the power of appropriating to themselves and assimilating the materials they need, each selecting from the surrounding elements whatever contributes to its well-being. Now, corals possess in an extraordinary degree, the power of assimilating to themselves the lime contained in the salt water around them; and as soon as our little coral is established on a firm foundation, a lime deposit begins to form in all the walls of its body, so that its base, its partitions, and its outer wall, which in the sea-anemone remain always soft, become perfectly solid in the polyp coral, and form a frame as hard as bone.

It may naturally be asked where the lime comes from in the sea which the corals absorb in such quantities. As far as the living corals are concerned the answer is easy, for an immense deal of lime is brought down to the ocean by rivers that wear away the lime deposits through which they pass. The Mississippi, whose course lies through extensive lime regions, brings down yearly lime enough to supply all the animals living in the Gulf of Mexico. But behind this lies a question, not so easily settled, as to the origin of the extensive deposits of limestone found at the very beginning of life upon earth. This problem brings us to the threshold of astronomy; for the base of limestone is metallic in character, susceptible therefore of fusion, and may have formed a part of the materials of our earth, even in an incandescent state, when the worlds were forming. But though this investigation as to the origin of lime does not belong either to the naturalist or the geologist, its suggestion reminds us that the time has come when all the sciences and their results are so intimately connected that no one can be carried on independently of the others. Since the study of the rocks has revealed a crowded life whose records are hoarded within them, the work of the geologist and the naturalist has become one and the same; and at that border-land where the first crust of the earth was condensed out of the igneous mass of materials which formed its earliest condition, their investigation mingles with that of the astronomer, and we cannot trace the limestone in a little coral without going back to the creation of our solar system, when the worlds that compose it were thrown off from a central mass in a gaseous condition.

When the coral has become in this way permeated with lime, all parts of the body are rigid, with the exception of the upper margin, the stomach, and the tentacles. The tentacles are soft and waving, projected or drawn in at will; they retain their flexible character through life, and decompose when the animal dies. For this reason the dried specimens of corals preserved in museums do not give us the least idea of the living corals, in which every one of the millions of beings composing such a community is crowned by a waving wreath of white or green or rose-colored tentacles.

As soon as the little coral is fairly established and solidly attached to the ground, it begins to bud. This may take place in a variety of ways, dividing at the top or budding from the base or from the sides, till the primitive animal is surrounded by a number of individuals like itself, of which it forms the nucleus, and which now begin to bud in their turn, each one surrounding itself with a numerous progeny, all remaining, however, attached to the parent. Such a community increases till its individuals are numbered by millions, and I have myself counted no less than fourteen millions of individuals in a coral mass of Porites measuring not more than twelve feet in diameter. The so-called coral heads, which make the foundation of a coral wall, and seem by their massive character and regular form especially adapted to give a strong, solid base to the whole structure, are known in our classification as the *Astræns*, so named on account of the little star-shaped pits crowded upon their surface, each one of which marks the place of a single more or less isolated individual in such a community.

# A WALRUS HUNT

## Elisha Kent Kane

*Elisha Kent Kane served as a surgeon in both the United States Army and Navy, visiting and exploring many out-of-the-way places in Asia, Africa, and South America. A member of two expeditions which searched the Arctic for the lost British explorer, Sir John Franklin, Kane made many valuable discoveries, although failing in his main goal. His books about these expeditions were immensely popular, for they told of a new and strange life and people, as in the selection from* The Second Grinnell Expedition.

I HAVE not yet described one of these exciting incidents of Esquimau life. Morton was full of the one he witnessed; and his account of it when he came back was so graphic that I should be glad to escape from the egotism of personal narrative by giving it in his own words. Let me first, however, endeavor to describe the animal.

The specimens in the museums of collectors are imperfect, on account of the drying of the skin of the face against the skull. The head of the walrus has not the characteristic oval of the seal; on the contrary, the frontal bone is so covered as to present a steep descent to the eyes and a square, blocked-out aspect to the upper face. The muzzle is less protruding than the seal's, and the cheeks and lips are completely masked by the heavy, quill-like bristles. Add to this the tusks as a garniture to the lower face, and you have for the walrus a grim, ferocious aspect peculiarly his own. I have seen him with tusks nearly thirty inches long; his body not less than eighteen feet. When of this size he certainly reminds you of the elephant more than any other living monster.

The resemblance of the walrus to man has been greatly overrated. The notion occurs in our systematic treatises, accompanied with the suggestion that this animal may have represented the merman and mermaid. The square, blocked-out head, which I have

[ 785 ]

noticed, effectually destroys the resemblance to humanity when distant, and the colossal size does the same when near. Some of the seals deserve the distinction much more; the size of the head, the regularity of the facial oval, the droop of the shoulders, even the movements of this animal singly or in group, remind you strikingly of man.

The party which Morton attended upon their walrus-hunt had three sledges. One was to be taken to a *cache* in the neighborhood; the other two dragged at a quick run towards the open water, about ten miles off to the southwest. They had but nine dogs to these two sledges, one man only riding, the others running by turns. As they neared the new ice, and where the black wastes of mingled cloud and water betokened the open sea, they would from time to time remove their hoods and listen intently to the animal's voice.

After a while Myouk became convinced, from signs or sounds, or both—for they were inappreciable by Morton—that the walrus were waiting for him in a small space of recently-open water that was glazed over with a few days' growth of ice; and, moving gently on, they soon heard the characteristic bellow of a bull awuk. The walrus, like some of the higher order of beings to which he has been compared, is fond of his own music, and will lie for hours listening to himself. His vocalization is something between the mooing of a cow and the deepest baying of a mastiff: very round and full, with its barks or detached notes repeated rather quickly seven to nine times in succession.

The party now formed in single file, following in each other's steps; and, guided by an admirable knowledge of ice-topography, wound behind hummocks and ridges in a serpentine approach towards a group of pondlike discolorations, recently-frozen ice-spots, but surrounded by firmer and older ice.

When within half a mile of these the line broke, and each man crawled towards a separate pool; Morton on his hands and knees following Myouk. In a few minutes the walrus were in sight. They were five in number, rising at intervals through the ice in a body, and breaking it up with an explosive puff that might have been heard for miles. Two large, grim-looking males were conspicuous as the leaders of the group.

Now for the marvel of the craft. When the walrus is above water, the hunter is flat and motionless; as he begins to sink, alert and ready for a spring. The animal's head is hardly below the water-line before every man is in a rapid run; and again, as if by instinct, before the beast returns, all are motionless behind protecting knolls of ice. They seem to know beforehand not only the time he will be absent, but the very spot at which he will reappear. In this way, hiding and advancing by turns, Myouk, with Morton at his heels, has reached a plate of thin ice, hardly strong enough to bear them, at the very brink of the water-pool the walrus are curveting in.

Myouk, till now phlegmatic, seems to waken with excitement. His coil of walrus-hide, a well-trimmed hide of many fathoms' length, is lying at his side. He fixes one end of it in an iron barb, and fastens this loosely by a socket upon a shaft of unicorn's horn: the other end is already looped, or, as sailors would say, "doubled in a bight." It is the work of a moment. He has grasped the harpoon: the water is in motion. Puffing with pent-up respiration, the walrus is within a couple of fathoms, close before him. Myouk rises slowly; his right arm thrown back, his left flat at his side. The walrus looks about him, shaking the water from his crest: Myouk throws up his left arm; and the animal, rising breast high, fixes one look before he plunges. It has cost him all that curiosity can cost: the harpoon is buried under his left flipper.

Though the awuk is down in a moment, Myouk is running at desperate speed from the scene of his victory, paying off his coil freely, but clutching the end by its loop. He seizes as he runs a small stick of bone, rudely pointed with iron, and by a sudden movement drives it into the ice: to this he secures his line, pressing it down close to the ice-surface with his feet.

Now comes the struggle. The hole is dashed in mad commotion with the struggles of the wounded beast; the line is drawn tight at one moment, the next relaxed: the hunter has not left his station. There is a crash of the ice; and rearing up through it are two walruses, not many yards from where he stands. One of them, the male, is excited and seemingly terrified; the other, the female, collected and vengeful. Down they go again, after one grim survey of the field; and on the instant Myouk has changed his position, carrying his coil with him and fixing it anew.

He has hardly fixed it before the pair have again risen, breaking up an area of ten feet diameter about the very spot he left. As they sink once more he again changes his place. And so the conflict goes on between address and force, till the victim, half exhausted, receives a second wound, and is played like a trout by the angler's reel.

The instinct of attack which characterizes the walrus is interesting to the naturalist, as it is characteristic also of the land animals, the pachyderms, with which he is classed. When wounded, he rises high out of the water, plunges heavily against the ice, and strives to raise himself with his foreflippers upon the surface. As it breaks under his weight, his countenance assumes a still more vindictive expression, his bark changes to a roar, and the foam pours out from his jaws till it froths his beard.

Even when not excited, he manages his tusks bravely. They are so strong that he uses them to grapple the rocks with, and climbs steeps of ice and land which would be inaccessible to him without their aid. He ascends in this way rocky islands that are sixty and a hundred feet above the level of the sea; and I have myself seen him in these elevated positions basking with his young in the cool sunshine of August and September.

He can strike a fearful blow; but prefers charging with his tusks in a soldierly manner. I do not doubt the old stories of the Spitzbergen fisheries and Cherie Island, where the walrus put to flight the crowds of European boats. Awuk is the lion of the Danish Esquimaux, and they always speak of him with the highest respect.

I have heard of oomiaks being detained for days at a time at the crossings of straits and passages which he infested. Governor Flaischer told me that, in 1830, a brown walrus, which, according to the Esquimaux, is the fiercest, after being lanced and maimed near Upernavik, routed his numerous assailants, and drove them in fear to seek for help from the settlement. His movements were so violent as to jerk out the harpoons that were stuck into him. The governor slew him with great difficulty after several rifle-shots and lance-wounds, from his whaleboat.

On another occasion a young and adventurous Inuit plunged his nalegeit into a brown walrus; but, startled by the savage demeanor of the beast, called for help before using the lance. The older men in vain cautioned him to desist. "It is a brown walrus," said they: *"Aúvek-Kaiok!"* "Hold back!" Finding the caution disregarded, his only brother rowed forward and plunged the second harpoon. Almost in an instant the animal charged upon the kayacker, ripping him up, as the description went, after the fashion of his sylvan brother, the wild boar. The story was told to me with much animation; how the brother remaining rescued the corpse of the brother dead; and how, as they hauled it up on the ice-floes, the ferocious beast plunged in foaming circles, seeking fresh victims in that part of the sea which was discolored by his blood.

Some idea may be formed of the ferocity of the walrus from the fact that the battle which Morton witnessed, not without sharing some of its danger, lasted four hours; during which the animal rushed continually at the Esquimaux as they approached, tearing off great tables of ice with his tusks, and showing no indications of fear whatever. He received upward of seventy lance-wounds—Morton counted over sixty; and even then he remained hooked by his tusks to the margin of the ice, unable or unwilling to retire. His female fought in the same manner, but fled on receiving a lance-wound.

The Esquimaux seemed to be fully aware of the danger of venturing too near; for at the first onset of the walrus they jumped back far enough to be clear of the broken ice. Morton described the last three hours as wearing, on both sides, the aspect of an unbroken and seemingly doubtful conflict.

The method of landing the beast upon the ice, too, showed a great deal of clever contrivance. They made two pair of incisions in the neck, where the hide is very thick, about six inches apart and parallel to each other, so as to form a couple of bands. A line of cut hide, about a quarter of an inch in diameter, was passed under one of these bands and carried up on the ice to a firm stick well secured in the floe, where it went through a loop, and was then taken back to the animal, made to pass under the second band, and led off to the Esquimaux. This formed a sort of "double purchase," the blubber so lubricating the cord as to admit of a free movement. By this contrivance the beast, weighing some seven hundred pounds, was hauled up and butchered at leisure.

## A Chanted Calendar

Fᴵʀsᴛ came the primrose,
  On the bank high,
Like a maiden looking forth
From the window of a tower
When the battle rolls below,
So look'd she,
And saw the storms go by.

Then came the wind-flower
In the valley left behind,
As a wounded maiden, pale
With purple streaks of woe,
When the battle has roll'd by
Wanders to and fro,
So totter'd she,
Dishevell'd in the wind.

Then came the daisies,
On the first of May,
Like a banner'd show's advance
While the crowd runs by the way
With ten thousand flowers about them they came trooping through the
  fields.
As a happy people come,
So came they,
As a happy people come
When the war has roll'd away,
With dance and tabor, pipe and drum,
And all make holiday.

Then came the cow-slip,
Like a dancer in the fair,
She spread her little mat of green,
And on it danced she.
With a fillet bound about her brow,
A fillet round her happy brow,
A golden fillet round her brow,
And rubies in her hair.

                              *Sidney Dobell*